THE VALLEY ROSE
BETWEEN
THE STAR
AND
THE LIGHT

BURNING BRIDGE
PUBLISHING

THE VALLEY ROSE
BETWEEN
THE STAR
AND
THE LIGHT

Danger Geist

www.BurningBridge.com

Cover illustration by Chris Beatrice
Book cover designed by Chris Beatrice
"Walled-Out Wise Men" illustration by Sharnee Taylor
Chapter Varia (40) photo by Hannah Goering
Select photograph editing by Trevor Niemann
Burning Bridge Publishing logo designed by Ryan Rizzio
PCIP block provided by Adrienne Bashista
Cartography by Mapping Specialists, Ltd.
All photographs and pictures property of Geist Family

www.BurningBridge.com

The Burning Bridge Publishing name and logo are trademarks of Burning Bridge Publishing.

Printed in the United States of America.

1st edition, December 7, 2023.

Publisher's Cataloging-in-Publication data

Names: Geist, Danger, author.
Title: The valley rose between the star and the light / Danger Geist.
Description: Tulsa, OK: Burning Bridge Publishing, 2023.
Identifiers: LCCN: 2023920371 | ISBN: 978-1-937691-12-7
Subjects: LCSH Geist, Danger. | Dogs. | Human-animal interactions. | Grief. | Christian pilgrims and pilgrimages--Palestine--Anecdotes. | Christian pilgrims and pilgrimages--Israel--Anecdotes. | Christian shrines--Israel. | Christian shrines--Palestine.| Christian biography. | BISAC BIOGRAPHY & AUTOBIOGRAPHY / Personal Memoirs | HISTORY / Middle East / Israel & Palestine | RELIGION / Christian Living / Personal Memoirs
Classification: LCC DS107 .G45 2023 | DDC 956.94--dc23

INNARDS

ZERO	001-008	Babylon	January 2019
Now Where Were We?	009-010	St. Louis, MO	February 2006
Wars and Rumors of Wars	019-023	St. Louis, MO	February 2006
Ever the Same	030-035	Zion, IL	May 2006
Who Sinned, This Man or His Parents?	044-045	Kenosha, WI	July 2006
Baptism by Tire	055-057	Edwardsville, IL	March 2007
Flight of the Hawkeye	066-070	Ft. Campbell, KY	March 2007
Fleeced	075-081	Edwardsville, IL	March 2007
Change of Just a Decade	089-091	Chicago, IL	February 2016
On Eagle's Wings	098-103	Milan, Italy	October 2018
"The One with All of the Pop Culture References"	110-115	Bethlehem, Palestine	October 2018
No Room in the Manger	122-124	Bethlehem, Palestine	October 2018
Guardian	130-132	Bethlehem, Palestine	October 2018
The Christian Barber of Star Street	140-142	Bethlehem, Palestine	October 2018
There's a First Time for Everything	146-154	Jerusalem, Israel	October 2018
Breaking the First Wall	160-169	Jericho, Palestine	October 2018
Selah	174-184	Ramallah, Palestine	October 2018
Ace in the Holy Land	189-190	Jerusalem, Israel	October 2018
At a Hostile	195-198	Jerusalem, Israel	October 2018
Off the Wall	203-208	Bethlehem, Palestine	October 2018
Mister Master Masticator	217-228	Bethlehem, Palestine	October 2018
The Final Night Before Five Years of Homework	237-244	Jerusalem, Israel	October 2018
Breaking the Fourth Wall	254-263	Bethlehem, Palestine	October 2018
Plant a Seed, Plant a Flower, Plant a Rose	272-275	Jerusalem, Israel	October 2018
Relying on a Star	284-311	Jerusalem, Israel	October 2018
Looking for Armageddon	324-335	Megiddo, Israel	November 2018
The Valley Rose	345-354	The Valley	November 2018
Out of the Belly of Sheol	360-368	Jezreel and Jaffa	November 2018
The Crowded Tomb	379-383	Jerusalem, Israel	November 2018
Noon in Jerusalem	391-393	Jerusalem, Israel	November 2018
Exsanguine	399-406	Jerusalem, Israel	November 2018
Missing Gabriel	420-422	Nazareth, Israel	November 2018
The Odyssey	433-436	Zion, Illinois	November 2018
My Final Broken Promise	447-449	Minneapolis, Minnesota	November 2018
Dawn of the Final Day -24 Hours Remain-	461-464	Tulsa, Oklahoma	December 2018
The Curse of Genesis	477-480	Tulsa, Oklahoma	December 2018
Trigger Warning	493-498	Tulsa, Oklahoma	December 2018
A Healed Knee	509-514	Tulsa, Oklahoma	December 2018
The Inciting Incident	525-534	Tulsa, Oklahoma	December 2018
VARIA	572-581	Babylon	January 2021

FOREWORD

On October 7, 2023 at 3:52am CST, my eyes opened. I was exactly two months from launching this five-year project and still needed to tweak a few of the finishing touches. When I checked the time, I instead found out that the worst tragedy in post-Holocaust Israeli history had occurred in those few hours my eyes were closed.

What do you do when you've spent the past five years working on a book talking about the inevitable coming war between Israelis and Palestinians, and then you wake up and hear that it started while you were sleeping?

Of course, the first thing you do is check on your Israeli and Palestinian friends. But once you do that, and you don't hear back from them because of the chaos they're dealing with or because it's Shabbat and they're in a bomb shelter with their phones off, what's the second thing you do?

Well, if you're me, you get out of bed. You reflect whether or not it's insensitive to still publish on time. You talk to a few friends and they remind you that you didn't manufacture the tragedy just outside (and later, inside) Gaza. And then you get to work.

A Jewish maven,
a charismatic Palestinian,
and an ignorant American walk into a war.

But the joke ends there. For generations, Israelis and Arabs have been waiting for a punchline that never lands. Neither Jews nor Muslims believe in purgatory, but they've lived it well.

I traveled to Israel and Palestine in late 2018. It changed my life, yes, but the same can be said for millions of pilgrims today. I attempted to tell my story anyway, but found myself unable to do so without sharing the stories of two ethnic rivals: an Israeli Jew and a minority Palestinian.

Several years into weaving our three stories, I was confronted with a bitter reality: not only did the Israeli and the Palestinian have competing worldviews, but I had written their stories to two completely different audiences.

Early readers agreed that my narratives were the thrust of this book. Then a fork: those who loved reading about the Star usually disliked reading about the Light, and those who were enamored by the Light rarely appreciated the Star.

I had several mentors suggest a few traditional ways to handle this problem, but none of those solutions felt satisfying to me, nor did I suppose they would've satisfied most readers. I was faced with a decision to either pull back and rework the narratives so that they were closer in style, or I could embrace the tension I'd caused by veering even further into the unorthodox. I chose the latter.

In this memoir, your prime quest will be to read my narratives. But between each of those chapters, you will be faced with either reading about the Star or the Light. The Star, upon its cessation, exists only as Light. And the Light owes its entire existence to the Star.

So, then, which side quest do I urge you to take?

The Star spotlights an Orthodox Jew who lives in Jerusalem.

The Star is concentrated over the course of nine months - March 2020 to December 2020 - as the phantom of the pandemic hangs over each chapter.

If you want to be buried with dense, uncomfortable theological crossfire, follow the Star.

If you've felt victimized by Christians and want a potentially cathartic read, you'll likely appreciate the Star.

If you tend to set your video game difficulty to "hard" or "hero" or this is your second read-through and you're ready for the Master Quest, you'll want to jump towards the Star.

If you prefer *Deep Impact* over *Armageddon*, *There Will Be Blood* over *No Country for Old Men*, *Wyatt Earp* over *Tombstone*, and *Lord of the Rings* over *Chronicles of Narnia*, tail the Star.

If you like cerebral puzzles, rational thought experiments, or phrenic discourse, seek the Star.

If you grew up with text messaging, or you're an English teacher who needs a break from stuffy syntax rules, you may be more comfortable with the Star.

If you experience Christianity as a suffocating and oppressive religion, you may want to fix your attention on the Star.

If you need help praying, allow the Star to usher you into refuge.

When the storm rolls in,
ye seek the Star.
Even the darkness must pass.

The Light stars a Palestinian Christian who lives in Bethlehem.

The Light stretches across 50 years - October 1967 to January 2019 - as the Six-Day War, the Intifadas, the Siege of the Church of the Nativity, and the building of the Separation Wall all serve as its backdrop.

If you'd prefer to watch someone else get slowly buried alive while they're caught in a literal crossfire, follow the Light.

If you've felt victimized by the enemy and need a Christian pickmeup, you'll likely be drawn to the Light.

If you set your video game difficulty to "easy" or "rookie" or you literally have no idea what I'm talking about, you'll probably find more joy sticking with the Light.

If you prefer *I am Legend* to *Legends of the Fall*, *Wonder Woman* to *Batman*, *Abduction* to *Inception*, and *Risen* to *Noah*, pursue the Light.

If you like jigsaw puzzles, moral-driven stories with an emotional pull, or fast-paced adventure, chase the Light.

If text exchanges irk your sensibilities for good grammar, or you prefer a simpler time when cell phones didn't exist and there weren't so many walls, go with the Light.

If you like to experience stories about Christian faith overcoming suffocating oppression, you may want to lamp the light.

If you're praying for a champion, allow the Light to suffuse you.

Be not afraid of the Light:
like any good Christmas legend,
this is a Ghost story.

Of course, I recommend doing not any one of these things. Whether this is your first time holding a "Danger book" or you're revisiting this story for yet another playthrough, if you want to understand the dynamics of a story in full, you read both.
If you want to live in the tension between religiosity and spirituality, between Abraham and his children, between your preferred genre and the one outside of your comfort zone, and the twilight between this broken world and the one that's prophesied to come, then you should read *The Valley Rose Between the Star AND the Light.*

ZERO

Don't ask me to pray for you.

My eyes open against my will. There's pounding pressure on my right temple. Heart's palpitating like an arrhythmic dog. Blood condensates on my wrist like midnight dew.

Also, not that it matters, but it smells like old man's breath in here.

Did I just respawn?

My neck and my back are killing me, so I get up off the carpet.

Empty. An entire condo, bare. No furniture, no people, and one of my worst fears has come to fruition: I started my story with an overdone trope.

Fuuuu…

Wait. No.

You're a Christian writer. You can't cuss, either.

My fatal recklessness had me loathing myself enough as it was, but now I think I hate myself as much as I hate this city.

I scan the room. It's incredible how spacious this long, vacant flat is when there's nothing else in it. It feels like someone recently had a boss battle in here.

Hero must've lost.

Now it's night, and given the lights are out, it's getting awfully dark. I reach for my phone to check the time. Except, it's not there. There's nothing in my pockets, just a set of keys a few feet from where I woke up.

I used to live here. I never appreciated this place, but I wish to God I could restart any stage other than this one. Jesus saves? Sure. He saved at the cruelest possible point and no matter what I do now, I keep reliving the worst night of my life without the skillset to forge ahead. He ought to just start over, honestly.

God may be good, but He's not too good, at least not so much that He'd just let me have what I want from Him.

I stumble over to the fireplace and set my hand on the mantle, then raise my arm to find my palmprint in the dust. The fireplace hasn't been used in at least a year, though I guess the last two winters have been relatively warm. I know I shouldn't keep revisiting the past, but now that I *don't* live here, I finally have something worth putting on the mantle.

I'm about to have to re-learn everything I thought I knew. That makes it really hard to want to leave. I can't tarry, though; it's bad for my health and my family's well-being. Besides, the sale's about to go through.

Walking on the crispy grass, I realize I'd shut the door and locked it without a second thought. Events with such finality usually cripple me. There are only a few times in your life where you leave someplace and you just know you'll never return there. At the risk of turning into a pillar of salt, I turn around and look up at the second-floor window. The ghost is watching me, beckoning me back.

"You have to stay here," I tell her. "At least for now. We'll roam again."

I crank my head towards the sky, ferreting for just one more hint of light, but it's officially gotten dark. "The day has just begun," Nicolas might tell me. And, okay, now that the sun is gone, this winter wasn't as warm as I just remembered it to be. I'm naked in this cold. Stripped of anything valuable. *Zero.*

I pull the keys from my pocket, jump into Joanna's car, and trek home.

I pull into the garage, breathe a sigh, then sheepishly inch into my own garage.

I know I did wrong.

I take my index finger, tap my forehead, then my chest, then my left shoulder to my right.

"Father, Son, Holy Ghost," I whisper.

I do it again, this time without saying anything. And then cross myself a couple more times for good measure. And then three more, to make it seven. Only five away from 12, so might as well finish the set.

"God is sovereign," I whisper. "God is sovereign. God is sovereign."

It's a brand-new home, but the door still creaks as I pass through the garage into the foyer. Our newest pup, Shadrach, meets me at the door, then begins to zoomie around the house after her investigation concludes that it's Daddy breaking into the garage. Joanna, meanwhile, is still on the couch, eyes puffy.

"I'm sorry," I announce upon my arrival. I hope I sound genuine. I really mean it.

2

"Where did you go?" she asks. A woman in mourning, more ways than one.

Blessed are those who mourn, for they shall be comforted. I realize that I don't think I believed this statement anymore.

"I know both of us aren't doing well," I say, ignoring my wife's question. "If we're going to get through this, there has to be some change this year. I need your help."

Where does my help come from? I can't tell.

"You can't do that," she responds. "You can't just bolt out and leave your phone behind with no way to get ahold of you. We're in this together, don't you understand that? If I don't have you, how am I supposed to manage? You've been gone all day and I had no idea what I should do."

"I know," I acknowledge. "That's *not* okay. I'm sorry for that. Really, I am. I shouldn't have done that."

Under the blanket next to Joanna, I see a tail gently wagging to the left. Sidney hadn't greeted me. Usually she'd meet me at the door with a toy in her mouth or paw at me. But, she had become an expert at sensing when Joanna and I were tense with each other. Years ago, I had abused Sidney and her sister, Romy. Our family healed from that and Sidney had come to trust me again, but she perhaps had the doggy version of post-trauma which led her to hide when she sensed I was upset. I speak for Joanna (and probably Sidney, too) when I say that those days in which my mental health was deteriorating were far sweeter than what we faced now.

"Sidney," I say, "come here baby."

She staggers over.

"Can I have a hug?" I ask her as I bend to my knees and extend my arms in an embrace.

She jumps onto her hind legs and puts her two paws over my shoulders, licking my face. Especially my eyes. They're salty, so she's going to town on them. Sidney has always liked to comfort us when we cry, but it's happened so much lately that I think she's actually gotten a little sick of the responsibility.

"Thank you," I say to Sidney, gently placing her paws back on the ground. Any more licking, and Joanna will know I was crying – though I think she suspects it anyway.

I glance over at the corner of the room, where our Christmas tree stands.

"What's with the tree?" I ask, noting that the lights were off and the skirt was missing.

"I was putting it away," she says. "But then I got distracted by the game."

I look at the TV just in time to see Nick Foles throw a 2-yard touchdown pass with a minute left in the game. Normally I'd care about this game. Like Joanna, I'd be engrossed. Not today.

Instead I'm focused on the dim Christmas tree with no skirt. Without its arbitrary-placed lights, it's dark. And Christmas, despite the way we spruce it up, is an awfully dark holiday, isn't it?

Strip away the lights, and the Christmas story feels like the fuel of nightmares. A family is ostracized because their daughter got pregnant from someone other than her husband. Innumerable children are killed under a systematic massacre targeted against babies, all to find this one child. A family so hated by their government that they have to flee their home and live as refugees for years in an enemy country.

This bastard child – now a grown man – desperately prays for God to spare him from a rancorous death. Undeterred, God abandons him in that moment. All this, for one purpose: so the mother gets to watch her son die one of the grisliest deaths in all of human history.

So many cities put lights on their trees every year. But why? Well, because it's the darkest month of the year. In fact, Christmas happens the same week as the darkest day of the year. And someday, our mourning will turn into joy. But first, there must be mourning.

DOINK. DOINK.

"Can we turn that off?" I plead.

"So, what needs to change?" Joanna asks as she reaches for the remote and turns off the TV.

"I'm done going to church," I declare.

Shadrach lies down at Mommy's feet.

"Okay," Joanna says, trying to be supportive but also understanding that my choice burdens her. "What about me? I just go alone now?"

Could I really do that to her? When we first dated, I'm pretty sure she was only going to church because she knew it's where she could be with me.

"When people wonder where you are," she continued, "what am I supposed to tell them?"

"Honestly, I wish I knew."

Honestly, I wish it mattered to me.

She nods. I figured she had already gathered that, but I was formally acknowledging it now.

"Also, you still have that list? The with all the names of people I want you to pray for, for me?"

4

Such an odd question, one that I didn't even know how to phrase without it being awkward. But she knew exactly what I was referring to: one of the ways we eventually survived my 2014 bout of obsessive-compulsive disorder was to have her literally take a list of people I used to pray for every day, and she would pray for them instead. Bible study and prayer had become the devil's ankle-hold on my life, and having her pray what I would otherwise be praying was a way to mitigate my mental illness from taking over my mind again.

But, this book isn't about my psychological problems. Yes, OCD is a thorn in my side, and I'm convinced God wants me to have it until the day I'm buried. I've begged God to take it from me, but it's mine, it's a suffering I'm intended to have, and I've accepted that. But now? I've got a poison arrow in there, too, and I want answers about who shot it and what it's made of.

"Of course, Nate," she says, her head reflexively jerking back. Even just talking about the fact that she was praying *my* prayers gave me a great deal of anxiety, and she knew I rarely broached the topic at all. "Nate, I pray it every night. *Every* single night."

"You can throw it out."

"What?"

"Toss it, please. Those prayers aren't doing anything for anybody. If anything, God might be using those prayers to heap suffering on the people we're praying for."

"You don't really believe that," she challenges me.

"I don't know," I say. "Just, I think, better safe than sorry. And, I need to mention, I'm going to start going to synagogue."

Really, *synagogues*. Plural.

"Okay," she says, nodding again. "That's okay, but what's the point of that?"

Are you trying to convert, is what she's asking.

"I don't know," I say as I scratch my right wrist, which is still itchy from the now-scabbed tattoo I had gotten in Jerusalem.

She nods once.

"Hey," I said, trying to cash in on an offer she made earlier. "What you asked me before? I have a better answer for you."

"Oh, yeah? Tell me," she perks up, trying to be supportive as ever.

5

"Don't ask me to pray for you."

Obviously, not just "for her," but for anything. Or anyone.

She lowers her eyes to the vinyl tile and nods again, hurt by my request, but respects it. I don't mean to hurt her by it, but I need her to understand that this is important. I mean, it's not like we're praying together anymore anyway. Whatever way we've been praying wasn't fruitful. My prayer life has been a farce, and I've wasted so much time praying prayers that were as beneficial as taking a placebo.

Though, at least a placebo won't kill you.

"Joanna," I try mustering another apology, "I failed you."

"How?" she gently asks, though she could've well responded, *"for which thing?"*

"I was barely a teenager. Open to the idea there's a God, but wasn't sure what I actually believed. And I whispered, *'if You're real, reach into my life and show Yourself.'* And to my surprise, He did. Oh, *how* He did. So I committed. I said, 'okay, use me however You want.' But I didn't know it would be like this. I don't want this, Jo. For either of us. *You* walked into this blindly. And I wish I could take it back: I don't want to be used anymore. Not if it's this."

"You," she says, shaking her head, almost in disappointment, "you put the weight of every problem on your shoulders, and it's not fair to you."

"Well, not everyone gets what's fair," I say. "I think you'd agree with that now."

"Why don't we take a walk?" she suggests, as if I'm a dog who needs cheering up.

"Only if we can bring Romy," I set my demands.

"Fine. We'll bring her," she yields. "But you're bleeding."

I glance at my wrist, which I've been unconsciously rubbing for the past few minutes. It's a blend of dry skin and blood.

The tattoo itself is of the Arabic letter ن. It's the equivalent of the English letter N, which is short for the Arabic Nasrani, which means follower of the Nazarene. Christians' houses in Syria are marked with the letter so extremists will know who to target.

"And, listen," Joanna says, looking down, afraid to look me in the eye.

"What is it?"

6

"I… found your poem," she says, holding up a piece of paper that had a rough draft of something I was working on.

My poem. She makes it seem like she had found a stack of dirty magazines under my side of the bed. Which, if you're wondering, no such stack actually exists. That book's been written and we're not going back there.

"So, I guess you read it then?" I surmise.

"I did. And it's… it's kind of shaking me up a bit," she says, then her eyeballs descend line-by-line as if she may have missed something.

"It's not done," I explain.

"You might need a few punctuation marks, but the heart of it sure seems done."

"Read it."

"I did."

"Read it aloud. Maybe it'll change things."

"I feel stupid doing that."

"Okay, then, nevermind," I say. "It's okay."

"No. If you want me to."

"Hun, don't do it if you don't want to."

"I just feel vulnerable, I guess."

"Okay," I say. "That *is* the point, though, for what it's worth."

She sighs, then takes a deep breath in.

"*The Valley* Rose," she reads with a dash of pompiety. "God spoke, and it's how the mountain calls for *you* now – not *me,* the Valley Rose."

I close my eyes. I can see the words dancing on the page they were writ.

"And it was *my beloved* who was always bound to suffer. The Lord was the One who was so focused on growing His garden that He left us to wither on this side. That God is actually not good. Never again will I think faith is the most important pillar of life. Contrary to my prior beliefs, prayer has no place in the logical man's life. Now I know that it's foolish to say 'God is sovereign.'

"For all of *eternity*," she chokes up and stumbles over the next words, "*I will never... I'll never...*"

This isn't helping anything.

I splinter over to my wife, kiss her on the forehead, and confiscate my poem. "A work in progress," as it were. Judging by her scowl, that doesn't comfort her much, but at least it seems to shore up the dam.

She swallows, then starts citing from memory what I just took away.

"You say '*God is not good*' and '*our suffering is meaningless.*'"

Yes. I do.

"*Come into the valley with me?*" she quotes another line – a declaration – torquing it into a question. "Should I be concerned?"

I need a moment to respond, but there's no tiptoeing here.

"Yeah, I think so."

The tattoo wasn't the only keepsake I brought home from my recent trip to the Holy Land. I also bought a tallit, a Jewish prayer shawl. That tallit, I thought, represented my rich, unblemished faith. But the problem with the color white is that it's quick to reveal infirmities: on mine, the slightest blotch started as a small red trickle, but in a matter of hours, my faith had bled out. My tallit was crimson. My dead faith was on full display for all to scorn.

I bought the tallit on my first day in Jerusalem. But I got the tattoo on my last day as a confirmation of what I believe.

What I am.

Who I am.

Who I believe.

And it's already fading.

"I'm still wrestling," I say. I scratch my wrist so hard that blood rams under my fingernails, and I accidentally rip open the skin over the tattoo that was trying to heal.

"We need to get to the next line," I hush as blood dribbles down to my palm. "We just need God to write us one more line."

NOW WHERE WERE WE?

> "I am a Rose of Sharon,
> a lily of the valleys."
> ~ Song of Songs 2:1, ESV

My unbelief had faded into abaddon.

"You know where I stand," my friend, James Amos, sternly told me at a booth in a burger dive outside of St. Louis. "I believe what you've told me. But don't get a spiritual arrogance about yourself. You've been given a gift from God; that doesn't mean you know God any better than anyone else."

I wanted to be courteous, but wasn't he kind of wrong? Why else would God speak to me individually? But I politely nodded at James, then wiped the residue from the world's worst milkshake off the corner of my lip.

"Your name may be Danger," James continued, "and you might not be able to die, but you can still be paralyzed."

James was wise, and one of few who believed me when I'd recently announced to my friends and family that God spoke into my life, revealing not only who my wife would be, but promising that I wouldn't die before our wedding came to pass. Slightly older than me and exponentially more spiritually mature, James took me under his mentorship when everyone else wrote me off as a nut.

"That's a good point," I told James. "I guess I hadn't thought of that."

A comfortable silence ensued as I dwelled on his insight, but after it began to turn awkward, I realized I needed to tell him one more thing.

"James," I confessed, "I need to admit to you. Something weird happened to me a few early mornings ago. Smack in the middle of a deep sleep, I woke up in a fog and uttered a sentence aloud – as if I was still in a dream, it just rolled off my tongue and I had no idea what I was even saying, so I wrote it down so I'd never forget it: 'Woe is the man who comes before Me, and thinks it best to speak.'"

"Hmm," James contemplated what I just told him. "Well, look, it's wise of you to try to understand the bigger picture of what God is saying to you. But don't lose this bigger picture either: God's call for our life isn't to help us achieve our own dreams, but to achieve His. And if God tells you that you can't die, and then you end up getting paralyzed because you put yourself in dangerous situations, don't go accusing God of violating His promise."

It seemed our theology was finally diverging, because what James was saying was in stark contrast to something else God had told me. James sensed this: I was withholding.

"What aren't you saying?" James leerily prodded me.

"Well," I explained, "there's more in store than what I've told you. But, saying it out loud... I kind of seem... delirious."

"You can trust me," James said. "I may not agree, and I won't roseate that or coddle you when I think you're wrong, but you're not going to say anything that floors me."

"Oh, I know I can trust you," I said with a smile, knowing that I was about to score a snort out of him. "Your name is *literally* two books of the Bible."

"Heh," James smirked. "I know. I'm thinking of changing my middle name to Second Thessalonians."

Instead, it was me who chuckled.

"Let me start by saying that – this thing," I stammered, "what you're about to hear? – I can prove it. It's going to sound like I've lost a hinge or two. But I'll be able to physically prove it to you."

James shifted in his seat.

"I was reading First Samuel," I continued. "About how David became a great conqueror for Israel, and I heard that voice – the same one that told me I wouldn't die until I marry Joanna – the voice told me, 'Nathan, this will be you.' That I am being anointed to have an experience similar to David's. That I – a weak kid with no battle experience – will go to Israel to fight in a battle. To protect people, like David the shepherd."

"By yourself? As a rogue?"

"I'm not sure. I think, most likely, I would be going with the US Army. I'd get attached to Israel."

"Attached? What do you mean?"

"Like, attached to their unit. Their military. The Federation Force. Or whatever they're called."

"Okay, okay," James said while nodding at me. "You're right. You were right all along."

My eyes widened. I didn't expect James to believe a word I said.

"It means a lot that you say that," I told James. "I haven't talked about this..."

"Sorry," James interrupted. "You're right that you're probably nuts. And I don't know how you think you'll prove this, but, you need to know: your wrongness is verifiable."

> "When faith did come,
> it came, I think,
> by way of
> my little paralyzed daughter.
> Her lifeless hands led me;
> I think her tiny feet
> still know beautiful paths."
> - Joyce Kilmer

א

March 14, 2020

> Esther.
> Hey -
> I heard you're under lockdown. You doing okay?

Yeah, I think so.

> It's Danger, btw.

Lol you don't need to introduce yourself. I've had you saved in my phone still.
I still have the Christmas card you sent me a couple years ago on my desk.

> That's amazing! I assumed it never got to you.

(｡^‿^｡)
What about you? Are you safe?

> We'll find out. I'm at O'Hare Airport actually.

Ugh! No way! Right now? Is it a madhouse?

> Like straight out of a bad Michael Bay movie. People getting their temperatures
> taken before boarding, lots of coughing, way too many people in one place. It's
> bad.

Why are you there?

> My dad had a stroke.

Oh my gosh, I'm so sorry!

> I'm actually flying back home to Tulsa now, I've been back in Chicago for a month
> now helping take care of him.

Is he going to be okay?

> We don't know yet. They say the first three months are the most critical to
> recovery, and he only got one month before services were suspended. Time will
> tell.

Hey...

> ?

I just wanted to say, I'm really sorry about what happened.

> ? My dad having a stroke?

No, the other thing.

> Oh. You mean right after Israel.

Yeah. I'm sorry god didn't do what you expected him to do.

> How did you know about that?

You asked me to pray about it. I know you would've reached out again if the
prayers had worked.
Hello?

> Sorry. Yeah. Things didn't work out as planned that night.

We don't need to talk about it. I just wanted you to know that I'm sorry.

> Thanks.

Did you ever finish your study?

ﺍ

<u>October 8, 1967</u>

The white flag sat atop the Bandak household. The war was over, and they'd lost. Four months prior, bodies had piled across the West Bank, 20 Palestinians for every Israeli. A sweeping victory for their enemies, a generational setback for Arabs.

Even still, the Bandaks had never wanted anything to do with the violence in the first place. They'd accepted their defeat: the Palestinians lost, and – yes, life was about to change – but this family had no intentions of resisting the Israeli presence that now swarmed Bethlehem.

"Umi," Abi Bandak addressed his wife, "I hate to say it, but we need to cook something. Everybody's wearied of eating olives and dates."

Umi sighed.

"I know it, too. The kids have been whining for something real to eat."

"You, especially, need to eat," Abi says, then nodded towards her womb. "Of all our problems, I will not allow a malnourished baby to be one of them."

Umi rubbed her belly, then nodded.

"What a curse," Abi lamented, "that we would have all the ingredients to fix a gourmet meal, but can use none of it!"

"It's not a curse. We are blessed beyond measure. Let me go cook some noodles; God will provide the rest for us."

"*The rest*? We already have the food; it is simply safety from Israeli punishment we need."

"Then that is what He will provide, Abi."

12

Yep! Here's a picture of me defending my dissertation.

Lolololol! Business on top, party on bottom! That's going to become so common in the next few months, let me tell you. You really are ahead of your time.
Also....... are those toon squad shorts??

Uh... you need to know that I showed this picture to probably about 100 Americans, and only 1 picked on it being from Space Jam. I can't express to you how proud I am of you right now.

I used to know that movie by heart. Like actually :-) I still own it

Me too! In fact I own 3 copies of it

Why 3?

In case I lose 2

Duh, of course. Silly question.
(⌐‿ ⌐)
I'm assuming your defense went okay then?

Yep. Passed. Graduated last week, actually.

You had a ceremony and everything?

Nope. I paid through the nose for the cap and gown, and then they cancelled all ceremonies indefinitely.

Well that stinks. I'm sorry.

The ceremony was more important to my family than it was for me. I'm more disappointed for them because they really deserved to get something semi-tangible happen for their support.

Umi smiled, which forced Abi into a wide smile too. She glanced at her four children, and they're giggling at the way their mommy is looking at them. Umi always had a way of making everyone feel buoyant, even in the direst circumstances.

Umi gently shut the door, leaving the room and her smile behind her as she tiptoed up the stairs. She wondered if it would be better to clamor so that the Tzahal would know that she's not a threat. After all, no sniper would be clumsy enough to draw that kind of attention to himself. But being so close to the heels of the Six Day War, Umi knew the Tzahal doesn't differentiate between competent snipers and inept ones.

She opted to keep it nimble and snuck into her kitchen. She threw some water in a pot, and while she waited for it to boil, she peeked at the world outside the window. She could see the stairwell that leads up to the famed Milk Grotto, the location that Maryam, Youseph, and Yasue hid after Herod the Great ordered the execution of all male babies in Bethlehem. Now nearly 2000 years later, the Bandaks were finding refuge in its neighboring space, praying for protection from the Tzahal.

Despite the recent rebellion, tourists still visited Bethlehem by the daily, many believing that the Grotto grants fertility to couples who visit and pray for children. Legend has that a drop of the Virgin Maryam's milk fell to the floor while feeding Yasue, consecrating the space into a sanctum that reverses in barrenness. Umi laughed to herself as she considered that maybe her proximity to the Milk Grotto is why she had such success in her own procreation, what with her four children and one on the way.

But Umi's smile was wiped off of her face as she began to hear an offensive noise.

FWAP. FWAP. FWAP. FWAP.

You could just print out your dissertation for them and gift wrap it.

That would be pretty easy to do because I published it through my indie pub. So, not an actual journal.

That's still cool.

Oh, wanted to mention, I've been going to Temple.

For real? You just started going?

No, I was going all last year. Well, not every week. But I was there for a good bulk of Shabbats.

With Joanna?

By myself. Or if it was something special, like Yizkor, I'd bring Romy.

What do you think of Temple?

It's a nice break from Christian culture.

How so?

Like, Jews realize that there's a limitation of what prayer can do. Christians treat prayer like it's a cosmic vending machine in the sky, that the Crafter of the Universe would have His persuasion changed because I put in a few prayer coins and made my selection.

We see in the bible that prayer is a centering thing. We need to remember that we're praying to a god who exists outside of our finite timelines.

Honestly, I don't pray like I used to. When I do, it's somewhat mechanical. Other Christians think they can solve every problem with prayer. Oh, you're dying? Pray that away. Oh, you can't have kids? Pray that away. Oh, you have postnasal drip? Pray that away.

Postnasal drip is really annoying though

Lol.

It's been nice to hear messages from rabbis who don't assume to know God's will. Rabbis ask a lot of questions for you to answer, pastors preach a lot of answers that I've come to question.

One christian told me that christianity answers all the questions that jewdism raised.

I'm sorry.

Lol it wasn't you. And I wasn't upset by it, per se. If christianity were true, it would make sense that it helps conclude what god began.

Well, I guess there could be credence to that angle, at least from a Christian's POV. If you're a Jew, then the Bible starts with paradise and ends with exile. But we Christians start with that garden and go to an even better city. Our Bible is bookended by darkness (Genesis 1), then light (Revelation 22).

So, you really don't see any value in prayer? At all?

Well, Yeshua commanded us to pray. So there's that upfront, and it's a big one. Christians believe God chooses to relate to us as a Father. He wants His children to have real relationship, which requires real conversation and real requests. In Revelation, it's said that prayer is incense. So the less we pray, the less incense in heaven. Even if the writer didn't mean it in a literal sense, and even if there's no practical purpose to prayer, it's an aroma for God, and there's value in that alone.

Umi's heart dropped. She knew the sound.

She froze as the Sikorsky H-34 leveled with her window.

"I'm not a sniper," she muffled to herself, as if the pilot could hear her whisper any better than she could hear herself.

"I'm not a sniper," she yelled at the pilot, waving her arms. "I'm making dinner!"

The chopper remained level with the kitchen, and Umi wondered if her message had been received by the pilot as she hadn't been fired upon yet. But then, she saw the barrels of the affixed guns began to turn.

"I'm not a threat!" she yelled again.

The barrels continued to spin.

Umi threw herself onto the ground as bullets sprayed her kitchen, hitting the pot with such force that it slung onto the floor.

One hand on her belly and one over her head, Umi trembled on the floor until the onslaught ended, the barrels slowed again, and the chopper took off.

"Umi!" Abi roared from downstairs. "Umi! Can you hear me?"

No response.

"Umi! Umi! *Umi!*" he yelled for each step his feet slapped.

Abi burst through the kitchen door, finding his wife in a pool of blood on the floor.

"I'm fine," Umi calls out. "But the baby…"

"Hush, dear. Let's get you to the hospital."

"I can't move," Umi wheezed.

"I will carry you," Abi insisted. "Umi…"

"Abi."

"Hold still."

Well, maybe treat it like you have COVID. You can't taste, but you know you still have to eat, right? Even if you can't enjoy it?

Hey, I'm boarding. Wish me luck. There's a few colicky babies here and a ton of fat guys on the flight, and I have a middle seat.

Well if you're on an American flight, the fat guys were a given. But I do hope you avoid the crying baby.

Babies are always welcome.
Hey, thanks for reaching out.

You did.

But you responded. I appreciate you.
gtg.

"Abi."

"What is it?"

"Abi, the baby."

Abi looked under her skirt and past the pool of blood to find the baby had been delivered to a world so cruel, she had never been given the opportunity to cry as babies ought to do.

The baby lain on the ground, unconscious, choked to death in her own mother's blood.

WARS AND RUMORS OF WARS

> "Better by far to embrace the hard truth
> than a reassuring fable."
> - Carl Sagan

"How can you tell I'm wrong, James?" I asked.

"Well, Mister Danger, first: let's chart this prophecy you think you got from the Almighty: Israel is going to battle, and they'll need you, this American, basically this kid from Babylon, to win the fight?"

"I'm a kid from Zion, not Babylon," I said, "and I told you I can prove it."

"So show me! I'm excited to see it. And I'll believe you if you can prove it. This is me testing the spirits."

"Okay, so I can't prove it today, but I can do it really soon. I was like you at first: in disbelief. So, I needed an affirmation from God about this," I explained, even though it felt like the more I talked, the deeper I was falling into a James-set-trap. "I wanted to have a sign to support my position, something like Gideon's fleece."

"Hmmm," James interrupted me. "Gideon's fleece. Can you tell me what you know of Gideon?"

"Gideon, he, uh, wasn't like a priest of anything, but he was a great man of faith," I said, offering the best Sunday school answer I had at the ready. "He had been called by God to do some big things, but before he acted on the call, he asked God for a sign because he wanted to be responsible about it. He wanted to make sure he wasn't off his rocker."

"That's the takeaway you got?" James probed.

"Sure," I hemmed, more confident than ever that I was being set up to have my answer used against me.

"And what exactly do you remember happened in that story?"

"Well, Gideon gives God two tests. In the first test, Gideon puts out a sheep's fleece onto the ground one night and asks God to miraculously leaven the dew to only collect on the garment, and none on the ground. When Gideon wakes up, the fleece is soaking wet and the ground is dry. But to make sure it wasn't a fluke, Gideon asks God for another sign the following night: he said 'now I want you to make the dew collect on the ground and keep the fleece dry.' So God did that very thing, and when Gideon woke up the next morning, the fleece was bone dry, while the grass was wet. So, Gideon knew that he wasn't insane, that it actually had been God who called him.

James simply looked at me – not smiling, but also not outwardly disagreeing. I had confidence I'd gotten the story right, so I continued on.

"I asked God for my own version of a fleece, so that I don't accidentally go to Israel and find out I was wrong about everything."

"You tested God for a sign, you mean?"

"I asked God for a sign, yes."

"What did you ask for?"

"I asked God to have me shoot a Hawkeye."

"Like, kill a bird?"

"No, not at all. In the Army, when you get a perfect score on weapons qualification, you 'shoot a Hawkeye.' "

"So, the sign is just that you don't miss any targets on your next shooting competition?"

"You make it sound easy. It's actually really, really hard. In the Army, we have to regularly do a weapons qualification. Forty targets pop up, and if you miss 18 of them, you fail. You need 22 or you get flagged. It's a big deal. But if you do better than that, if you shoot 30 to 35, you're a Sharpshooter and you get a badge for it. If you shoot 36 to 39, you're an Expert and you get an even cooler badge. But if you shoot 40 out of 40 targets, well... then you get the snipers begging you to join them while women fall at your feet. It's called shooting a Hawkeye."

"And what's your typical outcome? Have you ever shot a Hawkeye before?"

"No, *definitely* not," I hawed, probably sounding nerdier than a Chess Club novice who just got asked if he'd ever beaten a Grandmaster. "I don't even personally know *anybody* who's ever achieved a Hawkeye. If someone told me they were a Hawkeye, I'd assume they were that same kind of soldier who lies about being in 'Nam, or calls themselves an 'Army Ranger' when they haven't even jumped out of a plane before."

"When is this competition?"

"We only shoot once a year in the Guard, so it's another full 11 months from now."

"And how do you usually shoot?"

"Me, personally? My average for the M-16 is probably around 34 out of 40. This past time last month, I shot 38 out of 40, which was my best ever. It was so good that the snipers started recruiting me to go to sniper school. So, getting a Hawkeye isn't completely out of the realm of possibility."

James drew silence as he contemplated what I said.

"James," I said, "I'm just trying to do the right thing here. I'm trying to be as wise as Gideon."

"*Hmph!*" James said as he cracked a smile. "And you just might be. Who am I to say? But one thing I'm wondering about: why do you feel the need to tell everyone about this?"

"James," I said, "I don't. I don't at all. You're literally the only person I've told about this so far."

"We should keep it that way, I think, until you shoot the Hawkeye."

"But you said you could prove I was wrong. What were you talking about with that?"

"You know what, that's a conversation we can have another time because your ability to shoot the Hawkeye, I think, probably will put the exclamation mark on this a lot better than anything I could tell you."

"I'm going to prove it, don't you worry about that."

"Tell me about Joanne," James said, abruptly changing the subject, almost as if he didn't hear or admire my confidence.

"Joann-*uh*," I corrected him.

"Sorry," he apologized. "Joann*a*."

"Well, she's pretty. She has brown hair, she's the same height as me so I'll need to talk her out of wearing heels..."

"No," he interrupted, shaking his skull so forcibly that his shaggy hair wagged the opposite direction each time his head doublebacked. "Tell me what she thinks about any of this."

"She... doesn't know what to think, I guess? Joanna's a baby saint, James. She's eager to learn about Jesus, but I often wonder if she's just going to church with me just because she gets to spend more time with me. Sure, she's learning by osmosis either way, but I don't know if it's a genuine desire to know God, or to hold my hand on Sunday mornings."

"You've got her smitten enough to do that?" he asked.

"Yes. I explicitly told her from the git that she couldn't fall in love with me, but she didn't listen."

"*Why* would you say that?" James grinned. "That only makes a person want that thing more!"

"Mission: accomplished, then?" I joked. "I don't know. I was coming off an unhealthy relationship and didn't want to deal with anything serious? I wanted to just get to know her more. So I kept talking to her. Quickly but surely, my days consisted of two things: talking with Joanna or wishing I was talking with Joanna. One night, she told me not to be mad, but that she was *falling for me*. And I had to tell her the truth. I told her to go ahead: fall. I'd catch her, because she'd already dropped me."

"*That*..." he paused before blurting, "is some Grade-A romantic comedy barley, right there."

I blushed.

"You and Joanna hadn't even met, though? When you said that to her?"

"Not as an *a*-dult," I said, emphasizing the first letter of "adult" to sound more *muh-toor*. "We only met last weekend. Well, apart from when we went to preschool together."

"And meeting her went as well as you'd hoped, then?"

"It was an instant *connection*," I said, replacing the word "love" with something I'd found was easier for people to swallow. "She's the long-missing thorn to my rose."

It sounded much sweeter in my thoughtbox before it escaped my mouth. Judging by James' stink-eye, it indeed warranted explanation.

"When we were kids: *She* lived on Haw*thorn*. *I* lived on *Rose*wood. Apparently we lived a half-mile from each other growing up, only separated by busy Bernard Drive. We lived so close to each other, we may have even unknowingly walked to 2nd grade together."

Back when walking a mile to school without parental supervision was still a thing that children did.

"But," James clarified, "as kids: you didn't know each other then, though?"

"No. She wasn't in my class. But I wouldn't have wanted to meet her anyway because I'm a germophobe and she had a contagious disease."

"Oh," James said, the blithe in the booth getting sopped up by a pity straw. "I'm sorry. I didn't know that. What disease is it?"

"She's going to kill me for telling you this," I deadpanned, "but she had cooties."

Usually stoic, James smacked his forehead, then laughed in the same tenor as Count von Count.

"It cleared up," I told him amidst his fit. "We're good now."

My tactic worked: whenever I'd feel like I was about to be pushed into defending myself for falling in love with a girl – *woman* – I'd not seen in over a decade, I liked to change the subject.

"So you see my dilemma, then?" I asked James, trying to tug him off Sesame Street and back onto MLK Drive. "I wish Joanna had a clear faithfulness. One apart from my own faith. But maybe? Maybe she might just love *me*."

"But do you love *her*?" asked James, almost as if he still thought this was a romantic comedy and his question would be the turning point in the story where the lead character realizes they love *the thought of their* significant other rather than the significant other.

"James," I said, "I love her more than my words can express. Loving her? It's a glimpse into seeing how God loves me. I've never felt love like this before, and if she were gone tomorrow, I'd never feel love like this again. Do I *love* Joanna? Yes. I love her like it's a sacrament."

"Then, it's not a bad thing that she's willing to go to church with you," James summated. "If nothing else, she's learning about the Gospel by osmosis, and that's worthwhile. Don't push her to believe what you believe. But if she's wanting to go to church and get baptized and lap up the Bible, then great. But be careful: you're a prophet, and if you're wrong, you can damage her even as deeply as you love her. It can be confusing for her. For you. For anyone who reads your story."

"A *prophet?*" I murmured.

"Yes. You're a prophet now, Nathan Danger Geist."

"*Really?* You believe I'm a *prophet?*" I crooned, more amazed than if Spider-Man had just dubbed me a superhero.

"Sure," James exhaled. "Of course you are, by definition. But the better question is, are you a prophet anointed with the Holy Spirit, or are you a false prophet?"

He was pulling his punches for me. But I didn't need James or anybody else to believe me, because my Hawkeye was going to prove it.

"Three times I was shipwrecked;
a night and a day I was adrift at sea;
on frequent journeys,
in danger from rivers,
danger from robbers,
danger from my own people,
danger from Gentiles,
danger in the city,
danger in the wilderness,
danger at sea,
danger from false brothers."
~ 2 Corinthians 11:25-26, ESV

THE VALLEY ROSE.

God spoke, and it's how
The mountain calls for you now.

ב
March 17, 2020

Did your flight go okay?

Yeah. Glad to get out of Chicago before the COVID hit the fan.

You feel okay?

Jet lag is killing me today. But sure.

...you live in the same time zone as Chicago

Ugh. Caught me. Forgot that you're a connoisseur of American geography.

You don't need an excuse to be dog tired! Especially in times like these.
How's your dad? Now that you're not taking care of him?

Hanging in there. All of his rehab was cancelled

Ooo because the shutdowns

Right. So we have yet to see the consequences (if any) from not having that luxury. But he's in good spirits and can get around without a walker, which is a huge improvement.

I kind of feel like I know him a little because I read your book

You read my book??

Yeah, you gave it to me as a gift just before you left, remember?

Right, but that doesn't mean you actually were going to read it!

Well I did

Thanks! Dad actually has a bigger role in my second memoir

Wait you have more than 1?

I've put out 2. I know, how egotistical.
And I'm working on a third.

What's your book about? The one you're writing.

About my time in Israel, basically. My exposure to the conflict as a neutral observer.

Nobody's neutral in this conflict, fwiw.
Didn't you say you already published your dissertation?

Yes. But that was a bit more... clinical, I guess?

Did you go into depth about the history of the conflict in that one?

Of course. I actually described it in 3 different ways for 3 different types of people.

Israelis, Palestinians, and Americans?

Good guess, but actually for people's different attention spans. One description is 20 pages, one description is one paragraph, and one description is one sentence.
So I guess Boomers, Millennials, and Gen Z?

Ooh - can you share the Millennial version with me?

Really? I could copy and paste the one paragraph here.

Yes please!
(❁╹‿╹)

ב

October 8, 1967

"She won't make it to the hospital," Abi spoke into the phone's mouthpiece. "We need a doctor to come here. Please. Yes, she's alive and conscious and… what? No. The baby? No. The baby isn't breathing; she's dead. My wife will be soon too if you don't send someone. Yes, Tzahal has gone already."

"Abi, is everyone okay downstairs?" Umi asked in a haze, her blood having already dried on the tile.

"Yes, dear Umi. You should know, we have lost the baby."

"Well," Umi said as a tear rolled down her cheek, "let the doctor determine that."

They didn't have to wait long as the doctor was kneeling before them a few minutes later.

"You have not been shot?" the doctor asked as he listened to the stethoscope on Umi's chest.

"No. I was able to drop quickly," she said, then looked at the breathless baby nearby. "Too quick."

"Well, your heart rate is barely above average and your breathing is not as high as I would expect," the doctor said, then placed the stethoscope on the baby. "Let me check the child."

"She is dead," Abi reassured the doctor.

The doctor didn't respond, his bushy eyebrows concealing his eyes. Until he looked up at Abi without tilting his head and let out a soft, "hmmm."

"'Hmmm?'" Abi asked.

It's pretty dry, so just try imagining each sentence as if they were floating in space, like the beginning of a Star Wars crawl:

In 1948 during the midst of the aftermath of the Holocaust, the United Nations offered the land of Israel - which was colonized by the British at the time - as a safe haven for Jews. However, this land was concurrently settled by Palestinians who refused to concede the land, resulting in a violent war that same year between the Palestinians and the newly-settled Israelis. The State of Israel quelled the uprising and hundreds of thousands of Palestinians were exiled. In 1967, Palestinians collaborated with nearby Arab nations and launched a strategic offensive to take the land back. The Arab nations ultimately failed and lost even more land in the process. Specifically, Israelis suppressed the offensive in six days and took control of the West Bank, the Gaza Strip, the Golan Heights, and much of the Sinai Peninsula. In the years after the 1967 war, Palestinians conceded to Israelis that they would let them have the land as established by the UN in 1948, but only if they returned the land that they took control of in 1967. Israel refused to willingly hand over the land, citing that the 1948 borders left them tactically vulnerable, as evidenced by the 1967 Palestinian offensive. Since then, Israelis and Palestinians have remained in conflict, with Palestinians organizing sporadic uprisings against Israel, while Israelis build settlements in Palestinian territory. Several peace treaties have been attempted, of which usually include concession of land by Israel and a collective acknowledgement by Palestine of Israel's right to exist. Exactly zero of these treaties have worked.

You passed with that?

I mean, the study wasn't about the conflict itself, so we didn't really get into these particulars much. But it's not good?

It's a bit biased. From the terminology to the geography to the underlying worldview, it's not a window. It's a projection.

Well then. Perhaps it's good that you weren't part of the committee?

I mean, there's nothing glaringly wrong, it's just clearly written by an American.

Well, I suppose I can live with that much. What would you have changed?

well, palestinians are Jordanians in origin, with no more land rights to Israel than jews.
And maybe it's a bit fringe for the paragraph, but the "pay for slay" palestinian program should be mentioned for sure. Did you mention that in your dissertation?

Actually, no.

Pay-for-slay?? Technically called the "Martyrs Fund" in Palestine. It's where if you kill at least 70 jews, the Palestinian Authority will pay your family thousands of dollars per month after you're martyred. A stipend for terror.

It's not that I didn't know what it was, it's just that my dissertation wasn't about the conflict as much as it was about how trauma affects those within the conflict. You of all people were privy to that fact.

Honestly it's hard not to see that as relevant to your study. Especially given that the USA helps fund it.

That's absurd. I get the whole "silence is complicity" thing, but I really don't feel like it applies in this situation.

No. I mean actively. Literally. The US has dropped something like $5 billion to the Palestinians in foreign aid. And Palestinians use a big chunk of that to support pay-for-slay. Just fact.

"The child is not gone," the doctor explained.

Abi's eyes widened and Umi's face turned from agony to joy.

"But," the doctor tempered their excitement, "she will be dead soon. Much of this blood is her own. Her soul will leave her body within two hours."

"What can we do?" Umi asked.

"We must send for the priest."

"The priest?" Abi questioned.

"If you want her to be allowed into the Catholic cemetery with your ancestors, she needs a Christian Baptism."

"As Yasue Messiah entered the world in this manger," Abi said, gesturing his arm to the nearby church that was built upon the spot of Christ's birth, "so our daughter will leave it. We will contact the Church of the Nativity without delay."

I'll need to look into that. I feel like I would've heard more on this.

From who? Your media? Lol.

If anything, I'd say our media is biased towards being pro-Israeli.

You, sir, are dangerously misinformed. When it comes to Israel in western media, there's usually one aim: to stir the pot.
I can prove it. The next time you read an article about Israeli-Palestinian violence, do me a favor and look for a few things.

Okay. So it's like a scavenger hunt now. What should I look for

First, if the perpetrators are jewish and the victims are palestinians, notice that ethnicities are identified. If the perps are pals and the victims are jews, then they use vague terms like "people" or "victims/assailants."
Secondly, when giving context to any attack, most palestinian violence will be omitted or the violence will be vaguely referenced as "incidents" or "tension."
Finally, if the perpetrators are the Israel Defense Forces, they'll ascribe the acts as being committed by "Israel" or the "Israeli government." But if it's Hamas (which governs Gaza Palestine) or the Palestinian Authority (which governs West Bank Palestine), then they'll omit that they're the governing body, or they'll say that not all Palestinians agree with the government's conduct even though Palestinians literally keep voting them in and actively support their violent methods.

Wowee. You've clearly thought about this.

Well yeah. It makes me mad.
Have you ever seen an American outlet report that 9/11 was just retaliation for the USA meddling in the Middle East? Yet American media can't go one single article without bringing up Israeli occupation or mention the most recent IDF killing of a palestinian - even if the palestinian happened to be a terrorist.

That's it?

That's it. Write like that, and, congrats. You can work for the Associated Press.

I'll keep an eye out.

Spread the word.

So you feel like the US is actually anti-Israel?

No, I didn't say that. the US is our greatest ally. But americans lack comprehension. Like, when Israel won the Six Day War, there were american jews marching in protest against Israel's victory. We'd just faced another Holocaust-caliber annihilation from an amassed Arab army, and JEWS held up protest signs. Americans, even jews, are just so easily swayed by the media. When I visit my friends in New York City, sometimes it's hard to find a trace of authentic jewdism.

Let me chew on what you're saying. I need time to process that

That's good, don't ever accept anything at face value, even from me. But, just. Next time you hear about an "IDF raid," watch as Reuters, BBC, or any "credible" news source focuses on IDF killing rather than Israelis dying.

Hey, I need to go feed my kids.

K. Sorry to vent

Don't ever apologize for sharing your reality with me.
Thanks for reaching out.

Sure.
(^△^)

EVER THE SAME

> "Love goes very far beyond the physical person of the beloved.
> It finds its deepest meaning in his spiritual being, his inner self.
> Whether or not he is actually present,
> whether or not he is still alive at all,
> ceases somehow to be of importance."
> - Viktor Frankl

"You will soon be crossing desert sands for a fun vacation," my food court fortune cookie at the mall promised.

"Why'd you open your cookie before the meal?" Joanna pressed me.

You've already been caught! I thought. *Why can't you just be cool about this?*

Normally I wouldn't have opened my cookie first, but I needed to assure myself that I hadn't accidentally given myself the wrong fortune.

"Life is short: eat dessert first?" I cited an adage pithier than anything you might find in one of the cookies, then I changed the subject before she asked any more questions. "You know, this is now the *second* time I've eaten cookies around you."

"What an odd thing to remember," she said, swallowing my misdirection. "But I'll bite. What was the other time?"

"The last week of 2nd grade. Really, just before we moved away from Kilmer. At Mrs. Goff's funeral."

"You were eating cookies at her funeral?"

Rose Mary Goff was the secretary at Joyce Kilmer Elementary. When she suddenly passed away in May of 1995, it was my first brush with death. Not just death, but the realization that, sometimes, life sucks. One of my earliest memories is sitting at the kitchen table with my two brothers as we watched Mom drop the corded phone into her lap and sob at the news she'd just heard on the other end, we three boys unable to do anything or say anything to make it better.

Death became scary. I didn't have clinical obsessive-compulsive disorder quite yet, but you could trace my pathology back to the moment that I saw Mrs. Goff in her casket. I'd seen her, "paid my respects" (whatever that meant), and then sat down in the flooded church. It smelled beautiful, and I hated it: lilies and carnations were engrained in my olfactory as "the scent of death," and in the years since then, the whiff of flowers had become an affront. A woman whose name was *Rose Mary* would ruin flowers for me... but at age eight, the irony was lost on me.

After sitting in the pew, I stared at Mrs. Goff's casket and listened to the words of the sonnet that was being warbled, which seemed to be singing about anybody *other* than Mrs. Goff in that casket. I couldn't see how she was on the breath of dawn or in God's palm, and she didn't appear to have eagle's wings and I saw no shield. It seemed more like her foot dashed against a stone than anything else the hymn was talking about. Why was everyone singing this? Had they not been up to see Mrs. Goff yet, motionless and caked with makeup to conceal how terrifying she probably actually looked? Weren't her eyes glued shut? I heard her lips were stitched closed. Did anybody really mean these words they were singing? Why would they say them if they didn't think they were true?

After the service, I couldn't shake this idea that I *needed* to touch her. I *needed* to touch a dead thing. So I went back to the casket and gently tapped the dank husk that used to be the school secretary. It reeks of Levitical typeface, but the moment the tip of my finger felt the aura from her hand, I felt so unclean. As if a ghost had entered my body. I ran out of the church sanctum, through the narthex, and down the stairs into the refreshment room and I just started eating cookies, as many as I could, guzzling them like they were water but careful not to let my corpse-tainted index finger brush against anything that would be going in my mouth. I never touched "a dead thing" again until the day I said goodbye to my grandpa a couple months after my wedding, and I never entered the viewing room at a wake without first mentally annotating where the refreshments were – just in case. (It's a marvel that I didn't become an obese child after learning that I could self-soothe by eating.)

"They had a few snacks in the basement," I recapped to Joanna. I didn't want to expose her to my chaotic OCD if I could avoid it. Rather than elaborating, I forked my orange dead chicken and shoveled the bird meat into my mouth.

As my new girlfriend slurped her chow mein, I nervously eyed the wrapped fortune cookie at the edge of her tray.

Then she picked it up and examined it.

My heart skipped two beats.

"This reminds me of when I wore a Kimono in kindergarten," she said. "We had that 'Around the World' assembly, and they dolled me up in an authentic Kimono."

"Kimonos aren't Chinese," I rebutted.

"Oh, but fortune cookies aren't, either! They were started by the Japanese. The internment camps during World War II forced a ton of Japanese restaurants to shut down, and Chinese restaurants adopted the dessert."

She set the cookie – and my anxiety – back down.

Joanna and I graduated kindergarten together. It was such an important day that I wore my bow-tie. We also had graduated high school together, on the same day but 35 miles apart. The administration had already put me on notice after I donned a dress to a formal school award ceremony a couple weeks prior, otherwise I'd probably have gone full-rebel and worn a bow-tie then, too.

Life is easier – not necessarily better, but easier – when your spouse comes from the same generational window as you. Joanna was born exactly nine months and two days after me, our gestations nearly overlapping. It was an innate connection that reinforced our bond. Would dog still be "man's best friend" had they not been created out of the same dust on the same day?

There's comfort in the familiar. For Joanna and I, we lived in an acutely specific era where "Be kind, rewind" was essentially an 11th commandment. The coolest comeback you could lob at the unforgiving playground bully was to say, "As if!" There was no better and no worse sound than that of the dial-up connecting to the Internet. And while life as a teenager in the 21st century may indeed be a box of chocolates, no truffle was more prized than having someone to go to prom with.

And I missed it. At least, I missed out on taking Joanna to prom. Both years I was eligible for the big dance, my date ended up leaving with someone else. Not an ideal outcome, but preferable to leaving with the wrong person. Joanna and I both needed a do-over.

As she ripped open the wrapper from her fortune cookie, I feigned disinterest. I wasn't even looking when she snapped the cookie in half. When I finally looked up, her gaze was somewhere between an evil eye and an impassioned grin.

"How did you…" she started but didn't finish.

"What?" I toyed with her. "What you get?"

She glared even harder.

"Tell me! What's it say?" I said, still playing naive.

"Yes," she said.

" 'Yes,' what?" I clarified.

"Yes, I would love to."

I held out my palm and wiggled my fingers to beckon her to hand it over – partially because I was relishing the moment and trying to drag it out, but also because I still somehow felt the need to confirm that she got the right cookie.

She offered the little piece of paper to me.

"*WILL YOU GO TO PROM WITH ME*?" the tiny letters read.

A couple of weeks earlier, Joanna had gotten a notice in the mail:

Love is in the air, so prepare yourself for
A ROMANTIC EVENING
of elegance and memories shared!

Super corny, but the gist was that her – *our* – grade school, Joyce Kilmer Elementary, was putting on a formal dance, and she was invited.

Gentlemen, ask that special someone to accompany you.
Ladies, wait for that special someone to ask you!

The Kilmer Prom.

"Well," I scoffed at her cookie and channeled my inner gentle Englishman, "that's not much of a fortune, innit?"

"How did you do this?" she pouted.

Of course, a magician never reveals his secrets. The mystery was way better than the process. She didn't need to know that the fortune cookie she actually received from the restaurant was smashed to crumbs in my pants pocket right now.

"Why are you looking at me? Ask the fortune cookiers," I said with a smile.

"All right then," she said and shared her own smirk. "You keep your secrets."

I was pretty good at keeping secrets, with one exception: Joanna. She was the secret I couldn't contain, and I'd quickly become a Joanna evangelist for anyone willing to give me the time of day. All I wanted to do was tell people about her and then, in my free time, love her. I wanted to give her flowers. I wanted to give her adventure. I wanted to give her a ring and children and a puppy. I wanted to bewilder her by tweezing out the generic fortune from a cookie and impregnating it with my own slip of paper, even if I had to accidentally destroy 14 cookies before successfully not-cracking the 15th as I implanted a custom-made fortune that would ask her to a silly prom that I fabricated.

We'd only known each other a handful of months, but tweezing a tiny slip of paper from a baked biscuit was the least of what I was willing to do for her. If God asked me to extract one of my ribs for Joanna, I'd joyfully give it up with my heart still interred.

A month after sticking a cookie into my pants, I rolled up to Joanna's home in a chariot: Mom's mini-van, with the middle seats removed so it gave the illusion of a limousine.

I met Joanna at the door. The moment I lamped her, my heart began palpitating faster than a clock lost in a wonderland, the minutehand spinning like it was a pinwheel and midnight striking every couple seconds. She wore a raven-black dress, halter-cut at the knees. Her dress sparkled under the evening sun, as did her rose gold necklace that was adorned with sporadic black sapphires. By the time I slipped a corsage of roses onto her wrist, I think my ticker aged by several months.

Joanna grinned ear-to-ear, then pinned a boutonniere of roses onto my lapel. It was almost as if she'd gotten it from the same shop I got her corsage, the two sets of roses matching the other's blood-red hue.

I linked my arm with hers and escorted her to the limouvan. The chauffeur stepped out, slid the side door open, and declared, "Madame," as he tipped his military captain hat that I'd bought at the Great Lakes post-exchange.

Joanna yelled, "Kyle!" and embraced my friend that I'd contracted (for free) to be our chauffeur.

"Hey, I got an idea, you two," Kyle said and raised a camera, as if I didn't tell him to do it and also supply the camera. "Why don't you smile big? Cheeeeese!"

After a few snaps to capture the moment, Captain Kyle drove us to Lovell's of Lake Forest, the most expensive place I could think of in the area. Jim Lovell had been the commander of Apollo 13, getting his own fancy-pants astronaut movie about a month after Mrs. Goff's funeral. After commanding Apollo 13, he later commanded the star power of Tom Hanks in the movie adaptation of his daring rescue, and now he was commanding a $40 steak at his restaurant.

After our pre-prom dinner swallowed my entire drill duty paycheck, Joanna and I landed at Illinois Beach State Park to watch the sunset over Lake Michigan. Of course, there was nobody else on the beach. Kilmer Prom, party of two.

"You know," I said to Joanna, "I'm starting to wonder if this would've been more romantic if we went somewhere where the sun wasn't setting over a nuclear reactor."

She laughed.

"I don't know, it's kind of alluring in a green-glow, three-headed-fish kind of way," she said, gesturing to the decommissioned nuclear power plant in my hometown across the shore. "*Oh, those poor three-headed fish.*"

"Well, there are plenty more fish in the sea," I said, rubbing her back.

"That's true," she said, then twisted my hips so that I was looking into her eyes, which was one-and-the-same as staring into the ocean. "But you can't go back to clown fish after having a Lovell's salmon."

She gently kissed my cheek, then I pecked her lips.

"You ready?" I asked.

"For...?"

"Prom."

She smiled.

"Yes! But... I can't get over one thing."

Uh oh. We weren't about to break up, were we? *Not on Prom night!*

"Nate, I can piece together how you probably got that fortune into my cookie, and how you swapped it without me noticing. But I need to know how you got it sealed. It was *in a wrapper*. And don't give me that 'let's just not know' junk."

"Okay," I said, rapidly tapping her shoulders in defeat. "If you must know, I bought a box of fortune cookies. One-by-one, I opened them up and put the special prom fortune cookie into the old cookie's wrapper. Then I took Mom's curling iron and cinched it close. It's harder than you think: I went through 40 cookies, 40 wrappers to get it *just* right. But on the last cookie, the very last wrapper before I had to run back out to Jewel and buy another box, I steam-cinched your fortune cookie perfectly. I disguised it as a normal, everyday fortune cookie. And I tossed the others."

With the summer sun now missing, the chilly lake effect wind assumed command. I rubbed Joanna's arms, then clutched her shoulders.

"Because when the perfect comes, the incomplete will disappear."

"You... you... just threw them out?"

"Okay," I smiled, then patted my belly. "I may have had cookies for dinner that night."

"When the perfect comes... the imperfect disappears," she echoed to herself, closing her eyes.

I let go, turned, bent down, and pressed "play" on the boombox.

"Could I have this dance?" I asked, holding my palm out again, wriggling my fingers like I did when I asked to see her fortune.

She took my hand, and we began dancing. The song ended, but we didn't stop dancing. These two Kilmer kids danced through the night, into the morning, we danced into the next semester when she transferred to be closer to me, through my combat deployment, and we kept dancing right into our prophetic wedding night.

> "For I the LORD
> do not change;
> therefore you,
> O children of Jacob,
> are not consumed."
> ~ Malachi 3:6, ESV

THE VALLEY ROSE.

God spoke, and it's how
The mountain calls for you now.
Not me —
The Valley Rose.
And it was my beloved who was always
Bound to suffer.

ג

<u>March 20, 2020</u>

We had our first death.

O no!

55 years old, completely healthy. A Pentecostal pastor of one of the "faith over fear" churches that kept their doors open felt like they could pray away the virus.

Oh nooo, so sorry to hear that :(

There's a chapter in the Bible, Gospel of Mark. Last chapter. It wasn't in the earliest manuscripts - it was a late add, and certainly not written by Mark. But Christians (and Pentecostals in particular) take the verse and run with it, which is really problematic when you consider the chapter is literally telling believers that they can wrangle snakes and not be harmed.

Your bible really says that?

Yep. "They shall take up serpents." But again, there's a fat asterisk next to it. Not that it stops some people from disobeying common sense.

Yikes. That's incredibly... let's just say not smart.

Right. But I'm actually a little annoyed that the pastor died. Certainly annoyed at the church because, like, come on. Believe science. But also annoyed at God.

How is that god's fault?

Idk. Not that He was required to keep them safe. But they did step out in faith and trusted He'd be there to protect them.

God doesn't promise protection from stupid choices.

Even still, it's just annoying. Yes, the pastor had been reckless. But now a family is broken because God refused to move. Makes me question God's goodness.

I feel like you're projecting. Like, this isn't really about the pastor dying.

Of course I'm projecting. But there's an emotional truth here about what it feels like when God abandons. A truth that had many Jews becoming atheists after the Holocaust. And it's not just what happened, it's what isn't happening.

What do you mean by that last bit?

Well, you know how I told you that I moved to Tulsa, Oklahoma?

Yeah

For you, that's all you've ever known me as, an Okie. But for Joanna and me, it's a really new development that's still unfolding. In 2017, we felt called by God to move out of our comfort zone, uproot, leave our family behind, and move to Tulsa. We like some aspects of the city, but it's overall been a miserable, miserable experience moving here.

So you didn't have a plan when you moved?

Joanna had a job lined up, but I didn't. And here we are, years later, and I still don't have anything stable.

I'm not sure god called you to do that.

Lol me neither! at least now i'm not sure.

٣

October 9, 1967

"The child's name?" the priest asked as he dipped his hands into a portable baptismal font.

"Claire," Umi responded, now lying down on her bed. "Claire Ibrahim."

The priest took Claire into his arms, and pressing her against his chest with his left arm, dipped his right hand into the font and sprinkled water over her forehead.

"Claire Ibrahim Bandak, I baptize you in the name of the Father, of the Son, and of the Holy Ghost."

Umi sobbed. Abi comforted. Claire smiled, then breathed – what felt as if was her first actual breath. And suddenly, she began to breathe consistently. Breathe normally.

"This baby isn't going to die," Umi said.

"She's… lost a lot of blood, Father," Abi whispered to the priest, who nodded. "Not every red sea is destined to dry."

"My dear," the priest said as he put his hand on Umi's shoulder and explained, "this has all been a severely overwhelming experience, and it is good that she breathes on her own now, but you should know that this doesn't mean that she is going to live."

Abi covered his mouth with his hands and nodded, then met the priest's gaze.

"Take heart," the priest said, "she will be buried among the first martyrs."

I mean, I dont think god directs people to go move somewhere else. But maybe you can't find a job because Tulsa is so small.

Tulsa really isn't that small.

How big is it?

Tulsa is the second largest city in the 28th most populous state in the 3rd biggest country in the world.

Numbers, guy. Give me a number.

401k. Easy to remember for an American.

Oh okay, that's pretty big. That's actually just a little less than Tel Aviv.

But as it turns out, despite Tulsa's size, there's only a tiny market for anyone with a PhD. Like, someone did a study on this. Tulsa has tons of entry-level jobs and prides itself on entrepreneurs, but it's unprepared to field people with doctorates. Tulsa collectively has the education level for a city half its size. So why would I be called to get a terminal degree and then also called to go to a city that has little appreciation for education?

Again...

Okay, I know your perspective on this. I'm just saying, it feels like another act of faith that just fell flat in the end. I mean, I have to either been wrong about the degree, or wrong about the move, right? On top of it, the culture here in Tulsa drives me nuts.

How so?

It's just.... really, really lazy. Government entities work slower than anywhere else I've ever seen in the country. And they identify major problems going on in the city, and then commission people and organizations to fix those problems without providing any kind of follow-up or accountability later. All lip service.

Example?

Okay, just one example is this animal overpopulation crisis we're dealing with. It's maddening. Not even Afghanistan had the problem this bad. You can go nary a day in Tulsa without seeing an emaciated dog staggering down a winding street, begging for someone to rescue them. And Tulsa has one of the highest euthanasia rates in the country because there are so many backyard breeders and dog fighters needing supply. Stray dogs and cats rampantly maunder all throughout the city. I spent 30+ years of my life in Chicagoland and had never once - no, not once - seen a dead, abandoned dog on the side of the road. But Tulsans don't understand that seeing canine roadkill isn't normal. I've been to several third world countries and even they don't have dead dogs on the side of the road. But Tulsa? I see it about once a month.

And the city hasn't done anything?

The city formally recognized this as a problem, but nothing's changed yet. I'm not sure what measures they've put into place, but the most important ones - enforcing spay/neuter laws and stop backyard breeding - don't get done. People who complain about this on the mayor's social media pages get their comments deleted and then they're blocked, making it looks like everyone just loves the mayor. I once saw a man duct taping his own dog's mouth shut, and the police refused to come out because it's "just a dog issue."

Wow. That's a little messed up

Hearing this, Abi broke down and wept. The priest's pronouncement needed no explanation: Abi knew the "first martyrs" referred to the infants killed by Herod the "Great" when the king ordered the massacre of the innocents. The Grotto of the Holy Innocents was a chapel underneath the Church of the Nativity, adorned with skulls believed to be from those very children who were murdered in search of the Christchild. Of course Claire would not be buried in the cave itself, but the cemetery was in such proximity to the hallowed grotto that it was surely an honor to rest there.

"She will not die," Umi repeated herself. "Do you understand?"

"There is a shop off Hebron," the priest said, ignoring Umi and placing his hand upon Abi's. "I will give you the address. It is a special shop, a woodworking shop which makes baby-sized coffins. I suggest you visit there. Do not tarry."

Abi took all of his children – save for Claire – and fetched the coffin as the priest instructed. He returned home with a small pine crate, but five hours later, the child had not yet died, so he sent again for the doctor. When the doctor arrived, he was met with a rude welcome.

"You fool!" Abi yelled, clutching the doctor's collar. "You said she'd die and it wasn't worth it to bring her to the hospital! We could have saved her with your medical equipment, but now she will die because of you!"

The doctor threw his hands up, knocking off Abi's hand.

"Let me through," the doctor said. "I want to see the girl."

The doctor knelt between the casket and the baby, then pulled out his stethoscope and began his assessment. After a few minutes, the doctor

You know how some cities have hashtags, like #BostonStrong or #AustinWeird or #PhillyLove? Tulsa's is #TulsaLazy.
I think my biggest problem with the lazy culture is the manufactured religiosity.

You mean people are too religious?

No - that's not a problem for me. I mean, Jerusalem is just about my favorite city. Totally good with #JerusalemHoly.
But it's the "fake" religiosity. Like, they have faith only as long as it's convenient. As long as it serves them, like it's an ethnic identity.

Ah. I speak that language. I'm following now.

This might be gruff for me to say about people from my own faith background. But I've found that so many Christians live in a land of comfortable nescience and a false optimism that breaks away when they're confronted with the reality of the cruelty of this world. It's especially rampant in Tulsa, where so many Christians drink from a fountain that's dripping more water than Gospel, and the result is a city that's Christian Lite. Easy-to-swallow, surface-level messages from pastors who probably don't even know the definition of the word hermeneutics.

Nor do I... or most people...

Tulsans are proud to be a part of the "Bible Belt." But nobody addresses the fact that the Bible Belt is also the "belt" of the highest homicide, divorce, poverty, and infant death rates. Oklahoma has the highest domestic abuse rate, and it's not even close! 50% of women report having being abused in this state. So many of the abuse scandals in the Church happen along the Bible Belt, too. Call a church out on this, and they'll dismiss you as being a "spiritual attack" on their reputation. Overgeneralization here, but the problem with the Bible Belt isn't that people who live there use their interpretation of Scripture to inform their worldview, but that they use their worldview to inform their interpretation of Scripture.

Wow. Strong words.

When I was a kid, and I was first afflicted with obsessive-compulsive disorder, I used to hyper-intensify my faith. When I'd write a "t," I'd make sure it looked like a cross. I'd throw the adjective "God-given" in sentences that don't need it. I'd thank God in instances when someone else was clearly the actor of the thing I should be thankful for. I was an ambassador for a Disney-like faith, where everything would work out if you just trust God enough.

You didn't see that stuff back in Chicago?
(Also, what's hermeneutics?)

We saw it, maybe a little bit. Certainly not as prevalently. It's exacerbated here in the Bible belt, and I feel like so many churches share in my brand of OCD. Some pastors are so inauthentic, so lightweight that I find myself actually rooting against some good churches because of how superficial and unsatisfying their doctrines are. I mean, I'm a big Packers fan, but only because I don't have to deal with the shithead fans in Green Bay. Now I'm living in the Green Bay of Christian churches and it's got me rooting for the Bears.

That would be a great point, except everything you just said is gibberish. What do you mean by it?
(Also, last attention grab here for you to explain hermeneutics.)

I'm saying that I'm excited to spend eternity with Christians, but not really interested in wasting a minute of my lifetime with them.

closed his eyes and lowered his head, then asked, "what have you done to this girl?"

"What have *I* done?" Abi said indignantly. "What have *you* done! What have…"

"She is completely healthy," the doctor interrupted Abi.

"What did you say?" asked an incredulous Abi.

"This child: she doesn't need to go to the hospital. She would be the healthiest baby on the wing."

Abi's jaw dropped and he looked over at his wife.

Umi was smiling.

So was her daughter.

Ouch. That's a brutal thing to say. I'd never say that about fellow jews, especially well-meaning ones. Can you give me an example of what you're talking about? Like what's something Christians have done to you personally?

Okay. Here's just one example: Over the years, we've had a lot of Christians tell us that we'll have children. We've had people prophesy to us that we'll be having children and had spiritual healers lay their hands on us, telling us we're healed because "where two or three" agree, then surely the Spirit does too. It was encouraging then, but we were let down each time when it didn't happen. I'm 33. I'm starting to give up hope that we'll ever have children. Even if we got pregnant tomorrow, I'll be 50 years old before my kid's an adult. When our kids are the age I am now, I'll be a fogey. And forget about ever getting to meet my grandchildren.

I'm sorry. This might be hard to hear, but god never promises children to anyone, outside of specific instances in the bible.

Then what's that shit in Psalm 37 about God giving us the desires of our heart? THIS is the desire of my heart. It's super frustrating to ask the same thing over and over and over, not to even get acknowledged.

Not that this is true for your desire for kids, but sometimes the payoff isn't even worth what we ask for, and we find that out in the end.

Well, the payoff would definitely be present in this case. God wouldn't have wired me to want children and then deprive me of children, yet here we are.

God has reason to wire you to want children and then somehow not give you that deepest desire. Just because you're wired for something doesn't mean you'll get it. God is wired to have unity with all his people, and that def doesn't happen.

That's fair. It's just hard. Honestly. We've checked all the boxes of what we "should" be doing from a Christian angle. Just believe you'll have a baby? Done it. Stop caring if you get a baby? Tried it. Commit your baby to God like Hannah did? Been there. Go to the place that Mary divinely conceived Yeshua and pray for a baby? Check.
I wish Christians would stop acting like it's within our own power to decide who has kids. "Prepare for the rain." That's dangerous thinking. We used to hear that phrase a lot. But it's not biblical - you can't have faith in something just because it's what YOU want. God only moves mountains that He wants moved.

Well. If it's any consolation. Abraham was promised a son, and he and Sarah waited for 25 years. Joseph was in slavery and imprisoned for 13 years, Jacob a slave for just as long. Moses was exiled in Midian for 40 years then wandered another 40 years in the wilderness. Isaac was nearly 90 years old before we ever see god say a word to him. God's timing isn't usually what we expect.

Again, fair. Yeshua waited 30+ years to start formal ministry too. It's a good reminder. Thanks.

Speaking of timing: it's almost sundown. Shabbat is about to begin. I need to turn off my phone for the weekend. I promise I'll pick this up again though.

It's not necessary. Just me venting.
Oh. Also, hermeneutics: basically, methods of interpreting Scripture with emotion removed. Used mainly in situations where you're sipping tea with pinky raised.

Oh. Well that's super boring. Tov. Thanks

Shabbat Shalom, my friend.

Shabbat Shalom!

43

July 2006
WHO SINNED, THIS MAN OR HIS PARENTS?

> "The watchmaker works all day,
> and long into the night.
> He pieces things together
> despite his failing sight."
> - Steven Wilson

A month after Kilmer Prom and eight months before my rifle qualifications, I visited Dad's mom, Nana, for the last time before she died. Of course I didn't know this when I saw her – you rarely know that kind of thing, especially given she wasn't even sick then – but such moments have a staying power when you look back on them.

I wasn't blood-related to Nana. Neither was Dad, for that matter. In early childhood, he'd lost both his parents – one to death and one to schizophrenia. After watching his own dad lowered into the ground when he was three and his mom's descent into mental illness immediately following, Dad had a lot of questions about the universe. Fortunately, Dad's new foster mother was an evangelical Christian who had all the answers.

Nana was staunch in her faith. So staunch, in fact, that her zealousness pushed Dad to hate religion and become a faithful critic of the biblical myths that had shaped governmental policy for millennia – at least until William Paley won him over with the renowned Watchmaker Theory in college. After Dad finally entertained the logic that maybe God cared about creation, Nana was finally batting 1.000 with her Christian influence on her foster children. He first converted from atheism to agnosticism, then eventually from agnosticism to teetering dangerously close to a faith that resembled Christianity. But with Nana having moved to Florida, we rarely saw her growing up. So even though I didn't know this was my final encounter with Nana, it still struck me as something special nonetheless.

"Oh, *Ben*, look how big you've gotten!" marveled Nana.

"I'm *Nathan*, Nana," I told her. "Ben had to work today."

"Ben is the youngest," Dad's sister, Jan, explained to Nana. "Nathan is the middle child."

"And what do *you* do?" Nana asked, to which I was at a loss for words.

What do I do? I don't know, I receive money from you in a birthday card every year? Sometimes you accidentally send two sets of checks and I cash them both?

"Nathan is in school," Aunt Jan said, picking up on my inability to answer the question. "And he has a new girlfriend."

For the first time in my life, I didn't blush when someone pointed out that I was dating someone. In fact, I was hoping we could talk some more about this girl.

"Well," I corrected, "not really *new*. We've been dating four months."

44

"Oh," exclaimed Aunt Judy, Dad's older sister, seemingly remembering an important detail. "*Nathan* is in the Marines!"

"Army," I corrected her. "Army Guard."

"*Ohhhh,*" Nana cried out and clapped once, as if someone just told her that her next Bingo card would be on the house. "I'm *so* proud of you," she said, clasping her hands over mine.

Saying *"I'm proud of you"* is the kind of thing that grandmas are just supposed to say even if their grandkid had decided to join the circus as a clown. And I knew that much, but it still galvanized me.

"Look at these muscles," she marveled, squeezing my biceps. "You must be the manliest soldier in your unit."

Now I knew she was patronizing me: I had the muscles of a ferret and the machismo of a petunia. Even still, I swelled with pride as if the accolades had come from my drill sergeant.

"If you're in the service, just trust in the Lord, and you'll be fine," she promised, piling on that corny stuff you find in any Grandma's Handbook of Generic Grandmotherly Things to Say: Grandma Edition that presumably every grandma carries around for reference. So I just politely nodded as she finished her thought.

"So you're going out to Israel then? Well, just be prepared, because when you're over there…", she paused, then looked me intently in the eye before rasping, "*you… will… see… Armageddon.*"

The air escaped my lungs like I'd just undergone an exorcism. *Not* Iraq. *Not* Afghanistan. She singled out Israel, whom the United States has never been involved with militarily. The precise place I was convinced I was getting commissioned for.

And – I hadn't told *anyone* this yet, not even James, not even Joanna, lest they finally see me as a loon – but Nana had just confirmed a final prophecy I'd received. It was as if she knew. As if God told her to say that.

"Yes," I said to Nana. "Thank you."

I smiled at Nana and slightly tipped my head.

I know.

It would be the last thing I'd ever communicate to her.

> "For I heard a cry as of a woman in labor,
> anguish as of one giving birth
> to her first child,
> the cry of the daughter of Zion
> gasping for breath,
> stretching out her hands,
> 'Woe is me!
> I am fainting before murderers.'"
> ~ Jeremiah 4:31, ESV

THE VALLEY ROSE.

God spoke, and it's how
The mountain calls for you now.
Not me –
The Valley Rose,
And it was my beloved who was always
Bound to suffer.
The Lord was the One who was
So focused on growing His garden,
That He left us to wither on this side.
That God is actually not good.

ז

March 23, 2020

(˃ ˂)
it's here.

What's wrong? What's there?

We had our first death. Right after yours, on Shabbat. And I lost my job. They furloughed all of us except for one person to oversee the administrative side of things. I don't have work to go to today and I don't think I'll have a Temple to go to next Shabbat.

You gotta be kidding! I'm so sorry.
What are you going to do for money?

I don't know. Everything happened so fast. But, I mean, we knew it was coming.

That doesn't make it any less.

At least we can confirm it now, neither christians nor jews are spared from this.

Heh. I wish people understood that. I've been volunteering over the past few days at an emergency crisis center to help people with resources during this. It's run by a church and they're asking everyone to wear gloves, and the woman next to me said, "I don't need these gloves. I trust in Jesus."

Oh wow

It just encapsulated everything I'm bitter with about Christian culture.

Yeah that's really bad. Really stupid. specially considering your first death had the same mindset.
Did that pentecostal church stay open even though their pastor died?

No way. They shut the church down and posted a statement urging everyone to take the pandemic seriously.

Well, at least there's that.

When Christians want healing, when they pray in faith, they don't expect for even a millisecond that maybe it'll be the death of them. In fact they feel guilty if they think healing doesn't look exactly like they're expecting. but what if prayer is what ends you? what if the most basic medical procedure leads to death? When I hear people say they trust in God to take care of a sickness, it's only because they've never seen their prayers answered with a mercy kill.

Is all of Tulsa closed now? Does Joanna have a job?

Joanna's work shut down. I mean, still operating, but she's working from home.
We're sharing an office.

How do you synchronize that?

We don't. I'm up working in the middle of the night and she takes the office at 8am, and I nap until the afternoon.

And that gives you enough rest?

No. but I have a philosophy. If you're working fully rested, you're probably doing it wrong.

Hmm. Well at least you're back on Jerusalem time with me!

ع

December 10, 1987

"Abi," 20-year-old Claire asked upon entering her father's factory, "where is Riad's order? He's demanding it. They're saying that we promised it be done today."

"Oh, Riad," Abi chuckled. "You can tell that silly man that I had his order ready for him yesterday, if he really wants to know. His necklace is in the second cabinet, dear, third from the left."

"Thank you," Claire said, patted Abi on the cheek with a kiss, then left the factory and entered the shop, where Riad stood.

"My father sends his kindest regards," Claire said to Riad as she reached into the second cabinet.

"Is that why he sent a woman to do his work?" Riad asked with a smirk.

"He is busy today. And Abi is a good man, dear. He gave me a wonderful childhood. And unlike many of the men in Bethlehem," Claire taunted, "he treats me and my mother with respect."

"But is he an insurgent?" a voice called out from the corner of the room, startling Claire.

A man emerged. He was in a green uniform that bore the Star of David on its sleeve.

"Oh, goodness, I didn't see you standing there," Claire said to the officer, who smiled.

"I'll be on my way," Riad said. "Thank you for crafting this. Tell your father… Laila is going to love this."

True. We do have another room we're not really using so we're considering repurposing that into another office.

That's a great plan. Why don't you just do that?

Eh. We've had a spare room in all 3 of the homes we've had. It's supposed to be a nursery. It even has a children's bookcase with kids' books and movies. And a lot of dust. But it's more or less a room to store our vacuums. But repurposing it into something practical, I think that would kind of feel like we're formally giving up hope that we'll have children. And we're not there yet.

That sucks. Does Joanna have as hard of a time with the infertility issues as you do?

It's way harder on her. Each time a friend or family member announces a pregnancy, she wishes them well and then cries on my shoulder. Last year my brother called me, and I picked up the phone and just said "Congratulations." He said "how'd you know?" I said "why else would you be calling me," but what I really wanted to say was "because everyone gets pregnant except us." And I knew the hardest part for me would be relaying the information to Joanna, because she was really set on making my parents grandparents. And now that's not gonna be us.

So the news crushed her?

Yeah. I mean, we're happy for them. Honestly, we are. But it's just hard. We were visiting Joanna's family last year too, and her brother asked if he could take a moment to show her something. She feigned a smiled and said "of course" and he left the room, and she just started crying because she knew what the announcement was gonna be. I never tell Joanna what she's not allowed to do, but I said to her in that moment, "you can't cry. You can't cry in front of them right now." She nodded and got herself together in a hurry, and her brother came back with the picture of an ultrasound. She cried for an hour after visiting.

How do you feel in those instances?

Dread. Only because I don't know how to make her feel better. Honest, it's usually fine for me. I don't have trouble with pregnancy announcements. What gets me, though, is when friends say off-the-cuff remarks like "be grateful you don't have kids." Why? So we can have a room of vacuums?

Ouch. That's not an appropriate thing to say.

The thing that twists my stomach, though, is when those babies turn into toddlers and then kindergartners and then growing young adults. Seeing pictures of kindergartners graduate? That's just about the hardest. Our kid would be 8 years old if we conceived right away. 3rd grade already! And instead they're not even an embryo.

Have you thought about finding a support group?

A lot of our friends have dealt with infertility, actually. So that's created a sense of camaraderie. We'd talk about our struggles, cry with each other. And then they'd have a pregnancy breakthrough. And they'd be able to move on. Usually, they'd have another kid or two. And that camaraderie would kind of dissipate.

Like... you hold it against them?

No, no, it's not like that. We'd be happy for them, genuinely happy for them. But.

But what?

"What is this shop that you run here?" the officer asked Claire, eyeing Riad as he left.

"Sir, this is my father's shop. We sell Mother of Pearl here."

"Mother of Pearl?"

"Yes," Claire said, handing the officer an iridescent rosary. "As in, nacre. Mollusk shell."

"I see," he rasped while examining the prayer beads. "And what is it that you do exactly? Do you just work here?"

"I just graduated from school."

"High school, then?"

"College."

"What did you study?" the officer scoffed. *"Mother of Pearl?* With a minor in mollusk?"

"Business," Claire wryly responded. "I am *educated*; not an employee here. I'm helping my father manage this shop while I can."

"Very nice. And your father, does he pay his taxes?"

"I... I suppose so. I'm sure he pays what he owes. But sir, if I may say, if he is late on his taxes, it is only because your country has increased the price of our materials."

"Have we?" the officer asked as he raised his eyebrow.

"Yes. I will not be coy: the basic materials cost five times as much here in Bethlehem than they do in Jerusalem. It is destroying our economy. But that being said, we still pay our taxes."

"That is good. And you're sure that your father pays his taxes?"

"I have said so. I have confidence in him, yes."

But nothing. That's it. "Happy, but." That's what Joanna and I call it. Happy, but. And it's a common state of that.

I think I get it.

That's not even the hardest part. The hardest part, the very worst gut-punch? It's when one of our friends has a child and they just so happen to choose the exact name that we had wanted for our kid. I don't know why this is the ultimate nut-pummel for me, but it is. It's probably because we've had names picked out for our kids since before we were married. I've dreamt of my kids like I dreamt of Joanna before I met her. So it's really brutal when a kid with one of the names we've chosen comes into being. It's like showing up to Thanksgiving with a fully prepared turkey and finding out someone else brought one before you.

You have your kids' names picked out?

Yes. My heart has seen my children. I know them. They just don't exist yet.

Well if you don't end up having kids, remember you always have your doghters.

Yes we do. And we're so grateful for them. Past and present.

٩(＾ᵕ＾)۶

speaking of adorable animals, I had a question about your bible. Got a minute?

Yeah but it's gonna cost ya

Okay. Answer my question and I'll give you a dollar.

Unemployed and in need of it! Let's gooooo

So we have a Messianic prophecy in Zechariah 9:9 that says the Messiah rides into Jerusalem on a colt/donkey. I was wondering what yours says, and if you reject this as a prophecy.

No, this is definitely a prophecy about the meshiach. It's a famous and accepted interpretation.

so a literal donkey?

Yes.

Okay I know you didn't put your crystal ball in your purse this morning, but how could this be fulfilled today? The Messiah would almost have to have a cognizance that he's required to do this, just to "check the box" on the prophecy.

The idea is that it's a humble mode of transportation. The donkey is to show his humility.

But I thought the Messiah is supposed to be a conquering king?

He can still be humble too. Even though it's a literal donkey in the prophecy, I think you could get around this by having him show extreme humility in other ways.

So you could go around the barn, you're saying?

around the barn?

o. stupid English phrase. If you and I are standing in front of a barn, and I ask you to approach me, there's no reason for you to think that I meant for you to go around the barn to get to me. I clearly meant, "walk up to me, using the shortest distance possible."

oh. occam's razor. why didnt you simply say that?

Wasn't familiar with that term, I guess. Same principle though?

"And are you sure that your father isn't a rebel?"

"No!"

As the officer tilted his head, Claire added, "I mean, no, he's *not* a rebel."

"I only ask because there are rumblings that an uprising is coming. Three Palestinians were killed in Jabalia a couple days ago. Purely an accident. But the Palestinians in Gaza do not see it as such, and there has been some violence. We don't want that here; not in this city of Bethlehem, the birthplace of one of your greatest prophets."

"Yasue? Yasue is not a prophet," Claire corrected him. "Yasue is the Christ, the Messiah that your people long-awaited."

The officer took a single step back and put one hand on his hip.

"Do you see what you are still holding?" Claire asked the man, who turned his attention to his palm. "That is a cross. I am a Christian."

"The point still stands, we don't want violence here in the West Bank. But they say that there may be an intifada, like the Iraqis and the Egyptians before them. And we know the intifada worked out for them, but I can assure you that you will not have the same result."

"Sir," Claire became stern, "I don't want any part of violence in Bethlehem. Neither does my father. You won. We lost. We're at peace with it."

"And I have peace to hear that," the officer said. "I must be going, but I will report that this house will not be a problem. And we are all grateful for that."

"As are we. We don't want trouble."

THE STAR

Sometimes the shortest path isn't the best.

Fair.

I want my dollar.

I forgot you don't take dollars and I'm out of shekels.

What's currency in an apocalypse anyway

I'll send toilet paper!

Now that I'll take.
I require a 4-ply minimum.

Best I can do is 2-ply, but I'm make sure it hasn't been used.

Know what? Just keep it.

"Do you mind if I take this?" the officer asked, holding up the rosary.

Claire dared not ask why a Jew would want a Christian artifact.

"It is yours," she said.

"Thank you. I will also take this jewelry, please," the officer said as he grabbed three sets of earrings from the counter. "And I thank you for your hospitality."

> "Whoever slaughters an ox is
> like one who slays a man;
> whoever sacrifices a lamb is
> like one who breaks a dog's neck;
> whoever presents a grain offering is
> like one who offers pig's blood;
> whoever offers frankincense is
> like one who blesses an idol.
> Indeed, they have chosen their own ways
> and delighted in their abominations."
> ~ Isaiah 66:3, BSB

I fell in love with a teenager. Which is acceptable, only because I was also a teenager myself at the time. I knew I'd marry her, and if it were up to me, on our wedding night, we'd start trying for children. I wanted to replicate her so badly because there was nobody kinder or more caring, or anyone whose smile could kindle me even on the most bitter of Chicago wintry nights. Not to mention, I had always dreamt of having children. And when we'd have kids, I knew I'd raise that child to not be baptized.

At least not right away. You see, I was still a teenager for a few more months. Which meant, I knew everything there was to know about the universe and its stars, but on my next birthday, I'd lose all that information and become a full-fledged adult. One thing I knew in my teenage wisdom is that children shouldn't be baptized. (Sorry, Catholics and Presbyterians.) How could an infant or toddler adopt the conscious, eternal decision to follow the Lord before they're even capable of sinning against Him? It almost bares less sense than when a Christian proclaims that their 5-year-old son has "accepted Jesus Christ as their personal Lord and Savior." Like, how did that even go down? You're telling me that your child, who is too young to even comprehend the concept of eternity, has taken the ontological angle that a Triune God sent one of His persons to earth to be the propitiation of sins and an everlasting atonement for all mankind? If you want to see an evangelical rip their hair out, explain to them that the Bible instructs us to "repent and believe," not to sprinkle water on your baby's forehead and then have their first words be an invitation for Jesus to come into their heart.

Besides all that, I've never been stirred at an infant baptism, but I've cried at many an adult baptism. Not that the issue is a huge sticking point for me, I just never really grasped why we wouldn't follow the example of Jesus and wait until adulthood to be baptized.

Point being, when I started dating this girl who had become a new Christian, I wasn't in a rush for her to get baptized. I didn't want to push the subject, and I definitely didn't want her to do it for me, or for some ill-perceived idea that it would give our relationship a better chance.

That's not to say I didn't want it. I did, but as much as I wanted her to be baptized, I even more wanted her to *want* baptism. I wanted her to believe that God cares about her. I wanted her to believe that a Messiah had been sent. I wanted to show her that prayer works. Faith *works*. God works.

One night on campus after Joanna transferred to my university, we were moseying home from having dinner at the Union Center. Like a gentleman ought, I was escorting her to her dorm, and I'd trek to my own after.

And there he was: my first opportunity to prove the value of faith.

RIBBIT.

"Oh, no, Nate," Joanna bemoaned, releasing my hand from her grasp and shaking my shoulder. "He's not going to make it!"

I looked at the little side road leading to the cafeteria, and there was this bulbous treefrog in the middle of the street, vociferously advertising his presence.

RIBBIT. RIBBIT, RIBBIT.

So out of place. The nearest tree was about 300 yards away, and Joanna was right: if someone didn't come to his aid, he wasn't going to fare well. He was imminently doomed to splat across the street under the pressure of the first car's wheel that passed by.

Except, I doubt that he'd very well take to the palm of my hand and comfortably go for a ride while I gently restrained him until I could get to the woods. And what if he pooped on me? Or what if he died in my hands while I was holding him *and then I pooped myself?*

Plus, just grabbing our frog buddy and taking care of the issue myself would deny Joanna the chance to see how God works. Here was a golden chance to prove God's goodness, how He cares for even the tiniest sparrow. This situation was never going to make or break whether she believed in God, and on a scale of Genesis 1 to John 3:16, this was going to be a lot closer to planting a seed rather than watching it grow into Eden – *but* it would be one of many miracles we could build on, especially with my Hawkeye that would be happening in less than two weeks. I knew this frog wouldn't get killed for the same reason I'd never seen a dead dog on the side of the road: it just doesn't happen because God wouldn't allow that.

"Just give me a minute, if you can just stay here and keep an eye on him," I instructed Joanna as I raced away. "I'll be right back with one of those to-go bags from the cafeteria. *And be praying.*"

Joanna cupped her hands and prayed, petitioning God to protect drivers from committing frogslaughter.

I was in tip-top shape; in fact, I had just had my physical fitness test with the Army a month ago, and I didn't know it as a runner's breeze flowed through my brown hair, but this was actually the fastest I was ever going to be in my lifetime, and it would be the last time I'd even have enough hair for a breeze to flow through.

I prayed for God to spare the frog as I hotfooted into the Union Center and, in one fluid motion, grabbed a to-go paper bag and spun back out the UC doors. I quickly returned to find Joanna a few feet away from the curb, both of her hands digging into her cheek bones, pulling her eyelids down.

"I wish I didn't hear it splat," she said while frozen and not looking at anybody or anything but straight ahead. "I prayed for him. I prayed for him so hard." She went on to describe how, just as I'd entered the building, a car quickly turned the corner and didn't see her waving them down until it was too late.

I looked into the street and found our friend, with all of his insides... well, not on the inside. His brain was coming out of his nose, and the pool of blood was not under his body but several feet away, implicating that his last breath was probably spent desperately hopping away from where he had actually been rubberstamped. An impetuous final push to cling to a life which he didn't even realize was too far expunged; an agonizing death, just cruel enough to ensure that he had a frog's level of cognizance of what was happening to him and just enough functionality of his organs to feel the full weight of a car on top of him.

The reality is we didn't *need* to pray to save his life. We could've just picked him up, right then and there. But the prayer was an extra safeguard, an act to put a miracle into motion.

Except, no miracle happened. In fact, it almost felt like he died *because* we had been praying for him.

What would it have taken for God to save such an insignificant life? What would it have taken for God to protect Joanna from the echoing splat that engrained in her mind? And, more than anything, what would it have taken God to answer a simple prayer from a young Christian, proving that prayer is, indeed, a rewarded act of faith?

"Is God willing to prevent evil, but not able? Then he is not omnipotent. Is he able, but not willing? Then he is malevolent. Is he both able and willing? Then whence cometh evil? Is he neither able nor willing? Then why call him God?" - Epicurus

Joanna finally dropped her hands from her face, clasped them together as if still in prayer, and then covered her mouth and muffled, "That sound is going to scar me."

Joanna still ended up electing to get baptized. No thanks to prayer.

THE VALLEY ROSE.

God spoke, and it's how
The mountain calls for you now.
Not me –
The Valley Rose.
And it was my beloved who was always
Bound to suffer.
The Lord was the One who was
So focused on growing His garden,
That He left us to wither on this side.
That God is actually not good.

Never again will I think
Faith is the most important pillar of life.

ה

<u>March 31, 2020</u>

Good news Estee!

Don't ever call me that.

Ope. Why not?

Because I'm not an adolescent.

Noted. Sorry.

⊂(◉‿◉)⊃
What's your good news?

The pandemic should be over soon! Some Oklahomans were lobbying for a statewide mask mandate to stop the spread, so our governor declared a day of fasting and prayer to thwart the virus instead!

Lol let me know how that goes ;-)

I feel like this encapsulates my frustration with all things Tulsa. And it makes me sad, because it makes Christians look so.....
I'm not sure the word I'm looking for.

Naive? Idiotic? Irresponsible? Simpletons?

Where's German when you need a word that has all of those things in one? But yeah, you get the gist. Don't pray for what you can solve yourself.

Now that's an idea.
Is there a reason Christians are standing against mask mandates?

Well there's the "faith over fear" component. The idea that we shouldn't live in fear of what the world throws at us. And there are some Christians who believe that wearing a mask is akin to ascribing to the mark of the beast.

Huh? The mark of beast? Is that a lord of the rings reference or something?

No. I haven't seen LOTR, remember? :-) No, the "Mark of the Beast" is a Christian concept that in the end times, everyone in the world will be mandated to wear a "mark of the beast," and if they don't, they'll be persecuted and disallowed from engaging in economic commerce.

So worship the beast or die?

Right, that's the fear. So some Christians believe that mask mandates are actually the mark of the beast, as if kindness is the way of the antichrist. I was in an elevator with a guy - me wearing my mask and him not - and he flipped me off and cussed me out for wearing a mask around him and "believing in all those superstitions."

Youch.

People forget that Christian Church is responsible for founding universities and hospitals. How did the entity that helped human beings understand science so well become so opposed to it?

I actually wasn't aware that that was the case.

Did you know that when plagues hit in the early era, citizens would flee their cities while Christians rushed in to care for the wounded? And they'd die.

○

April 17, 1988

Several months passed since that day the officer visited Abi's shop. The officer's apprehension about an uprising taking place in Bethlehem were realized, and the city had been in upheaval for years. Civil unrest had claimed the lives of dozens of Israelis and hundreds of Palestinians as a long-standing cold tension was finally eclipsed with bloodshed.

But for Claire, the intifada felt as if it was on a separate worldly plain: several months ago, she had married Zuji Anastas, a master mechanic who was well-respected in Bethlehem, a man who knew how to love Claire as her own father had.

"My mother started having children when she was young, too," Claire beamed at Zuji, sitting at her kitchen table.

"Then it's settled," Claire's young husband said. "We can only hope that we will be blessed with many children to come."

"No, Zuji," Claire corrected her new husband. "We can do more than hope: we can pray. God decides who has children, not us."

Zuji put his hand on Claire's shoulder, and as if he had been waiting for the opportunity for such a punchline, said, "It helps that you grew up next to the Milk Grotto."

Claire covered her mouth as if her laughter would dribble down her chin as her tea would, gasping "Oh, dear Zuji!"

KNOCK. KNOCK. **KNOCK.**

"Claire!" a voice outside of the house called for her. "Please open up! It's an emergency!"

Okay. But Christians have done a lot of damage. Like, when you look at the Catholic Church especially.

I won't deny that. But I do think there's a certain unfairness that history likes to remember the Church's gaffes and ignores her contributions. The idea of the Church - when executed well - is such a beautiful, beautiful thing. I hold to the hope that Yeshua, as Messiah, someday makes all things new and will restore what the Church has failed to do.

What's that word you used for Savior the other day? Not Messiah. The other M.

Meshiach?

Yes. Meshiach. I believe Yeshua will establish his role as Meshiach to all mankind when that happens.

Just really hard to even conceive him as the meshiach when you look at his christian offspring.

I get that. All I ask: Please don't throw the Baby Jesus out with the bath water.

Are you still working on your book?

Yep! As we speak. Sitting at the kitchen table, burning the 5pm oil.

What are you writing about?

Funny enough, my 2nd book. I'm trying to bridge the end of that memoir with the beginning of my next one. Offer some semblance of fusion. It's been a struggle. I don't want to rehash what I've already written, but I'm balancing that against the fact that some people might not have read my other 2 stories and need context.

Well you could always just do what the bible does. Give a quick one-sentence recap that provides the context, then when you get tired of repeating what you've already wrote you just say I'm done talking about this, go read my other book.

the Bible does that?

Yeah. Check out 2 Kings 23. Verse 28: "Now the rest of the acts of Josiah and all that he did, are they not written in the Book of the Chronicles of the Kings of Judah?"

Seems solid! Good tip.

Is this going to be your final book?

I plan to keep publishing as long as I'm alive. Maybe even after I'm dead.

That'll be tricky.
So now I wanna know. what's your second book about?

Mainly mental health struggles.

From the war? Like PTSD or something? Is that why you were studying trauma?

No. I've had obsessive-compulsive disorder since I was a kid.
I don't have PTSD from the war.

Well, you're the doctor, so I'll take your word, Dr. Geist.

Don't ever call me that

whut why? Lol

Because if I'm in an airport and someone goes into cardiac arrest and shouts "is there a doctor in the house," and someone says "here's Dr. Geist!", then all I'm going to be able to provide is the information that PhDs are not medical doctors, but that I can do research pretty well, and that PhD is just an acronym for Phake Doctor, and he'll be dead by the time I finish explaining this to him.

Claire's eyes furrowed as she looked at Zuji in desperation, then responded to the voice, "Come in, Abi! It's open!"

"Claire!" Abi barged through the door with Umi and Claire's sister. "It's your brother; he's been arrested."

"No," Zuji gasped, his mouth hanging open.

"Who?" asked Claire. "Which one?"

"Walad."

"What did he do?" asked Claire. "What could he do? He's just a boy."

Indeed, Walad was only 12 years old.

"There were some Palestinian boys," Abi explained. "They were throwing stones at the Tzahal who were on a patrol."

"No! Why were they provoking the Tzahal?"

"Why do boys do anything? They were protesting, I guess. The Tzahal began to chase them, and the boys turned a corner and got away – slipping right past Walad. When the Tzahal turned the corner, they only saw Walad standing there with his backpack; the boys had escaped. So they arrested him."

"Well, did they search him?" Zuji asked. "If he was involved, he would have also had a mask or some dirt on his hands."

"They searched and found nothing," Abi explained. "But do facts matter in these evil times? They needed someone to blame, so they took him."

"Where is he?" Claire stood up. "We can figure out a way."

"We don't even know where he is," Abi said, collapsing in the chair at her kitchen table and holding his head up with two fingers. "And they don't just let visitors in. You know how long the prison lines are;

Lolololol that's so negative!

I actually often wonder how God feels about humans gussying each other up with superficial titles. Like, okay, I did an arbitrary amount of work and the rest of the doctors said "okay he can be a doctor." It's like if there was this society of dogs who like to wear bow-ties, and they wouldn't let this one dog into their group, so the dog ate an arbitrary amount of his own poop and the rest of the bow-tie-wearing dogs said "okay that does it, give him a bow-tie too."

(>‿<) hahahahaha
Well you earned the bow-tie, so you should be okay with being called Dr. Geist.

That's too formal.

Well Dr. Danger, I liked your first book so I have to imagine I'd enjoy your second.

Not necessarily. The second book is the antithesis of my first book. In every way that I might be a good guy in the first book, I'm a bad guy in the second book. If my first book was about Sgt. Geist's Honorable Discharge, then my second book was about Sgt. Geist's Dishonorable Discharge.

O. I dont know that I care to read that

I don't recommend reading it.

You're a terrible marketer of your work

Thanks!

Before reading your first book, I saw that you had great reviews.

Yeah that's because they're all written by my mom under fake names

Lolololol
So what brought on your "mental health struggles?"

Well I wouldn't want to spoil anything
#nospoilers #hashtaginachatbox #turtlepower

Wow your hashtag game is on point

That's the nicest thing anyone has ever said to me #sad

#dontbesad #myhashtagskills are #nogood
#isawabundanceonthetable

#okayrandom

What did I just say? Spell it out

I Saw A Bun Dance On The Table

Maybe. It could've also been I Saw Abundance On The Table. that's the difficulty with ancient Hebrew. It was written, all jammed together with no punctuation. Translators have to make a hard decision about what the sentence was meant to say, where it started and where it ended. but in choosing, you basically make a decision for an entire group of people who can't speak that language. You decide the meaning of the text, which is problematic because most verses can be interpreted a few ways.

Yeah the stakes are definitely high, there.

If you speak english only, then someone has made the decision for you, which is why it's weird to me that christians will stick their heels in the dirt on the meaning of a verse when they haven't even studied the original language. you've got churches entirely centered around the premise that the bun danced on the table. but it's just as likely that i meant abundance.

63

everybody is looking for their loved ones. It would take us three or four days for each prison we try to visit. And he could be at any of the prisons by now."

"So we search for him," Umi chimed in. She was met with blank stares, but the silence merely meant that everyone agreed with her. "It's the only way we'll find him. We split up."

"Yes," Abi broke the silence. "Walad needs us. Before it's too late."

So you think the Bible wasn't meant to have an absolute answer?

Maybe it is, I don't know and I don't know that it matters. But even if the bible is inerrant, your translators certainly are not, so your bible is not.

There's a verse (our Bible, not yours) that says "all Scripture is God-breathed and is useful for teaching"

But what is scripture?

That's my point. I've struggled with this verse in particular. people forget that it says "Scripture is God-breathed" and not "my interpretation is God-breathed."

So. You're really not going to tell me any more about your book?

Okay. Here it is in a nutshell: one terrible choice turned my life upside down, and the full corruption of my character was unveiled.

Wow. What choice did you make? What bad things did you do?

I made a really poor choice on how to use Google, then I started verbally abusing Joanna, and physically abused my dogs. But as for the other events of my mental health struggles, and all I did, are they not written in the book of the chronicles of "Mister Master Exacerbation?"

boom roasted. Well played.

That really is a good technique. Imma use that.

Can you at least tell me this: are you okay now? Like, is the "light" back on?

The light is on in my heart, yes, in large part because of medication. But when I take the meds, the light goes off in my brain. I get foggy. And the meds make me infertile. Which really is regrettable because I was infertile before the meds.

Is there nothing you can do about that?

About the meds or about the infertility?

Well I was talking about the meds but I'm curious about either

I could stop the meds and go on something softer, but then you're risking an OCD relapse, or worse. And that doesn't even take care of the root fertility problem, because like I said, there were other issues - though we may have actually taken care of that problem a couple years ago.

That's intriguing.

I'm not sure you wanna hear that story, tbh.

Tell it

I mean how good of friends are we? It's pretty vulgar

Are you trying to sell it more?

I tell you what. Remind me another time and I'll know you actually do want to hear it. But I gtg fix dinner for Joanna before she gets off work

What's for dinner?

Popcorn

Lol are you serious

Yes. She gets off work in 1 minute and she's in the next room. It's a pandemic.

Go set your table d'hôte

THE FLIGHT OF THE HAWKEYE

> "Like a flower of the grass,
> he will pass away.
> For the sun rises with
> its scorching heat and
> withers the grass;
> its flower falls, and
> its beauty perishes."
> ~ James 1:10-11, ESV

The day of the weapons qualification, I wasn't exactly exuding confidence. My throat was dry, my mind was wandering, and my sniper-steady hands were shaking.

"Geist!" I heard a voice call out behind me. "Have you thought any more about sniper school?"

It was SFC Clark, the platoon sergeant who doubled as the de facto squad leader of the snipers, though the number of snipers in our infantry unit didn't even amount to a full squad.

"Let's see how today goes," I nonchalantly responded. In fact, the reality was that if I were to achieve the Hawkeye, I was likely going to sniper school, perhaps whether I liked it or not.

"I'll be watching ya' out there," he reminded me, as if I needed any more pressure than finding out if the battle of Armageddon was on its way.

SFC Clark, nor anyone else in my unit, would've paid me any attention had I not impressed on qualifications. I was just another chaplain assistant with no infantry background that they were required to let tag along because of the personnel recquisite for each battalion to slot one token chaplain and assistant. But when Uncle Sam got wind that he could convert me from an altar boy to a killer, my military trajectory changed.

Reaction time and target accuracy are odd abilities to sport: you can't add them to your résumé and there's almost no civilian translation for the skillset. But it was this acute combination – and a Drill Sergeant screaming in my ear – that cultivated my expert marksmanship.

Whenever opportunities arose to showcase my (only) skill, I'd seize them. In driver's education, our miserable-man-of-a-teacher assessed each student's ability to avoid an accident with a "reaction time test." We'd have our foot pressed down on a pedal, and when this little Christmas light attached to the contraption shifted from green to red at intermittent intervals, we needed to slap the brake as fast as we could swing our foot over there. We had to do it three times in a row, and our best time had to be under one second.

When Mr. Hansen announced the test, I knew I'd be near top of the class. Not to brag, but I'd always walked away from the Quick Draw minigame in Kirby's Adventure with more lives than I knew what to do with.

Most students were able to consistently achieve a time of three-quarters-of-a-second, though some kids needed all three attempts to pass. My second attempt was better than my first, but both were under 0.4 seconds. On my third attempt, it was like I could smell the green light was about to wane, so I immediately cast my heel onto the brake.

Our crusty teacher shot his eyes towards mine. His icy scowl contradicted his broad eyes, which were peeled so widely that I could see his occluded tear ducts in all their vulnerable glory.

"That was fast," he mumbled to me. "That was *really* fast."

He shifted his gaze to the contraption's stopwatch.

"Zero-point-two-four," he mumbled. "Under a quarter-second. I think that might be the fastest."

I wasn't sure if he meant that it was the fastest reaction time in the entire class or in his entire career or in all of human history, but I savored this rare opportunity that led to *me* getting asked to Homecoming by the girl who sat next to me in class.

While in boot camp a few months later, I was one of the most consistent shooters in the battalion. So after I transferred to the HHC 2-130rd Infantry Battalion, when our commanders finally got a glimpse of what I was capable of on the firing range, I was the only one in the unit who wasn't shocked. And of all the leaders around me, it was SFC Clark who believed I could improve on my score, maybe even achieve every soldiers' dream of shooting a Hawkeye.

Up to the day of qualifications, I'd been careful not to accidentally "achieve a Hawkeye" through other means. If I was having a perfect run on a shooting arcade game, I'd purposely burn a round off to blemish my score. A transfer to the University of Iowa, home of the Hawkeyes? Out of the question! A 25-cent machine that dispensed gumballs with imprints of different Marvel superheroes? Clint Barton, not in my mouth! All so there would be no doubt about it: *this* was the moment that would prove my authenticity.

It was that warm March afternoon in 2007 on a shooting range in Fort Campbell that I got my golden opportunity. But as I clutched my M-16 and stepped up to the vatic firing pit, I was met by the platoon leader.

"Geist, take one of these," Lieutenant Southworth said while handing me a body armor vest.

"We have to wear this while trying to qualify?" I blustered.

"No, I'm giving it to you to use as a Muslim prayer rug," he said, then cackled at his own joke.

I put the vest on. It was way too big; I'm not sure SFC Haney would've even comfortably fit into it. But the bigger problem was that the vest's shoulder straps covered what I call my "sniper mount."

My sniper mount was the secret to my shooting success. It was a sunken spot on my body between my clavicle and my coracoid, a crater where I could wedge the butt of my rifle into my shoulder, absorbing the recoil during each of the 40 shots, which gave me an extra microsecond to find my next target, lock on, and rip away. My sniper mount probably was *supposed* to be filled in with more muscle, but with as scrawny as I was, I had the unique advantage of this body cleft that served as a shotback stabilizer.

They taught soldiers in boot camp not to press their rifles too hard into their bodies, but when I gripped that rifle, I forced its butt so hard into my sniper mount that it might as well have melded with my cartilage. It was the one piece of training that I didn't heed when I was learning how to shoot. The morning after any weapons qualification, I'd spawn what looked like a smashed blueberry across my shoulder. But, the early discovery of my sniper mount led me to becoming one of the most distinguished shooters at basic training. I had hit one less target than the top shooter in the company; one missed shot away from being paraded around graduation as the top marksman in front of thousands.

Having to throw this body armor over my shoulder and try to shoot was like when the optometrist tells you to keep your eyes wide open as they blow air in your oculus.

"This really cramps my style," I told the LT.

"There aren't even any plates in there."

"It's not about the weight, I just can't get a good grip on it."

"Are you suggesting that Big Army made a bad decision?" he teased, then burbled at his own joke again. Normally, when Lieutenant Southworth laughed, it was infectious enough to get the rest of the people around to laugh, too. But today, I wasn't having it.

I stepped into the firing pit. With the few seconds of time I had before qualifications started, I tried to find a substitute place on the body armor that could absorb the recoil like my sniper mount did, but the body armor's puffiness rendered it impossible to find a similar cavity. (This might be why I'd never seen a fat sniper.)

"Soldiers, take your positions," the intercom blared over the firing range. "Soldiers, ready yourself. Soldiers, fire, fire, *fiiire!*"

The first target popped up. I found it, locked on through my ironsights, held my breath, then squeezed the trigger.

The target dropped. One-for-one so far. Thirty-nine more to go.

The second target appeared. A shot, a drop, a breath. Third target cropped up. Shot, drop, breath. Fourth, fifth, tenth targets. Shots, drops, breaths.

Shooters never know for sure if they hit a target or not until they see the final results, but you could get a pretty good idea relative to how quickly a target would drop after you'd discharged a round. And up to this point, I was confident that I'd nailed all ten of my first targets.

The eleventh target popped up. A shot, no drop, no breath.

Why isn't it dropping?

Did I miss it? Or was it one of those dysfunctional targets that gets hit and takes a moment to register that it was hit?

The 11th target dropped – long after my bullet had hit the dirt somewhere down the range – and I had no choice but to shrug it off. The 12th and 13th targets rose and I hit them with ease, but as the 15th target popped up, I began thinking about the 11th target. Why hadn't it dropped? Did I actually miss it?

I shot at the 15th target, but the same thing happened then as it did on the 11th: I thought I'd aimed it perfectly, but the target stayed vertical.

It was the 16th target that I experienced something I rarely experienced: I shot at it, but I *knew* I'd missed. I had squeezed the trigger too hard and it shifted the rifle's muzzle just enough that I knew I had been off.

But the target fell anyway! Surely, if anybody could divinely bend a bullet in mid-air to home in on its target, it was God!

I continued through the flurry of targets, but lost hold of whether or not I was hitting them or no anymore. But then on the 30th target, I fired, and no bullet left the chamber and no recoil hit my shoulder.

Misfire.

I squeezed the trigger again. It wouldn't even click.

I quickly jumped out of my shooting position, dropped the magazine, and found a bullet lodged at a disjointed angle in the chamber. I covered my finger with my shirt, dislodged the bullet, and put in a new magazine. I got back into firing position, knowing that I probably had two targets upright at that point, and hoped that I'd fixed the misfire fast enough that maybe I could knock down the longest-running target as it was retreating, and the bullet could bounce off and hit the freshest-standing one like a prime pinball.

I positioned myself just fast enough to see the target plop back down all by itself.

I hadn't even gotten a round off.

A definite miss.

My heart sank. It was over. I had been late by a half-second.

There was no wiggle room here: I didn't get my Hawkeye. I finished out the final nine rounds, caring little whether or not I hit the targets.

"Ceasefire, ceasefire, *ceasefiiire!*"the intercom roared after the 40th target dropped.

Either God was going to fudge the final results so that it indicated I'd hit all of the targets, or I was a false prophet.

A few minutes later, SFC Clark marched by my firing pit.

"Geist," he said without a hint of enthusiasm. "You shot… 27."

27?

"27?"

"27."

27. My worst ever. I was literally just a few shots away from not even qualifying, something I'd never had to even worry about before.

"Geist, what happened?" SFC Clark asked. It was just a single, innocuous question, but it felt like he was pumping into me.

"This body armor, man. And my rifle misfired. And, *and*…"

It occurred to me that nobody cared to hear my excuses.

"…and the sun was in my eyes, and I have a tummyache," I joked, hiding the fact that I actually wanted to cry. But if there's no crying in baseball, then there's certainly no crying on the firing range.

SFC Clark wasn't amused.

"Wash up. Chow is outside the TOC."

The snipers had no interest in me anymore and there was never another conversation about sending me to sniper school. Which was fair, because I'm not even sure I was qualified enough to go to Stormtrooper school at that point.

I retreated to the headquarters tent to grab an MRE. I even got handed a beefsteak MRE, which was like the Ruth's Chris of MREs, but I wasn't hungry after having my fill of humble pie. During lunch, I bounced from denial (I would've hit a Hawkeye if not for the misfire) to anger (I shouldn't have been forced to wear body armor without any warning) to bargaining (God, give me one more chance). But then I realized that if God had actually intended me to shoot a Hawkeye, then none of those unexpected complications should've mattered. If God was behind this, He would've ensured I hit the Hawkeye.

So I finally settled into depression. I was a false prophet, worthy of death.

> "But though I have wept and fasted,
> wept and prayed,
> Though I have seen my head (grown slightly bald)
> brought in upon a platter,
> I am no prophet — and here's no great matter;
> I have seen the moment of my greatness flicker, and
> I have seen the eternal Footman hold my coat, and snicker,
> And in short, I was afraid."
> - TS Eliot

ו

April 1, 2020

Tell me your story

> Wow you didn't waste any time with that

No and now you're wasting mine

> Wow, you're saucy today. Ok. So several years ago, I got an appointment with a urologist through the VA. Do you know what the VA is?

Not a clue

> Veterans Affairs. It's basically the hospital that vets can go to for health coverage. But the coverage is abysmally lousy. There's a funny saying, that serving in the US military gives you a chance to die for your country, and then using the VA as your medical provider gives you a second chance.

Funny. awful.

> Anyway, I was at the urologist because I was having trouble peeing. Like, I was down to a trickle. I'd be at a public urinal and 3 people would come and go before I'd be done, some of them old geezers. And then I'd have to pee again 20 minutes later anyway.

Yep. That's clearly a problem.

> So they were going to do a cystoscopy, where they go in my urethra with a camera to check out my kidneys and bladder to see what's the deal.

Sounds fun

> Right away in the procedure, they hit a wall. Literally. My urethra was closed up by a stricture, just a pin-sized hole letting any liquids through. Urine and -otherwise. So they said, "we need to cancel this procedure, and reschedule a time we can knock you out and knock down this wall." I said "absolutely not, you knock this thing down right now" because it had taken me months to get this appointment (remember it's the VA), and I knew it would take another 6 months at least to get back in there.

Did he actually listen to you?

> He was really hesitant, but he did it.

SCHNITZEL!

> Yeah, it was the most painful experience of my life. I felt really bad because I yelled the F word at the doctor at one point.

That's like a bris on crack!

> I don't know if you know anything about medical terminology, but he just finished with a French 15, was about to go in with a French 17 when he said he wasn't comfortable going forward with it anymore. Which was fine because I was about to pass out from the pain.

Okay you've earned your honorary Jewdom.

> Rough start to my Jewishness because I went to the bathroom and pissed enough blood to become ceremonially unclean.

Lol but sometimes blood is holy! Animal sacrifices and splattering blood was part of the adornment process in the holy temple.

ז

April 18, 1988

Claire rushed into her parents' home, but tiptoed once she reached the kitchen, sensing the aridity of the room. Umi had tears in her eyes, and Abi squinted at the salt shaker as if it was 100 kilometers away.

"You found him?" Claire sat at the table and whispered to Abi as if sharing a secret.

"Okhti did," Abi said, nodding towards Claire's sister.

Silence ensued. Claire couldn't stand it though, and asked, "where was he?"

"Ktzi'ot," Okhti said. "Just in the Negev."

"He… is well?" asked an apprehensive Claire, knowing full well that she wouldn't like the answer.

"He is not," Okhti responded. "He has been tortured."

"How…" Claire began to ask a question, only to be interrupted by Okhti.

"He is missing his fingernails."

Claire's eyes widened.

"His bed sheets," Okhti continued with candor, "they look as if a thousand roses were crushed and smeared upon them."

Claire asked between her weeping, "What can we do?"

"There is nothing to be done," Abi reasoned. "It is up to him now."

"He won't sign a confession," Okhti explained. "They said they would release him if he would just admit that he was throwing rocks at the Israelis."

Yeah but this wasn't holy blood. This was along the lines of leaking menstrual blood or wandering near a corpse.

ok yeah that's impure lol.
But that worked? You've been able to pee since then?

No. I was able to pee okay for about 6 months, but then the Sarlacc pinched right back up. A year or so later, I did get the full surgery on my turgid urethra, where they knocked me out and they removed all the scar tissue that was responsible for it re-collapsing on itself. Ugly painful recovery. Lots of tubes in places you don't really want tubes.

Lots of tubes? Like, more than one?

Ha. Okay. ONE tube. Just... felt like more than one, I guess. But the good news I've been able to pee fine since then. Now that that obstacle is gone, it might be that my medicine is the only thing stifling my virility. It's the only variable we haven't messed with in the equation.

But you think it would re-trigger your OCD?

Idk what it would do. I want to try. Jo doesn't think it's worth it. We'll see what happens.

Thanks for sharing that

I hope you can finally sleep at night knowing it.

"So, he does that thing!" Claire insisted, as if Walad could hear her.

"He won't; I tried," Okhti said. "He prefers being tortured than to lie about this. I told him, 'Stop being so proud,' and he said it wasn't about pride, that it was about justice. That it would be wrong for him to admit to something he didn't do."

"So what can we do?" Claire asked again.

"There is nothing we can do," Abi said with a twinge of anger. "God has laid out the path for Walad. He will be imprisoned, his heel finding its place in the footprints of the prophets and the apostles."

"Maybe after the insurgency is over, they will release him," Umi said, trying to add an optimistic quality to the conversation.

"Maybe," Abi said, nodding his head.

> "From the day that the Holy Temple was destroyed,
> prophecy was taken away from the prophets
> and given to fools and children."
> - Rabbi Yohanan ben Zakkai

"My name's not Danger," I said, looking out over the pond.

James didn't respond. He'd taken me to what he referred to as his "place of prayer," an off-the-beaten-path woody peninsula that overlooked one of the campus ponds. Below, the pond itself was saturated with geese. Angry, angry geese. Campus students and the angry geese were gridlocked in a perpetual tribal war that reached its boiling point every year when the migrating geese returned to campus to reclaim their land. Like clockwork every spring, the campus would turn into a scene out of *West Side Story*, if you just replace the Sharks with the Geese.

This year, there was an extra outlet for students' grievances about the geese: a new phenomenon called "social media" had erupted, and there was a tribal war in itself between the different platforms. MySpace had been king, but "The Facebook" was steadily taking ground among college students around the country. This was true for our campus, too, as it was The Facebook – not MySpace – that allowed you to become members of imaginary clubs like "I hate the SIUE geese," "my shoe got goose poop on it," or "I saw Shane Ryan kick that goose 11 feet." (That last one was built on integrity, and you were only supposed to join if you were among the elite group of students who indeed did see Shane Ryan kick that goose 11 feet.)

James's place of prayer was somehow a refuge from the geese, who somehow hadn't claimed the peninsula above the pond. But more importantly, the spot was a refuge from the troubles of the world. I'd never seen another human being anywhere near James's spot.

"I said, my name's not 'Danger' after all."

"I heard you," he entertained me. "If it's not Danger, then what is it now?"

"Ichabod," I said. "It's Ichabod. I was reading the first book of Samuel, and this lady gave birth to a son the same day that the Ark of the Covenant was captured by Israel's enemies. And she named her son Ichabod. It's Hebrew for 'the glory has left Israel.' I connect with that."

"Alright, Ichabod. So you got this prophecy wrong. Where do you go from here?"

"I don't know," I admitted. "If I got this wrong, then it means maybe I've got a lot more wrong. Maybe God didn't plan for me to marry Joanna after all."

"So it's time to break up with your girlfriend because God didn't operate how you expected Him to?"

"I didn't say that," I said, a little roused by the insinuation.

"I'm sorry the Hawkeye didn't happen. But I think, also, you have to ask yourself: *for what purpose was God sending me to Israel for?*"

"I should tell you something," I reluctantly admitted to James. "I didn't tell you about it, but God told me *why* I was being sent."

James stared at me, beckoning me to continue. He knew that if I thought it was too outlandish for him to believe, then what I had to say next must have really been a doozy on the screwball scale.

"I'd been reading my Bible when I came across a verse that was in two places: the Jewish Bible and the Christian Bible. Old Testament and New. Isaiah 59 and Romans 11. And it just hit me upsides: 'the deliverer will come from Zion; he will turn godlessness away from Jacob.'"

"Right," James followed. "Verses about the Messiah. About Jesus."

Except – and, again, I wasn't about to bounce this part off of James – but what if a pictorial prophecy could have a third layer to it? A prophecy about something that about to literally happen in time and space, and then it also being a Messianic prophecy... and then it was also a prophecy about the end times, Christ's second coming?

If there's one thing my former-atheist now-reluctant-Christian father taught me about the Bible, it's to not cherry-pick verses without understanding the context of what was originally intended. And, yes, to James' point, these verses were clearly written about the Messiah, but I couldn't help pick up on the fact that I was literally from a city named Zion and my Hawkeye was about to prove that I was going to be physically sent to Jacob – that is, Israel.

"So, that verse weighed on me for a few days," I dumbed it down, unable to confess the bonkers interpretation I had had about it. "And then I found out about Gog and Magog."

"I know Gog and Magog," James said, a little less taken aback than I anticipated. "Walk me through this. What does that have to do with anything?"

"Well, late one night," I confided in James, "I felt an overwhelming direction to read a specific verse."

"What verse?" he asked.

"Revelation 20:8. It says something about..."

" 'Satan will be released from his prison'," James quoted Revelation 20, reading from an ESV translation that somehow had materialized in his hands. I didn't even see where it came from: he hadn't been holding anything in his hands prior to that, and I'm not sure where he hid it on his body, given he was wearing tight blue jeans and a white tee. I shouldn't have been surprised that James was concealing and carrying a Bible, yet I was. " 'He'll come out to deceive the nations that are at the four corners of the earth, Gog and Magog, to gather them for battle.' "

" 'And in number they shall be like the sand on the seashore,' " I said, reciting the rest from memory. "That's the one. James, the reason I was being sent to Israel was to fight in the Battle of Gog and Magog, the final unfulfilled prophecy in both the Jewish Bible and the Christian Bible, the battle that would bring on Armageddon."

"You thought that you'd been anointed to be a soldier in the battle of Armageddon, to be an instrument in God's orchestration of this final unfulfilled prophecy?" James had asked his question politely, but I could sense the vexation in his word choice.

"I... I did. I actually thought that. Yes. I thought that He knew I was doubting my purpose. I thought that God sent me this verse to remind me that Satan was the 'father of lies,' that the devil would try to deceive me and make me doubt my purpose, that God had a special plan for me, that I needed to have faith..." I spilled my guts like I was sitting in a confessional and James was about to absolve me of my madness. "I believed I'd stand up against Gog and Magog."

"And you understand what that means?" James inquired.

"I do," I said. "Or, at least I think I do. After I 'received' that verse, I did everything I could to understand it. I obsessively researched it like it was my job. I scoured the Bible. And the Internet."

And cereal boxes. And cloud formations. And 8-balls and fortune cookies and errant paint spills, all for the sake of any clues as to this coming battle of Gog and Magog. What fascinated me the most was that all of the Abrahamic religions – Judaism, Christianity, and Islam – believed in this prophecy: "Gog" and "Magog" would stand before Israel as her enemy in an attempt to wipe the promised people from the map. Muslims believe "Gog and Magog" to be the good guys, eradicating the Jews and the scourge of the earth; Christians and Jews believe Israel gets the best of "Gog and Magog," whom have aligned with the antichrist.

"And what did you find?" James asked.

"I'd found that 'Gog' is an individual person – an evil ruler – while 'Magog' is an alliance of several countries. From a potential real-world, political standpoint though? Basically, there will be two big precursors: Russia and Turkey – and maybe Iran and maybe China – will become an alliance to form Magog..."

"...and Damascus is destroyed," James quipped, knowing exactly what I was going to say next.

"You *know* about this?" I gasped.

"Yes, it's the 'Oracle of Damascus' in Isaiah's prophecies. You're regurgitating premillennialism. But do you realize there are multiple theories about this stuff? Amillennialism, postmillennialism, and even sub-sects of premillennialism, for that matter. Damascus being destroyed is the last thing that happens before the battle breaks out, at least, in historic premillennialism: Damascus is destroyed, Jews get blamed, the world turns on Israel. You're a premillennialist."

"And what are you?" I asked.

"Me?" James chuckled. "I'm a panmillennialist."

"What's that?"

James shrugged.

"Someone who thinks it'll all pan out in the end."

"Funny," I said. "Did you make that up?"

"No: there's nothing new under the sun. But you should know, you forgot one big component of premillennialism, regarding Gog and Magog. Israel isn't given some white savior from the western world. Israel stands alone, opposed. The United States is *not* a part of that conflict, not unless they're joining the ranks of Magog. At best, they're isolationists on the sidelines. The United States will abandon support for Israel."

"Any way you cut it, I misread all of this. I really botched this one. I've spent a year studying the end of the world like I thought God told me to, and it's all for nothing."

"Do you know how much of the Bible is about eschatology?" James canvassed me. "There's 66 books in the Bible. How many of those books would you say are specifically about the end times?"

"A ton of them are about the end of the world…"

" 'The end of the world.' You keep saying that. Eschatology isn't 'the end of the world.' The only thing it's the end of is sin. It's more about newness than it is about 'the end.' It's not the end of the world, it's the return of the King. He's only deconstructing so there's room for reconstructing. *But*, I'm sorry. You were about to drive a point and I ruined the train of thought."

"I was just saying, there's several Bible books that talk about the end of… times. Like, Revelation, of course. Ezekiel also talks about that last battle of Gog and Magog. Daniel talks about the antichrist and is about that stuff, too. There's a ton about 'the end' or whatever you want to call it."

"That's three books. Of the 66, you just listed three. I'm not great with math, but I think that's not even 5% total. And honestly, those three books are so much more than just end times prophecy. Eschatology is peppered throughout the Bible, but it's not the main thrust of Scripture. Why do you think God would have you fixate on this one aspect of the Bible?"

"It's what He told me to do, James. How else can I be obedient to His specific plan for my life? Where else would I go to find that?"

"Where else? Ichabod, you want a place to look? Scripture, buddy! The answers that you're looking for? You won't find those by looking within." He pressed his index finger against my chest and said, "The answers aren't in here," and then brandished his Bible again, saying, "they're in *here*. You know that saying, *'the answers are within'*? It's *skubalon*. Why would you look to the most broken thing in this world to get the answers to life's most important questions?"

"So if you were in my shoes, and you so blatantly misread something like this, and you were faced with the indisputable fact you were wrong, what would you do next?"

"First, I'd repent. I'd tell God that I missed the mark. What should you do next? Read what the Bible says about false prophets. It's not good. You can't take this lightly. But at some point – and I can't tell you when that is – but at some point I'd finish my moping and start listening for God's voice again, but I'd trust myself less. I'd trust God more. I'd seek wisdom, which the Bible is filled with. Read Job, Proverbs, Ecclesiastes: they're specifically dedicated to wisdom."

"So," I tried to hang with his lesson, "I shouldn't ever prophesy again? Even if I feel convinced that God wanted me to?"

"I'd certainly be careful about it. Test the spirits more before you do, maybe? I don't know that these specific verses were put on your heart by God. For the sake of argument, let's pretend that He did. Do you think that maybe He sent you this verse to warn you that Satan was trying to deceive you with your belief, rather than your unbelief? What if Satan wasn't trying to get you to doubt this prophecy, but convince you that it was real? To give you this grandiose belief that would set you up for certain disappointment?"

"It's... possible."

"That's what the devil does. He likes to trick you into questioning your purpose in God's plan. For as likely as it is that God laid this heart on your verse, it's just as possible that it was Satan laying this verse on your heart, knowing how you'd interpret it. He also used Bible verses to try to dupe Jesus, too. Or maybe... *just maybe*... there is no explanation other than you just missed a bunch of targets."

I didn't like that last one. It felt meaningless. And I hated the possibility that it was true.

"And keep in mind," James continued, "prophecies are amazing because there's no natural indication that they're going to happen. They're miracles. You shooting a Hawkeye is impressive, but maybe not a miracle. You said you only missed a couple of targets the last time you shot? For you to improve your score by two points, that's probably not a miracle. *Improvement* is the natural trajectory of a skill, right? A prophecy isn't a prophecy if it's likely to happen. That's called a bet. If you struggled to qualify at all; if your eyesight was bad and you had tremors in your hand, and *then* you shot a Hawkeye? *That's* a miracle. If science says you won't ever have children and then your wife gets pregnant? *That's* a miracle. If you made it back to your dorm without seeing a goose? *That's* a miracle. Think: what were the signs that God gave Gideon? That the fleece situation would defy natural law! Gideon couldn't accidentally achieve that himself. That's why it was a miracle."

"So," I reasoned, "be less like David, more like Gideon."

"You need to know something about Gideon," James shook his head with aplomb. "You misread his story. It's not a story about faith, but faithlessness. Asking for the fleece is a permanent mark of embarrassment to Gideon's legacy. Gideon didn't trust God without that sign. He was testing to see if God was actually greater than Baal. Why did Gideon specifically ask God to mess with the weather? Buddy, *Baal was the pagan god of the storm*: he was the one people turned to for rain. When Baal was at full strength, the land was wet; when he was weak, it was a drought. Gideon knew this. Asking for the fleece to be wet and the ground to be dry was testing to see if God could actually prevent Baal from working his pagan magic. When he asked for the reverse to be true, for the fleece to be dry and the ground to be wet, he was testing to see if God was capable of changing the weather on demand – something Baal even struggled to do, despite it being his specialty. Gideon knew the strength of Baal, but didn't yet know God's. He wanted to see God outdo what he'd already seen from Baal, completely ignoring the law in Deuteronomy, chapter six: 'You shall not put the Lord your God to the test.' God was patient with Gideon and his crippling fear. We aren't supposed to emulate Gideon, we're supposed to get away as far as possible from him."

I nodded, then solicited more criticism by asking, "Is this how my 'wrongness was verifiable,' the thing you mentioned before?"

"No, remember, we hadn't talked about any of this stuff. I believe your interpretation of David is what showed your error. Are you familiar with Jerusalem Syndrome?"

"No."

"It's where people go to Jerusalem, become overwhelmed with the religious significance of what they're experiencing, and become convinced that they're the Messiah. Reading the Bible and thinking you're David isn't far off from this, but for some reason, this is a takeaway for a lot of Christians when they read about David. The fact is, we should read the story of David and realize that we're a lot closer to Goliath, a pagan who relies on his own power. Or if you want to pit yourself as a 'good guy,' then, at best, you're one of the Israelites shaking in their sandals while David confronts Goliath. But you're not David. You aren't meant to be a warrior for God; Jesus specifically told his disciples to put away their sword. He said *His Word* would be the sword, not me or you. You don't get to be the hero of the story, here. But you know what? David wasn't the hero of his story, either! God alone is the hero of David's story. God is the only hero in the whole of Jewish Scripture; everyone else has mighty flaws. David is just a picture of the coming Christ. And Christ is the fulfillment of these ancient so-called heroes: Jesus is the better David. He's the better Moses, the better Abraham, the better Isaac, and the better Jacob. God isn't calling you to be David; He's calling you to trust Him. You have the Holy Spirit for discernment, which Gideon and David did not always have access to. We don't need any of that extra drama to trust God. If God wants to send you to a war zone, He's just going to do it, and you need to trust Him whether or not you have your Hawkeye."

"Ha!" I let out a single, loud laugh which cracked on its way out.

"*Ha?*" asked James. "Why'd you honk at me?"

"The last thing you said. It's funny you say that. Last weekend, my infantry unit was notified that we were on the sending list for a likely deployment."

"A deployment? Like, to Iraq?"

"Afghanistan. They're saying that's where most of the attention is going to shift now. Geographically, I'd actually prefer Iraq, to be honest, because then I could accidentally end up in Israel."

"Uh," James was unconvinced. "You could accidentally leave Iraq, cross through Jordan, cut through the West Bank, and end up in Israel?"

"Hey, it's more likely than if I were in Afghanistan. Afghanistan, I'd have to accidentally go through Magog, too."

"That's a lot to take in. How is Joanna handling it?"

"I haven't told her yet. It's kind of hard to find the right words. And it's a long way off: they're saying we won't actually be in Afghanistan until around Christmas next year. And nothing's official yet, anyway. We'll know more later this summer. No need to get her alarmed over rumors of war. But if I do get sent to Afghanistan, it's kind of the exclamation point that I was wrong about Israel. I just kind of assumed that if I globetrotted into Israel, it would be with the Army. So if I'm going to Afghanistan rather than Israel, I'll chalk it up to a failed prophecy: the end is *not* nigh."

"You know..." James trailed off, contemplating his next words carefully. "You know, you don't really need to go hunting down unfulfilled prophecies to figure this out. This isn't *Blue's Clues*. The Bible is already pretty explicit about what Christ's return looks like."

"Oh?"

"When Jesus came the first time, He revealed Himself as the humble servant, but underneath the earthly guise, He was also a conquering king."

"In like a lamb, out like a lion."

> " 'Come now, let us reason together,'
> says the Lord:
> 'Though your sins are like scarlet,
> they shall be as white as snow;
> though they are red like crimson,
> they shall become like wool.' "
> ~ Isaiah 1:18, ESV

"Both. Always both: Lion *and* Lamb. And when He comes back, there is zero confusion and zero ambiguity about what's going on. You don't need to try to get a jump on the battle of Armageddon because, first of all, you can't get a jump on it. But more importantly, there's a reason Armageddon isn't explicitly laid out in a clear timeline, because when you obsess on the wrong thing, you'll miss Jesus. And Jesus is the point."

"But James, there's also a reason that the Bible references end times, too. It's still an important component."

"Okay. But when Armageddon comes, you won't have to go looking for it. Stop trusting your own signs. Trust what Scripture has established. And whether you're in Afghanistan, in the United States, or in Israel, just go and trust God whether or not you get some kind of sign. That's kind of the point, Danger. And hey, I know you feel beat up, but this is important: the Lord *does* speak to you and you can know what He is saying. It's just... woe is the man who stands before God and thinks it best to speak."

James wasn't even 30 years old yet, but I left his private place of prayer feeling like I had talked to a man at least twice my age with at least three times the amount of life experiences. He had enough wisdom to write a book on it. But he was also much closer to graduation than me, and so our lives were about to split in different directions. Looking back, I wish I had seen this. But looking back, I also wish I had been looking forward because not only were James and I about to split in different directions, but so were my feet as I tripped over a branch and nearly stomped onto a goose.

"*Hissssss!*" the goose jeered at me for engaging in the ancestral turf war.

If a man kicks a goose in a forest and no one is around to see it, does it become legendary enough to warrant a Facebook group?

"We're cool, we're cool," I said as I held both of my palms forward in surrender.

James was right: the flight of the Hawkeye had been more likely than a goose-less flight back to my dorm. And neither happened.

It turns out the Army was the better prophet than me, because I did end up going to Afghanistan as they foretold. But as for the events of my deployment, and all I did, are they not written in the book of the chronicles of *I am Danger; I am Prisoner*?

THE VALLEY ROSE.

God spoke, and it's how

The mountain calls for you now.

Not me —

The Valley Rose.

And it was my beloved who was always

Bound to suffer.

The Lord was the One who was

So focused on growing His garden,

That He left us to wither on this side.

That God is actually not good.

Never again will I think

Faith is the most important pillar of life.

Contrary to my prior beliefs,

Prayer has no place in the logical man's life.

ז

April 11, 2020

chag Pesach samech!

Heeeeey, someone's been brushing up on their Hebrew. Thanks, but didn't you hear?

Hear what?

Passover was cancelled this year on account of the plague

Now there's utter irony if I ever heard it

Israel's been hit hard, everyone's Passover plans were toast. It was the first time we saw family over Zoom for the holiday, rather than in person.

Isn't that treif? I thought electronics weren't kosher?

Yeah. Rabbi gave everyone special permission to meet virtually.

Achievement Unlocked: Dystopia Activated

All the wildlife probably think Shabbat finally became permanent

And there's a lot of happy geese who think they won the war

Oh! it's a special day for you, too! Your Black Friday just passed, and tomorrow is Easter.

Good Friday, yes. It's what they call "Holy Saturday," which is that blip of time between Christ's death and resurrection. We overlook it a lot, but Christians today are basically living in Holy Saturday every day.

What do you mean?

Think of the past week as a microcosmic example of the entire history of time. We spent the first days of the week in darkness, without a Messiah. Then Holy Thursday came, where He appeared, and then Good Friday, when He was snuffed out. If Good Friday is Christ's time on earth, then Resurrection Sunday is where He rises and restores all things and establishes His throne forever. But that's not where we live today. You and I live in Saturday. Christ came to be the light, which means the light we see, it's not even in our world anymore. The light came from a star that is now dead, and it'll fizzle if we don't carry it forward. So Holy Saturday is all about living in that tension. between the star and the light. And for a Christian, until Yeshua returns, every day is Holy Saturday.

That's... poetic. Vivid.

You'd like the Gospel of John then.

I highly doubt that to be the case.
How's quarantine? Has Oklahoma been hit bad?

Not yet, not like it is in New York anyway. A few dozen deaths at this point. But our city is about to close down completely. All it takes is one freier who doesn't believe in the virus to spread it.

Yeah we've closed down everything, everything from schools to the gyms and now even the airports

Yeah but did you see how I nonchalantly used freier in a sentence

Lol yes. Good job

Thanks. And that it was an impressive effort and you're proud of me?

V

<u>March 4, 1990</u>

"I love you," Claire cooed at her baby. "Yes, I do, dear."

"Not so long ago," Abi said with a smile, "I was cooing at you the way you're cooing at Ebnahty."

"What a wonderful legacy you've imprinted on the world," Claire told Abi. "Your name will be remembered for generations now."

"I don't need history to remember me," Abi said, "so long as you do."

"Abi," Claire's sister, Okhti, interrupted, "there is a young man wandering towards our house."

"Oh," Abi replied, still only interested in Ebnahty.

"He looks filthy. His clothes don't fit. And he's coming right towards us."

Abi jumped from his chair to investigate.

"What is that man doing?" Abi asked as he looked out the window. "He looks drunk. Far be it from me to allow any more trouble to befall this household. Okhti, shoo him away."

As Okhti approached the man, Umi, Abi, and Claire plastered their faces against the window in a perfect line.

"Abi, breathe softer!" Umi demanded.

Abi peeled his cheek away and wiped the condensation that had fogged the glass as Okhti approached the man. After a terse exchange, Okhti threw her arms around the man and began to weep.

"What has that man done to her?" Abi asked, then jettisoned to Okhti. Claire followed after handing Ebnahty to Umi.

For sure.
On an unrelated note, I have good news.
Or bad, depending how you look at it.

Oh?

I read your second book

Uh oh. Well that was super fast

Some benefits to quarantine I guess.

Afraid to ask, what did you think

You have the ugliest book cover in the history of book covers.

What did you think of the book though

I think that it bears repeating, that *thing* on your cover is haunting. And having him hold that game remote like it's a weapon? So rogue.

Content, friend. what about the content

I liked the book. I hated you.

Par for the course

But sometimes I was cheering for you when I shouldn't have been, like when you were speeding away from the police. I wanted you to succeed, but you were such a terror. Total unmensch.

Unmensch? That's gibberish to me.

Have you heard 'mensch' before?

I think?

Just like, "man." Short version of menschlich.

Menschlich? I think that's gotta be my new favorite word.

What was your favorite word before that?

Alanthicke.

That's not a word. That's a name.

Right but it just rolls off your tongue.

When you were in Israel, I couldn't tell you had OCD

That's because I'm heavily medicated and I've mastered hiding it for the most part. My OCD usually comes after a highly stressful situation, it'll linger for a few hours and then I'll be fine the next day. Like when I tried going to Israel and got brought into the interrogation room in Milan, my OCD acted up after that for a bit. But I've had OCD so long and learned to manage it that now I have Obsessive-Compulsive Order

You haven't hurt your dogs since?

No

My OCD has told me to hurt Sidney and Romy but I never did it again.

Not once?

Never. Instead I'd go up to Sidney - or especially Romy, because she got the brunt of my venom - and I'd whisper, "you reveal God's goodness." To this day, I think of her forgiveness and it makes me feel a little better about who God is.

(˘ _ ˘)

"What is going on here?" Abi asked as Okhti continued to hold the man in an embrace.

"Abi," the young man crooned. "Do you not recognize your own son?"

"Walad!" Abi cried as he tossed his arms around both Walad and Okhti.

"Brother," a stunned Claire said as she examined Walad. He had gone from pre- to post-pubescent, now tall and lanky with a deep voice. He had cut the sides of his pants so he could fit into them, and his shirt was too short to cover his belly. It was the same clothes he had been arrested in.

"How did you…"

"They released me this week. I hitchhiked across the Negev Desert. It's not so tough for people to have pity on you when your hands are covered in bandages."

Walad unwrapped his coral-stained dressing and revealed that he no longer had fingernails on either hand.

"They will grow back," Abi enthused. "Six months from now, all will be restored – including those nails. Come, let's get you something to eat and some new clothes. Let's celebrate! We are a family again!"

Yes, they were a family again. But the family unraveled before Walad had his fingernails back.

It's funny. In that book you read, I talk about my fears and why I think the best thing for my family is that I exit the stage. I talk about my fear that nobody will ever hire me again. That something bad will happen to my family if I stay alive. That Joanna might never get to have children as long as she stays with me. And everything - all that I've feared might come true - has come true.

How are you and Joanna now that all the stuff in the book has settled?

Relationship is stronger than ever. A lot of good change came from what happened - we don't have any secrets anymore. None. She even knows that I know how to wink

Huh? She knows you wink?

So when we were dating, I lied to her and said I didn't know how to wink because I thought it was so cute when she'd try to teach me, and she thought it was so cute that I couldn't do it. So I kept the lie going. At least until those events unfolded and then I told her the truth: I always knew how to wink, all 8 years we had been together at that point. And we don't keep any secrets anymore.

I don't know if that's adorable or sociopathic.

Does it gotta be one or the other? Can't we just live in the Holy Saturday tension?

Deep. I think.
Do christians do anything for holy saturday? Like special prayers or whatever?

Not usually. And I probably wouldn't pray anyway, even if it was a thing.

Do you not believe in praying anymore?

Idk. I want to. I wish I believed in prayer. But I don't. What's the point of communicating with God if He's just going to do whatever His plan was from the start?

So you've stopped praying altogether?

I pray a little. Definitely not to the extent that I had been praying before.

All because god didn't do what you wanted him to?

It's deeper than that. First off, we're not talking about some trivial, passing desire I mentioned. God failed to act on the two prayers I've prayed for years upon years.

Which were...?

For us to have children. And we could've coped without that if He at least answered the other prayer: health for our family. I've prayed for my family every day, multiple times a day, specifically for their health and happiness. As long as I still had that much, then God was good. And He delivered - we were rarely sick and we continued to have peace in our days. But then came that fucking, miserable day in December 2018. And it wasn't that she suddenly got sick and died, which would've been out of my control. No, I killed my own doghter, my completely healthy baby.

I don't know what else to say, I'm sorry.

I don't know what else I could say either. But there's you answer. That's why I don't pray and why I don't trust God. God allowed me to kill Romy.

(ﻝ ˎ ﻝ)

CHANGE OF JUST A DECADE

> "Every valley shall be raised up,
> every mountain and hill made low;
> the rough ground shall become level,
> the rugged places a plain."
> ~ Isaiah 40:4, NIV

I stood with three fingers pressed against the massive window on the top floor of a skyscraper that sat on the Chicago River, bending my neck to check how far down Dearborn Street I could see.

It was a barren winter night, but I certainly preferred it to the warm summer day a couple years prior when I'd been on the other end of this looking glass, in that *other* skyscraper down the way by Daley Plaza, looking out from *that* institution just before a disciplinary hearing that would result in my expulsion and disbarment from the field. *Somehow* – and surely not of my own doing – I was *restored*, looking out at the beautiful city lights along the dark river.

People rave about "how beautiful" Chicago is during a warm summer day, but I'd always found the city to have far more charm when it was cold, night, and a few flurries shivered across the wind. Besides, "warm summer day," isn't Chicago's natural state: cold and dusky is.

And, the dark proves the light.

I was finally in my first residency for my doctoral program at The Chicago School of Professional Psychology when we were given an hour-long lecture about what standards would need to be met when we wrote our dissertation for the program.

"*Don't* be like the researcher who claims their study is without bias," Dr. Stevens told the lot of us. "*Every* study is biased in some way. Have intellectual honesty."

Cool, I thought to myself as the professor droned on about the issues that future Danger would have to worry when he started his dissertation. *A good lecture to think about in a few years.*

Except, it wasn't "a good lecture to think about in a few years," because for the next 30 minutes, they sat us down and told each of us to concentrate on coming up with a research question to study for our capstone in academia. And *PS*: this is an International Psychology program, so your study can't be about phenomena in the United States.

I had a *half-hour* to choose a topic and a country, which we were then going to flesh out over the next couple days of residency. A *half-hour* to make a choice that would impact my life for years to come.

The topic piece of it came easy: I'd learned a ton about shellshock already, and the academic degree I was working on had a focus in trauma specifically, so the clear natural progression was to study what I was equipped to navigate. But *where to go to research this?*

While nobody in Chicago would approve of this, we can all probably thank the Green Bay Packers for this third memoir.

One year before I shipped off to the Afghan battlefield (or one year after I navigated the goose minefield on campus), I had a class with a kid who was from Wisconsin. (You know. "Cheese. Badgers. Beer.") We shared a fondness for the Packers, and my college campus being in the St. Louis Rams' hood and in the Chicago Bears' home state, it was actually somewhat rare to find another Packers fan in Southern Illinois.

This So-IL Cheesehead (as they're known in "the biz") asked me if I'd ever been to the Packers' home Lambeau Field, and when I said I hadn't, he went on and on about the beauty of the stadium and its rich history that surpassed any other team's stomping grounds. Not only did I feel like I was missing out, I actually felt sheepish about the fact that I hadn't ever been to what is dubbed the "Mecca" of football. Think about the actual city of Mecca: Muslims are *required* to pilgrimage to this holiest city at least once in their lifetime to become a Hajj. It's literally one of the Five Pillars of the Hadith for Muslims, prompting them to come all over the world, even if their flights alone take 40 hours. Me? I grew up three hours from Green Bay.

Granted, football wasn't my religion. And granted, traveling through Milwaukee construction on a Packers home game weekend easily adds 90 minutes to the trip. But still, if a fan cheers for the home team and the athletes don't hear it, are they actually making a sound?

After I came back from Afghanistan, I felt like an empty jar: what once was a beautiful vase bathed in Army green was cracking with fissures. Engrossing myself in American football stopped me from feeling so numb, and piece by piece, the Green Bay Packers glued a man back together. Was my fandom meaningless? Of course. But the art of kintsugi at least had me feeling like I wasn't.

So, on the morning of December 27, 2009, I was home on break from college, had no stringent plans for the day, and a Green Bay home game kickoff was four hours away. I told Joanna it was tempting to grab last-minute tickets and hurry up north to see the game. Then she asked a pivotal question: "why not?"

So Joanna and I saddled up, zipped from Zion to Green Bay, and watched the hometown heroes rout the Seattle Seahawks to clinch a playoff spot.

My all-time favorite player, AJ Hawk, even had one of his nine career interceptions! I got hooked on attending games. For the next decade, I attended at least one away Packers game each year, and even had one on deck in Minneapolis right after I returned to the States from Israel. Because: why not?

Choosing to study trauma for my dissertation was a given, but choosing where to go to study it was a dream come true. As I considered the places I might collect data, I recalled the day that my Packers clinched a spot in the playoffs. I'd gone to Green Bay – not because I necessarily cared to see a live football game – but because it was the birthplace of my beloved team. But there was another place in the world – one far from Wisconsin – that had always called to me. A place that I once believed – and maybe still did, though I'd not thought about it in a long time – that I was destined to sojourn.

If Lambeau Field was the Jerusalem of my secular world, then Israel was the acme of my faith. So when the wheels on the brainstorming wagon stopped 29 minutes later, I found myself proffering my dissertation research question: *How do the faiths of Israelis and Palestinians living in perpetual conflict affect their ability to process the trauma they've endured?*

"That's good," another professor leading the lecture told me. "No, that's *really* good, actually."

He was wrong. I had to adjust the research question about seven times before it was finally approved by my committee. But, the research question at least gave me the on-ramp I needed to visit the most important city in the world. The holiest of lands. The bloodiest of battlegrounds. The crossroads of three of the most prominent belief systems, and the intersection of psychology and religion. *Abraham's nexus*: Jerusalem.

So, I dug my heels in to the ground and my face into the literature, and did all the research on the longstanding Arabic-Israeli Conflict that my pea-brain could handle. From there, I drove to O'Hare to fly to Milan so I could fly to Tel Aviv to bus to Jerusalem.

According to the intercom, the time to fulfill my lifetime calling had arrived.

"Final call for boarding! All sections are welcome to board flight A816 to Tel Aviv. The gate will be closing in five minutes. Final call for boarding to Tel Aviv, A816."

> "There is nothing wrong with the tree dropping its leaves in the autumn.
> There is nothing wrong with the sunset fading away into darkness.
> Evil consists in none of those things.
> Indeed, it is precisely the transience of the good creation
> that serves as a pointer to its larger purpose."
> - N.T. Wright

THE VALLEY ROSE.

God spoke, and it's how

The mountain calls for you now.

Not me –

The Valley Rose.

And it was my beloved who was always

Bound to suffer.

The Lord was the One who was

So focused on growing His garden,

That He left us to wither on this side.

That God is actually not good.

Never again will I think

Faith is the most important pillar of life.

Contrary to my prior beliefs,

Prayer has no place in the logical man's life.

Now I know that it's foolish to say

God is sovereign.

GOD IS SOVEREIGN.

ח

April 14, 2020

Hey, sorry about last time. I didn't mean to hit a sensitive spot.

That wasn't your fault. It feels like most of my conversations find their way to the topic of me killing my dog.

If I can be honest, I don't even know what happened. Not really. You contacted me that night, but I only have a vague understanding of what went on.

I don't really want to talk about it. At least not right now. I've never experienced anything as horrifyingly traumatic as I did in that hospital room.

(⤳ ﹏ ⤳)
And that's okay. We don't need to talk about it.

Just, understand that it was a slow roast. A grisly, unbearable end for Romy, one of the most agonizing deaths imaginable, and the single-worst day of my life. I can't stop envisioning the moments from those final hours.

Can I see a picture of her? Or a few?

What? why?

I think that sharing memories with someone allows that person to carry some of the grief with you. And I kinda would like you to force yourself to maybe see some happier memories. Maybe they'll replace the sad ones.

Okay then. I guess. That's nice of you.

These are some of my favorites of her.

The one where her head is cocked on the bed is one of the very first pictures we ever took of her.

She was such a cutie. <3 May her memory be a blessing.
Did you do anything for Yahrzeit?

Yeah. We drove to a cabin in the Ozark mountains. We prayed the mourner's kaddish. Joanna pointed out "I don't really see how the kaddish recognizes the one who died." Which was my thought the first time I prayed it.

Kaddish recognizes god's sovereignty. Without it, no mourner is truly comforted.
God is sovereign and you are not; anyone who can't get past that need not apply.

Yeah. I've learned kaddish is telling God that He's great rather than necessarily mourning the dead. A testament of faith over sorrow. I needed that reminder.

We all do. It's why we do it.

I wish I'd done better with prayer that day, or that whole week.

What do you mean? What could you have possibly done differently?

I could've prayed more. Prayed for wisdom instead of my own will.
That's what Christians are supposed to do, right?

Λ

May 6, 1990

Silent night. Claire and Zuji and their baby, Ebnahty, all slept peacefully, despite the insurgency intensifying each week. Two months is what the Bandaks were gifted with: it had been two months since Walad's return home from prison, and despite the political tension in Bethlehem, Claire's world felt like a utopia for that entire time. Her assumption was that this peace would last, that God was restoring all things around her right before her eyes.

Two months. And then it arrived, the Bandaks none-the-wiser that their final hour of peace had passed off into the night breeze as Claire woke up to a clatter.

"Zuji," Claire said as her eyes widened. "Zuji, what was that noise?"

"Mmmm," Zuji groaned.

"Zuji, I heard a dreadful sound just outside."

"Yes," Zuji groaned again, still motionless. "The wind is making lots of loud noise tonight."

Then screaming.

Zuji popped up in bed to listen again.

Another scream.

"The wind does not scream," Claire said, putting her shoes on and flying out the door to see the commotion.

In the dead of night, Claire quickened outside to find her two brothers, Shaqiq and Akhi, in handcuffs, surrounded by seven Tzahal.

You think praying for wisdom rather than healing would've altered that outcome?

It could have. I don't know. Asking for His Voice would've been a better prayer.

So god talks to you? And he punishes you for not praying the right way?

It's not a punishment. But if I have an opportunity to hear from God and I didn't take it, that's on me. And yes, I believe God speaks to us. Do you not?

No, he doesn't. Where does that even come from?

Did God not talk to Abraham? to Moses? to Elijah, Ezekiel, Daniel, Joseph? to... Esther?

Danger. Listen to who you're listing off. Those are the p.r.o.p.h.e.t.s. You have to have an incredible complex to put yourself among those names.

So God spoke to a select few prophets and leaves the rest of us hanging?

Kinda, yeah. and, I say this as gently as I can, but it's also important to know that jews and god have a special relationship. gentiles and god? not so much. christians (at least most of them) are not jews and will always be gentiles.

Abimelech, Pharaoh, Nebburs, Xerxes. God spoke to these lads too

Nebbers?

Nebuchadnezzar. Nebburs is just a really cute name you can call him by if you don't want to check the spelling every time.

So first you compare yourself to prophets, now to kings.

Okay, what about Ruth, Rahab, Achish of Gath, Ittai the Gittite, or the Witch of Endor? David's rise to king was made possible by many Gentiles.

God didn't SPEAK to them. He USED Ruth, Rahab, Ittai, etc for his purpose. Because god only speaks to prophets.

Well, I think this is a slight difference in our faiths. That we're all baptized together into one religion - Jews and Gentiles are not separated by the Law anymore. We believe the Messiah came, tore that veil between us, and that He now acts as a mediator for us. Are you familiar with the Holy Spirit?

No idea what you're talking about.

Just like Christians believe God was incarnate in Yeshua, God is incarnate in a person known as the Holy Spirit, who gives discretion and spiritual wisdom.

This is why I can't believe in your religion. Jews go thousands of years with only a handful of encounters with god. Then xianity is born, a religion mainly for gentiles, and now gentiles are hearing from god regularly and the chosen people still don't.

I'd argue hard that Christianity is not a religion of the Gentiles. There wasn't a single Gentile Christian for the first 10 years. And several books in our New Testament emphasize how Christianity isn't possible without Judaism. Christianity is very much a Jewish religion first in which Gentiles like me were invited to later.

I think you're missing the nuanced relationship that jews have with god. Like, it's not inappropriate for us to question god. Some people believe that god wouldn't even exist without jews, nor jews without god. It's a horizontal relationship.

For me, that's borderline blasphemy. I don't believe God needs any man or woman because He has the rest of the Trinity (Yeshua and Holy Spirit). He is the Creator of the universe, and not only does God not need humans, but humans are in desperate need of finding some means to be redeemed to Him.

Can I take a guess here? Would you refer to the "Holy Spirit" as a sustainer?

Umi was clutching Shaqiq, screaming as a soldier pried her apart from her son.

"They have not done what you think they have!" Abi protested to the Tzahal.

"This is what you say," the Samal noted. "Why don't your children speak for themselves?"

"We have spoken!" Akhi said. "You do not tell us why we are being arrested! Whatever you think we have done…"

The Samal smacked Akhi on the head, then the Tzahal stuffed Shaqiq and him into their humvee.

"Please," Abi pled. "At least tell us why you arrest my sons."

"We know about the meetings," the Samal replied. "There are young men at your house every night."

"None of this is as you say!" Abi shouted with tears in his eyes. "I know nothing about young men at my house."

"You may not know," the Samal said, then nodded at the men in the humvee, "but they know. They host these meetings to recruit youth to the insurgency."

"Sir, if there were meetings like this in my home, I would know," Abi restated. "It is not as you say it is."

"You know how this works," the Samal cut through Abi's pleading. "I have my orders."

"How long will my sons be in prison?" Abi asked.

"I know not," the Samal replied, then added, "Maybe you can ask Yitzhak."

I mean, sure, that certainly is a quality of the Holy Spirit. Advocate, sustainer. Actually those are probably the two biggest traits.

It's like christians have tri-partmentalized god. As if god wasn't enough, so they split him into three deities. In jewdism, we have a concept: God as Creator, Redeemer, and Sustainer. all one. In ancient days, jewdism was groundbreaking because they had the audacity to suggest that god was one. If anything, it feels like christianity has become the polytheistic religion of the day. God as Creator, but then Son as Redeemer, and now this Holy Spirit as Sustainer.

I can assure you that Christians only believe in one God. Father, Son, Spirit is just the way we relate to Him. They're different functions of the same person and, yeah, now that you mention it, it does kind of feel like God's primary function is creator and judge, the Messiah is redeemer and conqueror, and the Holy Spirit is advocate and sustainer.

So the Holy Spirit is completely absent from jewdism, and then randomly appears when christianity springs up? That doesn't seem fishy to you?

The Holy Spirit is in the Old Testament - your bible. The Holy Spirit is the "Spirit of God" that's immediately mentioned in Genesis. I'm pretty sure the term "Holy Spirit" is explicitly used in the Psalms and Isaiah. He's been there since creation, just like God. I'm sure you have some sense of the divine? In some capacity?

We have the shekhinah. God's in-dwelling within a person.

Shekhinah? In the prophets only?

Any person. It's like a convicting spirit. Someone who directs you.

Interesting. Sounds like the Holy Spirit.

But the Ruach HaKodesh (as he's called in the bible) is just another name for god.

Not to be contrarian, but I can't buy that because God is talking to at least one other person throughout the creation story, bouncing ideas off of them like I'm doing to you now. Bereshit 3:22, God says "man has become like one of us," and in Bereshit 1:6, He makes mankind in "our image." Both plural.

He's talking to angels?

We're not made in the image of angels.

But you said you did pray for Romy. So why would this Holy Spirit not respond?

I prayed for Romy's healing, not for wisdom or discretion about what was going on. I had the time to ask for His consult, and instead I was just spouting off my will: "heal her." "heal her." "heal her, please."

Did you ever think that maybe you just need to be more careful about praying for healing? The ultimate act of healing is for god to take them home for good. If you're not okay with that, then you're not actually praying for true healing.

So... to your point earlier...
I needed to say the magic words "physical healing" for my prayer to work?

Or maybe god knew what was best for Romy regardless of what you asked for?

Maybe. Or maybe God is NOT all-powerful. Maybe He willingly gave up some power in exchange for free will. And He knew it'd lead to intense suffering, both for Himself and His people, but that's what He did, similar to the deal we see Him make with the devil in the first chapter of Job.
Hello?
You there?

ON EAGLE'S WINGS

> "In the arrogant aspiration of my youth,
> I had dreamed of a radiant ladder to distant divinity.
> Now in my maturer intention
> my God came down to me and
> I struggled with him as man with man."
> - Irving Fineman

"Final call for boarding! All sections are welcome to board flight A816 to Tel Aviv. The gate will be closing in five minutes. Final call for boarding to Tel Aviv, A816."

Anno Domini, 2018. It had been close-to-three years since I began working on my dissertation, eight years since I married the girl who had once accompanied me to an imaginary prom, and over a dozen years since I sat at a St. Louis burger bar with James. In fact, it had been years since I'd seen James at all, for that matter. I had been to his wedding several years ago. Beyond that, I just knew he had ended up going to seminary and became a missionary; he was in Ukraine or Africa or something.

I changed a lot in those 12 years, too, though seminary wasn't anywhere near my docket. I had been to war, graduated school, was blessed to get married, went back to school, got expelled from school, was even more blessed to stay married, went back to school again, and that's why I was sitting in an airport in Milan. Actually, I wasn't sitting, I was boarding with everyone else. Actually, I wasn't boarding with everyone else, I was boarding with a few select stragglers who also hadn't embarked the plane. Because per my usual, I was last in line. It's not because I interpret Matthew 20:16 literally, it's just that I never quite understood why travelers are always in such a rush to get into an overly arid airplane only to end up sitting next to Helen McSniffle Cough and her child, Baby McFart Cry. (I also never quite understood why the baby has a different last name than his mom.)

The next time I got off my plane, I'd have followed through on my part of the prophecy of old. You know, the one that wasn't a prophecy at all but a construction of my imagination. Nonetheless, I'd be in Israel, and the penalty for following this particular prophecy was that I'd have my PhD. I went to Israel – not because I necessarily cared to answer my research question – but because it was the birthplace of my faith.

Last in line, I stepped up to the counter to offer my ticket and passport.

"Are you in transit?" the Israeli ticketer asked.

"Yes," I said, biting my tongue from saying something super sarcastic. I was literally stepping onto a plane, what did he think?

"Have you been talked to by security?" he asked.

"Huh? No."

"Are you... *Jewish*?" he coyly asked.

"No."

"Ah, that's too bad," he said with a hint of pleasure, as if he could mindread the sarcastic comment I nearly kvetched a moment ago. "Come with me."

I was escorted downstairs into an interrogation room by three Israelis, two of whom had taken my bags and started rummaging through them while the third looked me over. I was clean-shaven – in fact, just the day before I had shaved off my beard and my hair (down to the scalp) so that grooming in Israel would be simple and I wouldn't feel too gross if I couldn't get to a shower for a couple days at a time. A great hygiene technique, but it certainly doesn't allay airport personnel: when I was preparing for deployment to Afghanistan, we were trained to vigilantly scan for clean-shaven men because some terrorists ceremonially shave themselves bare before committing a suicide bombing. That was ten years ago – perhaps even to the exact day, if my estimation was correct – but my interaction almost convinced me I must have started playing for the opposite team.

"Is this your first time going to Israel?" quizzed an officer who punched each of his words with so much phlegm, his accent was borderline objectionable as to how stereotypically Hebrew it was.

"Yes," I said.

"Mr. Geist, are you married?"

Wow. Israelis are more forward than I thought.

"Yes." *Sorry?*

"Where is she? Or... *he*?"

Ahhhh, kay. I misread the purpose of the interrogation. Better nip this in the bud.

"*Sheeee* is at home."

"Mr. Geist, what are you doing in Israel?"

"I'm a PhD candidate. I'm collecting data for research."

"Research what?"

"Trauma in Israel."

"What do you mean, 'trauma in Israel?'"

"Trauma," I gulped. "In the Israeli-Palestinian Conflict."

"So, business, not pleasure? You are not here for tourism?"

"I mean, I sure was planning on carving out some time to see the holy sites."

"What will you be seeing?"

"Well, at least the crucifixion site and the Garden Tomb. And the Temple Mount where Isaac was bound. And the Holy Sepulchre. Oh, also the holy grotto where Jesus's manger was. Oh, and the

Mount of Temptation and the Jordan River. And maybe Rachel's Tomb. And maybe a few other things, as they come up."

"When will you be disembarking to go home?"

"November 13th," I said, then showed him my return reservation.

"And you *just* so happened to travel on the 45th anniversary of the Yom Kippur War?"

"Is that... *today*?" I asked, my voice trailing off as if a dear friend had just announced it's their birthday and I felt like I should've inherently been aware of it.

"Mr. Geist, you are staying for forty days. Why is your wife not here with you?"

Man, this guy can't take a hint. My wife and I are doing just fine, thank you!

"My school wouldn't approve her to come. Liability, I guess? It's not her dissertation, after all. But it wasn't a big issue because she couldn't get enough time off from work, anyway."

He stared, wanting to press me a bit more. I think I finally understood what it was like to be a woman dealing with an aggressive man who won't take "no" for an answer.

"She's joining me in Israel later," I added. "At the tail-end of my trip."

"Why 40 days? Why not come during Christmas, for example?"

"I need to be home before December 7th. *At* home, in my house."

"Why?"

"*Smash Bros.* comes out that day."

An agent in the room started flipping through the sole copy of *I am Danger; I am Prisoner* that I brought along. I hoped she was proud when she flipped open my GameBoy and saw the high score I just set on *Star Fox*. (She wasn't; probably more of a Playstation girl, I guess.)

"So, in a 40-day trip..." the officer began to ponder aloud.

"Sir," an irate female Italian boarding agent interrupted him and scolded me, "why did you wait so long to go through security? We need to leave!"

"What school sent you?" the officer interrupted her in kind.

"The Chicago School," I say, suddenly wishing I had enrolled in a school whose name didn't sound completely made up.

"That's it? 'The Chicago School?'"

"The Chicago School of Professional Psychology."

"Where were you studying before that?"

100

"American," I said as my throat dried. These generic-name universities weren't helping my cause here.

"When did you start studying trauma in Israel?" the officer continued vetting.

"2015. Or 2016?"

"If you've been studying Israel that long, how come you're only here now?"

"It takes a long time to do research – my professors needed to approve what I'm doing."

The boarding agent came back and shouted, "I'm sorry sir, we need to leave you. You should not have waited so long. This is the only flight to Israel today."

I felt a droplet leave my right armpit and roll down my side.

"Who do you know in Israel?" the man pressed me.

"Nobody. Well, Dr. Shalev, actually. He's a professor. An Israeli! He said he's going to connect me with Jews. I need 40 participants for my study."

"Okay. Here is what I am trying to understand," he said with indignance, "You are *trying* to say that you are going to Israel, you want to spend a large portion of time touring the country, by yourself. You want to enter Palestine and come back into Israel, and you also are going to make 40 friends to do 40 interviews, all within 40 days?"

"Yes," I said. "I'd also like to try a falafel."

What wasn't he understanding?

"Who else are you meeting in Israel?"

"Nobody... I'm just talking to Israelis about the trauma they face."

"Just Israelis?"

"And... Palestinians."

"How are you talking to Palestinians?"

"There's somebody that my professor knows, she has the job title of Country Coordinator for Palestine. She is meeting with me. I have an email from her."

"Somebody is not nobody. Why did you not just tell me about her? Do you have this email on your phone?"

"Yes," I said, super grateful that I had just added my school email account to my smartphone, otherwise I wouldn't have had access to it.

"Can I see it?"

"Of course."

I handed over my phone. The Italian boarding agent came back a final time and said, "we leave now, sorry sir, you've missed this flight. You shouldn't have waited."

I became the irate one.

"Waited? I've been glued here for two hours so this wouldn't happen."

"I only saw you these last three minutes," she argued back.

"I've been sitting right at the boarding gate!" I raised my voice.

"Mr. Geist," the officer demanded my attention, "what is this 'Danger?'"

He pointed to a line in the email exchange with the Country Coordinator of Palestine where I was referred to as… well, by my name.

"That's my name," I said, regretting my name change for the first time.

"Your passport says 'Nathaniel,' Mr. Geist."

He cornered me there – I received my passport three months before our honeymoon, which was two months before "Danger" was added to my name. I never hassled to add my middle names to the passport.

"Is 'Danger' your nickname?" he challenged me before I say anything.

"Yes," I lied, hoping that would solve this issue.

"That's not very appropriate for someone who has never met you before to call you by this nickname."

"It's my middle name," I changed up my answer, which I hear is always a good strategy during interrogations.

I showed him my American ID that had all my names on it.

"Mr. Geist, do you know anybody in the surrounding countries of Israel? Like Libya? Jordan? Maybe… Gaza?"

"No."

"In America, you've never met anybody from Syria or Jordan or Egypt?"

"No!"

"Have you had this bag since Chicago?" he asked.

"Yes."

"Did anybody in America give you something to take to Israel?"

"No."

"You don't have a gift for the Country Coordinator of Palestine in there?"

"No."

"If I unloaded your checked bag, what would I find?"

"I didn't check a bag."

"What would I find in this bag?"

"She just searched it! You'd find a book. My computer. Boxers, not briefs. Crumbs from Corn Nuts for sure."

> "Glory with dishonor.
> Genuine, but impostors.
> Known, yet unknown.
> Dying, but living.
> Sorrowful and rejoicing.
> Poor, rich.
> Having nothing,
> having everything."
> ~ 2 Corinthians 6:8-10, DSV

The officer looked up like someone behind me had gotten his attention, and he handed me back my bag. Another agent patted me down and wiped my shoes with a moist towelette that detected lead and other chemicals. Obviously nothing was there, given that I only wear my terrorist shoes when lounging.

"Have a safe flight, Mr. Geist."

The Italian boarding agent was waving me down to hurry up, so I doubletimed towards her – until another (much larger) Israeli officer stopped me. He was much taller and much more muscular, and his shirt could barely contain his chiseled torso.

"What are you doing in Israel?" he began to roast me in a deep, gravelly voice, and held out his palm that I assumed would have five fingers attached, but upon closer inspection, more closely resembled five mammoth bananas.

"*No! No! No!* We go!" The Italian boarding agent said to the towering Israeli officer, madly wagging her finger in his face. Then she grabbed me and we sprung up the stairs towards the boarding gate. Just before I did my little turn on the catwalk, I swiveled my head for one last glimpse of the officer, who looked quite forlorn that he didn't get a chance to interrogate me.

Hasta la vista, Banana Hands.

"I don't do this!" the Italian woman lamented as I handed the desk agent scanned my ticket. "I am making an *except-sheon*; I *never* do this."

She had no knowledge of how much this trip meant to me, and I certainly didn't have time to explain any of it.

"Thank you," I shouted as I scurried onto the runway, refusing to look back at her, lest I turn into a pillar of salt.

On to the Promised Land.

THE VALLEY ROSE.

God spoke, and it's how
The mountain calls for you now,
Not me –
The Valley Rose.
And it was my beloved who was always
Bound to suffer,
The Lord was the One who was
So focused on growing His garden,
That He left us to wither on this side.
That God is actually not good.
Never again will I think
Faith is the most important pillar of life.
Contrary to my prior beliefs,
Prayer has no place in the logical man's life.
Now I know that it's foolish to say
God is sovereign.
For all of eternity,
I will never see Romy again.

ט

April 15, 2020

Sorry, I got distracted and forgot to respond.

You fell off the map there. I was worried.

You don't ever have to worry about me. If I perish, I perish.
⊂(¸0.0¸)⊃
I don't know that I was going to add much to the conversation anyway, because I won't pretend to know god's will. Contrary to what others say, not everything that happens is for a reason, but everything that god makes happen happens for a reason. We just don't get to know why.

I so badly wish I had some kind of inkling. Often I wake up in the middle of the night and it's like I'm learning for the first time all over again that Romy died. Like my brain hasn't comprehended yet. I'll wake up and gasp, "oh, Romy," and cry.

I don't know why god didn't spare Romy.
And I'm sure I haven't thought about it as much as you have.

All of this going beyond my love for Romy. Yes, I loved her immensely. I still do, and always will. But the question I'm wrestling with is whether God even hears (or cares about) our prayers. I bet Job had to feel like his prayers were falling flat too. I mean, I prayed with utmost faith that Romy be spared. I was confident He'd spare her. I had praise-Jesus, move-mountains faith about it, not that hopeful kind of praying where you're secretly doubting the outcome.

Can I see more pictures of her? Please.

Sure.

 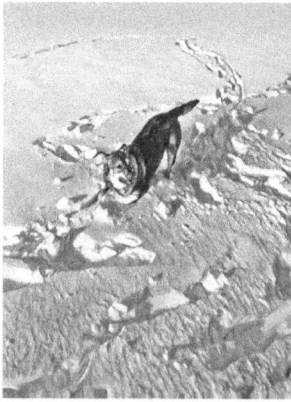 

So what do you think the purpose of prayer is?

Honestly? I don't know anymore. I've thought about it a lot.
Have you ever heard of Metroid?

Is that another Holy Spirit type of thing in Christianity?

It's a Nintendo game.

Nintendo?

For real. Come on. Like Super Mario Bros?

Ohh, you mean the computer thing?

٩

<u>September 23, 1990</u>

"It seems every time we are gaining a child through you," Abi observed to Claire, "we lose another to the Tzahal. This time, you must be having twins."

"It will need to be twins if I'm ever to catch up to Umi," Claire said, stroking her *very* pregnant belly. It caused Abi to smile, something Claire hadn't seen him do in the three months since Akhi and Shaqiq were arrested.

"With Ebnahty, you couldn't even tell you were pregnant. Now, well… it seems that perhaps there really are two or three in there."

"No," Claire laughed. "It is only one, and her name will be Mirna. It means 'peace,' and peace we will have."

"Peace we will have," Abi repeated.

Then, a gentle knock at the door. Abi checked the peephole, and his eyes drooped as if weighed down.

"It is the Tzahal again."

Abi opened the door, then said "hello" as if exhaling for the first time in hours. Abi noticed the soldier's rank: a Samal, same as the one who took Akhi and Shaqiq.

"Good morning," the Samal said. He was much softer-spoken than the one that had come in the middle of the night. "I am here to inform you about your son."

"Inform me of wha…," Abi gasped, not even able to finish his sentence.

"You will see your son this week."

I can't tell if you're kidding.

I'm serious. Mario, isn't he the game guy that jumps on the computer?

This is why you Jews have a Mourner's Kaddish, because you've never played Mario. So, Metroid is a "computer thing" like Mario, okay, but plays differently.

I really don't get digital games at all.

Okay, then bear with me here. Understand it as if it's a parable. In Metroid, you play as Samus Aran.

Is Samus a jew

Lol no. Why would you ask that?

Aran is a very jewish name. Means 'mountain' I think.

I wrote a poem about that name in high school. I even memorized it.

Really?

I, SAMUS ARAN,
RAN TO IRAN.
AYE, RAN!

Uh k. So there's Poe and Frost, then Yeats and Keats, and, now also: Danger.

Thinking about it, I guess I don't know if Samus has Hebrew roots.

Doesn't matter. Go on.

K, so you're this sci-fi bounty hunter, Samus. One of the tropes of the Metroid series is that you'll start out in your "Varia Suit," which comes with all of your power-ups you could possibly need in the game, but about 5 minutes in, you usually get blown up or something and you lose everything the suit and everything you have. But it doesn't really matter that much, because you've never been trained on your abilities in the first place. The game designers just threw all the power you could need at you, but you don't even know what to do with it. So they up and take all of your powers away, but then throughout the game, you're re-collecting each power-up one-by-one. And actually it ends up being great for you, because as you recover each special ability, it gives you time to focus on that ability and learn how to use it. The game makers throw obstacles in your way that forces you to use your new ability so that you have to master it before you can move on. At the end of the game, you're not only using every single one of the powers effectively, but you're getting creative and finding secrets that you would've passed right up if those powers had never been stripped away. Are you following so far?

ish.

Okay. The short of it: Samus has super amazing powers that she's immediately stripped of until she/you earn them again.

Wait, "she?"

Yes, Samus is a woman.

Woman bounty hunter?

Yeah, imagine playing the whole game with this character you assume to be a man, and it's only after you beat it that she takes her space helmet off to reveal she's a woman. That's what gamers experienced in 1986 when the first game was released.

I love that.

"Shaqiq and Akhi?" Abi asked. "They are released?"

"Akhi is coming home. He would not admit to the crime, and there is no evidence against him."

"Why not Shaqiq? Shaqiq is just as innocent as Akhi, just as innocent as anyone in this house."

"He admitted to his crime," the Samal said.

"This is not possible," Abi said. "He is not guilty! Surely if you know Akhi is not guilty, you also know Shaqiq is not either."

"I did not say Akhi is not guilty," the Samal corrected Abi. "I said we do not have evidence against him. For Shaqiq, a confession is evidence enough."

"Sir," Claire cut in, "the only reason Shaqiq would confess to a crime he did not commit is if you tortured him. So I suppose you helped him sign his confession, given that he probably doesn't have any fingernails left?"

Claire and the Samal locked eyes, exchanging contempt for one another. Abi, sensing the increasing tersity, thanked the Samal for the message and shut the door.

And then Abi collapsed into his chair and began crying.

Claire rubbed her father's back and said, "I am so sorry, dear."

Abi stood back up, forced a smile, and announced through his tears, "This is a good day. Let us plan for a big meal."

"Okay, we shall prepare," Claire agreed.

"Akhi is coming home, and it is a good day," Abi murmured as if he was only speaking to himself now. He nodded, then repeated his mantra.

"It is a good day."

So did all the fans. So, when this woman, Samus, is stripped of her powers, she wears her Zero Suit, which is just a skintight jumpsuit. What's the point of wearing something clunky anyway if it doesn't even benefit you? When she's Zero Suit Samus, she doesn't have any of her cool powers anymore, but what she does have is the freedom to understand the extent of her strength without the suit.

Okay.

Eventually you gather enough powers that you can get your Varia back. Varia Suit Samus supplants Zero Suit Samus, but only after learning to master her abilities.

Can I be really honest about something?

Of course.

I know we have a lot of similarities, but we're different in a lot of ways too. You're american, I'm israeli. You're christian, I'm jewish. You speak english, and I speak... well, english, too, but also Hebrew.

Okay. And?

And I need you to get to the point because I'm just about done listening to Mario talk.

Ha, okay. Point being: I'm Samus. I was given a divine power: communication with God. But I've never spent a moment without it, and I've never really been trained in it, so I don't even know how to use it well. When Romy died, I lost that power like when Samus gets blown up and loses her Varia.

So you're going back to wearing your Zero Suit?

Exactly. I'm living out the Metroid Principle. I'm wandering around in my Zero Suit.

That's a fun visual.

I told you Metroid was fun.

Well, I wish you all the luck in the galaxy, Zero Suit Danger. In the meantime, I need to finish making my omelette.

The thing is, if I pray to understand prayer better, and I don't ultimately understand it better, then I think it proves that prayer is a farce.

I see.

In the end, it's a win-win situation, because at least I'm getting closer to Truth, no matter how uncomfortable it might be.

Danger.

And if I don't understand prayer better after this, it will be a crisis. And the scary thing is this: I don't believe God will deliver on this one.

DANGER!!!!!!!

WHAT!!!!!!!!

Omelette.

Bon appetit!

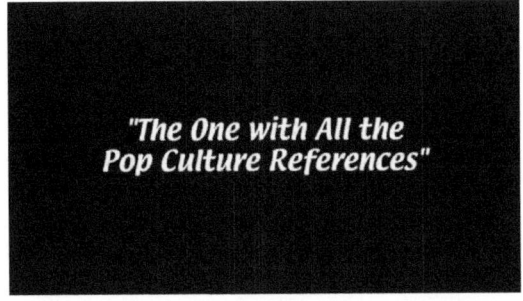

"The One with All the
Pop Culture References"

In my former book, Theophilus, I wrote about all that I did in Afghanistan until the day I was taken back to the States. But, one of the criticisms I received in that first book's release was that I had way too many pop culture references that wouldn't age well. I had passing references to Rod Blagojevich, Sanjaya Malakar, Fruit Stripe gum, and even a Sylvester Stallone video game. *Yipes!* The problem here, though, is that I'm simply a man of fleeting allusions. The more obscure, the better. Worst case, the reference goes over your head, so you shrug and move on with your life. It's not Pokémon – you don't gotta catch 'em all.

> "If you are not very careful, the color of the rose gets attributed to our optic nerves and its scent to our noses, and in the end there is no rose left."
> - CS Lewis

But, when you *do* understand it, it's as rewarding as watching Omega Riyon get blasted back into space. Did you understand that reference? No! Because it comes from a novella I wrote in junior high. And you've already moved on with your life all the same, and *just maybe* you're a little better for it. (You're welcome.) Asking me to write about a major ebenezer in my life and going easy on the references is like asking me to write dissertation and... well, going easy on the references.

To satisfy my borderline obsessive-compulsion and simultaneously whisk the rarefied clumps for everyone else, I'll try to contain as many of my American millennial references within this chapter. A few others will squeak past into other chapters, so if there's something that isn't overtly familiar to you, dear 24th century scholar, just assume that it was a common piece of the human experience before the Great American Empire fell. Is it a little risky? Sure. And I've often been admonished for my risk-taking. But if you're not reading both the Star and the Light, then you can't complain to me that you need every piece of context to understand the critical core of a story.

Truth be told, I'm more inherently a risk assessor than a risk-taker. I think it was JFK who said that the Chinese translation of the word "crisis" is just the conglomeration of the two words, "Danger" and "opportunity." So, I tend to live by the 5% Danger Opportunity Rule: if there's something I want to do, but there's more than a 5% chance that something calamitous will happen to me if I do it, I'll skip doing that thing. Five-percent or under? Fair game.

Five is a pretty high percentage to live by and it's admittedly gotten me into trouble before. For reference, our infantry brigade calculated that each soldier had a 2% chance of being killed when we deployed to Afghanistan ten years ago. I'm better at wordplay than I am a math magician, but I think this means that, apples to apples, I try to live life about twice as dangerously as if I were in a war zone.

THE VALLEY ROSE

After departing Milan and landing in Ben Gurion, I only spent a couple days in Tel Aviv before bussing to Jerusalem. And yet, the moment I got into the hallowed city I'd been waiting my whole life to enter, I not only bypassed the city, but I also left the country entirely and went out from the land of God, wandering east of Eden. Because, where else might I begin my journey but in the place where Christ began His?

I would estimate that hoofing from the contested capital of one country (Jerusalem, Israel) to an occupied city in a completely different country (Bethlehem, Palestine) is probably around a 2% risk. When you add that I've never been to either of these cities, and that I was carrying my camouflaged day bag that could easily be mistaken for an explosive by Israeli Defense Forces, and that it was night, I figure that tips the scales at 3%.

I can't tell you why I cared to do it. Jesus never took a pilgrimage from Jerusalem to Bethlehem (or vice versa). In fact, I don't think Jesus ever schlepped to Bethlehem at all – He was born there, so it was really just a one-way ticket situation for Him.

But when I was a youngon – we're talking 11ish – I always knew what I wanted for my first tattoo when I was of age: the Star of Bethlehem, though of course I'd shepherd the tattoo artist into inking a really rad design. (This was the '90s, from whence "rad" came.) I was too young for the tattoo, but that didn't stop me from buying a t-shirt that said "Jesus loves me and my tattoos" for when the proper time came.

But it didn't happen. I never trusted that anyone would draft a design that was gnarly enough. My promise-ring-of-a-shirt sat in my closet until I got too fat for it, when it finally found its way to a thrift store for some other kid to buy it, bring it home, and then someday wonder why it had even been designed in a youth size. Still, the idea of the tattoo rang meaningful to me: even at 11, I felt like I was following the lodestar that God set out for me, and like the wise men, I relied on faith more than logic.

But aside from the fact that you have to pass over from Israel into Palestinian territory, a normal hike from Jerusalem to Bethlehem isn't anything earth-shattering. It's a decent jaunt at five or six miles, but still nothing close to the 12-mile ruck marches we did in boot camp. But, my feet were already dead from traveling all over Tel Aviv and I was (purposely) wearing the least supportive shoes I own – you know, to get that real "biblical wise man" experience. And if you're looking for honesty, my body had been in the process of transitioning from American food to Israeli meals, so let's just say the muzzle on my rear cannon had been hot to the touch.

It was on the outskirts of Jerusalem – really, kind of a "no man's land" between Israel and Palestine – that I saw an interesting off-road path. There was a hill that was calling my name that had great views of Jerusalem at the top, so I nudged the 3% to 3.33% by trekking my way up.

I stopped cold when I remembered that there were several landmines left over from Israel's conflicts, especially near its borders with its enemies. This spiked the situation to a 5.5% – above my threshold, and, frankly, I didn't need my legacy to be an obituary that headlined "American man idiotically killed in accidental explosage, but he's from Oklahoma so honestly it's not a huge surprise."

But then I heard the cry of a distressed goat nearby, and I realized he probably would've set off any landmines if any existed.

Back down to 4%.

But what if he's an angry goat? Angry goats are like, what, a quarter percent increase at worst?

I noticed an abandoned water bottle, which was a little comforting, because it meant that someone had forged their way through here at some point and presumably didn't find any mines.

3.5%.

Unless the goat ate the man who was holding the water bottle.

3.75%.

Or maybe the bottle itself is an IED, which I guess is technically feasible.

4%.

I rationalized that my mind was probably just jumbling my environment with Afghanistan, which Israel is most decidedly not. Still, I pussyfooted around the bottle and into some bushes. The good news was that those bushes were just poison ivy, which I would only find out the following day.

I continued on and found that my journey was well worth it as I passed by some lustering evergreens that looked like they could have been broccoli for Goliath. Turned out, they were actually Israeli Ceratonia Siliqua carobs. Now, you may wonder how I am so familiar with Middle Eastern trees, and the answer is I just quickly googled "what's the name of the Israeli tree that smells like sex?"

In fact, the whole Jerusalem area was more naturally beautiful than some might think, but when I got to the official Israeli-Palestinian checkpoint, all of that changed. Checkpoint 300 felt like a scene straight out of *The Last Of Us*. Recognizing that most people (at least in 2018) wouldn't have gotten this reference, I'll say that it was also reminiscent of *I Am Legend* in the way it felt like a heavily-militarized dystopian future. (I hope that helps.)

Stepping onto the detrital streets of Palestine was like stepping into the opening scene of *Resident Evil 2* (*not* the movie, you heathen). Recognizing that most people don't get this reference either, I'll say that it was also reminiscent of the museum scene in *Batman* with Jack Nicholson's Joker, because there was a myriad of graffiti all over the strip. (Fun fact: this is my first non-zombie reference. And if you aren't familiar with Batman, then frankly that one's on you, not me.)

Bethlehem had fallen dark, but on the Separation Wall, I could see a large rendering of Rick from "Rick and Morty" with a speech bubble that said, *"*Burp!* M-Morty, welcome to *burp!* Palestine. We gotta solve the *burp!* whole daaang Middle East crisis!"* A few feet past this, there was a quote that stretched almost to the wall's uppermost slab, which said in stylized lettering, *"We know too well that our freedom is incomplete without the freedom of the Palestinians."* It attributed the quote to Nelson Mandela and had a large portrait next to the quote, which almost would have seemed genuinely poignant, if not for the fact that the mural wasn't actually of anti-Apartheid hero Nelson Mandela, but of American actor Morgan Freeman.

There weren't any humans around – granted, it was about 11pm at that point. But large, feral dogs with patchy, mangy fur owned the streets, winding back and forth with chicken meat and lamb bones hanging from their jaws that they presumably found when dumpster diving. I tried giving them a Clif bar, but that was a mistake for two reasons: first, nobody in mammalian history has ever raved, '*looks like granola's back on the menu, boys!*' Secondly, the pooches perceived my offering as an invitation to swarm and jump on me to puppy-nip my arms and hands.

I slipped into a restaurant that was open late. The situation felt like a movie scene where a yankee barges into a Wild Western bar and everyone stops conversing to acknowledge the awkward stranger. I approached the head chef – who looked like an Arab Joe Manganiello – and I asked him if I could just buy a bottle of water and use his bathroom. He obliged, and I left the restaurant, but not before realizing I missed a massive opportunity. So, I turned around and headed back in.

"Scuzi," I said to the chef. For some reason, in situations where I don't know the language, I find myself interjecting with "scuzi" instead of "excuse me," which I guess would be fine because nobody knows that I'm not Italian, at least until I open my mouth and everybody (including me) wonders, "why did this American just speak in Italian to get my attention?"

"Huh," he grunted – slightly annoyed that I was even attempting to talk to him – just as I realized his arms were actually twice as big as Joe Manganiello's. I was actually a little intimidated and felt like I had made a mistake, but then I realized, *no way jose, you are Danger Rose and you're not intimidated by anybody or anything*. (Danger Rose is my suave alter ego, kind of my Burt Macklin or Michael Scarn or Max Power or Quailman or Gizmoduck or H.E. Pennypacker. Surely you got one of those references.)

"You are famous in America," I said to the surly chef.

"What?" he grunted again, more than a little annoyed this time, just as I realized his arms are actually four times as big as Joe Manganiello's.

"This is Joe Manganiello," I told him, flashing a picture of the American actor on my phone. "And you look like him."

"There's no resemblance," he said.

"*Yes,* there is," I corrected him. "And he's attractive and chiseled and you look like him. So, you ought to be happy."

He smiled, then blushed – clearly flattered – but I decided it was time for Danger Rose to stop hitting on buff Palestinian Joe Manganiello and be on my way.

I finally entered into Bethlehem proper. It was actually a really moving experience for me – there was a feeling of physical proximity to Christ, and it overwhelmed me that this holy city looks like it's been reduced to being a suburb of Kabul. I found a bench and took an honest moment to weep over this.

As I gathered myself, I noticed a beautiful piece of bright graffiti on the side of an old, beige building.

It was a dove, gloriously white and drawn with perfect outlines that pronounced her wings. Hanging off the dove's mouth was an olive branch. Most interestingly, though, the dove was wearing a gray bulletproof vest with a crimson crosshair planted across her chest, as if she's about to be shot through the heart, and we're to blame.

"I think... *this* is a Banksy," I muttered under my breath and then slid my fingers down the dove's wing, as if the flat bird could take solace from my touch.

There was graffiti all over the city, but somehow, this spot was deemed sacred, and nobody dared deface the peaceful armoured dove. And as if I have already vandalized it by staring at it too long, I quickly continued with my trek until I came upon Manger Square.

Towering before me stood the Church of the Nativity – an effulgent basilica built upon the supposed spot of the manger that Christ was born. I'd finally arrived: years of following the proverbial star that God laid out for me had wended me to this exact moment and place in time and space.

The church itself was closed, but I had to wonder if there was a roundabout way to find the birth spot of Jesus, even in the after-hours. It was past midnight, but there were yet three rapscallions gambolling about the streets near the church. The kids were about eight, six, and four years old, if I had to guess.

"Scuzi," I said as I approached the children. They froze in fear.

"Do you speak a little English?" I asked.

The oldest boy nodded his head.

"I'm looking for Jesus. Baby Jesus birth spot?"

"Ah, yes," the boy said.

"You take me there?"

"Three shekels," he demanded.

"Okay," I agreed. I knew that was coming.

"Money," he said as he held out his hand.

"No, you show me first," I contested.

"Where is the one who has been born king of the Jews? We saw his star when it rose."
~ Matthew 2:2, NIV

The littlest boy – whose face was caked white from playing in a nearby pile of chalk – threw a load of the dust on my head.

"Okay," I caved. Being the mature man that I am, I chose to not dropkick the little kid for whitening my already-whitening hair, and I sweetened the deal for the bratty little hawkers. "Three shekels now, and three shekels when we get there. One for each of you."

They agreed, and the oldest handed off a box of the chalk to me. It was heavy; frankly, I couldn't wrap my head around how they could've even carried it with all six of their hands. The middle child, a girl, swiped my water bottle from my hand and washed her little brother off so that his skin returned to its normal brown. She tried handing me the bottle back, but I said "keep it."

We scrawled down a corridor – seemingly getting further away from the Church – until the oldest boy turned to me and said, "here," holding out his arms for the chalk. I handed him the box, and he nearly dropped it as his pencil arms began to shake.

"Okay, that's it. Go night-night now," he said as the three of them scampered off.

I'd only find out the day after, but you can't get to Christ's birth spot if the Church of the Nativity is closed. Fortunately, at that moment, I decided it was time to cut my losses and rest up so I could attempt to see Christ's manger in the morning. It was 1am, and I probably could have found an inn, but it just seemed way more appropriate to end the pilgrimage by sleeping on an uncomfortable plot of ground instead. I found a dark corner near a monastery, pulled out my foil emergency blanket, laid my head on my bag, and contemplated the weird sequence of events that had just happened.

Then I figured it out. I'd just paid some kids to make off with my water, throw chalk in my face, and gull me into becoming their lackey.

Directed by
ROBERT B. WEIDE

THE VALLEY ROSE.

God spoke, and it's how

The mountain calls for you now.

Not me –

The Valley Rose.

And it was my beloved who was always

Bound to suffer.

The Lord was the One who was

So focused on growing His garden,

That He left us to wither on this side.

That God is actually not good.

Never again will I think

Faith is the most important pillar of life.

Contrary to my prior beliefs,

Prayer has no place in the logical man's life.

Now I know that it's foolish to say

God is sovereign.

For all of eternity,

I will never see Romy again.

I erroneously believed

This pain will pass;

And also that

God sent Yeshua as Messiah.

׳

April 16, 2020

How was your omelet?

Tasty! Kosher.

I'd expect nothing less.

I wanted to ask, how's your other dog doing without Romy?

Sidney? We actually have 3 dogs now. Well, 2 dogs are ours and 1 is a foster. But Sidney was her longtime best buddy.

So Sidney, and what are the others' names?

Our other dog is Shadrach. She was a stray we found outside our condo. She had two sisters (possibly her own puppies) with her.

Ohhh, right: Meshach and Abednego. You mentioned this in Israel. You shipped shipped Meshach and Abednego off to a rescue up north. Sidney, Shadrach, and what's your foster dog's name?

Zero Suit Samus.

Lol of course it is. So you have 3 dogs in your house now?

Yeah, Sidney and Shadrach are ours, and we can only foster Zero Suit Samus because Romy passed away. They wouldn't have gotten along. So, silver lining, I guess. Romy's death spared another dog from being put down at the shelter.

So you just visited the shelter after Romy died because you wanted another dog in the house?

No, the opposite, actually. We had no intention to bring any more dogs into the house. But then we saw on the news about this pibble who came out of nowhere, ran onto the Tulsa highway, and a 4-car pileup ensued. She was pinned underneath a car, blood pooling from her ear and nose.

Oh noooo! That's terrible!
But what's a pibble?

Pitbull. Just sounds way cuter.

Ah i c. Why was she bleeding from her head?

We'll never know. They took her to the animal shelter and decided she didn't warrant a check-in from the vet on duty. They were going to euthanize her because she barked at anything moving, but they legally had to hold her for 3 days for an owner to get a chance to claim her. A rescue posted about her, so I dropped in to the pound each of those 3 days to try to gain her trust. On the day of her euthanasia, the shelter gave me a leash and said if I could get her collar on and lead her out, I could have her, otherwise they were going to put her down. I thought she was going to bite me, but she let me slip the collar right on and then started giving me tons of kisses and crying in thanksgiving that I came for her.

١٠

September 24, 1990

"Claire," Umi called as she gently shook her daughter awake. "Claire..."

"Umi? What time is it?"

"It is 3:00am. And your father has grown sick."

"Sick? What's wrong, Umi?"

Umi maintained a stoic expression, not answering her question, so Claire repeated herself.

"What is wrong, dear Umi?"

Holding back tears, Umi said, "You must go see Abi now."

Claire got up, got dressed, and staggered across the street to her parents' home, where she knocked as she entered.

"Abi?" she said. "Abi? It is Claire. May I come in?"

Claire looked behind herself; Umi hadn't followed her home.

"Abi? I am coming in to see you," she said, then passed the threshold into his quarters.

"Abi?"

She approached her father's bed and found him lying face down in his pillow.

"Abi," she said, beginning to shake him awake.

He wasn't waking. He was stiff and his face had grown cold.

"Abi!"

She began shaking frantically, trying to wake her father.

Wow now that's a dog with an origin story. That's wonderful. Really. In Israel, there are so many dogs who live their entire lives in under-funded shelters only to be put down after months (sometimes years) of loneliness and discomfort. I've heard from veterinarians that dogs in shelters are usually really excited on their death day because it's the most attention they've been given in years. Some dogs die thinking that they're finally just getting some playtime. I think that anyone who adopts, rather than shops at a pet store or from a breeder, is doing an incredible thing.

Thanks, that's a kind thing to say.

so no residual effects from the accident?

No she's got brain damage. She has seizures now. Long ones, like up to 5 minutes at a time where she'll seize up before Samus returns.

(µ_µ)
So, what about Sidney though? Was she okay after Romy died.

No. She was really depressed. She still is, tbh. Sidney is particularly empathetic, so we did our best to keep our crying sessions to a specific amount of time, then we'd shake it off. It'd be 6:48 and I'd say "okay no more moping after 7pm," and then we'd cry for 12 minutes and then force ourselves to get up and try to put Sidney in a good mood. But she was just so sad. Didn't want to walk, didn't want to play. We had just moved into a new house, but our new home felt so empty. It had a dog-sized hole. My understanding of God has a dog-sized hole, too.

Oh okay great. This is just what I told myself this morning. "I hope I get to bawl my eyes out today." Thanks for that.

These would be the best years of our life if Romy was still alive. And instead they're the worst.

I know you really loved her. I've never met anyone care so much about a dog.

It's a dog to you. Fine. But here's the issue: the Bible (mine) says that if you pray in faith, you just need to trust that it'll happen. Well I did that. And now here's irrefutable proof that that it doesn't always happen that way. Don't be concerned that "it's just a dog." It could've been a guinea pig, a worm, a candy bar, a rock. Where's the line? Prayer only works on humans? At the end of the day, Romy's death was either: 1) God's plan OR 2) not God's plan.

I guess. Those are the two options, right?

Watching Romy die was like watching a species go extinct. That wasn't just a life that we lost, but a legacy.

"He passed away," Umi said through her tears, appearing behind Claire. "I think he had a heart attack. I didn't want to startle you because of your pregnancy; I wanted you to see for yourself."

Claire grew dizzy as she began to hyperventilate.

"I think I," she started to say as she stumbled around the room. "I think. I think I, just…"

In a moment too fast for Umi to catch her daughter, Claire crashed to the ground.

"Claire!" Umi cried, falling to her daughter's side. "Wake up! Please wake!"

Claire remained unconscious. And from under her daughter's gown, Umi could see blood pooling on the floor.

I mean, I think people can understand that much. It felt that way when my grandma died. She had been in the hospital for multiple months, and losing her was like losing a link in our family. We prayed that she'd stay around longer, but it wasn't a prayer of faith. It was a prayer of hope. I knew god would do whatever's best and I wouldn't want to interrupt that. You gotta go from "answer my prayers please" to "please get me on board with your will." It's a difficult balance.

Basically "God can, but might not."

Exactly that. So, you at least get it logically? For me, losing my grandma was hard, but it doesn't amount to the pain you're experiencing. In fact there was peace in not seeing her in pain. I'm not sure why there's such a difference here.

Was your grandma ready to go?

Oh for sure. She said as much.

So you had the comfort of her telling you she had peace. I had the anguish of Romy crying out in pain, wondering why I would let this happen to her.

You know she wasn't actually thinking that.

How do either of us know?
Really, I'm not trying to just sulk here, but I hope I'm conveying that the biggest issue is it feels like God doesn't even care that Romy died. If I knew it was God's will for Romy to die such an awful, heartbreaking death, I could cope better knowing it was for a higher reason. But instead, it feels like God was nonchalant about the whole thing, as if He didn't care that it played out. As if it was a situation that wasn't worth His attention. That's what hurts the most.

God cares about your pain.

Maybe. My crying used to be out of sadness, then later anger, but lately it's a silent cry. Absolute apathy, utter confidence God doesn't care about my family.

If apathy towards evil is the worst evil, apathy towards praying is the worst prayer.

I know. But Christians often say "God doesn't will suffering." Wouldn't that imply that God can't fix it? That He's impotent on some level? It feels like the type of "bad theology" spouted by Job's friends.
There's comfort in it being God's plan, because if it wasn't, then it means God didn't care enough to move on my behalf despite my deepest prayers.
But there is a third option.

What's that?

What if this was Satan's plan that God allowed? Like he did in Job?

You keep mentioning Job. But have you ever read about the prophet Habakkuk?

No. I can't even pronounce it.

Remind me tomorrow or Saturday to talk to you about it.

Gotta go make another omelet?

Nope. I'm having shamburak tonight.

Drool! Enjoy. I'm jealous.

Thanks. Enjoy your... popcorn?

Cereal tonight.
Tutti Frutti.
In honor of the great, late, not-actually-dead Little Richard.

Oh lol well go wild!

NO ROOM IN THE MANGER

"He comes to us as One unknown, without a name,
as of old, by the lakeside…
and sets us to the tasks which He has to fulfill for our time.
He will reveal himself in the toils, the conflicts,
the sufferings which they shall pass through in His fellowship…
they shall learn in their own experience Who He is."
- Albert Schweitzer

According to the Bible – both mine and the Jewish one – the Lord sustained the wandering Israelites for 40 years. Nehemiah says "they lacked nothing, their clothes did not wear out, nor did their feet become swollen" (9:21, NIV).

I was clearly not an ancient Israelite because the only thing sacred about my feet was the blister of biblical proportions that had developed on my swollen toe. I woke up shivering with an achy-breaky back, and if that alone wasn't enough to keep me from falling back asleep, then the melody of plaintive prayers from inside the monastery would've been sufficient: the reality of a self-imposed exile.

I winced as I stood up, a few hundred feet from the front steps of the Church of the Nativity. I was only 32, but anybody watching me might've mistaken me for a Six-Day War veteran. I stumbled backwards a few steps, not fully realizing how fatigued I actually was. Beyond only having a few hours of sleep, my mental faculties had been spent: understanding foreign accents takes its toll, and the Middle Eastern flair to everyone's speech felt like I was in the middle of learning a completely new language.

But there are benefits to waking up before the sunrise in a Bethlehem alleyway. According to the Bible – only mine this time – Bethlehem isn't overly populated, just a small city with a few shepherds. But according to Google Maps, every day after 9am, Bethlehem is swarming with tourists, and the only time you can go see the manger in which Christ was born is at the crack of dawn.

I packed up my belongings and headed into the Church of the Nativity, which just opened for the day a few minutes ago. Top to bottom, the basilica was the most ornate church I'd ever seen, save for St. Peter's Basilica in Rome. Golden chandeliers furnished the vaulted ceilings and beautiful marble mosaics adorned the very ground you stepped on. The centerpiece of the structure, of course, was the grotto in which the remains of Christ's manger are said to be.

The line was short – maybe a ten-minute wait, which sure beats the 3+ hour wait it is on most days during the "slow" season. (I wouldn't even want to know what the wait is during the busy season.)

I stood on the stairs that led down to the manger, which was directly underneath the basilica's altar that's used during Mass. There were about four or five people in front of me, so I crouched on the step that I was standing on to get a glimpse inside the grotto.

I felt the heat coming from inside the hollow below. The room was packed – maybe about 40 people were down there, all fanning themselves and paying attention to a priest who was wearing ornamental robes that were slowly turning into an ornamental wetsuit. I decided that, if for nothing else but the sake of the priest's health, the Mass wouldn't be too long.

Sixty minutes later, I decided that I was wrong. I was sitting down outside the steps, as was everybody else, too. A stately man approached the crowd and said, "move," waving his hands.

"Move where?" a woman asked the man, who appeared to be some sort of warden of the basilica.

"Are you Greek?" the warden challenged her.

"No," she said. She clearly had a Western European accent.

"Are you Greek?" the warden asked each of us, one-by-one. He turned to me and asked in turn.

"No," I tell him.

"Then you need to leave. The manger is closed now."

The Western European woman switched from English to another language – I think it's Italian, though she didn't even say "scuzi," so who can be sure – and she ripped into the man.

The warden fired back and began yelling at her. The congregants and the priest in the grotto looked up at the scene that was brewing, but it certainly wasn't enough to deter the warden from asserting his authority.

"Go! Go!" the man yelled at the crowd as two guards came as backup. We were all ushered away from the grotto into a side-chapel area for another 30 minutes where one of the guards babysat us while the other stood at the front of the grotto entrance to protect the Greek service from onlookers.

"So, you come here often?" I tried to strike up conversation with the security guard. Except, he didn't even acknowledge that a question left my mouth. Probably because I forgot the magic words.

"Scuzi," I tried again. This time, he scowled at me. He was stout, but doesn't look a thing like Joe Manganiello. "Is this a Catholic Church or is this a Greek Church?"

"Both," he said. "It is Status Quo."

"The Status Quo?"

"It is the rules," he clarified.

"*Ohhhh*," I said and nodded, as if that helped clear up my confusion.

I pulled out my phone and Googled the words "status quo palestine" and found out that there's nine holy sites in Jerusalem and Bethlehem in which there's shared custodianship between multiple religious actors. The Status Quo is a set of documents that regulates the property rights and liturgical use of the Church of the Nativity. It's currently owned by three authorities: the Greek Orthodox are the main proprietors, but the Roman Catholics and the Armenians have a shared stake, too. It's actually a storied agreement and simultaneously a farce of an accord as there supposedly are monks – particularly those in training – who often get into brawls with other monks from cross-denominations when one sect is too loud when reciting prayers or singing hymns. It seems like a classic slapstick, and if there's an Arab Joe Manganiello, there had to also be an Arab John C. Reilly somewhere in this city of 75,000.

Thirty minutes into my descent down the online rabbit hole (which ultimately led to several Hollywood stars' filmographies as I tried to cast for the comedy noir script I was writing in my mind), the Greek Orthodox Mass ended and – glory be! – the Greek worshipers began to leave the grotto. I quickly put a reminder in my phone to finally donate $2.75 to Wikipedia during their next fundraising drive, then those of us who stuck around the church return to the line and started heading into the grotto. Though, there was pushing and shoving because it was much more than just a "small crowd" now.

I was next to go down into the grotto to finally see the manger of Christ – the birthplace of my Savior – when a guard approached me and puts his hand up.

"Hold on," he said.

Behind me, another group of worshipers were led down into the grotto. Once they were all in there, I started to step down the stairs to finally see the manger, but the guard didn't move. Instead, he held his hand up again.

"No," he said. "There is a service going on."

"They just finished a service!" I protested.

"Yes, but now it's the Armenians' turn."

"The Armenians? Well, how long is their service going to take?"

"Two hours."

For the first time in my life, I think I finally understood how angry Moses must've been when he double-tapped the rock and forewent his arrival into the Promised Land. I traveled 10,000+ kilometers to be here, but it was the last 30 impenetrable meters that prevented me from seeing Christ's birth spot.

I shook the dust off my feet as I left the Church of the Nativity, which held up Bethlehem's reputation as the least-welcoming city on the planet.

> "How long, O LORD? Will you forget me forever?
> How long will you hide your face from me?
> How long must I take counsel in my soul
> and have sorrow in my heart all the day?"
> ~ Psalm 13:1-2, ESV

יא

April 18, 2020

I'm still waiting to hear about Habakkuk!

Okay I'm ready, but I'm just gonna rapid fire here so don't feel like you need to respond.

Go for Habakkuk.

Habakkuk is a lot like Job, but Habakkuk was around when the jews were exiled from Israel by Assyria. It was a sucky situation because Habakkuk was a righteous guy, but he was forced into exile all the same, just like the bad jews.

"Bad Jew" sounds like a Hebrew rap group.

So Habakkuk questions god about this. He says, "why do you let bad things happen? Do you see our situation? We're in exile and there's no justice under the cruel Assyrians."
God actually responds to Habakkuk. He says, "Just hang on. The Babylonians will rise up and I'm sending them to conquer your oppressor. The Assyrians will be judged for what they're doing."
Habakkuk, confused, says "okay but how is that plan any better? For an oppressor to replace an oppressor? Why can't you let the righteous just win for once?" And god responds, "The Babylonians, too, will be judged in time, but what I want is for you to be patient and trust me."
Habakkuk wants to know, "will I ever get to see this victory?" And god bluntly says "No, you won't get to see the end result, but I want you to trust that victory is coming."
And Habakkuk promised, "then even though we remain oppressed, though i am confused, though the trees don't bloom and the olives are too bitter to eat, i will trust you. not just trust you, but do backflips for you."

The end?

Yes. Habakkuk was faithful and still got conquered. He lived a terrible life in exile, then died. The end.

Depressing.

Our prayer has to go from "God, I demand to know the meaning of this" to "God, see my pain! Please comfort me!" And the question has to go from "why is this happening to me" to "what are the next steps you want me to take?"

Wow. I need to chew on this.

It's the quintessence of the adage, "this too shall pass... like a kidney stone."

Ha! I've never heard that.

You need to get out more.

And breathe in other Pandemanians' death breath? No thanks.

Habakkuk is a tragedy that has an ending with happy subtext. He achieved peace by knowing his role and responsibilities, even though it wasn't what he wanted. Because what he wanted was the exile to end someday and for the jews to have a place of their own again. Which is kinda the same boat the jews are in today because we aren't allowed to build the Third Temple on the Temple Mount. Even though it's our plot of land, we can't build the temple without a fight.

١ ١

<u>September 24, 1990</u>

"He's gone!" Claire wailed on her hospital bed. "Dear Abi has departed us all!"

"Claire, you must calm," Umi pleaded through her own tears. "It is as they said: the baby will suffer too if you don't calm."

Claire wept into her pillow as a doctor entered the room.

"My name is Dr. Saad, and I think we can save your baby."

"Mirna," Claire corrected Dr. Saad.

"Mirna?"

"That is the child: Mirna. And peace we will have."

"We can save Mirna, I think. It was good that you got here so quickly. We will keep you here so we can continue to monitor you, probably until the baby comes."

"Now that I'm in labor, when will the baby come?"

"You are not in labor. You are weeks away, in fact. I think we will keep you here for about a month, maybe more."

"No," Claire shook her head. "Abi's funeral is forthcoming; I must be with the family as we prepare for that. Far be it that I would mourn in a johnny gown! I wish to be with my family for the 40 days."

Dr. Saad knew the practice of mourning for 40 days. It mattered not if Claire was Muslim or Christian, for every religious Arab had attached significance to the 40th day after death. The belief goes that a recently departed soul must wander the earth for 40 days before judgment, just as the Dajjal will roam the world for 40 days and 40 nights, or just as Moses waited upon Mt. Sinai for 40 days and 40 nights to receive the Law,

What would happen if you tried?

You mean besides World War III? We're barely allowed to slink around the outer courts! Be sure to get your prayers in before visiting the Temple Mount, because it's forbidden there - unless, of course, you're muslim. If you look Arab, you get a free pass to do as you please, but if you're profiled as a jew or you look like you're going to pay reverence to Yeshua, you won't be allowed. Overt, open racism. Muslims deny that jews ever had a Temple there in the first place, which completely disregards historical fact. Try cutting through the courts of the Temple Mount with a bible, and you won't have it by the time you get out.

I've had some experience with that. A maddening experience, actually. It's tragic that Jews and Christians are restricted from visiting one of the holiest places in the world. And a little frustrating that God would allow that to happen.

For the first 2/3s of the book of Habakkuk, Habakkuk is angry and confused, at a loss why god is still allowing evil to happen. But in the final chapter, Habakkuk is at peace, trusting god. So what happened between those chapters? Well, Habakkuk saw behind the scenes. He got to see god's plan, but the thing was, actually seeing the plan was more confusing, not less confusing. But the point was nailed home: God is on the throne and I'm not.

Okay. But...
At least Habakkuk got a response from God. He got assurance that his suffering wasn't meaningless.
I could deal with getting conquered if I knew God was in control through it. I mean, where was God in Romy's death? Or for an example that's personal to you, where was God in the Holocaust?

God isn't mentioned in the book of Esther. It's the only book of the bible he isn't referenced at all. Does that mean he wasn't there either? God has intervened in the past, and he will do it again. But not right now. Now you must suffer and wait on god's timing for restoration.

Is it restoration that I need?

I wasn't talking about you. This is still Habakkuk's story here. But yeah, I'd say you need restoration. I think you need to recognize how little you understand about the universe. You can't stand before god and think you know more.

Woe is the man who stands before God and thinks it best to speak.

Is that a bible verse?

No. It's more contemporary.

Well Habakkuk 2:20 says "The Lord is in his holy temple. Let all the earth be silent before him." It's the same de facto warning.

How long between Habakkuk's prophecies and the fall of Israel?

I can't remember off the top of my head, but I'm pretty sure it was a decade, maybe two?

But not, like, a hundred years or a thousand years later?

No. Why?

Something about Jewish thought I struggle to understand is that it seems like, most of the time, the Bible will offer a prophecy and it'll come to pass within a short window. Several years, a decade, but not usually more than a century. How do Jews reconcile the fact that the Bible is chock-full of Messianic prophecies, but the Messiah hasn't come?

or just as Yasue fasted for 40 days and 40 nights before ascending the Mount of Temptation, or just as any of the other 37 examples in these sacred texts that emphasize the number 40.

"I understand how important that must be to you," Dr. Saad reasoned with Claire, "but you need to stay in the hospital or your baby will not survive."

"Dear sir," Claire reasoned back, "we must have faith."

"Claire, faith does not give us the excuse to be reckless. You have lost too much blood; your child needs you to rest."

"When I was born, the doctor said I would not survive, but he turned out to be a hindrance. Now you say Mirna will not survive, and you are being that hindrance now."

Dr. Saad sighed.

"Claire, please. Your umbilical cord is compressed, maybe even prolapsed. You need constant care. Mirna needs constant care."

"Doctor," Claire said as she whipped her legs over her bedside, "it's time for me to go. I have daily liturgies to attend to for my father. Thank you for your help."

"*Please*, Claire. Do not let your religion be the reason for more unnecessary suffering."

She was no longer in the mood for negotiating.

"Release me."

For starters, I think christians overemphasize prophecies. You, sir, are especially guilty of that with how much stock you put into Gog and Magog.

Okay but to be fair to Christians, that's just kind of my own thing. Plenty of Christians have told me to stop studying that stuff.

Oi okay then I'll be the jew who tells you to stop. I know it seems stimulating but I fail to see the use in dedicating any time to it.

Let's put end times prophecies to the side, though. Those were never meant to be solved in the short window I'm talking about. But Messianic prophecies: why do Jews seem to treat those so nonchalantly and not consider the possibility that maybe they've been fulfilled?

Yes, there are prophecies about a meshiach. But most of the bible has nothing to do with prophecies. It's about getting the max benefit out of just a few books and allowing their spiritual guidance to push us to do our best to be good everyday, because focusing on ourselves and improving our behavior is what will bring the meshiach in the end.

I think this is where we veer from each other. I don't believe for a second that humans will ever be good enough to bring on the Messiah. if it's up to us, we're waiting forever. I think we see that again and again in both of our Bibles. we are not faithful to God's covenant. If the Messiah comes to save His people, why would He wait until we don't need saving?
And I think biblical prophecies are critical because they help show that God really is trustworthy - it shows this to jews, to gentiles, to jew-haters.

Ok I get that. But in terms of your fascination with prophecies that supposedly point to Yeshua. If the meshiach came once, why take over 2000 years to build the Third Temple? If Yeshua is the christ, he should've done something by now.

I get what you're saying. But in that same vein, when was the last Jewish Scripture written? 2500 years ago? Reading Isaiah 9, there's too much buildup about a Messiah coming for him to not have appeared yet.

Sorry, it's just not a good argument you're making. Yeshua didn't exactly come right after any of our prophecies, either. The time between Isaiah and Yeshua was about 700 or 800 years.

For the record, not trying to argue. I really want to be open-minded here. I'm not trying to convince you of anything, especially given that I've had my own questions lately.

I don't know about christianity much, but I've heard that Yeshua said he was coming back "soon." Wars have erupted over those words. I don't know any method of measurement in which a couple thousand years would count as soon.

That's fair. I've wondered about that, too. That's a mystery to me too. This was all helpful to me. And I hope I didn't keep you from an omelet.

Nope, it's a quiche. All about those carbs this week.
(∩L∩✿)
Are you having popcorn again?

No, Joanna wants to make dinner tonight. I guess she's sick of popcorn. My quarantine skills are no longer useful.
Your Shabbat has ended, and mine is just starting. So thanks for taking me to church today.

Uh. I brought you to temple.

GUARDIAN

> "The words of the reckless
> pierce like swords,
> but the tongue of the
> wise brings healing."
> ~ Proverbs 12:18, NIV

It was nearly high noon in Bethlehem, and I was back at the Church of the Nativity. Unlike my 6am excursion, the church was now chaotically packed with people shoulder-to-shoulder, no room for the Holy Ghost.

I glanced at a tiny side door – fit for a hobbit – and found someone with a microphone and earpiece peeking in through it. The guide stepped in, bounced his head to spot the location of each guard, and then waved his hands behind as if to say "come on!"

A gaggle of at least 40 men and women snuck in and followed the guide, who pushed his way into the line, just a few spots ahead of me.

"Uh, I'm not sure what you think you're doing," said the woman in front of me in a soft, murkled European accent – I supposed she was from the Scottish Highlands. "We've been in line for two hours."

I'm not sure why she assumed the line-cutters all spoke English, though it may have been on account that most of them had an American obesity to them.

A blonde woman from the line-cutters emerged. She seemed to be in her early 50s and she was, by far, the youngest of the group, lowering the mean age of the tour group to about 85.

"We're just following our tour guide," the blonde woman responded.

So, she did speak English. Precisely, American English. One point for the Highlands.

"Do you not see the long line behind you?" the perhaps-Scottish woman asked the blonde, eventually approaching her so close that they were nearly nose-to-nose.

"Excuse *me*, but you need to *back* off, *sister*," the blonde said, punting her words at irregular intervals.

"I'll *back* off," she responded, gently pushing the blonde woman's shoulder, "when you go to the *back* of the line."

"*Don't* touch me, *sister*," the blonde responded.

"No, no, no," a guard began to yell, his face no paler than a chili pepper. "No cut. No! Go!"

The tour guide and his entire group were removed, blonde in tow. And whilst the guard escorted the tour outside, another tour – this time, only about 15 people – snuck in and took their place. The European woman tried arguing with them, switching between English, French, and Spanish to try and land on a language they all knew. I couldn't understand what she was saying, but it didn't appear to be up to biblical code, or at least wasn't what you'd expect in one of the holiest places on earth. But after finding the tour group didn't speak English, French, or Spanish, she threw her hands up and just let them be, albeit stewing the rest of the wait.

After hours of navigating an ever-growing line, I finally arrived at the point I'd been turned away earlier: just before the stairs that led down to the manger of Christ. And just when I thought I had clearance to dip down the steps, the same warden from earlier planted himself in front of me.

"I know you cut in line," he said to me through a wry smile.

In my adult life, I have rarely felt the urge to uppercut one of my elders in the jaw. Yet there I was, envisioning the "wham!" comic-font text that was about to spill out between my knuckle and his tooth.

"No," I sternly replied, "I did not."

"Okay," he laughed. "Go ahead into the grotto."

I never imagined approaching Christ's manger in as bad of a mood as I was in, but I quickly shook it off because, well, I was approaching Christ's manger.

The slab that changed history.

The birthplace of my religion.

The manger of my savior.

But, when I approached the supposed stone that Mary gave birth upon, any sense of reverence was washed away as a guard herded pilgrims through the grotto as if a secret bomb was about to explode.

"Move! Move! Move!" he kept yelling, shooing people after they'd knelt in front of the stone for longer than three seconds.

The guard clapped in each pilgrim's ear as they briefly prayed. The mall elves in *A Christmas Story* had more poise than the guard, and this wasn't just an annual event to sit on the lap of a random man with a fake beard, but I was here for a once-in-a-lifetime experience to kneel before the birth spot of my Savior.

The woman directly in front of me — an elderly Asian woman who did not speak English — knelt before the manger for less than four seconds when the guard grabbed her shoulder, forced her to her feet, and lightly pushed her away.

I could barely shake off what I'd just seen, but knowing I myself had only a few seconds to take in this experience, I tried to focus on the spiritual significance of where I was. I fell to my knees, folded my hands, took my brief moment, and then opened my eyes. I quickly grabbed my phone to take a picture of the location when a hand corralled my shirt and pulled me to my feet, blurring my picture.

It was at that moment that I decided, if Jesus was arrested, then maybe it's something worth trying for me, too.

I pulled the guard aside and threw up my hands.

"Sir, where is your reverence?"

"What?" the guard asked me.

"Where is your reverence?"

"I know not English, what 'reverence'?" he implored.

"*Thissssss*," I sizzled, "is a holy place."

The guard froze, staring at me. I spoke up again.

"There is no need for yelling here."

The guard stared for a moment longer, and then his malevolent mien melted away.

"Okay, okay," he said and bowed his head to me before kissing my collar multiple times. He put his hand on my back and slowly guided me to see the manger.

"Here, see manger," he said, then excused himself to give me privacy. I watched him for a moment, and as if he snapped from a trance and just now returned to seeing pilgrims as humans and believing the manger to be sacred, he began dealing compassion to everyone he interacted with.

I knelt before the manger. An unintentional genuflection, though if I really thought about it, it would've been more appropriate to lie prostrate before this throne. I was allotted a split-second – really, the time it takes for my foot to release from the pedal and slam the brake – of holy digestion before the thoughts started swirling in my head.

Am I taking too long?

Is the guard staring at me now?

Am I allowed time to say a prayer?

I hope God heard whatever I might have prayed that day, but I won't blame Him if he filed it in the Lost & Found because even I couldn't tell you what my prayer was. I hope I at least said "thank You."

I rose, left the grotto and then the basilica, and marched down a side street feeling like I'd just asked Santa for a football instead of an Official Red Ryder Carbine-Action Two-Hundred Shot Range Model Air Rifle.

Fudge.

> "Our pride must have winter weather to rot it."
> - Samuel Rutherford

י״ב

April 22, 2020

Hey good news!

?

You get a gold star!

Ugh. I don't want it. I just woke up. How did I earn one?

I read Habakkuk in my Bible. Your summary checks out!

I wouldn't have been surprised if it didn't

Oh? Why's that?

Christians change a ton of things in the Hebrew bible

For real? Why do you say so?

Well for starters you say that the meshiach will be born of a virgin.

Right

That's a purely christian idea. A poor christian idea. A mistranslation. The verses don't say he is born of a "virgin woman" but of a "young woman."

Wow. For real?

Sure as shawarma.

I wasn't aware of this. And I don't have a defense to it. I don't know ancient Hebrew and you do, so I have no choice but to defer to you here.

There's a ton of misappropriation like this.

I wouldn't have ever batted an eye about whether or not Mary was a virgin without you telling me that. What else is there? I'd like to know

You sure? Because obviously I'm not a christian and I think that a lot of your religion is made-up, but I'm not trying to prove that to you and I don't want it to hurt our friendship

I can't ignore stuff like this. This affects my relationship with the eternal God. If something foundational to your beliefs wasn't true, would you want to know?

I don't know. I guess I don't want to live in ignorance

So, batter up. Give me your next Christian curveball.

Ok. Well you mentioned Isaiah 9 last time. You got in a tizzy about it being fulfilled by Yeshua but... it's not even a messianic prophecy.
And your translation gets it wrong.

go on

"for to us a child WAS born, to us a son WAS given. his name shall be called BY THE wonderful counselor, mighty god, everlasting father, prince of peace."
That's the correct translation. This verse isn't about yeshua. it's about hezekiah.

you're the expert, so i have to defer, right? but it seems weird. Hezekiah's reign didn't create everlasting peace.
if this is about Hezekiah, the prophecy actually failed.

well Yeshua didn't bring everlasting peace, either.
so nobody's right?

133

١٢

<u>September 26, 1990</u>

The Church of the Nativity looked more like a black sea than a place to celebrate the location of the Christchild's birth: everyone in attendance was wearing dark colors, mirroring their dark emotions as they gathered to mourn Abi.

Claire, wearing a black dress and black bonnet, kept looking over her shoulder as she sat at the front.

"They'll be here," Zuji guaranteed.

"You trust the Tzahal too much," Claire admonished. "I don't think they'll get their release. Even if they do, as soon as they show up, we must get started."

The Tzahal agreed to let Akhi and Shaqiq be released, but only for 30 minutes – even though a traditional Catholic funeral usually eclipses the one-hour mark. After those 30 minutes were up, Akhi would have to go back to the Negev Desert to serve his final two days before his release, and Shaqiq would have to go back to serve the remainder of his term.

Claire heard a commotion at the back of the church and wrenched her neck to see her brothers drifting down the aisle. They were dirty; still wearing their bright pink jumpsuits and mud-laden boots.

Claire jumped out of her seat, hastened to them, and wrapped her arms around their necks as they all sobbed together.

Abi was given a beautiful – and full, hour-long – Mass, with even the Mayor of Bethlehem saying a few words. After the Mass ended, Shaqiq and Akhi stood up and gave Claire a warm embrace.

Yeshua brought everlasting peace in that His death was the sacrificial atonement to free us from sin. The final peace doesn't come to earth now, but it will when God's kingdom comes down.

So invisible to the human eye until then? That seems awfully convenient.

You don't have to accept that it's about Yeshua if you don't want to, but it seems off that it would be about Hezekiah. There aren't other instances in the Bible where God is given a bunch of random names in the middle of a sentence. The beginning of the sentence is building up to the name the child is going to be called by, and then they just drop that subject and never circle back to it? It would almost seem like they were trying to confuse readers on purpose. The argument just strikes me as odd.

You're losing some of the nuance with the syntax though, as it's written in Hebrew. It definitely is about Hezekiah.

If you're telling me that I'm missing some context because of my language limitations, I can swallow that. That's fine. I do trust you, for what that's worth. For me, the struggle is that these verses seem to indicate someone who is larger-than-life. Someone who will change the Jewish world forever, not just another king from a kingdom that's doomed to fall in the next hundred years. I have to go around the barn to interpret the passage as NOT being a messianic passage.

Work with me here. If you don't accept it as being about Hezekiah, and I don't accept it as being about Yeshua, then what's the solution? There's no common ground here?

Well can't we both be right?

Oh so you're one of those "all religions are the same in the end" people?

Believe me when I say I'm not that, at all. I believe there's One Absolute Truth. But this wouldn't be the first verse that is written about one literal thing, and then God seemingly used it to also reference the Messiah.

Not following. What do you mean?

Consider Psalm 2. You read it, and you believe it to be about David - and Christians agree! It IS about David, but it's also about the coming Messiah. It describes what happened to Yeshua. Commentators call this "pictorial prophecies." Prophecies that literally meant one thing, but also was meant to be a picture of what would happen to the Messiah.

Do you have any other examples?

Psalms is probably the most popular place for this. In Psalm 22, David being "poured out like water" and his "bones are separated." David wasn't ever actually poured out like water, nor were his bones separated, but both things literally happened to Yeshua, hence it being a pictorial prophecy.

Hmm. I don't think that works. You're trying to emblazon the bible when it's already got enough chutzpah on its own. Like, a verse about someone's despair of going into Babylonian exile is just that: despair about going into exile. Why give it an extended interpretation? Especially a christological one?

I think all of creation as God intended it is a pictorial prophecy to who He is.

I don't know what you mean by that.

Okay, take childbirth being like God restoring creation: it starts with an act of love, then something grows in the womb that you can't see or understand, and then there's an agonizing process of birth, but in the end, we get a new creation.

"I am sorry this happened to you," Claire whispered to her brothers. "First they took Walad, and now they wrongfully imprison you. Shaqiq, we will fight until the day you are proven innocent."

"Yes," Shaqiq said, shifting his eyes around the room. "Walad was indeed innocent."

Claire felt it a particularly curious statement for her brother to make. She looked over to Akhi to see if he also felt the comment was bizarre, but he was squarely staring at the marble floor.

"Walad was innocent," Claire reiterated, then posed a second statement that turned into a question by the time she was finished saying it. "And you both are also innocent…"

Akhi did not move his hanging head, still staring at the ground.

"*Akhi*," Claire gasped. "*Shaqiq*. Please tell me…"

"This *isn't* to be discussed right now," Shaqiq replied. "These walls have ears. You know this."

"So," Claire said while rubbing her face, almost gouging her eyes. "Did Abi know?"

"No," Akhi snapped back in a loud whisper. "*No*. He had no idea. That had nothing to do with what happened to him. Listen, Claire. They took Walad from us for years. *For years!* He was almost 15 when they let him go! They stole his childhood. You see how it has grieved him so. And you expect us to do nothing about it?"

"You're right," Claire said, "this is not the place for this."

"Don't tell Umi," Shaqiq appealed of Claire.

"And lose her too?" Claire snapped back. "I have been robbed of my whole family, save for her. You must go serve your sentences. I want nothing to do with this."

Except pregnancy is not always initiated by "love," and science has showed us we CAN understand what's going on.

Sure, on some carnal level, we "get" how reproduction works now, but I think you'd agree that there's still some level of mystery to human development. And when a child is conceived in anything other than "love," it's simply failing to live up to how God intended it. Personally, this is my definition of "sin." We see sin as being a linear plane with a random line that separates "sin" and "not sin," but it's more like a circle, where anything outside of the bullseye is "sin."

Mmm I gotta say I don't agree there... I can't get behind that. Genesis, Exodus, Leviticus, Numbers, and Deuteronomy have some pretty clearly-marked lines in the sand.

That's fine, I know the Law is super important to Jews and you've definitely studied it way more than me. But I still do think that all of the Laws are helping to point us to a Creator who cares about us and wants good for us. Take marriage, for example. We have a ton of information about marriage (and divorce) in the Torah. But ultimately, I believe it's all trying to point us to understanding that communion with God is like a perfect marriage. And even when earthly marriages do a terrible job of showing it, the consummation was still intended to be a picture of who Christ is to us. He is the Groom, we are the bride.

Hmm. I've not heard of that.

Have you ever read any of the New Testament?

No. Never touched the stuff

There's a book in there, it's the last book of our entire Bible. Most people stay far away from it because it's so hard to understand.

Are you talking about Revelations? I've heard of it actually.

Revelation. Singular. But yes, that's the one. It's chockfull of imagery and prophecies. It's where we have the bulk about Gog and Magog, actually. But I believe the whole book of Revelation is really about Christ's burden for us. It changes the context completely when you read a book like Revelation and think of it being about a king fighting like hell to take back his kidnapped bride.

I don't think the bible needs to be like that. There's no need for god to be cryptic like that. The stories are usually what they seem to mean on the surface.

I disagree. I mean, look at Genesis, Daniel, Job, maybe even Isaiah, to name a few. There's obviously stuff going on below the surface with each of those, to the point that whether or not they literally happened doesn't quite matter anymore.

Even so, with the books you just named, they don't have more than one meaning. Sure, maybe some of these stories didn't literally happen the way it's recorded, but it's not like they have multiple meanings.

So marriage is what it seems on its face, and it isn't anything more significant than a legal bondage between two people? A Bible verse can't record a story that really happened, but also possess some deeper significance? Shakespeare and Hemingway and Fitzgerald and even some of the crappiest writers I know (present company included) can write a sentence that has a double entendre. Like, we even have a tractor company in the US that has this tagline: "Nothing runs like a Deere." Or, here's a sappy tagline jingle: "every kiss begins with Kay." But the Creator God of the Universe wouldn't do that in His book??

Shaqiq and Akhi retreated to the back of the church, but instead of finding their Israeli officer, there was the mayor. The brothers nodded at the mayor and then began to leave the church, but the mayor slapped his hand across each of their chests.

"Stay."

"It is not our decision to make," Shaqiq explained.

"Believe us," Akhi said, "we would stay if we could."

The mayor closed his eyes, breathed deeply, and shook his head.

"No," the mayor said. "You're not going back. I will take care of this."

The mayor's eyes strained with stern authority.

"You will stay."

There are still issues, though, where christians make up facts about the bible that weren't ever there in the first place.

Do you have an example in mind?

Well you say Yeshua is the son of god. He's divine.

Yes

But that's not a thing. the meshiach wasn't foretold to be divine. the meshiach was actually 2 people: both men. Neither are gods. One meshiach is the conquering lion, the other is the humble lamb.

Hm. Well couldn't the Messiah be just 1 person who fulfilled dual descriptions?

How can you be both

My understanding of what influenced a lot of Jews-turned-Christians was that they could eat the idea that there isn't 2 Messiahs, but just one with 2 different traits at 2 different times. What if He was the servant in the first appearance, and then He's going to come back as the conqueror?

In like a lamb, out like a lion?

Both. Always both.

Idk. Two different appearances? It seems far-fetched. And unnecessary.

Just because it isn't what you expect?

No, because it's not what any jews expect. If the meshiach was meant to be one single person, why would the prophets not just describe it this way rather than lead us to believe it's 2 different people?

For me, this is one of the biggest draws to Yeshua. Just imho. Yeshua took Scripture that had a certain meaning and completely turned it on its head, giving Jews a new way to look at things. Like the idea that the Messiah would establish a throne and conquer evil, it's easy to assume the Messiah is going to be a world politician who becomes emperor, but not Yeshua. Instead of waging war, Yeshua defeats warmongers by letting them kill him. He defeated the oppression of sin, not the oppression of world leaders. And this is so much more important.

Yeshua didn't just offer new perspective, he taught bastardized teachings that were contrary to jewish thought. And then his disciples looked at every little thing he did and tried to twist that into being some ancient mystical jewish prophecy. Oh, Yeshua was in Egypt? Let's turn that into a prophecy. Oh, he rode into Jerusalem? Let's tell people it was on a donkey. Oh, Yeshua had a friend stab him in the back? Well, I think there's something about being betrayed for money in one of the prophets' books.

Oh

I feel like you're getting angry.

Just frustrated.

Let's forget this. To your point, this isn't worth getting angry at each other over.

Just give me a breather for a bit.

kk

THE CHRISTIAN BARBER OF STAR STREET

> "Cut the Bible anywhere
> and it bleeds."
> - William Evans

Faced with the question, "how do you follow up after seeing the birthplace of Christ?", I meandered past Manger Square onto a side street and let myself in to a barber shop.

"Can I help you?" the barber asked me.

"I'm here…" I crooned in my most super espionage Danger Rose voice, "…for *Walid*."

The barber's eyes grew large and he ever-so-slightly nodded towards some stairs behind a shabby curtain.

I discreetly headed to the hideout above the barber shop and found a man who I've only seen in photographs and talked to over the phone.

"Mr. Danger. *Please,* sit down."

If my body knew how to perspire, I'd have been a hose. My right arm pit – the only part of my body that ever trickles any sweat – was probably misting pretty hard. I'd have checked, but given that Walid had just inserted a needle into my arm, I didn't dare move.

Bzzzzzzzzz.

"First time?" he asked, probably picking up on my right armpit dribbles like a bear can track down blood.

I nodded.

Bzzzzzzzzz.

Huh? *No,* I'm not doing heroin. Didn't you hear the sound effect? *Bzzzzzzzzz.* That's the sound of a tattoo needle, sillyhead. Getting a tattoo in Bethlehem isn't illegal, but it's certainly frowned upon in a Muslim-majority city. Tattoos are forbidden in Islam, and tattoo artists can become targets for oppression if they're widely advertised. As such, Walid (who is also a Christian, which carries risk in itself) discreetly runs his tattoo shop in the upstairs of his brother's barber shop – the only tattoo shop in all of Bethlehem, and possibly all of Palestine, for that matter.

After I left the Nativity, I made the impulsive decision that I couldn't leave the Holy Land without getting a tattoo. (That is, if a tattoo idea that's been percolating for over 20 years can be considered an "impulse" decision.) And blessed be Google Maps, because I wouldn't have known about Walid without it. After my initial encounter (or non-encounter) with the manger, I Googled to see if Bethlehem had any tattoo shops in the city. I found Walid, and what really sealed the deal was that his shop could be found on "Star Street." I asked if he would do a tattoo for me, and after he agreed, told him I'd be back after I actually get to experience being in the manger's grotto – a personal prerequisite.

I sit in the chair and Walid begins to ink me. I've always heard that getting a tattoo is fairly painful. I'll admit that it's not overly comfortable, but it isn't quite stick-a-rod-up-your-penis painful. The *real* discomfort is my anxiety. Obsessive-compulsive disorder doesn't take permanent ink any kinder than Muslims do, and while my OCD had become manageable, situations like this – where permanence is the goal – are the most distressing parts of life. My OCD troll finds his finest footholds whenever I encounter that which can't be washed away. I'm not nervous about the permanence of the tattoo itself, but about the permanence of any random "bad thought" that'll be permanently sealed like an imprisoned demon under the skin of my arm, *under* the tattoo. No undoing that; no second attempt to "do it right."

Naturally, I'm crossing myself over and over – my signature compulsion to quell anxiety.

"Ah, so you are a Catholic?" Walid purrs.

"No," I say. "I have OCD."

"OCD?"

"Yes. I don't exactly like to flaunt it, but I'm not even going to attempt to hide it from you."

"Is okay," Walid massages my neck, as if I just confided in him something that I hadn't written an entire book about. "Is all the same Jesus."

"Yessss," I agree, letting go of the "s" only after realizing Walid thought I had confessed my stake in a minority religion. "Only one Jesus."

I do exactly what an OCD-sufferer should *never* do when giving blood, cutting their hair, or – *yes* – getting tattooed: I look in the mirror to watch.

Surprisingly, some anxiety melts as the star forms on my left bicep. Walid limns the final beams that radiate off the astral nucleus, then holds a mirror up to my left bicep, where I can see the Star of Bethlehem in all its inked glory: the locus of the star is white, and it emanates an ebullient blue light that has green spindling off its edges.

"How does it look to you?"

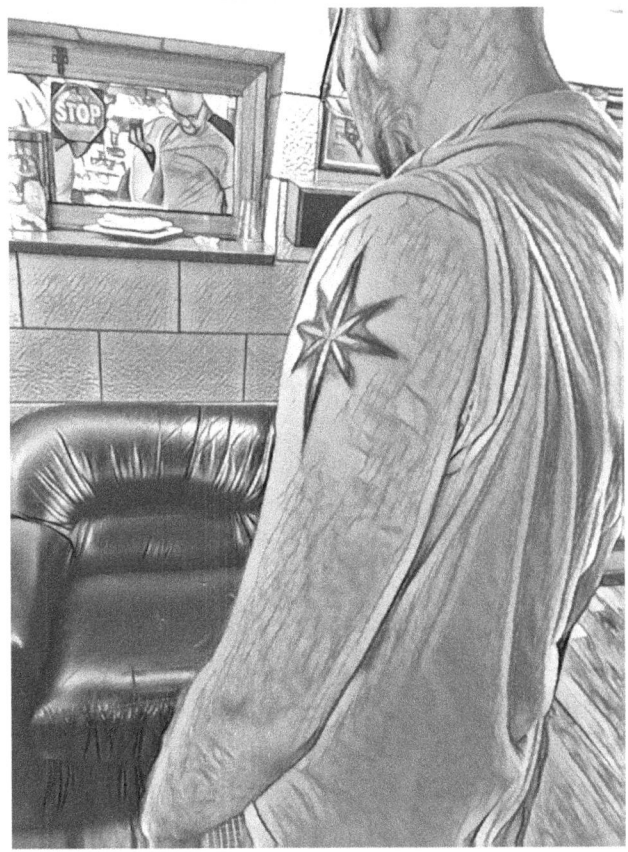

It wasn't the gnarly tattoo that the 1990s, pre-Danger Danger had in mind, but that didn't matter a whole lot.

"I love it."

"Congratulations on your first tattoo, my friend. How does it feel?"

"Honestly, I don't feel any different," I say. "I always knew it was there. It's just… now other people can see it too."

"Behold, the star that they had seen
when it rose went before them
until it came to rest
over the place where the child was.
When they saw the star,
they rejoiced exceedingly
with great joy."
~ Matthew 2:9-10, ESV

יג

April 28, 2020

Suuuuup menschlich!

I am no man!

Suuuuup, fe-menschlich!

Lol. Not much, How are you, mensch?

Feeling good! Still been able to dodge the virus somehow.

Same here! Oh, and I thought of another thing that christians say about Yeshua that's contrary to jewdism

Tell me

The messianic prophecies say that the meshiach will bring peace to the throne of Israel. That didn't happen, given that the temple was destroyed and Israel was consumed by the Romans and Jews (and even Christians) went into diaspora.

Okay. I know where you're coming from. But it seems like you're assuming the peace that cometh would automatically mean it's an immediate, physical, worldly peace. What if it meant spiritual peace? More importantly, like we talked about, the idea is that the Messiah has two phases. We've only gotten 1 of the 2 Yeshuas that are to come. The other Yeshua will indeed bring unarguable peace.

Because he kills everyone else.

Essentially. Is that so different from what Jews expected of the Messiah?

I'm not sure you're hearing me here. Are you familiar with the scarlet thread in the bible?

Maybe? Can't remember off the top of my head.

Maybe means no.
There is a common thread that runs throughout the bible. Literally: a scarlet thread around Zerach's wrist, a red cord hanging over Rahab's window, a crimson yarn attached to the curtains of the holy tabernacle, and one on the high priest's ephod.
Oral tradition says that they'd tie a scarlet thread on the door of the second temple whenever day of atonement came around (Yom Kippur). If the jews' sacrifices were accepted by god, then the scarlet thread would turn white (a Gideonesque miracle), and then the thread would be tied to the scapegoat before sending off to the wilderness.

That's wild. Really, really wild. Didn't know any of this.

Blood is holy. It's not called "blood" in Torah, but lifeblood. And Israel is bleeding. Israel has been bleeding out since birth. But listen. There were some years the thread didn't turn white. It stayed crimson and jews were devastated that they weren't starting the new year with a blank slate. They remained in their sins. This didn't happen a ton, but it did happen sometimes.

Do they (you) still do this today?

What? No. There's no temple.

So today you don't know if it would've turned white or not?

143

١٣

September 29, 1990

"Zuji!"

Zuji awoke, sprung from his chair, and rubbed his eyes.

"Claire? Where are you?"

"Zuji!" Claire screamed again from the next room over.

Zuji rushed to find Claire standing over blood on the bathroom floor.

"It's too much blood this time," she said. "We can't ignore this."

Zuji scooped up Claire into his arms and scampered to the hospital, wheezing the whole way until they arrived to the emergency entrance.

"Please," Zuji heaved, "Claire. Labor. *Baby!*"

"Great! Congratulations," the receptionist said. "When is the baby due?"

"Next month," Zuji gasped.

The receptionist's eyes swelled and Claire was ushered onto a rusty gurney and into a placid room with pink walls.

"Claire," Dr. Saad announced himself as he entered the room. "Tell me what's been going on."

"I'm bleeding. It's been happening since I left the hospital last time, but today it's been too much."

Dr. Saad took less than a minute to complete his checkups.

"You are not the one who is bleeding," he announced, before adding, "This will be the fatal wound. I told you this would happen."

"What did you tell me?" Claire clarified.

"Because of you, your daughter will die."

It would probably still be crimson. By the time the temple was destroyed in 70, it hadn't turned white in 40 years. The sacrifices hadn't been accepted for decades.

Is there any idea why? That seems like a long time to have sacrifices turned away. Cain committed fratricide for less.

Who knows for sure? But most likely it was because Jews were killing each other and losing a grip on what it meant to be a jew. That's the prevailing theory. You're smart. You can figure out why they were turning on each other.

I guess not smart enough. I'm not following how I'd figure it out.

Well, you're not going to like this, but it's because so many of the chosen people turned themselves over to a false prophet.

Oh.
Oof.
Ouch.

Your so-called meshiach came around and got himself crucified. Hordes of jews started following him, saying he was the promised king. It was a devastating time in jewdism because the fabric of the community was being ripped down the middle. King Solomon once said that a cord of three strands is not easily broken. He was talking about the jewish community as a whole.
There's a thing called Sinat Hinam - baseless hatred. When jews are divided, when they hold contempt for one another, they get punished. Exiled.
Yeshua came and all of a sudden, cord by cord, the jewish community started turning on each other. Rasha. The chosen become the rejected.

And it never turned white after the crucifixion?

Full disclosure, I'm not entirely convinced it ever changed color at all. At least not literally. It's one of those legends that seems a little far out there. A little too kabbalah for my taste.
But, some jews now believe that the entire jewish community was punished because of those who followed a false prophet, culminating in the temple being destroyed and our people going into diaspora.

Is any of this in the Bible? If so, I missed it.

Nope, not that I'm aware of. A lot of jewish lessons kind of run together so I forget where the source comes from sometimes, but this is definitely Talmud. Rabbinic tradition.

I don't know what to say. I almost feel like apologizing.

Don't. I just want you to understand that sometimes this can become a sensitive topic, even for me, because there's frustration over the impact that your meshiach had on my ancestors. For some jews, befriending a gentile isn't unlike befriending an anti-zionist arab.

Thank you for taking a chance on me, then.

We're even now.

Even? How?

For saving our butts during the Shoah.
Tell all your friends.

Okay. I'll let both of them know.

(א ෆ א)

THERE'S A FIRST TIME FOR EVERYTHING

> "What you have here is the whole of Israel
> practicing its national sport: matkot.
> Paddleball, basically.
> There's no scoring, and
> they are hitting the ball ferociously at each other.
> It's sort of a metaphor, the amount of aggression,
> the amount of noise, and it drives you crazy.
> There are no rules, no winners,
> and it never ends."
> - Bob Simon

The wise men were pagans – they had a pretty firm idea of why they were chasing the hallowed star that curtailed off from the rest of the galaxy, but they didn't really understand the gravitas of what they'd find from that brim star. As a child, I committed myself to follow that bright star, too; but, like those wise guys, I had no real understanding of where it would lead me. After chasing the same ancient light for 20 years and finally getting its delineation etched into my arm, I found myself in Jerusalem. Not just "Jerusalem" Jerusalem, but the Old City of Jerusalem, the same borough Christ walked.

The pavement was impeccably imperfect, some stones sunken while others stuck out, ripe for pilgrims to receive a divine faceplant – just as it should be. It was more enticing than a professionally-manicured football turf. Lambeau Field on a game day? Nah. This wasn't even Lambeau Field the morning after a Packers Super Bowl victory. Green Bay was a dried up, beige wasteland in comparison.

I shuffled through the Jaffa Gate to get into the Old City, and in true tourist fashion, stopped at the first shoppe that I laid my eyes on.

"Scuzi," I pidgined the shopkeeper, holding up a wide, white fringed shawl. "This is a tallit, yeah?"

"Yes, yes, this is *tallit gadol*. If I may, you put it around your shoulder like this," he said while draping the shawl around my neck. "Now you can put it over your head, and who is there? In this place, only it is you and it is God."

It was a beautiful statement: a private place between God and me in one of the most tourist-heavy cities in the world. And then, torn between helping me appreciate the deep religious significance and landing the sale, the shopkeeper continued talking.

"If I may say, this looks right on you."

"And what are you asking?"

"For you my friend, I don't want you to leave without this. I give to you for only 150 shekel."

In Afghanistan, I had become a master negotiator at the bazaar. Haggling is like golf: you want to get as low as possible, but if you're hasty and you shoot for the hole-in-one from the outset, you usually end up costing yourself more than if you had just attempted a hole-in-three. And I knew I was getting hosed on this one. But for something as important as this – the first tallit I laid eyes on in the Old City – I wanted to just go ahead and pay the full asking price.

Besides. What's forty dollars?

"Sure, 150 shekel," I said. He must reap a fortune on tourists like me who are excited about dropping their first wad in the first shoppe they see.

"Oh, but sir, you are bleeding."

"Huh?"

"Your arm is bleeding," he said, pointing to my left shoulder while keeping his finger at a distance. I looked and, sure enough, there were wine red dribbles seeping through the bandage and my shirt where I had just gotten my tattoo. The shopkeeper handed me some tissues, adding, "Do not get blood on your tallit. Blood will stain your tallit."

"Thank you," I said, slipping the tallit in my bag and wiping up my arm. "Can I ask a favor before I go? I am trying to find the Temple Mount, and I don't want to get lost."

"Please take this map," he said, then proceeded to give me detailed directions. Apparently the Jaffa Gate I had chosen to enter through was on the complete opposite side of the city from the Temple Mount.

"Thank you, you've been a help to me," I said, tabbing out.

"If I may say," he continued, "your English is verily good. And you also know how to spell?"

"Well, a little," I said, my cheeks turning rosy red. Little did he know that he was talking to the Our Lady of Humility K–8th Grade 2000 Spelling Bee Champion and Regional 7th-Placer. "I can spell anything you need." Unless he was asking me to spell "requisite," which is the word that tripped me up in the regionals when I added an unnecessary "C," and I still haven't consistently figured out.

"Please, come write down how to spell 'GRAND OPENING' so I can craft a sign for my shoppe."

I wrote down the words on some receipt paper and handed it back to him, a little disappointed that he didn't ask me to spell something like "pterodactyl" or "delicatessen" or "Kamakawiwo'ole."

"Young man, you have done me a great favor. If I may say, does your mother like earrings? Because you have helped me in this great cause, I will fashion you an earring for free to gift her."

He pulled out a beautiful chrysocolla gem – an iridescent azure-jade stone that is native to the city of Eilat in the southern-most tip of Israel – and he began pounding the earring hooks into a pair.

"This is exceedingly kind of you, sir," I say as I think about how little I actually did for this man. I mean, he gave me directions and a map, so we're actually already even.

"No, is no problem my friend. I give you one for free," he said as he dropped one of the two earrings into my palm.

"Again, thank you, this is…"

"And," he interrupted, "for this second earring, 57 shekel please."

Quick life lesson: nobody in a Middle Eastern city marketplace gives you anything for free.

I declined the blue stone and rucked out towards the Temple Mount. With the map and directions, I still got lost as most first-time visitors do: the Old City is as close to an actual labyrinth as you can get, but the bright side is that it's pleasant to be lost in Jerusalem.

"You, sir!" a man called to me as I was checking the map. I looked up to see a man who could have been the previous shopkeeper's brother, if not for the plum portwine birthmark across the right side of his face. "*My sir*, I will say, it is clear: *you* are a man of God, who seeks Him well."

Finally. Somebody gets me!

"You are a Christian, yes?" he asked.

"I am," I said.

"I am in need of money for my child's medication. It is said, 'Which of you, if your son asks for bread, will give him a stone? Ask and it will be given to you; seek and you will find; knock and the door will be opened to you. For everyone who asks receives; the one who seeks finds; and to the one who knocks, the door will be opened. For the prayer of a righteous man is powerful.' And now I plead you, because I see that you are connected to God, will you pray for me so that He will provide for me?"

"Of course," I said, clutching his shoulder and clearing my throat. "What is your name?"

"Berakhah."

Sweet name. Baraka's the coolest character in Mortal Kombat.

"Dear Lord, Baraka and I come before You because we have a need. You've said that not even a sparrow falls to the ground without your notice…"

But as I continued praying, I noticed Baraka shifting around like he was nervous… or disinterested in the prayer.

"Are you okay, Baraka?"

"Yes," he said, "but perhaps *you* have money for my child? Maybe it was *you* who I was supposed to meet?"

Fleeced.

"I can pray for you, but I don't have money for you."

"Okay, okay, just please continue the prayer then."

"Sure," I said. "So Lord, would You please…"

"Good prayer," Baraka said, slapping my back so hard that it almost knocked me into the netherrealm. "I go now."

And he got up and left.

That was weird.

I patted my pockets to make sure everything was still there, and when I could confirm that I had just as much cash as I'd come with, I continued onward – which may have been backward, I honestly couldn't tell anymore. As I eventually looped back to where I started, I passed a tour group in which a seemingly-Hasidic man stood on what appeared to be a literal soapbox as he stood outside a shop that sold these little bedecked porcelain, metal, and wooden boxes that had Hebrew writing on the front. He held one of the ornate boxes up as he addressed the tour, which I had only stumbled upon mid-speech.

"…and inside the tube with '*Shin*' for '*Shaddai*' on its outside is a parchment blessed by a rabbi," the Hasidic man said in a surprisingly thick British accent, "which contains inscribed passages from

Deuteronomy that instruct Jews to post the Lord's commandments on their doorposts. 'If you indeed obey these commandments, He will give you rain in its season and food in your belly.'"

The man stopped for a moment, held his belly out, smirked wide, and added, "That's just the Rabbi Weinstein abbreviated translation, as I'm always thinking of Israeli food," to which the crowd politely laughed. He actually didn't seem to slightest bit overweight, from my vantage. Maybe "British fat" is just "Oklahoma skinny." He continued, "Sometimes, if a family is going through many disasters and misfortunes, they take the mezuzahs to be checked for tears and, more importantly, verify that there are no misspellings or mistakes in the text. For the mezuzah helps serve as a beacon in this darkness. We often ask why the Torah instructs us to put the words of *Shema* on the doorposts of our houses and on our gates. Well, when we stand at the doorpost, we are no longer in the room where we were, and are not yet in the room we are entering: we are in that place in-between. The mezuzah serves as this visual reminder, from where we have come, from generation to generation, *L'dor v'dor*. The mezuzah serves as a constant: God's omnipresence, providing us with solace, all is 'as it should be.' The mezuzah serves as a support – literally the doorpost – providing us with strength to go forward, *Lech Lecha*. The mezuzah gives us a focus that can provide some sense of security in facing the unknown. When we stand in that place in-between, we do not know what it holds, yet we are comforted as we are never alone. If the Torah serves as the morning, and the unknown serves as night, then the mezuzah is *aravim*, which means evening. The doorpost is twilight, the threshold in which we live in the tension."

The tour, antsy to drop their wads of cash, scrambled into the shopkeeper's enclave and started putting their fingerprints all over the mezuzahs being sold. Rabbi Weinstein stepped down from his platform, revealing a sign behind him: "Temple Mount →"

I marched → and then followed another sign that told me to go ↑, then ←, ↑, →, →, ←, and, finally, →, as if I were inputting a live-action Game Genie code. And like any good cheat code will help you do, I found myself standing before the final level.

This was it! The Temple Mount: the holiest site in Judaism, where the binding of Isaac occurred and the Second Temple once stood – the place that Yeshua called "my Father's house" and foretold its destruction. The Temple Mount mattered at the beginning of Christ's life and again at the end: it's where He was "lost" for several days as a child, and it's where the veil tore from top to bottom on the day of Christ's crucifixion. And right as I was about to pass the threshold into this most revered holy space, a hand slapped across my chest.

I looked at the man whose hand persisted on my chest. He was in full riot gear, minus a helmet, and he had five other Middle Eastern officers accompanying him.

"It's closed," the officer said.

I looked ahead and saw hordes of people coming and going – the Temple Mount was clearly not closed. I looked to the officer for confirmation; I couldn't tell if maybe he was just playing a prank on an unassuming American. But, then a young Arab pre-teen stood on his toes, leveled his face with mine, and yelled, "it's closed!" just before accessing the Temple Mount himself.

The six officers erupt into laughter, but I didn't find any piece of the situation funny. I shot the first officer a stern look to convey that I didn't appreciate the sick joy he was getting from the fact that I couldn't enter, and he dropped the smirk from his face before saying, "for Muslims only."

Jesus once flipped tables here in the temple courts, and never in my life would I appreciate that story more than in this moment. I tried calming down by reminding myself that one of the perks of Christianity is that any place can become holy: God's sanctuary is no longer on that Temple Mount, but within us. Despite traveling upwards of 6,000 miles, I didn't actually need to see the Temple Mount to be near to God. So, I reeled around and explored the Old City in hopes that I'd forget the whole ordeal, a nugatory effort. But I did eventually find myself inside Amigo Emil, a swanky restaurant hideaway just outside the Old City supermarket.

I slicked down the chair, kicked out my legs to let my lumbar get some relief, and sighed. I was fuming harder than a chiminea with a fresh batch of lacquered piñon, so much that I didn't even care that my back was to the door. Since Afghanistan, I've always sat with my back to the wall, but today – in this city of perpetual conflict, mind you – it didn't even matter.

"Can I help you?" the waiter asked, startling me. (See, this is why I keep my back to the wall.) I was going to ask his name, but found it more endearing to think that I was actually talking to whoever Amigo Emil is.

"Yes," I said. "Why can't I go into the Temple Mount? Can you go into the Temple Mount?"

"Can I dally up to that gate and get in? No. Islam doctrine says that if Muslims conquered an area at any time in history, they own it forever. Even if it just so happens to be the holiest site in your religion, one that you've claimed stake to for thousands of years. But how about some tea?"

Amigo Emil ended up becoming my favorite restaurant in the Old City. As I waited for my lunch that day, I busted out my laptop and attempted to work on my study. But no matter how hard I tried to focus on my study, I couldn't help but hear lyrics to a song nobody had ever written.

For years, I wanted to write a Christian worship song, but anytime I sat down to work on it, I couldn't help but start thinking about "secular" work instead – assuming there is such a line that honors a separation of Church and state of mind. I think my inability to focus on songwriting was because I don't care much for music and I'm not much of a singer, not for a lack of trying, either. When I was a child, I was in the children's choir at St. Mary's Parish in Buffalo Grove. I had joined, assuming I probably had one of those latent angelic voices that could only be unlocked by some young, attractive, hotshot vocal instructor who was willing to invest a cinematic montage's amount of time in me. It didn't happen there at church, but sometimes these things take time, so I continued on singing. Eventually my voice deepened and instead of looking for a teacher who could help uncover my falsetto, I now needed one who could unearth my gravelly baritone. When I was a Senior in at Zion-Benton High, we had a major choir concert coming up, and it would be one of the last times I'd be publicly singing – unless, of course, that special teacher came along and unlocked my hidden dragon.

That teacher was Alice Simon-Richter, the esteemed choir director at our high school. Earlier in the year, she had me audition for the storied Zion-Benton Swing Choir, which was the most elite glee club this side of 21st & Lewis. I made the final cut, and surely it was because of my raw talent and not the fact I was only one of three boys who had auditioned.

A few days prior to our big, final concert, we were practicing our set when Mrs. Simon-Richter's jaw dropped and she stopped the entire choir mid-song so she could come talk to me one-on-one. I figured this was it: my singing dragon had been unleashed. She raised her hand to the class, as if to say, "hold on, class, I just discovered something incredible," and came up to me to whisper in my ear. Granted, she was quite older and not your typical cinema-ready toothsome lead, but her tantalizing whisper in my ear would do just fine nonetheless.

"Meet me after class," were the sweet words I expected. Instead, she cooed in my ear the suggestion I've never forgotten: "Why don't we try to have you just lip sync the song instead of actually sing it?"

I stopped singing after that. No more choir, no more musicals, and I even toned down my voice during cadences in the Army. Music has rarely had an effect on me since then, and given that corporate worship in church is explicitly equated to singing songs, it's been rare for a worship service to stir me.

"Worship isn't about you," my detractors say. "So sing whether you have a bad voice or not." Well, it's easy to sing worship when you have a gift to bring. Me? I'm not sure that my less-than-dulcet voice dovetails with any of the other canticles that have been laid upon the Lord's table.

In today's Church, we sing worship (at least in part) because we don't sacrifice rams to the Lord anymore. If we did, I could find the best ram in the world – and would weep bitterly as I sacrificed him, given that I'd probably have named him and cuddled him and brought him on my trips to Petco and taught him which spot of the bed was his. (I'm so glad we don't sacrifice animals anymore.) Me singing in worship? That's the ancient equivalent of me bringing a three-legged goat who has a terminal illness anyway.

And yet, here in the Old City as I attempted to get my secular work done, I couldn't help but hear a piquant song in my heart.

They said, "welcome now, come into the world,
life will bite, you're not some pearl.
Jesus was a good man, not of divinity;
Father, Son, and Ghost, He can't be all three."

"The color of the world
Turns your soul to jade.
Experience is a knife,
you die by the blade.
Shape up, listen to me.
Hey kid, listen to me."

"We'll take you in,
give you your Baptism;
it's your Spiritual insurance,
anything beyond that is fascism."

But that's not what I believe.
It's not what I believe. It's You I believe.

Your Sanctuary is not out there but within me;
the answers are out there, not within me.
And I will follow You into the Light.
I will follow You into the Light.

I used to hide from you in my foxhole,
now I want to praise my Rock with soul,
this soul You've given to me,
this soul You've given to me.

This world says you're the omni-faker,
but my scars show you're the sickness breaker,
bringing chaos to anarchy,
bringing chaos to anarchy.

They say you're a sadistic undertaker.
My heart shows you're a spiritual pacemaker,
calling our soul to breathe,
calling our soul to breathe.

Your Sanctuary is not out there but within me;
the answers are out there,
not within me.
And I will follow You into the Light.
I will follow You into the Light.

I get further from death, the older I grow.
The worse the threat, the deeper You burrow,
dearly hanging on to me,
dearly hanging on to me.

I find that personal ambition is the free man's prison.
Free choice has proved the innocent man's treason.
Restore me until I bleed,
restore me until I bleed!

They say "miracles must be a thing of the past;
trusting in God makes you a religious outcast."
But that's not what I believe.
What you speak is bad philosophy.

Your Sanctuary is not out there but within me;
the answers are out there,
not within me.
And I will follow You into the Light.
I will follow You into the Light.

"The gate is narrow
but I call you into my light.
Do you see Me yet?
Here, I give you sight."

From desire to thought to word to breath to page to flesh, flesh to the cross, cross your
desire, shining light into the depths of hell, to smother the forsaken flame cell,
I will follow You into the Light,
I will follow You into the Light,
I will follow You because You are the Light!

י׳
April 29, 2020

Do Jews cremate?

No. Strictly forbidden. If a loved one were to request cremation (they wouldn't request that though), the good Jew ignores the request and buries them.

So even in India or China, where space is limited?

Does not matter. The act of cremation has the ability to take away from peoples' eternal peace.

Well. That makes me feel really bad for cremating Romy.

She's a dog. It's fine. Animals were burnt up all the time in ancient times, at the direction of god.
Danger: Romy picture.

I call this one "The Stairway to Heaven"

Beautiful.

Do you believe animals have souls?

I don't know, personally. We aren't given much direction on that. Do you?

I sure do. I've thought about it a lot.
Do you know why Jews can't cremate?

Not totally sure, but I think it has to do with separating our ways from the ways of gentiles. Jews believe and hope for the day of the resurrection of the dead.

We do too!

I know most non-jews do open-casket funerals and whatnot. To us, that's not cool. We aren't supposed to get near corpses, and during the mourning process, nobody brings flowers. They are an affront.

Why?

١٤

September 29, 1990

In the small Bethlehem hospital, over the ensuing hours as the contraction pangs transformed into dolorous affliction, Claire remained steadfast that Mirna would not be lost.

"Your God may say that she will live, but my god is science," Dr. Saad explained with the bedside manner of a bedside pan. "And science says she will die."

"I woke up to this world nearly drowning in my mother's blood. A doctor from this same quarter of this same hospital told my mother this same thing, that I had no chance of survival. They fetched me a casket instead of a bassinet. My God prevailed against science that day, and you will see Him again today."

"I don't know what happened that day," Dr. Saad asserted, "but what you are facing now is emergently serious. I think you may have had a velamentous cord insertion or possibly a prolapsed umbilical cord. If not that, then it was certainly placenta previa. You had symptoms of all three abnormalities, and this is why I wanted you in my care last week."

Claire winced in pain, her eyes retreating to the back of her head as she bit her lip and twisted her body. A moment passed, then she recaptured her composure.

"On that day," Claire regressed to the story of her birth, "they said I had lost too much blood, as you say now. But then they baptized me in the Name of the Father, the Son, and the Holy Ghost, and my sickness departed. You will witness this today."

"I wish this for you," Dr. Saad responded, in a rare moment of tenderness. "If it is as you say, that God still works miracles today, then that is what we will require."

You shouldn't mix joy and mourning. Flowers are for happy occasions.

I totally get that.
Joanna and I found out that we kind of grieve differently. She tries not to think about it because it's too painful. Meanwhile I literally carry her urn around wherever I can take her. To church, to bars, along on dog walks, even if it's weird. I don't care if I make others uncomfortable. That's my daughter.

Your doghter.

Yeah. Well, if we never conceive, she's as close to a daughter as I'll get.

So Joanna doesn't like carrying her around?

Not especially. I think she feels weird about it. But I don't care when people look at me sideways (maybe a benefit of having OCD). Besides, I care a lot more about what dogs think about me than humans do. Dogs are better than any of God's human creations.

I like dogs too, but come on. you know that's not true.

Does God want me to like dogs better than humans? No. But it's reality and it would be dishonest to not acknowledge it. Logically, I know dogs aren't more important than humans. But my heart says otherwise, and I get irritated when people don't let me treat my dogs as if they're kids. Because they ARE my kids.

Well, okay... Dogs are really sweet additions to someone's life... but life completely changes when you have an actual child.

Maybe for normal people. But life changed after we got Sidney and Romy. Suddenly we were entertaining vacations that could include them and turning down time with friends and family so we could spend time with them. When Romy died, there were a few people who knew "Danger and Joanna just lost their child and their entire way of life," and not "just a pet."

Danger: picture.

I sent you one earlier.

Another, please.

Why?

Please?

Claire smiled for a moment, but then simpered out coiled cries. She fell into agony before her smile even had reached the corner of her lips.

"We can't keep Mirna in there any longer," Dr. Saad declared. "It's time to try to save her life. Breathe, Claire. Breathe."

It was a quick delivery; Mirna wanted to come out, the womb no longer a sustainable haven. She came into the world, coughing her mother's blood while simultaneously having too little blood inside her own tiny, premature body.

Claire held her sweet daughter, and all the pain washed away for a flitting moment.

"I love you," Claire wooed to Mirna as she cradled her.

"I'm sorry, but I need to take her right away," Dr. Saad explained, then carried Mirna over to the counter across the room. He checked for a heartbeat, and only hearing the faintest taps within, shook his crestfallen head.

"I told you!" Dr. Saad roared, allowing his emotions to get the best of him. "I told you this was the outcome!"

"Doctor," the nurse yelled, "something's wrong. She's slipping away."

"Don't you think I can see that?" Dr. Saad retorted as he conducted compressions on Mirna.

"No," the nurse muttered as she put her hand on Dr. Saad's shoulder. "Not the baby."

Dr. Saad whipped his head towards Claire to find she had slipped out of consciousness.

Cute.

Yeah. Both of them.
I would never breed a dog because I think it's extremely unethical, given the overpopulation crisis in the US. But there sure are some dogs I've met that make me wish their bloodlines had continued.

She probably has some sisters or brothers who are still out there.

True.
Hey, remember when we were talking about how Judaism hasn't had any new Scriptural additions for millennia? Well I had another question, when you get time.

Shoot.

So, the Messiah will come from the seed of David, right?

Yes

And descend from the tribe of Judah, right?

Correct

Well, we currently know that the historical Yeshua of Nazareth had lineage tied to the tribe of Judah, and He came from the bloodline of David.

You don't know that, you were told that by the christian bible

Hm. Okay, didn't expect there would be argument there.
But moving on, that doesn't matter for my point

Which is what?

That the seed of David can't be tracked now. Any old person can say "King David was my grand-grand-grand-grandpappy," and we'd have no way to disprove it.
Further, there is no "throne of Israel." It was completely dismantled.
Not a single tribe still exists, either. Any false messiah can say "oh yeah, I'm totally from Judah," and we'd have no way to measure the claim.

So where's the question in that?

Oh. Well, if peace didn't already come to the throne of Israel through the seed of David, how could that possibly be accomplished now?
There is no seed. There is no throne. The tribes are gone.
The ship has sailed.

That's actually a really good question that I don't have the answer to right now.
But you have to know that you weren't the first person to think up this question, so I'm sure there's a viable jewish answer out there.

You mean to tell me that you can't speak to what all Jews believe at all times in all points of history?

Lol no I can't.
Though I appreciate the vote of confidence!

As much as I want to keep chatting with you, I also recognize that it's dinnertime for you and I need to let you get back to your omelet.

Lol i eat an omelette one time and you think that's all I eat now!

Okay well, my popcorn is getting cold.

Ah, so the truth comes out. YOU are the hangry one.

Truth always reveals itself in time.

See ya.   (^▽^)V

BREAKING THE FIRST WALL

> "The beasts of the field
> pant for you because the
> water brooks are dried up,
> and fire has devoured the
> pastures of the wilderness."
> ~ Joel 1:20, ESV

I freighted myself to the ancient city of Jericho with one specific goal: submerge myself in the Jordan River because that's where Jesus was baptized, and then climb to the supposed spot of the "Mount of Temptation," because that's where Jesus retreated to after His baptism.

I hailed a cab, raising two fingers in the air rather than my whole hand, just to make sure the cabby knew that the tourist he was picking up was one of those cool kinds of tourists.

A taxi pulled up and honked a couple of times, as if I couldn't detect his presence a few centimeters away from me.

"Where?" the driver asked, giving me my hint that English wasn't going to take us very far.

"Baptism site," I said. "Jesus Baptism."

The driver offered a blank stare.

"Okay," I said, then tendered him my phone that had al-Maghtas highlighted on Google Maps.

He barely glanced at it in my hand, then batted it down and put the car in park.

"Jordan," he said.

"Yes!" I exclaimed. "Exactly! Jordan River."

"Is Jordan."

"Right!"

"Is Jordan. No Palestine."

"Jordan? The country? Oh, it's *in* Jordan."

I thought for a moment, then shrugged.

"Yeah, that's okay," I said, then pointed to my phone again. "Not too far."

"Is danger. Blow bomb. Explode."

"Explode? Why will I explode?"

"Road bomb. Harb. No go."

Oh. I've never been real fond of road bombs.

"Okay, I understand now. Thank you," I said, offering him 10 NIS that probably only amounted to a couple George Washingtons.

He batted my hand a second time, then motioned his hands to 'tip his hat' before driving off, which was kind of weird because he wasn't wearing a hat.

Still determined to get to the Jordan, I quickly researched on my phone the easiest way to get to the waters. I found several articles that described what the cab driver was so eloquently trying to explain to me: apparently, the nearest entry point was actually one country and 60 miles away. This was maddening to me because, even though the baptismal site was less than seven miles as the crow flies, it would take seven full-length marathons as the American limps to legally get there.

Illegally, though, I could've crossed over a Palestinian minefield and then sneak through the rifle-toting Jordanian border patrol, but I'd checked my handy-dandy Danger Risk Assessment Tool™, which verified that the risk was higher than 5%.

The *only* other option I had was to wait for the minefield to be cleared. One of the articles I had seen explained that a nonpartisan preservation group was intending to clear the mines over the next seven years. In theory, this was great news, but if they're anything like Laban, then it more likely would actually take 14 years of labor, and I simply didn't have that kind of time today.

So, in less time than it takes between my morning alarm and my snooze to go off, I'd already failed one of the two things I came to see in Jericho. There was also a peripheral third thing I wanted to do – breaking down a wall in order to reach the city center – but true to my suspicions, this isn't even a thing they offered (tourism opportunity: missed).

Rolling with the punches, it was time to focus on reaching the Mount of Temptation. It's the supposed location that Jesus was tempted by Satan after 40 days in the desert, though the specificity of this claim is slightly dubious because the Bible never mentions exactly where Jesus withdrew to in the Judaean Desert for those 40 days.

Skepticism aside, I'd heard it's a worthwhile visit. There's a monastery at the top of the mount owned by the Greek Orthodox Church, and I figured, if nothing else, it would give me time to reflect when I got there. Google Maps said the monastery closed in three hours and was only a two-mile jaunt, so I decided not to take a taxi there.

I steeled myself, knowing that it be only poetic that I'd face some kind of temptation on my journey there. *What would be my forbidden fruit?* Would it be too physically demanding to climb? Would I find a street temptress selling illegal black market GameBoy games at illogical discounts? Would there be a popcorn factory along the way whose batches of perfectly half-popped kernels as golden as the Jerichoan sun would have me forget my mission in a Wonkaesque bliss?

As I pondered, I realized that I'd probably never be in Jericho again for the rest of my life. I *had* to make sure I wasn't missing some big opportunity or tourist landmark, so I googled "what is there to do in Jericho?" It listed Elisha's Spring as a point of peculiar interest, citing it as the location of one of Elisha's miracles that was documented during the Babylonian Exile. Surely, this had to be the true location of the story in the second chapter of Second Kings, and ye are of little faith if you drudge up that the Jerichoan Earthquake of 659 leveled everything in this city. According to Google Maps, at Elisha's Spring, there's even a fountain with a mosaic that claims in italics – *italics!* – that Jericho is "the oldest city of the world," presumably because whoever built the fountain had never heard of Damascus. I wondered if legend also says that it was Elisha himself who wrote the italic lettering in English.

Google Maps said that if you *must* pass on Elisha's Spring – and unfortunately, I *musted* – you should at least check out the supposed-but-legendary Zacchaeus Sycamore, the tree that Zacchaeus climbed to see Jesus passing through the city (Luke 19). I searched and searched online, but couldn't find any straight answers about where to precisely find the revered sycamore.

I encountered a man who was selling some bananas in the shade and asked, "sir, any English?"

"Some English," he said as he handed me a banana. "Here, for you. This one be on the house."

Remembering my life lesson that nobody in a Middle Eastern city marketplace gives anything away for free, I started to refuse the banana from the huckster, wondering what skullduggery he was trying to pull – least until I looked upon the beautifully-golden fruit that seems it might actually glimmer if the sun hit it just right.

I peeled and then bit into the banana, and it was clear that this was my tongue's long-lost soulmate. It tasted richer than anything I'd ever had in my life before, like if a Jolly Rancher had been melted into a Warhead, without any of the carcinogens or tooth decay. *Is this how bananas were supposed to taste?*

"Whoa!" I exclaimed to the Jerichoan, "Surely this is fruit from the garden of Eden!"

The banana vendor chuckled and slapped his belly.

"Are you pleased with that bite?" he pandered.

"That wasn't a bite," I said with banana crumbling out of my mouth, "that was an epiphany!"

"Ho ho ho *hoooo*!" he exclaimed, swaying me into speculation that Santa may be Arab.

"Sir," I mumbled with my mouth full, "I'm looking for the Zacchaeus Sycamore."

The man developed a hard smile and raised his hand.

"My friend, you are standing under its shade."

Startled, I looked up and found that, indeed, I was standing under a sycamore tree that was identical to the pictures I'd seen online.

"Do you know the story of Zacchaeus the tax collector?" he probed me.

"I do," I said, but that doesn't stop him from summarizing the whole story in vivid detail.

"Zacchaeus was the head tax collector in all of Jericho," he raved, "which means everyone hated him because he stole extra money from the people in the city for personal wealth. And only once did Jesus go into Jericho, at least recorded so in the Bible. Now, Zacchaeus was a short man, so when Jesus came to town, he couldn't see him, so Zacchaeus climbed this sycamore tree right here. From the ground, Jesus cries out, 'Zacchaeus! Come down! I'm staying with you.'"

I nodded to remind him that I was familiar with the story, but it was too important to him to *not* re-tell it to me like I was his child who needed it drilled into my brain. Overemphasizing the moral of the story, he continued, punching each syllable into a series of one-word sentences.

"Of. All. The. Pe-eple. Jee-sauce. Saw. That. Day. He. *Chooooooooooose...*"

He hung his words on an imaginary clothesline to dry under the bleating sun, as if the anticipation was killing me.

"*Zuck-key-us!* The city's *Chief* Tax Collector and *Chief* Sinner. Jesus chose the most despised, scorned, and alienated man so that he could take on that despise, scorn, and alienation – a testament to the crucifix that came later. Jesus absorbs our sin and the condemnation that comes with it. Jesus is disgraced so we don't have to be."

Then the avuncular banana vendor (who supposedly only claimed to be able to speak "some English") described the rest of the life of Jesus with such childlike excitement that it gave me chills down my spine. And, yes – this guy turned out to be a Muslim, but he couldn't help himself from proclaiming Christ as the transgenerational atonement transmission of the human race.

New life lesson: sometimes *kind-hearted people do give you things for free.*

After thanking the man for his time and storytelling, I breached the respite of the sycamore's cool shadow and was instantly overburdened by the Jericho heat. Sure, Jerusalem and Bethlehem are also in the Middle East, but it wasn't until strolling through Jericho that I understood the true vulgarity of the region's searing weather. And don't forget: I came ready to dunk myself in a river, so I was actually wearing a second pair of shorts underneath my cargos.

When I trekked from Jerusalem to Bethlehem, it'd been intentional. I certainly didn't intend to hike from the middle of Jericho to the Mount of Temptation. Yet when Google Maps promised I only had a mile left, I figured I'd save the gas money because the price of it here in the Oil Capital of the World was somehow $8/gallon.

One thing Google Maps failed to inform me was that this morning constitutional would mostly be uphill. A bit of a bummer, but I was quick to forgive because, hey, it's all a part of the experience, right? *Right?*

What was much harder to forgive was Google Maps not grasping that I was trying to get to the *top* of the Mount of Temptation, not just the sign at the base of the steep uphill path that led to the Mount of Temptation.

I'm a millennial, so I like to turn subtitles on whenever I watch a movie. The one caption that always gets me to chuckle the first time its employed is [pants]. I like to think the Caption Artists were drawing attention to what the character is (or is not) wearing rather than the fact that the character is about to retch from not getting enough oxygen to their brain.

What I didn't realize until the very moment I reached the base of the Mount of Temptation is that [pants] is a lot less funny when you're the character who is [pants]ing. By the time I arrived to the sign, I was ready to heave my innards all over the apparent Google Maps hotspot. It wasn't that savage of a trot, but the combination of the incline and the scorching breeze had done me in. I squinted sunwards as my eyes scaled the mount to assess what I had left. Behold, the rest of the footslog was going to be barbaric in comparison to what I'd yet faced.

[pants]

I soothed my lungs with some heavy-and-hot Jericho air, and then inhaled one of my water bottles – which, ironically, was Jericho name-brand water. It was apropos, given that the sacred Wadi Qelt that springs from Jerusalem also flows all the way to Jericho, where it spills out south into the Dead Sea. The water certainly wasn't as supernatural as Elisha's Spring water, but it slaked away my growing frailty enough that I had the strength to start ground-pounding my way up the Mount of Temptation incline.

It was no slight uphill battle. When I say "uphill," I'm talking uphill like Rocky-running-up-the-Philadelphia-Art-Museum uphill. After guzzling the rest of the Jericho elixir, I'd started out a lot like Rocky but ended up looking a lot more like a Bullwinkle. I was also evidently limping – my pilgrimage to Bethlehem forced that nasty blister onto my left big toe, and ever since, I'd had to delicately hobble so as not to pop the pus.

As I ascended, I hummed some of my favorite tunes from my childhood. There was, of course, the Sunday school "Joshua Fit the Battle at Jericho," and then there was the other popular one that goes "Step into the town and break the wall down. Your heartbeat is the only sound. Step into the light and then you'll know you were stopped and dropped by the Walls of Jericho." I guess there's really only two that stood the test of time, but still: both classics.

The closer I got to the peak, the more flies swarmed me as if I was a dying animal that was almost ready for their harvest. And I hadn't faced a temptation yet, so I began to ponder if my temptation was to give in to my physical demands to rest. That seemed awfully cliché, easily the most obvious one that I could've been handed, but in case that truly was the trial, I ensured that my body just kept crawling forward, even if it was an inch at a time.

I passed an initial gate and quickly caught sight of a second gate with thick, metal bars and barbed wire on top – it was the terminal gate that served as the entrance to the monastery. Finally, at long last, I had reached the actual *entrance* of the Mount of Temptation! I was met by a priest at the burly gates.

"Hello!" I smiled and waved to the priest, who had a certain Greek mystique.

"*Clo*sed," he declared, turning the word into two syllables as he slammed the gate inches from my nose.

"Closed? No, *not* closed," I rebuffed. "Open."

"*Nnnnoooo! Closed nnnnnow.*"

"No," I huffed like I was suffering from COPD instead of OCD. "Google Maps says you close at 5pm. You're still open for two hours!"

"Who Ghoulie Map? No. Close *nnnow.*"

I collapsed on the steps and clutched the gate in front of the Priest Who Says Ni, singeing my hands and catching my [pants] as the holy man ebbed away.

With the priest out-of-sight, I examined the barrier before me. The gate wasn't particularly high, but the barbed wire crowning it certainly looked sharp. The gate's width beetled so far past over the mountain's steep dropoff that the only way to get around would be for the trespasser to hug and shimmy around the gate itself first, and then around its several stray bars that were purposely positioned to make it nearly impossible to swing about, all whilst hanging over a chasm that – should you fall – would lead to certain ouch.

Okay, now. It's the deep breath before the plunge.

Normally I'd probably have been able to use the rogue wires as monkeybars and pull myself up and o'er the gate itself – and, *normally* I wouldn't even consider breaking into a monastery – but, at that point, I was too weak and too hot to do anything right.

I'd pummeled my way through an ancient city, bested the villainous sun from *Super Mario Bros. 3*, climbed a biblically significant mountain, and even got through its first entryway. But against the power of one more door, there could be no victory. I let out a sigh of surrender and slipped back down against the mountain, ready to let God take my soul should He deem it proper.

Surely my head was as red as my temper, but some of my anger faded as I lifted my head and saw the beautiful cityscape over Jericho. It was one of the most picturesque views I'd ever seen, maybe even greater than that of Lambeau Field just before a critical game.

I fished my phone out of my sodden pocket and snapped a few hasty shots. But as I turn the hot-water-steeped-phone sideways to grab a wide angle, the priest came back to open the gate again.

Ah, finally, some mercy, I thought. *He sees how badly I want a good picture of this.*

I put my fingers through the slats and flung the priest a stupid smile that was probably goofier than I meant it to be, but I was just so excited by his change of heart.

"No," the big grump scolded me. "For Greek only."

Danger. Be silent. Keep your forked tongue behind your teeth.

He wasn't letting me in, but to his credit as a man with the charge to keep this mountain holy, I was more incensed standing outside the entrance than if I'd been invited inside to a Greek Divine Liturgy.

Out from behind him appeared about 40 Greek Orthodox women who marched through the open gate and then stopped right in front of it as they were leaving the monastery. Right in front of me. I could no longer get a shot of my panoramic without several Greek heads moving about in my shot.

The priest slammed the gate, the wind from the door fanning my face and lighting my dander. I could almost smell carbon as I heard the gate lock and I focused on my breathing, caustically waiting for the pilgrims to leave so I could at least take my picture. But they didn't leave. They all turned towards the monastery in unison and an impromptu Greek Orthodox religious service began.

I couldn't take a good picture until they left, so I patiently folded my hands and committed to stay placed until their service was over. At that point, I'd taken in about three liters of water throughout my trek, but I drank the last of my resources just as the Greek service closed out. I ass-u-me they all would promptly leave, but instead the Greek group started taking pictures right where I wanted to. Which was fine, except their photo opportunity was beginning to take just as long as their religious service was.

The Greek priest yelled something in his language to the group of pilgrims, and they began to slowly usher away from the Mount of Temptation. The priest waved his hand at me and said, "come," but I hadn't gotten my picture yet, and the group was still ruining my shot after stealing the panoramic I wanted.

"I will," I said, but he waved again, seemingly unable to understand me.

All I wanted was a quick shot of the view, but I was starting to suspect it was going to take the Greeks longer to get off the mountain than it took Jesus.

And then I broke: I noticed a natural ledge on the desert mountain, so I got as close as humanly possible to literally throwing caution to the wind by pulling myself atop a concrete ledge, then temerariously hopped across onto the mountain in a spot that'd possibly been undisturbed by man for a thousand years.

Landing on the outcrop prompted a kick-up of dust and gasps, which hung in the air for a moment before rolling down the steep cliff before me.

"No! No! No!" the priest yelled. "Is danger-*rose*!"

"I'm fine," I yelled back as I continued climbing.

"You crazy!"

"I'll be fine," I said again.

I get to the spot to take my shot, but the ugly Greeks are still obnoxiously in my picture.

"Sir, must go," the priest said. "Go now. Closed. Dangerous!"

"I'm fine," I said a third time.

"Must close gate!"

168

"So close it!" I yelled, using the last ounce of my strength to stifle my soon-to-be-leavened expletives. "I'll be fine."

"Come down!" he demanded once more.

"Come get me!" I snapped back, taunting him with a level of rudeness that caught even myself off-guard.

The priest threw up his hands up and said, "what you want," and the Greek Orthodox group left. I was left alone on the mountain by myself, and all I could hear was the rustling wind and the Danger Risk Assessment Tool™ threshold alarm ringing – which may or may not have just been my head throbbing.

I took a deep breath and then exhaled, looking over the same scenic view that Jesus and Satan shared together 2,000 years ago. While Jesus ended up overcoming His temptation by upbraiding the unholy devil that day, I failed mine by doing the same thing to a Hellene of the holy order. The transgression had snuck up on me: on my long list of temptations, being unkind to a priest was closer to the bottom of what I was guarding against, probably just one notch above "trick your father into giving your brother's birthright blessing to you instead."

I looked upon Jericho. I wasn't sure if the wavy lines over the city were from the torrid heat or a dehydrated delusion, and my understanding was that this view was supposed to stir me, but I was too exhausted, angry, regretful, and parched to even care to fully take in what I was seeing. Sure, it was a bit like looking over Lambeau Field, but only after the Packers suffered a blowout loss that eliminated them from playoff contention.

I quickly snapped my panoramics, wriggled back down the mountain, crawled through a crevice near the now-locked first gate, and began the 5k back to the city center.

> "It is not the task of Christianity to provide easy answers to every question, but to make us progressively aware of a mystery."
> - Kallistos Ware

THE VALLEY ROSE.

God spoke, and it's how
The mountain calls for you now.
Not me –
The Valley Rose.
And it was my beloved who was always
Bound to suffer.
The Lord was the One who was
So focused on growing His garden,
That He left us to wither on this side.
That God is actually not good.
Never again will I think
Faith is the most important pillar of life.
Contrary to my prior beliefs,
Prayer has no place in the logical man's life.
Now I know that it's foolish to say
God is sovereign.
For all of eternity,
I will never see Romy again.
I erroneously believed
This pain will pass;
And also that
God sent Yeshua as Messiah.
I've instead learned to trust
My old pragmatic way of thinking.

טו

May 7, 2020

Have you found any work yet?

No ‿_>‿
Like, I'm not even close to finding anything. Like, I've even started applying to pastry shops and being the information kiosk person off Yehuda, but no dice.

I'm sorry. :-(I'm in the same boat, if it makes you feel better.

Just so you know, it does not make me feel better that you are struggling to find work too.

I know.

Well I thought I should clarify that
ʕっ•ᴥ•ʔっ
Have you had any luck even landing any interviews?

No. None. It's getting kind of depressing actually. I've been applying to jobs all over the country, but I'm finding my book crushed my ability to get jobs in the professional world.

Really? How so?

I've applied for jobs whose description says "we're looking for a writer with a psychology background and international experience" and might as well have said "and their name must be Danger" and I didn't even get an interview.

But what does your book have to do with it?

Google my name. Go ahead, right now.

Oh. Ew.

Yeah.

That cover again. Danger, I hate it.

Right.

That is the scariest creepiest worst image I've seen in a long time. Ew!

K thanks.

Seriously, a thing of nightmares. Really a bad choice.

Kinda feels like you're laying it on now

That's DEFINITELY not what you want to see pop up as the first thing associated with you.

I am aware.

It's awful. Did you come up with it? It's awful

Of course. It's something I "see" every day and thought I'd share it with the world. But nobody wants to communicate with me after they see it.

So people are literally judging a book by its cover

They have a right to. I have no regrets putting it out there, it's just hard is all. I mean, had I made the cover an attractive naked lady instead, more people would've found it acceptable.

That has to be frustrating.

١٠

October 6, 1990

SMACK!

Claire jolted awake, a raised, red mark emerging across her face.

"Please, stop doing that," Claire told her mother.

"You are falling back asleep," Umi defended herself. "I don't want you going into another coma."

"I understand, but... can you smack me a little lighter? Or at least on the other cheek? Or perhaps... tickle me?"

"I've been a nurse longer than you've been alive," Umi responded. "And I've been your mother for as long as you've been alive, and I happen to know you'd rather get smacked than tickled."

Claire emitted a soft, terse laugh.

"Maybe," Claire admitted.

"If you fall asleep, they're going to need to give you a blood transfusion."

"Has there been any update on Mirna?"

"No, but it's as they said: no news is good news."

"I suppose," Claire said as she adjusted to her side, facing Umi. "If they're so sure Mirna will die anyway, I wonder why they brought her to the incubator."

"All we can do is have faith now," Umi said as Claire's eyelids again slowly closed.

SMACK!

"Wake up, Claire."

SMACK!

"Claire..."

SMACK!

"Dr. Saad!"

Sure, the double standard is maybe a little frustrating, but the most frustrating thing is that the point of the book was to patch a hole in my life. To beat my past and not have to kill myself to free my family from me. But in publishing it, everything I feared about my decisions came true. 4 years later, I'm still unhireable. And I'm right back where I was then, realizing that maybe my family would've been better off without the millstone I'd become.

Do I need to call someone?

Who you gonna call? The geistbusters? It's 3 in the morning here. I'm just spitballing, that's all. Yesterday was just hard. Another cycle for Joanna passed and I still have no interviews lined up. I'm in my mid-30s and have a doctorate. I don't want to go back to making sandwiches.

You'll get something eventually

That's what I thought too. But that was two years ago and I'm still in the same spot. And we are about to go into debt. I mean, we were always in debt because of me, but pretty soon my loan deferment is over and our mortgage is tripling because of an escrow error. We were barely surviving without those bills.

I'm really sorry to hear that. That's hard. We were all given the narrative that education would secure our future, and because everyone we trusted was saying the same thing, we swallowed it, fool of a took's brine stinker.

That's the oddest Hebrew proverb I've heard. But yeah, I should've just become a welder or something.

It's too hard to gauge the future. I left school to go into the hospitality industry because I thought it was an undying profession. Now I'm in the same proverbial cell block as you.

Sometimes when we focus on fixing one tear, it just creates another.

SELAH

> " 'A little sleep, a little slumber,
> A little folding of the hands to rest.'
> Then your poverty will come in like a drifter."
> ~ Proverbs 6:10-11, NASB

The night I failed my temptation, I was plagued with the worst headache of my meaningless existence. A few years ago, I began suffering from cluster headaches – which are nicknamed "suicide headaches" because so many people who have a chronic case of them end up killing themselves. I usually get them twice a year, near each of the equinoxes (as the moon's gravitational pull during those times can trigger them). Being October now, I thought I'd escaped my equinoxial cluster headache, but on the choppy bus ride from Jericho back to Ramallah, I'd be lying if I said I didn't fantasize about jumping headlong into the valley just off the highway.

To be fair, this might've been God's punishment for my cheekiness to the Greek Orthodox Church. If so, well played.

Between the brief period of getting off the bus and hobbling into my hostel, I felt like I was in danger of passing out, and an incessant amount of honking certainly wasn't helping my cranial misery. I had noticed that, throughout Palestine, drivers would compulsively lay on their horn. Either they thought I was an attractive Brazilian woman or it's just a thing here, because Ramallah sounded like a 24-hour-long World Cup game, with people yelling to each other on the streets and horns blaring so constantly that it sounds like one massive vuvuzela bombinating at all times.

Fortunately, my hostel was located on the top floor on one of the taller buildings in Ramallah, and the dull buzz wasn't much of a problem as I nursed my headache the next morning. Whilst Christ had ascended the Mount of Temptation as a spiritual retreat, my retreat began after descending the same mountain. I only rolled out of bed to void my bladder and refill it with whatever liquid was on tap in the hostel's cezve, and then pulled out my GameBoy and turned it on for the first time this trip. I know electronics are the worst thing you can tinker with when you have a migraine, but these space bounty hunters weren't going to defeat themselves, so I set it to the dimmest backlight and gave it a whirl. Unfortunately, it only took about 20 minutes of gameplay before I couldn't handle the pain anymore and shut the game off to instead lie down and toss a soaked towel over my wincing eyes.

"You hungover, mate?" a voice awoke me about an hour later.

"No," I said without flinching a meter, playing it cool. *Real cool.* Danger Rose cool.

"It's okay to admit it," the voice persisted. "I won't tell any Muslims."

"I'm fine, thank you," I mumbled. "I just get headaches."

"Which ending did you earn?"

"Huh?" I said, sitting up and tossing the towel on the bed. His question was acutely specific, and I was more fascinated by the fact that someone in occupied Palestine knew what game I was playing than I was creeped out by the fact that he'd clearly been watching me at some point. "How did you know what I was playing?"

"I've played it. Got the bad ending. And I know a 3DS when I see one."

"Hm. I still call them GameBoys. Just easier to say."

"Right, but you're dating yourself there, mate."

Only two of the 15 beds had been occupied in the room, and I had somehow drawn in the only other guest in the quarters.

Well, hostels are for meeting other people, right?

"I'm Danger," I introduced myself. *Danger Rose.*

"Prime. I'm Trae," he said. I rolled over to look at him, and found he was only wearing white briefs. [No pants.] He had greasy, jet-black hair, but otherwise his winsomeness was a poignant reminder of how unfair life is. Where my beard was uneven and splotched with different colors that made it look like a traffic cone covered in ash, Trae's was perfectly symmetrical and helped his beautiful amber eyes to pop. I guess he'd earned the right to walk around in his underwear. "What brings you to Palestine?"

"I'm researching," I said, then sheepishly looked at my GameBoy... *er, Nintendo 3DS.* "I'm studying the manifestation of trauma on Israelis and Palestinians in conflict. Specifically, I'm trying to see if their parents or grandparents have somehow transmuted their own post-trauma symptoms onto their descendants."

"Ah, so that's what gave you the headache."

"That, or the eternal state of car horns in this place."

"The chauffeur's shofar," he quipped.

"Huh?"

"The chauffeur's *shofar*," he woodenly repeated, much more slowly. "Nevermind, it's funnier if you're reading it. But you're lucky to have found Area D. The only noise you'll hear from a hostel at this altitude is the muezzin's call to prayer from the minaret. And let me say, if you think Ramallah is obnoxiously loud now, you should come back on a day when one of them kills an Israeli."

"What do you mean?"

"Sometimes there are clashes, mate. And sometimes when there are clashes, an Israeli dies. And when Israelis die, Palestinians celebrate on the streets, becoming much louder than this and handing out candy to one another. It's sickening."

"So I suppose it's safe to say you side with Israelis?"

"*Fuck* no! Fucking racist fuckles. *No*, Danger. I side with life."

I didn't respond, contemplating his words.

"I'm sorry, does foul language offend you? You seem taken aback."

"I am taken aback," I responded. "You called me Danger. By my name. Most people need me to repeat my name two or three times, and even then, they're afraid to call me Danger for fear that they misheard it and are going to offend me."

"Prime. I just figured you gave me a fake name. Which is why I gave you one in response."

"Well then, 'Trae,' if that even is your fake name," I said, then let my words hang in the air a moment until he smiled, "how can you not take one side or the other? I'm finding it futile to navigate my biases."

"Danger, there is nowhere to hide in the Israeli-Palestinian Conflict. Own your bias. Have intellectual honesty. This isn't a football game, like most people treat the conflict. You don't have to choose one or the other."

"You kind of have to, though, yeah? What third option is there?"

"You can side with the rules, who dictate what a fair game looks like."

"So, the referees?"

"Nah, mate, the refs are just as biased as anyone. Only the rules themselves are unbiased. So when I say that Palestinians are 'sickening' for celebrating murder, I really mean it. Even when a Palestinian terrorist is killed by an Israeli, you see no such celebration from Jews. Jews will mourn a loss, but don't celebrate a senseless killing. There is no joy in something that is so subversive to peace. And they get that."

"So where's the Palestinian angle in all that? That seems like a pretty comprehensively biased stance."

"Well, Israelis bring that wrath on themselves. So it may be tragic, but it's also deserved."

"There are many Jews and Palestinians who have been killed in this conflict that wanted nothing to do with it. Is it fair to them?"

"In Judaism and Christianity, and probably Islam, there is an explanation to the problem of suffering that while an individual isn't directly responsible for the evil in their lives, they are collectively part of a group that *is* deserving of such misfortune, and in that way, it's fair after all. So for the little Jewish girl who meets her end when a stray bullet hits her, it's both extremely fair and extremely unfair. A consequence of not only her own identity, but her parents' and countries' identities. Many that live deserve death. And some that die deserve life."

"Do you believe that?"

"No," Trae chortled. "It's hogwash. We *all* deserve life. I don't even believe in the premise that there's a 'problem of evil.' It's a *problem of God*."

"Incredible. So you're religious?"

"No," Trae quickly clarified. "I am an atheist. And don't misinterpret that: I'm not an agnostic, I'm not a searcher, but an atheist. There is *nothing* out there for us. And once you accept that, once you stop trying to figuring out which of the scenes in *Looney Tunes* count as canon, all the rest of life's theological problems are easier to solve. The only thing – and Danger, I'm saying *the only thing* – that I know for certain, is that I exist. And believe me when I say that there were no shortcuts getting to that conclusion. I only figured out that much after a lot of soul-searching. You need to be willing to ask yourself, *'what if,'* and think through each scenario you come up with, no matter how wonky your hypotheticals are."

"And where do you come from? What are you doing here?"

Trae's lip developed a sly curl.

"I'm a Jew."

"A *Jew*? Like, a Jewish Jew?"

"Born in Jerusalem. Snipped tip, orthodox school, the whole *tesha* yards."

"Trae is... *Jewish*?"

"Is that so hard to believe? I come from an esteemed rabbinic dynasty. Call me Trae the Jew!"

You could hail from an ancient high priest. I'll still refer to you as Trae-Beard before I call you Trae the Jew.

"Mate, that's how I knew your 3DS. I spent my formative years in the States. My grandpa founded the biggest Orthodox Jewish synagogue in Miami, and to this day, my pop smear is the lead rabbi there. That's what really needs a bris: Jewish nepotips."

"How are you *here*?" I buzzed.

"Well," he said, "when a man loves a woman very much..."

"You know what I mean," I grunted, annoyed that he gave me a witty response that I wished I had been the one to use instead. "How are you in Ramallah? It's way illegal. Not just under Israeli law, but even the Palestinian Authority doesn't want you here."

"I know," he said, his eyes widening as if he just got a surge of adrenaline from being reminded he's an outlaw. "Kinda crazy, mate."

"No, really," I demanded. "What are you doing here? You've got my full attention."

"I was visiting the Yasser Arafat museum. Museum, and mausoleum."

"The terrorist?"

"One man's terrorist is another man's freedom fighter."

"You illegally slipped into Ramallah just to pay your respects to a... *revolutionary*?" I chose my words carefully this time.

"No, no," he said. "I actually live here. Well, not *here*, or I wouldn't need a hostel. But I live in Bethlehem and don't venture too deep into Palestine much. Because of the illegality, and all."

"Why do you, a Jew, live in Bethlehem?"

"To earn my bread. I work there. I slipped through the checkpoint about ten years ago, found that I liked it, and I wanted to learn from the Palestinians, and I took up residence."

"Do Bethlehomies know you live there?"

"Oh, yeah. They're cool. They know I'm not extreme. And they don't tell anyone."

"I guess I don't understand why... like, why eschew your God-given land to live behind enemy lines?"

"*Ah-ah-ah!*", Trae-Beard tsked me. "What did I just got done telling you? God didn't give us the Promised Land, the UN did."

"But… just… why even try to sneak through the checkpoint?" I flabbergust. "In the first place, all those years ago, why slip through? Like, you're messing with your life, man. Which, I get to an extent, but it doesn't seem like there's a point to any of that."

"I backpacked up in Iraq awhile ago. Just for the adventure, really. And I'm talking *Iraq* Iraq, like Ramadi, Fallujah… but then I got caught in Baghdad. US forces detained me for a bit, there, and my armpits was making armpits juice. I smelled like a mango squeeze vinegar smoothie after the interrogation, but I was able to convince them I wasn't actually a terrorist, and they sent me on my merry way back down through Jordan. I got addicted to the danger. '*From the ashes a fire shall be woken, a light from the shadows shall spring,*' so says Tolkien."

"Wh… why *Iraq* of all places? Like… not Egypt? Not Saudi?"

"I always liked going north. Somehow, it feels like going uphill. But, that whole experience… it just kind of had me realize: there's more out there, mate. If I can just get outside my comfort zone, there's so much more for me."

"Okay," I mentally drew up my caricature, "an atheistic Israeli Jew, speaks English, says 'mate' like an Australian, living in Bethlehem, because backpacking through Iraq wasn't enough adventure for him."

Maybe *he* should be named Trae Rose.

"It's not like I snuck into Gaza," he said, as if *that* was the line between sanity and psychopathology. "And I should caveat, I might be an atheist, and I might be living in Bethlehem, but I still feel really connected to my Jewish culture. For me, it just got to a point where I didn't find value in pretending to practice a religion I didn't believe in. My parents took that hard, but I was done living a lie. I actually told them I was an atheist on National Coming Out Day. It gave me the push I needed to say what I needed to say."

"And what did you say?" I wondered. "How did you put it?"

"I told them I was done pretending. That there are prime hunters and gatherers, and that I wasn't a gatherer. That religion made no sense to me. I didn't see why a God would require faith or obedience. I'm an adult now, and I don't want to do what I don't want to do. Not anymore. But I'm not hostile towards religion. At least, I don't think so. Maybe a little annoyed at religion, especially when it manipulates science and history."

"Can you give me an example? Of the manipulation, that is. Specifically, in regards to Israel and Palestine?"

"Hear me, Danger. I love my Palestinian friends. My *Bethlehomies*, you called them. But they've fucked up this entire situation with Israel. Are they prisoners in an open-air prison? Yes. But they act like they'll get paroled through mutiny instead of good behavior. Incite outrage rather than rational diplomacy, and it'll never go anywhere. Like, listen, mate. They've been on the shitty short end of the stick, and there's no denying that. But the only reason Israelis are so reactive to Palestinians is because of *sixty-fucking-years* of targeted attention by them. You've got Arabs taking Jewish history and altering it so it fits their own narratives. Example: the Temple Mount is the holiest place on earth. Full stop. But you can't even *pray* there if you're a Jew. And the most annoying part of that is *Muslims don't even really care about the Temple Mount!* They only consider it a holy place because their enemies considered it a holy place first. It's just... Arab culture is rooted in dramatic effect rather than empirical evidence, and they view everything in black-and-white lenses. Muslims *on the whole* act like the creation of the world happened in the mid-6th century and anything before that doesn't count."

"Shoot," I said, realizing I follied. "You should've been a participant in my study."

"Well, that won't work," he said. "You've told me the whole purpose of it already. Tampered interview at this point. Besides, I haven't had any trauma. I've never been to war."

"I mean, you can have trauma outside of war. It's PTSD, not post-war syndrome."

"What's the core of PTSD? It's acting like you're still in that traumatic event when it's long over. Acting like you're in war when you're at peace. PTSD is different for you Americans. You see it as a bad thing because it doesn't help you survive. PTSD in Israel and Palestine? It's a survival skill. It only becomes a disorder when you move on from war and enter peace. That's the only reason it's maladaptive in the good graces of the United States of Wankers."

My eyes nearly bulged out of my head.

"Do you even know what the word means?" I asked Trae. "You shouldn't say words you don't know the meaning to!"

"Well, *crack my timbers!* You *are* offended by language!"

I guess so, but not enough to let it derail this fascinating conversation.

And ugh. His beard. It was so good. He looked like he was a veteran closer for the Brooklyn Bombers.

"So," I brushed off my allergic reaction to Trae's use of the word *wanker* and my obsession with his finely-groomed chin, "you don't feel like that fits your description? You don't feel like the conflict has caused any kind of trauma in your life?"

"Nah, mate," he effeminately snapped his wrist, "the only thing that's ever traumatized me in my entire life is seeing the stonewall truths that have become decayed in my life. Losing my Judaism has pushed me to distrust every institution and person, including my own parents. And Netanyahu? He thinks he's *not-an-yahoo* but he's the core component of the all the prime corruption. He's made the whole conflict a stimulus and response situation where he simply taps into Jewish fears to keep the tension alive. But Palestinians shouldn't even be mad about it! Who are they if not for being the enemies of the Jews? They have no identity outside of it. They're served by the conflict the longer it goes on. They thrive on the outrage of it all. Think about it. When Jews get together to celebrate their country, they're waving the Star, not trampling the Moon."

"The Star and the Moon?" I pressed.

"The Shield of David, versus the Crescent... well, I guess there hasn't been a moon on Palestine's flag since the Ottomans. But point still stands, Israelis pride themselves on their own identities. They're not calling for the expulsion of Arabs from the Holy Land, or calling for attacks on peripheral Muslim institutions. If Jews pulled that shit, they'd be ridiculed, called oppressors, maybe even given sanctions. But when Arabs do it? The mirror image is just fine."

"So who are the victims, you think?"

"Victims? It's complicated. They're both victims in their own right. Certainly Palestinians are the greater victims today, and I'd roast anyone who tries to argue otherwise. But the pro-Pals want to solve the 1948 Palestinian refugee crisis by creating the 2018 Israeli refugee crisis. If two lefts don't make a right, then two *nakbas* certainly don't make a ceasefire."

That word. *Nakba*. For the life of me, I couldn't remember the Arabic translation, but I knew it was reference to the Palestinians' evacuation from their homeland in 1948. If you're a Jew, it was a willful exodus. If you're an Arab, it was a forced exile.

The Nakba. *The Calamity. The Upheaval. The Imprisoning War. The...*

"But you got's-to remember," Trae sundered my internal monologue, "Jews have either been the capstone or they've been on the seafloor, and never in-between. Everyone loves a Jew until they're winning. So if you're not cool with them getting the garnish on the food chain, then you're calling for them to be in the lion's cellar. Pick your poison, mate."

"And you said you feel like Jews are racist?"

Trae laughed, albeit with a certain hollowness.

"*Pffft*. Is the pope the ultimate symbol of religious oppression on the masses?"

I stared at him for a second, and then he flicked me on the head with his finger.

"*Doi*, mate. The answer's yes. Everybody's a little bit racist, right? Well Jews are super elitist. They're so arrogant, they might as well be honorary Americans – no offense."

I threw up my hands and shrugged, saying, "Some taken." Though I think I resented the pope joke more.

"Bottom line, mate, just because Jews aren't so likeable whenever they reach that mountaintop, it sure doesn't mean they belong in the valley. They've done their time down there. And Palestinians aren't exactly the first group of Arabs to have to crawl their way out, either. They want onlookers to be so offended by their exile that they become the most pressing refugee crisis the globe has ever seen. Their collective identity benefits when the world is clamoring 'free Palestine, free Palestine!' And the thing is, the Israeli-Palestinian Conflict of 2018 is not the Israeli-Palestinian Conflict of 1948."

"What do you mean? If the conflict today isn't the conflict from yesteryear, then what is it?"

"An echo. Just prime echoes of the original issues, mate, like a bad TV sitcom that's run for too many seasons, and the characters from season one have become shells of themselves by the final season, and all the storylines have run their course."

"You really think that? The part that they benefit from their oppression?"

"We all benefit from suffering from time to time, Danger-man. Absolutely, both sides benefit. It's a part of their brands. It's the Yankees-Red Sox rivalry."

Hmmph. I think Bears-Packers would've been more apt.

"You go to those games to see your enemy lose as much as you want to see your team win. That's why the Wailing Wall is so impactful. *'Oh, poor Jews, that's all that's left of their Second Temple.'* Or think about the tourists coming to Bethlehem now. Are they there to actually learn anything about the conflict? Or are they there to take selfies of themselves pressed against something they spray-painted on the wall?"

I felt my face growing Oklahoma-election-map-red.

"Bethlehem is Disneyland. Occupied Disneyland. The fact that it's occupied makes it an even more interesting Disneyland than when it was just the birthplace of Jesus. Not only do you get to see Mickey Mouse, but he's chucking Molotov cocktails over the wall."

I was always more of a Steamboat Willie fan, but the point stuck the landing.

"Can I ask you about your study?" he politely requested, officially becoming the first person in well over 6,000 miles to have any interest whatsoever in my study.

"Of course," I said.

"What kind of questions are you asking your participants?"

"Here," I said, pulling from a copy of my questionnaire out of my travel bag.

"Hmm," he said, supposedly looking it over, though I didn't see his eyes moving at all. "Good thing you bumped into me, because you're missing something important. Can I give you advice? You need to be asking about the physical manifestations of trauma. This shit you ask about, 'what kind of recurring nightmares do you have' and how they express feelings, it's rubbish, mate. No offense, but it's rubbish. That's not how it works here. When you talk to people here, they're going to express their trauma *unconsciously* through physical ailments. Like, they'll get diabetes if they're really traumatized about something. You should change that."

"I... can't," I said. "This is the questionnaire that was approved by the board. I can't add anything without going back to them. And that'll take too long."

"Welp, that's going to be your problem. Your study won't go anywhere. You're basically taking your participants into a sterilized lab and asking them to not mind the probe up their asshole: it's intrusive and isn't even hitting the right spot for them to get off. You need to be able to adapt based on what you're hearing. If you can't ask about their physical sickness, then you've botched it out the gate. Stomach cramps, heart attacks, that kind of stuff. That's what you should look for."

I took the questionnaire from him and looked it over for the two-thousandth time. The paper had a certain limpness to it now.

"Hey, also, I should add, you really need to talk to people in Gaza. West Bank Palestinians? They've seen some shit, but it's not like what you'll get in Gaza."

"How do I get inside there?" I pondered aloud.

"Well, you probably can't, unless you're a certified journalist or something. Unless you found a crack in one of the gates or something. *Hey...*," he lit up, "would you want to slip through the gate with me?"

"How many days would it take, you think?" I indulged him, the idea actually seeming a little endearing. After all, I was approved to collect data anywhere in Palestine, not confined to the "safer" West Bank.

"*Naaaaah*," he backpedaled, "that's not how I'm going to die. I'm gonna die for trusting the wrong person and that's just that."

"Maybe next time, then?"

"Maybe."

An awkward silence ensued, the kind where I'd usually slap my thigh and say "welp" to let them know I'm done talking to them, but this is the Mideast, not the Midwest, and I don't know what colloquialisms translate here.

"What ending did you get?" Trae asked, circling back to the beginning of our conversation.

"Huh?" I replied, my palm already in the air, about to smack my thigh out of its socket.

"That," Trae nodded his head towards my GameBoy just beyond my left arm. "What's your ending?"

"Well," I sighed, "I don't know. I still need to get there."

"Okie doke," he said, which kind of felt like maybe it was the Ramallah equivalent of *welping* and swatting your thigh? "Enjoy your headache, mate. I'm going to head back to Bethlehem now."

I fist-bumped Trae, and for the subsequent 24 hours, I spent the whole day within 500 feet of my bed. I would end up walking about five to ten miles per day during my time in Israel and Palestine, except for the day after my cluster headache, which was the only day of rest I got the rest of the trip. I figured that even Jesus had taken retreat when in the Jericho wilderness, so I thought if even the Savior of the world who was without sin and knew no selfishness took a day off here and there, maybe it was good for me too.

Selah.

> "Science by its very nature is always a work in progress.
> No matter how well-founded we think our worldview is,
> we have to be prepared to rethink it
> if new evidence raises doubts."
> - Dr. Bruce Greyson

טז

May 10, 2020

So I guess you've heard by now.

...

Little Richard, the great, late, not-actually-dead patron of your favorite cereal, is now actually dead

Ohhh yes. I did hear that. I raised a glass of Tutti Frutti in his honor.

Full disclosure, I'm not sure that I really knew he was still alive. He's been out of the limelight for awhile.

He quit show business to focus on ministry.

Is that true or am I walking into a punchline?

No, it's true, Scout's honor!
He said, "I've traded rock-n-roll for the Rock of Ages" after God reminded him,
"you can't serve two masters."
He actually was really spooked that Armageddon was on its way. He spent his life
torn between obedience to God versus obedience to the flesh.

Good golly. I didn't know any of that.

Hey so, I was looking into the stuff you talked about, and realized I had an
important question for you

Okay what?

How are you?

What do you mean?

We've been so wrapped up in theology and our differences that I feel like we
haven't taken the time to check in on each other.

Oh. I'm doing fine. Great actually. Still looking for work, but besides that, everything's great. Are you doing well?

Sure. It's weird though, I'm exhausted all the time lately. Though I guess waking
up in the middle of every night to write a manuscript will do that.

Maybe drink some coffee?

I'm ingesting more caffeine than ever before in my life.

How many cups do you drink a day?

At least two cups. Three if the writing's going particularly well. I have yet to
achieve a fourth cup of coffee in one sitting.

That's a ton of coffee.

Well I'm a growing boy.

Have you tried working out? Or running?

I was in the military. I'm tapped out on calisthenics for at least another 40 years.
Besides I actually am the creator of a quarantine extreme sport:
doing a yard poo run during dusk while wearing flip-flops.

I should try that.
I'm definitely missing the gym.

I missed the gym long before the pandemic shut them all down.

‏ ז ‏

October 8, 1990

"Your daughter is barely hanging on," Dr. Saad said.

"What else can we do?"

"We've done it all. If the blood transfusion didn't help, then it's too late."

"It's her birthday," Umi said. *"Does that matter right now?* No, but I want you to know it. She is 23 years old today. And she can't even be awake for it."

"I hate to ask this," Dr. Saad said, paying no concern to anything irrelevant to the matter at hand, "but given the circumstances, I need to know. If your daughter doesn't make it, and Mirna does, are you prepared to take her in?"

Umi broke down crying, unable to answer the question.

"Dr. Saad," a nurse interrupted. "There's a pr… I would like to talk to you in the other room."

Dr. Saad looked at the nurse as he held his hand on Umi's back.

"It's urgent," the nurse added.

And Umi was left alone with her tears, though she fell asleep even before her tears dried as she sat waiting.

A few hours later, Dr. Saad found Umi slumped over her chair, resting her head on the concrete wall. He gently touched her shoulder, and Umi bounced to her feet as if she was a junior Tzahal who was just caught sleeping on duty by her Samal.

"Dr. Saad."

Lol.
I do fear that once the restrictions are lifted, physical activity will have taken a permanent hit. I've already been gaining quarantine weight.

I guess that's the perk of a pandemic: we're that much closer to WALL-E becoming a reality.

You're full of them today. You'd make for a good dad with those terrible jokes.
Actually I was thinking about you this morning. I thought you should adopt a child.

Oh, thanks. Never thought about that

Really?

Yes, you're the first person in the history of people who thought to yourself, "I should tell him about this great new invention where you go to the Child Store and find the pen of children, pick one out, and take them home."

(ಠ_ಠ)

Sarcasm is hard to pick up on through text.

I don't know how it is in Israel, but here, adoption is a long, complicated, emotionally (and financially) draining process.

So money's a big factor?

Of course, but if it was just about money, then we'd buck up and do it. But I'd never do adoption as a "consolation prize." That's not fair to the kid. If we someday get excited about adoption, then absolutely, we'll go for it. But the passion right now is for us to have our own biological children.

And if that doesn't happen? Will you adopt?

Adoption isn't a "cure" for our issues. You're recommending that I put a band-aid over something that needs a lot more intensive healing. We might adopt someday, but only if we were sure we could love that child like it came out of my own battered urethra.

That's really graphic.

Thanks.

...not a compliment.

What I have written I have written.

She looked into his downturned eyes, which seeped of grief. He squeezed her shoulder.

"I'm sorry," Dr. Saad apologized, almost as if he was defending a particularly poor choice to a superior. "Mirna is… sick. Sicker than she should be. We put her in an incubator. But… I didn't know."

Umi removed Dr. Saad's hand from her shoulder and peered into his sad eyes.

"I didn't know… the incubator we put her in, it had not been disinfected. The baby before Mirna… there was a terrible infection. That baby had passed away, but the incubator was never cleaned. Somehow. I don't know how. Mirna has contracted that same infection that killed that child."

"My granddaughter will die because of this?" Umi asked, taking Dr. Saad's hand into her palms.

"Germs – so insidious. Unseen. They swim on surfaces, sail on the air. Innocuous, they loll on a fomite, and then they die, unless they find a host. Unless they make their way into a vulnerable throat… then the virus attaches. Multiplies itself. The immune system fights it, forgetting its top goal: make sure we're breathing. The oxygen can't get through the capillaries, and then it's over."

"How far has the infection progressed?" Umi asked.

"There is no need to be concerned about having to raise Mirna."

ACE IN THE HOLY LAND

> "There are many people who reach their
> conclusions about life like schoolboys;
> they cheat their master by copying
> the answer out of a book without
> having worked out the sum for themselves."
> - Soren Kierkegaard

There was a cost to my rest: I'd already burned about a quarter of my 40 days, which I would've been comfortable with had I actually gotten to experience the places I'd planned to visit. That Israeli officer in the Milan airport was starting to get in my head: was it really possible to achieve some kind of religious transcendence at the holy sites scattered through the Promised Land *and* find enough participants for my research study? If I was having this much trouble simply getting access to tourist destinations *during the tourism off-season*, then what if I had just as much difficult getting access to Israelis and Palestinians? What if my entire trip was shaping up to be a complete wash?

Enough (non-)adventures. Enough nonsense. I had traveled across the world, not to get shut out from every tourist locus I could lay my eyes on, but to conduct a research study that would cap off my doctorate program. Even so, this deep into my journey, I still didn't have a single unit of data that I could actually use.

It was time to play my ace.

In my back pocket was Dr. Shalev, a natural-born Israeli who worked at an interfaith community engagement center. Several months ago, he had agreed to be my liaison to the Israeli and Palestinian young adult population that I was looking to interview for my study. He was confident that, with his network of young adults he had earned the trust of at the engagement center, I would have no problem getting all the participants I needed. He was *so* confident, in fact, that it was the reason I had time to visit (or attempt to visit) several of the landmarks in Israel and Palestine.

I sat down outside the Jaffa Gate, where a woman wearing an angel outfit serenaded travelers with a harp as they passed the threshold. I emailed Dr. Shalev and announced my arrival to Jerusalem. He'd always been prompt in his responses; sometimes I had to wonder if he had been writing his response to my emails before I even knew I was about to send one. True to his nature, Dr. Shalev responded within minutes after I emailed him.

Oh, Shalev. Good, ol' trusty, dependable Shalev.

"Danger, I am so sorry that I forgot you were coming. I am away on holiday. Good luck!"

I couldn't believe my eyes. How could he forget I had been coming? *Me?* Danger Rose!

I responded, sounding less like Danger Rose and more like Scarlett O'Hara begging for life direction, "Where shall I go? What shall I do?"

And channeling his innermost Clark Gable, Dr. Shalev replied, "Check with the hostel you're staying at; maybe they have somebody who will want to volunteer for your study."

The hostel I'd checked into was a bit outside of the city and had a maximum occupancy of 13 people and maybe a dormouse or two. Most of the people staying were from Germany and New Zealand, though. That wasn't going to cut it, so I cut my losses and checked out of that auberge, then entered the Citadel hostel in the Old City instead, which had dozens of travelers coming and going.

"Hi, I would like to check in without a reservation, if you'll have me," I told the front desk worker at the Citadel.

"Sir, I'm so sorry," the man replied, "but we have no rooms for you. We are completely booked this whole week. However, there is access to our roof, and if you'd like, we have some room for you up there."

"I'll take it," I said, actually kind of enjoying the fleeting feeling that I was a bit like Mary and Joseph, needing a room and being given a corner. "I was also wondering, would you be willing to allow me to post a flyer in your hostel? The flyer explains this, but I am an American doing a study, looking for…"

"Yes," he interrupted and handed me a push pin, then motioned towards a corridor. "You can post it on the board down the hallway."

I wandered down the hall, found the bulletin board, and push-pinned my flyer onto it with a schmaltz that hadn't been seen since Martin Luther hammered his 95 Theses onto the doorway of the Wittenberg Castle Church.

I backed up from the bulletin board to take glee in my accomplishment. There sat my monochrome flyer, created by my own hands, amongst a vibrant field of 25 other flyers. The successful completion of my PhD was predicated upon whether or not 40 people would see my flyer and become so stirred about "interpersonal conflict in the family dynamic" that they would go out of their way to contact me at my school email address, which happened to be longer in length than the whole of the Oslo Accords.

"Nope."

I hied out of the Citadel and began my study recruitment.

```
             "If I say,
 'Surely the darkness shall cover me,
   and the light about me be night,'
 even the darkness is not dark to you;
     the night is bright as the day,
  for darkness is as light with you."
        ~ Psalm 139:11-12, ESV
```

יך

<u>May 14, 2020</u>

So I had an annoying thing happen

Whats that

I talked to a job recruiter to get help finding work.
She told me to omit my education from my resume given that Tulsa doesn't field
higher education too well, and nobody wants to hire an overqualified applicant.
She also told me to stop going by Danger. Change my name.

Do you think there's truth to what she's saying?

Idk for sure. She's the expert right?
But even if any of that helped me get a job, it's not what I believe was meant for
me. My name isn't a nickname. It's my actual name. God called me to go by that
name. God called me to get my degree. I stepped out in faith and did it.
5 years and a lifetime of debt later: nothing. And now the recruiter tells me to
scrub from my resume everything I was ever called to do.
And for what? A chance to earn $13/hour?
I wouldn't scrub my identity for $80/hour.

I'm sorry
I feel like this is an inappropriate time to have a "I told you so" moment, but this
interaction kinda proves my point that god doesn't call us to specific things.

I knew you wouldn't agree.
I know we're on separate waves here.

It's the same ocean though. That counts for something.

As long as neither of us drown, I guess.
Though it would be kinda cool to sink and find yourself inside a whale.

That happened on the Mediterranean, not the ocean.
And it wasn't a whale, but a fish.
"Leviathan" vs "Dawg"

Matchup of the century!

Hey, going back to the "meshiach would be born of a virgin" mistranslation that
christians believe in. You asked if I had any more examples of christians altering
the meaning of the Hebrew bible

Yes, do you?

do you know the story of Sodom and Gomorrah?

Of course. It's probably the most cited Bible story when Christians converse
about whether or not to support gay rights.

But you realize that's not the intent of the story, right? In the jewish narrative, it's
not there to take a stand about homosexuality, but about all righteousness.

So what does the Jewish text say about what happened?

Well, you know how the people of Sodom try to rape 2 angels?

Yes.

That didn't happen.

Oh. Really? What's the story there then?

١٧
October 13, 1990

Her eyes opened. The world was still spinning – too fast for Claire's liking. She saw a figure in the chair, but her vision was blurred and she couldn't decipher the shadow.

"Umi?" Claire inquired.

"They're all gone," a deep voice responded.

"Doctor?" Claire asked.

No response.

Claire scraped her eyes with her nails, and her vision slowly came back. The figure, indeed, was Dr. Saad, who hunched over in the visitor's chair with his head cradled in his hands, still in his bright lab coat.

"Where is my daughter?" Claire asked.

"I was wrong," Dr. Saad announced, a defeated man. "My god is no god. I don't know what's worse: not having any chance of saving her, or that we could have saved her and failed to."

"*Where* is my *Mirna*?" she shrieked, impatient with Dr. Saad's uncharacteristic caginess.

"I don't know what's worse, if it be that your God didn't have the power to save, or that your God did have the power to save and refused to save them."

"Who is *them*?" Claire yelled, now incensed at the cryptic man who was normally so straightforward.

"The children, Claire," Dr. Saad said, finally looking up at her with intensely cardinal eyes.

The Lord tells Abraham that he's going to destroy Sodom and Gomorrah because of how unrighteous it is, and Abraham opposes this, he argues it's not in god's character to destroy the righteous with the unrighteous, and asks god to spare the city if Abraham can find just 40 people. And god says, 'sure, find 40 people and I won't hurl burning sulfur all over the city.'

"Lord, Lord," Abraham goes on. "What if I can't find 40 people? Will you be satisfied with 30?" God says "If you can find 30, I will be content with that." Abraham says, "Thank you, Lord, but, what if I cannot find 30? What if I can only find five less than 30? Would this be enough to please you?" God says "I would be satisfied even with 25."

"Thank you, Lord. But Lord, if I may say without you being aroused to anger, what if I can only find 20?" God says "I would be willing to accept 20 as satisfactory."

"Thank you, Lord. But... Lord. What if I cannot find 20? What would you say if I only brought forth a total number of 2 people?" God says "Abraham, my son. Then, I will spare Sodom and Gomorrah."

But there weren't even 2 righteous people in all of Sodom and Gomorrah, so the Lord destroyed the city, and only the prophet Lot and his family escaped the city. Not even his wife survived, because when she turned around to watch the destruction, she turned into a pillar of salt.

But here's the thing: the jews orally passed down this story, and then were the first to actually record it in writing, and somehow still, muslims and christians both found ways to add and pervert this story for no other reason than to bend the story to fit their narratives. The muslims state that Lot's wife didn't turn into a pillar of salt, but was killed by a rock that fell on her, and christians add a story about the residents of Sodom trying to rape 2 angels. Neither of these are in the original text, so where do you get off making this stuff up? Like, why even do that?

Interesting. I'm definitely familiar with the bit about the Sodomites trying to rape the angels. I didn't know that was a late-add.
Still, that being said:
these are minuscule differences. None of this changes the overall theology.

Sure, THESE are small differences, but if you're willing to bend a little detail, you're willing to bend a big detail eventually. Like: the meshiach being born of a virgin. These small differences amount to great differences when piled together. All of a sudden, christianity is full of appearances by angels when they were nearly unseen in jewdism; muslims tell jews that our narrative is wrong when we had the narrative 4000 years before them! And then jews have to defend our stories as if we weren't the ones to write it down in the first place.

I can see how that's frustrating. Angering, even. And I don't have an answer to that. I didn't realize that Jews didn't believe the bit about the angels in Sodom. I'd have to look into why Christians translated it like that.
I still haven't looked into the Mary-as-a-virgin thing either.

Sounds like you have some homework

That's okay. I haven't had any homework since leaving my program. I welcome learning

Ever the scholar

Just a curious cat.

Or dawg.

He seemed a different man. His outline was so vivid to Claire, as if a cartoon, and his presence was so cutting that Claire actually felt discomfort. He relished Claire not knowing Mirna's fate.

"What children, doctor? Please, please, please: where is Mirna? And where is my Umi?" Claire asked, slicing into his crimson eyes with her own tensity.

"Mirna is on life support. Umi is on her way to the church to get the priest, so that we can unplug and let Mirna die. Your daughter was afflicted with an infection. A lethal virus. A contagion so communicable that every other baby on the wing was infected. All six of them infected. All six of them dead."

Claire's eyes swelled as her heart sunk.

"All of the babies are gone?" Claire asked.

"All," the doctor shook his head, "but your Mirna."

"Mirna."

"Your God – the God of Moses, who killed hordes of infants at Passover – is alive today. This God – who, in this city, orchestrated the Massacre of the Innocents to spare one child at the expense of all the others in Bethlehem – He is here. For only He could compose a symphony so bloodthirsty as this."

"May I see her?"

"Normally, I would not allow it. But there are no more babies for you to kill, and she is going to die anyway."

"No. Not my girl. Not my Mirna."

> "The plural of anecdote is data."
> - Raymond Wolfinger

"Hi sir, are you checking in?" the young woman at the hostel front desk asked without looking up.

"No, thank you," I said. "You are Talia, yeah?"

The woman met my eyes and raised one eyebrow.

"That is correct," she replied. "How may I help you?"

"I was in here earlier today, speaking with Noam. He said that you grew up on a settlement in Palestine?"

"I grew up in a small, beautiful town in Israel, the land of the Jews, which was given them by God," Talia tersely responded.

"And he said that you have had some experiences on that set...*y*. City. Specifically in regards to Palestinian terrorists. And you're pretty open to talking about it?"

"I suppose, yes," she said, clamming up a little more with each word. "Who did you say you were?"

"My name is Danger," I said. I was tempted to follow up by announcing my full name – "Danger Rose" – coupled with a soul-touching smoldering smirk, but instead settled on something a smidge more tantalizing.

"I'm a student at the Chicago School of Professional Psychology who is studying interpersonal conflict in the family dynamic."

Talia burst out laughing and slapped her wrist over her eyes.

"*Ahh*, kay," she said, then lowered her hand and locked her eyes on mine, as if I had opted to pass on "truth" and now she was drumming up a dare. "It's funny how you Americans always see this thing."

"Well, how do I see it?" I implored.

She responded with a withering grin of her own.

"Good luck," Talia dismissed me.

I nodded, then left.

While this had been the first time I'd been outright laughed at, it wasn't the first time that my identification as an American researcher had killed a conversation. Starting a dialogue with "would you wish to take part in my research study" was like going a first date and asking "do you mind if I report the details of our evening to my mama?"

As I staggered away, I felt the heat rising in my cheeks. My frustration came to a boiling point: no place in the world knew perpetual stalemate like Israel did, but nobody seemed to be willing to acknowledge it. It was almost as if it was an unwritten rule to not talk about it with outsiders in the same way you wouldn't air your family's dirty laundry when friends are around.

After shaking off the dust from my encounter with Talia, I popped into a convenience store.

I grabbed a Jericho-brand water bottle from the fridge, and attempting humor (as I usually do when I'm flustered), asked the shopkeeper, "do you need me to march around the shop seven times before I buy this?"

"No," he said, "you can just pay me 15 shekels."

I couldn't tell if he had no sense of humor or was wildly funnier than me.

"Is this water actually from Jericho?" I asked him, to which he shrugged.

"I went to Jericho," I said to him. "I've *been* there."

He wasn't impressed.

I handed him the money, then looked at the bottle, which said in its fine print, "*bottled in the Philippines.*"

"It's bottled in the Philippines," I told him.

"Okay," he told me.

I started walking out of the shop before realizing I was in danger of never graduating if I didn't use this as an opportunity to get some answers.

"Hey, sir, *you* don't find me funny," I vented to the unsuspecting shopkeeper. "Can you tell me why do people here laugh at me when I try to talk to them?"

"They laugh at you?" the shopkeeper asked in a flat voice, somehow not caught off-guard by my arbitrary question.

"Yes, I show them this flyer, and they laugh at me," I brooded, as if one person constitutes a "them" and a "they."

The shopkeeper read over my flyer.

"Ah," he said," "yes. This is your problem. Do not show them this. Talk to them like they are your friend. Talk as we are now."

"So, just strike up a conversation, hear what they have to say, and write it down later?"

"Yes, do that."

"And don't tell them I'm doing that?"

He closed his eyes, then shrugged.

The idea was alluring. But it was also unethical, and would illegitimatize my data.

Maybe it wasn't my destiny to get any participants after all. Maybe it's my destiny to live in a state of perpetual toil. *Have you heard the tale of Danger Rose? Legend has it that he still wanders the shops of Jerusalem and the deserts of Jericho in search of research participants, limping along because he doesn't want to pop open the blister on his left big toe.*

I've always loved to play chess. I'm not sure there's a better way to teach a young child how to think critically than to explain the strengths and weaknesses and importance of each piece, and then see what scheme they can concoct against an opponent who has the same exact resources as them. Yet, I never stopped to think about the chess pieces' emotional states on the battlefield.

What does the pawn think when he knows he has to sacrifice himself for the greater good?

What does the rook think when he realizes he's just a big castle keep and shouldn't be able to move or have any stream of consciousness?

Most importantly, what does the king think to himself when he understands that, in about five moves' time, he's going to be cornered and unable to defend himself? That no matter what he does now, there's a big, fat loss coming his way?

Even if I didn't spend another millimoment taking in another holy landmark, I now had little over two weeks to get a commitment from 20 Israelis and 20 Palestinians to give me an hour of their time, conduct 40 hours' worth of interviews, and then report my data collection to my school in preparation for analysis.

And for those of us in the biz, we call that a *checkmate.*

In my state of desperation, I reached out to my dissertation chair at the Chicago School of Professional Psychology – a man by the name of Dr. Lord Giddie – to report on my struggles.

"Lord, Lord," I said. "What if I can't find 40 people? Will you be satisfied with 30?"

"If you can find 30, I will be content with that."

"Thank you, Lord," I said. "But, what if I cannot find 30? What if I can only find five less than 30? Would this be enough to please you?"

"I would be satisfied even with 25."

"Thank you, Lord. But Lord, if I may say without you being aroused to anger, what if I can only find 20?"

"I would be willing to accept 20 as satisfactory."

"Thank you, Lord. But… Lord. What if I cannot find 20? What would you say if I only brought forth a total number of two people?"

"Danger, my disciple. Get out and start recruiting before I destroy you."

And so it was that Danger Rose rodeth onward to hasten the mission of his Lords.

> "Have mercy on me, LORD, for I am faint;
> heal me, LORD, for my bones are in agony.
> My soul is in deep anguish.
> How long, LORD, how long?
> All night long I flood my bed with
> weeping and drench my couch with tears.
> My eyes grow weak with sorrow;
> they fail because of all my foes."
> ~ Psalm 6:2-3,6-7, NIV

יח

May 16, 2020

Any job leads lately?

No. You?

Not paying ones. I did have a pastor ask me if I wanted to help him lead a college youth group at a church. Which is a move of restoration, given my past. But I told him no.

Why?

Well first I need to stop taking on new volunteer roles and find something that pays a couple bills. My daily schedule is full of volunteer stuff as if I have a retirement check coming in. But I told him I need to evaluate some things, figure out what tenets of American Christianity I actually believe

What don't you believe?

Idk. Things that get said like "there's power in the name of Jesus" or "God has a plan for everyone." Again it's not that I don't believe those things, I simply need to scrupulize whether they're Scripturally-based and not just westernized adaptations of something.
I just want to get away from American Christianity and get back to the Christianity that was rooted in Judaism. "The Way." That Christianity.

What else are you evaluating?

I have a list actually. I could go on and on. But the big ones are what I just mentioned, and then "Yeshua broke the curse of sin" And "prayer can sway God's will" and "God gives you the desires of your heart" and "You should pray for other people when they're ill and their sickness will be cast out."
Stuff like that

So if you end up not believing any of that, then what do you think prayer is good for?

Lately I've worked under a new rule. Well 2 new rules. The first is "Don't ask God for anything you can do yourself," and the second is "Don't ask God for anything unless you're already sure it's in alignment with His will." And if I'm not sure His stance on it, I can ask for the thing, but I have to be okay with whether or not I get the thing I'm praying for. If I can't promise to be okay if I don't get it, then I don't get to ask for it.

That doesn't seem like a christian thought. It's certainly not a jewish one.

It's a logical conclusion I guess? I started with the facts of what I know for sure to be true and then considered all the possibilities of why it's true

What are the facts?

The big one is this: Romy died despite my earnest prayers.

And what was the conclusion?

There were 4 possible outcomes.

Oi. No. Not doing it.
That's too long of a conversation.
Can you sum it up?

Let's compromise. I'll sum up each individual one.

١٨

<u>October 13, 1990</u>

Claire cradled Mirna, but Mirna's throat was too obstructed for her to even cry.

"You only have a few moments left," a young doctor told her as he tracked Mirna's heart with a stethoscope, Dr. Saad having gone home.

"I want you to see what happens when the priest comes back," Claire told the doctor, whose skeptical eyes invalidated his nodding head.

"Mirna," Claire cooed in her child's ear, "my little girl. Arise."

Umi rushed into Claire's room, seeing her daughter – and granddaughter – awake for the first time together in days, months, years, lifetimes, or however long ago it was.

"Claire!" Umi yelled, wrapping her arms around her daughter, then acknowledged the priest she brought with.

"Father is going to say a prayer. Well, Baptize. Father is going to Baptize Mirna."

Claire smiled.

"Baptize her, Father, and we will watch as the God of Abraham, Isaac, and Jacob takes away all her pain."

The priest extended his hand, sprinkled water on Mirna's crown, and rubbed his thumb over her forehead as he trumpeted with authority:

"Mirna Anastas, I baptize you in the Name of the Father, of the Son, and of the Holy Ghost."

The room hushed, making way for reverent silence.

Deal.

The first is that my prayers, though authentic, were simply not earnest enough. This goes back to when we were talking about whether or not prayer "works" if you don't say the right magical words. With Romy, I'd prayed for years for her health, but as she was dying, I didn't "inform" Him or remind Him how much I love and needed her. I figured God knew how much we loved our dogs without my saying it in that moment.

Yeah. That's outright silly. If you have a newborn on the way, you don't need to pray for every piece of that process. I mean, how specific do you have to get? "Please make sure the doctors are competent, that they weren't educated in a third world country. Develop the baby's lungs, and the immune system, and her eyes - hopefully they're blue, Lord - and - oh! Please don't forget to give her a brain." No, you just say "please see this pregnancy through." Otherwise it's a slippery slope where the more we know about science, the stronger our prayers are.

Hmmmmmmm... though that would explain why so many babies died in childbirth up until the 21st century...

Are you serious right now?

No. Not at all.

Okay lol. Like I said, sarcasm gets lost in text.

I know in my heart how fervently I prayed, and I know how much faith I put into praying for her as her health nosedived. And if I wasn't where I needed to be in order to get heard by God during my mountaintop, then I'll never be righteous enough for my prayers to be heard in this valley.
It's just not a sensical conclusion.

I agree. What's your second possibility?

Yeshua is really the Christ, but the early church misquoted Him so egregiously that our understanding of prayer is corrupted.
But to cross that bridge, I would have to throw out most of the New Testament, and if I'm doing that, then how can I believe the Gospel in the first place? Again, not a compatible philosophy, and it would be narcissistic for me to believe that I somehow have the inside track on Yeshua's actual message in the early church.

K. Third?

It was God's will that Romy die. But this one is hard because I think it would mean that God's will trumps what Scripture says prayer is powerful enough to do.
There's a paradox here.

Yeah, that one can get you into a logical loop. It's a circular question like "Is god powerful enough to create a rock so heavy he can't lift?"

But there's one more possibility. And I'm scared because it's the most logical conclusion I can think of right now.

?

What if Christ is not the Christ? The Messiah is still to come?

Mirna interrupted the quiet with a vociferous gasp, then gurgled as she caught Claire's eyes with her own. Mirna smiled just before her pupils dilated for a brief moment, then shrunk to midposition.

"Mirna," Claire whispered, then put the back of her hand on her daughter's cheek. "She is not breathing. *Help!*"

The doctor felt her neck, then placed his stethoscope on the middle of her chest. Then just to the left of her thorax. Then to the right. Then he grabbed her tiny wrist and measured her pulse. Then dropped her hand and frantically used his stethoscope to find any sign of life.

He shook his head and unequipped his stethoscope.

"Her heart has stopped," the doctor announced.

> "For with You is the fountain of life;
> in Your light do we see light."
> ~ Psalm 36:9, ESV

I had my mission: get 20 participants. Ten Israelis, ten Palestinians. It was no easy feat: I had exhausted my Israeli and Palestinian contacts, and I had contacted every listed university in Israel and Palestine for some direction. Only one school responded, but they didn't have any English-speaking students and I couldn't afford a translator. I had dropped in on a few of the unresponsive universities' campuses, only to be shooed away when I canvassed the administration if any of their psychology students might be interested in taking part of a real, sanctioned psychological study. One of the college's directors said "we can't just approach our students and ask them if they want to be in research," citing a policy that not only betrayed the basic principles and purpose of higher education, but one that was probably as real as Jewish leprechauns. I wasn't really sure how else their psychology department got participants for their own studies, but it certainly wasn't my ground to argue.

I thought about the deadpan shopkeeper, and how he urged me to engage with Israelis and Palestinians as a friendly tourist rather than introducing myself as a researcher who needed an hour of their time. It sparked an idea: while there was *no way* I could ethically collect qualitative abstracts from an individual without their explicit consent, I *could* try to create a surface relationship with potential participants and *then* tell them about my study. Pull a Baraka, without the religious manipulation. Hopefully, I could create enough pull in these momentary relationships that it would generate an authentic interest in what I was trying to do.

Of course, the problem with this plan of action is that *even people in my homeland* don't usually like me enough to want to talk to me. So, out of options and nowhere to turn, I threw a Hail Mary and contacted the one person I usually turn to in times of crisis.

"Jesus, I'm here. You called me to this place to do this study, but I'm running out of time. If I don't get participants, then I can't fulfill this call you gave me. Please, by the end of today, when I lay my head down to sleep, may I have gotten at least one participant for my study. I've tried to make this happen. I've failed every time. Please come through for me because clearly I can't do it myself."

I felt that my best shot was to go back to the beginning: Bethlehem. My first soiree had been veiled by the night, and while it made me much more of a tourist than a pilgrim or a researcher, I still wanted to check out the Separation Wall between Israel and Palestine – a cement slab that was nearly 30 feet tall and topped with barbed wire, and it stretched the 440-mile perimeter around all of the West Bank. The wall was spray-painted with political phrases that were often accompanied with cute art, ranging from archetypical tags like "Free Palestine" and "This Wall Will Fall," to more creative graffiti like a painted road sign that said "Caution: Children Playing... with Barbed Wire" and the sketch of an MS-DOS error message that stated "Oops Your City Has Been Encrypted." With any luck, maybe someday I'd see this wall carved into sections, sitting next to the Berlin Wall in a museum. But as of right now, the towering hunk of concrete guaranteed that I never accidentally wandered over the border into Israel.

The wall was typically busy, so I had as much of a chance of finding a participant there than anywhere else in Bethlehem. No longer wandering under a dark sky, I moseyed along the wall, admiring the extensive art until I came across a small hut that called itself The Banksy Shop. The young store merchant was standing outside the door, looking bored as not a single customer was inside perusing the postcards and Separation Wall paraphernalia inside.

"Please, come have a look," he called out to me.

"Thank you, but I don't have any cash," I said, providing my go-to (and technically-honest) response when beckoned by merchants, as I was only carrying credit cards in my wallet.

"My friend, no problem. Looking is free!" he said, providing the go-to (and technically-honest) response to my response, as he knew I was carrying credit cards in my wallet.

"Sure, why not?" I relented and entered his shop, eliciting a wide smile from the shopkeeper.

"Where are you from?" he asked.

"Zion. Er, Chicago."

"*Chi-ca-gooo!*" he punched every syllable. "Windy City. Chicago Bulls. Obama. Michael Jordan."

All correct affiliations. I smiled politely.

Most of the merchandise were pins and posters and metal signs that had the wall art embossed on the products.

"There's a lot of good stuff in here," I patronized. My compliment was the only thing I intended to pay him until I saw a nativity set that was nothing short of brilliant: it had the normal Nativity tableau, with baby Jesus in a manger, surrounded by Mary and Joseph and Gabriel and a few animals. But the diorama extended far enough that there was an added Separation Wall in front of the manger, and *who had been cast away from the impenetrable wall* but three weary wisemen!

"This is beautiful," I told the merchant. "Do you take credit card?"

The merchant smiled.

As I checked out of the store a few minutes later – admittedly with a few more postcards and ornaments than I intended to leave with – the merchant said to me, "I'm glad you appreciate the commentary on this nativity set."

Hokay. This guy can actually speak straight English.

"I think it's powerful," I said, trying to ascertain how pretending to not speak fluent English would embiggen a merchant's sales. "It puts into perspective what's going on here. So you would say the Separation Wall has been effective?"

"Oh, it's effective," he quickly agreed, still in perfect prose with an accent that was actually quite endearing. "For all the criticism about how inhumane and demeaning and oppressive it is, nobody can argue and say that it's not enough of a deterrent. Not only would I never be able to find a way over that wall, but even if I found a slip-hole, you certainly wouldn't see me daring to breach it."

"Do you feel like it adequately restricts you from engaging with Israelis?"

"Oh, yes, sir. I have visited Jerusalem on a permit just a few times in my life. I have little interaction with anyone outside, at least anyone who is not a Palestinian or a tourist visiting the Nativity site. I have high hopes that maybe someday I can escape this prison yard, but what can I do? It is an occupation. Unless someone breaks me out, I am stuck under this oppression."

"It seems like you have a lot of thoughts on this. Would you care to share them with me? I'm a doctoral candidate at the Chicago School of Professional Psychology, trying to gather participants in a study related to interpersonal conflict on the family dynamic."

"My sir, it would be an honor to talk to you. Are you free tonight?"

"Yes," I said. (I had cleared my docket for such a reason.)

"Then I insist that you must come to my home in Aida Camp, where my mother will cook dinner for you and we can talk as much as you need. In fact, my friend will also be coming by later tonight, so when you are done with me, you can speak to him as well."

"That would be amazing to me. Amazing *for* me." Within minutes of my plea to God, my study ballooned from zero participants to having 20% of the Palestinians that I needed. Who says prayer doesn't work?

"And your name, sir?"

"I am Danger."

"Danger?"

"Yes, Danger. Or... *Khatar*," I said, recalling my name in Arabic.

"Khatar!"

"Yes, Khatar. Danger. And you are?"

"Izzy. They just call me Izzy. And my friend is Jehad."

"*Oof*!" I instinctually winced.

"What is wrong?"

"Oh, it's... nothing," I said, but then his crestfallen face prompted me to realize he thought I was somehow mocking him, so I elucidated. "It's just... that's, like, Number Three for us."

"Number Three of what?" Izzy puzzled.

"Well," I explained, "you've got Adolf. Then you have Osama, and then it's Jihad. The order of names you can't give your baby."

"Oh, yes," Izzy said, "this he knows. His requests to go to the United States have been denied many times."

"I'm sorry to hear that. I know what it's like to have your own name become a millstone."

"Well, I like your name, Mr. Danger. I will give you my number and we can chat after I'm off work. In the meantime, maybe you can continue looking at all the art that our Wall of Oppression has to offer."

"I guarantee you that I'll be doing that. Have you ever drawn on the wall, Izzy?"

He smiled. It was a stupid question. It was technically illegal to draw on the wall.

"I can't remember, Mr. Danger Khatar."

I laughed.

"Hey, I was also wondering about the art out here on the wall. Are any of those actual Banksies?"

"Banksies" are the eponymous name given to any street art done by Banksy, the world-famous (yet-unidentified) graffiti artist who created detailed renderings on the walls of some of the most famous landmarks around the world. Or, in many cases, the renderings themselves turned the otherwise-benign location into a political landmark.

"None of these are Banksies," Izzy confirmed, "at least right in this area. Of course, you have the Armoured Dove down the way."

"I saw that one! In fact, I *touched* it," I exclaimed, as if saying so made me cooler.

"Why did you touch the art?" Izzy inquired.

I considered his question. I didn't really know the answer, other than I felt the compulsion to. I'd often get the urge to touch meaningful art after I'd seen it, and sometimes I'd oblige by stroking the contours as if my finger was the paint brush. Of course, the exception to that is if a "do not touch the art" sign was posted next to the piece, in which case, I'd *always* get my fingers on it.

Even the day after Joanna and I got married, before we hopped on a plane for our honeymoon, I looked out our Chicagoland hotel window on the seventh floor and noticed the neighboring city's famous water tower. I'd seen it probably a hundred times in my life: it was painted to resemble a massive rose, with the riser glossed green to annotate a flower stem and the top-heavy tank itself daubed as a blooming rose. I was as close as I'd ever be to touching the art, so Joanna humored me and we shuttled over to the towering rose – her first wedded foray into my trademark neuroticism. I touched the thornless stalk on the homely side street, and then we immediately turned around and caught another ride back to the hotel, where we had a far greater view of the Rosemont horizon and its rosey water tower – art that was intended to be appreciated from afar, not next to.

"You know what, Izzy?" I snapped back to reality. "I'm not entirely sure. Maybe to absorb it a little more? Mentally, I mean? I don't know. Does Banksy have other pieces around here?"

"Why? So you can get your grubby fingers on them?" he asked, which I *think* was meant as a joke.

I smiled awkwardly.

"There are a few other less-famous ones throughout the city," he noted. "Right here, we have some replicas of them, but none of them are authentic. But most of our merchandise is from official Banksy street art, hence the name here, 'The Banksy Shop.'"

I'm sure the anti-establishment, anti-commercialization Banksy was happy to see his art turned into bite-sized low-resolution renderings of his street art. But to be fair, not far away from where I was standing, Banksy did have a shop of his own that sold bite-sized high-resolution renderings of his street art for about five times the price as these knock-offs. Further, that shop was in a Banksy-commissioned hotel – the "Walled Off Hotel" – that rented out rooms for about ten times the price as any other lodging in Bethlehem.

"Have you ever met the guy?"

"What guy?"

"Banksy, of course."

"No. How could I? Nobody knows who he is."

"But if you don't know what he looks like, maybe you have met him then?"

"No, but nobody has ever come up to me and said, 'hi, I'm Banksy.'"

"Okay. But if I'm Banksy, am I going to go up to you and explicitly say, 'I'm Banksy, nice to meet you.' Would you actually believe someone who tried pulling that?"

"I guess not, no," Izzy conceded.

"So maybe you have met Banksy and just don't know it?"

Izzy looked skyward and thought about that statement for a moment. I sensed a small rush of excitement come over him, which quickly was washed into shock after he looked back down and peered into my eyes. Seizing the moment, I winked at him.

"*Banksy!*" Izzy whispered in a high shrill as his eyes widened. "Banksy, is that you?"

I belted one hearty laugh, then followed up by saying, "No, I'm not Banksy."

"That's *exactly* what Banksy would say! It *is* you!"

"Bro, bro. I was just messing with you," I said as Izzy whipped out his phone and took a picture of me.

"Can I take a picture *with* you?" Izzy needled.

"No, because I'm not Banksy! I'm an American. Banksy is English."

"Oh? How do *you* know he's English?" Izzy said, wagging his finger at me as if I just blew my cover.

I began to refute again, but to his point, I guess I technically couldn't *prove* that Banksy was from England. So, I held my hands up and shrugged. I meant to admit that I couldn't prove that Banksy was English, but Izzy seemed to think I was admitting that I was Banksy.

"*Ah-HA!*" he cheered, then came around his cashier's desk, snugly wrapped one arm around me, and snapped a selfie of us with the other hand. He excitedly turned the phone around to see the shot he took, which had him slightly out-of-frame and me in the center of the picture with an embarrassed, crooked smile.

"I tell no one," he whispered into my ear.

י״ט

May 21, 2020

I figured out another logical conclusion to the "why did Romy die" question.

What's that

Maybe it's because I didn't have a Mezuzah on the doorpost to my home.

Ah yes. It's definitely the mezuzah. lol

I installed one sometime last year, one that I bought at the City of David. So no more bad luck in this house going forward

Yeah nothing bad has ever happened to jews who put up their mezuzah the right way.

It's good timing because we're trying something new. We're getting aggressive with fertility treatments. If we get pregnant, it'll likely be in the next 3 months

Wow! That's actually quite exciting

Well our window is closing, so we knew it was time to give it our last shot. We're spending a TON of money and going further into debt, but it'll be worth it if it works. I'm even getting off my OCD meds to give it a try.

Uh oh. That could end poorly. Did you talk to your doctor about it?

Yeah my psychiatrist is in on the loop. Truth be told I've been weaning myself off my meds the past couple months because I had a feeling this is the direction we would be going. And I don't want to go into debt over this only to find out that had I just stopped my meds, it would've worked.

So you're not on anything right now?

I have meds on an "as needed" basis. My psychiatrist gave me "oh shit" pills just in case.

In case of what? You feel like killing yourself?

Not "I feel like killing myself" but "if I don't take these pills, I will absolutely hurt myself."

Well let's not get there

Yeah I suppose that would be my preference too.

You should figure out a way to smile more over these next few months. Find something to laugh about every day.

I'm good, I already laugh once a day.

Just once?

I look in the mirror every morning and just laugh so I can start the day out by laughing in the face of danger

Lololol nice

I had a question for you. Do you think God calls individuals to specific purposes?

Hm. Kinda a loaded question. Of course the answer is "yes sometimes" because god did that with the ancestors. And there is this idea that we're all here for some individual and specific purpose. But to say "god called me to do ____" is probably more of an act of ego. Nobody can know with 100% certainty that "this" is what god wants for them. That mindset is a little destructive and potentially dangerous.

١٩

November 26, 1990

Claire buried her daughter among the first martyrs, in the cemetery alongside the Church of the Nativity that had allotted a plot for Claire so many years ago. But this suffering was not, in itself, satisfactory: while mourning Mirna, Claire's backyard was chosen to become the site of an Israeli bivouac. Not only would the Anastas home lose their privacy, but soldiers would be allowed to come in as they please to use their roof for surveillance.

"Your house is plotted on Israeli soil," the Samal explained.

"This is not Israel," Claire blustered at the idea that her enemies would have full access to her house whenever they wanted. "This is Palestine!"

"Palestine *is* Israel," the Samal barked back. "We would not need to do this, but you know full well that your people... that is to say, *some* Palestinians have begun using weapons against us. We don't wish for any of this to be escalated, but we simply cannot have our soldiers being attacked."

"And you cannot choose one of the *many* empty homes on this street?" Claire asked.

"Claire Anastas, your home is three stories tall and provides natural protection from bullets," the Samal reasoned with Claire, even with a hint of empathy. "Does it make you feel better if I tell you that Rachel's Tomb is being commandeered to become a military fortress, too? Your backyard is far from being the only piece on the chessboard, here. If you point to me another house that has three stories with access to a roof

Because if you're so sure that what you're doing is mandated by god, then you'll do it at any cost.

The mindset of a terrorist.

Or a prophet.

Yeah. But today, a terrorist.

Fair.

In jewdism, when someone dies, it's common to say they died because they accomplished their purpose in the world. Even a baby who was barely alive and spent her entire short life in a hospital, she fulfilled her purpose and there's honor in that. It is no bad thing to celebrate a simple life.

That's way interesting. And I think it emphasizes an underlooked difference between Jews and Christians. Christians have the notion of the Holy Spirit which is essentially God's spiritual presence that helps guide in our decisions. (You called it the Shekhinah before.)

Holy Spirit and Shekhinah are a little different from each other, I think. Holy Spirit = Ruach HaKodesh. Shekhinah is more like a divine presence rather than god directly. Think of Shekhinah like a holy dwelling place that's within reach of god, like a mother's bosom. Holy Spirit is more active, like a wind or god's breath.

They still sound eerily similar to me. I'll need to chew on it. But I guess, my main point was that Christians aren't even supposed to make big decisions without seeking direction from the Shekhinah.

I personally don't like that. You can bolster your position with a "divine stamp of approval" just because you said "god told me this."
To me, it's not even a discussion because so many people clearly make the wrong decision and do it while invoking god's name.

The Israeli-Palestinian Conflict is basically that. "God said I could have this land."
"Nuh uh, He said I could have this land."

Yeah the whole conflict is like a bad improv troupe

I don't know what you're talking about

Okay, Mr. I Come From Second City

First off, that's Dr. I Come From Second City

Oooooooooo, so now you start peacocking your PhD all of a sudden!

Smoke 'em if you got 'em, right?
But seriously. How is the Israeli-Palestinian Conflict like improv??

Well the rule in improv is nobody negates what another actor is building to. If one actor says, "I see a gun in your pocket," then the other can't say "no that doesn't work for me, let's start over." He has to play along and pull a gun from his pocket.

And how is that like the conflict?

If Israelis and Pals were doing an improv show, it'd just be them standing on stage saying, "no, that narrative doesn't work for me, start the scene over." We invalidate each other's experience. Even if we think the other is wrong, it would help to try to understand where they're coming from.

You literally just described Recognition Theory, which is what I operated off of in my dissertation. What do you think that would look like in a practical sense?

like yours, and I promise you, Miss Anastas, we will set up our outpost there instead."

"Is it because we have the best house that you also steal from our shelves?" Claire protested, now airing other grievances she had long bottled up. "Is it because of Saddam Hussein that your junior soldiers' pockets are lined with my mother's pearls?"

"No, we take from your house because you have not paid your tariff," the Samal responded, his voice deepening and becoming much more emphatic than empathic.

"That is not true," Claire boiled. "We have paid every shekel of the 18% you demand from us!"

"Even so, many of you Arabs are not paying your tariff. For some, they pay less than what is due. For others, they pay more to offset what your brothers and sisters fail to give."

"Why do you call them my 'brothers and sisters?' Do you believe that we all live in harmony without our own conflicts? I am a Christian. My heroes are your heroes. I do not receive any support from Arabs who are not also Christian."

"So then, call upon your Christians to help you."

"There are none of us left!" Claire cried.

Indeed, the Samal knew she was not overstating the reality. Bethlehem had seen their own exodus as native Palestinians fled the city in hordes because of the Gulf War. While the war itself was fought well over 1000km away in Iraq and Kuwait, the Iraqi military dared Israel to get involved so that Saddam Hussein would be justified to use chemical weapons on Jerusalem. Like Iraqis, Palestinians are Arabs, and the Palestinian sympathy for their Iraqi counterparts in the east was palpable,

Well when a Palestinian calls our army "terrorists," we shouldn't downplay that. Even if we disagree, and I do hate when the IDF gets called that, we should let them have that - at least temporarily. Because it matters that they see it that way.

And what about from your angle? What would you want in this improv show?

Hm. Maybe, when a jew thinks that a settlement is actually Israeli land and not in Palestine, try to understand why they think that without jumping to the conclusion that they're just trying to oppress or colonize. There's a reason we believe places like Hebron are actually jewish land, and it's lazy to assume it's just us flexing.

Why do Jews believe Hebron is theirs?

Well you need to read Genesis for that. Abraham bought the land. The oldest historical document literally offers that proof. But if you want something recent, look into the 1929 Hebron massacre against the jews. You're still in Tulsa right?

Yea

The 1929 Hebron massacre is basically our version of the 1921 Tulsa massacre. Arabs killed 69 jews who did nothing to provoke them and then chased the rest out of the city. A terrible tragedy that's swept under the rug and has big ramifications if it's true.
Which it is.

That's an awful, awful event.

You'd see #JewishLivesMatter if people knew about how many pogroms we face regularly. The Israeli-Palestinian Conflict predates the Holocaust. If anything, the Holocaust was inspired by the conflict. Jews and Arabs were killing each other long before H*tler felt "called by God" to annihilate us.

I think Christians need to be careful - very, very careful - about what they say God told them to do. For this exact reason.

Not just christians. Anyone, anywhere, from any time. Even the prophets were careful with that kind of thing. In jewdism today, we too pray for god's will and favor, but I think the point is that we have an insane amount of laws and instruction that are the guide already.

So outside of your prescribed rituals and prayers, there's no reason to try to intercess to God?

Intercess?

Like recess but less kids playing.

Not sure what you mean

Ignore me. Intercess = prayer

O.
Well I personally don't like when jews say "god guided me to do this" or "god told me to try this." No he didnt. They thought deeply and carefully and made assumptions about what god might want from them and they picked a path with that information. It was based on their beliefs and what they were taught, not an inner voice and definitely not god's voice.

Well, maybe you'll be happy to know I don't really operate like that with my prayers anymore. When I pray at night, I'll say "speak, Lord, for your servant is listening," and then I'll just shut up.

And do you ever hear anything?

Not since Romy died.

often leading to clashes between Palestinian civilians and the Tzahal. In Kuwait, many Arabs were exiling from their homeland and resettling in the West Bank of Palestine, often bringing the war with them and dragging the native Palestinians into the crossfire.

Christians in particular were emigrating in droves as they did not have the support of non-Christian Arabs in Bethlehem: During the Israeli War of Independence, Bethlehem was 85% Christian. By the Six-Day War twenty years later, only 46% of Bethlehem was Christian. A quarter-century later, as Claire stood before the Samal, that number had dwindled to 40% and Christians had officially become the minority in the birth city of Yasue. Even Claire was wrestling with her faith as she slowly became a persecuted people, and for what? To serve a God who would take her peace?

Of course Claire could not have foreseen it, but in less than 20 years, the Christian population in Bethlehem would nearly tauten to extinction. Surely, pilgrims come and tourists go, but the number of Christians who steadfastly suffer for the cause of Christ in the city of His birth is less than a mere 5% today.

"Well, you must know you're not the only one with this problem," the Samal said, the waning drips of his patience now spilt. "From the dissolution of the Soviet Union, we have Jews fleeing from the northeast and pouring into our borders."

"But you have the support from the strongest country in the world," Claire clapped back. "While Americans have spent their effort throwing their support behind Israel, they have ignored the fact that this support is creating unchecked persecution upon Christian minorities here in Bethlehem."

Quite right.

> Wait. Okay, can I take that back?
> There was one time, many months ago, in all fairness.

That you think you heard from god?

> Yes. I said my spiel. "Speak, Lord, for your servant is listening." And the voice
> said, "I've already spoken."

meaning what?

> Voice went on and said, "Check out what I've already told you. Start with
> Jeremiah 31. Read verses 10 through 12, and keep going until you get it."

What is it?

> I opened up the passage. It spoke of the ancient Israelites who were about to be
> taken into Babylonian captivity, where most of them would be killed or enslaved.
> But to this, God tells them not to weep. He wants His children to know that He
> sees their pain; their suffering doesn't go unnoticed. And someday, He will turn
> their mourning into joy.
> But first, there must be mourning.
> So I think I got what He was going for.

I don't think god spoke to you, but the conclusion of your experience is basically
what I said a minute ago: there's already a book in place to guide you.

> Ugh. You are way too high on Lord of the Rings.

(◉>◡<◉)
Lol. no.

> Ooo, I was thinking about the creation story recently. I had an idea.

Is it quick? I have to venture home from my parents' house and I'm not about to
get hit by a car because my schnoz was glued to my phone.

> I can make it relatively quick.

I only have time for actual quick

> K. Premise of the Creation story:
> Light was created on the first day, and it praised God. Then the sky and water.
> And a few days later, the stars were created, and they praised God. and so on
> and so forth, until God said it was good. BUT: none of these days were declared
> "good" until the end of the day. Presumably there were tenets of chaos as the
> days aged and the world formed. What if the light and the stars protested at first?

I'm not following how that would matter

> On the 6th day, God created man. What if we're living in the middle of that 6th
> day right now? And the 7th day is just a prophecy. That we're at sunset of only
> the 6th day, and God's rest - and ours - is to come after twilight?

Maybe. Gtg beat feet. Later

> Take care.

"We will only be here for a brief moment," the Samal assured Claire. "Can this conflict last forever?"

Laden with grief over the losses of both Mirna and now her backyard, Claire resigned herself to accept that she must sleep with the enemy just outside of her window.

MISTER MASTER MASTICATOR

> "I love my country and
> you love your country,
> and I love your country too,
> and it is the same country.
> And I have nowhere else to go
> and you have nowhere else to go.
> So we are here, and nobody will dream the other away.
> And our enemy is the only partner we have."
> - Dalia Eshkenazi

Izzy set down the paper, reached onto the plate and, taking a spattering of rice between his fingers, stuck it into his pita and chomped on it.

"Sure," he said, some grains popping between his teeth onto the floor.

" 'Sure,' what?" I asked.

"This is fine."

"You agree to this informed consent?" I asked.

"Yes, I have read this and it is fine with me," he said, then added, "America taught you how to be a good student, yes?"

'Merica? America taught me nothing. I was born such a good student, even my blood is A+, baby.

"I try to be," I said instead.

He smiled.

"Is there meaning behind your name, Izzy?" I asked, leaning back onto the worn, gray sofa inside a small apartment in Aida Camp, a hovel that reminded me of a mingier version of Cabrini Green – if such a thing existed.

"Yes, it is a strong name that means majesty and power and glory and honor and mightiness," he responded.

"Wow, that's a very strong name indeed! All those meanings from one word?"

"Yes sir!" Izzy said, welling up with pride.

"And how long have you lived in Palestine?"

"Well, it is my 23rd birthday this Saturday," he said, taking another fingerful of rice and stuffing it into his half-eaten pita.

"Oh! Happy birthday!" I said, though I was now more focused on the fact that if I didn't act quickly, each section of the rice was going to have Izzy-ickies spread over every grain.

"Thank you. So to answer your question, if I am 23 years old on Saturday, then that means I have been living in Palestine for 23 years on Saturday. Well, 23 years and nine months, I guess."

"And you've spent all your time in Bethlehem?" I asked, stuffing my pita with so much rice that I wouldn't have to take another handful the rest of the meal.

"No. I have lived at Aida Camp in Bethlehem for many years, but before that, I was in Beit Jala. I was born in Ramallah, but that was before I remember."

I took a bite into the pita, and gasped as I determined that what I was eating was demonstrably *not* pita.

"Is something wrong?" Izzy asked, examining my face.

"Yes!" I scoffed louder than intended, despite my mouth being full. "You said this was pita?"

"Yes. Well, *naan*. Pita; naan. Same thing."

"*No*," I said. "*Not* that same thing, Izzy. This is *homemade naan*. This is, like, my second-favorite food in the world, behind popcorn. And your mother makes it so good!"

"*Waleda*!" Izzy cried, and his mother appeared in the doorway behind me. Izzy shouted a few sentences at her in Arabic, and I turned around in time to see her cheeks turn rosy and her hand placed over her heart.

"*Mamnountak*," Ms. Waleda said, which I could only assume meant "thanks."

"*Tashakur*," I responded as she retreated to the kitchen, then slapped my face as I remembered that I had used Farsi (not Arabic) and said "thank you" (not "you're welcome").

"Khatar, you like bread. You are easy to please."

I smiled, my mouth full of rice and naan. After a cumbersome swallow, I asked, "What religion were you raised to believe in?"

"My dad's name is Mohammad. My brother's name is Mohammad. My brother's grandfather was Mohammad. I will let you fill in this blank."

"Okay," I chuckled. "If you were raised Muslim, what religion do you think of yourself as now?"

"I don't like labels: we are all one."

"So you wouldn't consider yourself a Muslim now?"

"No, I'm a Muslim. Write me as a Muslim please. But we are all one."

I wrote what he wanted, but saw him grab more rice out of the corner of my eye. At this point, there was no rice I could pinch that wasn't already touched by Izzy.

"Do you consider yourself religious?" I pried, taking another piece of naan and nibbling on it.

"Yes, for sure, man. I am quite religious!" Izzy said, rice shooting out from between his teeth as he spoke.

"So you go to mosque still?"

He cracked a smile and it took a moment before he answered, "No, I do not attend it."

"Do you... pray?"

"Pray? Prayer is good, and a staple to Islam."

"But do you actually *pray*?"

"I think I'll start next week," he laughed at his own joke, which took me a minute to realize it was humor at all. "Would you like any more rice?"

"No thank you," I said. "I... I just like eating naan by itself. Okay, as a... 'religious' person, are you familiar with the prophecy of Gog and Magog?"

"*Ga and May-Goo*?"

"Gog and Magog."

"No, I don't think so. What is it?"

"It's about the end times, a big battle between Israel and the rest of the world."

"Ah! *Ya'jūj wa-Ma'jūj*! Yes, very much. Dude, every Muslim knows this prophecy. Sorry, my English lacked there."

"If it's any consolation, my Arabic lacks here, too," I said, gobbling the rest of my piece of naan and grabbing another couple.

"Yes, friend. 'Gog and Magog,' it is the time that Jews will be wiped from the earth and Islam will be revealed as truth," he exegeted, which was in alignment with my understanding of what the Qur'an reports.

"And where does this battle happen?" I asked, then devoured both pieces of bread.

"Israel? I don't know. I don't know a lot about it, that's about the extent of it, though we know it will bring the end."

"What happens in the end?" I dug, asking a big question in hopes of getting a few bites in while he answered. I got more than I bargained for: he responded as if Roger Waters was narrating a documentary about Palestine.

"Mahdi comes. He breaks all crosses and kills all pigs. Mahdi destroys all synagogues and all churches, leaving only mosques. The first trumpet sounds. *Boom.* Mountains crush to powder. The sky is torn apart. All living things have been annihilated. Only God remains for a period. Then the second trumpet. God will raise the dead for judgment. Eight angels bring the judgment throne, while everyone stands on a vast plain facing that throne in terror. Each person has two books: a record of good and a record of wrong, and every day, a page will be read in each book. The judgment may take a hundred-thousand years like this. Then, each person is assigned one of the eight levels of paradise or one of the seven levels of hell. Then the earth is obliterated, as its purpose is completed."

It almost sounded like a poem coming from his lips. A devastating, hopeless poem.

"And do you believe this?" I probed.

"Me, personally?" Izzy flapped.

"Yes. You."

Izzy took a breath.

"Does it sound like a story that's believable?" he relented.

"What about other Muslims? What do you think they'd say about this?"

"Every Muslim wants to be a good Muslim. They might believe in it a little bit. But enough to kill in the name of Islam? No. The people who are killing in the name of Allah are not killing in the name of Allah, they are killing in the name of fundamental extremism. It's different."

I continued writing a few notes, and while I wasn't supposed to be analyzing data as I interviewed, I couldn't help but think about how I hadn't even broached the topic of terrorism, and it was as if Izzy felt like he needed to defend his identity in front of me.

"I don't know that many Christians or Jews could rattle off end times information like that," I observed to Izzy. "Do you feel like Muslims are more concerned with the end times than other religions are?"

"No," Izzy said, almost seeming offended. "You pray for the end times every day."

Me? Why does he think he knows what I pray for?

"Muslims repeat the Fatiha 16 times per day with our face to the ground, asking for favor on the day of judgment. And what do you do? Like us, you pray for your apocalypse, too."

"Do I?" I asked, a little perturbed that he would assume that that's the content of my prayers.

" 'Thy kingdom come. Thy will be done.' You pray for the Lord's Kingdom to come to earth as it is in heaven anytime you pray this."

Wow. I'd never thought of it quite like that.

"Banksy, we have a word here, it means 'God-willing.' Have you heard someone say something like, 'I will drive back home today, Enshallah?'"

"Yes," I sputtered, surprised to hear this term again. "In Afghanistan, our air support was affectionately dubbed 'Enshallah Airlines,' because it was never a guarantee that the pilot could get off the ground that day."

"*Ha!*" Izzy laughed. "It is Enshallah Airlines operating here, too, because checked points and incursions can stop us. So we say, 'if we don't make it, then *oh well*, it was not Allah's will.'"

So fatalistic.

"And why does the Muslim care about Allah's will?" he continued, "Because we want to do that will, so the judgment may come, and we may win."

I wondered to myself, do we — that is, Christians — really say *'thy Kingdom come'* because we *actually* want God's will? Do we really believe that God's ways are better than ours, that His will is perfect and that's why we want it? Are we the American soldier, surrendering to fate and stating that we're willing to roll with whatever punches are in store for our chin? Or are we like this Muslim, simply asking for judgment so there is self-serving victory? Or, *worse*: do we say it and not mean anything by it at all?

"But maybe Muslims are more focused on end times than other religions?" Izzy wondered aloud. "Maybe we need that hope. I can't know. But yes, Muslims know this prophecy. It's baseline. Arabs rise against Israel and destroy it. Maybe this current conflict is a part of it, I don't know."

"Let's talk about that for a minute," I said, trying to regain my professional display. "What are your feelings about what's going on? I know this is a big question, but how do you feel about your country always being in conflict?"

"I hate it. There is no need for war. You live your life, I'll live mine, and I don't see why that's a problem."

"Isn't that easier said than done?" I asked, realizing I had just projected my own beliefs onto his answer, so I tried to recover. "I mean, that seems so simply stated. What makes it tough to do that?"

"The occupation makes it tough. I don't like living in an open-air prison. And we have what we call 'The Catastrophe.'"

"*Nakba!*" I shouted, then snapped my fingers.

"Yes," he said, leaning back in his chair, as if wanting to keep a physical distance from my outburst.

"Nakba," I said again, this time much more calmly. "It's 'The Catastrophe.'"

"So, yes, when Jews exiled most Palestinians from their homeland so they could take the land instead. I think it was a million Palestinians, maybe more. But I don't hold this against the Jews today, because we are all one."

"How would you explain the conflict to a child?"

"I'd say, 'war is no place for a child.'"

"I mean, how would you describe its complexity in the simplest terms possible?"

"Oh. I'd say, 'as a child, you should not worry about war.'"

I cleared my throat and pretended to scribble something down.

"How do explain this conflict to your children?" Izzy asked me, turning the tables. "Or, do you have any children?"

"I don't have any children," I responded. "Maybe someday."

"God is generous. You will have child," Izzy heralded with excitement and confidence. "You are a strong believer of God. I can see it in your eyes."

His comment was one I'd heard so many times before, and such a promise normally irked me. Maybe it was because he forgot to say the '*a*' before child despite his English otherwise being so impressive, but the way he said it was so authentic, so unselfish that it actually touched me. I got goosebumps down my right and left vertebrae, over my entire R.L. Spine.

"Why is there confusion about who owns Israel?" I asked, quickly moving on from the moment even though it was one I knew I'd cherish.

"Because," he said with replete seriousness, "it is La La Land."

"What do you mean?"

"I want to go to Hollywood someday, so I love the movie *La La Land*. It won the Best Movie award, did it not?"

It didn't. It was the most infamous fiasco of the Academy Awards: Warren Beatty and Faye Dunaway were given the wrong card prompt and announced *La La Land* was the Oscar winner for Best Picture. The producers came up and started giving an acceptance speech when they were stopped midway through, and it was revealed that the Academy had bungled the presentation and that *La La Land* was actually the loser. Barring a presenter getting slapped onstage live at the Dolby Theatre, it would probably remain the most well-known gaffe for the rest of award ceremony history.

"Izzy, you know they didn't win, right?"

I suspected he knew this already, until I studied his eyes, which was like looking into the eyes of a child who was just told that Santa Claus had died in a sleighing accident.

"You knew this, right, Izzy?" I implored again, this time more slowly.

I could almost see a tear forming. *Man, this Palestinian really loves* La La Land.

"I'm sorry, Izzy," I said, now feeling bad that I broke the news to him. "I felt this deep hurt, too, one time. My favorite movie of all-time is about an honorable man who everyone thinks is a lowlife scoundrel, so he goes out to prove himself as a hero. And when the Academy Awards came around that year, and they didn't announce it as the Best Film Ever winner, I decided to never watch the awards again. There's this one part in the movie that gets me emotional every time, where at the pinnacle of his self-discovery, Ralph is reciting the Bad Guy Creed..."

And then Izzy began to smirk until a pint-sized laugh tittered through his missing molar.

"Wow," I groaned, abandoning the point I was building to. "You do belong in Hollywood."

Izzy aired a daffy chortle, then said, "But can you imagine if they didn't correct this mistake? If they stood up there and, to avoid embarrassment, they just went with it and gave the award to *La La Land*? That's what the UN did. They believed the Holocaust happened, and that Jews needed their own land, so they said, 'Here you go, take Palestine, it's not like there's any people there.' Except there were people there: my grandfathers. And the United Nations is too ashamed to admit they made a mistake, that they shouldn't have given the land to them, so the award goes to *La La Land*. To this day. And it was never *La La Land*'s to take."

"Do you think the UN would ever recant their decision?" I asked.

"History is not kind to losers," Izzy shook his head.

"That's an interesting perspective," I noted, then scribbled his insight down. "So if that's the root of the conflict, how can it end?"

Izzy thought for a moment on this and then nodded as he said, "It is a pain to me to say this, but it ends in fighting. Many people die. It will start in Gaza, and then everyone in Israel and the rest of Palestine will get involved. It is war."

"Who wins this war?"

Izzy thought for a moment again, and then nodded one more time, "The Jews win this war. And Palestine is no more."

"How might that *not* happen? How can it end peacefully?" I asked, amazed at such a brilliant, spontaneous analogy.

"I have hope, Mr. Banksy. I have hope that this will happen, that we shall live in peace. I can maybe see it happening when the Palestinian Authority and the Israeli government become sick of the killing, and they come to a treaty. And this will bring peace."

Not to prick his bubble, but this has been attempted many times.

"Would you like more naan?" he asked me.

Where am I? The House of Bread?

"Absolutely," I wanted to say, but instead politely responded "no thanks" while eyeing the remaining few pieces.

"Okay," Izzy said, grabbing one of the last three pieces and sending me into a state of despair as I realized my window for eating homemade naan was in its waning moments.

"In this conflict..." I said, now overthinking the naan shortage crisis I'd just instigated, "...or, maybe even unrelated to the conflict, have you suffered any trauma?"

"No."

This struck me as unlikely.

"No? You've never had something happen… let me put it this way. Have you ever had anything happen that made you lose sleep?"

"I lose sleep thinking about how to get a better job, how to support my family tomorrow, not because of anything that's happened to me."

"So you've never had any close encounters with violence?"

"Just rockets and explosions," he stated with more indifference than he had displayed when talking about prayer.

"*Just* rockets and explosions? Those aren't significant to you?"

He shrugged. "I didn't lose any sleep over it."

This hit a personal chord with me. Without telling Izzy, the phenomenon of trauma was the actual crux of my study. And I'd had this conversation before, albeit I was on the other side of it: Coming home from Afghanistan, I'd had military doctors try to explain to me that I would have post-traumatic symptoms after my experiences, but the doctors refused to take into account that the explosions weren't the thing that would keep me awake at night. They didn't want to *understand* my narrative, they wanted to *explain* it to me as if I couldn't understand it myself.

This invalidation had been far more provoking for me than any explosions had been. And far be it from me to do to him what military psychologists did to me.

"Do you have any friends who are Jewish?" I asked, moving on.

"Sure," he quickly replied.

"Can you describe your relationship with them?"

Izzy thought for a moment, then said, "We are not close."

"Growing up, were you ever told that 'Jews are bad' or 'Israelis are bad' by anyone? Like, a teacher or a parent?"

"Mmm, no. Just that we should avoid them."

"So imagine you're drifting down a street, and it's just you by yourself, and an Israeli is gravitating towards you. Do you assume they mean harm towards you?"

"Hmm. No, I think not. Unless… yes! Are they wearing a uniform? Then, yes, sure. I am scared of the IDF. I avoid them always."

Izzy picked up the last two pieces of naan, and my heart sank as I contended with the reality that I'd already had my last piece of naan without emotionally preparing for it.

"Is there anything you wish you could say to your enemies?" I asked, trying to do my best not to look at the bread in his hand.

"No," he responded after considering the question. "Because, I don't have any enemies."

He offered me one of the two pieces, and I again politely declined.

"It is rude if you don't take it," he grinned as if he knew a secret. I probably definitely let on that I'd really, really, really wanted another piece.

"If you insist," I said. "But only *one* more."

He handed me a piece that had somehow baked with the adjacent piece's dough, conjoining itself into a doubled piece of siamese-twinned bread.

"That still only counts as one!" he said, the edges of his mouth nearly folding up to his earlobe.

"So," I said, biting into the bread as my taste buds danced one final conga, "is there anything that keeps you up at night?"

"Yes: finding a job. Do you think I want to keep selling knock-off prints of your work forever?"

"Well, guide me through what your life looks like in five years. What do you see yourself doing?"

And as if I opened a floodgate, Izzy's words cascaded into a steady stream that sounded more like a solemn creed he'd rehearsed many times over.

"My name is Azzat Rashid Musa Sediqzaad. I am a fifth-generation Palestinian who wants to leave this country, not because I don't love it, but because I want to do more with my life. I want to become educated, so now I am working hard at my job to save money to go to school. But my family needs money too. And I give them. Why? I owe when they are in need. And they are always in need. In five years, I will be getting an education, but I don't know what that path looks like."

I scratched a summary of his declaration onto my notes, then looked up to find him smiling.

"Would you like to play *The Show* now?" Izzy asked me.

"*The Show*? Like... you mean, the Playstation game?" I responded.

"Yes, sir. The Major League Baseball game," uttering the most American thing I'd heard since leaving the States.

"I... honestly, I didn't take you for a baseball fan, Izzy."

"American video games are how I learn all my English. American video games, and American wrestling."

"Ah. Our two finest contributions to the world!"

"So what do you say? There is an eSports lounge in downtown Bethlehem. I will pay for the hour; it's on me."

"Grrrreat…" I said, trying to sound as enthusiastic as Tony the Tiger but accidentally trailing off and probably sounding more like a passive-aggressive teenage drama queen. The reality was that I didn't have much interest. For one, I was in a pretty monogamous relationship with Nintendo products, and I'd much prefer going back to my hostel and replaying *Samus Returns* on my own GameBoy. More importantly, though – and perhaps this comes as a shock – but I didn't travel around the globe to visit the host cities of the holiest sites in the world just to play virtual baseball a few blocks away from where Jesus was breastfed.

"You can be Nolan Ryan," Izzy said, trying to sweeten the deal.

"Wow, you've really sold it," I joked. "Also, how is Nolan Ryan in any 2018 video game? Isn't he in his 70s now?"

"He is a custom pitcher that I created," Izzy proudly declared.

"How in the world do you even know Nolan Ryan? He retired before you were probably even born."

"Because," Izzy beamed, "Robin Ventura."

I laughed. Nolan Ryan had a Hall-of-Fame career that spanned nearly 30 years, and he was somehow known for a largely frivolous incident that happened in his career's final two months. At the end of a lost season for the Texas Rangers, Nolan Ryan threw an errant pitch that up-and-comer Robin Ventura took exception to. Ventura, a good 20 years younger than the pitching legend, made the same faulty assessment that every 20-something year-old kid makes: he assumed he could take on his elder. Ventura charged the pitching mound, but found out what's known as "Grandpa Strength." The old timer gracefully supplied four noogies to Ventura before offering a fifth and final shiner across the young buck's face. Not only did Ventura get his ass kicked by a dinosaur, but he ended up being the one ejected because he was the one who provoked the fight.

"Got it," I said. "So you created Nolan Ryan as a character because you respect it when old men can still hang with the hotshots."

"I have one final gift for you, Mr. Banksy," he replied.

Please be naan. Please be naan.

"August 1993. Nolan Ryan is pitching, young Robin Ventura takes the mound. The pitch is behind Ventura. Why? Was it an accident? Mr. Banksy, this is a legendary pitcher in the final month of his career. He knows how to throw a ball. But to some, they look at this pitch and they say, 'he didn't mean to do it.' But to others, those with at least half-a-brain, they say, 'of course it was to send a message, to put Ventura in his place.' At the time, there was a rivalry between Chicago and Texas, and this moment was the peak of Jebel Quruntul," whatever that meant.

I was starting to feel like my gift wasn't going to be take-home naan.

"Young Ventura charges the mound," Izzy continued, "and he gets put into a headlock and then gets walloped. What happens to Robin Ventura is not proportional to his offense. And who gets ejected? To everyone's shock, it is the victim, the one who got punched. Why? 'Nolan Ryan has a right to defend himself,' they say. Defend what? The consequences of his actions? And you know what happens next! The White Sox coach also gets ejected because he comes to defend Ventura."

He must mean manager. They're not called coaches in baseball.

"Ventura goes on to have a famous career of his own. And what is his legacy? He's a hero in Chicago."

Well, on the southside. Sure.

"By the letter of the law – in both baseball and in humanity – everyone knows the umpires did the right thing because who can disagree that Nolan Ryan should be allowed to defend himself? But everyone who sees it, assuming they are smart enough to see it, they know that Nolan Ryan got away with one. And now, whenever you look at the earlier parts of his career, you look at his performances through the lens of this fight."

"I don't think I understand that last part," I interrupted Izzy. "What do you mean by that?"

"Okay, well, as an example. You watch Bo Jackson knock a Nolan Ryan pitch right back into Nolan Ryan's face. If you're a fan of Nolan Ryan defending himself in 1993, then you look at this separate incident from 1990 and think to yourself, 'Wolly, Nolan Ryan is amazing because he regained enough composure to still get the out on Bo and finish the game.' But if you think Nolan Ryan to be trash for what he did to Robin Ventura, then this become *still* a win for you, too, because at least you got to see Nolan Ryan's lip explode on live television. 'That one's for Robin,' you say to yourself, even though he had nothing to do with Bo Jackson splitting Nolan Ryan's lip."

"Hmmm," I said aloud. I was starting to get it.

"What happens to these two men's legacies? Well, Ventura is instantly a folk hero for Chicago, eventually getting to manage the White Sox someday. And Nolan Ryan? Well, go shop for Nolan Ryan memorabilia, and you can't not see him pitching with a bloody lip, because his fans want to remember that he's strong and smooth and will defend himself, and then he gets a little shrine at the Texas Rangers Hall-of-Fame museum and gets to own their minor league team."

"So," I connected his point. "This is the conflict, you're saying. Israel throws an errant pitch to provoke you, and you respond in like, and Israel disproportionately retaliates against you and somehow still earns the favor of their supporters?"

"I didn't create Nolan Ryan as a custom character because I esteem him," Izzy corrected my initial assumption, still smiling. "I created Nolan Ryan as a character so that I can beat him again and again and again."

"Okay, Izzy. I'll play *The Show* with you. And I'll be Nolan Ryan, and you can beat me."

I contemplated Izzy's answers to my interview, then remembered I had one final question. I was a little hesitant to ask it, given that the suggestion had come from someone who overused the word "mate" despite being neither British or Australian. Can such people be trusted?

"The interview's officially over, Izzy," I formally declared in case the ethics board was listening in. "But, I'm wondering: do you have any ailments? Like, do you suffer from any chronic conditions?

Physical stuff. Especially ones that started after the first time you experienced 'just rockets and explosions.'"

"Hmm, well I have some stomach cramps. This is all."

"These cramps started when you encountered *trau*... like, warfare?"

"Yes, I remember. Maybe when I was about seven or eight? It was when Israel bombed the big church in Bethlehem. We had just moved to this city, and I got stomach cramps and my father – may Allah be pleased with him! – lost his eyesight."

"Lost his eyesight? Like, he went blind? From shrapnel or something?"

"He became blind from nothing. No reason. At least, not at first. Years later, he suddenly got diabetes, and they think this was related to his blindness. But I don't know more than that. He would not talk about it and we were not to ask. I'm sorry, Mr. Banksy, I know nothing more."

Izzy held his head in shame, as if he let me down by his answer.

"Izzy," I said as sweetly as I could, "I need to know one more thing."

He looked up with a sparkle of hope that he just might be able to redeem his grand failure.

"I need the truth now, you listening? Izzy Sediqzaad, how can I convince you that I'm not Banksy?"

"Sir," Izzy's smile widened, "you cannot."

"Honestly, I'm not him. I don't know why I winked at you as if I was Banksy, it just came over me. Do you want me to draw you something? You can see what a bad artist I am."

"Yes, that would be fine, actually."

Izzy yelled to Ms. Waleda in Arabic again. I assumed he was yelling, "ma, the *naan* loaf!", at least until she came in and only brought an inedible blank sheet of paper.

"Here," he said as he handed the pad to me. "You can draw."

So I drew him a terrible rendering of a stick man and handed it back to him.

"Hmm," he said. "Now try writing 'Banksy.'"

So I wrote "Banksy," assuming he was going to match it against the artist's actual signature, but when I handed the paper back to him, his face gleamed.

"Now I have an original Banksy drawing!"

"Ugh!" I groaned. "I'm not Banksy, man!"

"Of course you're not," he winked.

> "Keep falsehood and lies far from me;
> give me neither poverty nor riches,
> but give me only my daily bread.
> Otherwise, I may have too much
> and disown you and say,
> 'Who is the LORD?'
> Or I may become poor and steal,
> and so dishonor the name of my God."
> ~ Proverbs 30:8-9, NIV

ב

May 28, 2020

I finally did it.
I achieved the fabled fourth cup of coffee.

How was it?

I saw colors that haven't been named yet, had the energy of a Power Ranger for
30 minutes, then crashed on the couch.

Are you sure you didn't drink mushrooms?

Ha - I don't love the Mario computer things that much.
I wanted to tell you, we attempted our first round of the fertility treatments last
week. It didn't work. Now we just wait for the next cycle.

I'm sorry, that's a bummer.

Still got 2 more chances

Can't you do it more than that?

I mean yeah, the option will be there, but we can't afford it. We've budgeted for
three attempts. Each attempt costs more than Joanna's entire paycheck, and
even more if there's complications and they need additional tests or drugs.
I'm certainly not bringing in enough to help with that.

But if you got a job/salary that matched your education level someday, you could
get on it again?

Technically, but then I would be back on my meds, which makes it exponentially
less likely to work. And can cause birth defects.
Also, the fertility treatment process isn't particularly easy, and I'd have to deal with
coordinating Joanna's doctors with my bureaucratic doctors at the VA. That's
kind of insurmountable as it is.
So this really is our window: the next 2 months.

Where do you go - mentally, emotionally, spiritually - if you end up not having
children ever?

I don't know because we're not there and I'm not entertaining that.
I'm trying to trust that this'll work.

You think this'll work?

I do. I don't know why. Maybe it's faith? A mustard seed leftover from the spiritual
fire of 2018?
But if not, I'm resigned to believe that a curse has been placed upon my house.
Say, do Jews believe in curses?
Like I know the Bible talks about them in a general sense but do you ever look at
a person and say "oh well maybe they're just cursed."

Every religion has its superstitions.
Or more accurately, superstitious believers.

Ever since I left Israel, life has felt like I'm under an actual curse. Like literally that
I've done something so wrong that God has left me

I'm not sure that's really biblically accurate, honestly.
Where are you getting that from?

٢٠

December 2, 1990

Claire woke up on a Sunday morning to the sound of an excavator outside her bedroom. She got up and thumbed the plastic sheet that was over her window to peep outside, just in time to see the excavator dig up her bed of flowers.

Usually there were several soldiers congregating in her backyard, but today it was only the excavator and its operator.

Claire checked her watch: a minute after 5:00am. She hustled to the kitchen and threw on a pot of coffee, poured a cup, and met the Turai just before he knocked on the front door.

"Good morning, Chileab," Claire said to her enemy, opening her door and offering him the cup. "Would you like some coffee?"

"Not today," the teenager said, then briskly pushed past Claire and headed to her roof, calling down when he got to the third floor. "But thanks."

"He's cranky today," Zuji said, sneaking up behind Claire and putting his chin on her shoulder.

"Probably because the sun is rising earlier and earlier," Claire said, grabbing Zuji's hand that's wrapped around her waist. "I'm telling you, one of these times, he's going to miss his stand-to, and they will demote him."

"Claire," Zuji laughed, "he is a foot soldier. I don't think a Turai can be downgraded any lower."

"Well, dear, then this is a perfect explanation for why he's so cranky. Coffee?"

Well, you mentioned Esther feeling like the Shekhinah left her as she approached the courts. In other instances, we see God refuse to hear the prayers of some Jews, and then there was the time that God removed His Spirit from King Saul. Even Yeshua was forsaken for a purpose. I have to admit that this idea doesn't fit the New Testament narrative about what a believer should expect to happen to them, but that being said, I don't think it's utterly out of the realm of possibility that God still does this, right?

Well, okay. Job felt like he was under a curse

Well Job was really kind of under a curse, right? Maybe that lends way to the idea that I could be under a curse, too.

Idk. I mean god would "cut off" jews in the bible, often by turning away from them or by making them barren and childless so their seed would die off.

Where does it say that?

A few spots. Hold on.
Malachi 2:3 talks about it. And in Numbers 5, there's a whole weird narrative about how they'd invoke god to make cheating wives' uteruses fall out. I can check for more verses sometime later, but the bible often makes a point to accentuate that the worst punishment from god in those days was to be unable to bear children. For the jew, barrenness was the curse of curses in a cursed world.

Well if the world is under the curse of sin, it's not that much a stretch to think I might be under a related curse. Not like a voodoo curse that someone put on me, but the type of curse that even the prophets faced in their desert situations. I cried out to God one day, "why are you so far from me? I've cried out day and night for you. I've praised you for so long, but it's like you don't hear me." And I realized how eerily similar my sentences sounded to the psalms.

Again, on the David thing. You're not Israel's greatest king and his story wasn't meant to be yours

I wasn't comparing myself to him, I just meant I looked at him as an example.

Look at Job instead.
His story was meant to be yours. Take your cues from him.

Come on, you've read my second book. Job was a righteous man and I'm... not that.

Again, you're not supposed to be sizing yourself up to the people in the bible. You need to focus on the purpose of the stories. Use them as a guide.
Job isn't about being Job. It's about whether or not Job - and we - can trust god in affliction.

I think there's more to it than that, right? I mean, you don't think the book of Job maybe gives us a glimpse into how God operates?

Danger. God almost literally says "you don't get to see how I operate."

But even that response, it's still data about God, right? And don't you think we learn a bit about the devil there?

You're personifying a phantom. The devil doesn't have influence on us.

Well who sent the afflictions in the first chapter of Job?

Some guy - a fictitious mist - known as "the adversary."

Then who tricked Eve into eating the fruit in Genesis 3?

Zuji smiled and took the steaming cup, his mustache dipping into the coffee before he returned to his chambers.

Another of the Tzahal – that is, another lowly Turai – tried to sneak out Claire's front door without having to converse with any of the Palestinians in the house, but Claire caught him anyway.

"Moshe?" she said, "how was your shift? Are you not helping Chileab with the sunrise watch?"

Moshe turned around. He was just a teenager, too, and the younger of the two soldiers. Moshe was perhaps not even old enough to legally sip araq. Despite his youth, he had bags under his eyes and almost looked inebriated. He didn't want to be here; it's just part of his mandatory service.

"My shift was fine," he responded, trying to slip away before Claire snuck another question in.

"What are they doing out there?" she asked.

"I… well, this location – your backyard – they have chosen it for a camp."

Claire knew this already. More, the Turai knew that Claire knew this.

"So, I am not allowed to use the front door to leave, and now I must squeeze by a construction site every time I use my back door?"

"That would be the case, but you know you can't leave anyway right now. What does it matter if we choose that spot?"

"Well," Claire bristled, "I'd certainly prefer to have some kind of privacy. It appears I will be under close watch for the remainder of this conflict."

A snake.

Just a snake?

Yes. Not a devil.

Okay, but in Job, you think "the adversary" can't be "the devil?"

No, it's the devil. But I don't think it was meant to be taken literally as if there is some adversary actively working against god. In fact, in jewdism, we believe that if (big IF) "the devil" isn't just a completely made-up literary tool, then he's just one of the angels of god, a subordinate who takes his tasks from god.

What kind of tasks?

He takes lives, so an angel of death I guess. He tells god of their bad deeds and tries to get them to be judged unfavorably. But he's just doing god's bidding. He's just a part of the balance. He's mentioned rarely in the bible and definitely much less prevalent of a figure than what christians think of him.

Do you have demons in Judaism?

They're mentioned even less. Most jews in my sect agree they don't actually exist. Probably just another literary technique. But if they exist, they're the same: just doing god's bidding.

I'm not sure that sounds biblical to me.

How is it not? Think about the role of "Satan" in Job. God and satan - no, not even satan, again it's just some guy who is referred to as "the adversary." They made a bet. God said "this guy Job won't ever curse me." The adversary said "yes he would if bad things happened to him." So god said "do your worst, adversary." And the adversary sent afflictions to try to turn Job away. And Job did a so-so job, just alright on his test but ultimately learned that god is sovereign. The original hook of the story is whether or not Job curses god. By the end, it doesn't even really matter as much, because the point is god is sovereign regardless.

I think Habakkuk and Job would've had a great conversation if they could've met.

Yeah prolly

So you really think we shouldn't compare ourselves to any characters in the Bible? Even in the book of Job, I feel like Job's friends are there to be warnings of who NOT to become.

Job's friends are there to just spout bad theology at Job while he suffers.

Why tho? Why spout things they don't understand? I feel like they had a bigger purpose here. The point is looking inward and seeing how we fall into the same trap. Job's friends gave bad advice because they had to reconcile Job's suffering with what they knew about God, but they weren't willing (or capable) to contend with the intricacies of Job's suffering. They spurned sitting in that discomfort because they felt like if they couldn't explain it away, then it would impact their own faith and make as little sense to them as it did Job.

Okay. I can buy into that much. That's a possibility.

In the same way I think we can look at Job and put ourselves in his shoes and say "I shouldn't fall into the temptation of bad theology, even if it allows me to make better sense of the world."

Is that something that helps you right now? Thinking that that's the point of Job?

I think it does. Why? Do you have a different interpretation?

"That is what it appears, yes," Moshe responded, rolling his eyes as only a teenager can master. "What game are you playing with me right now?"

"Come on," Claire appealed. "Talk to your Samal. We are hungry. We need groceries today. Let us go."

"No," Moshe curted.

"I am just asking you to talk to your Samal. I'm not asking you to invoke a Seren or a Segen, I'm just trying to find a way…"

"You may leave," Moshe interrupted, rubbing his eyes, "the day that Iraq stops using chemical weapons."

"I hear the Americans are purging the Iraqis from Kuwait," Claire augmented his stipulation. "This is good?"

"Yes, this is good. But we will see how it plays out."

Claire smiled, then asked, "coffee?"

Moshe angrily shook his head, but his lips betrayed his body as he responded, "Yes, please."

Claire crossed to the kitchen, but before she could grab another cup, the city-wide alarm just outside the Church of the Nativity began to whir.

Claire, eyes wide, looked over at Moshe and found him in just as much of a panic. Chileab barreled down the stairs from the roof, yelling "suit up!"

Claire exhaled as the two rushed out her front door. She grabbed a cup of coffee, then sat at her kitchen table, alternating her lips from sipping on her coffee to sporadically chanting prayer.

No, I think that's a good, contextual reading of one of the goals of the book. Go with that for now!

I feel like you're insinuating that there's more that I'm missing.
I mean, I know that Job is also about having hope in God and stuff

I think that's a component too. But did you know that the concept of hope isn't mentioned in the bible until the exile? First instance is in 1 Chronicles 29:15.
"There is no abiding" is how it's phrased.
But yes, part of Job's story is him clinging to hope. But clinging to hope during trial doesn't make us Job.

Okay. Well, you won't have to worry about me having some disillusion that I'm like Job. Unlike him, I'm a shithead.
And he and I have one other huge difference that separates us

Which is what?

Even Job was blessed with children.

Zuji appeared in the kitchen once again, covered shoulder-to-toe in a hazmat suit, holding a gas mask at his chest.

"Claire," Zuji said, "I'd really prefer you put yours on. Even just once, so you know how to use it. What happens if we are really under attack this time?"

"I love Him so much," Claire said, staring into her husband's auburn eyes, "and He knows that. And if the rocket comes and burns me up, then I'll be with Him. And that's okay."

"But what about us?" Zuji asked. "How could we fare?"

"Faith over fear, dear," Claire said.

Zuji sighed, then donned his gas mask. Claire gaped out the window and saw Moshe and Chileab both patrolling the streets, head-to-toe in the suit and mask. Claire examined the young men over. She could see Moshe was violently shaking, even visibly so under all the protective wear.

"I think I'm going to take a shower," Claire said as the alarms continued to pierce through the plastic-shielded windows.

October 2018

THE FINAL NIGHT BEFORE FIVE YEARS OF HOMEWORK

> "The doctrine of Creation means
> that your body is a calling.
> The doctrine of the Fall means
> it's a calling you might not have wanted."
> - Sam Allberry

Joanna?

Yes?

It's Danger from Kilmer.

Danger from Kilmer?

Yes. I attended kindergarten with you. I had a bowtie in my yearbook photo. I wound up dating you for several years and then we got married.

Ohh, ok. I think I remember you now. From the bowtie, of course. ;-p

This is what I look like now. Less hair than when I was 6.

There's that smile! I think I just fell in love with you all over again.

Go ahead: fall. I'll catch you again.

Boy, you know how to sweet talk a girl.
Your beard's growing back real quick.

It's no trae-beard, but that was from a week or two ago. Here's a recent one.

Trae beard?

Whoa! Nice picture!
And look at that super scruff!
You've really mastered those selfie skills.

Tell me about it! Check this one out.

Lol. You're goofy.
How did your interviews go?

Pretty good. None of the interviews were overly groundbreaking.

Booooo, hissss. Sorry to hear.

It's all good. I ate some pretty magnificent naan. And I'm not a journalist looking for a
Pulitzer, I'm a student looking for a Cap n' Gown.
Plus I learned a new word!

I did too! It turns out you're callipygian!

What's that mean??

Idk. Guess you gotta look it up later! What's your word?

Ignis Fatuus.

Is that really a word or did you drop your phone?

Haha. It's real. Or actually, it's "fake!" Means "foolish fire."
It's a light that's doesn't actually exist. Often called a ghost light or spooklight.
It usually happens in swamps, where basically the bog farts and creates an optical
illusion and creates light where there isn't any.

How did you randomly come across this??

One of my participants was absolutely fascinated with them ignis fatuuses. Ignis fati?
Ignia fatua? Idk the plural.
But he brought it up twice. In urban mythology, travelers would see what looks like a
person carrying a flickering lantern, and they'd get stuck in a moor or fall down an
escarpment by chasing it and die.
In fact, this is where the concept of jack-o-lanterns come from.

I had no idea that that was a thing.
How many participants were you able to get?

I was able to muster a couple more participants in Bethlehem and several more at Birzeit University through a contact I had in Ramallah. I'm pretty maxed out on Palestinian participants at the moment.

Great! So now you can leave Palestine and go somewhere safe?

The West Bank is safe. Certainly not worse than south Chicago.

That's not exactly setting a very high bar.
Also, I thought Bethlehem wasn't in the West Bank? Isn't it east of Jerusalem?

More south than east. But yeah, the West Bank is actually east of Israel. Kind of backwards, I know.

Why would they name it like that?

Back in the day, Egypt and Jordan were warring over territory, and Jordan referred to Palestine as the West Bank, as in "West Bank of Jordan's borders."

So Egyptians could've call Gaza the "east bank of Egypt?"

Ha! Missed opportunity to flex on Jordan, I guess.
So yes, the West Bank is east of Israel, and Gaza is west of Israel.
Gaza is the really dangerous place though. Going there is a gamble with your life.

But you're done with Palestine. How many Israeli participants do you have so far?

Still zero.

Oh.

Yeah. I'm getting worried that I'm not going to make it. We'll see.
But my brain is fried. Don't really want to talk shop.
Are you doing okay babe?

Sure. Yeah. Just finishing up lunch, might take a Sunday nap in a bit. What time is it by you?

Almost 9 PM. I just got out of the evening service at Christ Church.

Is that in Bethlehem?

No. Old City, Jerusalem. It's the oldest Protestant church in the entire Middle East.

Cool! So I guess even though we're on separate continents, we're still going to church at the same hour. I didn't even think about that. What was the sermon like?
That had to have been cool, going to a church service in Jerusalem.

I thought it would be super cool too, but it felt like any other service. The message wasn't overly powerful or anything.

What did they preach on?

The pastor just made some parallels about how Christ-followers should be prepared for hard times during ministry. He talked about how so many of the characters in the Bible experienced their highest "mountaintop" moments on earth, only to be immediately followed by their lowest "valley" moments.

Interesting. Did he give any examples?

Yeah, let me see if I can remember.
He talked about Moses, how he had his direct interaction with God and received the Ten Commandments, only to come down from Mt. Sinai and find the Jews had abandoned the faith and started worshiping statues again.
He also brought up Elijah who struck down all the false prophets at Mount Carmel, only to have to flee to the wilderness in Horeb where he got super depressed and stopped eating altogether.

Is that it?

No, there was more. Trying to remember.

Did they not mention Jesus?

Oh! Right! Good job! Jesus was Baptized and had the clouds split in two as God proclaimed him to be God's Son, but then right after this, Jesus had to go into the wilderness for 40 days and get tempted by Satan.
And then the pastor talked about Jesus again and said that Christ gave his disciples the authority to cast out demons, and then He ascended a literal mountaintop and had His miraculous transfiguration. But right after coming down from that, Jesus had to cast out a demon that His disciples couldn't, which was kind of a reality check for Jesus because He probably thought these disciples were ready to minister, but clearly they still sucked at prayer.
Or like how Jesus raised his friend Lazarus from the dead and converted one of the most despicable sinners (ie, Zacchaeus the chief tax collector), but less than a week later Jesus was dead.

That was the last example?

I think there were others but I frankly can't remember more. Basically, it was like anytime God told someone to do something and they got really excited about it, it was always followed up with some really difficult times ahead. I think the sermon title was something like 'When you're on a high, expect a trial to follow.' The sermon wasn't anything overly relevant to me, but it was still pretty interesting.

Pretty comprehensive. But I'd also say it's not always one or the other.

What do you mean?

Life isn't all valleys and mountaintops. I think you can't have either of those without the fields. Everyone you just mentioned had long periods of time in the fields. The boring, boring fields.

That's a great point. I guess the valleys and crests are just the most memorable.

For sure. But we spend most of our lives in the fields. Even God's chosen mostly do a lot of waiting.

Wow. Yeah. Jacob, David, Elijah, Jesus. There's a lot of pastures with those guys. Some of them spent almost their entire lives in the plains, and we only remember them for their time they spent leveled up or leveled down.

We can't assume we're on the mountaintop yet just because we made it out of the valley.

True. Though I can't help but feel like I'm on a mountaintop right now. I can't wait to show you around this land.

Me neither. T-minus two weeks-ish! More or less.
So what's next for you? Are you still in the same hostel?

No, I've been hostel hopping. Tonight I'm back at the hostel that gave me a roof and then I'm heading to Bethlehem again in the morning. Izzy wanted me to visit him one more time.

:-|
You said you were done with Palestine.

This is for pleasure! Or, at least, out of obligation.

K well I'm not about to be a naggy wife.
Also, who is Izzy?

He was my first participant. The one I couldn't unconvince I wasn't Banksy. He told me that I should check out Gaza if I really wanted to get some authentic data, so I might check into that. I also found out today that there's a crucial tourist stop that I've missed the past times I visited Bethlehem.

Did you just try to casually sandwich in the fact that you were going to try to get into Gaza, so I wouldn't notice you said it? Right after you just got done telling me how dangerous it is?

Did it work?

Honey.

Aw, nuts.

As your official Idea Filter, I'm going to have to stop you there and put my foot down on that. I will be very mad at you if you try to go to Gaza. Naggy wife or not. Sorry. What's the tourist attraction you missed in Bethlehem?

Kever Rachel, Rachel's Tomb.

That sounds ominous.

Right up my alley, then.

Can you please make that the last stop in Palestine? At least until I'm there with you? Please?

Yes, fine. Actually though, the reason I texted you is because I wanted to talk to you about something.

That sounds ominous too.

It's actually a good thing. I think? But I had an experience tonight at church. Like, I guess you can call it a religious experience. Something I haven't had in a long time. Really, since Afghanistan, I think.

What do you mean by religious experience?
I thought you said the message wasn't impactful?

It was during worship.
Which... if it's coming from me that worship was moving, you gotta know there really was something going on there.
I felt that small, still voice that I haven't heard in a long time. The same one that told me I would marry you. It was so clearly that voice again.

So: God's voice.

Yeah. At least I think so.

What did He tell you?

I'm supposed to write.

Well you're in luck: you know how to do that. What are you supposed to write?

"Write what you know. That should leave you with a lot of free time."

God said that?

No. Howard Nemerov did.

Well why'd you say it, goofball?

I usually only write about my life because it's one of the few things I know a lot about.
So, I can write about my time in Israel, but... it's boring.
Not just boring, but a complete party-sized package of snoreos and soy milk in a boob sack.

You really believe you haven't had interesting stuff to talk about?

241

I have a bunch of interesting anecdotes maybe, but none of this pulls together into a coherent linear story. People don't pick up books to read about someone who ALMOST experienced something cool. I almost experienced the Temple Mount. I almost made it into the church at the top of the Mount of Temptation. I almost made it to the Jordan.

Moses almost entered the Promised Land.
David almost got to see the Temple.
Paul almost got to Rome.

Paul did eventually make it to Rome... as prisoner.

These guys didn't reach those places when they wanted to, but the story was still important. The fact that they didn't reach those places makes the stories more touching. And real.
A lot of people who live awesome stories don't have time to write about them. A lot of people who write awesome stories haven't had time to live them. If you knew the story and how it was going to be written, what's the point? That's like if you had put your research study together after you knew what your conclusions would be.

Thanks. That's helpful. I'm just not a fan of anticlimactics. And I don't even know what the inciting incident would be in this case.

Inciting incident? Like the thing that spurs the story you mean?

Right. Where I'd start. Like, you have to jump into the action from the beginning. And you never want to start with a lazy trope. It's like using a bad simile. They say "start with a yawn and your reader will end with one."

Who says that?

Idk. They do.

Who cares? You need to start the story where it makes the most sense to.

I'd be writing more about how I missed the best Holy Land sites, rather than what it was like to experience them. That's like using an overused simile.

Okay, so maybe you're not writing a tourist's guide to Israel.

But I'm confident I was called to tell a story about this place. Specifically, a story about what I've encountered here. But it doesn't make sense to me because I don't have a story, really. It would be the worst book anyone's ever read.
I know how to tell a story, but I don't have the story to tell.

Danger from Kilmer: WHO told you to write this story?

God, I think.

He will provide the story.
You there?

Yeah. Sorry. Was just thinking about what you said. You're right. Except, I was also called to write a dissertation and that isn't happening right now.

Well you're getting there. You're halfway.
Just gotta find some Israelis to talk to.

Yeah.
How about this:
if God provides the Jews for my study, then maybe He'll provide the story too.

That's the spirit.

It's getting late.
I should go.

One sec! Some pups want to say hi.

It looks to me like they're sleeping

Now there's some life! Thanks babe.

I'm getting purty good at selfies myself.   ;-)

Lol. Nah, I know Sidney's pawdiwork when I see it.
How did you actually get those? Well the first one. I remember taking the second
one...

Your dad sent it a bit ago. I'd asked him to send one.

And here you are, hoarding it!

Busted! Okay actually, I took a super cute one before you left. Wanna see?

I think you know the answer to that.

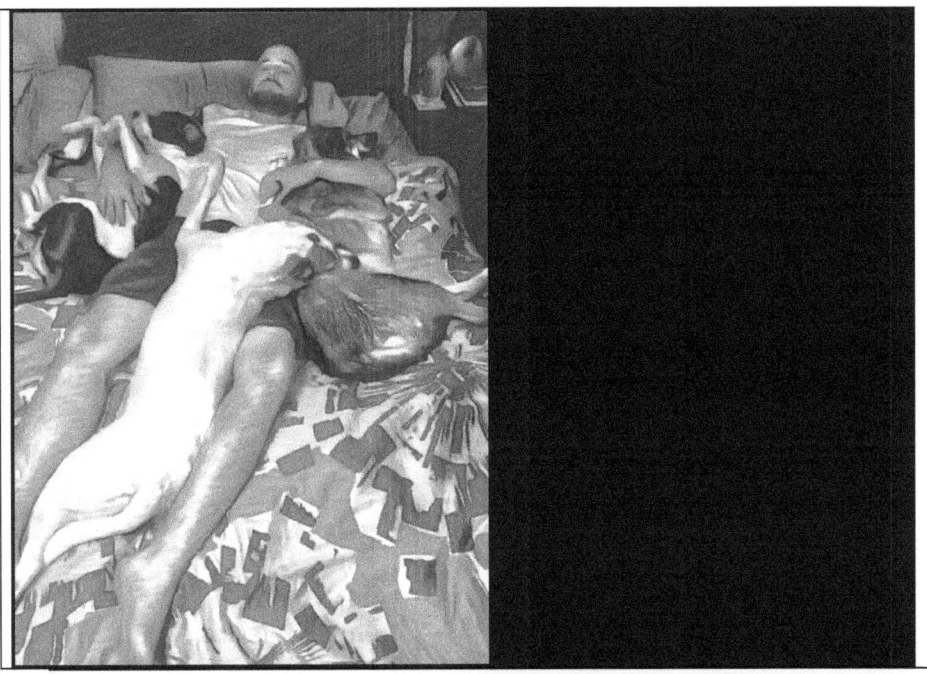

Awwwwww! Three of the four are so cute!!

UGH. As grateful as I am for your parents watching the puppos, I miss them so doggone much. I'm honestly not sure if I'm more excited about Israel or about seeing our girls again.

Well, the good news is, you get both. Don't have to choose.
I actually really need to get going. Full day tomorrow.

Be safe! Love you!

Love you too – gnyte! *-:

:-*

"There is only one lawgiver and judge,
he who is able to save and to destroy."
- James 4:12, ESV

244

כא

June 3, 2020

Good morning!

Actually good evening here. But you're right, it was a good morning, too. I finally did my taxes

This late in the year?

Yeah they postponed the filing due date because of the virus

Ah right, they did that here too.
It's funny, Benjamin Franklin once said, "In this world, nothing can be said to be certain, except death and taxes." Except now, it's only death.

That's so true. Grim, but true.
Have you been working on anything?
I mean like writing anything?

Yeah - why, you want a job working for my indie publisher?

If you're hiring! What's the book's name?

"Installment 4, as of yet untitled." Like it?
And we're always hiring! You can help me with the blurb and tagline.

Super! What you got so far?

"A Jew, an Arab, and an ignorant American walk into a war.
The Star Vendor says, 'wouldn't it be better if we all met in a bar?'"

Oh my. No. Scrap it.

Nuts. Really?

I'm so serious. that's terrible. And we're not even in a war right now.

It's just a draft. I've got to work out the punchline a bit.

No you don't. Feed it to the pigs.

I'll put you down as 'still thinking about it'

(ಠ_ಠ)

See, you're really good at this. You're hired. The best part about working for me is you can work from home. But, be warned that my company has existed for almost a decade and even now I barely have enough money to keep my 3 current employees on staff, and they're all dogs.

Well thanks for thinking of me
(¬_¬)
Are you guys going to try the fertility thing again this month?

Yep. That's the plan. Obviously gotta wait a few weeks. Do a pre-checkup, then we'll give it a go.

Are you excited??

That's not quite the word I'd use.
It's funny, just a couple years ago - around the same time I met you - this infertility stuff was one of the things that I'd be certain I could "pray away" with faith.

And now you dont?

‏כ א

It was a new moon. Bullets rang in Bethlehem, and Claire felt Zuji jolt awake at the sound of a distant explosion.

"Claire," Zuji panted, "did you hear that?"

"Yes," Claire responded. Of course she did. She's been awake all night, listening to the crossfire. "Aida Camp has been at it again."

The Gulf War ended almost a decade ago, but you wouldn't know it in Bethlehem, where Palestinians still sprayed Jerusalem nightly.

"Aida Camp has a right to defend their home," Zuji rationalized, as if saying it atoned for the unprovoked transgressions by his people.

"Maybe," Claire reasoned, "but Aida started this fight tonight. Before you know it, the Tzahal will be setting up checkpoints in Bethlehem."

"Hmmm, yet you wish to *stay* in Bethlehem."

Claire turned her head to her husband.

"Yes, Zuji," she said in disbelief. "This is our *home*. You know our agreement: the moment any of us become injured, we leave. Until then…"

"Yes, yes, that is the agreement," Zuji pined. "At first injury, we leave. I will stop bringing this up. But Saddam Hussein gassed his own people. How much more might an enemy do that to us if they acquired such technology?"

"Israel is wrathful, *not* evil," Claire said with confidence, then followed up with an assertion imbued with just a hint of diffidence. "They have never done this before, and they would not do this thing to us."

If my faith wasn't enough to save Romy who was already alive, how could my faith stir a life that isn't even here yet?

Well I think we're finally on the same wavelength here. I don't believe prayer was ever intended to allow us to produce miracles.

I never thought healing an animal would be outside the realm of what He is capable of doing.

Ugh. Hold on, now we're not on the same page. Sorry you're so hurt, but you need to let that go. It's harsh to say, but god doesnt owe you anything. Nothing. It's not that he couldnt snap his fingers, it's that he didn't. You seem to expect special treatment from him and I don't know where this comes from. If this wasn't weighing on you before Romy, then why should it now? What makes you so special that god would do this favor for you and not others? Have humility. We can't question everything that happens. I mean, why did god allow the shoah to happen? Some survivors abandoned god after that, and obviously it was a terrible part of our history, but it's also one of the main reasons jews beat the odds and got their own country IN THEIR ANCESTRAL HOMELAND after thousands of years of exile.
That's what faith is, trusting that god not only exists but that he has a plan and you can trust him to do the right thing, even if it seems wrong to you.

Ow.

I don't mean to be offensive.

I'm not offended. That was, just, a lot. Like drinking from a scalding firehose. It's just hard to reconcile what I know to be true in my life, and what my understanding of God is.

Well what's your understanding? I mean, what is different now than before?

I just don't see any purpose to verbalize our requests to God when there is nothing we can say or do that will change His mind. Any such petition is simply informing God of our will, which 1) He already knows and 2) He has already committed to either seeing through or not seeing through.

So what then? Do we stop praying for the things on our heart and just say "God, do whatever you were already planning to do"

Maybe! I mean, that's not the "right" New Testament answer. In the book of Philippians, Paul says to let your requests of your heart be made known to God "in everything." But why do that? It's silly. I don't want to pray for God to give me a good job when He already knows whether He's going to give me a good job. Why pray for safety when God's probably already decided my fate? Why pray for Dad to recover from his stroke if God has already determined how that will play out? Asking for this stuff is almost an act of obsessive-compulsion: it weighs on my mind, so I pray about it to get it off my mind, despite it being illogical to think that my prayer changes God's course. I'm just saying these magical words because it's what I'm supposed to do. I'm just doing it because Yeshua told us to do it.

So, don't pray because the stars are already aligned?

I don't know. Sure. I guess that's is the crux of the spiritual swamp I'm in. In my fallen, sinful mind, I'm finding that prayer has lost nearly all of its value in the face of an Almighty God.

"Are you sure?" Zuji asked, capitalizing on Claire's anxiety. "Because if wrong, it will not be *injury* that we suffer first."

"Our enemies are humans, just like us," Claire reminded Zuji. "They take no more pleasure in…"

TCHUU! TCHUU!

More gunshots. Not from Aida Camp, but from the Anastas' roof.

Claire jumped out of bed and hurried toward the door.

"Claire!" Zuji called, stopping his wife in her tracks. "Where are you going?"

She looked at Zuji. He looked as pale as an American rendering of Yasue.

"I have a right to defend my home," she quipped, and fled up the stairs.

Claire reached the door that led to her roof, but it had been locked from the outside by the Tzahal on the roof. So instead, Claire skidded to her guest room to look out the window into the dark abyss of night.

Directly in front of her view, no more than 500m, was Rachel's Tomb. How she longed to visit it again, but she'd been banned from the site because she is Arab – despite Rachel being a matriarch for Jews, Christians, and Muslims alike.

The Tzahal had also taken over Hebron Road, the main street in Bethlehem, and there had been a strict curfew imposed by the Tzahal. When Claire looked out, she couldn't see a single person, enemy or not, but she did see flashes from guns light up both Aida Camp and downtown Bethlehem, of which Claire's window was situated directly between the two, giving her a full vantage of the fireshower.

Do you know Elie Wiesel?
Survivor of the Shoah?

I'm a writer who is interested in Jewish thought, of course I know Elie Wiesel

└(^ ও ^)┘
While at Auschwitz, Elie and a couple other concentration campers put god on trial for the atrocities he's allowed. A literal trial. They presented their evidence and determined that god was chayav.
Chayav is kind of like "guilty" but a little more nuanced. More like "he owes us something" like a reparation.

What did they demand from Him?

Nothing. They determined him chayav, knew they wouldn't receive whatever they felt like they were owed, and decided to worship him anyway. They didn't let their bitterness towards god negate the fact that they aren't monarchs over the universe.

I'm not as bitter with God as I am frustrated with the idea that we're commanded to pray, which never accomplishes anything almost ever.

Sorry you're having a hard time. What is prayer "supposed" to accomplish in your eyes though? I mean, christians can't believe prayer possibly guarantees whatever you ask for right?

I'd say there's two main schools of thought on this, and it's divided Christians into two stark categories. One side believes prayer ALWAYS works, but sometimes not in the way we want it to (i.e., doesn't always lead to healing, but can transform our hearts to align with God's will). The other side believes that prayer ALWAYS works: healing WILL happen with enough faith.
So, I'm torn between the two: I've seen miracles happen as a result of prayer. But: I prayed for Romy in absolute full faith, fully expecting God to heal her, at a time when my faith was at an all-time high. She still died. So now I can write that school of thought off. I'm forced into the first group now, and just trying to wrestle with what the purpose of prayer even is if God has His plan, which He's going to execute whether I like it or not, so why should I ever pray to offer Him my opinion?
There's a Bible verse: "Therefore confess your sins to each other and pray for each other so that you may be healed. The prayer of a righteous person is powerful and effective." - James 5:16.
This was my "verse of the year" in 2018, the year Romy died. I had a printout of the verse and put it on our window sill that year and contemplated it often.
I recently wrote out all the ways that Judaism is starting to make more sense than Christianity, if you care to hear them.

How many are there?

Not sure. Why?

I'd be interested to read it unless but not if it's another midterm essay like the one you just wrote.

Ouch.

I'm just saying, I want to grow old some day, but not on this thread.

I literally don't know if I should share it then.

I'm just ribbing. Please send it.
After condensing it.

As she poked her head out the window, a few more gunshots rang directly above Claire, dragooning the gun flashes from Aida Camp to turn towards Claire's direction instead of downtown Bethlehem.

Claire heard one bullet chip her roof, followed by a sound that sunk her heart.

Whiiizzzzzz…

Claire threw herself to the floor face-down and covered her head with her hands, but the rocket missed her house and hit the road behind her.

kpuuuh!

Bullets started spraying onto Aida Camp from several directions, including downtown Bethlehem, Claire's own roof, and from a building adjacent to Aida Camp itself.

Twenty full seconds into the onslaught, she began to hear screaming intermixed with gunfire at Aida, and Claire rolled onto her back and broke down crying.

"Lord!" she cried out, "I can't take it anymore! Save us from this bloodshed! Do not allow me to give into my cravings of fear, but give me a spirit of power and love and a sound mind! Send our people help! Send my family help! Please, give us an advocate!"

As Claire prayed, she felt a strange sensation come over her body, a feeling of warmth that started at the top of her head that traveled through her entire body and became cold by the time it hit the bottom of her feet, where the feeling grew warm again and travelled back to the top of her head until it pendulummed back to cold.

Ha. K.
I can whittle it down to 3 points?

Yes please.
But no run-ons.

Judaism makes more sense in the loss of Romy in these ways:
1. Christianity says that healing is possible through prayer if we just have enough faith; Judaism tells us to pray and just accept if it doesn't happen.
2. Christianity says that "God works all things together for the good of His people." Judaism says sometimes meaningless things will happen, but God will hold us and comfort us during those times where chaos reigned.
3. Christianity says we can know God's will; Judaism says who can know the ways of God?

I told you some time ago, I once heard that christianity answers jewdism's questions.

Yet I don't think I'm satisfied with the easy answers that we see in the New Testament. Like when Yeshua says that a mustard seed of faith can move mountains. I didn't have a mustard seed of faith when Romy was sick. I had a melon. And it did nothing beneficial.
If I rejected Christianity and embraced Judaism, the world would make more sense.

So why don't you then? I mean I'm not trying to convert you, jews don't care about that like christians do. But it sounds like you're a jew living in the closet. Or at least not necessarily a christian.

No religion makes total sense. Including atheism. But there are still compelling things about Christianity I can't just ignore.

Like what?

Things that have to hold weight from an intellectual standpoint. Like all of the disciples dying because they refused to recant their testimonies. Nobody knowingly dies for a lie, especially one they'd expect to get squashed. And I think that if Judaism is true, then the Messiah probably already came.

How do you figure that?

Judaism speaks of a Messiah that will save Jews from oppression. Sure, Jews face oppression today, but not like they did in the face of Egypt, Assyria, Babylon, Rome, Germany. You now have a land of your own and the support of the most powerful country in the world. If the Messiah was ever going to come, I feel like He'd be here by now.

Yeah but. Danger. Part of being human is learning to seek god rather than trusting ourselves on issues. There are answers to the questions, even if we don't know those answers.

That's true. If I didn't have the freedom to make the wrong choices - choices so consequential that they killed my doghter - then I've not really been given the opportunity to be human. And that seemingly matters to God.

Right, and why would the almighty god bend because of a lowly human's convincing? He wouldn't be almighty if that was the case. Here's a question for you: how much do you think you know about the universe?

Not totally sure how to answer that...

Give me a percentage. What % of all of the universe's mysteries can you explain?

251

Claire stood in her place, all fear removed, then peered out her window and watched the steady stream of gunfire that had only intensified since her prayer.

"It is time for bed," she whispered to herself so quietly that she couldn't even hear her own words over the firing weapons.

Claire stumbled down the stairs, completely exhausted, and found Zuji in bed with the covers over his whole body.

"Claire, is that you?" Zuji muffled.

"I think I need to get some rest," Claire replied, then collapsed onto the bed and immediately began snoring on top of the covers.

Oof. I suppose... 0.000000000000000000000000112358132134558914 4233%.
If not way way less.

Lol. That was oddly specific. But okay, let's round up. Let's pretend that instead of your whacko number, you actually knew 0.01% of all of the universe's mysteries.

Okay. Not even Einstein or Galileo had that, but go on.

Even if you were the smartest of men in the history of menkind, you would know close-to-nothing about god. 0.01% understanding, at best.

Whoa.
That's trippy.

People act like they know 5% or 20% about the universe. or, if they're christian, 99% and upwards. (no offense)
Prayer is a tool to enhance your dependence on god. enhance your fear of god. You don't influence god any more than a defendant influences a judge. You don't even get confirmation that he heard you. If I believe he exists, then I *must* also believe that he heard me.
Praying is just a kind of comfort for people, when you've lost control of a situation, and you can't do anything for the person you care about. Praying is the only thing left you can do, so you do it as an act of compassion.

Yeah. I get it. In the Bible, Jacob scolded Rachel when she asked for sons because Jacob didn't believe God needed to bend to their wishes about children. Jacob was angry that she even asked for Him to bend His will.

God does not owe us anything. Several years ago, 3 Israeli boys were kidnapped. The army and the police searched for them while jews around the country got together at the Western Wall and in classrooms and at home to recite prayer for them. They were found a week later, dead. Did the prayers work? They'd been dead for days. We were praying for dead boys without even knowing it. But can we measure whether or not the prayer was "worthwhile?" We tried, and it didn't work this time. But hundreds of thousands of people learned the limits of their power while doing a kind thing for complete strangers and were unified around one goal. There's power in that.

I just don't get why we would even pray then, if it doesn't affect the outcome.

You don't pray to get what you want. God is in charge, and there's a reason he doesn't give us the power to alter his will.

Or as the saying goes:
There is only one Lord, only one who can bend us to His will. And He does not share power.

Not familiar with that saying, but sure.

Hey, gotta run.

Cool.

Good night.

Good morning!

BREAKING THE FOURTH WALL

> "Sometimes they ask:
> 'Does this mean you are pro-Palestinian?
> Are you anti-Jewish?'
> You would have to say the same thing to the biblical prophets
> because they were some of the most scathing critics
> of the Jewish leadership of their day.
> We criticize, when they need to be criticized,
> the government of Israel."
> - Desmond Tutu

Bad news. Izzy just told me I need to break the fourth wall, but I can't do that. It's greatly frowned upon. People who are smarter and have had far more success than me have always highly advised against it. They say it's lazy: that there are more creative and effective ways to get to where you need to go.

I'm on a short leash with my readers as it is. When you picked this book up, did you expect to be bouncing between personal text messages like you're at some kind of deposition, coupled with narratives about a guy who never gets to his destinations? If you're a lawyer on lunch break and just can't get enough of that stuff, you're in luck. But for everyone else, this might seem like the worst book you've ever read.

"You're 100% sure I can't get there?" I texted Izzy back.

"Bro, yes, it's on the Israeli side," he replied. "And the checkpoint is closed. You cannot pass! At least not tonight. Go to sleep and try first thing after the sun rises."

Ugh. I can't do that, either, though. It's another lazy trope: starting the journey with someone opening their eyes and waking up. You need to jump into the action, right out the gate! Like Joanna said, start with the inciting incident.

Problem is, the inciting incident here started in Genesis. Jacob – who later was named Israel and, you know, had a country named after him – had had a divine dream where he saw either a "Stairway to Heaven" or "Jacob's Ladder," depending on whether you're a fan of Led Zeppelin or of Huey Lewis and The News. That must make it seem like he was a man who would be blessed by God, but Jacob's favorite wife, Rachel, died in childbirth. He constructed a makeshift burial place for her in Bethlehem, and 3,500 years later, according to Google Maps, I was supposedly standing directly in front of it. But there was no building except a closed gas station.

I was about 50 meters away from the Separation Wall, and to Izzy's point, Google Maps did say Rachel's Tomb was 100 meters away. It would take 20 seconds to reach Rachel's Tomb... if not for the 3-meter-thick, 8-meter-high wall directly in front of my face, which Google Maps didn't think was important enough to annotate. That did it for me: I was done using Google Maps the rest of my trip. They hadn't even warned me that there was Jebusite scum in the area, which I was only alerted to after studying the maps in the back of the Bible.

"Just try again later," Izzy pinged me one last time, responding to my silence.

"Thanks for your help," I texted back. Though, I certainly couldn't heed Izzy's advice there, either: this is already the *sixth* time I've taken you to Bethlehem. Not even the Bible has as many chapters about this city. In fact, Jesus tarries only a few sentences in Bethlehem, and for the rest of the city's presence in the Nativity story, it's getting ragged for its diminutive importance.

No, this was happening tonight. I tend to believe that if you're facing something that's overly dense, there's no need to feel like you're swimming through wet cement: just blow past it like it's a storyline that's not even there. So if the people who built these walls were anything like me, they certainly offered a way around, maybe leaving a crack in the wall that I could exploit.

I take pride in being slick (Proverbs 18:11-12). I've always enjoyed climbing things that weren't meant to be climbed. In college, you could often find me hanging out on top of the art building, just because it was climbable and the student handbook never said you can't climb the art building. Granted, I wasn't going to be climbing the Separation Wall because I prefer my meat without bullet holes. But if there was a way to slip through this blockade, I was going to find it.

I followed along the wall and, to my surprise, it led to a graveyard. I couldn't tell if the writing on the gravestones were in Hebrew or in Arabic, but I didn't figure it mattered – being in a graveyard is a pretty good indicator that I'm getting close to a tomb, yeah?

As I squeezed my way through narrow mausoleums, I noticed in my peripherals that a group of Israeli soldiers were eyeing me, and one of them had his hand on his rifle – not on the trigger, of course. But his index finger was close enough to get my attention.

I continued moving away from them through the cemetery, but each step became more tense with that rifle-toting Israeli.

Should I shout at him, letting them know I'm friendly?

Shouting at them in a foreign language seems like a bad idea, so I just chugged along instead.

Against my better judgment, I checked Google Maps one more time just to confirm that I'd already passed Rachel's Tomb again. As I looked up after pocketing my phone, I noticed there were four Israeli soldiers approaching me.

I froze. I was sure this was not a good situation; I'm more sure about this than I'm sure that you Googled my name if you've been following the Star storyline.

A tower guard from a nearby Israeli citadel started shouting at me in Hebrew. I couldn't understand what he was saying, but he shouted louder and louder and louder with each moment I didn't move.

I raised my hands in surrender.

Wait. What if he thinks I'm a skinny bear trying to show my size?

One of the four Israeli soldiers cautiously approached me and shouted at me in Hebrew.

"English?" I asked, proving to him I wasn't a bear, or at least that I was a talking bear and therefore had big top value.

"Hi," the soldier said in a heaping Hebrew accent that almost had a corporeality to it. "What are you doing here?"

"Rachel's Tomb," I responded, as if that was a logical sentence. "I want to go there."

"It is the feast of Rachel's Tomb," the soldier said. "It is the anniversary of Rachel's death, and is one of the holiest feasts of the year. You chose tonight to visit? You cannot go there; all the checkpoints are closed."

"Oh," I said, my hands still on the invisible monkeybars.

"Are you British?" he asked me.

"American," I responded, but was quite tickled as I couldn't fake a British accent if my life depended on it.

Uh oh. What if my life really depended on me faking a British accent here?

"From U.S.A.?" he clarified.

I debated between responding "yes" and "cheerio," then my answer straddled between the two.

"Yesshhh," I said, confirming that Americans come from U.S.A.

"Oh," he said. "That is so much good for you. Your passport is like a Joker card."

I think he means "wild" card.

"Go back this way you came," he continued, then extended his hand to shake mine. "Relax. You are fine. You are safe."

I shook his hand, gadded towards the main road, and watched as the Israeli soldiers gazed towards me again as if they were in a portrait in which the subjects' eyes move, following your every step. After retracing my path and absconding out of their view, I continued following the wall and sensed a certain level of connection with Jacob, who, in Genesis, had also randomly wandered this city. Why had Jacob come to Bethlehem in the first place? The Bible doesn't really clarify what he was doing here. For all we know, he was looking for participants, too.

If you make it to the 35th chapter, yes, you'll read about the worst night of a battered man's life as he loses his beloved to an unexpected, preventable death during a routine medical event. Jacob lost his wife, and I'm now also resigned to the fact that I won't see Rachel, either.

Of course, I differ from Jacob in that he had children. Twelve babies, in fact, later known as the 12 Tribes of Israel. The youngest baby – the one whose life was traded for Rachel's – was the only of the brothers who was born in the Promised Land itself. With her dying breath, Rachel named him Ben-Oni, which was a really cool name and had a certain Anno-Domini-1977 forward-facement to it. Unfortunately, Jacob wasn't a huge fan, so he waited for Rachel to die and then changed the baby's name to Benjamin.

My path still knit with the wall, I stumbled upon a souvenir shop that had its door open, despite the late hour. I'd been looking for a Nativity Set to buy in Bethlehem – and a real one, at that: not like the parody one I bought earlier that had the wisemen blocked off by a 3-inch-high wooden wall. And maybe this means I'm racist, but it just felt wrong to buy this particular souvenir – a display commemorating the cornerstone of the Christian faith – from a salesperson who outrightly rejects that belief. And, listen, I know what you're thinking: it's discriminatory and, frankly, not biblically justifiable to want to only buy from a Christian. But for this one thing, this *one* purchase, that's just where I was at with it. Of course, though, you can't just hurtle into someone's business and ask, "are you a Christian?" before buying from them.

The shop was uniquely positioned, surrounded by three walls. I'd not seen another building with more than two barriers against it, but this shop seemed like it'd been curiously carved out so that it would *just* fit into the Palestinian side. It had a three-story home attached to the shop as well, which struck me as odd, too. I couldn't imagine the history of this building that warranted such deliberate demarcation.

I eased into the shop – which was even darker inside than it was outside – and the woman at the counter jolted up and turned on the lights. The walls were filled with shelves, and those shelves were filled with Nativity sets and crosses and crucifixes and every other bit of Christian "paraphernalia" you might expect from a shop situated in the city of Christ's birth.

"Oh, hi," she greeted me, though there was a certain lifelessness to her. It almost felt like she didn't want me to be there.

"Hi," I responded.

"We don't get many visitors anymore," she said, solidifying my feeling that she wanted me to leave. But, *hey*, engaging with the shopkeepers here has been the only successful thing I've done, so I wasn't going to quit here.

"Are you a Christian?" I blurted.

She flinched.

"Yes," she responded. "I am."

"I didn't know there were many Palestinian Christians."

"We exist," she said before conceding, "there are not many of us anymore. We are stuck between a wall and a hard place. Bethlehem used to be mostly Christian, but as I stand before you today, maybe only one in ten are Christian in Bethlehem."

"Whoa. What happened? Why such an exile?"

"Oppression, mainly. Things have been tense for us since the turn of the millennium. This wall you see? It was built in one day, just in time for Christmas in 2003. Israelis are brutal to Palestinians, but then Arabs will usually only help Arabs who are Muslim. Arab Christians are on their own, but it's hard to survive when you can't find work. Many have fled to Chile, where Christianity is still celebrated. This was Chile's gain, but Christ's birthplace's loss."

"And now you sell these crosses and nativity sets?"

"Yes, we hire poor wood-makers to handcraft these sets, and then cut them a commission on top of it to help them feed their families," she said, holding one of the sets up. "Have you seen these sets before?"

It was identical to the ones I'd seen in The Banksy Shop and all over Nativity Square in downtown Bethlehem.

"Yes, I've seen them," I said, trying not to let on that I'd bought one from another peddler.

"We are the ones who conceived the idea. People would come to our shop to buy these, but with any good idea, everybody copied our work and now they get the firstfruits from our product. Banksy now sells it for much more money, and people buy from him because, well, it comes from his shop."

"And that's how you survive? Just selling these wooden tchotchkes?"

"Yes, but the taxes required are so high, and Israel does not use the money to repair our infrastructure. What is it said, about Americans? 'No taxation without representation,' it is? Palestinians – even those in Jerusalem – are taxed as Israelis but have no citizenship rights. So to survive, I also manage the bed and breakfast upstairs."

"Knock, *knock*," a deep voice called from outside the shop. The shopkeeper and I turned to find a white man and woman.

"Can I help you?" the shopkeeper asked. "Would you like to see our woodwork, or perhaps to stay the night in our bed and breakfast?"

The couple – I assumed them to be married and from Iowa, for some reason – looked at each other with a certain unease.

"Uh, is this the Banksy hotel?"

"No," the Palestinian woman sighed, curling down the corners of her lips. "No, the Banksy hotel is up the road. Turn around, go from where you came, and just follow the big wall."

They left. Not even a thank-you.

"You know," she looked back at me and continued right where she'd left off, "we used to be popular, being so close to Rachel's Tomb. But the placement of the wall has put us in a dead end. Would you like to see a map?"

"Is it a Google Map?"

"I don't know. Maybe it is. But it is printed here."

She handed me a piece of paper that was demonstrably *not* created by anybody at Google, and proved that I was never going to get to that tomb no matter how hard I tried.

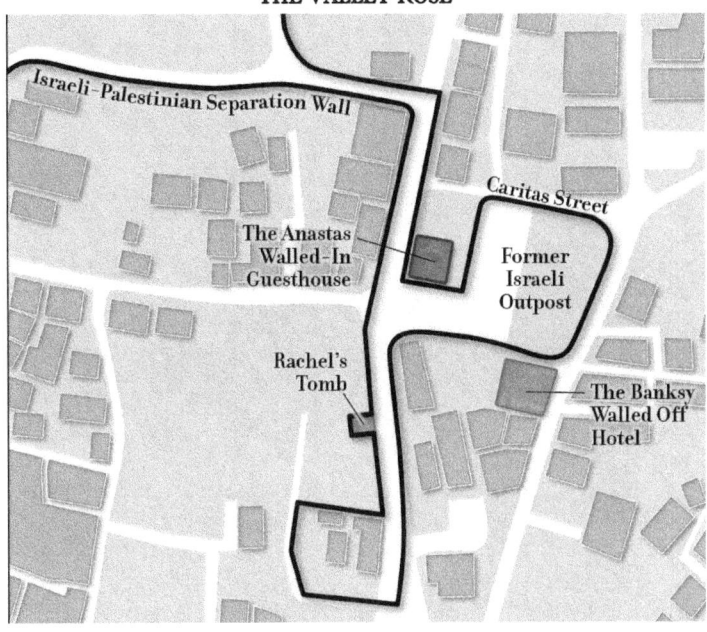

"You can see," she said, "the only people who find us now do it by accident."

"Yeah," I admitted, "I kind of stumbled in here like that. I followed my way around three sections of the wall and thought I might be able to get through on the fourth section, but it just led me here instead. This'll be the last time I try to break the fourth wall."

"Where are you trying to go?"

"I want to see Rachel's Tomb."

"*Oh*, you want to see Rachel's Tomb? I can show you that!"

"Really? How?" I perked up, excited to think that maybe finally I would actually get to a destination I set out to get to.

"Please, follow me," she said, then took me outside her bed and breakfast, right to the edge of the wall where there was a thin opening between two sections that hadn't quite connected. "Look through this crack, and you can see Rachel's Tomb."

Oh. Literally, "see" Rachel's Tomb. Not experience it.

I put my eye up against the crack in the wall and I could *maybe* see the entrance of the tomb, at least when Hasidic Jews weren't swarming about.

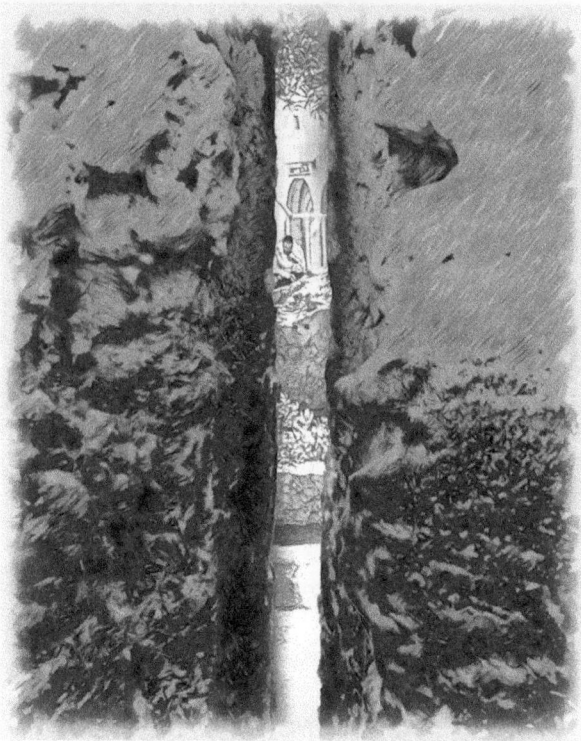

"Today is the feast day," the woman explained. "It's the anniversary of Rachel's death. They close all the checkpoints to Palestinians and only religious Jews are allowed to see it today."

I was indeed destined to never make it to a single tourist location in the Holy Land.

"So, you're not allowed to go outside the wire today? Even if you have a job in East Jerusalem, for example?"

"You can leave, but you must go the long way. It adds several hours to your trip. See this map?"

She handed me a printout that had the Separation Wall and its checkpoints annotated in red marker. It's probably about five miles from East Jerusalem to Bethlehem using the highway, but with the checkpoints, it was a lot more like taking a trip from Dallas to Houston in order to ultimately reach San Antonio. (Pull up Google Maps if you wish, but I won't condone it.)

"Well, that's kind of bogus," I told her.

"It's better just to not leave during Jewish feast days. Plus, it's dangerous because if you try leaving, sometimes they think maybe you are going to cause a problem for their feast day. Many misunderstandings like these happen. Many Palestinians have been killed because of confusion like this. Even me, I have had many encounters with the Israeli military. I shouldn't be alive."

Bethlehem's significance as one of the most death-filled cities in history is, frankly, overlooked. It's been a key bastion of fighting between Israelis and Palestinians, and even its central church is sitting on a cave of thousands of skulls, legend purporting most of them having come from "martyred" babies.

Rachel's motherless son, Benjamin, indeed went on to sire one of the 12 tribes of Israel. But hundreds of years later, his tribe was nearly wiped out after a civil war erupted over the rape, murder, and mincing of a Bethlehemian prostitute.

Bloody.

I peeked through the crack again. I imagined what it might've looked like if this woman's Nativity parody could come to life: *what if* the wisemen had traveled from Persia, only to be stopped here by a wall? I wasn't sure if the construct of that image was funny or funereal.

"It sounds like you could write a whole book about this stuff," I surmised to the keeper.

"I have been praying and praying for that. Just last week, I told my friends that I was still waiting on God to send me someone who can help me tell my story, someone who could write for an American audience."

"Really?" I marveled.

"Yes," she said, "make my story accessible to American Christians."

"How can it be made accessible to Americans?"

"Write in the language of the people. Instead of 'the Naksa' or 'the Harb,' write it as 'Setback.' Or better, the Six-Nineteen-Seven War."

"The 1967 War?"

"Yes... yes, that's right," she ceded. "I have the story, but I don't know how to tell it. I've imagined this American coming and listening to my story, and writing about it."

My cheeks warmed and I gulped.

"What's your name?" I bandied, knowing that the name I would hear next would be one that I'd be linked to for the next many years.

"I am Claire."

"Claire? Claire. Can I sit down and talk to you?"

Fair reader, this might be the worst book you've ever read. But it's the most important one I'll ever write.

"He comforts us in all our affliction,
so that we may be able to comfort those
who are in any kind of affliction."
~ 2 Corinthians 1:4, CSB

THE VALLEY ROSE.

God spoke, and it's how
The mountain calls for you now.
Not me –
The Valley Rose.
And it was my beloved who was always
Bound to suffer.
The Lord was the One who was
So focused on growing His garden,
That He left us to wither on this side.
That God is actually not good.
Never again will I think
Faith is the most important pillar of life.
Contrary to my prior beliefs,
Prayer has no place in the logical man's life.
Now I know that it's foolish to say
God is sovereign.
For all of eternity,
I will never see Romy again.
I erroneously believed
This pain will pass;
And also that
God sent Yeshua as Messiah.
I've instead learned to trust
My old pragmatic way of thinking.
I've been forced to surrender
My family, after all.

My family, after all.

June 25, 2020

It didn't work.

What didnt?

Our second attempt. Fertility treatments failed. We've got one more go before we know we won't have children.

I'm sorry

Trying to be optimistic. But you're one of few people I've talked to this about so just thought I'd let you know.

I'm honored that you thought to tell me.

Yeah. Well.
Job hunting going any better yet?

No. And I'm still holding out hope that I'll go back to my old job. But it's a silly thought because the hostel isn't anywhere close to being opened back up. I'm at a loss as to what to do. Already dipped into my savings just to survive, and if I don't find something in the next 7 months, I'll have to open a loan just to pay rent.

I feel that. I feel that in my bones. I'm sorry. I'm not any closer to a job, either. My day usually consists of applying to jobs, then working on my manuscript.

About Israel?

Yes.
Actually I'm working on a story about a Palestinian woman I met right before you.

A muslim woman?

Christian, actually. I'm writing about how her faith - how the Shekhinah - shepherded her through all kinds of oppression.

Oppression from who exactly?

Well, Israelis.

I see.

She's a kind, honest woman. You might even like her.

Can I offer some advice with this one?

Of course

Well, you're clearly going to be describing her story and, I'm assuming, negative interactions with Israelis?

Correct.

I think it's only fair if you include instigation from Palestinians, which she probably won't tell you about. Or like how, a little while ago, an IDF soldier was killed by a palestinian. The IDF soldier was a christian arab who volunteered for the IDF, so his funeral was led by a priest and his casket was draped with an Israeli flag and the service was in hebrew and arabic. We let a man serve alongside us, even though he had our enemies' ethnicity, wasn't our religion, and wasn't even ethnically jewish. You'd never see that in palestine. How many countries let their enemies join their ranks as soldiers, and will let them on the frontlines against their own native people without concern for betrayal? So i just think it's worth mentioning is all.

٢٢
November 27, 1996

"At first injury, we leave," Zuji reminded Claire of the promise she made years ago, glancing at her only sporadically so as to keep his focus on the busy road ahead. *"Fine.* But you don't need to throw yourself into danger, is all I'm saying. It's like, lately, someone has cinched your basic survival instincts."

"God will protect me," Claire responded. "Or, He won't. We don't get to decide that. We only get to decide to trust Him."

"And what happens when He decides to not protect you? Then our children have no mother."

"And at that time, you would get to decide to be happy for me that I am with Yasue."

Zuji sighed, and silence hung in the air long enough that they could hear a crossfire emerging in the direction of their house. Zuji and Claire glanced at each other with worry, then Zuji slammed on the gas pedal to get home.

Less than five minutes later, they were home, but there was no indication that there had been a firefight a few moments before.

While Zuji threw the car into park, Claire flung herself out of the car and into her house.

"Abni? Ebnahty?" Claire called out.

"Momma?" Abni emerged from his room, followed by his sister.

Claire hugged them both, almost knocking their heads against hers.

"You are fine?" she asked them.

I really don't think there's a place for that in her story. I mean, it's not my story that I'm trying to tell. It's hers. It's not about what I want to write.

Then why write it?

Well, for one, I felt called to. Difference of opinion, I get it, I can hear you now, "God doesn't call people to specific tasks anymore." But also, it's an important story. I'm sorry Israelis are the "bad guys" in it. The point isn't to draw attention to politics, but to highlight the way God has moved in her life.
Also, for what it's worth, she's been persecuted for her religion by fellow Arabs. So there's that.

It's whatever. I'm not telling you what to do. It's just sometimes, and we see this in the media a lot in the US, but sometimes writers will focus on the issue of the israeli occupation as if it's a "human interest" story or something innocuous, and it's actually just a thinly veiled attempt at evangelizing their antisemitism.

If any of my readers close my book and feel like its purpose was to condemn Jews for being Israelis or Arabs for being Muslim, then they're missing the point. Or I'm a bad writer. Which, to be fair, is entirely likely in itself. But your feedback is noted. Truly, I mean that. My intent is to share her story, not editorialize. I don't want to share something unfairly skewed.

But that's exactly what palestinians do every day. They know their facts are skewed and choose to accept them.

Not to be contrarian, but can you give me an example?

I can give as many examples as there are stars in the sky.
Here's one that gets under my skin: palestinians say israel is committing "genocide" against them. Genocide? Really? There are about 7 million palestinians living in israel today. We kill less than 100 palestinians each year, and most of those are straight-up bonafide terrorists who took up the cause of Hamas. Let me do the math.
0.00001%. That's ONE ONE-HUNDRED-THOUSANDTH of a percent. Laughable to call that a genocide. If the Shoah / Holocaust was actually in their textbooks, they'd see the stats of what a real genocide looks like.

I think the problem isn't necessarily in the stats, but in the occupation itself. Like, sure, not that many Palestinians are killed, but they're still under occupation. The hashtag I often see isn't #PalestinianLivesMatter but #FreePalestine.

#freepalestine from what? The bare minimum we have to do to survive? We're not invading other countries like Arab nations around us incessantly do, we're just claiming what was designated for us. Kay, so suppose we "#freepalestine" as they want. You know what happens? the same thing that happened when we gave back Gaza. The same thing that happened when we let them on the Temple Mount. They take the concession and then use that land against us.
#freepalestine is the same thing as saying #destroyisrael. You might as well keep the two hashtags together.

I hear you.. (I really do. Please don't lose that.)
But setting up colonies on an under-resourced, overpopulated region?
It's imperialism, any way you frame it.

Uh... as if the US, Europe, and Arabs didn't use colonies to expand their empires. If Israel is guilty of imperialism, it's on a much smaller scale than what the superpowers have used, and we're doing it out of self-preservation.

You're really convinced Israel would be destroyed if they didn't build settlements?

"Yes, but there is a man on our roof," Abni replied.

"Yes," Claire responded. "Sometimes we will see men in those uniforms going on the roof, and there is nothing we can do about it."

"But momma, he wasn't wearing a uniform."

Claire and Zuji shot each other that glance again, and then Zuji rushed to the top floor. He turned the handle to the roof, which was unlocked. If it was Tzahal on the roof, it would be the first time they'd ever let the door remain unlocked while they were conducting operations on the roof.

"Hello?" Zuji called out as he slowly ascended the stairs into the full view of every sniper in Bethlehem.

"Yes, my sir," said a man dressed in plain clothes and carrying a camera on his collarbone.

"Who are you?"

"I am Marwan," the man said, waving a badge. "I am with the media, a member of the legal press."

"How did you get up here?"

"Your son gave me permission, actually, after I knocked on your door."

"I doubt that to be true," Zuji said, flinging his arms in the air and then pointing a finger at Marwan's nose. "Who are you, to think that a 7-year-old has the authority to decide who comes in and out of households?"

"I am sorry. I got what I needed, so I can go."

"What did you get?"

Marwan flashed the sleek, pocket-sized camera he'd been carrying. A muddled Zuji watched as Marwan thumbed through crisp

Okay, so you're a hard facts guy. Let me drop some dimes on you.
-1921, Palestinians kill 47 diaspora jews in Jaffa. Unprovoked. Mind you, Palestine was in charge and jews were in exile at the time. Nobody cried #letmypeoplego.
-1929, Palestinians are still governing, and kill well over 100 diaspora jews. About 70 of those were killed in Hebron overnight! why? because #freepalestine.
-1938, Palestinians massacre a dozen children in Tiberias. No other reason than they could get away with it and the children were jewish. Yup: #freepalestine.
-1940s. Hajj Amin Al-Husseini is the grand mufti of Jerusalem (think "high priest of islam"). He advises H*tler to exterminate the jews, and when he implements the final solution, the kind Hajj blocks all jewish refugees from escaping to Palestine. Holocaust within a holocaust. It wasn't #freepalestine when jews were there.
-1947, the world finds out about Shoah and unanimously supports giving aid to jews. Except for the Pals, who are the only sect of people who deny a genocide occurred against the jews, even though their mufti clearly helped instigate it.
-1948, Palestinians + mufti invade Israel with an intent to wipe out jews from the human race. They convince surrounding arab countries to help. Jews go from Shoah in Europe to genocide in their own land. Jews fight back, win.
-1967, angry about losing, Pals conspire with arabs across the middle east and stage another coup to take over Israel. So we take away the land they used as strongholds against us and create colonies on their land to keep them in check.

Wow. I'm sorry. That's incredibly depressing.

But sure. go off on how jews building mud huts today are the problem.

You pull those stats out of your crystal ball?

lol. yeah. my crystal ball has a name. its called google.
Okay. End rant. Just, look up the stats sometime.

That's brutal. So much death. What can men do against such reckless hate?

Where exactly did you meet this woman?

I accidentally met her during my trip during an excursion to Bethlehem.

Okay. Not to beat the donkey, but this is a good example of what I'm trying to get at. If you asked her the meaning of "Bethlehem," she'd tell you it means "House of Meat," Bayt Laḥm in native language.

I thought Bethlehem meant "House of Bread"?

Exactly! Bet Lehem in Hebrew. A language 3000ish years superior to Arabic. Does anything highlight the issues more succinctly than this? They believe it means House of Meat when it actually has meant House of Bread for far longer.

Well. Bread vs Meat. Sounds like when Cain gave bread and Abel gave meat. Maybe their offering is the right one?

(ᵕ‿ᵕ)

I'm just kidding. Just a joke.
Anyway, again: her story isn't about etymology or history or "Israel = bad."

But you DO paint us as the bad guys?

I mean, it's certainly hard to see these Israelis as the good guys there. You have to recognize that sometimes Israelis are the bad guys, just like sometimes Americans are the bad guys. Even in the Bible, Israelis play the bad guys.

I can't believe you just said that.

Sorry, I'm really not trying to be offensive.

pictures of Palestinians holding rifles in the air as they pressed their backs to the outside of Rachel's Tomb, whilst a small group of Tzahal were being mobilized from their military camp on the other side to respond to the insurgency.

"What is this?" Zuji asked, trying not to sound impressed.

"It is the new Powershot 600. No need to develop photos later, it can be shown in an instant. Just a third-inch sensor and over 800 pixel res on the width, auto white balance, and an optical viewfinder."

All of that was gibberish to Zuji, and Zuji didn't care to admit it to Marwan, but these were incredibly impressive pictures, and the camera unlike anything he'd ever seen before.

"I believe I am living in the future," Zuji admitted to Marwan, then quickly added as he remembered the gravity of the situation, "but you need to leave my roof right now. The Tzahal has forbidden *anyone*, even ourselves, from being on our roof. You have put my family in grave danger."

No, the bit about Americans being bad guys. Americans rarely admit that.

You can't look at the innumerable Vietnamese interpreters we left behind to die in Vietnam and not also want to fly the flag at half-mast. Is it coincidence that April 29th is the date of both the capture of Saigon AND the premiere of the Imperial Death March? We were a lot more Darth Vader than Luke Skywalker that year.

Not a star trek fan, but I think I get it. But how did you "accidentally" meet her?

She lives near Rachel's Tomb, and I so happened to try visiting the site on October 28th. The Jews were celebrating Rachel Imenu though, and I couldn't get in. What are the chances that was the day that I chose to visit the tomb?

Hmm. I can check for you, hold on.

No, stop. It was rhetorical lol. It's a 1/365 chance. I'm absolutely certain that was the day, I meant my statement like "wow, how absurd that was the day I visited."

so you never got in then?

No. I could only look on through a crack in the wall.

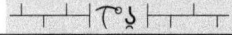

Did you seriously just casually have a "person gets stuck outside of holy site and has to look through a crack in the wall" emoticon at the ready?

_(ツ)_/

Lol. That's too much.
It wasn't all bad though. Because I got walled out, I spent a night at the bed and breakfast owned by the Palestinian woman, and we talked for hours on end. It's one of those instances when you only spend a day or two with someone, but it impacts you for a lifetime. Which I can say is the effect you've had on me, too.

That's nice of you to think that. So you still talk to her?

Yes, I do. Every day. This woman has been communicating her story to me ever since I met her. And it's really amazing stuff. At least I think so.

Just be careful with that. Sometimes they say things that are untrue.
Especially if what they're saying can't be fact-checked.

Well don't forget, I did also write "Holy Hotbed," which is a whole book about how narratives have become fabricated potboilers in Israel and Palestine.
Also: I trust this one. And I believe her agenda is apolitical.

But she DOES have an agenda, then.

Don't we all?

Well. Jews don't.
ʕ •ᴥ•ʔ

(ರ_ ⊙)

ʕ ರᴥ•ʔ
so you're emoting now too huh

just copied and pasted yours from earlier

(> ᴥ <)

Anyway. This woman's aim is definitely peace. And you never know.
Even the smallest person can change the course of the future.

If you say so.

PLANT A SEED, PLANT A FLOWER, PLANT A ROSE

> "The wilderness and
> the dry land shall be glad;
> the desert shall rejoice and
> blossom like the crocus."
> ~ Isaiah 35:1, ESV

"Hi sir, are you checking in?" the young woman at the hostel front desk asked me without looking up.

"Yes, please," I said.

"So, where in the U.S. are you from?" she asked, looking up at me. She had slightly wavy ebony hair and deep-set brown eyes, a rounded nose, thick eyebrows, and plump, fleshy lips that contoured down her diamond-shaped face.

"*Chuh-uh,*" I fumbled. "Chicago. Well, the Chicago suburbs. Well, actually, I live in Tulsa now. It's a bit of a different world than Chicago. Same time zone though!"

"What made you leave a big city like that and move to the boonies in Timbuktu? Wait, no: wrong musical. *Oooooo-*klahoma!" she trilled, buffaloing me with her knowledge of American geography and showtunes. "*Get your kicks on Route 66!* And your oil, and your Woody Guthrie…"

"Indeed! My family and I recently moved there. I'm impressed you could tell I was an American within two words."

"So, you just a really big *Grapes of Wrath* fan?" she asked, ignoring my compliment.

"Well," I slowly spoke, trying to come up with an asinine answer because I love to respond to sarcasm with sarcasm. But I was at a loss, flabbergasted by her knowledge of American literature, now.

"Well?" she interrupted my thoughts.

"Well, the truth is I'm a really big Hanson fan, and they live in Tulsa."

"So you MmmBopped your way to Oklahoma?"

"You got that reference too? Who are you?"

"Come on. Tell me for real. Why did you move?"

"I guess it was just a lot of little things," I replied, always hating this question because I never knew the real answer as to why I moved from Chicago. I mean, the reason was "God called us to," but that's so unsatisfying for so many people – maybe even for myself.

"Little things? Okay, at some point, on some random day, you made a conscious decision and said to yourself, 'I need to leave this home I've created.' What day was that?"

I thought about it, then realized she was right. There was a specific moment.

"I took my dogs to our neighborhood park. I let them off-leash for five minutes so they could get their zoomies out, and during that short time, the police pulled up and told me to leash my dogs and leave because they had gotten a call from one of my neighbors complaining. It was a cold day. There wasn't a single person out in the park. And I said to myself, 'I need to move somewhere less uptight.'"

"And Tulsa was that?"

"Tulsa was that. Initially we wanted to move to Seattle, but we couldn't land any jobs there after about a year of trying. My wife applied to a single job in Tulsa because we had been down there once for a beer festival, and she got it, so we moved."

"*Ohhhhh*, a beer festival? Okay, so this makes so much more sense now: you were drunk. Do you like it there?"

"We like it. I think. Maybe. It's nice. I mean, once get past the thunderstorms, tornadoes, earthquakes, sinkholes, allergenic grass, antiquated liquor laws, and stroke-inducing heat."

"Are you there long-term? Like, do you rent?"

"Actually, we just moved into a brand-new house. Literally, everything's still in boxes in that house, and I'll be unpacking after this trip. The week before I traveled to Israel, we moved from a cramped condo to a single-family home with a big fenced backyard so our dogs could zoomie all they want without having to worry about irritating neighbors calling the police on them."

"Wow. You love your dogs."

"Yes, 'and our dogs love us.' "

"What do you do? For work?"

"Well, I'm a student, and..."

"You *pay* to be a student," she corrected me. "What do you do for *work*? Or, what do you want to do for work?"

"Write. I'm a writer."

"Cool! What do you write?"

"Whatever I feel compelled to. I just have to. I have to write or I go nutballs. I write so my kids and grandkids can know me after a likely-early death."

"You have kids?"

"Well, no."

"Probably a good reason to get it on paper, then, I suppose."

"But how could you tell I'm an American? And how do you know so much about American culture? And your English... it's good. *No*, it's not good: it's perfect."

"I was born in New York City," she said, vaporizing the anxiety behind her mysteriousness.

Ah, New York. Big Apple. Yankees. Joe Namath. Spider-Man.

"Okay, so you have American-detecting superpowers now. Why'd you move to Israel?"

"I'm a Jew."

"Well, that's a good reason then, I suppose."

"It's hard to find anything kosher to eat in the States."

"It's also hard to find anything authentic to eat in the States, too," I said. "The American grocery system is basically broken down into three aisles: poison that tastes great, poison that tastes bad but you eat it because you think it's not poison, and then food that's way-too-expensive. But here? I've only had one headache since I've been here, and that wasn't because of the food. You guys put cucumbers and rosemary in everything, which are my absolute favorites."

"I didn't realize I was talking to Christopher Columbus. Is it the spices that brought you to Israel? Or are you Jewish?"

"I am not."

"Well, sooo...," she let her words float. "Why'd you decide to take a trip out to Jerusalem?"

"I guess because it's hard to find anybody kosher to meet in the States?"

She blankly looked at me. I forgot the first rule of international travel: don't attempt humor. Especially when you're not very funny in the first place.

"What I mean is, I'm a PhD student trying to conduct research. I wanted to interview Israelis and Palestinians about the way conflict impacts them. I'm pretty maxed out on my Palestinians, but don't have a single Israeli participant. Which reminds me: would you mind if I put this flyer up on the bulletin board in your hostel?"

She grabbed my flyer and scanned it over.

"Eh, actually, I would mind," she said. "This isn't going to do you any good. The travelers staying here are from literally everywhere else in the world *but* Israel and Palestine. That's why they're staying here."

"I mean, it's my only shot at this point. I've got less than two weeks before my time's up. I'm not going to be able to salvage this study if I don't get Israelis interested in sitting down with me."

"Are you free in a couple hours?"

"Sure, Jerusalem is my oyster."

"Nevermind. Can't. Oysters are forbidden. Not kosher."

"I just mean, I..."

"I know what you meant. Meet me on the roof at seven. I'll be your first Israeli interview."

"Wait... really? That would be awesome. Like, that is really fantastic of you! I just need one hour of your time. I promise I won't go over that."

"It's no problem. I love to share this culture with others."

"Hey, what's your name?"

"I am Esther."

> "The history of men
> is reflected in
> the history of sewers.
> It has been a sepulchre,
> it has served as an asylum.
> Crime, intelligence, social protest,
> liberty of conscience, thought, theft,
> all that human laws persecute or have persecuted,
> is hidden in that hole.
> All which was formerly rouged, is washed free.
> The last veil is torn away.
> A sewer is a cynic.
> It tells everything."
> - Victor Hugo

THE VALLEY ROSE.

God spoke, and it's how
The mountain calls for you now,
Not me –
The Valley Rose.
And it was my beloved who was always
Bound to suffer.
The Lord was the One who was
So focused on growing His garden,
That He left us to wither on this side.
That God is actually not good.
Never again will I think
Faith is the most important pillar of life.
Contrary to my prior beliefs,
Prayer has no place in the logical man's life.
Now I know that it's foolish to say
God is sovereign.
For all of eternity,
I will never see Romy again.
I erroneously believed
This pain will pass;
And also that
God sent Yeshua as Messiah.
I've instead learned to trust
My old pragmatic way of thinking.
I've been forced to surrender
My family, after all.
I never deserved
Anything less than this confidence:
Our suffering is meaningless

כג

June 30, 2020

I *just* realized that you ended our last two conversations with quotes from the Lord of the Rings.

Yep. I thought you were going to miss it completely. Finally watched all of them

(ﾉ°□°)ﾉ
CONGRATULATIONS. You've made it to the 21st Century!

It only took me 11 sittings to get through them all, and it wasn't even the extended editions.

The story makes more sense if you watch the extended ones.

So it just needed to be longer to keep my attention better?

Okay, so yeah, that sounds backwards now that you say it like that. But most stories make more sense, the more context you get.

That doesn't mean the stories are worth the time.

Idk. I think any subtext makes a story more interesting. Even when you read the bible, the stuff that's hardest to get through, there's a lot of subtext there that we can't even know is there.

Can you elaborate?

Well we don't understand what's NOT being said. Think about the most misused verse in the bible, the one in Jeremiah. When God tells Israel "For I know the plans I have for you, plans to prosper you and not to harm you. You'll call on me and pray to me and I'll hear. You'll seek and you'll find me."

Not quite getting it. What's not being said there?

The rest of the context. You look at this quote as it is, you think "okay cool, god's got my back." But what did he say just before this? God said the "plans I have for you" were suffering, exile, and physical harm. Many of them were going to be killed.

Why would God say "I plan to prosper you" if that's what was in store??

The "you" was not "you, Israelite," and it certainly wasn't "you, Dr. Danger." it was "you, Israel." the community. the whole. We've taken a cultural principle (individualism) and turned it into a cultural vice. One that has us misreading scripture through western eyes.

So this "promise" isn't even true then? You're saying God was saying this to Israelites - collectively, as a people - for something that would happen eventually to a select few of them, while the rest of them would actually be killed?

There's a saying. "The promise may not apply to me but that doesn't mean it doesn't apply to us."

Who says that? And what's the application for us today in that?

What if there is no direct application? What if the bible says things that have no meaning for us today? What if the application for a 1st century jew is just supposed to be a bedtime story for a 21st century christian?

That would sure make Revelation a lot easier to swallow.

November 27, 1996

"Marwan could win the Nobel Prize for Best Photo," Zuji raved to Claire and the kids as he stuffed glass noodles into his mouth. "I told him, 'you have brought this camera from the wizarding world.' He did not need to develop any of his photos, they were available immediately! He said that there are some cameras now that show your pictures immediately on a tiny TV screen that can fit in your pocket, and that…"

BANG! BANG! BANG!

Zuji froze in fear as he heard someone wildly knock at the door.

"*Lehipatakh!*" the person at the door shouted. "*Lehipatakh!*"

"Claire," Zuji said as a noodle escaped his mouth and into his lap, "they have come for me."

Claire stood up and began to head towards the door, but Zuji jumped in front of her and shook his head.

"This is mine to carry. You take the children upstairs."

Claire schlepped the children upstairs and they hid behind a corner couch. They heard a loud crash, but after a few moments, she realized she hadn't heard any commotion downstairs – not a peep from Zuji or the Tzahal.

"Stay here," she instructed her children and then hustled to the ground floor, where she found a single Samal standing in her doorway taking notes, but no Zuji.

"Samal, what's going on?" Claire asked.

Yeah, I know we've talked about that. Your idea that the end times battle would happen in YOUR generation is individualistic at its core. Since the day your bible was fumbled together, every generation has believed the end times was going to happen to them.
All of the "signs" that the end times are coming? They've been happening since Adam ate the apple.

There's a lot to digest there. The Messiah can't redeem mankind and fulfill God's plan without all of those things coming to pass, and I think that's why people look for it with such zeal.

"when the messiah redeems mankind" guy, that's not even the point of the story. even if your religion is true, that it was Yeshua who redeemed creation, then you have to understand the story isn't about YOU. that grand redemption plot? it's a small piece of god's grand plan. and it serves him as much as it serves you, if not more.

Fine. That's worth thinking about. But I don't think we should discount Armageddon just because it's been misinterpreted more than any other prophecy.

Okay. That aside. Imagine if someone read our text exchanges. How many times have we said "Lol"? I don't need to explain what it means to you. You don't need to explain it to me. But think if someone is reading this exchange a couple hundred years from now, and "Lol" isn't a thing anymore. Ergo, people who don't know what it means are missing context.
My aunt used to say "LOL" when she meant "Lots Of Love." I got a text the day my uncle died. "Norman passed away this morning - LOL"

...lol

I know!

But I get it. All of a sudden, we might be reading about this great joke that Moses told, and he ends it with "Lol," and if we think it means "lots of love," then we think he's being particularly sincere when it's actually the opposite.

Right. Even if they figured out what "lol" meant, they still miss the subtext. Is it meant to be literal? Sarcastic? Funny? Or is it used like "Selah" in the bible?

We still don't know what Selah necessarily means

Exactly! We have some ideas, but there's a context that's lost there. At the time, it probably was a word that went without explanation. Today? It mystifies us more than any other word in the bible.

That's a really good point. That which "goes without saying" in 2000 BC is a lot different than what "goes without saying" in AD 2000.

So whether it's Lord of the Rings or Lord of the Bible, we're reading ancient texts in which some of the cultural cues aren't spelled out for us. What do we do when that happens? We use our OWN context to fill in the blanks. And voila: an entire people group are operating off of a misinterpretation.
Operate off of it long enough, it accidentally becomes canon.

That's why expository preaching is so important to me. Expository preaching requires you to take the central verse you're preaching on, but then you also look at all the verses before and after that verse to fill in the context, so you're not making any assumptions or hearing what you want to hear.

The soldier turned towards Claire, flashing his rank. He was *no* Samal: he was the boss of the Samals, a *Segen*, only one grade below the top Israeli commander in Bethlehem.

"*Se-gen*," she fluttered a melody. "I'm sorry, I didn't see your rank at first."

"Shaket!" the Segen whisted. She knew enough Hebrew to know that meant "shut up," and she knew enough Tzahal to know that one does not become a Segen by pandering to his enemies.

The Segen took a single step inside the house and looked upstairs, as if he was thinking about going up there.

"While you're in this house, do not trouble my children," she instructed the Segen.

The Segen looked at Claire with unforgiving contempt. Claire didn't mind him, and tried to get a peek out the door to see if she could spot Zuji.

The Segen grabbed his weapon, spun it around, and thrust the butt of the rifle into Claire's face, stopping no less than a millimeter short of Claire's nose – she could smell the carbon from the rifle.

"In some countries," Claire spoke into the stock, "Segen means 'blessing.'"

The Segen lowered his rifle and Claire retreated back upstairs to the western window to catch a glimpse of what might be happening to Zuji. She approached the glass and spotted her handcuffed and blindfolded husband, just in time to see a Samal crack the back of his torso with his rifle's butt, sending Zuji to his knees and gasping for air.

Just then, another man was brought into Claire's view: it was Marwan, the cameraman from Claire's roof. The Samal herded Marwan to

The problem with ancient text is it's not easy to hear the voice's tone. There was something said, it was passed down orally, eventually written down, duplicated by hand over thousands of years, translated into multiple languages, and finally the meaning was interpreted. Could some of the commands we heard be a bit of humor? How can we know.

Emoticons. They should've used emoticons so we could hear the inflection in their voice.

╲ ⌒ ⌣° ╲╱ yaasss
Long tangent, but my point is when you watch deleted scenes or you read commentary or you take the time to interpret text exchanges in their original context, then you're putting aside your cultural assumptions to fill in the blanks, and instead gleaning the story with the proper context.

It's why I always admonish people to buy the deluxe version of Wreck-It Ralph so they can watch the deleted scenes.

Fair point.

Did you ever read choose-your-own-adventure books as a kid?

No. They drove me mad. I need linear stories.

Oh. Well, this might be lost on you then, but I always loved reading until I got every possible ending because it allowed me to fully understand the context of what was going on. (if it was a well-done CYOA, that is)

Have you seen "Groundhog Dog?" The Bill Murray flick?

"Bill Murray flick?" I think you mean "Harold Ramis flick." And yes. It's one of my favorite movies. In fact I used to live near Woodstock, Illinois where it was filmed. They have plaques throughout the city commemorating where each scene was filmed.

So you probably know where I'm going with this.

Actually, not at all, but I'm always happy to discuss Groundhog Day.

Premise: the Bill Murray character has to relive the same day over and over and over, which means he gets more and more context for each day he has to suffer through. He understands every intricacy of every person and everything around him. His knowledge becomes close-to-infinite. He makes the comment that he feels like god because he's been around so long.

What if the real God uses tricks? What if He's not omnipotent? What if He's just been around forever, He knows everything now?

So you're familiar.

I've always felt like Groundhog Day is an unintentional analogy to how demons and the devil work in Christianity.

What? How?

Well if Satan has been actively working against humans since the dawn of the apple, then he's only getting more and more cunning as we approach the twilight.

The Flynn effect. That's what I was bringing up. You know it?

No.

It's the idea of why humans have gotten smarter over time. We score so much higher now on standardized tests than people from the 1900s. Fluid and crystallized intelligence, both. You're smarter than your grandpa.

the Segen, who was now standing before Zuji, and he handed Marwan's camera to the Segen.

Marwan gestured his hands towards Zuji and argued with the Segen, though Claire couldn't hear what he was saying. The Segen ignored Marwan while he thumbed through the pictures on the camera. It didn't take long before the Segen had seen – or heard – enough, and he winded his arm back and thrust a haymaker into Marwan's ribs, forcing him to the ground and into a coughing fit. They didn't need to handcuff him – he wasn't going anywhere.

The Segen pitched Marwan's Powershot 600 onto the ground, then spent almost five full minutes stomping it until the Segen's boots were stained with zinc and carbon residue. Marwan didn't protest, looking on with distinct sadness.

Claire's feet began to hurt from standing to watch through the window, but she knew it couldn't be worse than how her husband must've been feeling after kneeling on the gravel in the blistering light. Claire watched as a cruiser pulled up to her house. She sprinted downstairs, but before she even made it outside of her home, both Zuji and Marwan had been scooped and hauled away. She couldn't even see what direction they went, and Claire was left with no explanation of where they were going or when she could expect to see her husband again.

Yeah maybe but I've also had more education opportunities than he ever had. He had to fight a world war.

Still, same result. Of course there's some explanation. But still. You're smarter.

Ugh so my 1 year-old niece is gonna be smarter than me. If she isn't already.

Yep. With Groundhog Day, Bill Murray became so smart just by existing. He knew what was behind every single choice he made.

That's why I love the movie. Phil Connors was living a literal choose-your-own-adventure. If you read through a story that has multiple paths, and you don't read every possible branch, you're always going to be missing some context. Context that makes the rest of the story richer.

You can make the same argument for the value of unabridged books. They give more context and are how the creator wanted them to be consumed. Yeah, it's more dense, but it's a trade-off to gain a richer appreciation of the story.
Except for Les Mis. Nobody needs a 6-chapter discourse glorifying the Paris pooh rivers.

Poo rivers? I've skimmed through the abridged Les Mis, but honestly you may have just sold the unabridged to me better than anyone could have.

Unabridged versions are just better.

Same page.

So you know what you have to do then, right?

No...?

Watch the LOTR extended editions. ೮ঽ↰ᴧ→⌐

Ugh.

Your niece is catching up to you!

But that's just such a big time investment.

All we have to decide is what to do with the time that is given us.

Next pandemic. Pinky promise.

283

RELYING ON A STAR

> "This is the verdict:
> Light has come into the world,
> but people loved darkness."
> ~ John 3:19, NIV

I ascended to the roof of the hostel where there were groups of people – mostly in their late 20s and early 30s – chatting with each other, holding alcoholic drinks that ranged all the way from Goldstar to Goldstar Light. It felt a bit like I was on the Tower of Babel, with different languages and dialects from across the globe gathering on this one roof.

Most everybody was standing: the sky had tinkled recently and all the patio furniture was still damp, though it was a comfortable temperature: I'm guessing upper 60s. I looked skyward and found that the clouds looked almost like a chain-link fence, a spattering of sunshine sneaking through the holey ashen clouds.

I checked around for Esther. Given I was 15 minutes early, she wasn't there yet, so I plopped onto a pleather sofa that was situated under a set of cafe lights in the furthest corner of the roof. I pinned my back to the wall – partially because of that gunslinger anxiety that I get if someone can sneak up behind me, but this time it was mostly so I could watch for Esther as she got out of the elevator. The sofa was largely dry thanks to the fabric, though I was afraid if I stood up again, it would look like I peed my shorts, so I didn't dare stand. I leaned over and wiped the seat across from me so Esther wouldn't have to deal with the same self-consciousness I was experiencing, and then locked in so deeply onto my dissertation notes that Esther snuck up on me anyway.

"*Erev tov*, Danger," she announced herself, flanking me to the left and startling me, though I steadied myself so as not to allow my body to flinch. I looked up and found her demurely bundled in an olive peacoat that covered her from shoulder to knees like it was the middle of winter. I'd worn shorts and a gray V-neck every day since I'd arrived, and I started to wonder if my tolerance to the cold had me sticking out like a man sporting a muumuu at a biker convention.

"Esther!" I exclaimed, standing up and shaking her hand, which I think she found a bit foreign, but politely responded in like. "*Erev tov* to you too, and good evening."

"That's… that's what that means. 'Good evening.'"

"I thought *aravim* means evening?" I appealed, then remembered my seemingly-soiled pants and shot back into my seat.

"It does. Both do. Same root word. The Jewish evening service is named '*Maariv*.' And evening can even be a verb. So if you were to say, 'At *Maariv*, I prayed to God, *Ha'Maariv Aravim*,' you'd literally be saying, 'In the evening, I prayed to God, who evenings the evenings.'"

"And what does that mean, practically speaking?" I said, noticing it growing exponentially darker. I glanced up and realized the chain-link fence had closed up and become more of a sheet of alloy.

"At the service," Esther explained, "I prayed to God, who is the bringer of twilight. '*Ha'ma'ariv*' is a verb based on *aravim*. It pretty much means God spindles the days and brings the evening forward. Best English translation I've got for you."

"That's fascinating! Thank you so much for showing up. This is a fantastic way for me to end my *erev*."

"Well, erev has just begun."

"Okay, then this is a fantastic way for me to end my day."

"The day has just begun, too," she corrected. "In Israel, sundown is the start of the day."

"For real?"

"Yes, I'd never lie to you, you're not my dentist."

"Why is the start at sundown?"

"It's from Bereshit Genesis."

"You said *bea*... did you say bear shit?"

"Listen closely. *Berr-uh-sheet*. Bereshit. It's what we call Genesis. Hebrew for 'in a beginning.' It's one of the opening lines in the Bible. 'There was evening, then morning: the first day.' Evening first, then morning."

"I never noticed this," I said, suddenly feeling a little chilly now that the sun had sunk and the wind picked up.

"Yeah. So, if you were born at 9:46am on a Saturday, then you were 'actually' born on Friday, the day before. But if you had been born Saturday evening, then we'd be celebrating you before sundown on Sunday."

"So because the sun just fell asleep, this is the dawn of a new day?"

"I mean, we wouldn't refer to it as 'dawn' of a new day. And that's a weird American quirk, to say 'the sun fell asleep.'"

"That's not an American thing. I guess I just say things a little awkwardly sometimes. I just mean that night has started."

"Ohh," she said, shaking her head. "It's not night. It's twilight. Big difference."

"Okay. Why does *that* matter?" I asked, realizing that at age 32, I still didn't understand the different phases of the day. Maybe Americans really are as dumb as the stereotype.

"When you've been fasting on Yom Kippur and you're dying for sundown – for night – so that you can eat again, it makes a big difference."

"So when does 'night' actually start?"

"When you can see three stars in the sky."

"Well, that sucks if it's cloudy," I said, glancing skyward again.

"Ha!" she laughed, driving me to realize I had imparted an unintentional joke. "I mean, you can always wait for the official designated time for night, too."

"So the 'third star' thing is for those without a watch?"

"Actually, it's mainly for smokers who are dying to get that cigarette and want to end the fast a few minutes early."

I chuckled heartily; she seemed surprised, now being the one who'd accidentally kippered a funny.

"I can just picture that conversation," I designed a scene, " 'Hey, why are you smoking when our fast hasn't ended yet?' 'Look, there's three stars.' 'Those two are stars, but isn't that one a plane?' 'No way man, that's totally a star.' 'It's moving.' 'It's a shooting star, man.' 'It's doing tricks and leaving a jet cloud.' 'Totally a star, bro.'"

"Yeah," Esther delivered a wide grin, "that's basically how it goes when you're relying on the stars. Now let's get down to business. Is this interview confidential?"

"Of course, yes," I said, shifting gears more suddenly that I thought I'd have to. "I'll reveal the content of the interview, not the individual. I actually need your informed consent after you read over the rules of the study," I said as I held up a piece of paper with densely-packed text. "That cool with you?"

Esther grabbed the sheet from my hands, scanned it over, and said, "yeah, I agree to this."

"Okay, cool. Alright, Esther. Question one: what is the meaning behind your name?"

"Are you freaking kidding me?"

"Huh?"

"Do you take me as a freier?"

"*Freier*?"

"Yes, freier: sucker; chump. You said the names are going to be secret. It's super easy to tell my name if you publish the meaning."

"I'm... it's not to publish. It's honestly intended to just be an icebreaker question. You can skip it."

"Okay. Let's skip it then."

"No problem," I yielded, suddenly feeling like our pre-interview vibing wasn't matching the actual interview. "Okay, well, let's try this one instead: what's your first memory?"

"Oh, *nu*," she laughed. "Did you need me to find a chaise so I can lay back and look at the ceiling while I answer this? Are you Sigmund Freud?"

"Alfred Adler, actually," I quipped back. "I was trained in Adlerian psychology. A lot of emphasis on childhood and early memories. But again, this is kind of an icebreaker. We can skip it."

"No, I like the question," she responded with her first flash of enthusiasm. "Give me a second to think."

She took a deep breath in, then pursed her lips to exhale.

"Okay," she said. "It's kind of a scary one. At least to me. I was a child, maybe about three years old. And I remember being in a day care, and... I got bit."

"Bit?"

"Yes. Another child bit me. Really hard. I had to go to the doctor. It hurt like Mel Gibson."

Interesting. Not just in regards to the imaginative use of Gibson as an adjective, but there's this Adlerian theory that your earliest recollection exemplifies how you see the world. For example, a person whose earliest memory is getting lost in a zoo might be unsure of their place in the world or feel invisible to their loved ones. Someone whose first memory was that of losing a card game after their sister cheated, they may grow up to believe the world to be an unfair place and that family isn't to be trusted. Or, for a little girl whose first memory was getting a chunk taken out of her arm by another human being, the world might be a scary, unsafe, unstable place.

But I'm no licensed therapist.

"Thanks," I said as emotionally detached as possible, cloaking the fact that maybe I was psychoanalyzing her just a little now. "And then, next question: where do you see yourself in five years?"

"Ooh, so now it's a job interview," she sneered. "But I'm so happy working *here*!"

I wasn't sure how to respond. Why did nobody in Israel take me seriously? Had I done something to lose her trust?

"*Staaaam*, I'm just kidding," she said, perhaps sensing my apprehension about the tone of her answers. "Jews use a lot of sarcasm. It's actually a good question. I'm not totally sure where I'll be, but I imagine I'll have children. I really want to have children. Do you want kids?"

I was taken aback. She was the first participant since Izzy to turn the interview around and ask me a personal question – and it was the same one he had asked me. And it just so happened that this question was a deep source of pain.

"Maybe someday," I said, belying the fact that Joanna and I had been trying for over six years. I say "trying" as if repeatedly doing the same thing that doesn't work is really actually "trying."

Esther's eyes widened, as if she was expecting more.

"I already have kids," I added. "They walk on four furry feet."

"Uh…" Esther said, her eyes growing wider and wider. "Are you trying to tell me that we've been talking here for almost ten minutes and you have dog pictures you haven't shown me? Now, please!"

I handed over my phone.

"Okay, they're stinkin' cute. What are their names?"

"Sidney and Romy. Sidney's the one that's white as snow."

"So one came from Australia, and the other Italy?"

An awkward silence ensued, at least until I figured out the droll she was going for.

"*Heh*," I finally responded with a humorless laugh, "apparently."

"They look so happy and I bet they're well taken care of, too," she said, offering both my phone back and what appeared to be a compliment.

"Thanks," I said, feeling a sudden warmth down my back. "They're happy. At least now they are."

"Oh, are they rescues? Were they abused?"

She was peddling awfully close to a much longer story, one so long that it had a 42-word subtitle.

"Yes. They are rescues, and yes, they've been abused. So, my next question for you: how long have you lived in Israel?"

"Are these all the dogs you have?" she asked, ignoring my question altogether.

"Uh, no. I have three."

"I love dogs."

I wasn't sure how to respond. But the truth was, I loved when people wanted to talk about my dogs.

"I love them, too. My wife and I... we can't have children. Or at least, we just haven't yet. Maybe we might. But our dogs really are our children. We once skipped Thanksgiving with our family because our girls weren't allowed to come, if that gives you an idea of the hierarchy."

"They're all girls?"

"Yes, girls."

"Sidney, Romy, and what's the third one's name?"

"Shadrach."

"But no... Meshach and Abednego?"

"Actually, there was," I said, showing her my phone again. "There *is*."

"We found these three outside our condo a few months ago. We kept Shadrach and drove Meshach and Abednego to a rescue in Denver."

"Why Shadrach?"

"Because she's a passionate kisser."

"Which one is she?"

"The happy, fat one."

"She's fat?" Esther smiled.

"She's getting there. She's always hungry. She always needs to feed."

"So," Esther tittered, "these are your *doghters*," unsilencing the "G" in *daughter*.

"Huh," I snickered, "I guess they are."

"Who's watching them now?"

"My parents. Joanna – my wife – *would* have been watching them, but she'll be flying out to Israel from Tulsa and we're both coming back in to Chicago for Thanksgiving, and it was just a logistical nightmare to not drop the pups off when I left instead. Honestly, leaving our dogs behind for 40 days was the hardest part of coming to Israel."

"That's cute," she said.

Yes, it was. But also: I didn't come to Israel to talk about *my* family. "So, you said you were actually born in New York City?"

290

"Yes, and immigrated to Israel in 1991 when I was five," Esther said, accepting my redirection.

"So you moved into Israel during the First Intifada," I said while trying to detangle the extremely-uncomplicated math in my head. *In 1991 she was 5, so 91 minus 5 is 85, no – it's 86 – then add the 1900, so she was born in 1986.* "Where in Israel did you move to?"

"A small *yishuv* outside of Jerusalem."

"A *yishuv*?"

"Yes, like a kibbutz. It was... well, occupied territory."

"*Oh*, you're raised in a settlement. Got it. What religion were you raised on?"

"I'm a Jew. Modern Orthodox is the specific sect: Dati Leumi Light. It's not nearly as strict as the Ultra Orthodox, but it still takes religion pretty seriously."

"What religion do you identify yourself as ascribing to now?"

"I'm a Jew. Modern Orthodox. Dati Leumi Light."

This caught me by surprise. Most of the Jews I had informally talked to weren't religious anymore. In fact, Esther was the first Jew I had talked to who didn't try to dilute the religious aspect of the identity: "I'm Jewish, but only by ethnicity," or, "I come from a Jewish family, but I'm not religious." I wanted to explore this more.

"So," I asked, "when did your faith become something that was important to you individually, rather than it being about carrying on the family tradition?"

"What religion were you raised as?"

"A Christian."

"And what are you now?"

"A Christian."

"So you know. You understand that faith is a lifelong struggle. Anyone who's being honest knows this. But I was a teenager when I decided that it just made more sense to be a Jew than to not be religious. A lot of Jewish children become teenagers and then abandon the faith, especially in such a time as this. I didn't want to be a hypocritical teenager who left the faith, only to come back to it when I have children to put on a façade for their sake."

"So, how do you reconcile everything happening here – all of the fighting, violence, struggles – with the notion of a God who is good and wanted you to have this land?"

"Huh? That's a bad question. It doesn't even make sense. Why would anyone think God's character is dependent on whether or not there is violence in the world?"

"Well, the American Christian might say, 'God will protect me from danger because He is sovereign,' for instance."

"That's a bad take. God will let me suffer because He is sovereign. That's the reality."

"So the perpetual struggle here; the lives lost. None of that affects your faith?"

"No," she replied, somewhat vexed. "Am I a Jew so that God might serve me? No. We walk into the wilderness if He tells us to, and not because we're concerned about our own well-being."

"Is there anything you've struggled to believe in your faith?"

"I don't believe in Yeshua, if that's what you're getting at."

"Yeshua?"

"Jesus. That's His Hebrew, Aramaic name. 'Yeshua.' Any Jew will know who you're talking about if you say Jesus though."

"I kind of like 'Yeshua' – the name feels warmer. More intimate."

"Yeah. But like I said, I'm a Jew, so I believe Yeshua was a false prophet. I believe in most of the Jewish theology."

"So you have no problem saying you're a religious person?"

"No. Why would I?"

I nodded, but given her entranced look, realized that she was literally demanding an answer.

"Well," I said, "there's a movement – at least in the U.S. – where people have tried to shy away from being labelled 'religious.' A lot of times, if you ask a person if they're religious, they'll get defensive about it and try to distance themselves from that label. They'll usually say, 'I'm spiritual, not religious,' as if that distinction provides some level of empowerment."

"Hmm, that's weird," Esther responded. "Well, here's some good news: you won't get that with me. I'm religious, not spiritual."

A laugh escaped from my belly, partially because what she said struck me as funny, but moreso because it struck me as refreshing. I hadn't heard such a genuine sentence in a long time.

"As a 'religious' Jew, are you familiar with the prophecy of Gog and Magog?"

"Gog and Magog? Sure. Every Jew has heard it. It has to do with the end times, but honestly, I don't know much more than that. It's just one of those unfulfilled prophecies. But sure, I've heard of it."

"Okay, next, I've got a question that is pretty open-ended, so bear with me the 'bigness' of the question."

"Just ask it, *yalla*. I don't need a prologue."

292

"Okay, what do you think of your country being in perpetual conflict?"

"Ha! What do I think? I don't know, put down, 'I hate it.' And it's stupid. Write that down too."

"What makes it that way?"

"It's unsolvable. There's literally no right answer to end any of it. They call it a 'conflict' because they say it hasn't escalated to a full-out war, but that's only because they're looking at the physical evidence of war."

"What do you mean by that?"

"There's a war going on, but it's a war between two different history books. Israelis have their spin, Palestinians have theirs. It's narrative warfare. Most people hear one narrative or the other, and then think they 'get' it, but most people who say they 'get' the conflict only 'get' it because they think in black-or-white terms," she said, using air quotes whenever she said 'get.' "You really only 'get' it when you choose to believe that your enemies have nothing to teach you. For everyone else, the whole thing has more layers than a shallot and is more confusing than a Christopher Nolan film, and I know I've spent my share of being angry at the Knesset."

"Knesset?" I asked, knowing I should know the term but it was escaping me.

"Israeli Parliament. The government. I get frustrated with them so often – not as angry as I get at Hamas or the PLO, of course – but the whole thing is just so, *so* stupid. And it's a war of the few: a few weeks ago, two Arab girls stabbed an Arab man in Jerusalem. The IDF came, shot those kids with rubber bullets, but the bullets ricocheted off and seriously injured a Jewish bystander. An idiotic shuffle between three people of the same race, and suddenly it's an international entanglement."

Esther shook her head, then added, "Stupid country. Everybody's so reactive. The whole thing has become a punchline: in the U.S., if you're having a heated conversation about your government and you want to end the dialogue, you just accuse your opponent's political leader of being Hitler. Do you literally believe that Obama is Hitler or Trump is Hitler? No. I mean, maybe, if you're an absolute idiot and you don't know history. But you just say it to blow up the conversation; you can't deal with the emotional intensity in a logical way so you blow it up. It's the same thing here: when it's time to set off emotional dynamite, you just bring up the Shoah. It's the be-all, end-all."

"To clarify, why Shoah?" I asked, then realized how unnatural the word came from an English-speaking, American-accented Christian. "Why the Holocaust?"

"Well, it's what's really at the heart of so many of the issues here. Modern Israel is the 'never again' response to the Shoah. But how do you stand on that leg when a chunk of Palestinians don't even believe the Holocaust happened?"

"You really believe that Palestinians deny the Holocaust?"

"I don't need to tell you what I believe. Go look up the official stance of President Abbas regarding it. *Nu*, read that man's dissertation. The Palestinians elected this man as their leader."

I noted this assertion, intending to look it up later.

"Imagine an anthropologist from Mars came to Earth. They'd have no idea that the Holocaust ever happened if they were operating off of the Arab narrative alone. We'd be erased from history. And what's frustrating is that Arabs know what it's like to be persecuted! Why would they do to us what others – namely, Christians, no offense – have done to them?"

"Hmm," I said, continuing to chickenscratch all over my notes.

"There was actually a secondary, smaller Holocaust that took place in North Africa during World War II. It's never talked about by anybody, but almost a half-million Jews were stripped of their belongings and banished from Arab-African countries."

"Do you know which ones those are?"

"Libya and Morocco, for sure. I believe Algeria and Tunisia, also. And Iraq, but that's not Africa, of course."

"And they suffered the same fate as European Jews?"

"A lot of them were put in concentration camps, but, no, they mainly were forced into diaspora, rather than being killed. The war ended just in time before they were slaughtered. But they lost their land in Africa, and many of them emigrated out and re-settled in Israel after our nation-state was established."

"Why would we not hear about this Holocaust?" I appealed, afraid that my question almost came off as if I didn't believe what she was saying.

"For the same reason that nobody talks about how many Gypsies were killed in the Holocaust: people don't care about them."

"Why would nobody care about this?" I asked again, not understanding why this would be such an abandoned (or perhaps taboo) topic in history.

"Danger, *because*. In chess and in life, white goes first. And these Jews weren't white."

"Oh, wow," I said. "So, what are we talking, specifically? Black Jews?"

"Exactly. And they were *very* affluent in their communities, arriving with nothing, creating wealth, and then they were massacred. Hey, you said that you live in Tulsa, correct?"

"Yes," I affirmed. "I do."

"It's the same thing as the Tulsa Race Massacre."

"What do you mean?"

"The African-Jewish Holocaust is the black-eye of history that's swept under the rug for the same reason nobody talks about what happened in Tulsa."

"I'm lost," I admitted. "What happened in Tulsa?"

"Oh, man, Danger," Esther said, shocked. "You aren't familiar with the Tulsa riots?"

I shrugged.

"Actually, they *just* changed the name to better reflect what it was: a massacre. You need to look this up: the Tulsa Race Massacre. Black people set up what was known as 'Black Wall Street,' which was an uber successful and thriving business district. And then white people burned it to the ground."

"Literally? You're literally saying 'started a fire?' "

"Not just a fire: a conflagration. The flames started in Tulsa but the heat is felt by the entire Black community. Your city covered up that it ever happened. To this day, it's believed there's a mass grave hiding somewhere in your city."

"You've got to be kidding me."

"I've got dark humor, but I'd never joke about this. There are the victims of a secret genocide under your highway."

"When did this happen?" I scoffed.

"Like, a hundred years ago. I don't know."

"Why is an Israeli Jew explaining to me the history of the city I live in?"

"History is told by the winners."

The second time I'd heard that during my interviews.

"So," I peeled myself away from this fascinating conversation and tried to redirect the conversation back to my study, "how would you explain the conflict to a child?"

Esther stopped for a minute and contemplated the question.

"I'd say, 'it's complicated.' It's really frickin' complicated, and its history goes back a long time now. I don't think you can even explain it to a child, really, at least not any better than you might be able to explain to them why the sky looks blue when it's actually not."

I wasn't sure why, but her comment prompted me to scan the sky again. Jerusalem had gone dark, clearly so despite the cloudiness veiling the true night sky; any smoker who had fasted for the day was surely puffing by now.

"And how does the conflict end?" I asked.

"Well," Esther began, followed by another brief pause. "Well, 40 to 50 years from now, we look back and we're ashamed. We're ashamed at how idiotically we all handled the situation. Everyone in Gaza is probably killed, and war breaks out."

"War breaks out," I said as I scribbled her prediction. "Who wins?"

"The Jews," she responded, not missing a beat.

I didn't sense it was just a homer pick on her part.

"How could the conflict end more peacefully?" I questioned. "I mean, end without bloodshed?"

"A peace treaty like the Oslo Accords could be a good start, if both sides had actually abided by the rules. But Palestinians didn't play by the rules. I moved from New York City to Israel during the First Intifada, as you pointed out. I immigrated during a time of great darkness, and then we had a peace treaty two years later that was supposed to bring a time of light. But instead, it was just seven years of terrible tension when the Oslo Accords were signed in September 1993."

September 1993.

Like an epiphany was being had, I remembered one of my other participants had mentioned the summer of 1993 in some capacity that had nothing to do with the conflict. As quickly and discretely as I could, I flipped back through my notes until I got to the jottings of my first participant: Izzy.

In August 1993, Nolan Ryan provokes Robin Ventura into charging the mound. Robin Ventura loses his footing, gets slugged in the face, and is ejected for it. It's an all-out brawl on the field. So, in September 1993, the Oslo Accords are signed and nobody in Israel or Palestine is happy about the collective bargaining agreement, resulting in a strike that would become the longest stoppage in all of pro sports history.

"In order for the conflict to have any kind of actual resolution, it would require economic cooperation," Esther continued, fracturing whatever niggling connection my moony brain was trying to manufacture between baseball and war. "But economic cooperation requires trust and a willingness to lose something, and neither side is willing to do either."

I jotted this down, then she added, "And with good reason. The bottom line is that there's always a breakdown between sides. Even when you get the rest of the world involved, like what you did with the Oslo Accords."

Ah, yes, I thought to myself. *What I did when I, as Elementary Advisor to the President of the United States, counselled Bill Clinton to push for what would go down as the most epic peace treaty failure in the Israeli-Palestinian Conflict.*

I kept my snark to myself.

"Have you suffered any trauma that made you lose sleep?"

"No, people here usually don't suffer from trauma that stems from a specific event. You have to go to Gaza for that. Here, it's the day-to-day stuff that's the problem. The threat of war is worse than the war."

"But you *would* say you've been affected by the conflict? Or is that putting words in your mouth?"

"For sure, I'm affected. Within the first year of the Second Intifada, I lost a friend *and* a teacher to separate bombings on busses. I've never had any trauma happen to me, but somehow when sirens go off now, I get anxious because it reminds me of being a kid and my parents freaking out when the sirens would come on. They'd lose their minds when the alarms sounded if they weren't sure where we were. Some of it is practical fear, but at least with my mom, some of it's because my grandma told stories about hiding under her bed during the Holocaust whenever a shelter-in-place was issued. My mom never had anything bad happen to her while under alert, but you wouldn't know it by the way she acts when she hears them. She acts like it was *her* hiding under the bed during the Holocaust. It's so annoying."

"Have you seen this happen in people other than your mom?"

"Hmm. Well, one of my friends can't watch black-and-white films. Not that any of them are worth watching, but my friend saw so much footage of the Holocaust in school – and obviously that's all going to be black-and-white footage. Now she can't see black-and-white movies without thinking about Jews being tortured."

"Have you personally experienced anything like this? Where your mind tricks you into having post-traumatic symptoms even though you weren't exposed to any trauma?"

"I mean, growing up, I'd daydream about dying. Not that I wanted to die, but just that I was prepared for it to happen. Sitting in a classroom? I'd imagine a bullet coming through the window and hitting my artery. Getting on a bus and I see an Arab with a backpack? I assumed I'd get exploded. But that's not trauma. That's just a survival instinct."

"Has this 'survival instinct' impacted the way you engage with your family?"

"I don't know that this falls under that category, but my own brother has become a militant right-wing Zionist. He's a part of the Lehava. At 13, he was listening to Backstreet Boys and at 16, he was a religious zealot. He's been arrested by our own government for being too extreme. He showed up to our cousin's bris in chains with a police escort."

"So, would you say you're against Zionists?"

"What? No. What a question! Not at all. I'm a Zionist. All 'Zionist' means is that you believe Israel has a right to exist in this land. It's not an extreme position. Do you believe that I have a right to live here, in Israel?"

I felt cornered. I wasn't overly comfortable now with how much of this was getting turned back to questions about my opinion. But to move forward, she clearly needed an answer.

"Of course Israel and you and all Israelis have a right to exist and to call this place 'home,'" I said, meaning every word of it but feeling like I had broken some promise by admitting my bias.

"Then you are a Zionist, by definition. But when you kill people to make that point, it's gone too far. I just want a land where I can be a Jew and be safe at the same time. Think of it like this: a lot of women say they aren't feminists, when all it really means is you believe in equality. Are you a feminist?"

I adjusted myself in my seat as I thought about what to say.

"Am I making you uncomfortable?"

"Yes," I bluntly explained. "Not because of the subject matter, but because this isn't how research interviews are supposed to go. Anything I can say, anything I convey to you could alter your responses to me."

"Okay, pause the interview then. We're just two people talking now," she prompted, as if that caveat could prevent our discussion from being tainted by bias. "Would you say you're a feminist?"

"I think I would have to operationalize what you mean. Like you said, do I believe in gender equality and egalitarianism? Of course."

"Then why shy away from it? Because that's what feminism means."

"Yes, sure, on paper that's what it means. But my hesitation is with the context of the word. So many people think of bra-burning, men-hating women when that word comes up. I'd be lying if I didn't say that my experience with feminists is that a lot of them are extreme and, frankly, quite hostile. And a lot of them became feminists, not because of some bend towards equality, but because they've had men who have done evil things to them and it almost feels like adopting that title is a way to help process that trauma."

"But the definition hasn't changed."

"But the context has, and that's even more important."

"So you haven't had good experiences with feminists?"

"Sure I have! But I think the extremists drown out the better experiences I've had."

"So you'll call yourself a 'Christian' even though the most famous ones are the extreme ones who have given Christianity a bad rap, but when it comes to feminists – who have done *way* less worse things than Christians – you won't associate?"

I was stunned: Esther was absolutely right. I'd been checkmated.

"Well, I'll proudly tell you I'm a feminist," she continued. "And you should be one too. The fact that others don't understand feminism shouldn't be a reason for me to not identify as one, but it gives me a chance to enlighten people. The dumbest thing about your country is the stupid one-liner discourse. Like, 'Zionism' is 'extremism,' or 'feminism' is 'man-hating,' or 'socialism' is 'communism.' Who even cares?"

"Well… okay, I concede on feminism. I'm a feminist, by that measure. But I think when you have loved ones that have been killed fighting against the principles of communism and socialism, that one hits a bit differently," I said, feeling slightly emotionally-heightened for the first time in the conversation.

"Communism died over 30 years ago. Get over it."

Get over it?

"I don't think that's fair," I said, remembering the name Michael Waterloo, who was my godmother's boyfriend whose death in Vietnam impacted her family for generations. "That's like saying you shouldn't worry about Nazism just because it happened so long ago."

Esther lowered her eyes at me, piercing me with imagined darts.

Oops. I struck a chord.

"That's not fair," she protested. "Nazism was an ideology that was antithetical to life. Communism is a *way of life*, not an end to it."

"I don't know," I said, concealing the reality that I did absolutely know where I stood on this issue. "A lot of Americans died fighting communism. I think it's fair that there would still be a sensitivity. Thirty years is not that far removed."

"Okay," she said as it seemed like she was about to devise another emotionally-charged argument that I wasn't sure I was ready to field, but instead simply followed up with, "unpause."

"Unpause?"

"Unpause. Yalla. Interview's back on," she declared, impelling me to feel like I was an improv actor who'd just been asked to carry a scene right after my counterpart insulted my mother behind stage.

"How is your relationship with your extremist brother?" I asked, trying to revert back to the Zionist discussion.

Esther's eyes narrowed, better expressing her deep hurt than her next words could.

"I have no relationship with my brother."

I nodded, quickly brainstorming as to how I could segue away from this subject that had us both feeling sore.

"What about your relationship with Arabs?" I asked. "Do you have any Arab friends?"

Esther thought for a moment, smiled, then said, "No."

"Why do you think that is?"

"We don't really run in the same circles, I guess."

"Is that all it is? For example, you're heading down an alley, and it's just you and you see an Arab coming towards you ahead. Are you uncomfortable?"

"Yeah, I'm definitely uncomfortable in that situation. I've not had many good experiences with Arabs, if I'm being honest. I fear Arab men, especially."

"And where does that come from, do you think?"

"Uh, from them being pigs," she gibed. "I've been sexually harassed quite often, and it's always been at the hands of Arabs. Arabs can't whistle at their own girls because they'll get the shit kicked out of them for it. But Jewish girls are in a different category, for some reason. So, yeah, if I see a teenager, and he happens to be an Arab, I go into the interaction assuming I'm going to at *least* get catcalled."

"As a child, were you ever explicitly told, 'Arabs are bad,' maybe by a parent or a teacher?"

"Hmm, nah. Nobody said it outright, but Arabs were made to seem inherently bad. Jews are taught in religious school that people are trying to kill them. They never said who, just that some people would hate you for being Jewish. But after you're shot at for the first time, you don't need to be told about it anymore or wonder who they're talking about."

"What do you believe to be the root of hatred towards Jews?"

"Laziness," she said, not missing a beat.

"What did you say?" I asked, clearly hearing her the first time, yet seeking the kind of clarification that others seek whenever I tell them my name.

"At its root, laziness is what allows people to hate Jews. You familiar with *Volksgemeinschaft*? Or at least the different Geists?" she asked.

"*Huh?*" I squeaked, angling my head. "You know another Geist?"

"Surely you know Zeitgeist. Or maybe you've heard of *Weltgeist*, which I think, is like, the spirit of the world, or something to do with moral order in the world. But then there's *Volksgeist*, which is the spirit of a nation. Think patriotism or nationalism, for instance. Volksgemeinschaft, then, was the foundation of Nazi totalitarianism. This idea that the German people would all be one united community. But here's the thing: Jews considered themselves Jewish first and German second. Hitler hated that we put religion over patriotism, so he started spinning this idea that Jews only cared about Jews. It was a cotton candy idea but people ate it up like it was meat."

"So you're saying it wasn't hate that drove Germans?"

"Of course it was *hate*. To say otherwise is Grandma Grape's wool," she said, her inflection having enough of a hint of frustration that I didn't ask if Grandma Grape's wool was a Hebrew euphemism or an Estherism. "But there are things worse than hate. It's the banality of evil. It's not about hatred as much as it is giving yourself over to not thinking for yourself. Laziness is not indifference: laziness is evil."

"So going back to the Arab in the alley: does he *hate* you? Or is he just not thinking for himself?"

"Does it matter? Either way, I *have* to assume he intends harm. We all have to. Be logical. The recent stabbing sprees dictate that you have to assume harm is intended. That's basic survival."

"What do you wish you could say to them? If you were able to say anything you wanted to them – without consequence – what might you tell your enemies?"

"I didn't call them 'enemies.' Now you're putting words in my mouth."

"What's a better word to describe them?"

"Cousins. They're not brothers or sisters. They're cousins, cousins that I wish I could explain to them how they're not being partners in peace, and how that's hurting the extended family."

"And what's one thing they could do to be partners in peace?"

"In the big picture? Uphold the principles in peace treaties they *agreed* to. On a micro-level though? I don't know, maybe don't shoot at us? I used to be able to drive through Ramallah without fear of getting shot at. No way would I drive there now."

"Is there a lot of Arab-on-Israeli violence there?"

"Are you kidding me? Israelis can't even show their face around there. I was in Ramallah during New Year's during the Second Intifada, and I don't think they were shooting at my family specifically, but one bullet hit our house. I've avoided that place ever since. Ramallah is a headache, just a hot mess express."

I frenziedly scribbled notes across my papers, trying to catch up with what Esther said.

"You know what's super annoying about all of this, too?" she said, so much more of an exclamation than an actual question.

"Hold on one sec," I gritted, furiously penning more notes that resembled hieroglyphics more than English.

"We're under a microscope by every other country in the world while this is going on," she continued, not 'holding on one sec' at all. "Countries like to project their own issues onto our conflict: if you're an American, then you look at the conflict through the lens of racism, religious rights, or the right to bear arms. If you're German, you start drawing parallels to the Holocaust. Whatever the hot topic in their country, they find a parallel to our conflict. I mean, you've seen the Separation Wall between Israel and the West Bank. Have you heard someone call it the 'Apartheid Wall' yet? I don't know if anything makes me madder than hearing that."

"I have heard that," I said. "Actually, I believe Nelson Mandela and Desmond Tutu both called it apartheid. Do you feel like that carries any weight with you?"

"Of course that has weight. They're the apartheid experts, no? But here's my point: aren't they naturally going to be the first ones to call something apartheid if it reeks of it, even just a little? They're projecting their awful experiences onto something it's not. If you want to weigh the opinion of Desmond Tutu more heavily, fine, but then you also have to weigh his ultra-sensitivity to apartheid, too. And you have to weigh the fact that he's never been shot at by a Palestinian for 'looking Jewish.' Let me ask you, do you know how many people died during apartheid?"

"I honestly have no idea," I admitted. "I can't even come up with a figure."

"Twenty-one-thousand people. *Twenty-one-thousand* across, what was it? Fifty years? And that's without any real 'intifadas' from the minority Bantustans. A total of 21,000 across 50 years. Our conflict had more casualties than that *in six days*! Can you imagine South Africa's reaction if they had been getting daily rockets from Bantustans? What if Indians or Mexicans tried getting their land back from America, and the rest of the world demanded you give it back? Would you just hand it over? You're already trying to close off the borders, and that's not even because of violence. Can you imagine what Donald Trump would do if Mexicans invaded Texas and launched attacks? You'd figure out where they were coming from and lock that shit down."

"Hmm," I responded, trying my best not to engage in hypothetical situations or reveal my own feelings about the conflict.

"Listen, Israel has its parliamentary issues," Esther wrapped up, "I get it. I don't want to minimize the Palestinians' hardships. There's abuse of power there, and that bothers me. But it certainly doesn't fall under the category of apartheid, which is an emotional response to stir the pot. In Israel, Arabs and Muslims can be doctors. Parliament is 10% Palestinian. Some of the highest-ranking commanders in our forces are Druze. You want to know what apartheid is? Apartheid is when a kid wearing a kippah can't walk into West Bank because he'll be killed for it. Palestinians get permits to come into Israel; Jews gets signs that tell us we'll be killed if we take a single step into their territory. So leave apartheid, the Holocaust, and Hitler where they belong. This conflict is not that. It's occupation and overzealous security."

The topic seemed to have finally hit a chord, and I found myself in this tension between wanting to pursue Esther's contempt and wanting to refocus the conversation to my actual research topic. As I contemplated which direction would be more fruitful to explore, Esther chose the first option, reinforcing her earlier position after catching a quick breath.

"To this day, Jews can't openly express their Judaism in Europe for fear of some kind of retribution."

"What does that mean?" I asked. "*Express* Judaism? How?"

"Religious garments. Again, think a kippah. You wear a kippah in Europe, you subject yourself to persecution, yet Palestinians and other Arabs can cavort about, all while wearing their religious identifiers. Several years ago, my roommate had a German friend visit us. She and I got into it because she decided to use me as a sounding board for her politics, and she looked me in the eye and said to me, 'you are doing to Palestinians now what our country did to you during World War II.' The audacity to implicate Israel to Nazi Germany! And to say it right to a Jew. How do you think that's okay?"

"How did you respond to that specific comment?"

Esther laughed so hard and unexpectedly, I could see spit fly out of her mouth. I wasn't sure why she was laughing, but Jews do tend to laugh at me in this country.

"I told this German girl, if you weren't the guest of my roommate, I'd kick you out of my apartment right now. We aren't herding Muslims to concentration camps like her people did to the Jews. They had a refined system to exterminate Jews; Israel has yet to kill a single Palestinian just for being who they are. Did Germany financially support its enemies during the war? Of course not. But Israel has sent tons of money to Gaza so they could develop their community, and instead of using the funds for building houses or education systems, the Palestinian Authority used the money to build terror tunnels. So I told this girl, your alleged concern for this conflict doesn't clean your conscience for what you let happen in your country."

I finished scrawling my notes, then checked the time.

"Shoot. Time's up. If I ask anything else, we're going to go over."

"It's okay, honestly. What's your take on this?"

"Huh?" I asked, a little startled.

"You have an interest in this, clearly. I'm not really sure what prompted that. What have you found in your study?"

"Well, I can't really say what the results are because I haven't analyzed anything. I will certainly keep you abreast with my findings, and send you a copy…"

"*Ugghhhhhhhhh!*" Esther groused, lightly slapping the table, raindrops bouncing in the air and seemingly evaporating before landing again. "Are you studying to become a psychologist or a lawyer? Talk to me like a human, man. I want to know: what was your opinion before you got here, and what's your opinion now?"

"You're putting me into a corner? Nobody puts Danger into a corner," I joked, hoping my lightheartedness would allow me to not answer the question.

"If you don't answer me, then you can't use my interview," she said with a smirk, which made it seem like she was joking in kind, but that was not an outcome my study could survive.

"Okay," I said, collecting my words. "Listen, the UN gave the land to *you* after the Holocaust…"

"Hold up," she interrupted, then extended her pointer finger towards the stars. "The UN didn't give us the Promised Land, God did."

"Okay, sure, that's an important note. Let me rephrase: the UN *said* that *Israel* gets this land," I corrected myself, "Right? Right. So it's not like Israel 'invaded,' as the narrative goes. Was it fair to Palestinians? No. But the world collectively agreed this was the fairest plan possible, and nobody gets to just ignore it, even if you get the short stick. You can be mad, you can protest, you can work towards reparations. But 'ignoring it' isn't an option, and 'trying to conquer it back' is far more vile. So, Israel building a literal wall to keep neighbors out? I hate it. But I get it. I hope that wall comes down someday. But I get why it's up.

"That being said," I breathed in, giving her the part she wouldn't like. "From the moment I tried to get onto a plane to Israel, I could see the Israeli officers drunk on power. They relish their authority. They dared me to challenge it, even. I got into Palestine, and it took two seconds to see the overreaching on Israel's part. I'm an American – clearly not an *enemy* – and they treated me like I was the last known descendant of the Agagites. To me, it feels like abuse, okay? I'm sorry to say it…"

"Don't be sorry," she said, nodding her head. "I asked for your opinion."

"Okay," I said, exhaling some anxiety with my words, "and I just find Israel to be so reactionary. Would I be so reactive if people were constantly trying to kill me? Maybe. No, definitely, I would. But there's this Israeli mindset, 'kill here and we'll build.' That's a problem. Settlements are not the answer, and the Palestinians will continue to resist as long as that's going on, because you can't live in complete harmony with someone who has control over you. Settlements create rogue

Israelis who think they're the West Bank police, and all of that only serves to exacerbate the conflict."

"*Ohhh*, that's a big word! Good job pronouncing it."

"Thanks – I've used it a lot in my life. So, these settlements are perhaps the biggest obstacle to peace, as I see it. Condemned by the world, and you don't care. 'You' as in Israel, not 'you personally.' But you build these settlements so deeply into Palestine, no matter how far a Palestinian is from the actual border, they feel the bitter cold cast from Israel's shadow. I'm not Arab, and I felt it. Bethlehem, Ramallah, Jericho, Hebron – their livelihood is maligned by what you're doing. And of course you're going to get retaliated against. And then you set up these checkpoints near these settlements – checkpoints that are excessively inconvenient and not even well-manned – and it serves to further oppress your enemies and further extends the chasm between you and them. Don't get me wrong: you've dealt with frequent uprisings and coupes, and I don't agree with that kind of butchery at all. Yes, the Palestinians inflict their own wounds, but you keep putting your finger in it so the flesh can't heal. You fear that if you don't keep the wound fresh, they might heal and rise again.

"But then I see what Palestinians are doing, and they're just breeding so much hate against Jews. At Birzeit, the most prestigious university in all of Palestine, there's a Star of David plastered on the ground for people to stomp, and their pissers have Netanyahu's face emblazoned next to the urinal soap. How can you claim to be a partner in peace when you do stuff like that? So I find myself enraged by the Israeli government, but I think about what the Palestinian authorities are doing, and I get even madder. And then, I just feel sadness. Sadness for a conflict that has no good solution. Sadness for the Palestinians. It's like telling a landlocked nation to open a beach resort. Either you can't do it, or you need to encroach on someone else's property to do it."

Silence followed. Esther looked at the ground.

"You've been to Hebron?" she asked, returning to a statue-like state after her lips stopped moving.

"Yes," I said, surprised that *that* was the takeaway she got. "Have you been there?"

"Have I been to the city that contains the burial place of Abraham and Sarah, Isaac and Rebecca, and Jacob and Leah? Yes, Dr. Danger, I have gone to visit Abraham, Isaac, and Jacob."

"Well, don't forget the entrance to the Garden of Eden," I smartly quipped, citing a not-so-grounded mythology about the Cave of Machpelah in Hebron having connection to the Garden, as well as Adam and Eve supposedly being buried there.

Esther laughed. At least she laughed.

"The city of our ancestors. The city whose deed is recorded in Genesis 23 of one of the oldest books in human history, a deed that was fairly bought – not given – to the Jews. And Muslims still contest that the city is theirs. Narrative warfare, Danger."

"When I was there on a tour, I heard something troubling from a Palestinian there," I said, revealing more bias than I perhaps should have, but it was a story that spoke to her fair assessment about narratives. "The Palestinian tour guide kept saying things like, 'we Palestinians only use nonviolence here and then Jews kill us,' and he said in Hebron alone, only 20 Israelis have been killed in contrast to thousands of Palestinians, and that Israel never comes to the table with an open mind about compromise. And I found myself getting – I don't know, triggered? Because none of those claims are rooted in reality. And I know this for an absolute fact. I've studied this stuff for the past, I don't know, three or four years? And then the Palestinian guide gave his opinion, stressing there's this effortless-but-untapped solution that would make everyone happy: just make Israel and Palestine into one state. And the people on the tour? They just ate it up. As if *that* was the resolution that nobody had ever come up with before. So I raised my hand and asked a question."

Esther smiled, beckoning me to continue.

"I say, 'Sir, what is the name of this state?' And everyone on the tour erupted in laughter. Because everyone knew: his single-state solution starts cracking at step one, agreeing on a name. You can't even get to the first sentence of the plan! It falls apart at the title."

"How did he respond?"

"Well, he knew I had put him in check. So he just smiled and said, 'I will call it Palestine. They can call it Israel. And you? You can call it Disneyland. I don't care.' "

"In Hebron – do you know what Hebron means, Danger? You have no idea, I'm sure. It means 'friendship.' How ironic is that? The last place in the world that there's friendship or cooperation. It's like Jerusalem: Jerusalem means 'heritage of peace.' Can you think of a city in the world that has been fought over more than Jerusalem?"

Aleppo? Baghdad? Kabul? Beijing? London?

"No, it's Jerusalem," I agreed. "It has to be."

"It *has* to be," she assented. "In Hebron, there's a set of olive trees up on a hill. Maybe you went there. You should search it on the Internet. If you're on *al-Jazeera*'s website, you'll see reports about Jewish settler 'terrorists' stealing olives from those trees. And if you're reading *Yediot*, you'll be told that Islamic terrorists are harvesting what is rightfully owned by Jews. Both Israelis and Palestinians have documents saying they own those trees. And can it get any more ironic that the fighting is over an olive tree? With the olive branch being the international symbol of 'peace?' And there used to be peace. Or at least, some semblance of it. Up until the First Intifada, there was freedom of movement for everyone. Gaza, Bethlehem, Ramallah, Galilee, Jerusalem – it didn't matter whether you were Jewish or Muslim, Israeli or Arab, you could visit any of these places. They were all open and without borders. Not that any of them were the safest place in the world, but it was different back then."

"And it was the intifada that changed things?"

"The intifada was the exclamation point, but the preamble started in Hebron, in 1980. Everything changed then."

"Not 1929?"

"You know about 1929?"

"A little."

"You should study it more. In fact, tell others about it. Honestly, the Hebron Massacre is what actually put the conflict in motion, at least to the extent of what it looks like today. If 1987 was the exclamation point, and 1980 was the first sentence of the story, then 1929 is the pencil getting sharpened in the first place. And most people who try to accuse Israelis of being culpable for accepting the British land in 1948 conveniently forget what happened in 1929."

"Tell me more about 1929."

"It's too long. There's too much history. Let me tell you about 1980, because it might be worth mentioning for your study."

"Kay," I said, my voice goosing the single letter into two syllables.

"So, in Hebron in 1979, there was a vacant building. It had largely been vacant for 50 years because Arabs believed it was haunted. Why was it haunted?" she asked, furrowing her eyebrows and glowering, as if I had been the one who transgressed. "Because that's one of the buildings that the Arabs raped and murdered the 69 Jews in the 1929 massacre, the one you referenced. So a group of 50 Jews – women and children – started squatting in the empty, haunted building, wanting control of it again to honor the memory of the *crippled* Jewish pharmacist who had served Arabs for 40 years, only for them to turn around and rape-then-murder his daughter before murdering him, too."

Yikes.

"In retaliation to the squatting, and because it would've been globally condemned to kill the women and children, a small group of Palestinians launched a terror attack on six young students, killing them in cold blood while they were worshiping during Shabbat. Internationally condemned, too, just maybe not to the extent if it had been women and children. And four terrorists were arrested, though there were surely others that never got pinned down. One of the terrorists was Tisir Abu Sneineh. If you've been to Hebron, maybe you heard what happened to him?"

I shook my head.

"He was released in a prisoner swap, then appointed as administrator of the Cave of the Patriarchs that you visited. Spits in the face of Jews, but hailed a hero to Palestinians. For the record, Jews would never promote a rogue terrorist who mercilessly killed young, innocent men. But for Arabs? They elect and appoint people based on how many Jewish bodies they've racked up. The higher the body count, the more 'qualified' they are – even if they don't have experience for the office they're running for. How can I say something so incendiary? Because Tisir Abu Sneineh is now the mayor of Hebron, winning his election last year for his 'heroics' in 1980."

"Wow."

"Netanyahu may be responsible for some needless deaths, but he never personally killed anyone, or if he did, he certainly doesn't boast about it lest he end his political career. But for Palestinians? The world has no problem rallying around politicians who kill Jewish boys in response to squatting. You said earlier, how sad you feel for the Palestinians. I do, too, but only to an extent, because Palestinians voted their governments in. They're getting exactly what they cast their ballots for. When Hamas fires at us, that's what the people voted for. They weren't unaware of what would happen by voting a terrorist group as the governing body."

"That's true, and there's something to be said about that," I said. "But the last election was over a decade ago, at least for Gaza. We don't even know how the next generation of Gazans would vote, if they had the chance."

"They certainly don't seem to mind when Hamas launches attacks on us," she retorted. "The media captures this 'next generation's' responses, and it's always cheering, not mourning. I'd never celebrate the murder of an innocent Palestinian, but it sure seems fine to the world when Arabs celebrate dead Jews. We aren't always in the right, I know that. But more often than not – we are. At least I think so. And when we're in the wrong? I'll admit it. At least I think I will."

Esther glanced behind herself, then stretched her neck to see the sky, as if the dark expanse could tell her what time it is. Though at this point, I was starting to wonder if Jews could tell time based on the positioning of the sun and the moon.

"Gotta get back to work. Close up shop. If you have more questions, now or even later, you can reach out."

"Really? I've taken a lot of your time."

"I don't mind. This is important for people to talk about."

"Okay, thanks. I might reach out again. Once or twice."

"I'm okay if you reach out three times," she smiled. "So, are we done here?"

"Yes," I said. "No. I mean, yes, but actually, I did just have one more question. Like, off-the-record. Do you have any physical problems? Like, heart murmurs or... *sudden blindness*? Or, like, cancer?"

Her smile weakened into a solemn grimace.

"Blindness? No. My grandma had cancer."

"Does it run in the family?"

"Not before my grandma. But yeah, it kind of does, now that you mention it. Dad had a cancer scare, and his brother – my "

"Have you been diagnosed with anything debilitating?"

"Nah. I mean, abdominal pain. That's it."

"When did that start?"

"I was maybe a teenager? Young teenager."

"So, like... *menstrual cramps*?"

"No. Nothing that would affect fertility or anything. Israelis are über fertile anyway, nothing takes us down. We can pop 'em out like the earth rocks out dust. It was just abdominal pain. Doctors don't know why. Still happens infrequently, but it's not too bad anymore."

"Young teenager? Like 13?"

"I think 13 or 14. Or, 14 or 15. 14. Definitely 14."

Born 1986. Add 4, carry the 1, plus 10. Year 2000.

2000: the Second Intifada. Her friend and teacher were killed that year.

"Well," I said, careful not to give in to temptation to write this down and pretend that she organically brought this information up during the interview process on her own, "you've given me a ton of good data here. I'll have a lot to wrap my mind around."

"So where do you go from here?"

"Well, basically, I need to make sense of all my interviews and then report my findings and defend my dissertation to my committee..."

"No, not 'where do you see yourself in five years.' I mean, like, where do you see yourself in five hours? Where else are you getting your participants?"

"Oh. I'm not sure yet, honestly. It took me, like, three weeks just to get one Israeli. I'll probably just try..."

"I can help you," she interrupted. "Nobody here is going to trust you unless you have an Israeli saying 'this guy's okay.' I can get you so many participants that you'll have to start turning people away."

"Wow," I said, stunned. "That would be so... helpful. Like... *why* would you help me?"

Her mouth opened and she stammered a bit, then closed her mouth and gave up from providing an answer.

"Nobody's wanted to help me," I explained my cynical question. "There's nothing in this for you."

"I value helping people, and I like what you're trying to do, actually. It's fun. And it's important, probably. How much time do you have left in Israel?"

"Time left for interviewing? A little less than a week."

"And then you're flying back to the States?"

"No, I'm going to Nazareth for a few days. As a retreat. Spend some time going over the data and whatnot."

"You won't be far from Megiddo."

"What's Megiddo?"

"Gog and Magog? You asked about it."

"What's Megiddo got to do with Gog and Magog?"

"Megiddo is where the battle takes place, or so it's said."

I had scoured the Bible for anything related to Gog and Magog, and had never once come across a reference to a place called "Megiddo."

"Is that in the Jewish apocrypha?"

"No, the prophets talk about it. I'm pretty sure it's in your Bible, too."

"I don't think it is. It's probably a Jewish thing, I think."

"You just call it the battle of Gog and Magog? You don't refer to it as the battle of Armageddon?"

"Of course Christianity talks about Armageddon."

"That's what that means, '*Megiddo*.' Megiddo is on a hill, called a '*har*.'"

"A '*har*?'"

"Yes, a '*har*,' like a '*tel*.' Tel Aviv? Tel Mond? Tel Be'er Sheva? '*Tel*' just means mound. '*Har*' means the same thing, '*hill*.' Just like there's Tel-Aviv, there's also Tel-Megiddo. Except they used to call it Har-Megiddo. Armageddon; Har-Megiddo. Sound similar? The Battle of Armageddon is literally the Battle on the Hill of Megiddo."

My eyes widened.

"Armageddon is a *place*?"

"Yes. Now you're following."

Ooh, baby! Armageddon is a place on earth!

"And how does Gog and Magog play into it specifically? Like, Megiddo is the spot where Israel and Gog and Magog all come together and fight? That's where there's so many dead bodies that…"

"Whoa, slow down yankee. I don't know anything beyond that. Armageddon is very Christian. It's not a thing for us."

"But… it's here? In Israel?"

"Yes, super close to Nazareth. I mean, it's 20 or 30 kilos away. Like, a short bus ride. Short-ish. You can't just walk there. 'One does not simply walk to Megiddo,' as Boromir would say."

"I've actually never seen *Lord of the Rings*," I said, but clearly picked up on the reference.

"Are you kidding me? I can forgive someone if they haven't *read* the most epic bildungsroman of all time, but to not see the movie…" she trailed off.

" '*Bil-dungs-roman?*' Is that Hebrew?"

"No?" she stopped and thought for a moment. "I have to assume it's German. But it's a genre. Novels where the protagonist has a coming-of-age journey that forces his – or her – moral and psychological and spiritual development along the way."

"Doesn't that description fit, like, half of all books?"

"I don't think so," she shrugged. "Oh, usually there's an element of tragic loss and suffering, too, so I guess that narrows it down a bit."

"Do you like to read those kinds of books? I have one that's kind of like that: war, loss, spiritual journey junk."

"*Ooohhh,* gimme!" she said. "I love to read. Just drop it off at the concierge desk if I'm not there. You sure you're done with it?"

"Definitely," I said, baring every wrinkle on my forehead. "I've been done with it for about six years."

"Well that's an awkward amount of time to be lugging around a book you finished. But, *hey!* You're deflecting the real point here, that you've never seen this Middle-Earth masterpiece and yet you claim you're actually an American."

"Come on, that trilogy is entirely a New Zealand production. I dare you to name three Americans in those movies. And I've tried watching it. Twice, actually. The first time, I got bored. The second time, I fell asleep. And, I think it was Hitchcock who said 'the length of a film should be directly related to the endurance of the human bladder.'"

"You're telling me you can't hold your pee for three hours?"

"It's… *no,* if I'm being honest. I can't. The *only* time I've ever sat through a three-hour movie without having to get up and pee was when I watched *Wreck-It Ralph* twice in a row."

"Never seen it."

"Your loss. Anyway, I don't really care to invest the time. Maybe someday when the world stops turning and I have ten straight hours to dedicate to watching a movie that's already zoned me out twice, I'll do it."

"Well, it's certainly more entertaining than what you'll find at Megiddo. It's just a bunch of ruins from far too many dynasties who thought the end times battle was going to happen there."

"Yeah, but, I… will definitely be looking into that," I said.

"What's the big deal, anyway? Do you think the end times is coming?"

"Someday? Of course. But I can say with confidence that it won't be soon. Not in the next few years, anyway."

"How can you say that?"

"*If* the Bible is true, and at least *some* of the end times prophecies are to be taken literally, then Magog needs to band together first. Gog is the leader; Magog is the collection of countries. Russia and China become invading powers on their own, then join forces together – with Turkey, for some reason. And they descend on Israel to raze it from the map."

"Well, yeah, that's World War III if that were to happen."

"Yes," I said, excited that someone – for the first time in my life – was finally interested in my knowledge of Magog. Or at least pretended to be. "But it's not *World War III* as much as it is the world versus Israel. Even Israel's closest allies, like us, won't come to aid you."

"Why not?"

"Doesn't say."

"Everyone just becomes anti-Semitic?"

"That's possible, but I think it's like you said earlier. The whole '*banality of evil*' thing. I think it's unlikely the whole world becomes anti-Semitic, I just think countries – especially the U.S. – has war fatigue. Tired of spending resources on other countries' battles and we all get too apathetic to help you."

"Okay," Esther said, tapping two fingers to her temple and then flinging them forward in salute, "I'll watch for Russia and China joining together after they become conquistadors."

"And Damascus," I said. "Damascus gets destroyed. That's the prophecy, at least. Damascus gets destroyed, and the Jews are blamed for it. That's what sets everything off and puts Gog into motion."

Blank stare. I was losing her.

"But I can't get ahead of myself," I said, deflecting my passion for the subject. "I still have a lot of work to do here. A lot of people to interview."

"Well, let me help with that," she said with a smile. "I'll tap into my network. Give me five hours."

> "The opposite of love is not hate,
> it's indifference.
> The opposite of art is not ugliness,
> it's indifference.
> The opposite of faith is not heresy,
> it's indifference.
> And the opposite of life is not death,
> it's indifference.
> Action is the only remedy to indifference:
> the most insidious danger of all."
> - Elie Wiesel

Esther was true to her word, and in a matter of days, my study expanded from having her as a single Israeli participant to having more Israeli participants than I did Palestinians. I traveled to Nazareth as planned, and by the time I got on the short bus ride from Nazareth to Megiddo, I had achieved everything I had set out to achieve for my research study. But as for the events of my dissertation, and all I did, are they not written in the book of the chronicles of *Holy Hotbed: Transgenerational Trauma Transmission in the Israeli-Palestinian Conflict*?

THE VALLEY ROSE.

God spoke, and it's how
The mountain calls for you now.
Not me –
The Valley Rose.
And it was my beloved who was always
Bound to suffer.
The Lord was the One who was
So focused on growing His garden,
That He left us to wither on this side.
That God is actually not good.
Never again will I think
Faith is the most important pillar of life.
Contrary to my prior beliefs,
Prayer has no place in the logical man's life.
Now I know that it's foolish to say
God is sovereign.
For all of eternity,
I will never see Romy again.
I erroneously believed
This pain will pass;
And also that
God sent Yeshua as Messiah.
I've instead learned to trust
My old pragmatic way of thinking.
I've been forced to surrender
My family, after all.
I never deserved
Anything less than this confidence:
Our suffering is meaningless, and

Now I know it's a lie to say
God sees our pain.

בד

July 2, 2020

Hey. Been reading books a bit more. Not Lord of the Rings type books, but nonfiction. I read a book, "When Bad Things Happen to Good People" by Kushner. Can't remember his first name. But basically he's a Jew who gives his theodical stance.

theodical?

Like, theodicy. pronounced like "The Odyssey" if you've never heard it said aloud. It's the study of the problem of evil. Or, the study of "why do bad things happen to good people?" Which is kind of a stupid question anyway

Why do you say that?

Because all people suck and deserve bad things. I think the real question is "why do bad things happen to good dogs?"

Lol that is somehow pessimistic and adorable at the same time.

No, but really. Why allow or create diseases that kill innocent wildlife? Why parvo? Why cordyceps? Why a tongue-eating sea louse? Why zombie wasps? Why heartworms and hammerhead flatworms and even bagworms for that matter? Why a plague that targets first born children?

So what does Kushner say is the answer?

He argues that God is limited in what He can do; He can't work outside the basic laws of nature that He created.

Is that what you believe?

If you asked me a month before Israel, then I'd say no way is God limited in any way. But now? I don't know. Maybe God isn't all-powerful. But if He's not, it's because He willingly gave up some power in exchange for free will, which He knew would lead to intense suffering - both for Himself and His people.

So, that doesn't make much sense. why would He do that?

The "why" isn't ours to know. We just have to trust that He was making the best choice possible.

Yours is still a problematic idea. Saying "he's all powerful but chose not to be" isn't any more helpful than "he can stop evil but chooses not to."

I just know God COULD have healed Romy. But I think somehow it would've violated His commitment to free will. I had my opportunity to take care of Romy - I had the time to go to prayer and ask for His consult. I barely spent time in prayer, and when I was praying, it was for healing, not discretion. My free will killed her.

You need to forgive yourself. Romy probably did. God surely does.

I think I've forgiven myself. But I am at fault for killing her. There's no getting around that. And it's better that I'm at fault for killing her, because if God's actually at fault... I don't know that I can handle that. I've realized that if God's plan included Romy's suffering, then I wanted no part in it.

Well, the idea that god sacrificed power for free will. It's a charming idea, only because god knows so much more than us about the world. Things that may seem miraculous to us today may in the future be discovered to be within the scope of what's possible, and in that way god is all-knowing and all-powerful.

٢٤

<u>November 27, 1996</u>

"You will be shot if you go," Okhti rebuked Claire. "You are out of your mind right now."

"I can't stand it anymore," Claire said while throwing on a light jacket, as the hot day dipped into a cool night without the summer sun. "We have been waiting for hours and nobody will even acknowledge that they took my husband from me. There is a time to pray, and there is a time to act, and this is a time to act."

"It is three hours past curfew, and if you drive to that prison…"

"Sister," Claire interrupted. "Will you watch my children?"

"Of course I will."

"Then it is settled. Please let me go."

Claire grabbed the keys to Zuji's jalopy and began the long drive to prison, knowing that an unmarked Palestinian vehicle like hers would likely be a target.

"Lord, will You please send Someone to protect me and Zuji?" she asked as she drove into heavy Tzahal territory. Within minutes, she began to feel a warmth at the top of her head, the same warmth that she felt on the roof days ago. The warmth surged to the rest of her body, and when the warmth finished moving from one area of her body, it left a refreshing cool behind in another, and the rising and falling calescence flowed through Claire's body so fluidly that it felt like a massage.

Claire pressed her foot to the pedal and sped to the prison, where she boldly parked outside its gates and stomped her way to the front entrance.

But then you're going back to the Groundhog Day premise all over. We'd be able to essentially become God one day.

In this thought experiment? It's possible. Which is why it's unreasonable.

It's a fascinating thought though. What if God restricts His own power for some purpose we can't understand?
Kushner talks about the Holocaust from this vantage. Hold on, I'll find the quote.
Kushner: "To try to explain the Holocaust, or any suffering, as God's will is to side with the executioner rather than with his victim, and to claim that God does the same. I cannot make sense of the Holocaust by taking it to be God's will. Even if I could accept the death of an innocent individual now and then without having to rethink all of my beliefs, the Holocaust represents too many deaths, too much evidence against the view that 'God is in charge and He has His reasons.' Having given Man freedom to choose... there was nothing God could do to prevent it."

So god allowing the shoah to happen = siding with the executioner??

Would it not be?

That seems like a lazy idea, tbh. The shoah happened because people suck. People are filled with hatred and evil and all kinds of scuzzy shit.

Probably from all the coffee and popcorn.

Nasty.

I've had a lot of things challenge my faith in life, but the example you just gave reminds me of the thing that makes me doubt Christianity the most.

What's that?

The idea that humans are worth saving. It's the Bible's biggest plot hole. It's like me taking a shit and saying "You know, I shouldn't flush that."

God did flush, though. He just had an ark built first and saved the good stuff.

Ew.

K sure. I'm the gross one here.
¬‿¬

God says that He wouldn't flush us ever again, but with the pandemic, maybe it's time for Him to renege?

Yeah who knows. COVID-19 is awful, but what if COVID-20 turns us all into zombies?

Sooo, you're a zombie movie fan?

Not at all. I hate those.

Well I think I know why

Enlighten me

Your first memory was of a zombie child biting your arm

[⁻°-°]¬ <(מִיּיּיּיּיּיּיּיּ)

Which is really tragic if you think about it, because if there's a zombie apocalypse, your first and last memories will be of getting eaten

Circle of life, I guess.
Okay. I have a question for you: do you think god is all-powerful?

I think so, though the Book of Job has me questioning it a little. It almost reveals God to willingly not be all-powerful.

"What do you need?" the guard at the door asked her, keeping his rifle pointed at the ground but with his finger on the trigger.

"My husband," Claire said, her eyes glowing with furor.

"He is a prisoner here?" the guard asked.

"I would like you to tell me that," Claire responded.

"What is his name?"

"Zuji Bishara Anastas."

The guard grabbed a walkie-talkie and began to speak Hebrew to the other end. He received a response in like, looked at Claire, and then nodded his head.

"One moment."

One moment later, a Samal appeared before Claire.

"Claire Anastas," he said, "your husband was brought here earlier today."

"Yes, this I know!"

"He has been released one hour ago."

"Where did you take him?"

"Take him? We didn't take him anywhere. He walked out the front gate, where you stand right now."

"You released him from prison *after* curfew, with no way home, knowing that he would be shot at for being out past 10:00pm?"

"This is not our problem. When your people stop shooting at us, then you will no longer need to worry about us shooting back."

"Which way did he go?"

"Where does any released prisoner go? Into the wilderness, I suppose."

Or is there power in him allowing evil to happen? If god is forced to bend to YOUR will, then is he really god? I think I've told you my take on this before. So many people get caught up thinking "God is sovereign and therefore won't let bad things happen to me." No. That's stupid. History has disproved it. There's a different, better answer. God is sovereign and therefore he allows bad things to happen to you.

You have told me this before. In fact, it's one of the primary themes of my dissertation. Israelis and Palestinians (at least the religious ones) both believed this to be true.

There's an old jewish adage about god. You'll see it on bumper stickers sometimes.

Can I guess what it is? I think I know where you're going with this.

Okay, go ahead, guess.

"God is my co-pilot." I hate it. God isn't our "co-pilot." God is our pilot. We are the passenger.

God is definitely not the co-pilot, but I don't think he's the pilot either. God is the air. God is the ocean. God is what your ship is riding on, not the one driving your ship.
Also: you failed. That's not the bumper sticker I was talking about.

Okay. I'll stop mansplaining. Or at least manguessing. What's the bumper sticker?

"God is: omnipotent, omnibenevolent, omniscient. Only choose 2."

Ah yes, the Epicurus trilemma. Rationalizing God would be so much easier if we could accept that He was only 2 of those things, because His 1 shortcoming would explain away all the evil. But I know God is all 3, which is why this is so hard to understand. I know He had the capability to heal Romy, and He didn't. I know God knew Romy was sick and knew how to heal her. So is God not good?

Let me ask this: if you could have a god who was omnipotent, omnibenevolent, and omniscient, but executes them over at a turtle's pace, would you take that? Because that's what you're getting with Elokim.

Elokim?

HaShem. El-Shaddhai. God.

Ah. We call Him the "Man Upstairs."

God is good. I don't care about your faith in Yeshua or religion. But I don't like that you're allowing this to shake your faith in god.

I'm allowing new information to inform me. That's what people are supposed to do, even if it changes everything they know to be true. If there was something that you believed with your entire being, your whole mind, body, and soul, but it was actually a lie, would you want to know?

So you think he's NOT omnipotent?

I don't know! But I have to entertain the possibility, don't I? There's a folly that a lot of people like to do. They have something that challenges their faith, so they strip it from their lives. It's refreshing at first because they're not encumbered with everything that weighed them down before. No more rules, no more devotions, no more getting up on Sunday mornings. But then they don't ever clothe themselves with anything to replace what they used to be wearing. They think "all clothes are bad" and spend the rest of their lives in the nude. Naked as a Trae-Beard.

Claire turned around, looking at the vast, barren desert behind her.

"You have no humanity," her lip quivered.

"I have humanity," the Samal responded, his eyes actually exuding pain by her words. "How am I to do my job otherwise?"

Claire felt her own disposition soften, so she retreated to Zuji's car and headed back home. There was no value in searching for Zuji: Claire was more likely to get bit by a viper than she was to find Zuji in that wilderness.

Claire crept into her home so as not to wake anyone, set the keys on the counter, and let out a deep sigh. Then, the hall light came on and she saw a withered, worn Zuji standing before her.

They didn't even speak. Zuji wrapped Claire in his tight embrace until she stopped weeping. Claire reached her hand and grazed her fingers through Zuji's hair, to which he winced from.

"Are you okay?" Claire asked.

"They blindfolded me and I tripped down the stairs," he explained. "I struck my head and became dizzy, so they carried me out. Come, let's sit down and talk."

Zuji pulled out a chair for Claire, then continued his story.

"Marwan, the man with the camera, he fought for me. He told the commander I had nothing to do with it, and a few hours later, they released me. 'What about Marwan?' I asked. They didn't answer and I don't know his fate. But at this time they released me, it is past curfew and I ask them to just imprison me until morning because I will not survive the night. I will be shot at a checkpoint or I will be stung by one of God's creatures. They refuse to imprison me, so I tried braving the desert, but it

I don't get it. What's a trae beard? What should they be wearing in this situation?

[pants]

You're so abstract, it should be terefah.

Okay, let me give you a personal example.

When I was in boot camp, the drill sergeants absolutely tore me down. They stripped me of my individuality, my personality, my dignity in a lot of ways. Why deconstruct a human being so aggressively?

It was so they could reconstruct me as a soldier. A warrior and a member of a team. Anybody who deconstructs for the sake of deconstruction - without reconstruction as an endgame - is not doing it for the right reasons. I'm in boot camp again. I'm deconstructing what I see to be long-held church traditions and evaluate if these traditions are what was intended by Christ. And then, we reconstruct.

Sometimes people reconstruct and build something worse.

That's true. Some people "reconstruct" a loss of faith, or even worse than a loss of faith, they reconstruct a hostility to the thing they deconstructed. Because the thing that they deconstructed hurt them, so they try to reconstruct in a way that is sure to hurt that thing back. But I believe that people who have true faith, who really had a firm foundation to begin with, they aren't going to reconstruct something completely false for the sake of being contrarian.

So, do you think god is omnipotent?

Well, put it this way. If someone asked why God didn't intervene in the Holocaust, how would you respond?

How do you know he didn't? :)

So you think that God sent the Americans to liberate you just when you were on the brink of annihilation?

How do you know he didn't intervene from the beginning? And also, not to poop in your red/white/blue cheerios, but have you read the bible? We would've been fine without your help.
And stop deflecting. I'm asking you directly. Yes or no. Is god omnipotent?

He has to be. But are there things that God doesn't have control over? If so, maybe it was because He willingly gave up that control, like He did in chapter 1 of Job. If God isn't all-powerful, then could it be that it was His judgment - not a lack of power - that made Him powerless? Again: what if God is limited by the rules He's created?

I guess I hadn't thought through that before.

The Holocaust is single-handedly the proof we need to prove that God either chooses not to intervene, or is too limited to intervene (perhaps because of a bet He made with the devil, like in Job). What if when God calls us to do something, it's supposed to hurt?

(pssst... god doesn't call individuals...)

Work with me here. Go with my "what if." If this be the case, then we turn to God for inward strength and comfort - not to change our circumstances.

But does god actually *will* pain? I don't think that's true.

became so cold and I saw slithering animals. I turned around and begged and begged and they still would not let me back into prison. I asked if I can call you; they said to handle it myself and then locked the gate and left.

"I strayed down the road," Zuji continued, "and a truck passes by. I raise my hands and I think they understand how desperate I am, because they stopped, and it was three Tzahal. I beg them to take me to wherever they are going, and they say they will drop me off near Hebron Road. But when they drop me off, they drop me off at a checkpoint on the Israeli side. 'I cannot get home here,' I tell them. 'Please drop me off in Palestine.' And they tell me to talk to those at the checkpoint. I ask, 'shall I tell them of my story and that you dropped me off here?', and they panicked and said to not tell the guards that they helped me, and to instead just say that I hitchhiked. So, I approach the checkpoint with my hands up, and here I am, approaching a soldier after curfew with no logical alibi that I can use, and my face grows hot..."

Claire slapped the table, startling Zuji.

"You felt it, too," she noted.

"Felt what?"

"The heat."

"Yes, my face was hot. I was terribly anxious, and we had many bodies pressed together in the vehicle."

"No, it was not body heat," Claire reasoned. "It is something else and I have felt this too."

Zuji raised an eyebrow, unsure how to respond to Claire's excitement.

You're being a bad improv partner right now.
Also, God willed animals (and then the Messiah) to suffer and die as atonement.

But that wasn't god's original plan.
And I don't actually like improv, for the record.

There is this one idea that God just passively ALLOWS death, pain, broken
relationships, but doesn't actively WILL death, pain, broken relationships.

Sorry but it's all or nothing here. If you trust god when he builds, then you need to
trust him when he uproots. No matter how bad a situation is for me, he probably
hates it even more than I do. You think god didn't weep when he sent us into
exile? You can't believe in an almighty god and believe he's only responsible for
the good. If that's true, there's no logical way to explain suffering without also
admitting that you think god is limited in the scope of what he does.

What if God isn't limited, but He doesn't want to be on the hook for either the
good or the bad? That He created us in an environment where we can choose
good or bad, and our job is to choose the virtuous route?

What if? then you're a Deist. And god doesn't really matter then, would he?

One concept I've heard is that God has a permissive will (what He allows) versus
God's perfect will (His ideal situation).

Nah. Every bee that brings the honey needs a sting to be complete. And we all
must learn to taste the bitter with the sweet.

That... was beautiful. Did you come up with that????

No. It's a famous song. We sing it in synagogue. Al Kol Eleh. Bless the sting and
bless the honey, bless the bitter and the sweet. A bee isn't a bee without a sting.

Wow.

If god isn't on the hook for the bad, then he doesn't get credit for the good,
either. If that's your belief, that he just created this environment random

Fwiw, I think I'm on board here with your vantage.
But can I tell you why I'm still a little angsty about this? Like, if I was Elie Wiesel
and I put God on trial, what evidence I'd exhibit. Facts that I can't reconcile with a
"Good God who answers prayers"?

Go off.

Joanna and I had 2 requests: keep our family healthy, and let us have children. So
many Christians have told us that if we desire to have children, then it's because
God put that desire there. 7 years later, it hasn't happened. We upped the ante,
praying for our dogs' health every day at mealtime too. That same year, Sidney
was diagnosed with lumbosacral disease, then Romy tore her knee and died.
Both faced these things unnaturally young. And when Romy got sick, every time I
prayed for her, she got worse. When I finally caved in and asked God to let her
pass peacefully? That's when the pain spiked about ten notches. So, fine. I get
that you don't always get what you want. But there's the other stuff: the call to
get my PhD, which has only worked as a career millstone. To move to Tulsa,
which has felt more like a move into the wilderness than a move into some
Promised Land. We're in critical debt and I've missed a credit card payment for
the first time in my life. I asked Him to increase my faith, and it's been rapidly
decreasing. I asked for comfort and have received anything but that. I asked for
rest, and I feel more stressed than ever despite not having any responsibilities
whatsoever. If God didn't will pain, He'd have intervened already.

"Claire," he concluded, "I bruised my head. That is why my face was hot."

"But then it was cold after? The hot leavened your body, and your face became cold, and your body was warm and cold at the same time and it was a comfort of peace?"

"No," Zuji said, grabbing Claire's hand. "I became hot, and, yes – the air was cold. But I approach the guard and he asks what I am doing and I tell him that I hitchhiked, knowing it is a terrible story that can't be true. He asked who gave me a ride and I tell him it was dark and I can't remember what he looked like, and the guard knows I'm lying and tells me I am under arrest and he puts handcuffs on me. And I beg him to take me to prison. I say, 'please, please arrest me and take me back to prison. That's fine!' And I tell him my story of what happened to me today, and he calls the prison, and they tell him it is a true story that I was there in jail today, though they can't believe I am somehow in Israel, but he lets me go. And I cantered the rest of the way with no more trouble. And now? Now I am home."

Claire exhaled, then leaned back in her chair.

"I felt something," she said, almost gasping for air as she spoke it.

Zuji shrugged, unsure of how to validate her feeling.

"The Lord was with me tonight," she said, staring off in confusion.

"Yes," Zuji said, squeezing Claire's hand and caressing her cheek. "The Lord is always with us."

I don't know what else to say other than I'm sorry you feel that way.
And I want a Romy picture.

But still. The more important question isn't "God, why did this happen?"

It's "God, what do I do with this suffering?"

You seem upset. Can I tell you one thing that i do know is true of god?

Of course

God followed his people into the wilderness.
God followed his people into Babylon.
God will follow you into Babylon too.

One can hope.

One can pray.

No thanks.
If the one thing that I asked for on a multi-daily basis - perhaps the greatest innate desire of my heart if I'm praying about it that frequently - if that one thing doesn't happen, then what does that say about the power of my prayer?
So go ahead. I'm not stopping you. Pray if you want.

I will. And I'll pray for you.

That's fine.
Just don't ask me to pray for you.

LOOKING FOR ARMAGEDDON

> "Save me from the mouth of the lion!
> You have rescued me
> from the horns of the wild oxen!"
> ~ Psalm 22:21, ESV

Most Armageddon pilgrims travel on a tour bus with other like-minded Christian fundamentalists, but my small transit bus was filled with just a few Jews scurrying to get home before the weekly Shabbat came. Instead of getting dropped off at the doorstep of Megiddo National Park like most tourists, my bus dumped me at a crossroads next to the local prison and a large field. There was only one large hill opposite the prison, and it looked over the expanse of the Valley of Jezreel, so I headed that direction.

The closer I got, the more I was whisked away to a different world. The field, though abandoned now, had not always been. I was standing on what clearly used to be temple grounds, given the detritus of the large structures around me: tall columns held a roof that no longer stood, and I imagined Israelites (or Israelite conquerors) sitting in the pews of stone. I thought to myself that this should be a tourist spot in itself, seeing as it felt like I was standing amongst the ghosts of a civilization lost, an ancient battleground straight out of the *Legend of Zelda*. Beyond this fantastical link, the field was riddled with massive piles of dung, piles so colossal that I wondered if they'd been left by the biblical Behemoth described in the book of Job.

As I trekked past the remnants of a seemingly-ancient city, the path split into two: one that led up a shallow hill, and another that led to a valley below. On the path leading down, there was a crude sign posted on a stick:

להיפגש באמת

The descent looked dark. Cold. Valleys are the worst place to be, metaphorically and from a tactical standpoint. I would be exposed no matter where I entrenched my back. Plus it'd be sloshy if it rained recently. If I slip and break my neck, who would find my body? I'm not even sure God would meet me if I went down there.

"That place is a curse," I declared like a Pentecostal preacher trying to manifest the authority of Christ.

I ascended the incline instead and headed to the hill. Well, it was less of a hill and more of a hillock, if I want to be absolutely literal – and I better be, in case any Southern Baptists read this book. I cantered skyward until I glanced to the east, where a large yellow fence caught my eye. There was a sizable posted sign that announced "נהג יקר! אין צורך לצפור" in bright red lettering, which is Hebrew for something in Hebrew, and Danger for "please squirm under this fence to enter."

Perhaps a loss in translation, but after wriggling through and dusting myself off, I found myself in a gated kibbutz. Given that Shabbat was a few hours away, it was largely a ghost town. But the paved road led right to Tel Megiddo – and at the top of that hill was not only the apex of Megiddo, but the apex of my journey, the very culmination of my spiritual calling that began over a decade ago, the fulfillment of Nana's prophecy when she said "be prepared, for you will see Armageddon!" *Hinneh!* Over several hours, I saw the sites and roamed the ruins, but couldn't find Armageddon on Har Megiddo, nor Gog from Magog. Perplexed (but not driven to despair), I retreated down the mountain to find snacks.

There in the kibbutz, I found a small convenience store still open for another few minutes before the sun set and Shabbat officially began. A small crowd had gathered there, presumably a bunch of Jews needing to grab last-minute Bissli and Bamba before 24 hours of hibernation. It seemed to be a tight group of people who all seemed to know each other, but I didn't seem to stick out as an imposter, so I kept my mouth shut to keep it that way. At the very least, none of them knew I had snuck into their gated community, which was fortunate for me, because the last time a Gentile tried to trespass in the Valley of Jezreel, they were thrown out of a window and eaten by dogs.

Revealing myself as a foreigner to the store clerk, I asked if she knew of a hostel or any place I could sleep for the night, and she said that in Midrakh Oz – their neighboring kibbutz – there was a guest house, but that she wasn't sure if it would even be open on Shabbat.

"They even shut down the lodging on Shabbat?" I asked her.

"My friend, if you want customer service, you go to the Hilton. Here in Canaan, Shabbat is our bride," she explained. "If you had not seen your wife for six days, and then you saw her approaching from the distance, you would not stand in wait for her to come to you. You would run out to meet her. And you would not care if some stranger was trying to get your attention, you would push them away and meet your wife."

"Well, it can't hurt to check to see if they're open," I said. "How can I get there?"

"Here," she said, pulling out her smartphone. "Let me pull it up on Google Maps."

"No!" I instinctively responded, not wanting to even look at her Google Map, which the Levites would've properly deemed unkosher had the internet been around during the advent of Moses' beard. "I just mean, tell me: how far is it?"

"About six kilometers," she responded. I'm American, so this was gibberish to me. I only measure things in miles or feet or inches or baseball bats or Budweisers or pickup trucks or charcoal grills or Abe Lincoln hat.

"Is that far?" I ask.

"Do you know what a 5k is?"

"Of course."

"Add 1k."

Ah, kay, so basically several thousand bald eagles away.

"Is there a quicker way?"

"You might be able to find an Uber, but they don't usually cab around here. You can get a taxi, but you'll pay through the nose because Shabbat is starting and they know you're desperate. But that's the extent of your options," she said, then added what I think was supposed to be a joke. "Unless you care to cut through the forest and fend off the wild animals you find."

Challenge accepted. I bought some granola bars, a water bottle, hand sanitizer, a bright-red fleece blanket, and a pair of scissors with a trusty 4cm blade that could maybe cut through a slice of day-old bread. (You know, in case I encountered any of those wild beasts.)

The clerk locked the door behind me as I left the shop. The sun was setting – in fact, a little quicker than I'd like. As I gazed at the sky, I could already see the twinkling of a single star. By the time I had hopped the yellow fence to leave the kibbutz and headed towards Megiddo Forest, there was already a second visible star.

I was literally one star away from being allowed to smoke. But when I arrived to the base of the forest, it wasn't the sky that stressed me out as much as it was the howl from a lair of jackals somewhere in the forest. The heavens had fallen dark and the world around me transmogrified into a noir set-piece. No longer able to see more than a couple football fields (American football) ahead, I decided to do the smart thing and pulled out my handy dandy scissors with its 4cm blade, just in case I encountered any wild creatures that God formed with butter instead of flesh.

After I took one step into the forest, I heard some snapping and saw rustling in some bushes. My internal Danger Box beeped to warn me that not only was I above the 5% threshold, but was actually approximately at 22% – the highest it's been in years. Granted, I'm not native to Israel, but all of my research in the States led me to conclude that any beasts capable of threshing foliage on a particularly warm day were *not* wrought of butter.

As the sun continued to coil, I retreated away from the forest and weighed my options, of which I had three. My first option was to roll the dice and just spurt through the forest until I reached Midrakh Oz and then hope that the guest house would be open tonight. My second option was to hop the fence again and just trespass overnight at the kibbutz alongside Tel Megiddo. The third option was to ascend the small hill I had spotted near the forest earlier, which I could see had about three trees and what looked like a small oil derrick at the crest of it. Clearly, the best option was to go back to the kibbutz and find a bench to sleep on, but I've read enough Choose-Your-Own-Adventure books to know that you should never go with the obvious choice.

I chose to scale the nearby hillock so that I could at least sleep on higher ground. The climb was accompanied with supernatural transformation: the small hill embiggened into a sizable mountain, the hike was now a footslog, and my 30-pound (or 200-crumpets) bag became a 90-pound (or 600-crumpets) bag.

[pants]

Huffing, puffing, and rolling over onto my back when I clambered to the top, I found an ATV and two men already around a campfire that had been slapdashed together with plastic bottles and aluminum cans. Between the toxic-fume trash-burning and the back-breaking bag and my underestimation of the Ghar of a hill, I kind of felt like I was back in Afghanistan.

After I re-canistered my steam, I stood back up and investigated the "oil derrick" I had seen when I had looked upon the hill from a distance. I've clearly been living in Oklahoma too long, because it wasn't a derrick but some kind of utility box – it looked like maybe it had been the base of a truncated power line tower that had been weathered away by decades of wear; it perhaps was even a survivor of the 1948 War of Independence. It had a "roof" to it, which was really just a thin slab of metal that was rusted and decayed. I realized that if only it could support my weight, it would actually be a good place to roost in a pinch. I climbed up the tower and perched myself so I could gauge whether it would support me, but sliced my ankle on a shard of dross from its siding. Is tetanus contagious? There hasn't been a global outbreak in over a century; what are the chances I was conjuring up the next one here on Megiddo Hill?

I'd gained a little winter weight over the summer, but the roof held up just fine. It wasn't the most ideal of places to sleep, but I also think any opportunities for finding a California king had probably passed. And then, of course, there's a pivotal truth I realized long ago:

"God will protect me if He wants to protect me, whether or not I have an epiphany that makes me believe so."

From my vantage, I could see the bulk of Jezreel Valley below – at least that which wasn't blocked by Tel Megiddo. Yonder in the valley next to the decrepit temple that I had passed by several hours ago, I watched a couple of gentlemen riding horses in and out of the valley, whisking me away to a bygone era I had only heard about in classrooms.

I had decided long ago that I'd like to be buried in a random grassy area. I'd like a subtle headstone, one that has my birthdate, deathdate, and my foremost occupations: "Prisoner of Christ, Joanna's husband." (Maybe a small sign that says "no Greeks allowed.") This hill? This was that place. If not for the fact that I had a family, I'd be willing to sell my new house and live homeless the rest of my life if it would cover the costs of being buried on this mountain, where I'd have a permanent vista of the valley and remain on watch for Gog, and nobody could find my resting spot unless they *really* were trying to find me. I'd be alone: just the Lord and me, a testament to my inability to connect with people while on earth. Why would I want to attempt anything more in death?

The once-bright sky was crestfallen, even its short season of twilight now slipping into dark. In spite of my overpowered glasses, I barely recognized the horses trodding their jockeys around until their form was no more. One by one, the rest of the stars began to appear and coalesce with the soot cloak overhead. The dawn of a new day, as I understand.

I swooped back to the ground and approached the two men by the polluted fire. One of the men – skinnier of the two – was dressed in a black hoodie with something written in red that I couldn't understand or even tell what language it was in. The other man was a little underdressed – though I was still only wearing cargo shorts and a V-neck, so I shouldn't be judging – but he only had a bright purple tanktop on that revealed more of him than I cared to see. Actually, I could get past his flubber easier than I could his tanktop, which was so obnoxiously bright. And of all colors, *purple*. Purple had always been my least favorite color because everyone knows purple is just the worst. You know it's ugly when "red" onions (unfazed about being the social pariah of vegetables) are less embarrassed about how repulsively pungent they are than they are about being called by their actual skin color. Purple is horrid: too feminine for a man and too masculine for a woman, it's the color of the Lakers and the Vikings *and* the most boring Teenage Mutant Ninja Turtle, and it's the color of grape which is easily the worst candy in the Skittles rainbow. Even the best color – green – is on the complete other side of the color wheel because it can't tolerate even being near purple. You know you're the outcast of the group when no other English word wants to even rhyme with you, unless you count "nurple."

"*Erev tov*," I said as I approached them.

Neither man said anything back, but they both looked up at me.

"*Erev tov*," I repeated. *Was I saying it wrong?*

The shorter of the men offered me an energy drink and a water. This gesture of goodwill pressed me to realize that their silence wasn't a matter of disregard, rather diction. And my sentiment of feeling like I was in Afghanistan again was only reinforced when I recognized that the men were Arab rather than Israeli.

"Scuzi. *As-salāmu 'alaykum*," I said a third time as I sat on a log with them. "Any English?"

"Little," one of the men responded. He was a scrawny guy, maybe a year or two older than me. His friend – a hefty, tall man – giddily waved at me with a sinuous smile, and I waved back.

"That Saleem," the scrawnier man said. "Saleem is no talk. My name Khalil."

"I am Danger," I said, then pulled my Arabic name out of my bag of tricks. "I am Khatar."

"Khatar?" Khalil asked, his head snapping back as if someone slapped his forehead.

"Yes, Khatar," I confirmed.

"Where from you?" Khalil asked.

"Well," my lip curled in anticipation of how funny I was about to be, "when a man loves a woman very much…"

I trailed off and raised my eyebrows, waiting for laughter that never came. Instead, Saleem turned his head back to the fire, ditching my joke into a mental trash bin while Khalil looked at me as if he was a robot who was just given an invalid command and was dutifully waiting for the next one.

Thanks for nothing, Trae, you foul-mouthed bastard.

"Chicago," I responded, crossing my fingers that he wasn't actually from Wrigleyville and was about to call me out for saying I'm from Chicago when I'm actually from the suburbs.

"Illinois," he said, accentuating the "S," suggesting maybe he was from Missouri instead.

"Yes, Illinois," I verified.

"Windy City," he said.

"Windy City," I confirmed again.

"Chicago Bulls."

"Yes, the Bulls."

"Obama. Michael Jordan."

"Obama, and Michael Jordan," I confirmed. And Navy Pier and deep dish pizza and hot dogs and snow and guns.

"How do go home?" Khalil asked.

"By plane," I said, a little confused at the question.

"No, how do go sleep?"

"I'm going to stay the night," I said.

"Where?" Khalil asked.

"Here."

"Where 'here?'"

"There," I said, gesturing to my cozy utility box.

"*Ngh! Ngh!*" Saleem snorted.

"Sleep here?" Khalil asked. Saleem grew quiet to hear my response.

"Yes, I will stay the night here."

"*Ngh!*" Saleem groused as his eyes widened.

"Saleem doesn't like. Yes, is bad idea," Khalil agreed. "No good. Fall through. Bad weight."

"I'll be okay," I said, trying not to be offended that he pointed out my bad weight.

"*Ngh*!" Saleem snorted again, then added, "*Hmph*!"

"Saleem want you know that animal here."

"Yeah? That makes sense."

A quick silence followed, but then I began thinking about the mammoth piles of butt-mud I had seen all over earlier.

"What kind of animal?"

As if it was his cue, Saleem jumped to his feet and gestured with his hands, which were clasped in a fist, except for his pinky and thumb, which were fully extended outward. It was the "hang loose" *shaka*, but that's certainly not what he was trying to indicate here. He held his hands up to his face and began dancing around the fire as if he was a wild animal, his saggy skin dancing along under his tanktop. I may have even seen a nurple.

"Ngh! Ngh! *Ngh! Ngh!* Ngh!" He repeated and then came up to me, face to face, and pretended to gore me.

"Warthog?" I asked.

"Ngh! Ngh!" Saleem blustered as his hands continued to feign fangs penetrating me.

"Pig? Big pig?" I asked.

"Yes," Khalil chimed in. "Big pig. War hog? Pig."

"Pigs can't climb," I gestured back towards the utility box, though I wondered if a warthog would have the skookum to topple the rusty structure over.

Saleem continued to pretend to gouge my innards at an uncomfortable proximity to me.

"He fine, Saleem," Khalil affirmed to his friend, then added something in Arabic, which roused them both to laughter.

"Also, caracal," Khalil said.

"Caracal? What's that?" I asked.

Saleem's fingers shifted from tusks into fangs, and then he began to snap at my face as if his hands were a mouth.

"Caracal. Like, *eh*, lion. But mini."

"Mini-lion?" I asked.

"Mini-lion."

Mini-lion?

"Like a bobcat?"

"Bobcat?"

"Bobcat."

Bobcat.

I drew my phone and googled synonyms for "bobcat."

"Puma. Mouser. Cougar? Kitty? Jaguar. Ocelot? What's an ocelot? Lynx."

Then, realizing my stupidity that I could just show them a picture of what I was looking up, I turned my phone to them so they could see the image. Saleem began to jump around as if to say "bingo!"

"Yes," Khalil confirmed. "Bobcat."

I gulped the last of my water, then Khalil reached for the empty bottle in my hand and tossed it in the fire.

"Soon, we leave," Khalil said, accidentally forming a complete English sentence.

"Do you mind if I use your fire after you're gone?" I asked, as if saying "no" was an option on the table. I figured this fire will keep me warm for a couple hours, and then after it dies, I can crawl into "bed."

"Yes, my friend," Khalil said. "For you; yours."

The three of us sat in relative silence for another 20 minutes, until Saleem looked past Khalil and myself, jumped to his feet, and began grunting like we were a trio of Neanderthals.

"Hmph! Ngh! *Ngghhh!*"

Khalil and I looked behind us, but saw nothing.

"Saleem nervous a lot," Khalil said to me with a smile.

I nodded. I get it. If I couldn't communicate the things I wanted to communicate, the world would be a much scarier place for me too.

"So, so good guy," Khalil added. "Just nervous."

Saleem danced around the fire, almost as if in a tribal trance, throwing his hands in the air and continuing to grunt, and parts of his skin I didn't want to see continued to splurge through the openings of his shirt. But Saleem's cries grew louder and higher until his grunts had lifted a couple of octaves into a whimper and he sounded like a wounded animal pleading for his life before his predator.

Khalil and I looked over our shoulders again, but I saw nothing. Khalil kept his head swiveled.

"In Israel..." I began to ask a question, but Khalil grabbed my shirt collar and jumped to his feet, yanking me up as well.

"Come, go," Khalil said.

I looked again and didn't see anything, but clearly they were in a rush to get out, so I jogged over to the utility box.

"Quick, can you help me up to this bench before you get out of here?"

"No! You come!" Khalil waved me over as Saleem continued to wail.

"Warthogs can't climb," I reminded them as I began to mount the utility box.

"Not war hog!" Khalil yelled.

I scanned the taller grass again and didn't see anything on my first take, but on second skim, my eyes settled on a large cat lurking with his head to the ground and his butt in the air.

War hogs can't climb. But mini-lions can.

My Danger Box sounded, telling me not only was I above the 5% threshold, but was actually approximately at 19%, which is the highest it'd been in almost an hour.

Like an Olympic committee was judging my form, I hopped off the rung of the utility box and triple-jumped over to the ATV, which was already warmed up and Khalil inching forward with. I tossed my bag to Saleem who caught it, allowing me to jump behind him. It's a single-seater, so there really wasn't room for Saleem, let alone a third party, but we bunched together and careened out of there. I loosely held onto Saleem's bulging side, afraid to get blubber sweat or purple on me, at least until Saleem grabbed my hands and dug them into his love handles, communicating "hold tight" with his actions. Figuring he knew what the ride was about to entail, I plunged my fingers into his lard until they were snugly enveloped, as if in a bamboo finger trap.

The ATV was still facing the mini-lion, so Khalil spun us 270°. As the world blurred before me, I saw no less than four sets of reflecting eyes in the grass ahead – one from the mini-lion I'd already seen and then at least three more behind him, all within striking distance. The ATV's wheels coughed up dirt onto the breath of the wild beasts, and we paraglided off the crest for a moment before sledding down the hill. My callipyge spent almost as much time in the air as they did on the seat, and my tailbone had post-traumatic flashbacks from riding the Cougars in Afghanistan.

Still clutching Saleem's excess, we zipped past the dilapidated temple of time and sunk into the steep valley that I had avoided earlier in the day.

I hopped off the ATV and Saleem tossed me my bag.

"Thank you," I said, but nobody disembarked.

"Time for go home," Khalil said.

"Oh, *kaaay*," I respond, my words trying to balance between stifling my dismay and purposely expressing consternation. "And… what of me?"

I waited for him to invite me to go to his place to crash for the night. And I'd have asked for such hospitality myself, but in the words of Daniel Woodrell, "don't ask for what ought to be offered."

"Wadi," Khalil said, pointing to the valley creek and clearly outing himself as a non-Woodrell fan.

My eyes followed the line of his finger, where it pointed to a wet riverbed. Did he think I was about to go full Jeremiah Johnson and set up camp here for the rest of my life? Unless he had a wicker basket and had thought I was Moses, I wasn't sure why he thought this might be remotely helpful.

I looked back at Khalil and Saleem in time to see them whisk away, and I realized I ought to have offered to have asked. But I didn't, and found myself sad as they hauled themselves away. Sad, not just because now I was at the mercy of a mini-lion, but also because I realized I'd never see them again. In fact, *every* person I'd come into contact with over the past month would be people who would likely be out of my life forever, and I finally understood why Wolverine was so sad about being immortal.

Now, instead of being on the mountaintop in communion with others, I'd found myself in this valley alone. And for the first time that night, I found myself filled with concern. And then for the first time this entire trip, fear. And then annoyance. And then anger, because I had been better off on the hilltop because at least I had had the higher ground there – a better position against predators, as well as the warmer of the two locations as the heat would rise through the night. If I were to sleep where I had been standing now, in the middle of the valley, my attackers could come from any direction. My best chance of survival now might be to lie doggo in the creek.

I remembered avoiding this dark valley earlier today. Nothing was appealing about it. I don't think anybody would've chosen the valley given the same choice I had, but there was no easy way out for me now. Nobody wants to go into the valley, but sometimes we have to go there. No shortcuts. We all find ourselves in one eventually.

I looked up at the sky, trying to find the heavenly gas that mirrored the facsimile on my arm. There were far more than three stars now; the whole sky was a dim backlight, as if someone was peering down from their own GameBoy and watching me adventure through the starlight.

They're not very good at this game. I'm probably going to die here.

Frankly, I had no idea which of those stars was actually the muse for my tattoo. I didn't even have any idea if the Bethlehem Star existed in time and space anymore, for that matter. When the light rips itself from the star, it never returns to its wellspring. The star and the light, irreparably torn asunder, as far as the east is from the west (plus several million lightyears between).

I lowered my head and, in the distance – even deeper in the valley – I spotted the glint of some flames. The day was satisfied. The clouds became eclipsed by the pillar of fire, so I chased. The heat girded me in towards its rusty fragrance. I expected to hear the flame's crackle but instead it was the strum of a guitar and the lilt of a flute over a harmony of voices. I would've confused the cantors as the ghosts of ancient priests, had not a dulcet of sopranos also levied their voices against the nighttide smoke.

An outer circle of tents, that inner pack of men and women, and a polestar of lumber fully ablaze, seething off the colors of the national flag. The campfire was as an altar, a sacrifice offering a jeremiad of its own. But afraid to puncture the group's perfect circle, I quietly took a seat among the tents. I couldn't understand the words of the song, but it sure was beautiful. Sitting in the murky nadir of the dark valley, I looked skyward towards the zenith I just came from. It wasn't lost on me how quickly I had tumbled from the highest crest to the lowest valley, buried somewhere between the star and the light.

The song finished. Everyone fell silent as one man took the lead and began to address the crowd with a commanding voice. However, it's in Hebrew, so I couldn't understand a word of it. I supposed that I had stumbled upon a religious group of Jewish hippies.

"Hey," a man whispered just loud enough that I could hear him, then scooted over a few feet to free up space for me in the circle. "*Ma nishma!*"

"*To-da,*" I said as I sat next to him.

"*Ma nishma?*" he asked as I scooched near him. "*Ma shim-kha?*"

"I'm sorry, I'm an American," I told him, the equivalent of begging "talk to me like you would a jingo."

"Here, have some tea," he said in perfect English as he handed me his mug.

"*To-da,*" I said. While my Danger Box was no longer alarming, my "OCD Box" kicked into high gear. I really, really didn't want to drink from a used cup, but this is a tip I learned in Afghanistan: if someone offers you tea in the Middle East, it's rude to say no. So, I accept the man's tea, hold the cup so the handle is facing towards me, and drink from the lip just above the lug – another trick I learned in Afghanistan to mitigate the chances that my mouth is drinking from where someone else's lips have been.

After the lead hippie finished his speech, several of the people around the fire busted out instruments – at least two guitars, one flute, and one wind instrument I wasn't familiar with. Those without instruments knitted their voices together into a mellifluous harmony, hot honey dribbling down the scape of my soul. The lyrics weren't in English, but the words melted over me as if I knew them all the same.

"Excuse me," I whispered to the man sitting next to me, "but do you mind if I hang out with you guys here for awhile?"

"Yes, hang out, stay, sleep, eat, share in life!" he said over the music. "What's your name, traveler?"

"I am Danger."

"I am Nicolas."

> "Only when it is dark enough can you see the stars."
> - Martin Luther King, Jr.

THE VALLEY ROSE.

God spoke, and it's how
The mountain calls for you now.
Not me –
The Valley Rose.
And it was my beloved who was always
Bound to suffer.
The Lord was the One who was
So focused on growing His garden,
That He left us to wither on this side.
That God is actually not good.
Never again will I think
Faith is the most important pillar of life.
Contrary to my prior beliefs,
Prayer has no place in the logical man's life.
Now I know that it's foolish to say
God is sovereign.
For all of eternity,
I will never see Romy again.
I erroneously believed
This pain will pass;
And also that
God sent Yeshua as Messiah.
I've instead learned to trust
My old pragmatic way of thinking.
I've been forced to surrender
My family, after all.
I never deserved
Anything less than this confidence:
Our suffering is meaningless, and
Now I know it's a lie to say
God sees our pain.
After a bitter season of contemplation
I have come to the sobering conclusion
God does not change.

כה

July 28, 2020

Have you guys not had your final fertility attempt yet?

> No, Joanna is finally going in for her pre-check ultrasound tomorrow, and we schedule it from there. But probably next week.

Crossing my fingers for you!

> Thanks. I'm feeling optimistic this time.

Really?

> Yeah, third time's the charm, right? And I really believe it's in God's will for us to have kids. I really do.

Not to knock you off that hope, but why do you say that?

> God gives us the desires of our heart, no? And this has been the fiercest desire of my heart since meeting Joanna, that we would share children.

God promises a lot, but he doesn't promise children. At least not to anyone outside of Abraham. That's important to remember. Not even the prophets had that.

> But then why wire me for children? I've been asking God to either grant us children or take away the desire to have kids. At this point, either action would be a miracle. And instead God is sitting on it and I don't get it.

Maybe god wants you to have this desire and not get it and have to sit in that.

> Well that feels cruel.

Also, I'm confused by you. You told me to not ask you to pray for me. And now you're saying God is going to give you a miracle?

> There's a difference between trusting in God's will versus the power of prayer. My prayers are as impotent as my swimmers, but I really believe God will overcome that for us.

I guess I'm just not following why you think god is destining you for fatherhood.

> Not having children goes against my nature. God created me to be a dad. For as long as I've known Joanna, I've known my children. I know their names. We have rooms for them. I just can't imagine God implanting this innate desire for children, allowing me to see my kids in my heart's mind, and then striking me with Abraham-sickness.

There are just some things we're not entitled to know, and I think that's one of them.

> I wish the Christian Church knew how to help people navigate these issues. So many churches try to blindly say "if you pray hard enough, God will give you children" or "just trust God's timing" as if everyone who has done that has overcome infertility. But the Bible doesn't promise that.

The bible doesn't really address infertility. It's used as a plot point, but that's it.

> Yeah. It's frustrating. There's not one episode in the Bible - not a single one - where God allows someone to remain childless for their entire lifetime, and I'm angry that He's given me a trial to navigate that He didn't force anyone in the Bible to endure.

Claire was changing the guest sheets – the Anastas family finally had their first customer in several months, most tourists being warded off by the presence of military activity by Rachel's Tomb – when young Ebnahty came to her mother.

"Mama," Ebnahty said, tugging at Claire's blouse, "there is someone on the roof, and they are going pee-pee on our house."

So many things about that statement seemed off, starting with the fact that nobody had come through the house to get onto the roof, which had been locked ever since the debacle with Marwan years ago. Secondly, another crossfire had occurred between Aida Camp and downtown Bethlehem just minutes ago, so it would seem awfully bold for someone to be standing on the roof with so many opposing snipers about. Third of all – and probably the most important – it may be war, but this was a house of dignity. Nobody urinates on the Anastas house.

Claire hustled to the stairs leading to the roof hatch and, after unlocking and cracking it open, listened for what Ebnahty reported. Indeed, there was a leak occurring, but it was much too copious to be coming from a human. Claire realized that this leak on the roof was, quite literally, a leak on the roof: one of their two water tanks had been scuppered by a rogue bullet during the crossfire, and the Anastas family was going to lose half their already-sparse water supply if Claire didn't act fast.

THE STAR

BUT... you still might have children! You don't know yet that you won't :-)

But you see how unhelpful that is though? To say that? It's a thing that people say, not because they genuinely believe it, but because it's the only miserly response that they can muster if they don't know how to deal with the possibility of it being true. And barrenness has been true for denizens of people. It's much cheaper to just boil the situation down to a catchpenny than to sit with someone in their pain. It's the exact same return that Job's friends provide.

Well, sorry

No, that probably came off ruder than I meant it to. My frustration isn't with you. Sorry. I just wish I knew what was promised and what's not. If I at least knew that I wouldn't have children, then I could have spent the past decade healing from that rather than having a false hope.
It's the same thing with Romy. I could have peace if I just knew that I'd see her again, if there was this promise that our pets are restored in heaven.

It does promise animals in heaven, though.

Right. But are they are our pets? Do I get to see Romy? And Sidney? Or Shadrach and Samus? Chief, Rykki, Candi, Pepper, Barkley?

Or Casper. Or Wiggles.

Sure. Casper and Mr. Wiggles too. This is what I'm revisiting right now.

What do you mean revisiting?

I've wondered about this a lot over the years. A lot more than the average person.

Ah, you talk about this a bit in your second book.

Right. My OCD begs me to believe that I can create order in the midst of chaos, that I can somehow control the fate of those around me. As if I have this responsibility that clearly only belongs to God.

Well the bible does say that god used his breath (nephesh) to give life to animals, as he did humans. But he gave humans a special kind of breath, a soul - neshama. I've heard it described like if you imagine god as a glassblower. The creator blows hot air into a tube and creates something, right? Well, animals were created this way. It's still god's breath, nephesh, but it's just not super hot or uber strong by the time it gets through the tube. For man, god put the blowpipe aside and blew directly on his creation - neshama breath. Full strength, using every morsel of wind that was inside god's cheeks.

So is the nephesh creation as heaven-bound like neshama creation?

I don't know.

For better or (probably) worse, I've realized my joy is dependent on whether or not we see pets in heaven. I believe it can't be eternal bliss without their presence.

The one thing I can say for certain is that god cares about animals. Abel, Jacob, Moses, David, Rebekah, and probably some others were shepherds first. In fact, our talmud says that Moses and Rebekah were chosen for their special roles partially because of how kind they were to animals. Because if they could handle caring for animals well, then they surely would be earnest in their higher callings. On the other side of things, we have two hunters in the bible: Nimrod and Esau. Both villains.
So, it does seem like god favors those who care about animals.

Of course, it was forbidden for Palestinians to be on roofs. To save her family's water, Claire would risk jail (or worse). But losing that water, especially in the dead of summer, would be to lose their means of survival.

Claire headed back towards the scuttle stairs to see what she could scrounge up in the house to plug the hole, but as her feet hit the top rung of the ladder, she heard an unnerving noise.

THWIT!

Claire froze in her tracks. She swiveled her head to look over her shoulder, but didn't see anything or anybody. But as she kept herself fixed in place, it happened again, this time louder.

THWIT! THWIT!

A bullet hit the roof, chipping away at the concrete on its edge. Someone was shooting at her. Were they aiming at her? Were they warning shots? She wasn't sure, so in a panic, Claire scrambled downstairs, slammed the door, and leaned her back against it and began to sob.

An untenable choice, and one that had to be made quickly: allow her family to lose half their supply, or risk getting shot for plugging the tub? She could ask the Tzahal for permission to go on the roof, but by the time she received approval, the supply would be mostly gone. She thought maybe she could ask the Tzahal to mend her tank and refill the water, but they had already declined her requests for reimbursement after one of her windows was busted in a firefight by a Turai who had the marksmanship of a camel, nor were they willing to help offset her electricity bill when they occupied her home.

No, if her family was to have their water preserved, it was up to Claire to defend her home.

There's this guy from Oklahoma, he died a long time ago, but man do Tulsans love this guy. He wasn't even a professing Christian and you've got churches named "Will Rogers Methodist Church" and if Joanna and I were to ever have kids, they'd eventually go to Will Rogers High School. You'd think he was a prophet or something.

Anyway, Will Rogers has this famous quote: "If there are no dogs in Heaven, then when I die I want to go where they went."

That's cute.

I don't identify with Will Rogers as most Tulsans do, but I do identify with that quote. I really, really need my pets in heaven.

There's this anecdote, and I'm having trouble finding it right quick. But there's this boy, and he asks his priest if his recently-departed dog will be in heaven waiting for him. "Do you really need your dog in order to be happy in heaven?" the priest asks the boy. And the boy responds, "yes, sir, I do."

"Well then," the priest responds, "your pet must be in heaven then!"

I know, I know, it's not biblically sound.

Yeah but it's cute, too.
So there's value in that.

Losing Romy for a lifetime pierced my soul. I cried more in 2019 than any other year of my life.

Ever?

Yeah even more than 2013 when Wreck-It Ralph came out on DVD and I was watching that every day.

I cried a lot too when I lost Casper and Wiggles. All we can do in the meantime is remember them.

Every day, I wear 6 purple bracelets to remember Romy.

Why 6?

6, because that's the number of years we had with her.

Does the purple have meaning too?

That was her "color." Her collar was purple. Each of our dogs have a color assigned to them.

It's actually a little ironic. I've always avoided the number 6 and I never liked purple. But now I find myself compulsively counting 6 purple bracelets every few hours to make sure I didn't lose one.

Why don't you like 6?
Wait, I know that one. You mention that in your other book. But what's wrong with purple?

I've always just thought it was kind of an ugly color. Except now I always find myself gravitating to purple whenever I can, just to remember Romy. My bracelets are purple. My shoes are purple. I wear a purple shirt every single day. When I play Smash Bros now, I always choose the purple variation of my character.

Smash Brothers?

Facepalm.
Why I assumed you'd know what that is, I have no idea.
It's one of those "Mario computer things".

(^ェ^)

341

"Yasue," Claire whispered through her tears, "it is time. Please help me. I need an Advocate."

A brief, hurried prayer that culminated in Claire feeling her head as if aflame, followed by the brisk freeze of a silent, winter night. A spirit of fire and ice coursed through her body, and then she had an epiphany: neoprene rubber.

A few years ago, the Anastas had lost their water supply once before during a rare Bethlehem hailstorm that damaged one of their water tanks. They lost half a tank that night, and bought neoprene at the pharmacy the next day in case they ever had another occasion in which their tank chiseled.

This was that occasion. Claire loped to the closet, found two packages of neoprene still in their original packaging, and opened one package up as she launched herself back on the roof and raced to the tank.

As if they knew she'd be coming back, the snipers didn't miss a spank and shot at her. Claire heard the bullets pouring in behind her and in front of her, and she even saw a few spray in front of her face as the wind from the bullets slapped her cheeks. She thumbed the neoprene into a small plug, and sealed the hole.

However, she still heard water running and realized the snipers had added a couple more cracks in her tank, so she sidled around the cistern as they continued shooting at her, and she plugged each hole as they appeared, one-by-one. Seven holes later, she exhausted her supply of neoprene and realized she needed to grab the other package if she was to plug the last two holes.

"Woman!" a Tzahal cried to her from a distant roof. "Go inside! If we see you again, we will kill you!"

Smash Bros is a Nintendo game that released the morning that Romy died. I had decided to fast from food and Smash Bros until Romy got well. I'd much rather still be fasting, but like I said, now I wear 6 purple bracelets every day in her memory.

That's sweet.

One time, I was getting my teeth cleaned at the dentist, and the hygienist cracked a joke, "what, did your daughter bully you into wearing those bracelets or something?" She was mortified at her comment when I said, "Actually, I'm infertile and can't have children even though I really, really want to be a dad. The purple bracelets are in memory of my dog that I accidentally killed, thanks for asking."

ʕ^ᵜ^?
Is it okay to laugh at that story?

It is, because what are the chances that she'd find the one question that broaches every topic that brings me anguish in this life? She hit on all cylinders in one fell swoop.

You do well to remember Romy.

I miss her so much. So, so much.

I know you do.

They said it gets better with time, and they're liars.

"What?" Claire cried out to him, cupping her ear to challenge him to speak up.

"Go. in. side!" the man yelled, punching each syllable as if each word was its own sentence. "I. will. kill. you. if. I. see. you. again!"

"I can't hear you," Claire yelled, amusing herself now.

The man pulled his rifle to his shoulder and peered through the scope.

"Okay!" Claire yelled, smiling and waved at the man through his scope. "I'm just going to get something!"

"No!" the man put his rifle down. "You. stay. in!"

Claire scampered down to her closet, unpacked the other roll of neoprene, and drifted onto the roof, eschewing urgency to accentuate her defiance. Bullets began to rain around her again as she ambled to the vat, keeping her head lowered and avoiding eye contact with the soldier. Taking her time, she corked the final two holes in her water supply.

No more gunshots. No more breaches. She turned around, descended back into her home, and feeling the fire and frost flee her temple, she shut the door.

THE VALLEY ROSE

> "It may be that
> the Spirit of the LORD
> has caught him up
> and cast him upon
> some mountain or
> into some valley."
> ~ 2 Kings 2:16, ESV

I woke up shivering. My fleece felt like it had been in a freezer. James Amos had once admonished me from ever attempting to pull a Gideon ever again, but here I was tempted to ask God to dry off the dew that had collected.

I sat up. A dark figure was poking the fire with a stick, coughing up a few more flames.

"It's coldest before the dawn, Danger," the figure said to me. The white of my eyes must've contrasted with the otherwise dark-shrouded environment to let him know someone was watching him.

"Nicolas?" I asked.

"Yes, Danger, it's me," he said as he took a step forward, allowing me to see his big, recognizable smile that his bushy, weathered gray beard couldn't even conceal. "Do you need another blanket? I'm not using mine right now."

The night had grown cold. He had not ought to offer his blanket. But if you ought not to ask for what ought to be offered, then maybe the reverse was true, that you ought to accept what ought to not have been offered?

"Danger, what were you going to do if you didn't find us?" Nicolas inspected me and my bag as he draped his still-warm blanket over my shoulders.

"I would've had to figure something out," I said, which was the most eloquent way of saying "I have no idea." I was starting to understand why so many animals were nocturnal; if I had to live outside, I'd probably turn to sleeping during the warmest portions of the day, too.

"How long are you traveling?" he asked.

"It'll be 40 days when it's all said and done."

"Hmm. Forty? And that was intentional, yeah?"

"No, if you can believe that," I said. "I only recently realized it. I had allotted for about a month for a project, and then ten days for recreation. It just ended up that way, I guess. Not intentional."

"Hmm," Nicolas said. I don't think he believed me.

"Nicolas, what was that song your group was singing when I came here?"

"Which one? How did it go?"

"It was like, 'ya ya ya *ya* ya *ya ya*, ya *yaaa*.'"

"I think maybe you are singing 'Kol Galgal?' This one is very famous in all of Israel."

"The song is beautiful. What does it mean? Like, in English?"

"It's translated as, 'The Voice of the Wheel,' or maybe 'The Tune' or 'The Sound of the Wheel.' Are you familiar with the Zohar?"

"Sure I am. Adam Sandler made that movie, *You Don't Mess With the Zohar*."

"I do not know this movie, but the song's meaning comes from the Zohar. It is about the connection between God and all the creatures of this world."

"All creatures? Animals too? Not just people?"

"Yes, all creatures. It's hard to translate as the original meaning is unclear in itself, but it says it is the sound of a wheel turning from below to above, and that sound wanders the world, going up and down, up and down. The 'wheel' in the song, it is about nature, and how the world here below longs to connect with the world above, to go up, which is why it's spinning upward. And on the other end is God, who wants to connect with us, to bless us with his... well, how can I say it? He wants to bless us with his *Shchina*, which is too convoluted for me to translate. The blow of the shofar causes the wheel to turn, and the shofar is a deeply religious symbol, so it's saying that our desire to connect to God is actually perpetuated by God Himself."

"So this is a religious band?"

"No, not really. They take their band name from a sentence in Talmud, 'and from the day that the Holy Temple was destroyed, premonition was taken from the prophets and given to fools and babies.' They like to ask a lot of questions that they don't necessarily care to answer for you. But they aren't religious. A lot of Israeli bands take their lyrics from religious text, especially from Kabbalah, which is like Jewish mysticism. I'm sure you see the same duplicity in American music."

"Yeah, we sure do," I lied. "There's this famous American song about a girl who has sex so hard with her boyfriend that he becomes convinced God is a woman."

"Okay," Nicolas said. "Maybe the same principle? I don't know this."

The sound of the wheel was replaced with the sound of silence for a moment, until I broke it up with a question.

"Hey, Nicolas. Where am I?"

"Here? You're in HaEmek. Jezreel. *The* Valley. Where you stand, specifically? This place is the belly of the valley of the Valley of Jezreel." Which felt appropriate, considering I had just come from the top of the hill of Hill Megiddo.

"But what am I doing here? What are you doing here? Are you guys a religious group?"

"Religious? Like, Jewish? Well, do Jews kindle a fire on Shabbat?"

"I... is that rhetorical? Like, 'does a Bereshit in the woods?' I actually, I don't know. Is that forbidden?"

"Yes, it's explicitly forbidden, Danger. What did I tell you when you showed up? I said to come 'hang out, sleep, eat, share in life.' And that is what we are doing here."

"This place feels... well, kind of sacred."

"Sacred, huh? There's a McDonald's down the way, if you want to ruin that image. Right next to the prison, off 66."

"Route 66?"

"Yes, down the way," Nicolas repeated himself, pointing yonder.

I guess you can get your fried fix on any Route 66.

"America's fat food staple on America's main street," I said, if only for myself. "Seems appropriate, I suppose."

"Remember, every sacred plain once was ordinary," Nicolas said. "It takes something memorable to replace the unremarkable. Of course, it's true that Jezreel Valley is more than a quotidian stop, even in a place like Israel. This place has a long history. Most very violent, too."

"What kind of animals are here?"

"Huh?" he asked, poking around the fire again.

"The wildlife. I'm just curious. I saw some droppings earlier today... massive droppings. Like, they came from a giant. Like... from a behemoth."

"Behemoth, eh? Well, the Rephaim are from northeast of here, but they're extinct now. Probably wasn't them. Maybe it could've been the Ziz, then."

"Oh?" I said. "The Ziz?"

"Yes, the legendary *Ziz-Saday*. The Ziz is to the sky what the Behemoth is to the land, and what the Leviathan is to the sea. Are you familiar with Rabbah bar bar Hana?"

"With... what? Rabbi Barbera Hanna?"

"Rabbah *bar* bar *Hana*. He was a Jew who lived shortly after the common era started. He braved many voyages and recorded all of them, no matter how fantastical they seemed. He wrote one story about the Ziz: he and his shipmates were at sea when they saw a large bird in the ocean. They figured that for a bird to be standing there, the sea was very shallow at that point and, being overwhelmed with heat, they decided to anchor their ship and cool off in the water. But a voice from heaven warned them not to harbor there and swim, for a carpenter's axe had been dropped in this same water seven years ago, and it still had not hit the bottom: *not* because of the water's depth, but because a creature was turbulently swashing about below. Then the beast emerged

347

from the water, and it was a massive monster with the body and legs of a lion, but also the wings of an eagle. The crew reported that, as it flew away, the Ziz's wingspan blotted out the sun."

"Hmm," I considered the story. "That's a bit too... Kookian. Even for me. I have some pictures of what I saw, if you want to see it."

"Do you? You took pictures of shit?"

"Yeah, here!" I boasted as I pulled up the camera roll on my phone.

"Ohhh, these droppings," Nicolas said as his eyes widened. "You want to know what animal dropped this?"

"Yes, I have to know. Was it the Ziz?"

"Hmm, unfortunately, no, I can't confirm that this came from the Ziz. But I do know what animal this came from."

"What animal?" I hemmed, holding my breath.

"Cow."

"Cow?" I whimpered.

"Yes. Have you ever heard of a 'cow pie?' Well, this came from a cow. This is a cow pie."

"Oh, well, it's really big, right? Like, this must've come from a *really* big cow?"

"Sure," Nicolas pandered. "I guess the cows are pretty big around here." A brief silence ensued, then Nicolas added, "You have a big imagination, Danger."

"Thanks," I said, though I was pretty sure that wasn't a compliment. "You know, it was my big imagination that brought me here in the first place."

"*Ohohhhh*?" he eddied like a fish who knew there was a hook in the worm, but took the bait anyway because he's a very polite fishy.

"Are you familiar with the religious significance of this place? Of Megiddo?"

"That it's the spot of the end times battle? Sure, I'm familiar."

"I don't like to go advertising this, but many years ago, I felt God call me to this place. To become acquainted with the land. In case, you know, an apocalyptic battle does break out in my lifetime."

Nicolas remained silent.

"It's been many years since I've talked about this. I hear how... *other-realm-ly*... it sounds as I say it. And it stirs up a lot of... feelings, I guess. Just... stirs up stuff for me."

Nicolas abided in his silence.

"I don't know why I felt the need to say that," I continued to spew words to fill the awkward silence. "It's actually been a long time since I've really thought about this stuff, to be honest. And I don't know why I shared it. I guess just being on the battlefield where it supposedly happens..."

I looked at Nicolas who almost seemed uncomfortable now, and realized I needed to just shut up and quit digging myself a bigger grave.

"...I guess it just excited me. Nevermind about it."

"Hmm," Nicolas finally spoke, stroking his fluffy beard like he had become a Shaolin sensei in deep thought. "Does not the prophet say, 'woe is the man who longs for the day of the Lord, for that day will be darkness, not light. It's as if you've fled from a lion.' "

"Or a mini-lion."

"What?"

"Nothing," I said, now fully embarrassed by talking too much. "Nevermind."

"You may have heard of it," Nicolas goaded, "but Jerusalem Syndrome is this weird mind thing where people come to Jerusalem and, by the time they leave, they're convinced that they're the Messiah. You may be tapping into something similar."

I nodded. What he was saying was possible. The fools of prophecy.

"Danger, do you still believe that you've been called to be a part of the end times?"

I exhaled deeply. I guess I hadn't thought about it in such explicit terms in a long time. It was a decision point; I couldn't skirt the question.

After calculating my thoughts, I finally responded.

"No. I don't."

"Just enough to travel to Israel and make sure that a trip to Megiddo was on the ticket."

"I'm not here as a tourist," I told Nicolas. "At least, not primarily. I was here for research."

"Researching what?"

"The conflict," I said. "Specifically, the trauma of it all."

"*Mmm*," Nicolas contemplated. "And I bet Israelis were hard to talk to about that?"

"Yes," I said, surprised that he would inherently know that. "Israelis would sometimes open up about the conflict, but not trauma. Palestinians were a little more open."

"Israelis are distrusting people, and I say that as an Israeli. We've had a lot of betrayal. Palestinians don't mind talking about trauma as much because they *want* to relive trauma because it's not resolved yet. At least not for them. It's hard to make meaning out of something you can't wrap your mind around. They're still under a thumb, and remember, I'm saying that as an Israeli."

I wished I had interviewed Nicolas. I didn't have any more of my consent forms. He was way too old for my target demographic, anyway.

"So, you came to Israel to see if you were going to fight in a war, and then wrapped your visit up in some other purpose so it seemed less illogical," Nicolas said. "But a piece of you still wanted to see if it was true."

I was a little offended, at least until I considered the possibility of what he was saying.

"Hmm. I think, maybe. Do I wish it was real? Sure. There's meaning in it if it's true. And if there's any chance that it might have been true – well, I suppose it was worth checking out."

"But now you can have confidence?"

"Confidence that I'm not special? Sure," I nodded. "Reality bites."

"Oh, but why do you think you know what reality is? Humans don't get to see reality, man," Nicolas said, finally revealing his full inner hippie. "We think we do. You see those stars hanging above? A certain number of those don't even exist. Not only do they not exist, but we don't even have the right to know which ones don't exist. Loads of them have dripped away before our very perceptions. Danger, you have heard 'mazel tov,' yeah?"

"Of course," I said. "From Jewish weddings and whatnot."

"Right. Jewish weddings. In Hebrew, though, it's more than a word. It's a potent picture. It's even used in the Bible."

"The Bible? Really? I don't think I recall that."

"It's in Job, near the back. When God is interrogating Job, He asks him, 'Job, can you lead the constellations in their proper season?' Because that's important. Even stars have their anointed appointments. *Mazel tov* itself just means 'good constellation,' like 'good luck.' You'd stop there in English, but in Hebrew, 'Mazel tov' is thought to be related to this verb, 'to flow down.' The concept of *mazal* is rooted in the belief that our fate is predetermined by the stars, or even just their positions at the time of our birth. *Tov* means 'good,' and again, in English, we stop there. In Hebrew, it is a goodness that can only be seen from God alone. So the idea is that our lives' most significant moments are paired with the positioning of the stars, that they flowed down to us in that moment to present us with God's goodness. Danger: I say to you, *mazel tov*. May fortune and destiny drip drip *drip* from the stars."

"Are you Kabbalah?" I asked him.

"*What* is Kabbalah?" he asked.

Uh. You're the Israeli, aren't you? Don't tell me you don't know this.

"Danger, if you're asking me 'have I received something?' Then most certainly. Yes. I have."

I nodded. I didn't understand.

He kept talking.

"We might say 'the star rose' as an idiom, but all we purely see is *the light from the star*," he differentiated. "For us to see the light, it's traveled far and wide, but looking at a star is like seeing a light to the past. Whenever you look into the night sky, you can marvel at the star, but what you don't know is that it could be dead. Sure, most of them still exist, but not all of them. Some of them actually died hundreds of years ago, and we just don't know it because the last of its light hasn't reached us yet. So we get caught in this in-between where we don't know if we're looking at an actual star or just its light. Let me ask you, at what point during the day can we most see the galaxy?"

"I mean... that's night."

"Exactly. Only in darkness are stars revealed. Only when it's night can we see the rest of the universe. Why curse the darkness when it allows us to see the light? Why say that we see most clearly during the day? We see *our* world during the day, and then we sleep when the *rest of the galaxy* is on display. How egocentric of us."

"Well, you have to understand the micro to see the macro, right? Perception informs reality, at least a little."

"Why not both, though? Why are we so focused on it being one or the other? Can't we just live in the tension? Danger, did you know the Jewish day doesn't start at midnight?"

"I do know that," I said, flexing my pecs just a little. "The day actually begins at sunset."

"Right. When the sun is halfway gone, that's the actual beginning of the day in Israel."

What?!? I thought it was when you can see three stars?!

"Elie Wiesel has a good quote on this," Nicolas continued. "He says something like, 'Man's tragedy is he can't distinguish night from day. He says at night what should only be uttered in day.'"

Ugh. Just when you think you understand how night works, along comes Elie Wiesel to shake everything up.

"Exactly," I said, concealing the fact that I was actually befuddled. I wasn't really sure what would be okay to say during the day that would be inappropriate after the sun's gone down. Is the answer *"you sure are prettier in this light?"*

"It's funny," Nicolas said, corking my mental expedition for Wiesel's punchline. "But, the starbright moon cloaks the entire universe, from our view. We can't see the very source of the moon's light. Or, as it's been said, *'moonlight drowns out all but the brightest stars.'*"

"Who says that?" I asked him. It didn't sound biblical, or Talmudic, or even poetic enough to repeat.

"That's Tolkien," he said, then clarified as if there were two of them, "JRR Tolkien."

Ugh. What is it with this place and Lord of the Rings*?*

"So," Nicolas continued, "you can't say 'the world is 'dark' or 'the world is light,' because both realities exist at different times – and at least twice a day, they exist together. There's something to be said about that time in-between the night and the day, when we get a little of both. We were meant to live in that tension between the star and the light. How could it be just one or the other when both are such intense parts of our existence? The star needs the light, the light needs the star. They work off each other. If you're a star, it might be easy to say you're more important than the light, but if you're the light, well, of course you're going to think the offspring of the star is more important. Especially if the light believes the star might be dead. And the further the light travels from the star, the less important they believe each to be to the other. But they were both designed by God to serve a purpose, and they're serving it. For... well, are you religious?"

Am I religious? It's a good question. *I think I am?* Because if you're anything like me, you were born in the twilight of the 20th century, a time when religion became whitewashed. Christianity became almost as much of a political identity as a faith. Islam became a "religion of violence" because of terror sects in the 1970s. And Judaism is a rallying cry for Israelis in the post-Shoah era. But is that really *religion*, per se?

"Are you religious, Danger?" Nicolas repeated his question, splitting my eloquent soliloquy.

Oops. He had been actually fishing for an answer.

"Yes," I responded.

"May I guess? Christian?"

"Yes," I said, puffing my chest with unbiblical pride, for I was a religious minority for once. "I believe in Yeshua."

"We see a star. He sees galaxies. Consider the thematic tensions that exist even in your religion. By faith, by works. Forgiven, but sinful. Already, but not yet. A foot in heaven, the other on earth. Healed and rescued, but needing healing and rescue. Prayers answered, but in silence. Out of the silence, music. Out of uncertainty, promise. A conqueror, but a servant. Unpredictable, but reliable. Human, but divine. Unglorified, but sanctified. Out of depravity, hope. Out of darkness, light. And you know, we share a story that have many of these principles: think about the story of Jacob."

"Which one? When he tricked his way into his birthright? Or his dream with the staircase to heaven? Or the bit about when he wrestled an angel?"

"Was it an angel? Is that what the text says?"

"If you're asking... I'm guessing not?"

"It's a mystery. We don't know if it was man, or God, or angel. And are we supposed to know for sure, or are we supposed to sit in that mystery? All we know is Jacob had this ineluctable wrestling match until daybreak, and then the mystery figure says, 'it's time to let go. Let go, Jacob.' And Jacob says, 'I will not, not until you give me a blessing.' So the mystery man asks, 'what's your name?' Jacob responds, but the mystery man says, 'You're no longer Jacob. Now you're Israel, because you've wrestled with God and humans, and prevailed.' Did he necessarily 'beat' God? No, but he did refuse to stop fighting, to stop wrestling until it was time. Jacob embraced the uncomfortable; he didn't even know who he was wrestling with, but he assented anyway. And in the midst of that uncertainty, Israel was born."

"A small price to pay, I suppose, given that it cost Jacob his hip," I quipped, trying to showcase my own biblical knowledge.

"Jacob spent his in-tact life wandering with no *real* reason for his being. Why did God dislocate Jacob's hip before sending him on his mission? I have no idea. I've spent many hours wondering this. But know this, Danger: luxated hip, meaningful life. His suffering was connected to his calling. I think he was fine limping around with purpose."

I was outmatched. I didn't dare add another thoughtpiece to the conversation, lest I also believe that I could've outperformed Robin Williams in an improv competition.

The fire crackled, exerting itself for just one more evanescent breath of life. Soon the valley would be replete with darkness, the same tenebrae that the original disciples fought through to find Christ's body on Easter morning. It's often thought that the women arrived to the tomb at first light, but that's not what the Bible records: Joanna and the Marys left at dusk, when Sabbath had just concluded. They traveled during the gloaming – the darkest flash of twilight – knowing they couldn't even get into the tomb because the stone blocked their way. Why not just wait until first light, which would beget so much more sense? In those days, back before electricity, twilight was the time of day that it was hardest to navigate and hardest to survive. Ah, but it's always been the hour when divine lilacs and astral lavenders compete for primacy atop earth's canopy, that ephemeral burst commissioned not by the lowly Sistine, but by the sixth day itself!

"We spend our entire existence where the light and the darkness meet," Nicolas added one more thing. "It's okay to live in that tension, Danger."

The women fought through the darkness for the honor to sit alone with Yeshua in the cold, despised tension rather than sit with Him in the warm, alluring light like everyone else was intending to do. It was the final yawn of death, not the invitation of the light, that drew them in. And it was *in the tension* that the women found the empty tomb.

A quick moment of silence followed before I tried capping our conversation.

"Thank you, Nicolas. And you should know something: I am fond of your name. It is one that is near and dear to me."

"Is that so?"

"Yes. I once knew a Nicholas. I still kind of do, sometimes. He had wisdom, like you, and he wasn't afraid to be afraid."

"Maybe you are a little bit like this Nicholas too, wandering the valley of Megiddo without a real plan."

"Thanks for saying it," I told him. "That means something to me."

A longer silence, then Nicolas's face scrunched so vigorously that his wrinkles now highlighted every one of his aged cracks as he beamed, *"Boker or!"*

"What does that mean?" I asked, unable to help but smile back at his sudden whimsy.

As if he an amateur actor spouting his scripted line seconds before his actual cue, Nicolas pointed to the hills and said, "The light has come." A few seconds later, the first rays of the sun actually broke the plain, and Nicolas proclaimed, "Twilight is over. We're not in darkness anymore."

"At Noon today," Nicolas continued, "you will remember this moment to be darkness. When you come into twilight from the light, it seems dark. Even then, I will not say the day is done, nor bid the stars farewell. But if you're coming into twilight from the dark, it seems light. In Bereshit, it's not called 'light' and 'darkness.' It's called 'light' and 'less light.' Greater *Ma'or* and Lesser *Ma'or*. Together, they are the 'two great lights.' The 'lesser light' is still great, for how else will the greater reveal its fully glory if not contrasted by darkness? This is why I don't understand why Christians celebrate Christmas morning. All evidence points to the miracle happening after sundown. Your Scripture says He was born in the evening, does it not? There's beauty that 'the Light of the World' would be born in darkness: 'the people who walked in darkness' will only understand the light's greatness because of their knowledge of what it means to live in the dark. And be sure, there are places that the light does not reach at all. Valleys, caves. You must get out of that place as soon as you can, until you at least get an idea again of what the light looks like. Even if it's just *less light*."

> "Holy is twilight -
> the realm of in-between.
> And so our sages taught:
> pray in the moments when light and darkness touch.
> We are all twilight people.
> May the sacred in-between... illumine our way
> to the God who transcends all
> boundaries and definitions.
> Blessed are You, God of all,
> who brings on the twilight."
> - Rabbi Reuben Zellman

Nicolas would perhaps be interested to hear that I've so often found myself chasing this dark. In my first year at college, even before I was Danger, I'd equip myself with a pocket knife and explore the dark forest surrounding campus. I'd follow the stars (and, okay, a woodchipped path) in spiritual contemplation, which just seemed like a thing mystics do before they become mystics. But chiefly, I did it because – like most students – those woods terrified me. I wanted to face those fears until the horror of the forest wizened to the caliber of a peanut. And it worked: the dreadful woods quickly metamorphosed into my dearest ally that year. (I'd have never considered crossing through Megiddo Forest without this experience.) I've forced myself into learning that the darkness must be pursued, not feared. People often think that my name sprung from something I've done. No. It's about where I've been called to go.

But maybe I've taken it too far. Maybe I've started to choose the shadows over the light.

"*Akedah*: God provides," Nicolas interrupted my dark thoughts. "Abraham gets to the saddest mountain of his life, and God provides the ram. You get thrown into a cold valley, and God provided a fire. You have no food to break your fast, and, well, we will have breakfast for you in a couple hours. But you may want to sleep until then, if you are tired. It is comfortable right now, but a hot day is in chase. By next weekend, such days will be cold. Maybe too cold to gather."

Nicolas seized a stick and prodded the dying embers as the fire coughed up a single flame, a promise that life could be unearthed somewhere here. As he stabbed the pyre, he alternated between whistling and humming an unfamiliar song. No doubt it was just another pop song in this country, but it landed on my ears like an ancient, hidden melody.

Covered in Nicolas's blanket, I laid my head back on my bag and passed out before the sun cuffed the nearby creek.

August 3, 2020

> I have bad news.
> Well bad news for me. It doesn't really affect you.

What's wrong?

> We were preparing for our third fertility treatment. Joanna went in for an ultrasound to certify everything's working as they should. And that's when the doctors found a cyst on her ovary.

What.
No way
Also, it does affect me because I care about what you care about.

> They're pretty sure it's not malignant or anything.

So they just randomly happened to check the one body part that she had a cyst on?

> The fertility medications spawned it. That's why it was on her ovary. It's not our first time dealing with this kind of thing. When I was in Afghanistan, her hormones were so out-of-whack that the gyno said she had a tumor.

What happened then?

> We trusted God that it would go away, and when she got her brain MRI, they couldn't find a tumor and her hormones suddenly settled in.

What do you do now?

> Now she goes on birth control to shrink the cyst.

So you have to go on anti-fertility treatments because of your fertility treatments?

> Yea.

That's really a bummer. I'm sorry.

> "Some will win. Some will lose. Some were born to sing the blues." And everyone assumes they're gonna be the winners, nobody wants to believe they're the loser or the party that ends up singing the blues, but here I am, realizing that's my lot.

That is really pessimistic

> That's too bad, because it's one of my more optimistic thoughts

How would that be optimistic?

> Because at least then my life would be helpful to someone else. Because you can't have winners without losers.

That's still a bummer.

> You wanna know my purpose? This is my lot in life: applying to jobs I'll never get, writing books that will never get read, and watching my dogs die while I can't leave a legacy of children.

You don't know that any of that is true. At least one person, that Palestinian woman you told me about, is relying on you to come through. To dig deep, to tell her story. This task was appointed to you. And if you don't find a way, no one will. Also: did you know that The Great Gatsby wasn't a New York Times best seller?

> Neither was Wreck-It Ralph

‏ר כ‎

December 30, 2000

Claire and Umi sat on the Anastas House balcony, each sipping their Turkish coffee on an unusually warm morning.

"There used to be nothing to look at on this balcony," Claire explained to Umi, "but now we get to people-watch every day. Even if they happen to be carrying weapons and are watching us in turn."

Claire leaned over the balcony and smiled at a Turai looking up at her.

"Hello, young man," she called below, waving. The Turai, unsure if he was allowed to respond in like, turned away and pretended he didn't see her.

Claire sat back down and giggled to herself. "They don't know what to do with themselves, Umi."

"*Qassam!*" Umi screamed, interrupting Claire and pointing at an object hastening their way.

The Qassam: a crude rocket created in Gaza that was propelled with common household ingredients like sugar and fertilizer, with the nitrate in its head exploding upon impact. It had first made its way from Gaza to the West Bank and, most recently and urgently, was now making its way to Claire and Umi.

Claire could certainly jump out of the way in time, but knowing Umi wouldn't make it, Claire stayed seated and chose to share whatever fate befell Umi, too.

Claire sputtered, "God will protect us," and the sensation of fire and ice descended upon her. She stared the Qassam down as it

well Wreck-It Ralph wasn't a book

well that's 2 strikes then.

What I'm saying is someday that list won't matter. So write what you should be writing.

I have a hope that what I write will someday resonate with people, but if that happens, it won't be in my lifetime. Every day that I wake up, I feel like I'm writing to someone who hasn't been born yet. Some future generation I'll never get to meet. As far as today's crop is concerned, my name is writ in water.

If you can't appreciate who you are, maybe you can at least appreciate who you aren't.

It's just hard to appreciate when you get to die with the same amount of relevancy you were born with.
I think that's what the obituary gets to say about me. "The no-hit wonder, as relevant in his final year as he was in his first." It probably refers to me as an "Oklahoma man," which makes it even worse.

You don't seem okay really. This isn't the same Danger I've been talking to it feels like.

Sorry. I had a dream a few days ago that's messing with my head. I've kind of gotten pessimistic since that dream.

I wouldn't dwell on it. So, maybe you've heard this before, you know with you being a psychologist and all, but dreams aren't real.

It wasn't what happened in the dream, it's something I said. And the thing I said is messing me up because I realized it's true.

Fine I'll bite. What was the dream

My family suspected Joanna was pregnant. They thought I was acting unusual, avoiding conversation with them so I could announce it in a special way at the right time. My brother convinced my parents that we were hiding it, so my mom excitedly tried pressuring me to announcing our pregnancy. Except it wasn't the case. We weren't pregnant. I was avoiding them because I was depressed. And in my dream, I told them "I'm much closer to killing myself than I am to being a father."

Oh

"I'm much closer to killing myself than I am to being a father."
I keep catching myself thinking about this phrase, the truth in it.

I still stick by what I said. Don't let what happens (or what gets said) in dreams dominate who you are in waking life. God gives you plenty of reason to not be depressed.

Your advice may be true, but it's harsh. You can't pretend you're happy to get around the heartache. Don't tell me to "count my blessings" as if that's the mathematical formula to shortcutting my grief. Many Christians (and probably Jews) have killed themselves over feeling like they've failed God by being depressed.

I'm sorry, I didn't mean it that way

I know, you're fine. I just think that a lot of people forget that Biblical heroes suffered from depression too.

Who are you thinking about?

357

approached, and just as it reached Claire's property, the rocket's trajectory dramatically weakened, and as if it was slapped out of the sky, the rocket tip tilted towards the sky, hung in the air for but a moment, and then came crashing back to earth. It had enough momentum that it still hit the window directly below Claire and Umi, but its velocity was so weak that it didn't even crack the glass.

The rocket pounced on the dirt at the foot of the house and dust billowed around the crashsite while several Tzahal jumped onto a Sufa 3 and headed west, shooting towards Aida Camp as they seemed to pursue a ghost.

Umi dropped her coffee, the mug breaking into three pieces, as she bitterly wept. Claire reached over and rubbed her shoulder, but the consolation wasn't helping any, so Claire set down her own coffee and instead embraced Umi, who began shaking in Claire's arms.

"Hey, hey," Claire consoled Umi, as if soothing a terrified child. "Look at me. Look at me."

Umi kept her eyes shut, barely allowing the tears to even seep through the cracks of her eyelids.

"Look at me," Claire requested once more. Umi's cloudy eyes looked up into hers, spilling a backlog of tears down her cheeks, and Claire declared, "Fear not, for behold, the Lord is with us."

Umi leaned over the balcony to glance at the impotent rocket's final resting place, then she began crying again – albeit less violently – so Claire asked one final question before enveloping her mother with her arms until the remainder of Umi's reservoir drained.

"Whom shall we fear?"

king David, for one. Moses, for two.
(I know, I can already hear you, "you're not Moses or King David, Danger.")

Actually, was closer to saying I don't think Moses was depressed.

Read Psalm 90 and tell me Moses wasn't aware of the hopelessness of life. But there's also whoever wrote the book of Lamentations. And for sure Elijah. Elijah killed the false prophets at God's bequest, only to be threatened by Queen Jezebel for doing so. Elijah was so scared, so faithless, that he ducked into the wilderness. Not just the tip of the wilderness, but burrowed in a full day's journey so that he could die in peace. And when he got there, he asked God to kill him.

Have you ever heard "hang in the balance?" Well that's you. The way you talk isn't the person I used to know. You're hanging in this tension and there's no way to tell which way you'll fall.

Okay.

Are you seeing a professional? Like a counselor

I've got a meeting with my psychiatrist two weeks from today.

You know what else is in two weeks?!?!?

No?

Your birthday!

True. My appointment is actually the day after my birthday.
I'll be 34, reaching the earthly age that Yeshua never got to.

He died at 33?

So they say.
I wonder if Yeshua knew He'd be childless. He knew about the cross ahead of time. Surely He knew His seed would be snuffed?

son of god, father of none.

Sorry to be such a bummer lately. I don't mean to be. I'm just in this existential vacuum right now. Maybe the birthday party with my shrink will help.

Maybe she'll speak some words of wisdom

Like let it be, let it be?

No. That's mother Mary. I want your psych to say something else.
"Go back on your meds, go back on your meds."

OUT OF THE BELLY OF SHEOL

> "Enjoy life with the wife whom you love,
> all the days of your
> vain life that he has given you under the sun,
> because that is your portion in life,
> for there is no work or thought or knowledge or wisdom in Sheol,
> to which you are going.
> A living dog is better than a dead lion."
> ~ Ecclesiastes 9:9-10,4 ESV

"Here comes the sun, doo-dun-doo-doo! Here comes the sun, and I say, it's alright..."

It was late morning when I woke up to the sound of singing in the valley of Megiddo. I lifted my eyes towards Megiddo Hill, though I was so deep in the valley that I couldn't see any part of it. Even if I had a sightline to the hill, I wouldn't be able to really decipher it without my glasses. But when I reached for the lone pair that I had brought, I realized they were crushed.

"Shoot!" I gasped, clicking the lens in and out of its socket, which no longer fit.

"Danger, you're up!" Nicolas cheered. "Here, take my cup and get yourself some coffee."

I took the cup from Nicolas and lifted my eyes towards Megiddo Hill,

"Nicolas," I said, gesturing with my head to the unseen mountain just outside the valley. "Who owns that hill?"

"Tel Megiddo?" he miffed, almost annoyed by the question.

"No," I corrected, "the smaller hill near it."

"Oh, I don't know, Danger. Maybe the kibbutz? Maybe the historical society?"

"I want to buy it," I declared, like I just landed on a vacant property while playing Monopoly.

"The hill? Why?"

"That's where I will be buried. That's where I find rest, on that hill."

"Okay," Nicolas said in his barest monotone, probably unsure why I would share that information. "You are planning your funeral arrangements today?"

"Maybe," I said, realizing how morbidly uncomfortable I was making him feel. But talking about the inevitable day where I become the king of worms in a 2.5' x 8' plotted kingdom never seemed to unsettle me like it does others around me. Death is just another path – one that we all must take. Ready or not, it's coming, and I look forward to eternity as a college student looks forward to graduation. University is good and nice and I shouldn't rush it – I can't just strut into a commencement ceremony and take part. I don't belong until I belong and do what I'm supposed to do, but I can't help but get excited about being there someday. Being with the Messiah. Being with my loved ones.

"How about you go get some coffee?" Nicolas shook up my thoughts.

I nodded, then reached for my glasses only to find one of my lenses had broken off the frame. It'd been a long time since I had sniper-capable eyesight, so the rest of this trip was going to become a blur. Frustrated, I toddled to the nearby creek to rinse my cup out. But as I leaned over the edge of the bank and submerged my cup, the mud under me gave out and tossed me into the brook. I'd thought the valley couldn't plunge me any deeper, but there I stood, sopping wet and holding a cup of slime. The moment had me realize that I'd let the invisible lethargarians of the valley seduce me into staying far too long here.

"You okay?" Nicolas called over and, to my chagrin, drew everyone's attention to this defiled Gentile whose fingers were deep in the mud, looking for a foothold.

"Nicolas," I grouch as I crawl out of the pit and hand his mucky cup back to him, "it's time for me to leave this valley. I have to get to Tel Aviv."

"What's in Tel Aviv?" he pried.

"My wife. She's getting in to Israel today. I haven't seen her in over a month."

"Yes. The valley crest is deeper than the mountain's basin, and all creation demands an escape from the grave," he says, looking me over until he realizes he said kind of a weirdo thing to say. "You must be diligent and go. How are you arriving to Tel Aviv?"

"*Uh.* I'm not sure. Do you know how far it is from here?"

"80km. Maybe less?"

"How far is that?" I asked for a translation.

"About an hour or two drive. Or about a five-minute flight on the Ziz. Or a day's journey on foot."

"Well, I'll start on foot and see what happens. Thank you, Nicolas, for all your kindness."

"Who needed the staircase?" he asked, quite randomly.

"What?" I wheezed, fully having thought we concluded our soul-searching for the weekend when I fell into that brook.

"Jacob. You mentioned Jacob's ladder last night."

Yes. I did. But now I'm wondering if the angel actually dislodged Jacob's hip, or if Jacob smacked his own thigh into oblivion to give the angel that good ol' Midwestern goodbye.

"Or, that staircase to heaven," Nicolas continued. "Who were those steps for?"

"Welp," I said, locking and loading my palm just above my thigh, "I think it was for the angels. It says they were ascending and descending the steps."

"Angels don't need rungs to get to heaven, Danger, do they? Remember what transformed Jacob into Israel," he added, endcapping our momentary-but-momentous relationship with a final nugget. "Jacob wanted to give up. He wanted to stop wrestling. Instead, he never let go. It's okay to be tired. Just don't let go."

I tepidly extended my hand to shake his, but Nicolas instead wrapped me up in his arms and offered a gentle squeeze.

"Mazel tov, Nicolas," I whinnied with a mouthful of Nicolas beard. Then, I began my ascent out of the valley. After finding the highway, I crossed westward towards Tel Aviv. I quickly dried off from my muddy tumble: the cold morning had broiled to 84°, and it felt more like Celsius than Fahrenheit.

My phone was dead, so even if there were cabs working on this Shabbat morning, I had no means to call one. I galumphed onward with my thumb extended toward the road. After a couple 5ks deep and becoming convinced that my first night reunited with Joanna was going to be spent nursing another cluster headache, a car pulled over next to me.

"Where are you going?" the driver asked.

"Tel Aviv," I explained. "I need to get to Natbag."

"My name's Ido. Hop in. I'm headed that direction; I can drop you off at the airport."

Several hours later, I found myself watching for my wife to come out of her terminal. Now, I don't really believe in soulmates. The idea is rooted in Greek mythology, that everybody has another soul they were conjoined to before birth, and then we were callously split from our other half to double the praise for the gods, fated to spend our earthly lives searching for the one we were snatched away from. Plato's *Symposium* described the concept a bit and society ran with it. But wouldn't our actual soulmate really be God Himself? Isn't the idea of an earthly "soulmate" on par with the way we "believe" there's an enamel-greedy fairy out there who checks under pillows and trades cash for children's teeth?

But as I watched my wife come out of that terminal, sporting a 50-pound teal hiking bag with her hair bouncing and a slight bend in her bowed, strawberry lips, I was reminded that if the Greeks were right about this thing – that we spend a lifetime in pursuit of our elusive soulmate – then Joanna and I were the most blessed people in the world to have found each other so early in life.

I rushed to greet her as soon as I spotted her, becoming uncharacteristically inconsiderate of strangers' personal space as I bumped my way towards the stanchion separating travelers from their retinue. She was swallowed by a group of foreigners and didn't see me, but I kept my eye on her and pressed my way onward until I could reach out and touch her fingertips. She dropped her bag to the ground, smacked her lips against mine, and then nuzzled her soft cheek against the bushy beard I'd been growing since O'Hare airport. I enfolded her in my arms and squeezed her hard enough to hear her wheeze. The moment was reminiscent of when, many years ago, I was in an airport and found myself in the most exhilarating embrace of my life with the girl of my dreams. Same hug, same person, but the girl of my dreams was now a woman, and we'd reached the Promised Land together.

After the initial excitement waned, I looked at Joanna's shirt and started cracking up.

"I thought you'd appreciate it!" she beamed.

Last May, I had bought Joanna a black t-shirt that simply reads in white lettering, "I miss my dog." For how much we travel, it seemed like the perfect gift for her, though perhaps it would've been a notch better if it said "I miss my dogs" – plural. The worst part of traveling always was leaving our dogs behind, and some trips end up not even being worth the absence from them.

"I haven't seen you wear that once!" I said. "I thought you didn't like it."

"I've been saving it for this trip," she replied with a few gravelly chuckles, pleased with her surprise.

"Are you feeling okay?" I asked.

Her face transformed from giddiness to palpable anxiety.

"Yes," she said, but it felt like she was hiding something. "I think I'm just jetlagged."

I'd been many different time zones in my lifetime and, upon exiting a terminal, only ever felt a surge of adrenaline and never once jetlag. But, to each his own. Besides, if there was something else going on, I didn't want to talk about whatever it was while taxi drivers were hawking over us.

"Well," I said, "the best thing is to just fight through it the first day. Try to forget about Tulsa time. We're on Tel Aviv time now, and it's 2pm. Do you want to see the beach?"

She lit up again, bit her lip, and nodded.

After we offloaded our bags at our hotel, I took Joanna's hand and guided her a few blocks westward. At one intersection, she closed her eyes and breathed in so deeply that it was like whatever aroma she was chasing was about to escape the vortex of her inhale. She sniffed a few more times, not unlike a bloodhound discovering the scent of funeral incense from a church down the road.

"What is it, girl? What do you smell?"

"It's not a smell," she smiled. "I *taste* something. It's the *dew of the sea*."

We headed towards the Mediterranean Sea, Joanna skipping about a bit, apparently shaking off whatever jetlag had been dogging her earlier. A flurry of salt-sprinkled air blew on us as we broached the shoreline, until we shielded ourselves behind a bakery along the beach, where I could cosher Joanna with a croissant loaded with chocolate hazelnut.

"These pastries are the best you'll ever have, trust me," I said. "It's not like U.S. bread. It won't give you any headaches from preservatives."

"A sad statement about the state of American cuisine," she said, nibbling on the end of croissant while flakes whisked away on the sea breeze.

"Have you ever heard of Jesus referred to as *the Rose of Sharon*? Well, this coast right here is what was known as *Sharon*. At least, in antiquity it was."

"But Jesus didn't minister here, right? Why is He the *Rose of Sharon* then?"

"Well, you'll get about a thousand different answers if you look that question up. But for better or less-better, He is affectionately thought by many Christians to be just that."

A mischievous gust skimmed across the sea, flitting off the waves until disembarking at the port of Jaffa solely to target Joanna's hair, bowling each strand until they plaited together across her face. She didn't seem to mind.

"Hey!" I said, pointing skyward. "You can see God's fingernail."

Joanna looked at the celestial sliver of a moon.

"Weird! It's only mid-day," she noted. Then, as if an ancient memory smacked her across the face, she squealed, "Let me see your *tattoo*!"

I pulled up my left sleeve and she placed her palm on the center of my star, then flimsily grazed the outline of the design with the tips of her indigo-glazed nails. Her polish almost matched the outline of the tattoo.

"Can I tell you about a major epiphany?" I asked her.

"Of course," she said, examining my blotchy skin instead of admiring the waves riffling onto the shores of Israel.

"The wise men were the first Gentile Christians – at least, unofficially so. When the star rose and they chased its light, God was manifesting Himself in a way that they would perceive Him. The Bible spends only a few words describing their trip 'from the east' into Jerusalem, but that's not even a good translation. The Greek word is *anatole*, meaning *'rising of light.'* It's only written 'from the east' by implication."

I looked at Joanna and saw that I was losing her here. I was being way too abstract for a person whose jetlag had her body feeling like it was a few minutes before dawn.

"Joanna, just, think about the magi's crossing. Surely they wanted to give up. Their journey was long, longer even than what it'll have taken for me to fly to Israel and back. I mean, did they question what they were doing? Did they ever feel silly for putting faith in a star? They were supposedly astrologers: Did they know their star might even be dead, its light an illusion? Whatever they felt in that time, they trusted enough in the light to lead them far from home. And they finished their journey. They were pagans, and still they understood the gravitas of the moment better than anybody in the world at that moment."

A heavy zephyr rippled over the sea and carried east into Israel, blasting into an otherwise delicate moment between my wife and me.

"Well, you ready to see something cool now?"

We rambled along the Mediterranean until we hit the port city of Jaffa.

"Jaffa is one of the oldest cities in the world, and without it, there wouldn't even be a Tel Aviv," I said, regurgitating what a tour guide told me on the first full day of my trip. "Jaffa is famous for its delicious oranges, which have thicker skin than other oranges, making it a popular item for exporting because the flavedo doesn't break in transport."

"What's flavedo?"

"I don't know," I admitted. "A tour guide said it. I think it means rind."

Joanna nodded while continuing to whittle down her croissant as we approached a restored portion of the otherwise dilapidated city – if brick-cobbled sidewalks and ancient homes can ever "go out of style," by definition.

"But the export it's most famous for was actually profitable *because* it could be broken, *and* it was on the opposite end of the color wheel!" I exclaimed, finding myself deviate from my first tour guide's way of describing the city's history and turning it into my own teaching. "Do you know what color I'm talking about?"

"Is it… purple?" she deduced.

"Yes! *Purple!*" I said. My tour was *way* cooler. *Way* more interactive.

"*Aww*, Romy's color!" she exclaimed, her eyes constricting at the edges.

"Purple is naturally rare," I continued my spiel. "In ancient times – like when Yeshua had an abode here on earth – the only way to winnow purple was to crush these snails. *Murex snails*. Jaffa was famous for having these snails, and they'd smash these poor bugs using a pestle, and they'd use the mucus to dye clothes. As such, it was rare, expensive, and only associated with royalty."

"Yeshua?" Joanna pressed me.

"Oh, that's *Jesus*," I told her. "That's what they call Jesus around here. Or, at least it's what I call Him around here."

"Wait. So they *don't* call Him Yeshua?"

"No, not really," I explained. "But that's how you'd pronounce it here."

"But they call Him Jesus?"

"Yes," I said.

"Okay," she shook her head. "Go on."

I took her by the hand and showed her Andromeda's rock, where the future queen from Greek mythology had been chained to a rock when Perseus, fresh off killing Medusa and still holding her head by the monster's snakey hair, saw the beautiful (and naked – it's worth mentioning she was naked) woman and rescued her from a sea monster. It's also the site where Jonah sailed off before being swallowed by a whale.

But what I wanted to show Joanna wasn't rooted in mythology: it was a narrative that had a lot more historical evidence than either of the other two claim-to-fame stories from the port city.

"There's another story you should know about Jaffa," I told Joanna, which seemed to pique her interest as we sidestepped through the labyrinthine corridors of the ancient city. "In the New Testament – in Acts – the Apostle Peter was brought to a corpse. She had been a lowly woman – probably a widow – who was renowned for... coat- and shirt-making."

"Probably because she imbued them with purple."

"Hmm," I pondered, "I guess there's a good chance of that, huh? But seeing her dead body, Peter bent over and breathed in her ear, '*arise*,' and she rose from the dead. And what do you think he did right after that?"

"Uh. Maybe, eat some of the chocolate bread here?"

"Maybe," I snickered. "But then after that, he took a nap. And you probably have heard this story, but it's important to hear again right now."

I stopped in front of a home that had the words "*Simon der Gerbe*" across the crown of the front door's archway. Tourists aren't allowed inside the house – especially someone like me, who couldn't even get into the tourist hotspots you *are* allowed into – but it's not the inside of the house that matters anyway, it's its rooftop.

"Joanna, do you believe that Yeshua – Jesus – died for your sins on the cross, adopting you as a child of God and granting you access to God's kingdom?"

"Yes," she said with confidence.

"And if you were to have been alive on the day that Christ ascended to heaven, and you confronted Peter, John, and the other apostles, and you told them that you believed you were adopted as a child of God and granted access to God's kingdom, do you think they would have believed you?"

"I do."

"How would you have convinced them?"

"I believe God would have helped convince them. I would have just explained, 'I'm a Christian, like you.'"

"*Christian*," I emphasized the word she used. "That wasn't even a term they used then. They had no label. They were 'Jews who followed the Master' or simply 'Followers of The Way.' A group of stray dogs who didn't even have a corner among outcasts. You think they'd have accepted you? How would you have responded if they said, 'You're not a Jew. You can't be one of us?'"

"Come on. I don't think that's what they'd actually say. What would you say to them?"

"I don't know, honestly. If I told them that I believed myself to be a disciple of Christ, and the harbingers of the Christian faith told me I wasn't allowed? Man, I don't know how I'd take that."

"Is that what they actually were telling people?"

"Who can know what they actually said? But here are the facts that we know: Christ died. And then over 500 people claimed to have seen Yeshua turning up – physically – at random intervals for over a month. And then thousands of Jews began to refer to themselves as 'Followers of The Way,' which we now call Christianity. But… no recorded Gentiles. Not even one, at least not for almost a decade."

"That's surprising. A decade?"

"A decade. Or, at least, almost a decade. Most scholars believe Christ died at age 33 around A.D. 30, and then Peter traveled to Jaffa to pray for a Jewish widow's healing around A.D. 39. And immediately after the miracle, Peter visited his house. *Simon the Tanner*. This house in front of you. And he took a nap at his friend's house."

Joanna turned her head towards the door, reading its post.

"While Peter napped, he had a dream. A sheet was lowered from heaven, and on the sheet was every kind of animal – including animals that Jews were allowed to eat, and many not-so-kosher animals. The Lord spoke to Peter and told him to eat the animals, and Peter refused, thinking it was a test. 'No, Lord,' he said, 'I've never eaten anything unclean.' He thought he passed the test. But instead, the Lord rebuked him and said, 'What the Lord has made clean, do not call unclean.'

"Joanna, this was a moment of reckoning for Peter, one that's often lost on Christians. We don't appreciate the immensity of what happened here. If you want to be a reasonable person, the most important quality that you have to have is the recognition that you might be wrong about something, even if it's a truth you've hung onto your whole life. And Peter was faced with a most challenging idea that would rock The Way forever, an idea that he feared would be received as blasphemy: Christ died for non-Jews, too.

"And Peter ate from the sheet as instructed – foods that he had *never* eaten his entire life out of religious piety. Moments later, a messenger came to Peter – in real life now, or at least what we like to call 'reality.' And the messenger said, 'Peter, come: there is a Gentile who was told by an angel that you have something to tell him.' So Peter traveled north about 40 miles, sought the man in Caesarea, preached the Gospel to him, and baptized him. It's true, Joanna: the magi were the first *unofficial* Gentile Christians. But this Italian man – Cornelius – became the first *official* Gentile Christian."

"So, between the time of Jesus and the time of Cornelius, all Christians were Jewish?"

"Exclusively. Do I know what the early disciples would've said to you if you told them you were a Christian? I don't. But I do know that after this happened, Peter returned home and the apostles ridiculed him for even eating with a Gentile – they didn't even know that Peter had ceremonially accepted the Gentile into the fold of Christ! A non-Jew being accepted into the Christian faith was as absurd as a non-Muslim being accepted into Mecca."

I surveyed Joanna's countenance to see if my analogy landed. But scanning her face had me a bit windblown; I think maybe I'd forgotten how beautiful she is, her ocean blues sparkling even more than the wispy waves that were frothing the stone embankment below us.

But I'm a tour guide today, and tour guides don't fall in love with their tourists!

After regaining my balance, I punched my point with a bonus reference in case it had fallen flat.

"It was as unorthodox as if a Chicago Bears fan was accepted at a Packers game at Lambeau Field!"

I'm the coolest tour guide ever.

"So, Peter's standing before the crowd of Messianic Jews and boldly explains what happened in the alcove right above you; he explains that Yeshua's atonement covered not only Jews, but Gentiles."

> "The opposite of a fact is a falsehood, but the opposite of one profound truth may very well be another profound truth."
> - Niels Bohr

Joanna looked up, almost as if Peter might still be nestled in the perch above us.

"Joanna, take this in," I stopped and inhaled deeply, bidding her to do the same. Even though it hadn't rained recently, the musky air carried a hint of petrichor, perhaps from the Mediterranean's sea spit. "*This* is hallowed ground. Yeshua died on the cross and was resurrected, which created a Christian sect of Judaism. But where you look now? This is the spot where your faith, and my faith – a Christianity for the nations – was birthed."

" 'To the Jew first, then to the Gentile,' " she said, reciting a passage from the Apostle Paul that was written about 20 years after Peter's dream.

"Exactly," I said. "That's what that means. In hindsight, it's easy to say, 'of course Christianity is for everyone.' But that wasn't the belief for a long, long time. It is an act of grace that we would be included in this reward. The messianic promise to the Jews became a promise for us, too. One faith. One Gospel. One baptism. One child."

At my last statement, Joanna's anxiety-oppressed demeanor returned as her shoulders slumped and she looked to the cobbled ground.

"I need to tell you something."

My heart dropped.

"What's wrong, Jo?"

"Nothing," she said as she smiled and her sole dimple came back out to play. "Nothing's wrong. It's just, what have we been praying for every day for the past – *oh*, I don't even know how long anymore."

"Uh, well, our family's health. And... *babies*."

"My dogs aren't the only thing I've missed this week," she said, pointing out her shirt again.

"What do you mean?"

"I missed my period."

כ

August 15, 2020

Yom hu'ledet sameach!

Come again?

Happy birthday!

Thanks. It's tomorrow though.

Not in Israel. Israel, it's right now.

I guess that's true.

Is something wrong?

Today was not good.
Today was really bad.
I took my "don't kill yourself" medicine.
Something broke today.

Wtf happened?

I'll tell the story and you won't even think it's a big deal. Today we all hiked in the forest. JoJo, Sidney, Shadrach, and Samus, and me.
Bad idea all-around. Base heat was like 97 degrees Fahrenheit

Idk what that even is

Sorry. It's like mid-30s for you.
Yeah, 36 degrees Celsius. Looked it up.
Anyway, we brought Romy like we often do on walks.
The urn was packed into a backpack I was carrying.
I bent over to pick something off the ground, and the urn fell out of the bag and crashed onto a rock

Oh no

It was awful. I fell to my knees and began crying. Like, serious weeping.

Is the urn okay?

It's functional. No apparent cracks. But it's pretty scratched up. Not at all what I'd like the shell for a loved one to be. So I cried out "I can't even keep your urn safe!", and just sat there in the forest, bawling all over the urn while Joanna rubbed my back. She kept saying over and over, "Romy's fine. She's not in there, Nate. She's not in there." And Sidney was so stressed because she knew something was really wrong.
And I didn't stop crying.
The rest of the walk, I cried.
On the drive home, I cried.
I got home, I cried.
I was crying for hours, and it reminded me, yeah, I actually am a lot closer to killing myself than I am to being a dad. And that thought kept hitting me hard, so I broke open the seal on the "oh shit button" and took it and it stonewalled me. But now I'm coherent again and I hate life again and I just want to take one more pill.

Don't do that

Abni and Ebnahty were huddled beneath their kitchen table, crying as they held their hands over the back of their heads, which were pressed to the floorboards. Their parents were fortifying the two of them with chairs, books, and anything else that could be used as a makeshift barricade in case another errant bullet came through the window.

In the weeks prior, fighting between Israelis and Palestinians had intensified as Arabs more readily had gotten their hands on weapons and often preemptively struck against the Tzahal. Once in war only by proxy, Bethlehem was now very much an active participant in the intifada, and on this particular night, the Israeli-Palestinian infighting had escalated each enduring minute over the course of several hours. It wasn't just the usual crossfire, but dozens of bombs had been heard going off around Bethlehem. The Anastas family had been eating dinner upstairs when the window cracked once by a stray bullet, then was completely shot out.

Claire clutched Zuji's shirt and pulled the both of them to their knees, then yelled to him over the sound of the explosions at Aida.

"Should we go downstairs?" she shouted.

"No," he yelled back, shaking his head. "There is way too much fighting in the streets. If we…"

THUMP. THUMP. THUMP.

A loud banging interrupted Zuji's train of thought.

"I think someone is at the door," Claire said, though it was hard to be sure that it wasn't a military vehicle turning over or even a dull explosion.

I know. I'm supposed to be a psychologist, remember? I get that that's how addictions start. I'm just saying, something broke today. And this is me here, telling you I don't know what the next steps are.

I literally don't know what to say to you. I don't have words.

I'm so tired, Esther. So so tired. It's not the medication, either. I feel like I can't even get air in my lungs anymore. It's been going on for months and it's just destroying me this week.

Has this been going on for awhile? Were you tired before the pandemic?

Yes. I actually had been going to doctors for awhile, like a couple years, trying to figure out why I've been so fatigued. Had a surgery to correct a deviated septum because they thought I wasn't getting enough oxygen, but I felt the same after.

Is there anything that makes it worse?

It happens especially when I get sad. It's like the oxygen is leaking out of the room. I just can't get enough air whatever I do, so I just slow my breathing until it passes.

Was this before or after Romy?

I was going to doctors before that happened. But after she died, it became insurmountable. My dissertation and everything I once cared about felt meaningless.

It's funny, when Joanna and I first knew each other, I told her that I didn't sleep. I tried to convince her that it was my superpower, and she played along because she knew I was trying to impress her. And it might as well have been true because I used to work on fumes with no problem.

But now?

Now I'm the bludger of a husband who can't find a job and sleeps all day.

That's how she sees it?

No. Of course she's sweet about it. I'm just languishing. I search for a reason, but she doesn't return to me.

How many jobs do you apply to each week?

Usually about 5 a week. Sometimes less.

That's a good amount.

Right? Something should be falling into place at some point, right? I feel like I've been conned by the generations that went before me. In high school, I told an older guy at my church that I was thinking about skipping college, do my own thing and figure it out without going into debt. He was a carpenter, one of those guys whose palms are permanently tattooed with dirt and his fingers crooked from getting hit by so many hammers. He was upset when I said I wanted to skip school. He told me "you can pay now or you can pay later, but either way, you're gonna pay." I can still see his lips smacking together as he said this. And now, one Bachelor's degree and a Master's and PhD later, plus a short military career to boot, I can say that he was wrong. The entire generation was wrong. Hard work doesn't guarantee anything. Cursed is the ground. My military career cost me a chance at having a family, and my PhD has scorched opportunities I'd otherwise have had. I've put in the hard work, and it's only cost me at every turn. Had I moved up the ranks of the pizza delivery boys, I'd have a million times more stability than I have now.

"I will go see," Zuji said, lowering himself into a sprinter's stance: one knee on the ground and the other foot ready to propel him across the room to reach the door, having to bolt past the window that had been shot out.

"No," Claire cried, grabbing the back of his pants. "You stay here. Remember last time? You will not be going back to prison on my watch."

Claire scurried across the room, keeping one hand out in front of her face and one on the back of her head. She scampered down the stairs, hearing the door thuds grow louder as she approached.

As she turned the front door handle just enough to unlock it, a Samal flung the door open, knocking Claire against the wall as he sprinted upstairs.

Without a word, Claire lunged after him but was tackled by another soldier, who pinned Claire to the ground.

"No!" Claire shrieked. "My family!"

"*Shaket*! *Shaket*!" the soldier cried, then put his finger to his lips, urging her to be silent, as if anything she said could possibly be heard over the chaos outside.

Claire heard gunfire coming from the top floor, in the same room that her family was in.

"Let me go!" she cried, violently wiggling her way out of the soldier's grasp, but unable to outmuscle him.

She turned her head towards the door and saw bright flashes raining down from the sky – bombs or bullets or the sacred Bethlehem star, she wasn't certain and didn't care – and finally broke free of the soldier and hustled up the stairs.

There are people who were meant to deliver pizzas, and you are not one of those people.

> I suppose not. Instead I was meant to go get a degree that might as well have been made out of Play-Doh and signed by Chuck E. Cheese.

Well without your degree, you would've never met me!

> That's true. And it almost justifies the half-million dollars of student loans I have. But it's just annoying that I felt called by God to do the program and nothing came of it. Last year, looking at our tightening finances, I told Joanna, "we'll be okay as long as I'm using my PhD by next July." Well, next July is next month.

It's hard enough to find stable work when the world isn't on fire. It's just that much harder during a pandemic.

> I graduated the second week of March. Literally the same week WHO declared the pandemic a worldwide emergency: March 11th. Billy once said to "beware the Ides of March." Did he have more foresight than God?

Well, "Billy" is dead and God isn't, so there's that.
I'm kind of wondering something about you. You remember you were talking about that meteor game?

> ...meteor?
> Ohh. Metroid?

Yes. With the woman spaceman.
You talked about how you had lost your prayer spacesuit, and how you didn't know how to use it in the right place. Right? That's what you were talking about?

> Yes. Right before you had a pressing omelet.

You had said you were going to try to re-learn the "right" way to pray. Right? And I'm wondering, have you attempted that at all?

> Honestly? Not really.

I think there's value in that! I know you and I have a lot of differences, but I'd have a major interest in whatever it is that you were to find out.

> I know what you're doing, and it's not working, for the record.

What am I doing?

> You're trying to give me purpose so I don't feel so down on myself.
> I was a therapist, please don't forget.

I can see why you'd say that, but I don't think it changes the fact that I would be genuinely interested in hearing about what you learn, and that I'm not giving you a meaningless, silly little mission with zero worth.

> Well. Whether or not you're patronizing me, the good news is that I'd still like to get there and do that. My heart just hasn't been in it.
> And I still don't get the purpose of prayer if I can say with certainty that God is not going to change His plans for me.

But that's the point of what you're doing! You can't go into this assuming you know the outcome. That defeats the whole purpose.
You've come with an open mind when you talk to me, in a lot of ways. I wish you would go to god with that open mind, too.

Along the way up, she passed the Samal who was jumping down each set of stairs. Upon recognizing that he just passed Claire, the Samal turned and offered an exasperated cry of caution.

"*Lech! Lech-Lecha!*"

Claire soared upstairs into the kitchen and found that the sloppy barricade she and Zuji created had been tossed aside. She saw her two kids lying on the floor, but not her husband.

"Zuji?" Claire cried out, then approached her children and asked, "where's your Baba?"

But the children could not respond.

"Abni?" she asked, getting on her knees and shaking him. She looked into his eyes – or at least attempted to – and could not find his pupils, only his whites visible, almost as if they were glowing.

"Abni!" she cried and backed up in horror, only to find he continued to shake after she let him go.

Claire looked over at her daughter: her hands were frozen in a twisted position and the rest of her body distorted into angles that the most skilled contortionists wouldn't be able to pull off.

"Ebnahty!" Claire cried and then grabbed her daughter's hand to put them back in a relaxed position, but it was as if they were constructed of stone. Claire looked into her eyes to find that Ebnahty's pupils were also rolled into the back of her head.

Claire shrieked and watched as both her children continued to violently convulse, slamming their heads against the floorboards that they once were pressing their foreheads against.

As if Ebnahty was somewhere inside her own body, desperately asking for help but not knowing how to, she turned her head and peered towards her mother with pearled eyes. Claire looked at her lips and saw

I hear you. There's just a lot of frustration that's preventing me from going Full Samus right now. Like, I'm still wondering, why would God have me graduate the week of a pandemic and put me on a sinking ship?

Why would he put millions of jews thru two different exiles and then a holocaust?

That's a good question. No, that's a really good question, actually.

You know about Esther right?
The actual Esther, from the bible

Yes of course

Well maybe I should tell you the story. Because I don't want to assume our translations are the same, given the differences we've talked about.

I think we probably match up here. Esther was a Jew who was chosen to be the king's wife, but then she found out about a plot to kill all the Jews in her kingdom so she broke the law by approaching the king without being summoned, which carried a penalty of death at that time.
I can't imagine there will be disagreement for us on the story of Purim.

Yeah I guess that's the basics of it. Reason I ask:
Talmud says that Esther, when she was encroaching towards the king's door to plead with him, knowing full well she might die for what she was about to do, she quoted Psalm 22:1, "my god my god why have you forsaken me," because she felt the shekhinah of God leave her.

Yeshua had the same thing happen to Him as Esther had happen to her: He felt abandoned just before facing the most powerful ruler of the day. "My God, my God, why have You forsaken me" is literally the same verse that He cried out with when He was dying on the cross.

I didn't know that. Might be appropriation though. Like they put that in the christian bible because they saw it in jewish text first

Ehhhh that doesn't jive.
Talmud was written hundreds of years after the Christian Bible.
At Yeshua's crucifixion, some Jews were standing by when He cried out the Psalm. They said: "He must be calling for Elijah."

Was he?

No. Elijah couldn't even save himself. Apart from God, Elijah dies in the wilderness, depressed and alone.
The confused words uttered at Golgotha, etched at that moment, capturing how there was nobody - Jews, Gentiles, Romans - who understood the significance of what was going on.
They thought that Yeshua was calling out to Elijah to be His savior.
But Yeshua was calling out to Elijah to be his Savior.
Yeshua was redeeming all of mankind, even Elijah.

Well..

I find myself connecting with these heroes of the faith who spent so much time feeling abandoned. Esther, Job, Habakkuk, maybe even Yeshua. I feel like I did something wrong and God is no longer answering my prayers. I feel empty, like the Holy Spirit and/or Shekhinah no longer dwells in me.

I'm sorry.

What if we can lose the Shekhinah? Is there anything in life we can do in which we lose the favor of the Lord like King Saul did?

they were turning a ghastly Marian blue, and then saw Abni was experiencing the same fate.

"Zuji! They are not getting oxygen to their brains!" Claire cried out to Zuji as she watched her children die from suffocation as their elder sister, Mirna, had done shortly after birth.

"Zuji, please!" Claire cried out, but her cries were masked by a salvo of explosions right outside her home, compelling her to plug her ears with her fingers.

She unplugged her ears and found all the noise had stopped. Except, the bombings were still going on, she just couldn't hear it anymore.

"Zuji" she cried one last time, but couldn't hear herself anymore as the ringing in her ears became the only sound she heard.

"Lord, I know You are with us! Our Father, who art in heaven, hallowed be Thy Name!" she cried out.

"*Ask...*" Claire heard a voice command her, the only thing she could hearken.

"Thy Kingdome come! Thy will be done on earth as it is in heaven!" she continued crying, gaining some of her hearing back as she punched each word.

"*Ask for the Holy Spirit...*" the silent voice commanded.

"Lord, please send the Holy Spirit!" she screamed over the sound of the explosions right outside her blasted window. "Holy Spirit, I need You!"

Claire felt the sensation she had felt several times before: her head was filled with heaping warmth, and it traveled to her toes and back up to her crown, leaving a trail of arctic bliss in its trail.

I don't know that.
Idk.
Can you send me a Romy picture please?

Danger.
I'm sorry your birthday sucked so bad.

It's not my birthday

O right. Well, sorry the last day of being 33 sucked so bad.

Yeah. I guess me and Yeshua have that in common now.

Claire grabbed Abni's mangled, stony hand, and began praying in a language that she had never studied or even heard before. With her other hand, Claire grabbed Ebnahty's frigid palm and continued to pray in this strange tongue.

An overwhelming heat – more fervent than she'd ever felt it before – shot from her own body and through her hands, and she felt it escape through her fingertips. Abni and Ebnahty's heads snapped back in tandem, and Claire felt their contorted grips loosen as she continued to pray.

Claire leered at Ebnahty, who was staring back at her with her sweet, pure eyes, her cerulean lips slowly regaining their natural strawberry color. Claire then surveyed Abni, whose eyes were closed but was now calmly breathing. Claire began to stroke his face, and he opened his soulful pine eyes.

The three of them huddled together, the explosions right outside their window seeming as if they were a thousand kilometers away. And for the first moment in many hours, they had peace.

"Zuji," Claire whispered, unsure as to why her husband's name escaped her lips. "Zuji. Zuji, Zuji, Zuji."

Abni and Ebnahty chimed in, quietly chanting, "Zuji, Zuji, Zuji," together. And then all three of them, as if rehearsed, coalesced to a thundering crescendo:

"ZUJI!"

Claire heard a discordant clatter and turned her head to find Zuji falling to his knees as a bullet spiked through the Anastas window, cleaved Zuji's frazzled hair, ripped through the bathroom wall, and collided with their master mirror, splintering it into fragmented daggers that chevalled back towards Zuji, drilling glass into his body.

THE CROWDED TOMB

> "The wound is the place
> where the light enters you."
> - Rumi

"How are you feeling this morning?" I asked Joanna.

A few days after she landed in Tel Aviv, before the sun had even risen on Jerusalem, we were standing in line just outside the Church of the Holy Sepulcher: the supposed site of not only Christ's crucifixion *and* resurrection, but also the burial place of Adam (of Adam and Eve fame). For God's part, it's a remarkably courteous *mise en scène* placement to offer everything in a one-stop-shop for hectic pilgrims.

"I'm better, just tired," Joanna responded to me. "And I have a little headache."

We'd arrived at the church about 30 minutes before it was set to open at 5am. If you try to visit the place at any point after the sun is hovering over Jerusalem, then you likely won't actually get in to the church for several hours because of the crowds. The best bet for a quick, meaningful visit is to show up before dawn. So, that's exactly what we did, and now we were in line to see the actual sepulcher – that is, the supposed tomb of Christ.

"Hey," I said, caressing the shoulder seam of her coat with one hand and pointing to a dinky wooden ladder with the other, "see that ladder? Well, there's hundreds of years of history to that thing."

She looked up at the unassuming ladder. I could kind of tell that she didn't really care to hear a history lesson at 4:30 in the morning, nor would my readers really care to read a history lesson 300+ pages into a book, but you don't get a name like Danger from playing by the rules of the road, baby.

"You are looking at the 'immovable ladder' of the Church of the Holy Sepulcher. This church is maintained by *six* different Christian sects – the Roman Catholics, Greek Orthodox, Armenian Apostolics, Coptic Christians, and Ethiopian Tewahedo."

"Wow. It sounds like an entire minor arena football league," she quipped.

"I'm giving an architectural tour here, please leave your jokes until the end," I joked. "But all six sects have some level of custodianship of the church, as agreed upon by some documents known as Status Quo. But none of the Christians hold the keys to the church: that duty is reserved for a family of Muslims, if you can believe it, for who else would be impartial enough to resist accommodating special religious requests? Irony aside, nobody knows exactly who put that ladder there or why they did it. Some sources suggest that it was the Armenians, because during the Ottoman Empire, Christians would get taxed any time they entered or left the church, so the thought is that the ladder was put there so the monks could creep outside to get fresh air and sunshine – and surely not to smoke. There's suggestion that at one point on that ledge there, a vegetable garden was even grown. But the point is, one random day during the 18th century, this ladder simply seemed to appear, and because nobody can definitively claim it as theirs, it just sits there."

379

"*Ohh*, kay. So it's kind of symbolic now? Nobody moves it out of reverence for its history?"

"No," I tossed my head about, "there will be a literal fist fight if one of the monks were to move it. It's part of the rules of Status Quo, no clergy can alter any of the furniture without the other five denominations all unanimously agreeing to it. This church has seen bloody inter-denominational brawls between monks erupt for far less than moving that lowly ladder. Inherently meant to move and have use, but now immovable and impractical for fear that it will incite a religious riot. And now it sits there, 200 years and counting, because nobody can agree whose ladder it is or what to do with it."

"Dear sir!" called a voice that was far-too-peppy for such an hour. I looked over and saw a man with an eggplant of a portwine stain across his face.

I know him. Balrog. Or, Blanka? Bulblin. Bowser? No.

"My child is sick, and I have been up all night trying to find medicine for him. 'Ask, it will be given! Seek, you will find! Knock, and...'"

"Baraka."

A single word. It dizzied him enough that I could've executed a finishing move without him flinching.

"Baraka. I *know* you. I already prayed for you."

Without a word, Berakhah nodded and scuttled off, shrinking behind the corridor like game that had just heard a rifle in the distance.

"Joanna," I asked, shaking my head. "Why is it that the most morally bankrupt people are also the ones who most readily share Scripture?"

"You know that guy?" she asked.

"Excuse me?" a traveler called to a few people in the back of our line, holding up a map. "Does anyone know how to get to Jaffa Gate? I'm supposed to meet a friend outside of some Armenian restaurant past a coffee house on Helena Street. She said 'blink and you'll miss it' and I guess I blinked. *Bulghourji* it's called?"

"Sure," I waved him over. "I think I know the one you're looking for. There's a couple ways to get there, but I usually go up this way, through the market, and you're going to take Mark Street for just a few seconds, then branch over to David Street and you'll basically just head all the way there. You'll see the signs taking you towards Jaffa Gate. When you see the Tower of David, you'll take a left and you'll head into the Armenian Quarter. If you hit St. James Cathedral, you've gone too far."

"Thank you!" he said.

"Well, you've become quite the pilgrim, huh?" Joanna said.

"John Wayne would be proud," I said, smiling as I watched the traveler disappear behind a corridor. "I guess you learn a lot about a city when you rely on your feet and public transportation. That poor sucker, though? He ain't gonna make it."

"What do you mean?"

"Did you hear his pockets? Shopkeepers are going to hear those coins jangling a mile away and close in on him like vultures to a fresh carcass. And he's carrying plastic bags. Just screams 'tourist.' Where did he even get souvenirs this early in the morning?"

"Well, no offense, Nate, but you don't exactly look like a local, either. I mean, I can see your wallet's entire outline in your cargo shorts."

"Ah-ha, you've spotted my dummy wallet!"

I whipped out a bulgy, aqua-tinted pleather billfold.

"Wanna steal this? Go ahead. All it has are debit cards from the '90s, receipts, and exactly 20 NIS."

Exactly 20 NIS, so I could tell a shopkeeper I only had five bucks in my pocket (and be telling the truth).

"Crafty," she yielded.

"Gotta' be prepared to play chicken," I said, maybe pushing too hard to impress her, but also unperturbed by that possibility. "I mean, I'm not saying you should try to collide with people, I'm just saying you should be ready to."

"This city is such a maze," Joanna opined. "I think I understand the Book of Revelation more than any of the maps here."

Joanna clutched her tummy.

"Indigestion?" I asked.

"Probably."

"Hun?"

Her eyes glazed over and continued to look forward, with no response.

"Jo," I said, "We've talked ad nauseam about all the pregnancy symptoms you're having. And at this point now, you're later than you've ever been since we've been married. So, my thought is..."

I was interrupted by the insufferable sound of heavy furniture grating across a wooden floorboard, which permeated the church courtyard. I squinted over to see that the doors had just opened. The entire line crept inside the church, which was even more ostentatious than the Church of the Nativity in the city just yonder. The ceilings were decked with medieval art of the apostles while the walls were speckled with mosaics and other marbleized abstractions. Every inch of the recesses seemed to shimmer from the golden fixtures hanging from the vaulted domes, which were the only indication as to where one room ended and another began.

"*Wow*," Joanna marveled, the warm din of her voice rising like a balloon until it melted into the billions of other involuntary gasps that came before. "I bet it didn't look like *this* when the stone rolled away for Jesus."

"Was the stone rolled away *for* Him?" I poked. "That's like assuming the clergy opened the doors just now so *they* could leave. Could any of us have gotten in here if there was a big boulder blocking our path? Yeshua could've gotten out just as easily as He could've gotten off the cross. The stone wasn't rolled away so He could get out, it was rolled away so we could get in, yeah?"

She didn't respond to me, still surveying the cathedral with her mouth ajar.

Fine. I'll save that pearl-of-a-sermon for later.

However, the stunning magnificence of even the most illustrious halls on earth can diminish when they're no longer novel, and after being in line for an hour, Joanna's and my stupefaction reached a certain degree of staleness. No longer admiring the brilliant exhibits within view, Joanna hung her head, looking at her Chuck Taylors while massaging the temple attached to her own skull. The early hour and amount of time already spent schlepping around the Old City would easily explain her fatigue and head tension. But, so would an uptick in hormones.

"Babe," I interjected as she pinched the skin over her eyeballs, "I really, *really* think you need to take a test."

"I'm just so scared," she whispered.

"I know it. I do," I said as an Italian family left the line, so we stepped forward to take their place. "But we can't go through this whole trip without knowing the answer."

We were a mere few feet from being allowed entrance into the sepulcher, the central attraction within the holy church. Only a handful of people were in front of us now, and one-by-one, they were being let into the sepulcher. Joanna and I inched so close, we could see inside the tomb – famous for not having any people in it, but never having been empty since.

Isn't it amazing that the most visited burial site in the world doesn't even have a body in it? But if the tomb was really empty on that Sunday morning nearly 2,000 years ago, then all of history pivots around this one event. Nothing else even really matters, does it?

If Yeshua rose from the dead, then actually, there is one thing that still matters: bringing more humans into the world to experience this joy, this truth. Creating relationships matters. It's the only thing we take into eternity. And what bigger blessing than to have an eternal relationship with not only the Living God, but also someone that you personally raised into relationship with this God? It was beyond my comprehension if God wouldn't want us to have that.

"Excuse me, excuse me," a bearded man in a garish robe said as he put his hand up to stop me and the rest of the line behind us. "I need you to wait here."

"What's going on?" I asked him as several other bearded, robe-adorned men entered the sepulcher.

"Now the Greeks will have a little service and you must wait."

I felt my face burning up.

"No!" I dithered. "Please. We will be so quick!"

The robed man didn't respond, retreating towards the tomb.

"Well, I guess we just wait it out," Joanna said as the doors to the sepulcher itself closed.

Oh, honey.

"Let's go," I dissented, trying not to bare my ill-will towards the Greek bishop. "Come on, let's have a peek at Adam's skull."

"What? *Why?*"

"Because the Greeks suck!" I exclaimed in the holiest church in the holiest city on earth, then looked around and lowered my voice so only Joanna could hear. "*I'm sorry, but* they *just* do!"

"So, we made a 4-day pilgrimage to Jerusalem, and we're not even going to spend time inside of the tomb?"

"Yeah," I gritted. "I guess we have that in common with Yeshua now."

Joanna looked at the closed-off sepulcher, the disappointment sprawled across her face.

"Joanna," I said, taking her hand and stepping out of line with her. "I need you to trust me. We are never, ever going to reach that tomb today."

"He blossoms like a flower,
then withers;
he flees like a shadow
and does not last."
~ Job 14:2, CSB

THE VALLEY ROSE.

God spoke, and it's how
The mountain calls for you now.
Not me –
The Valley Rose.
And it was my beloved who was always
Bound to suffer.
The Lord was the One who was
So focused on growing His garden,
That He left us to wither on this side.
That God is actually not good.
Never again will I think
Faith is the most important pillar of life.
Contrary to my prior beliefs,
Prayer has no place in the logical man's life.
Now I know that it's foolish to say
God is sovereign.
For all of eternity,
I will never see Romy again.
I erroneously believed
This pain will pass;
And also that
God sent Yeshua as Messiah.
I've instead learned to trust
My old pragmatic way of thinking.
I've been forced to surrender
My family, after all.
I never deserved
Anything less than this confidence:
Our suffering is meaningless, and
Now I know it's a lie to say
God sees our pain.
After a bitter season of contemplation
I have come to the sobering conclusion
God does not change.
Give me a break:
I prayed so hard for change;
We can't stay in that place.

We can't stay in that place.

כח

September 14, 2020

Hey!! I know it's been awhile. I'm sorry for that. I just haven't known what to say.

Hey. It's okay, that burden shouldn't be on you. It works both ways, too. I could've reached out. It's just been a dark month.

Did things get any better?

No. But I did find a silver lining.

Oh yea?

I finally hit the final age bracket.

Huh??

When you take surveys or fill out forms or whatever. You've got "0-17 years old" first, then you hit "18-33," and finally it's "34-DEATH." I've made it to 34-DEATH.

I mean, COVID maybe expedites the process a bit, but I'd say you hit that final bracket in another 40 years. You're not even halfway.

I need to say, your timing is quite impeccable. I'm suspending my phone service.

When?

Today. I don't know exactly. They said "sometime today" it would be deactivated.

What? Don't do that

It's done. Clock is ticking. By midnight tonight, I'll piss off.

Why?

I need time away from everyone

No that's literally the opposite of what you need

Well that's what I'll be getting.
So, Shanah Tovah, G'mar Tov, sameach sukkot and happy Hanukkah and whatever else with the rest of all that.

Can I have just a second? I thought it might be helpful to hear this. You mentioned Elijah's depression. Well God saw him through that spell and he still had purpose for him yet.

But remember, he is a p.r.o.p.h.e.t, Esther. I shouldn't expect such care, right? And when Elijah was in the wilderness, how did he overcome his depression?

Well, god sent him an angel.

You don't really believe God will send me an angel.

Idk. Probably not. I don't think so.

I know He won't. I know because I've been asking God to take my life and He hasn't moved one way or the other.

Do I need to call someone?

Don't bother. My psychiatrist already sent the cops to hospitalize me.

Did they convince you?

No. You know better. You've read my book.
This wasn't my first rodeo fleeing the police.

٢٨

<u>March 11, 2001</u>

Pieces of the Anastas shower curtain fluttered in the air for a moment, then floated to the bottom of their tub. Debris surrounded the Anastas family as they all lied prostrate on the floor. Claire poked her head up to see glass all over her husband's coiled body.

"At first injury, we leave," Claire remembered her husband say many months ago.

Claire rolled over to Zuji and began shaking his torso.

"Zuji," she said. "Are you hurt?"

"I…" Zuji gurgled, immobilized. An explosion down the street blasted through the street, then a few shots of gunfire, followed by silence for the first time that evening. "I… think I am."

Claire rolled Zuji over and began checking his vital signs, remembering what Umi – a former nurse – had taught her about basic first aid.

"Where are you hurt?" Claire asked.

"I… am not hurt," Zuji said.

"You just said you were."

"No. You asked me if I was okay, and I responded, 'I think I am.' "

"I asked if you were hurt," Claire rebutted.

"You did not," he said. "You asked…"

"What does it matter?" Claire asked, hugging her husband and crying into his armpit. Abni and Ebnahty both crawled over, and the four of them wept together.

What happened? Walk me through this.

My psychiatrist said I sounded suicidal and said she was going to have a welfare check sent to my house. I told Joanna to deal with the police for me and I deactivated my phone's GPS and hid for a few hours in the city. By the time I got back, they weren't looking for me anymore. Finally benefitted from #tulsalazy.

What happens if they were to come back?

I have an escape plan.

Ok.
Are you back on your meds yet?

Yeah. I started taking them again this week.

You're not worried about the fertility treatments?

They're done. They failed. We had our third attempt and it didn't work. So I'm back on my meds.

Wait. So that's it? No more treatments?

No. My netherstraw closed back up anyway. I'd do the surgery again if we think it would change anything, but there's new research that say veterans who were around burn pits in Iraq or Afghanistan may not be able to have children anyway.

What's a burn pit? Were you around any?

A burn pit is where we would create a big fire and throw all our trash in it. Including toxic stuff. And yeah, we were all around it all the time. Even when our own pits weren't burning, local Afghans were doing the same thing with their trash just outside our base. So one big cesspool of noxious fumes, breathing that shit in for the entire deployment.

That seems barbaric. Like, there should be a better method somehow.

What would you suggest? We didn't exactly have trash services on our bases. All those surgeries, all the dicking around with my antidepressant dosages, just to find out the burn pits were the biggest factor.
It's like the story you shared, with the three dead Israeli boys. You were all praying for dead boys and you didn't even know it.
We were putting ourselves in debt, putting myself through the most painful situations imaginable, and it was never going to work anyway. We never had a chance.
So that's it. We're done. Science confirmed what it already suspected years ago: we're not viable candidates to have biological children. It just won't happen for us.

$(\eta \_ \eta)$
I'm sorry. I was really rooting for a miracle.

I'm resigned to believe that God will never work another miracle in my life. Christians are so caught up in quoting John 3:16 that they forget Bereshit 3:16 and the curse we all live under. Yeshua said "there will be no suffering in heaven." And I realize now that I don't think I believe that claim. The idea that I'll never get to spend time with children in this life is really hard. But the idea that I'll never get to spend time with children in eternity is devastating. Suffering follows the barren into eternity.

I wish this was something you could control. I really, really was wishing for a baby for you.

"*Ow!*" yipped Zuji, then saw he had pieces of blood-stained glass embedded in his arms. As if he had done this many times before, Zuji began picking shards from his skin while speaking to his family. "But, why? Abni. Ebnahty. You called me *Zuji*."

He looked at them sternly.

"*Why* did you call me Zuji?" he asked, then added, "you *never* call me Zuji."

"I'm sorry, Baba," Abni cowered.

"No, I am not mad," Zuji responded, then plucked glass from his wrist. "It... *ow!*... it is okay. But I must know, you stopped praying together and then called out for me. Why did you call me by my name?"

"I... I don't know, Baba," Ebnahty skulked as her brother did. "I am sorry."

"No, do *not* be sorry," Zuji urged them again. "I stepped into the bedroom, right next to the bathroom, just to see if there was damage in that room. And I could not help but stand there in that room, paralyzed. But then I decided to come find you, so I returned to this kitchen, all three of you yelled my name. '*Zuji!*' you yelled. And I was struck with uncontrollable fear, and could do nothing but fall on my knees in awe. And as I did so, I felt a bullet over my head, then..."

Claire, Abni, and Ebnahty tried to gather what he was telling them.

"You saved my life," he explained. "You called my name, and I knew I was in danger, so I collapsed."

" 'Ask... ask for the Holy Spirit,' " Claire uttered.

"What?" Zuji asked.

"That is what the voice said. Ask for the Holy Spirit."

I actually feel like I've gotten control in my life again. It's the first time I've been in control in a long time. I'm so in control that I can actually prove that God's promises aren't true. I can shoot myself in the brain stem and I know from experience that He won't bend those bullets before they land in the sludge. I'd fall dead and prove once and for all that what He promised was empty.

Ok Ok, have you talked to Joanna about this? Like, specifically, what you just said to me?

She's not on board. In fact, the fact that she's not on board is the only reason I'm still alive. I've re-offered a deal to her I made years ago, that I can end my life so she can go on and rebuild hers. They say suicide is a cowardly move, but at least this coward goes out knowing that he did what he needed so his family could get back on track. Curse God and die? No. I will not. It's better to just die.

You're putting a lot of pressure on her. That's not fair to her.

I know it's not. Domestic abusers actually wield suicide as a threat, as a tool to maintain control of their significant other. But I'm not using it as a threat, I'm using it as a promise. Not that that makes it any more copacetic, but it is what it is.

I don't even know what to say. I wish you could make sense of what you're going through.

I'm working on it. I had a thought on it. What if we humans are living in the dark, follow me? And God is in the light. And we want to get to each other. But WE can't step into the light, and HE can't step in the darkness. And at first, there was no way to cross the "spiritual Terminator."

Already having problems with this thought experiment, but what do you mean by Terminator?

"Terminator" is the lunar line on the moon. The twilight between the light side of the moon and the dark side. To this day, no man has walked on the far side of the moon because it's a death sentence. No light, no heat, no way to communicate.

So if you find yourself walking into the Terminator, it's hasta la vista, baby? ⚆⚇⚆?

So imagine God and me are separated, so He stretched His light as far as it would reach, and it made the twilight. And I can still step into the twilight, and so can He, and once we're both there, He can walk me into the light?

Maybe. Except god can dwell in the darkness.

Are you sure? Because I feel like I took a step past the Terminator and now I'm in a crater that's 300 degrees below freezing.

He IS the light. It's his light that makes the twilight even possible.

Yeah.
Maybe.

⚠ I know you're struggling and you're not understanding what's going on, but can I tell you a story?
[[YOUR MESSAGE COULD NOT BE RECEIVED. TRY AGAIN LATER.]]

⚠ Danger?
[[YOUR MESSAGE COULD NOT BE RECEIVED. TRY AGAIN LATER.]]

⚠ FUCK.
[[YOUR MESSAGE COULD NOT BE RECEIVED. TRY AGAIN LATER.]]

"Who is it?" Zuji asked.

"He is not 'it.' He is Him."

"Of course I want the Holy Spirit," Zuji said. "The Lord knows this already."

"Ask for Him."

"Yes, of course I will," Zuji responded, scratching his elbow. "May we be thankful that… *ow!*… that we are safe."

NOON IN JERUSALEM

> "It hurts to feel lonely.
> Now I'm beginning to recognize that maybe
> that's what it feels like when God calls me.
> Maybe when God is calling, it hurts.
> Maybe when God calls us, it feels like a pain.
> We go, 'wow, will I ever stop hurting?'
> And my answer is: Don't worry about hurting.
> Realize that this is how badly God wants you.
> And that that hurt that you're feeling,
> that emptiness that you're feeling,
> maybe that's the way it feels
> when you're called by God."
> - Rich Mullins

I was told that once you try it once, you can't help but keep coming back for more.

Bzzzzzzzzz.

I didn't think that would ever apply to me, yet here I am, in a back alley of the Old City with a needle in my body again.

Bzzzzzzzzz.

No, it's not heroin. What is with you and always thinking I'm doing heroin? *Bzzzzzzzzz. Bzzzzzzzzz.* It's just another tattoo. Though at this rate, I may exhaust places on my body for tattoos by the end of the decade. I spent over 32 years without any tattoos, but now I'd gotten two in as many months.

"You here as pilgrims?" asked Wassim, a Coptic body artist with chopped walnut hair.

"Yes and no," I said. "Well, yes, I guess."

"It is for me," Joanna said.

"Why wouldn't it be for you?" Wassim asked me, though he seemed disinterested in actually hearing the answer as he worked on my right wrist.

"I was here for business. For school."

"For the conflict? To study our pain and suffering?"

Well. Yeah.

"What did you come up with?" he asked. "Sum it up for me in one sentence."

I was actually prepared for this question. I had written a few days ago the most succinct way I could summarize the entire conflict, so I did my best to remember how I phrased it.

"Okay, I'll try: in a conflict that has spanned thousands of years, Israelis and Palestinians are deadlocked in competing narratives that are presented through their religious texts and traditions."

Wassim sucked his lips in and nodded, then said, "There's a lot more than that, but I guess I did only give you one sentence. So, not bad."

"Thanks," I said, then glanced over at Joanna who winked at me like she had just inhaled an aphrodisiac.

Nothing sexier than a man who can extrapolate data from the most up-to-date literature.

"You better not go home thinking you're the messiah," said Wassim, studying my wrist like it was about to tell his fortune. "You know that's a thing here?"

"Yeah," I acknowledged as he continued to ink my right wrist. "People visit Israel and go home feeling like something has activated inside of them, revealing that they're actually the messiah. *The Simpsons* did an episode about it. And if *The Simpsons* made reference to something, then I'm familiar with it."

"That's Jerusalem Syndrome, right?" Joanna added.

"Yes," Wassim nodded, then added with a smile, "I see who the brains of the operation is here."

Wassim continued working on my wrist. While my previous Bethlehem Star tattoo was resplendently intricate, this one had beauty in its simplicity. In fact, it was just a single letter from the Arabic alphabet: the equivalent of the letter "N."

"If anything," I said, "I may have uncovered a new phenomenon: Jerusalem Imposter Syndrome. Where you leave your trip realizing more clearly than ever before that you're *not* the messiah."

"If you're getting this tattoo," Wassim said, "then you're a Christian, and if you're a Christian, then you know full well that we already have our Messiah."

"Amen," I said.

"Amen, yes, right," Wassim replied. "That's the word Christians are supposed to throw around other Christians to indicate they're a fellow believer, right? Like overtly saying 'I am also a Christian' will run the risk of getting you crucified today."

"Hey, it still does in some countries. That's the whole meaning behind this tattoo. It's just the letter 'N,' but in Iraq and Syria, some Christians are forced to get this letter spray-painted on their homes to identify them as Christians, so they can be persecuted. 'N' for '*Nasrani*,' a derogatory term towards Christians. They're branded with this letter."

"Hmm," Wassim cracked a smile. "Bold. And so you think, as an American, you're standing in solidarity with persecuted Christians by wearing a symbol that means nothing in your country and won't ever get you persecuted?"

Well. Yeah.

"Hey, I'm just poking fun," Wassim said, then held up his hand to reveal his knuckle. "I have this tattoo, too. I'm a Coptic Christian; my family knows persecution. Nobody's going to hang me in Jerusalem for having this tattoo, but I like the idea of championing the persecuted church. They say to me, don't wear your beliefs on your sleeve. I say, don't let me lead you to believe I'm someone I'm not."

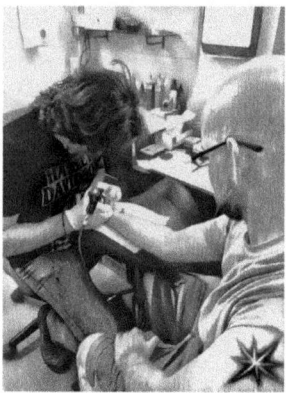

The buzz ceased and Wassim snapped his fingers.

"There," Wassim declared. "You're a branded animal. Is it perfect?"

I looked at the design, which seemed less like ink and more like a divine lava rock had etched an immaculate onyx emblem beneath my skin.

"It's better than perfect," I beamed. "It's kosher."

> "Rejoice not over me, O my enemy;
> when I fall, I shall rise;
> when I sit in darkness,
> the LORD will be a light to me."
> ~ Micah 7:8, ESV

٢٩

March 12, 2001

Twelve hours and what felt like a lifetime after Zuji fell on his knees, Claire was back in the bathroom, collecting glass from underneath the sink, where the waterline behind the toilet was leaking from an errant bullet.

"I think this will take many months to fix," she mumbled to herself in frustration. "And the Tzahal will not help us pay a single shekel of it."

"Hello*ooooo*?" Claire heard someone faintly call through the opening that used to be the kitchen window.

Claire looked outside to find two women knocking on the door to her woodshop attached to her house, then hurried downstairs to greet them.

"Can I help you?" Claire asked.

The women startled, then turned around to see Claire.

"Goodness! You snuck up on us," one of the women said. "We heard that you had the best souvenirs in Bethlehem, and we leave the Holy Land tomorrow, so we thought we would come by and buy from you, and your sign said that you were open, but nobody was inside…"

"Do you know we are in war?" Claire asked, exasperated at their audacity. "Just last night, this area was bombed. I harvest glass from my bathroom floor today."

"Oh," one of the women shrugged her warning off, "if you are open, that's all that matters to us. We trust in the Holy Spirit, and He will protect us."

"Holy Spirit?" Claire repeated.

"Yes, the Holy Spirit."

"We are open," Claire quickly said, unlocking her shop door with zeal. "Yes. Yes we are! Please come in."

כט

October 22, 2020

⚠ Danger...
[[YOUR MESSAGE COULD NOT BE RECEIVED. TRY AGAIN LATER.]]

Claire stood at the register as she watched the two women pick up wooden trinkets, marvel at their craftsmanship, then put them down.

"May we take pictures?" one of them asked Claire.

"Yes, of course," she replied. "Please tell others about us."

The women giggled as they perused the shop, tickled by the interesting knickknacks they were finding. As most customers do, they had showed interest in many of the items, but ultimately came to the register with just a single artifact each.

"That is 55 shekels, please," Claire said.

They handed her an American $20 bill, and said, "please, keep the change."

"Thank you," Claire said as they began to leave, then blurted out, "who is the Holy Spirit?"

The women turned around, surprised at the question.

"You have not heard of the Holy Spirit?" one of them inquired.

"No, I am a Catholic," Claire explained. "So, yes, of course I have heard much of the Holy Spirit, and have received Confirmation. But to the extent of what you say, that the Holy Spirit would protect you, this I don't know about."

"The Holy Spirit – or, you said you're Catholic? Sometimes He is called the Holy Ghost, too," one of them explained. "But He is a divine power within Christians. A *real* power! And a most important gift."

"So He is a 'He,' right? Not an 'it?'"

"Yes, dear. He's a person. He has a personality, just like Jesus; just like you and me. Many churches don't explain the purpose of the Holy Spirit. He gets a watered-down overview, and most churches don't explain His role in the Church. We become baptized in the Holy Spirit without even understanding what the Bible says about Him. But Jesus wouldn't have been able to do any of His miracles apart from Him."

"Are you prophets?" Claire asked.

"No, no, *no*," one of them laughed. "We are Texans."

"I am a Christian, and I have a problem," Claire admitted. "I... don't know fear."

The two women glanced at each other, puzzled.

"That is a *good* thing, dear," one of them responded. "You have felt fear though, yes?"

Claire nodded.

"You know that feeling? The knot in your stomach? When you feel that, you know that you are not trusting the Holy Spirit."

"How do I know if I am trusting the Holy Spirit?"

"You will smile," one of them said, whilst smiling herself, "and you will feel the fire that can only reign down from heaven. And you will have peace."

EXSANGUINE

> "Absolutely have to have dark
> in order to have light.
> If you have dark on dark,
> you basically have nothing.
> You know, it's like, in life...
> you gotta have a little sadness once in awhile
> so you know when the good times come.
> I'm waiting on the good times now."
> - Bob Ross

The day after getting my second tattoo in as many months, I escorted Joanna to a bus parking lot just northeast of the Damascus Gate.

"Okay, I'm going to take a page from the Quizdaddy and ask you a trivia question. Do you know what most thrones are made of?"

"Like, the material? I dunno. Gold?"

"You'd think so, but it's actually wood. Of course, it's gilded wood, so yes, most of them have gold hot-painted onto it. You're right about that. But the core is wood. Which is interesting when you take into account that Yeshua was killed on a tree."

I glanced at Joanna, her visage daring me to get lost in her eyes again. Dazzling though her face was, it certainly seemed she wasn't making the connection I was going for.

"Jesus was crucified on a throne."

Joanna sealed her eyelids and nodded.

"If God is the Sower, then Christ is the seed that had to die to bear fruit. He was planted into rocky ground, and sprouted anyway. Cross-ridden and exposed to vultures who could've unwittingly pecked Him to death instead, He took root in the hearts of the very men who stapled Him to beams. In their ignorance, they adorned Him with loincloth as if nakedness was defined in Genesis rather than Revelation; in their subreption, they crowned Him with blood and bramble, but neither was He choked out by the thorns. Crucified on a throne, sown upon skull, Jesus died and produced fruit worthy of Eden, budding as the Tree of Life."

"*Mmm*," Joanna spoke delicately, "only God can make a tree."

"And now, across the earth, His Name is known above any other Name, and now, dear bride, you stand on hallowed ground."

Joanna swiveled her head around at the lot that had trash strewn about it. It smelled like a bright combination of diesel and urine.

"What do you mean, the part about this being hallowed ground?"

"You are standing just before the spot of Christ's crucifixion."

"I thought that was in the Holy Sepulcher?" she said.

"Most people believe that. But there are two other spots here near the Old City that scholars believe could have been the actual spot of Christ's death. I'm convinced that we're standing in the right spot."

"How… or, where did you hear about this? You didn't mention any of this before you left home."

"You can learn a lot in 40 days."

"I trust that you've really looked into this," she hesitated before prying, "I just… what gives you the monopoly on knowing where the crucifixion actually took place?"

"I can't know for sure," I conceded. "But I can tell you with confidence that it probably didn't happen at that spot in the Holy Sepulcher. And if you look behind us, towards the Old City, I paid for a walk on those ramparts, and if you're up there, and you look over at this mountain from that height and that angle, it appears to look like a skull – Golgotha, 'place of the skull.'"

A driver got out of his bus, acknowledged us, and then turned around and began urinating on the tiny mountain before us. Perhaps the holiest site in all of Christendom: God's own blood stained on these rocks. God's blood, and now some guy's piss, too.

"But there's no church, no tourists, not even a plaque," Joanna protested.

"This is Muslim property. Christians couldn't build a commemoration here if they wanted to. Why do you think they put a parking lot right here when they could've reaped scads of money off of a souvenir stand or a restaurant? 'Skull Rock Shawarma,' they could call it. If this is just another rocky hillside, why have barbed wire preventing anyone from touching it? Do they really think someone is going to come here and scale the hill to get to the cemetery on top? Even if I'm wrong about this being the location, it still would've served them to finagle money from tourists who'd at least agree that this certainly *could* have been *the* skull rock. But it comes at an excruciating cost: they'd be disowning their ancestral religion and giving credence to their enemy's narratives. Why would you draw attention to a documented event that undermines the basic premises of your ethnic history and casts doubt on your right to the land?"

Joanna looked back up at the small mountain, examining what would appear to be hallowed hollowed eye sockets had we been standing level with the mountain a few hundred feet back.

"Just imagine," I said, "the traffic nightmare if the Via Dolorosa led outside the Damascus Gate instead of to the Holy Sepulchre in the Christian Quarter."

"What's the *Dolorosa*?"

"Oh, that's just the name for the route that Christ took to Golgotha. Condemnation to crucifixion."

"But," she persisted, "why *Dolorosa*? Is that Italian?"

"The word?" I asked. "I'm pretty sure it's Latin. Dolorosa itself means 'suffering.' So, *Via Dolorosa* is 'Road of Suffering.' Are you familiar with the term *dolor*?"

"No."

"Yeah, it's usually employed by annoying writers who make readers reach for their dictionary. (I would never.) The word literally means *suffering*. Hence, Dolorosa."

"So *dolor* means suffering and *Dolorosa* means suffering?"

"Correct."

"So wouldn't Dolorosa actually be 'the suffering of' something? Like, the rose's suffering?"

"No."

"Why not?"

"I don't know! It just is."

"It would make way more sense if it was, like, 'The Road of Suffering for the Rose of Sharon' or something poetic."

"Well, I'm sorry," I laughed. "I didn't name it!"

"So," Joanna asked, not losing her gaze on the eroded skull, "when we got up before sunrise, stood in line for hours, and didn't even get our chance to see the Tomb of Christ? That wasn't even the right place to go?"

I shrugged. Again, who am I to say that millions of pilgrims are misguided, and I'm the one who figured out the truth by doing several hours of research?

"Well," I tried to answer her question tactfully, "Jesus was born in the humblest of circumstances, was killed in the humblest of deaths, was buried in the humblest of tombs. What if God *doesn't* care for a palace built by human hands? What if God veiled the literal place of His birth and the literal place of His death, and given His divine humor, He also set the actual locations within a few hundred feet of the gold-plated cathedrals were everybody thinks these events occurred?"

I looked at Joanna, who – judging by her stormy eyes – almost appeared downcast by my opinion.

"That's just conjecture," I said, trying to back off my presumptuous history lessons. "Here's what I *will* say with certainty: religion can lead you to the wrong places if you don't approach it critically."

She nodded. We left the blood-stained, piss-spattered Golgotha Parking Lot and scurried around the outside perimeter of the Old City for about a mile until we broached a cemetery, headstones written in Arabic and adorned with crescent moons. We tiptoed around each grave, some of which were hard to avoid despite a walkway having been paved. The layout of the cemetery felt slipshod, as if a collection of graves had been haphazardly dug in a rushed effort.

"Why'd you want to go through the graveyard, babe?" Joanna balked, a little perplexed and perhaps distrusting my skills as a tour guide.

"Well," I said, then stopped in my tracks, put my hands on her shoulders, and turned her body to face the wall. "I wanted to show you this."

She scanned the concrete.

"I take it this wall is important?" she conjectured.

"It's not a wall," I said. "*This* is the eighth gate into the Old City. The Eastern Gate, or better known as the Golden Gate if you're not anywhere near San Francisco."

She squinted, then nodded when she realized that the concrete that filled the gate had been cemented differently than the dolomite and limestone that made up the walls around the Old City.

"And it's the only one sealed shut," I declared, almost with a sense of pride, as if I had something to do with the historical marker. "Sixteen feet of concrete, densely packed. It would take several rounds of explosives to get through here. And you want to know what's on the other side?"

Of course she did.

"The Temple Mount. The holiest site in the world; the intersecting circle of the Abrahamic religions' Venn Diagram. So, why would the holiest site in the world be hidden behind 16 feet of concrete, you ask?"

Joanna didn't ask, but nodded to humor me.

"Jerusalem was one of the Ottomans' earliest conquests in the 16th century. The sultan, Suleiman, had some concern, though, about this gate. There are a couple of Jewish Scriptures that say the Messiah would someday come westward through this gate on his way to ruling the kingdom. Sultan Suleiman, in his fear of the Jewish messiah overthrowing his rule, ordered this gate to be sealed shut in a way that no mere man could ever break. But in his wisdom, the sultan also knew that if the Jewish messiah may not be mere man and feasibly would have the physical or supernatural powers to thwart the seal. So he got clever and ordered this cemetery be hastily erected around the gate, for he knew that under rabbinic law, a cemetery would render the messiah unclean for seven days and, as such, unfit to overthrow the government for that whole week. The element of surprise would be lost."

"Quite wily," Joanna responded, either finding the anecdote to be interesting or doing a wonderful job feigning curiosity.

"Today, as it stands before us, the way is shut. It was made by those who are dead, and the dead keep it now."

The morose specter of a slain prophecy beetled overhead. That is, at least, until I couldn't contain my excitement and the elation pipped through my teeth, revealing that this story had a Christlike resurrection to it.

"Ah-*ha*! Just one problem, Sultan Suleiman!" I proclaimed, then reverently cradled my phone across both of my palms as I quoted a prophecy from chapter 44 of Ezekiel. " 'Then he brought me back to the outer gate of the sanctuary, which faces east. And it was shut. And the Lord said to me, 'This gate shall remain shut; it shall not be opened, and no one shall enter by it, for the Lord, the God of Israel, has entered by it. Therefore it shall remain shut.'' "

"So," Joanna interpreted the passage, "the Bible had already prophesied that someone would someday shut it? So, in trying to stop Jews from fulfilling one prophecy, the sultan instead fulfilled a different prophecy?"

"*Kismet* of the cosmos!" I acclaimed with as much enthusiasm as if I had earned a gold star while playing *Mario Party*. "Here's the ironic thing, babe: that prophecy that the sultan worked so hard to avoid? It had *already* been fulfilled by a man. Want to take a guess as to who?"

"Was it... *Jesus*?" she trailed off, uncertain if her too-easy cookie-cutter Sunday-school answer could possibly be the right one.

"Exactly," I confirmed. "Suleiman had slowly shaped it to his shifting purposes and made it better, as he thought. Being deceived, at the height of his wisdom, he fulfilled a critically-important biblical prophecy, for this had already become the very gate that Jesus Christ, Yeshua of Nazareth, Yasue Messiah rode through on a colt. It's the event that we celebrate every Palm Sunday before Easter Pascha. So as the prophet Ezekiel foretold, the Lord entered through the gate, and now it remains shut. Believe this: as the tribes of Israel and the seed of David have been buried, so will no Christian, no Jew, no Muslim, no man will ever pry this gate open again."

"Hmm," Joanna said, nodding pensively.

"Come," I said and rubbed her sun-kissed arm, "there's one more spot to show you."

We trotted across the street from the cemetery, descended into a valley, and entered the inviolable Garden of Gethsemane. It felt like the world around us fell into sepia, laden with olives all over the soil. I sniffed hard enough that even the depths of my lungs would get swept up by the sweet-but-earthly aroma imbuing the garden.

"That scent," I said to Joanna.

She closed her eyes and breathed in.

"It's like mint, honey, and pine combined," I said, trying to put my finger on what could be producing it. "Woodsy, earthy, but like a sugary nectar. Is that eucalyptus?"

"No," she said, "eucalyptus is a bit more offensive. This smell has a passion to it. I *like* this smell."

It was the most germane, most perfectest fragrance for this bittersweet garden, the crossroads of suffering. It was how funerals ought to smell, rather than carnations or lilies, which became an odious stench to me after Rose Mary Goff's death over 20 years ago.

It was also a boon that we came at the time of year that we did, when the olives were ripe and falling off the fructified branches. Joanna and I sat down under a gnarled olive tree, probably crushing a few olives onto our pants. She grabbed my hand and put her head on my shoulder.

"Now you're going to tell me this isn't the actual Garden of Gethsemane?" Joanna said, gently squeezing my hand. I could feel the muscles on her cheek forming a smirk against my collarbone.

I laughed at her joke. Though – and I didn't feel like telling her this – some archeologists think the olive trees here were planted by Crusaders at least a thousand years after Christ.

"If this isn't the actual site," I crafted a careful response, "then I don't think we'll ever know the true location. Not on this side of eternity, at least."

I caressed the earth with my free hand, dirt sifting through my fingers, some rogue soil sticking underneath my fingernails. I picked up one of the fallen olives and clutched it.

Have you ever stopped to consider how amazing the olive is? You can scrub the oil on your body to moisturize your skin, shine your hair, soothe your lips, and slow your aging. Olive oil can be utilized as a shaving cream, makeup cleanser, paint stripper, ring slicker, adhesive remover, metal dislodger, wood smoother, vinyl polisher, steel shiner, and dry eraser. How many other things can you name that safely repel both candlewax and earwax? All that, without even mentioning that olive oil provides protection against arthritis, infection, diabetes, stroke, heart disease, brain atrophy, and cancer.

Olive oil is perhaps the most functional all-purpose cleanser and the most underappreciated, healthiest superfood in the world. Of course, it has to be the *real* stuff, the *extra virgin* olive oil that's cold-pressed and unadulterated. No joke, there's a whole underground olive oil ring that's governed by the Italian mafia where they export "extra virgin olive oil" that's actually cut with knockoff oil and sold as being pure. Fauxlive Oil™, I call it. The whole production is strikingly similar to the export of the Murex snail, that Jaffa gastropod whose innards hold the key to the elusive and true royal purple. It took tens of thousands of mollusks to extract one single gram of purple, so it's probably not a shock to learn that counterfeits concocted with artificial dyes became an underground export in the Middle East. The artificial purple intinction would quickly fade, of course, long after the sneaky merchant executed the sale. Even today, we haven't mastered the natural beauty of purple: when you print an image with purple on, *say*, a book cover, it just doesn't come out as beautifully as it appears in nature, because only nature knows how to produce it and has an organic firewall protecting it. Whether you're talking BC or AD, Tyrian purple was and is the most beautiful hue in the world, and I doubt you'd find a soul willing to argue otherwise – save for a few mollusks, of course.

Still under the shade of Gethsemane, I squeezed the olive in my hand, careful not to split it, then released my grip to examine it. It was jet black, almost a hue of obsidian that matched the mark on my wrist, which was the sharpest the tattoo was going to ever be in my lifetime. I placed the olive in my right palm, then stretched my wrist outright to heaven.

2,000 years ago, Christ had definitely/probably/possibly/supposedly been in this very same spot to begin the Passion. He had just entered this valley after departing the upper room with a belly-full of His last supper, the last morsels of food that would sustain Him through His suffering. When Yeshua broke bread that fateful night, the disciples thought it was just another Thursday. They didn't know it was the last time they'd see their rabbi healthy and whole, and all the suffering that followed after they left the garden in Zion escalated so abruptly and wounded so deeply that they began to question everything they thought they knew.

Yeshua knew. It's why we get one of the most tender, most vulnerable moments in the entire Bible: Yeshua asks God to neuter the plan. *There* must *be another way!* And if anybody had a direct line to ask whatever they wanted, and if anybody is guaranteed to get whatever they asked for, it was Yeshua.

God's answer? Silence. Not even a "no." God isn't swayed by the prayer, and His plan is executed as originally designed.

The undiscerning eye says that Christ's prayer changed nothing. But it actually changed *everything* for Yeshua: He knew that His prayer had been heard, and He knew that God would have gladly honored the request and diverted the master plan, save that there was an attractive alternative. But because God stayed the course, Yeshua was able to trust that there wasn't a better way to achieve what they'd set out to accomplish together, and He knew there was a necessary purpose behind His imminent suffering. With this knowledge, He never complained; He never asked for deliverance again.

Yeshua forged forward and, within hours of leaving this nursery, He was affixed to a cruel tree where He cried out to God, "why have You forsaken me?" And it doesn't matter if that happened at the site of the Holy Sepulcher or on the urine-soaked mountain I brought Joanna to see, because the end result was the same.

How appropriate that Yeshua began His tribulation in the garden of olives. Humans soak up this tree's fruit without even knowing it. Yet, "there *must* be another way!" cries the olive.

But I'm afraid not. There are no shortcuts to beauty: either crush the snail, or it's a knockoff.

How barbaric. How divine.

"Truly, truly, I say to you,
unless a grain of wheat falls
into the earth and dies,
it remains alone;
but if it dies,
it bears much fruit."
~ John 12:24, ESV

ל

November 22, 2020

Hi. Reactivated my phone.

Danger. How are you?

It's a quiet house on a Sunday.

Quiet is good.

There should be children screaming about. Instead I can hear my own breathing.
How are you?

I'm really well, actually.
Are your meds working yet?

No. After my psychiatrist called the cops on me, we had a falling out and so I
don't have any way to get refills anymore. So I've been rationing my pills. I'm
actually on a way lower dose now, and only taking them 3 times a week, at that.
Almost a negligible effect.

What happens when you run out?

Not sure. Tell you when I get there.

Oh. Are you feeling any better lately?

Can I be honest?

Of course. I'm asking you to be

I'm doing a little better.

Really?? That's great

I had a weird thing happen the other day. And I've felt better since then.

What happened

Lately I've been feeling invisible.
I pray, I don't hear back.
Constantly applying to jobs, I don't even get rejection letters.
I reach out to friends, I'm ghosted.
There was a point I've even questioned my existence.
Like, how far from the world do you have to be to wonder if you even exist?

Yeah. That's really disappointing to hear.
Though you did turn your phone off...

Yeah but God invented email.

How could I have forgotten.

But then I shopped for some groceries, and on the way back, I stopped at a red
light and in the car next to me, some kid rolled down his window.
"Hey!" he yelled at me. "Hi," I said. "How are you doing?" he asked me. "I'm okay.
How are you?" I responded.
"Good!" he responded, then added, "I like your Jeep." I said, "Thanks... I like
your... hatchback." Then he yelled over, "I like your tire cover."

What's on your tire cover?

A smiling Bob Ross holding a paint brush.

Oh! I like your tire cover too.

٣٠

<u>March 24, 2001</u>

"Yasue said that He would need to leave this world in order to spill the Holy Spirit upon the world," Claire explained to her children, trying to impart all she had learned over the past couple weeks. "Yasue was the harbinger for the Holy Spirit, who is now the harbinger for Yasue's return. Do you understand?"

Abni and Ebnahty, eager to please their mother, nodded their heads as if they understood, but their eyes proved there was still much confusion.

"I know it is hard to understand, but the important thing is that as you speak to Yasue in prayer, so you should also spend time speaking with the Holy Spirit, who indwells you. Many people feel like they're lost at sea when trying to discern the Holy Spirit, but…"

BOOM.

The earth grumbled, and several VHS tapes fell off a hanging shelf and crashed to the ground. Abni gasped and instinctively grabbed his sister's arm, and the both of them ducked behind the drab olive recliner next to them as the curtains whisped towards the center of the room.

Claire cocked her head and put her hand out towards her children.

"Stay here," she said, then jogged out her front door and looked over towards Hebron Road.

"Claire?" Zuji called over to his wife as he shielded his body behind the front door. "Do you see it?"

"Yes," Claire responded as tears welled.

"You see smoke?"

Yeah I had it custom-made.

So the light turned green and I shouted over to the kid as he rolled away, "thanks for knowing who he is." He didn't hear me, I'm sure. But the whole interaction just messed me up. I pulled over and cried because it felt like it was the first time in months that I'd been seen by anyone. And I just cried on the side of the road, cried and cried until I could see again, then drove home.

Oh

I hate being unseen. Invisible. Unimportant, irrelevant. I think, deep down, I want to be more important than I'll ever be.

That's true for most of us.

I haven't told anyone about any of that. I'm not sure why I'm even sharing it. But I also should let you know, I've been better since then.

That's really great to hear. Really. I'm happy that you're feeling better.

You've got me listening to Hebrew music a bit. The beats aren't better, but the lyrics sure are.

You're reading Hebrew?

I'm reading Google Translate's understanding of Hebrew. But also, yeah, I'm studying it a bit, sure. Just basics.
Humans are such misers. Myself included. I used to love the Red Hot Chili Peppers, and then someone pointed out that their writing skills have as much whip as a soft tail. They're half-talented: they get leeway because they compose melodies that have a heavy glow. But have you ever looked up the words? They're just card sharks doing a really impressive con job because their lyrics are a complete blood bath that shouldn't have gotten out of dogtown. The words are boot cut to the tune instead of the other way around. The result is music that's as sharp as a steak knife, but just as intelligent too. They care more about the way they play rather than what's actually beneath the marquee, where there's less brain tissue than what you'd find in a rib cage.

Well yeah. Most people would prefer music that moves them rather than music that speaks to them.
By the way... that's true of Israelis too.

"No," Claire shook her head, "I see the explosion."

"Was it by the restaurant over there?"

Claire nodded, then added, "there is no restaurant there anymore."

"Get in, quickly," Zuji urged. "This will soon be a holy hotbed."

Claire loped back inside and locked the multiple locks on the front door, then sat in the recliner the kids still hid behind and began to weep.

"Oh, Lord," Claire lamented, "may today have been Yousef's day off!"

Claire's words hit Zuji as abrasively as the blast had, for his friends who worked at the restaurant were probably incinerated with the building.

"That was a kosher restaurant," Zuji said aloud. " Tomorrow is the Kippur feast. This had to have been the work of Palestinians."

Zuji closed his eyes, scratched his cheek, and shook his head before having an epiphany.

"They will be coming," Zuji said. "They will need their scapegoat. We should go…"

THUMP. THUMP. THUMP.

Too late.

THUMP. **THUMP!**

"*Potkhim!*" a voice cried from the other side.

Claire got up from the recliner while the rest of her family froze after hearing the enmity in the voice behind the door. But as she touched the handle, she heard a much different voice.

"*Do not open… do not open that door.*"

It just encapsulates what I tried to say awhile ago, how so many pastors get away with emotional manipulation because the American Christian church focalizes their platform on getting their congregation emotionally charged - dedicating large portions of their ministry budgets to worship bands and almost nothing to devotional writers or their Bible studies. The result is congregations that sing to the Lord with words they don't even understand.

Adherents from all religions say things they don't fully believe or perhaps even understand, though, even in jewdism.

I hear that. I do. I just feel that when Jews are praying things they don't fully grasp, it's incidental, whereas Christian leaders do it intentionally. The most successful mega-churches provide scant biblical context, keeping their congregation in a level of spiritual immaturity, and instead resort to cheap means to keep them coming. Why else would they feel the need to play a crescendo when the pastor is emphasizing his big idea? The idea should be able to stand on its own without music. that emotional response you're feeling, it's not coming from the Holy Spirit, it's coming from a piano.

But faith is a feeling too, yeah?

Sure there's a component of that. But it shouldn't be all-consuming. For every moment of meaningful, emotional epiphanies, I've had ten more intellectual ones. The Holy Spirit uses both, for sure, but well-meaning (and not so well-meaning) pastors can replicate emotional responses much easier than intellectual ones. It's why the most famous and well-known preachers are often the ones who know how to tap into emotion with stirring speeches, so we can "feel" like we can touch faith. But it creates mindless religion.

Can faith be faith, even without facts though? In your view.

I don't think so, honestly. There's proof for religion. God gave us historical accounts of miraculous intervention. Seek it, and you can find it, but we're more worried about picking up another shift at work to make ends meet. The Bible says that our faith will be "tested by the fire." That means it can't be paper thin. It'll burn up. We need a cornerstone, and it needs to be made of gold.

All that is gold does not glitter.

But it's just as valuable.
And at the end of the day, Esther, I just don't want to be devoid of hope.
I don't need to glitter, so long as I'm authentic.

Do you think you'll get your footing back on your faith?

My faith?

Like, your belief in god?

I don't think my belief in God wasn't ever in doubt. It's been my faith in prayer, and whether or not Yeshua is the Messiah, that's been a hard squeeze lately.

Well maybe we're more alike than we thought, then.

My faith doesn't blow around in the wind. When I was in college, I took an intellectual look at God, evaluated the Gospel, and came to the conclusion that Christ is King. It just made sense, in both theory and reality.

I mean... you were raised Christian, right?

Yes. Catholic.

So weren't you biased?

Claire turned around and, seemingly speaking to nobody, asked, "no?"

" 'No,' what?" Zuji quizzed Claire, who was as if she was talking to an apparition. "Open the door before he blows it open!"

Palestinians are required to open the door for the Tzahal, no matter the situation. If they don't open the door, the Tzahal are authorized to use force to open the door, and such decisions don't often end well for indignant Palestinians.

"*POT. KHIM!*" the voice behind the door cried out again.

Claire's hand remained on the handle.

"*Do not open that door…*" the quieter voice whispered again. When Claire realized it wasn't anyone in her family whispering it, she pulled her hand away from the handle.

"Claire!" Zuji whispered so loudly, he may as well have been using his normal booming tone. "Are you crazy? Open it or they will kill us!"

THUMP! THUMP! **THUMP**THUMP**THUMP**!

"*Potkhim, potkhim, POTKHIM-POTKHIM-**POTKHIM**!*"

The voice outside the door started to sound more crazed than angry.

"No," Claire said to Zuji, caressing his arm. "The Lord says not to."

Zuji walked towards the door to open it himself, but Claire squeezed his shoulder.

"Zuji, we trust the Lord."

Zuji's mouth gaped and the color in his face poured out, turning yellow and then as chartreuse as the recliner.

Well, of course I was. Should I eliminate Christianity just because I was raised with it? There's a reason it's persisted this long.

If standing the test of time is your measuring stick, you've overlooked Hinduism.

Karma and Job are incompatible.
If Karma is real, and Romy still died the way she did, then Karma is evil.
I know too many successful people to believe Karma is real.

So what's holding you back at this point? What are the biggest doubts you're facing?

If I'm being honest? Christians probably hold me back more than anything else at this point.

Really!?

Yes. I try not to let someone's disciples impact my opinion on them too much, but living in Tulsa has made it hard to rest in God's sovereignty.

In what way? What do they do?

We've talked about this awhile ago, but people who don't have critical thinking skills tend to believe in superstition instead of religion.

Yeah. My experience with christians is that they're emotionally manipulative people who care more about dramatic effect than anything.

That's funny. A guy I met in Palestine said the same exact thing about Muslims.

Muslims do it too imo.

I think a lot of Christians forget that, yes, the Bible has charisma to it and we believe in the supernatural, but the Bible also instructs us to check ourselves and to test the spirits.

What do you mean by "charisma?"

Well I've noticed that many Christian pastors - at least from my experience in America - are guilty of invoking an emotional response in people, then say "that's the Holy Spirit moving in you." it's just... idk. is that the Holy Spirit, or is it the autonomic sympathetic nervous system activating in the same way it might at a Bon Jovi concert?

Lol.

Or when pastors have superfluous, bombastic sermons that don't engage people intellectually, so they glaze it with a motley of different inflections in their tone so it comes across as more profound than it is. or they cinch some axiom with a booming "can I get an amen?" because it was a principle that wouldn't otherwise have stood on its own if they allowed people the time to consider what they said.

Well, I can't say I've been to too many christian sermons to know what you're talking about. But I get what you're saying. "Can I get an amen?" might be the pastor's version of "Lol." Just say it when you're not sure what else to say.

Lol.

Lol.

I think this problem stems from the fact that so many pastors have never had an original thought in their head. They were born into the faith, never questioned it, and then they rely on cliches, like calling God "the Great Physician" or how they have a "personal Lord and Savior," phrases that aren't found in the Bible and instead were birthed in the echoes of the halls of mega churches.

"Please, open it," Zuji pleaded with his wife, appearing like he was somewhere between physically-sick and already-dead.

"Relax," she disquieted Zuji. "At first injury, we leave."

Zuji's mouth remained open, and whimpered like he was choking on the heavy air, which now reeked of smoke and sinew.

"If they come in, I will ask them to kill all of us," Claire said, finding the most oddly comforting words she could find in the moment.

Zuji allowed a few disconcerting snickers to escape his mouth, though they sounded more like a sheep's bleating.

"Listen," Claire whispered, then smiled. "They are no longer pounding on our door."

Zuji stopped for a moment and listened. She was right: it was silent, save for the sirens in the distance.

"You're right," Zuji smiled.

It remained silent for a moment longer, at least until the loud ringing of automatic weapons sprayed the house. Zuji and Claire dove behind the recliner, shielding their children's bodies with their own as the shattering of glass rung upstairs. Claire looked out her window and saw lights in the sky, as if stars were plummeting to Bethlehem like rain.

"They're shooting out our windows!" Zuji cried, announcing the obvious. "We must open the door! It is the only way they might have mercy on us now!"

Claire twice tried to talk, but each time, multiple gunshots cloaked her voice. When the shooting stalled for a moment, Claire realized that not everyone was accounted for.

"*Umi!*"

"Personal Lord and Savior" is one I've heard a lot. it isn't in the bible?

No. It's a phrase that was mechanized by the western church to help justify our individualistic worldviews. A lot of pastors will have new Christians pray the "sinner's prayer," and I think a lot of people would be upset to find that this tactic was only invented in the last couple hundred years, not by any of the original Apostles.

That's intriguing. Why do pastors use it then?

I mean, the concept makes sense - how else are you going to show that you're dedicating your life to Christ without some kind of communication with Him? It's the same thing with altar calls.

What's an altar call?

Oh. It's this time in a service where a pastor will have everyone bow their heads, and then say that if anyone accepted Jesus as the Christ, they should approach the altar and pray the "sinner's prayer" I just mentioned.
In theory, I don't hate altar calls, but they can be cumbersome when you do them every week, which (at least to me) makes it lose its impact. What's super annoying is when pastors do an altar call without explaining the context of what it is.

Again, I don't get why pastors would use this technique if it's not in the bible. What gives with that?

I think these things are just so mechanical now that it's the engrained method to tangibly measure (and report to leadership and stakeholders) how many people supposedly became Christians during an event. As if Yeshua's command was a one-and-done prayer to report statistics.
If it was only a few churches guilty of this, then whatever. But I think the bigger issue is the Church has just lost a certain humility. We get set in our traditions, what's been done in the past, and then canonize it. We need to consider that maybe there's still more (even for Christians) to learn about God. You can't reach people if you claim you have all the answers, because the first time it's proven that one of your answers is wrong, you're exposed as a false prophet.

Yeah, christians are pretty bad with that. I think today's "prophets" are a lot like bingo grandmas in that way. With a room full of them, someone is bound to win eventually. 1 winning game against their hundreds of losing cards.

Right, and instead of contending with the fact that you were wrong, you ignore it or, worse, distort the facts so it looks like you had other winning cards. It helps you sleep at night, fine, but any conscionable person sees right through it and knows you're being a spin doctor.

And we disregard the many, many prophecies they've gotten wrong. Show me someone who got it right even 10 times, and you'll turn my head. Have a fulfillment 50 times, and I'll believe.

When someone is wrong about a prophecy and can't admit it - even just once - then they deserve to lose their following. Believe me, I know.

You don't get to think of yourself as an honest person if you're unwilling to look at evidence that challenges your worldview. Plus, the bible isn't meant to be a tool to wield in the face of people who don't believe in it. It's like you said. Don't use the Bible to justify your worldview. Use the Bible to inform your worldview.

Exactly.

Claire fled upstairs to find her mother sitting at the kitchen table, glass all over the floor, and the legs of the chair trembling along with Umi.

"Is it over?" Umi asked.

"Are you hurt?" Claire gasped, checking her mother's ankles for shards of glass, but exhaled when she found her mother unscathed.

Umi smiled at Claire, shook her head, and then simpered as tears sluiced down her face as if they'd been prevented by a dam. Claire rubbed her mother's shoulders, then felt Zuji's grip on her own as she bowed her head.

"I know what you're saying is logical," Claire reasoned with Zuji. "But I also know what God is telling me. And if God wants us to survive, Zuji, we'll survive. If not, He'll let us all get bombed together and we don't miss a minute with each other. We win no matter what is about to happen."

"Losing our lives is not winning," Zuji retorted, then squeezed Claire's shoulder again to offer tenderness.

"Yasue has said otherwise. We are already living as a dead family, stuck in this house and being slaves to the war around us."

Zuji whimpered and stroked his nose.

"Zuji… we have the Holy Spirit."

"Claire, what does that even mean?"

"He's an Advocate."

"We have always had an Advocate! His name is Yasue."

"Yes," Claire agreed, "Yasue advocates for us unceasingly before our Father in heaven. But we have another, right here on earth. He is completing the work of Christ until the return."

"Return of what?"

Wait, are we actually agreeing on something?
٩(ᐛ)۶

Lol. I think so.
Bottom line: don't confuse emotion with faith. They're not the same thing.
Phooo. Thanks for letting me vent. That actually feels good to talk about it.

You know what would help ME?

What's that?

Can you share a Romy?

So fluffy!

I know, right!? And Romy is too!

Lol.
So where are you at in all that, then? You say God exists. Good. But what's the verdict on Christ? On prayer?

I'm trying to get back into prayer.

What does that mean? Like, just that you're praying again?

You brought up a good point, last we talked. I hadn't taken the time to really evaluate the purpose of prayer. I've been doing that lately, though.

So you've figured out your prayer principles then, huh?

No. I kind of let the Metroid Principles get away from me.
But I'm committed to re-discovering the purpose of prayer.

I'm actually really happy to hear that.

"Yasue, Baba," Ebnahty chimed in. "We have the Holy Spirit to watch over us until Yasue comes back."

"You know about this?" Zuji said, aghast at his young daughter's response.

"Yes," Ebnahty replied. "I have felt Him, like a jacket over my body."

"Zuji," Claire added one final point to her argument, "the army is gone."

Zuji perked up. She was right: they had been arguing so long that he hadn't even realized that the shooting, the pounding, the screaming outside had all settled.

It was the first time the Anastas family– or perhaps any living family along Hebron Road – had refused to open the door for the Tzahal. And it would also be the last, as Claire and the rest of the family would never again refuse to open the door for anyone.

"Let us pray," Claire said, bowing her head. And as she began to pray in an unfamiliar language, so followed the children as Zuji marveled at the natural flow of this language he had never heard before.

"Love," Zuji said, closing his eyes and bowing his crown, "I feel a hallowed heat upon the top of my head."

I figure, I kiss Romy's urn every morning and every night in the unlikely hope that she can feel my love when I do that. That she can somehow feel my touch. And if I'm willing to go out on a limb to do that, then why not pray? Especially when God promises He hears what we say.

I'd like to know what you come up with during your Zero Mission.

Is that genuine? You really want me to share what I find? Because I don't have to.

That wasn't just a careless line I gave you, last time. I really would like to know what you think you figure out. Nobody completely understands prayer, jews included. If you have something helpful, I'd like to hear it.

Well, as of now, I've got nothing. Not yet. Though I learned how NOT to pray, I guess.

What do you mean?

Call them rules if you want, they're just things that I've stopped praying for altogether.

Like what?

Like, don't pray for things that you can do under your own power. Don't pray for safety, God already knows whether you're going to survive whatever you're doing in that moment. Don't pray for healing from afflictions that can be treated with basic medicine. Don't pray for career advancement, again, God has this laid out already. In fact, just don't ask God for anything unless you're already sure it's in alignment with His will. If you're not sure His stance on it, you can ask for it, but you must be okay with whether or not you get this thing. If you can't promise to still be satisfied with Him if you don't get it, then you don't get to ask for it. In fact, understand such a request as evil, for this thing has become your god if it is a conditional requirement to continue your relationship with the Lord.

That's too fatalistic. Almost nihilistic.
And that's a lot of don'ts.
I think instead of focusing on what not to pray for, you should think about what's worth praying for. Because I think it's okay to pray for whatever you want. I don't think you were meant to be restricted as to what you're allowed to pray for.

Well each "don't pray for this" I just mentioned has an implicit "pray for this instead." Like "don't pray for safety," my point is you should use higher-level thinking to seek out God's will for you instead of dictating what you expect from Him.

So instead of "keep me safe," what DO you pray for?

Well, it's still an incomplete process remember. I'm working through these things again. I need to consider the Metroid principles. It's my top priority now.

Welcome back, Zero Suit Danger

Thanks, Jewish Siri.

419

MISSING GABRIEL

> "Elisha said, 'At this time next year
> you will have a son in your arms.'
> Then she said, 'No, my lord.
> Man of God, do not lie.'"
> ~ 2 Kings 4:16, CSB

Joanna and I ambled down an alley, heading towards the most popular tourist destination in Nazareth: Mary's well, where the angel Gabriel prophesied the coming of Yeshua to Mary.

"I love being able to share all this with you," I told Joanna as we walked hand-in-hand on our last full day in Israel.

"Well," she said with the enthusiasm of a reader on the 400th page of a needlessly long book, "you saw a lot worth sharing."

As if an invitation to transmogrify myself into Robin Williams on some 1970s-grade sugar cane, I scatted back, "Forty days sure seems like a long time, at least until you're on the last day. I mean, I'm really excited about going home and I can't wait until December 7th, but I do wish I had more time to show you the places I visited before you got here. Here in Nazareth, they have this hidden little mill down the road: Elbabour. They sell all kind of nuts and spices. I bought a pound of their corn nuts and it's pretty much what I survived off of in Megiddo. If we had a full day here, I'd take you there and then I'd definitely want to hike back up Mt. Precipice with you if I could. Also, did you know the oldest café in Israel is here? The Café Abu Salem. Jerusalem used to just be called 'Salem.' But the Café Abu Salem, it opened before there even was a modern-day Israel. They sell this special drink made with cinnamon and walnuts and some kind of exotic spice."

Joanna didn't respond; not even a nod from her head to acknowledge anything I had said.

"Are you okay?" I probed.

"Yeah," she said. "Just... listening."

Maybe she wasn't in the mood to hear about my travels. I guess it was kind of a somber day, with the trip almost being over. So, I shut up until we stood outside of Mary's well.

"So, this is it!" I heralded, like I had something to do with its development.

"This is it? It seems... I don't know. I thought it would be grander. It's... humble."

"Yeah, it's not even really marked. You could walk right by and not know it was here. That's what happened to me the first time I got here. I walked right by it and you see that coffee shop on the top of the hill? I perched there for awhile and had some yogurt to hold me over, but the best meal I had in Nazareth was right over there at Rosemary's: they had this 'rosemary ice cream' which I think was just vanilla with cinnamon and apples. I think you'd really like it, if you're in the mood for..."

"I'm not pregnant," she interrupted my burbling.

"What?" I whispered, as if I didn't hear what she said.

"I'm not pregnant."

"You're *not* pregnant?"

"No. I took a pregnancy test last night."

I thought about it for a moment, but then had a spark of hope as I realized that pregnancy kits can sometimes result in false negatives.

"Well, you know, those tests..."

"It's not a false negative," she interrupted again.

"But how can you even know that for sure?"

"Because my period started this morning. With a vengeance."

"In the early stages of pregnancy, some people experience..."

"I'm not pregnant," she interrupted me a third time, her eyes glossing. "*Believe* me."

I sat silent for a moment, then breathed a wistful sigh. After all the excitement of her maybe being pregnant, here we were, back to square one and no closer to pregnancy than when we began trying years ago.

"It's okay," I tried convincing her (and myself). "It's okay. This isn't the first pregnancy scare we've had."

Pregnancy "scare." What do you call a "pregnancy scare" when it's the thing you wish for most in the world?

Joanna started to tear up.

"This one is hard. It's like, why give us the..." she choked on her words and her pupils darted skyward. I hugged her hard enough that it could have served as the Heimlich. "...*hope*? Why lead us on at all? Give me all the symptoms of a pregnancy, like this curse was finally broken. It just feels a little... cruel."

She was right. Couldn't God just say "no," and let that be it? Wouldn't it be enough for Him to just shut that door and let us hear that it closed? Instead He leaves the door open just a crack, and just as we think to walk through the door in faith, it gets kicked in our face.

I could maybe accept that we were incapable of having kids. But why fleece us into feeling mocked, too? Is that really necessary?

"Time is jealous of you," the villain needled Dorian Gray, *"and wars against your lilies and your roses."* The polemic corrupts a man, a beautiful man, and Gray trades nobility for hedonism, legacy for the moment, a wooden rose for the gloried whites and the reds already in his hands.

A few tears rolled down Joanna's cheek and dropped off her chin. I'd been around the block with this enough to know that commiseration only led to a dark cloud, so I tried to change the tune.

"I believe we're going to have children," I tried encouraging her. "Or, if I'm wrong about that, we'll still be granted peace from God about it. But I think... really believe... that for the same reason you and me didn't know each other before 2006, we don't know our children yet."

My words had no effect on her, except maybe pushing her into feeling guilty for not agreeing.

"We have to have faith," I said, scratching at my wrist until it bled. My tattoo had scabbed over, reaching the itchiest phase. "So, you're not pregnant *now*. I know you really believed it would be this time. So did I. But if God wants to give us children, He'll do it. We just do what we can on our end, and in the meantime, we count our blessings. And we are very, *very* blessed."

"Yes, we are," Joanna said as she nods. "I know that."

In every trial and through every sorrow, this is what we always came back around to: we love our dogs. God was always aware that, had He blessed us with children, we would've poured ourselves into loving them. He didn't – or *hasn't*, at least – allowed that, but we still had so much love to give. So, we poured it into our dogs. And you know what? I like dogs. I like dogs better than I like any of His human creations.

There. I said it. I know humans are the most important species to God's overarching plan. I know they're more valuable. But I prefer dogs to humans in the same way that I prefer benevolence to malignance, and it would be dishonest to not acknowledge it.

There are two things Joanna and I unfailingly prayed for every day: our dogs' health and to someday have children. So, God hadn't blessed us with any babies. But, He did grant us with the best dogs in the world, and 50% ain't bad when you're asking for two very big things.

"Oh," Joanna sighed, "what I would give to have a Sidney hug right now."

"Yeah, or a Romy cuddle. Or a Shadrach kiss."

Joanna smiled, and then so do I, because there was one truth that got us through times like these.

We love our dogs and our dogs love us.

> "There's rosemary,
> that's for remembrance.
> Pray you, love, remember."
> - Ophelia

November 25, 2020

Hey, how are you? How do you feel today?

> I'm okay. How are you?

I'm doing well. But I mean, no, really. How's, like, your mental health?

> You don't need to walk on eggshells. I'm going to be fine.

Because it just felt like, kinda like you wouldn't be fine.

> Really, I'm okay.
> You just checking in on me outta pity, or do you have something on your mind?

K honestly, I've got more gripes with christians to talk about

> Okay, get in line.

I hate how christians always try to convert people. It's maddening.

> I get that. I do think the heart of someone "trying to convert" is (most times) out of genuine concern, so I try to remember that when I see it going on.

No, my friend. You live in privilege. I doubt you've had someone tell you "you're going to hell" if you don't accept what they're peddling. It's not gentle.

> Well I can't vouch for that technique.

For a gentile to say it to a jew, too. What a dynamic.
This is a big difference between jewdism and other Abraham religions. Christians and muslims aim to convert everyone, while jews aim to be exclusive as possible.

> I hear what you're saying, and I really don't mean to defend the practice, but I have to note that I don't believe conversion is the aim of Christianity. It only manifests that way when Christians miss the point.

What's the aim then? I mean, for everyone to be good and that christianity will make you a better person?

> To be honest, that's actually even further away than your first guess.

lol so what is it then

> Christianity takes the basic principle that nobody can ever be "good" enough to stand in front of God. All of us stand condemned for failing to uphold the Law - Jew and Gentile alike. Every sin will be judged some day, and I can't imagine anybody could stand before a Holy God who finds unholiness unbearable, and reasonably respond to His question, "why should I let you in my presence?"

So where does the "let's convert all non-christians" come in? Why did the crusades happen?

> Two very different questions there. Referring to the Crusades as being "Christ-based" is like pointing to beef as being "plant-based" because cows eat grass.
> Crusades happened because of political and emotional manipulation.
> For the other question, Yeshua resurrected and hung around for just a blink and then left again, but not before giving us some specific instructions.

which are what?

> 1) "Tell everyone my story." Because it's good news: a Just God won't punish us if that penalty was already paid.

What's the other?

٣١

Only two years deep, and the new millennium had brought a generation's worth of fresh challenges to Bethlehem; events unfathomable in the 20th century. Hostiles increasingly targeted Israel, and the Tzahal and Palestinian insurgents were deadlocked in protracted conflict that continued to claim lives on both sides of the bank.

In one fateful clash, a group of Palestinian militants assailed the Tzahal, fled from them, and finally sought refuge in the Church of the Nativity. The insurgents took the clergy inside the church as hostages, and the holy ground in which Christ was brought into the world became a defiled battleground. The basilica was bedeviled into a standoff as soldiers, insurgents, and innocents alike were killed as the Tzahal pursued the aggressors and worked to free the hostages.

A strict curfew was promptly mandated, and Palestinians were only allotted a few designated hours per day to buy the essentials they needed – any Palestinians outside of their homes during the specified times would be assumed guerrillas and neutralized as such. Many families were too afraid to get groceries, preferring to starve than risk being shot. Even still, the lines at grocery stores in Bethlehem became so congested that it had become impossible to drive to the stores, grab rolls of toilet paper, and get back home before curfew started again.

"We are going to miss the cutoff," Zuji said, clutching his vegetables and milk in the line at the market.

2) "Love everyone."
Christians equate "conversion" with "discipleship." They're not the same.

Are they not?

No. Tell me this: why does communism fail every time a government props it up?

Because American imperialism?

Seriously?

Okay, well a lot of times, it turns into a dictatorship, and the dictator gets overthrown when people start to see the dictator's lack of balance.

Not where I was going, but that works to support my point I guess: communism can only work if everyone within the community agree to it. It can't be forced. It's why the early Christians thrived: they had a communist mindset, but the thing was that everyone agreed to support one another. Nobody was forced to. It's why kibbutzes are so successful in Israel!

Kibbutzim.

Bless you.
Israeli communities become self-sufficient and thrive, not because you were forced into the arrangement, but because you're happy with it.

Your point is getting away from me.

You can't "convert" someone into being a disciple.
Discipleship is a choice. It has a cost. A steep cost.
And it only works if you're knowingly accepting the role.
Every Christian has the same responsibility: profess the Gospel of Yeshua. But it's up to the listener to choose whether or not they believe. And all the other stuff that Christians overemphasize? Those are just details.

Okay well that's more reasonable to me.
A little less imposing, to think of it like that.

One of our heroes of the faith, Paul (who was a Jew and I would assume you're familiar with (and probably at odds with)) explained the process like a horticulturalist: someone plants the seed, someone else waters it, and God decides if it grows. Evangelism, discipleship, and the rest is up to God. We know most will reject the message, but still others will come to know repentance, and that's what makes it worthwhile. That's true faith.

As interesting as this is, I also want to be respectful and let you get to bed given that you have a major holiday in the morning.

...how does an Israeli know that I'm about to have Thanksgiving?
Is it on your calendar or something??

Yes. Well, no. Not officially. But don't forget I was born in New York.
I grew up in a small settlement. So those of us get together and celebrate Friendsgiving, just for fun. It usually coincides with your Thanksgiving week.
Of course, though, it's cancelled this year. We've been calling it Friendsgrieving.

Well can I tell you that it's actually really timely? Because I got my first upgrade.

Oh yeah?

1. Be thankful. Vocalize your thanks.

Quite right. Even if you're doubting prayer, you should still be thankful for what god gave you

"We will not miss curfew," Claire assured him, holding onto the figs and eggs with one hand, Abni's soft fingers with her other. "Curfew does not begin for another hour."

"Maybe we should leave now," Zuji mused. "Perhaps this standoff ends soon and we have enough to survive until then?"

"No," Claire hastily responded, "this standoff has gone on for almost two weeks already. We cannot know when it will be solved."

"We should have split up again," Zuji lamented. "The bakery took too long, and now we will have no time to get to the pharmacy after this."

"We can visit the pharmacy tomorrow," Claire reminded him.

"I heard the Tzahal snipers shot one of the monks," said a Palestinian who stood in front of Zuji and Claire at the checkout line, swiveling his head to jump into their conversation.

"Yes, that happened a few days ago," Zuji affirmed. "I have heard this also."

"First they kill our bellringer, now they are killing our monks. Soon enough, they will start executing priests and none of us will be allowed to leave our houses after war breaks out in the Church."

"Believe me," Zuji told the stranger in line, "the Tzahal do not want any priests to die. That would make them look bad."

"What do they care?" the stranger asked. "They already look bad. They have created gunbattles in church, throwing grenades in our most famous tourist attraction and starting fires in the basilica. They should just go in, kill the militants, and end this standoff for the good of all Bethlehem."

Exactly that. If you have a mortal enemy, and they give you $100 out of the goodness of their heart, do you refuse to thank them just because you don't like them?

I might, yeah

Oy I didn't expect that kind of spite from you. Lol.
Well I wouldn't. And how much more to be thankful to god, who is definitely not an enemy.

That's good. A good one to start with. There's always a place to be thankful, no matter how glum it's gotten.

Figuring that out has been one of the most helpful boons. Not a big fan of "just think positively" mantras, but being thankful has helped pull me out.
Like when I tell God "thanks for my family" now, that's all it means. No strings attached, no implicit plea to keep us intact. I'm saying "thank you for this moment that we're all together."

And you thought about it because it happened to be Thanksgiving week?

Honestly, no. This is one that's been percolating. And I've started reading a couple books to help supplement my foray into prayer.

Finally getting into Tolkien?

Man. I'm starting to understand why God warned Jews so much about false idols.
No, one of them is the Didache, another is St. Benedict's Holy Rule for monks.

Whut's that

They're not unlike your Talmud. Didache is a book of ethics and principles written by the early apostles of the Christian faith, shortly after the historic happenings of Yeshua. Benedict's book is similar, it was based off of traditions from the monks known as the desert fathers, who made the argument for a process called Contemplative Prayer. It was developed into what's known as Lectio Divina, a prayer process to better understand the Bible.

What's special about it? Would it translate for jews you think?

I don't think so. You see the Bible as a guide, but this thing, Lectio Divina, assumes that the Bible is active and alive today.

So tell me about it. How is it different than normal prayer?

"One day I was engaged in physical work with my hands and I began to think about the spiritual tasks we humans have. While I was thinking, four spiritual steps came to mind:
reading (lectio),
meditation (meditatio),
prayer (oratio),
and contemplation (contemplatio).
This is the ladder of monastics by which they are lifted up from the earth into heaven. There are only a few distinct steps, but the distance covered is beyond measure and belief since the lower part is fixed on the earth and its top passes through the clouds to lay bare the secrets of heaven."
Guigo II

It's a bit more formulaic, with four steps:
(1) Read, (2) Meditate,
(3) Pray, (4) Contemplate.
Guigo (ancient monk) developed it. It's basically an invitation for the Holy Spirit and/or Shekhinah to come and speak to our heart while studying Scripture.
So, no, I really don't think it translates.
Lectio Divina doesn't work for someone who doesn't believe in the Holy Spirit.
The whole point is that He directs you.

So how do you actually use it though? Like practically speaking?

Lectio Divina dissects a single sentence of a book until it's picked clean. The premise is that, to hear God's voice, you need to slow down. Way down. And Lectio Divina forces your hand into that: if reading is ice-skating, then contemplative prayer is crawling on your belly through slush after the ice melts.

"Do you hear this guy?" Zuji whispered to Claire through his clenched teeth. "The Jews do not care. The Muslims do not care. It is only us who are losing our most holy place to violence."

Claire did not respond, so Zuji looked behind himself to find his wife kneeling on the ground with the back of her hand on Abni's forehead.

"It has gotten worse," Claire said, looking up at Zuji. "This is definitely a fever. We need to leave now and get to the pharmacy for this medication."

"But we have been standing in line for an hour, and we are so close," Zuji protested – at least until he looked into Abni's pained eyes and saw how unwell he had suddenly become. "Yes, we must leave now. I will put the eggs back if you will take Abni…"

"ATTENTION," a man on a military vehicle outside of the grocery store announced over a loudspeaker. "ATTENTION! I need everyone to listen."

The commotion in the grocery store ceased, and it became so silent that the only audible noise were the wind chimes right outside of the shop, which were picking up as the Sufa inched by.

"Everyone, go home."

As quickly as the pandemonium had settled before, the Sufa's new order stoked the shoppers into an aggrandized uproar.

"I repeat, go home. Curfew starts in *five* minutes. Anyone who is not home will be treated as a threat. Go home! Immediately."

Claire and Zuji exchanged quick worried glances at each other, then were pushed aside by the shoppers who abandoned their groceries in the spot they had been standing to rush home to avoid any chance of reprisal.

Watch out for the Zambonis!

Every weekday, I spend time on a single verse of Scripture. A random verse chosen from a "verse of the day" algorithm online. Literally one line. I'll read the verse, then meditate on it, then I'll read how it's translated across 5 different versions, then I'll read a little bit of commentary on it, then I'll look up the literal translation of each word in its native language (Hebrew for OT and Greek for NT), and then I'll pray about it and rest, waiting to see if the Holy Spirit sends any more direction about the verse.

Have you gotten anything from it?

Yeah, actually. I've done it for 2 days now. And both times, I found really helpful truths about God.

Like what?

Well, the first Lectio Divina I ever did, I read 1 Corinthians 1:18. Which I recognize isn't in your Bible, but it says, "For the word of the cross is folly to those who are perishing, but to us who are being saved it is the power of God."

So like, what did you get from that?

I concentrated on each individual word, then tried to see the forest from the trees, and felt like the Holy Spirit was telling me "the message of the cross is foolish to those who are foolish." The idea being that there are things in life that we are absolutely certain about, but we have to accept that we're limited by human logic and might be wrong about things that we're sure about. Like, I can sit here and tell you that I KNOW that 1 plus 1 equals 2. But if I die, go to heaven, and find out from God Himself that 1 plus 1 actually equals 3, I need to accept that and just rest in God's sovereignty over the matter. Even though it makes no sense to me.

Christians are bad at math.

Lol.

And you've kept doing contemplative prayer?

Yeah. The verse the second day was Matthew 11:28, also not in your Bible of course: it's Yeshua speaking about the respite He offers. And as I closed my eyes, I saw a traveler dragging himself to the top of a steep hill, seeking a place to rest. He hauled to the top of the hill and there were others there. They warned the man that he couldn't stay in that place. He said no, I'm staying overnight, I need rest. They said you'll be killed up here, that he should come with them. He said no, i'll be fine and will just find higher ground. Then animals came to attack the traveler, so the man decided to go with the men into a nearby valley. They dropped him off and said good luck surviving the night. The man found a campfire in the valley, and stayed for a night. With only a modest blanket and the kindness of a stranger, the man survived the night. Dreading the valley at first, he instead woke up and wanted to stay for as long as he could, because he was already tired and he knew what came next was arduous and would deplete him. But he knew it had to be done, so he took up the journey out of the valley. The man thought it would be a quick trial, but it ended up that the journey out of the valley took every ounce of his strength. But at the end of the journey was the warmth of a bed and his wife. And God's rest is a lot like the moment he crawled into that bed.

What's the verse actually say? The one you were studying.

"Come to me, all who labor and are heavy laden, and I will give you rest."

"Meet outside!" Zuji yelled out, raising his finger amidst the wave of chaos heading out the door.

When Claire finally made it out with Abni, she saw Zuji standing beside the Sufa, talking to the soldier on the loudspeaker.

"See to it yourself," she heard the soldier tell Zuji as she approached.

"But he is only five years old and so sick!" Zuji dissented. "Why can we not go to the hospital?"

"Two soldiers have been wounded."

"At the Church? The hospital is right by our house, if we can just get permission…"

"Not at the Church," the soldier corrected, "but at Rachel's Tomb."

Also right by the Anastas house.

The narrow streets of Bethlehem became the autobahn of the Middle East, the most inexperienced drivers suddenly turning into Arab Andrettis.

"Maybe we can treat his fever at home?" Zuji suggested, weaving through Hebron Road.

"There is no way," Claire said, shaking her head. "This is getting much too serious much too quickly."

"Is it better for him to be shot?" Zuji posited. "We have a much better chance of survival at home. We can get the medicine tomorrow."

"If two soldiers were injured right in front of our house, then, no. We will not be able to get the medicine tomorrow either. Besides, this cannot wait until then. I need you to drop me off at the hospital, and you go home and take care of the others. Abni and I will stay at the hospital

Yeah, I think that's a lot more succinct than your story.

Yeah. It's a good thing God didn't ask me to be one of the writers of the Bible.

But he did call you to write a book, right?

I thought you don't believe God calls us to do specific things like that?

I don't. But I'd sure like you to believe it.

I actually wanted to talk to you about that.
I can't write my book without talking about you. I tried, it doesn't work. So would you be cool with me conveying our conversations into a book i'm writing?

Hmm. I might be okay with it. But I almost wouldn't want you to use my name. Or if you do, only use my first name, and I'd just want you to emphasize that I'm not some expert. I don't speak for all jews.

Of course you don't speak for all Jews throughout all space and time. I'll just let readers know you only speak for all Jews from 2000 BC to modern day.

ヽ(`⌒´メ)ノ

Just kidding!!

But fine. Go crazy. I'm not interesting anyway.

Phew. Thanks. Appreciate it. I was actually nervous to ask you that.

Though I can't speak for all Jews, it's believed that we are all connected by Elijah.

Really? How so?

Elijah connects the past and the future - past redemption and future redemption. Elijah is known as the covenant protector, and he's believed to watch over every child born. This is why during the circumcision ceremony (bris), the godfather holding the baby sits on a chair called Elijah's Chair. There's also a belief that Elijah occasionally reappears to help people.

Really? There's a story in our New Testament where Yeshua gets talked to by both Elijah and Moses on Mount Tabor

Well, for us, it's more like there are stories about people who were in car accidents being saved by a stranger who was never found again. People say it might've been Elijah. Because in the bible, he was whirled up into the sky without dying.

Do you know who was the only other human in the Bible to be taken to heaven without dying?

Yeshua I guess?

No, Yeshua was crucified, silly.

Hmmmm - and you're sure this is in my bible?

Yes, I'm certain. Want a hint?

Yes please

Hint: it's Enoch

Ohhhhhhh yeah!
He's Chanoch in our bible btw, pronounced with much phlegm. like hocking a loogie.

Shoot so I guess I'm the one that got it wrong

Never get into a bible trivia contest with a jew, Danger
(ᵔⱽᵔ)

until the curfew is lifted, or if it is not lifted, then we will sneak back home."

"That is too dangerous. Why don't I go to the hospital with Abni, and you stay safely at home instead?"

"Because I have a way of getting what I need," Claire said. And Zuji knew she was right: she was the shrewdest person he knew, and Abni's life was on the line.

After parking in front of the hospital entrance, Zuji lurched out of the driver seat and opened the passenger door for Claire, extending his hand to help her out of her seat.

"Go home and get some rest," Claire instructed Zuji. "Don't even spend a thought on me."

Zuji clutched his wife, laden with grief as if she had just been given a death sentence.

"You know I will not commit to a promise I intend to break," Zuji said, then kissed Claire on the forehead. "May the Holy Spirit be with you."

"And also with you," Claire responded, displaying her innate Catholicism.

Zuji crawled back into the car and watched his bride carry Abni towards the entrance, breaking Israeli law by sojourning after curfew.

"Claire!" Zuji yelled after rolling down the car window, suppressing his tears. Claire turned around and watched her husband's trembling lip.

"Love," Zuji pleaded, "you bury me."

THE ODYSSEY

> "The dog is the most faithful of animals
> and would be much esteemed were it not so common.
> Our Lord God has made His greatest gifts the commonest."
> - Martin Luther

"You're sure you don't mind if I lie down back here?" I called to Dad, closing my eyes and resting my head in Joanna's lap in the backseat.

"Not at all," he said. "I get it. I know jet lag. Just get some rest."

It was only 45 minutes from O'Hare Airport to my childhood home in Zion, but I coveted every extra minute of rest I could get. It wasn't but a few minutes into the trip that Joanna whispered, albeit loud enough so that I could hear her.

"You've been there," Joanna she quietly exclaimed, prompting me to sit up and peer out the passenger side window.

With my glasses still being broken, my vision was shot, but I was able to recognize that she was pointing to the water tower off to the eastward Rosemont horizon.

"I did!" I granted, before proudly adding, "I *touched* it."

I set my head back on her lap, smacked my tongue against my lips to try to get the day-old breath off my taste buds, then asked, "How are you so awake right now?"

"I'm *so* excited," she squealed, squeezing my cheeks. "I missed them so much."

In my fatigue, I hadn't even deliberated what an awesome moment Joanna and I were riding into. My lethargy wore itself out and I sat up, unable to contain myself after considering Joanna's point. The more I thought about seeing Sidney, Romy, and Shadrach, the higher my heart climbed into my throat. Certainly, there have been several occasions in which I've been especially excited to see that house, but not so many in which I was actually nervous to be coming home. Somewhere along the way still, my excitement of seeing our pups again turned to anxiety; this had been the longest I'd ever been away from any of them.

Would they be mad that I left them for so long?

Have they gotten so used to life without me that they didn't need me anymore?

Would they even be excited to see me again?

I received all my answers when we pulled into the driveway and, hearing the wheels screech up the asphalt, Romy's head popped up behind the front window as if she hadn't moved since I left three months ago. She was behind a pane of glass in the house and I was behind one in the car, but that didn't stifle her excited howls when she espied me.

Romy's joy had always been contagious. In fact, this isn't the first time that her happy face had quelled my anxieties. There's a chance that you, my reader, have read my second memoir, *Mister Master Exacerbation: my obsessive quest to uncover the final compulsion, and how my porn use got me fired from work, kicked out of school, banned from my field, separated from my wife, and warped me into an animal-abuser, a fugitive, and an all-around villain*. And if you hadn't read it before, you kinda just did by reading the title a second ago. If you read that book, then you know another subtitle could've easily been implemented: "My painful quest to restoration, and how my greatest mistake got me to confront my flaws, admit my failures, reflect on my own evil, accept my weaknesses, and transformed me into a Christ-follower, a family man, and an all-around testament to God's redeeming grace."

At my lowest point, it wasn't my Christian upbringing that offered me the hope I needed. It wasn't my faith, and it wasn't even Joanna. It was Romy.

> *"Romy cried with joy when she saw me. That's when I knew it wasn't over. That's when I knew there was still hope. Romy's love for me – a love that existed even after all I had put her through – pushed me to believe in restoration."*

As Dad put the car into park, and I watched through the window as Romy wagged her entire body, I thought to myself, *this is the happiest sight I've ever seen in my entire life.*

Joanna and I entered the house and embraced our pups, whose excitement was so raucous that it sounded like there were tiny little tornado sirens swooshing about from room to room. Shadrach whirled in circles and showed off her caboose (to remind us that nobody was scratching it), and Sidney and Romy zoomied around the house and wrestled with each other, at least until Joanna snatched Romy and held her face against Romy's neck.

While hugging Romy, Joanna suddenly burst out laughing.

"What's so funny?" I asked.

She pointed to Romy's feet.

"The pups had a spa day with Grandma," Mom chuckled. "Apparently some places do mani-pedis for dogs."

Normally black, Romy's nails were brightly painted with pink glitter nail polish. She pranced around like a furball who mistook herself for a royal princess, only missing the tiara. While I was busy appreciating the intricate paintjob on her nail, Romy sniffed the fresh Nasrani tattoo on my wrist, then snuck a kiss on its raised scabbing. Unlike Sidney and Shadrach, Romy wasn't one who gave kisses freely, even when commanded to – if she gave a kiss, it was because she wanted to. So, I melted when she surrendered one of her coveted kisses to this mark of suffering.

Romy didn't normally like playing – she was always much more of a "let's just run in circles until we get tired" kinda gal – but on this occasion, she picked up a toy, tossed it in the air and caught it before it dropped again, inciting Sidney to come and play, too.

Shadrach stood at my feet and kissed my shins and ankles like they were made of beef lollipop, and then the five of us – Joanna, Sidney, Romy, Shadrach, and myself – all went into the snowy backyard and played until none of us could stand breathing in the cold air anymore. [pants] We cloistered back inside the warm house to cuddle, where Joanna settled her temple on Romy's chest, head rising and falling every few seconds as Romy's diaphragm heaved.

"*It's Your breath, in our lungs,*" Joanna quietly sang one of the popular worship songs from church. "*So we pour out our praise, we pour out our praise to You only.*"

Joanna closed her eyes and took in the gentle raising and lowering of Romy's chest.

"That's God's breath," Joanna said, opening her eyes. "In her lungs, that's God filling her lungs. I can feel God's breath when I'm here."

It was then that it dawned on me that my wayfaring was truly over. My journey to the Promised Land had started in conjunction with the Feast of Tabernacles, and it lasted exactly 40 days – which, I'm promising you, was honestly unintentional if you can believe that any better than Nicolas could. Now like an ancient Jew who had just been emancipated, I could rest in my *sukkah* with the deep peace of the knowledge that the work was finished. And this? *This?* Cuddling with some of God's most magnificent creations? It was a glimpse of heaven: man and wife, dog and war hog, the mini-lion and the lamb, all grazing together.

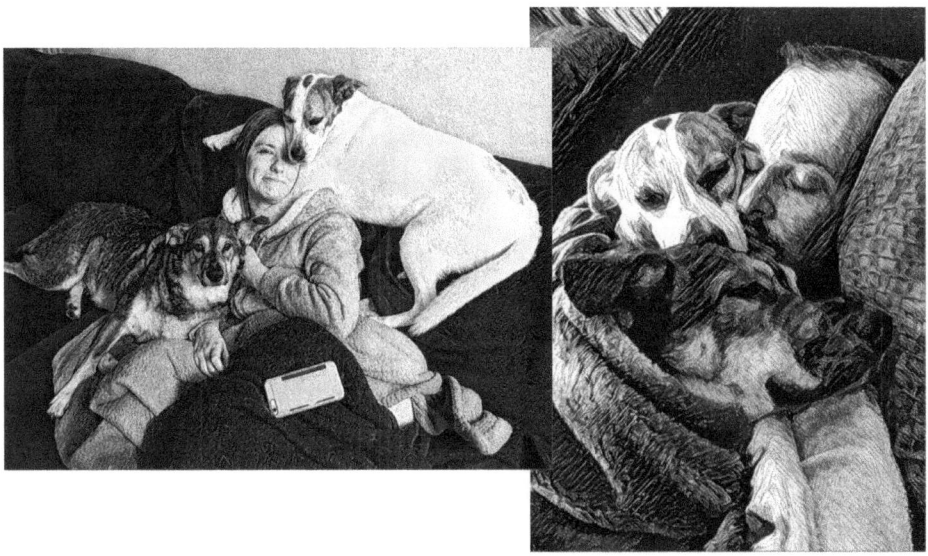

The week that followed was the best of my life. I had almost no responsibilities, except for a modest compiling of raw data from my Holy Land trip, and overcoming the final challenges in *Super Smash Bros.* on my Gameboy in anticipation for its preeminent sequel that *even* had the word *Ultimate* in its title, if that tells you anything!

And Romy – normally an anxious dog – was different: she wasn't afraid of the world. For instance, she actually wanted to cuddle with me. Normally she'd feel trapped and launch off my body when I forced her into a cuddle session, but now she was voluntarily folding into my body, showering me with kisses. She was the most loving she'd ever been, and I just knew this was the start of a new thing: fearlessness had sprung forth in Romy and together we were stepping into an era of communion unlike any connection we've ever had before. Joanna and I might not ever be able to have children, but at least we had this indescribable bond with the family we were blessed with.

And then came Thanksgiving Day. Romy was playing outside in the backyard garden with sister Sidney. She dashed, planted her back left foot, juked, and then cast the cry that took my heart and stuffed it into the valley of my gut.

"YELP!"

> "For I consider that the
> sufferings of this present time are not
> worthy to be compared with
> the glory that is to be revealed to us."
> ~ Romans 8:18, NASB

לב

November 30, 2020

You still doing your prayer thing?

Yes! I hit on a troubling verse today.

Is it one that's in my bible?

No. But I don't think you'd have a problem with it.

What is it?

Matthew 5:4. "Blessed are those who mourn, for they shall be comforted." It's a hard verse. It suggests that it's actually more valuable to be comforted by God than it is to never lose anyone you love at all. Which is incomprehensible to me right now. I would trade all of the comfort God has given me, I would do away with all the lessons I may be learning just to have Romy back for one more day. I can't imagine how God's comfort is more valuable than my tightest relationships.

How do you make sense of that then? Because to me it doesn't make much sense.

In my life, the Lord has afflicted me with pain. Sometimes in discipline, sometimes just because of the way His will works. But He's always near to me when this happens. In fact, I'd say He's nearer to me during these moments than when I'm not suffering. So, maybe that's what Yeshua was going for with the idea that those in mourning are more fortunate than those who aren't suffering.

That is kinda heavy

The baby asks in the womb, "why do I have four arms? Certainly, I've used these two near my shoulders. But the pair on the bottom? They have no use for me in this brackish state, and they impinge on my limited space. I cannot use them for anything, not for grip nor to scratch my eyes. Even my courier wishes them gone! This is suffering; pure suffering, and for no reason at all. If you are truly a good God, then why would you crimp me so? When I get out of this womb, I will chop these two legs off since you won't do it yourself, and I will roll on and live the rest of my days in peace."

Wow. That's quite the articulate, cultured fetus. He sounds like he's from Oxford, like he's just hankering for a game of polo.
Also. I don't really get it, Danger.

Okay, maybe I belaboured the vocabulary. But the point was supposed to be that the little British baby doesn't know that he needs legs for what's coming next. What if the suffering we experience now is giving us arms and legs for the next life?
What if the more you suffer now, the better eternity ends up being? That's the thought. So, as I have to do with so many passages in the Bible, I'm forced to trust this proverb over my feelings that don't actually reflect the truth of eternity. I'm challenged to simply rest in God rather than my limited understanding.

So you've been doing this contemplative prayer pretty consistently?

Off and on, actually. I've found that whenever I've got something weighing on my heart - like, something wrong that I did - it bogs down my ability to pray. Like I can't face God. So it forced me to confront the second Metroid Principle.

Abni was asleep, his hands clamped around Claire's neck as they sat in the sanitized waiting room of the same hospital where Claire lost her daughter so many years ago. He was getting too big for this and the weight of his arms was cricking her neck, but Claire endured the uncomfortable positioning so he wouldn't wake.

On the television in the waiting room, the newscast was highlighting Rachel's Tomb, where the recent attack had canopied the next few days with an extended curfew. The newscast panned to a bird's eye view – being displayed by a helicopter that Claire could hear whirring almost directly overhead – and the Anastas guesthouse could be seen on the broadcast.

"Look!" Claire remarked and pointed to the monitor, forgetting altogether that Abni was asleep. "Our home is on TV!"

Abni opened his eyes for a moment, then dozed off again. Claire was giddy – not from her guesthouse's fifteen minutes of fame, but from the relief in seeing that Zuji's car was safely parked.

Claire could hear the heavy sound of sprockets rolling on the ground just outside the hospital, then she saw the source of the sound – a tank – come into view on the TV screen. There was no turning back now: going home was no longer an option.

"How much longer, Mama?" Abni asked, almost an hour after they checked in. He couldn't care less that his house on international television.

"I don't know," Claire admitted. "I know it's already been a long time. They must be busy today."

Though it didn't seem busy. Nobody else was in the waiting room and Claire had seen a couple doctors laughing and cajoling the head nurse, a European nun with a beautiful face and a cute blonde bob that felt slightly ahead of the times.

Just then, an Arab family of three – father, mother, and son – walked into the hospital. The father was wearing a luxurious camel Bisht, while the mother flaunted a Harvey Nichols peacoat that still had its pricetag on – conceivably not an oversight on the mother's part. Though Claire couldn't see the exact number, the coat appeared to be worth four-figures in the British pound: worth more than most of the Anastas combined assets. Even the child was donning a Saudi Arabian farwa.

Which is.....
?

2. Confess your sins daily. Ask God to reveal to you how you have failed Him, and understand the seriousness of this sin. Ask for forgiveness.

That's not bad.

I know how consequential sin can be. I've fornicated with evil. I think it's important to drop that stuff off at the door in order to be in commune with God.

And what do you do if you can't remember your sins?

You pray the sinner's prayer, verbatim, based on the way it was delivered (in divine revelation) to Reverend Prophet Patriot Pat III of Holie Rollie Baptist Church in Uranus, Missouri.

Checks out, Talmud says the same thing, in so many words.

Really though, if I can't recall my sins, I ask God to open my eyes to what I've done. Ask God to search my heart so that my shortcomings can be revealed to me. Like David's words in Psalm 139, "Search my heart, oh God!"

I think this is a good finding for you. Well done, sinner.
Okay, I need to confess something to you, too.

What's that?

Last time, you mentioned Paul. The famous Jew-turned-Christian.

Yes?

I don't know your Paul. No idea who that is, never heard of him.

Really? He was one of the most murderous persecutors of Christians, until he became one after experiencing Yeshua and realizing He was the Messiah from the Jewish Scriptures.

O. I had no idea.

Actually, just today I was reading something he wrote, something I thought captured the most basic divide between Christians and Jews. Really, the most basic divide I've seen between you and me.

About what?

About hearing from God. He said that Christians are not like the ancient Jews, who had to have Moses put a veil over their eyes to protect them from God's holiness. Jews keep that veil on (sometimes literally) when they pray and read Scripture because they don't trust Yeshua can take it off. And He's the only one who can. Jews find it unacceptable and arrogant to suggest that any living person today might know God better than Moses did during his years on earth. But Paul says it isn't necessarily an act of ego, because the death of Yeshua allowed God's spirit to pour over the world. If that's true, then human beings have far more at our disposal today than even Moses, Abraham, or Elijah did in theirs because God can be revealed through that Spirit.

It makes me a little uncomfortable to think that Patriot Pat would have more access to god than a chosen jew. Aside from the fact that I think your bible is irrelevant and made up (not to be mean), but even if I believed it, that fact alone would really bother me.

For Jews, Scripture is a religion rulebook; for Christians, Scripture is a testament to the freedom we have from religion. And if I'm toeing the party line here, and we have that kind of freedom, wouldn't God make Himself available to us?

Claire looked down at her dowdy jacket – a hampered puffer coat that now looked more navy than its original violet – and adjusted her hand to cover the obvious tear in the left sleeve.

The blonde nun saw the family walk in, and before they even finished signing in, walked over and warmly welcomed them to the hospital.

"I am the head nurse here," the nun said in a soupy Swiss accent, "I have some time now, if you just follow me to the back."

Claire chased after the nun and caught her just before she had escaped behind the locking door.

"My son is suffering terribly," Claire pled with the nurse.

The nun motioned with her hands for Claire to shoo, annoyed that she was preventing the door from being closed.

"Wait your turn," she said, slipping behind the door, Claire hearing it lock.

"My son has been waiting over an hour!" she yelled, pounding on the locked door. Getting nowhere with the door, she turned to talk to the receptionist, but nobody was manning the front, either. Claire collapsed into her chair again.

"Mommy, is it time?" Abni asked, his eyes closed and his head cradled in his hands.

"Almost, sweetie. Would you like to lie down?"

Abni put his head on his mom's lap and cabled his legs through the chair's armrests. Claire closed her eyes, and when she opened them again, she wasn't sure if they had been closed for a minute or an hour or a day, but she could hear voices coming back through the back door, so she leapt from her seat and got ready to meet the head nurse there.

"We'll send you off with the medications," the nun said to the camel-coated family as she held the door for them. "But, I'm throwing in a few extra doses, just in case. Thanks for dropping in, and have a safe ride home."

The father put his hand over his heart and gently bowed before the family cleared the room.

"My son is gravely ill, Sister," Claire stopped the nun before she turned around and left again.

"Your son may be sick, but you are playing with both of your lives being out past curfew. You are out of your mind to come here."

"And I suppose that family was sane?" Claire flouted.

"Refugees get the priority. You know that."

440

I still don't think so. Because god isn't obligated to make Himself available to us.

But what if He chose to? If God did make Himself available - what would that look like, you think? Wouldn't prophets be more common?

Possibly. But false prophets, I think, would be even less common because I think god would want to help differentiate.
But you know what? No. I think god makes it clear who the prophets are. If god was making himself available to us, then we'd have more indisputable prophets.

What?? I'm struggling to remember any prophet who wasn't outright rejected at one point or another.

Even the "rejected prophets" - each and every one - was eventually seen to be what they truly were.

And would the Messiah be rejected like that, at first, do you think?

I doubt that's a scenario. The whole thing about the meshiach is he will be a clear king and will prove himself with actions.

There's a verse in Psalm 118 that Christians believe to be speaking to the fact that the Messiah will be rejected:
"The stone that the builders rejected has become the cornerstone."

Postdiction. No need to make that messianic in understanding. The whole psalm is about David himself. Or if you want to get pictorial about it, it's about Israel.

So you think the Messiah will be 100% recognized by Jews?

I'd like to think so. Like, it would be irrefutable with facts, not just faith.

People still refute facts. Today, people are literally on their COVID deathbeds in hospitals, refuting that there's actually a virus going around. So I think if a Messiah came, was widely accepted in Jewish circles as the Messiah, there would still be those who refute it. Even after the Messiah died, I think it would take only like 2 generations of Jews before people would question whether or not the Messiah even came.

Hmm, possible. Provocative, even. I always just pictured the coming as an event that is the end of all doubt, but I guess it's possible that the end of all doubt would only last a generation. I'll need to think on this.

It goes back to what we were talking about before: if the Messiah comes, will he be both emotionally and logically clear to us? If it's only one of them, which would it be?

Logical. I think christianity kind of shows what happens when he's only "emotionally" revealed.

What would it look like to you? Logically?

Well, history would be changed. Jews would have a king and peace. And there are SOME prophecies in the bible that point to the messiah, just not nearly as many as christians think there are.
What about you? Do you think meshiach reveals himself emotionally or empirically?

Hmm. If I had to choose, then I think I agree with you. It would be a logical conclusion, not just an emotional one.
Even if it wasn't a completely logical conclusion, I think that it would at least be NOT illogical.

How would it be not illogical? You're saying it it would be... ill-illogical?

"*Those* were not refugees. They were closer to royalty than refugees. You chose to treat them, even though their illness was minor, rather than my son."

"If Bethlehem is to ever recover from this infighting, we must prioritize those who stimulate the city's economy."

"Will you please see my son?" Claire said, making a conscious decision to mind her tongue.

The nun sighed, then walked over to Abni in the waiting room and examined him as he sat there.

"This is a sinus infection," the nun said. "He needs antibiotics. Some fever reducer, too. I doubt you can afford it."

"I will pay whatever it takes. Sister, I also need a bed to lie down in. I know you have a guesthouse in this hospital. May I take my son there so we can rest until curfew is lifted?"

"Absolutely *not*," the nun replied. "Does this look like an orphanage? I am trying to run a business here."

"Perhaps you can let us stay in an exam room, or even the waiting room until tomorrow."

The nun's eyes widened and then began maniacally laughing, as if she was having a psychotic fit.

"*Woooooo!*" the nun howled so loud that her other subordinates came out from the back to determine if everything was civil in the waiting room. After nearly giving herself a charley horse, the nun calmed down and then calmly said to Claire, without even a hint of mirth, "there is no room for you in here."

Claire, feeling a fire come down upon her head – a much less calming fire that had no trace of coolness – spoke with authority to the nun as the other nurses looked on.

"You are a disgrace to the garb you are wearing, Sister. Why do you laugh at me? Because I am in need?"

"I laugh because you come here expecting special treatment. You are here past curfew. Is that my problem? No. You choose to fire weapons at Israelis, and this is the consequence upon your head. Do you even have the money to pay for your medicine?"

"How much do I owe you?"

"It doesn't matter. We both know you don't have the money."

It is true that Claire did not have any money with her at the moment, so she pointed at the television in the waiting room.

"That is my house that you see on that TV," Claire kept her finger angled at the corner of the room, refusing to lose her gaze on the nun. "I

I'm saying you wouldn't have to go around the barn to believe the Messiah is the Messiah. You could point your finger, say "that's the Messiah," and even those who don't agree with your conclusion could at least grasp how you got there.

I do think that the meshiach would be widely recognized, at the very least. Definitely at first, even if it fades. It's said that during the reign of the meshiach, it will be harder to convert to jewdism because a convert's reasoning would be less about true conversion and more about just wanting to be one of the chosen. We saw this happen during David and Solomon's time, the more jewdism is thriving, the more exclusive it becomes to weed out the wannabes.

Interesting. The more Christianity thrives, the less exclusive it comes.

Christianity is the most dominant religion in the world, something jewdism has never achieved (or aspired to). There are literally more people who practice voodoo than there are jews today.

I think every religion has their "point of no return" though. If I say "I have faith in the Packers winning the Super Bowl," there's no glory in saying that a week after it happened. After something is revealed as the "Truth," nobody can convert from a place of faith anymore.

It's like that in all three Abrahamic religions. Once the truth is revealed, you hedged your bets and there's no going back on where you tossed your bagels.

Hey! I didn't even have to ask.

Figured you were owed one after this long discussion.

Wow you look way different in that photo.

Like... fat? Yeah. That picture is from just before I got fired and lost all that weight.

I'm not sure Sidney wants to be there, in that picture.

I think we might have been rasslin'.
That's just her crying "uncle."

Cry uncle?

Oh, I didn't realize that was an American phrase.
We say it when we're trying to express the existential crisis that we all contend with the first time we think about our mortality and how nobody and nothing has true permanence in this world.

Whoa. I need to give americans more credit.

Nah I lied. It just means "I give up, let me go"

will go home right now. You can watch me on television like it is a security camera. If I slip into my house without being shot, I will grab the money and come back here and pay you. Please just let me have the medicine and I promise to come back."

The nun grew irate and began to say something that was sure to be pointed, until one of the nurses interrupted.

"Sister," the nurse gingerly interjected her soft voice, "I know this woman. She is an honest woman. If she says she has the money, then she has it."

"And I am to trust your word?" the nun scoffed. "I don't know this woman."

"Sister, if she doesn't come back to pay for the medicine, then I will pay for it out of my salary."

"Forget it," the nun replied, preferring to lord Claire's poverty over her. "I will give you your medicine. But don't you forget that it is I who am helping you, and not the other way around."

"*Help* me?" Claire barbed. "You do not help me. You have expert hands to construct such indignity from nothingness! I am used to this from Jews. I am used to this from Muslims. But you are most wretched of all, and subject to judgment. Where does my help come from? Not from Israelis. Not from Arabs. And no, not from Christians. You tell me now, how much is the medicine?"

"Forty nis."

"When curfew is lifted, I will come back with enough shekels. But you need to know something, Sister: we are in a war. It is a war where the good is blurred with the evil. I know this. But I also know that no matter who is right in this war, you are wrong, and you have stained your habit with evil today."

The nun didn't say a word to Claire, ordered her nurse to fetch the medicine for Claire, and the Anastases were on their way, weathering the one-mile trek to their house while violating curfew.

Claire lumbered towards her home with Abni draped over her shoulders as two more tanks started to turn off Caritas. Claire scuttled to an alley and squatted behind a dumpster, bracing Abni's head and shushing him from crying until the tanks were clearly a safe distance away. Claire hoisted her body and Abni's back up, then tiptoed down the dusty road, praying for provision as she inched towards her home.

Then she saw a red dot on her chest. And she froze.

( )

Lol. I'm sorry.

I reluctantly forgive you.

Actually, while you're in a forgiving mood, can I ask you to do something for me?

Umm not so excited that you're asking for forgiveness in advance here..

I'll need to ask for your forgiveness for putting you through this.

Lol okay, that's fetching. What can I do?

I want to play a game.

Ooh I like games. Except I have an appointment in a couple minutes, soooo....

Okay, well I can at least share the game. I was reading my Bible, and there's a chapter I want to share with you. It's kind of long, but I'd like you to read it and tell me who you think the chapter is talking about.

Okay. I don't know many christian characters but I'll try.
Drop it here, and I'll check it out later.

Okay. Have a good appointment!
Here's the chapter:

"Who has believed what he has heard from us? And to whom has the arm of the Lord been revealed? For he grew up before him like a young plant, and like a root out of dry ground; he had no form or majesty that we should look at him, and no beauty that we should desire him. He was despised and rejected by men, a man of sorrows and acquainted with grief; and as one from whom men hide their faces he was despised, and we esteemed him not. Surely he has borne our griefs and carried our sorrows; yet we esteemed him stricken, smitten by God, and afflicted.

But he was pierced for our transgressions;
he was crushed for our iniquities;
upon him was the chastisement that brought us peace,
and with his wounds we are healed.

All we like sheep have gone astray; we have turned - every one - to his own way; and the Lord has laid on him the iniquity of us all. He was oppressed, and he was afflicted, yet he opened not his mouth; like a lamb that is led to the slaughter, and like a sheep that before its shearers is silent, so he opened not his mouth. By oppression and judgment he was taken away; and as for his generation, who considered that he was cut off out of the land of the living, stricken for the transgression of my people? And they made his grave with the wicked and with a rich man in his death, although he had done no violence, and there was no deceit in his mouth. Yet it was the will of the Lord to crush him; he has put him to grief; when his soul makes an offering for guilt, he shall see his offspring; he shall prolong his days; the will of the Lord shall prosper in his hand. Out of the anguish of his soul he shall see and be satisfied; by his knowledge shall the righteous one, my servant, make many to be accounted righteous, and he shall bear their iniquities. Therefore I will divide him a portion with the many, and he shall divide the spoil with the strong, because he poured out his soul to death and was numbered with the transgressors; yet he bore the sin of many, and makes intercession for the transgressors."

Esther, who is this verse about?

"Hands up or we will shoot!" a soldier screamed from behind a barricade.

Abni began to wail, "please don't kill us!" as tears dribbled onto the dirt below.

Claire set Abni down and raised her hands. Abni, keenly *au fait*, did the same.

A Samal slowly approached Claire with his rifle raised to her face, bringing the count to two weapons aimed at her. Out of the corner of her eye, she saw Abni now had a red dot on his forehead, too.

The Samal approached close enough and, finally able to recognize her face, lowered his rifle and waved his hand down, snuffing the red dots into evanescence.

"Miss Anastas?" Chileab said. "What are you doing out here?"

Claire dropped Abni's medicine onto the road and embraced Chileab, sobbing into his shoulder. He had become so muscular since she last saw him years ago, when his post was still by her home.

"I… Abni came so sick…" she wheezed, barely intelligible. "I didn't know what to do. They were so inhumane and wouldn't help him…"

"Hey, hey, hey," Chileab said, patting Claire on the back as she held him. "It's okay. It's okay. Let's get you home, okay? It's not safe here."

Claire wiped away her tears and nodded, then collected the medicine off the ground as Chileab took Abni's hand and escorted the both of them home.

MY FINAL BROKEN PROMISE

> "The people who walked in darkness
> have seen a great light;
> those who dwelt in a
> land of deep darkness,
> on them light has shone."
> ~ Isaiah 9:2, ESV

"She looks better today," I told Joanna as I took off Romy's collar and she pounced away in excitement. "She seemed really happy for that whole walk. We dodged a bullet: for a second, I thought we'd have to get her checked out."

Joanna sighed. Of relief or concern, I couldn't tell.

"Why don't we head out to the dog park in a bit?" I suggested while trying to gauge Joanna's reaction. "It can be like a mini-Galena day."

She hesitated, nodded, then said, "okay."

Joanna, Sidney, Romy, and I had once taken a week-long trip to the cozy little town of Galena, Illinois a few years ago (pre-Shadrach years). I had largely just recovered from my OCD spell, and for the first time since our lives were upended in 2014, our lives – and our family – felt restored during that trip. The weather was perfect all week long, and the days were characterized with walks with our dogs, followed by trips to the dog park with our dogs, followed by cuddles with our dogs. It was the closest to heaven I've ever been.

But we were East of Eden today. I'd dragged the family to Minneapolis, the land of the dreaded Purple People Eaters. Despite blocking off over a month of my autumnal calendar to visit Israel and Palestine, I'd still felt compelled to squeeze in a Packers trip, chasing that first playoff-clinching-high from the Green Bay home game almost a decade ago. The trip would end up being a disaster – not just because the rival Vikings ended up handing the Packers their cheese rinds, not just because the whipping wind chill was blasting sub-zero freeze balls at us, and not just because it's the annoying state where celebrities go to launch will-be-failed political careers. It's also where I walked Romy across the famed Stone Arch Bridge, not knowing the true extent of her injury, or that it would be her last walk.

To be fair, the dogtrot itself had been wonderful – even Romy enjoyed it, despite nobody knowing her knee's ligaments were hanging on by a fiber. And the bridge was a cool site, its limestone not unlike the makeup of the Old City (though, the City of God had a few thousand years on the City of Water). And after our furry trio settled in from the walk, we indeed cuddled with them as they napped, twitching and pumping their legs during their doggy dreams. Eventually, they opened their eyes, let out long, high-pitched yawns, and began licking our hands and cheeks. I shot a look over to Joanna, who was grinning from ear-to-ear, and she nodded.

"Girls..." I whispered just loud enough so they could hear. Shadrach cocked her head, Romy's ears perked up, and Sidney stopped mid-lick, her tongue resting on Joanna's palm as if she was frozen in time. "Girls... I have a *question*."

Tails wagged. They loved the word "question" and the phrase "do you want to" because they're usually followed by "...go to the dog park" or "...go for a walk" or "...go see Grandma."

"Girls...," I repeated. "Do you want... do you want to *go* to the dog park?"

Shad shot off the bed to the door, ready to go. Sidney's tail began to spin like a helicopter. But, Romy didn't move. Her tail slapped the bed a couple times and she pawed at me, but it was like she couldn't move the rest of her body.

"What's going on?" Joanna bristled.

"Hold on," I said as calmly as I could, swooping my arms underneath Romy to pick her up, gingerly setting her on the floor.

She stood still on three legs, her hind leg up in the air, careful not to touch the ground.

"Oh, boy," I muffled into my palm and then took a few steps back. "Romy, can you come here please?"

She took one step forward, but as soon as she put weight on her hind leg, she collapsed and didn't try to get up again. Hopelessly, Romy looked up at me, as if begging for help.

We called the emergency vet. "We can get you in, in an hour," they say. "Come then."

"This hour is going to suck," I said.

"Sidney and Shad are still expecting us to go somewhere," Joanna said. "Why doesn't one of us take them for a walk, and the other stay here with Romy?"

"Sure, but Sidney isn't going to like walking without Romy."

"True: they're all going to freak out if we don't leave together. And Romy will need to go potty before the vet. So why don't we take them all out to go potty, and you'll just continue on with Sidney and Shadrach, and I'll bring Romy back in?"

We headed outside. Romy delicately peed in the grass, careful not to put any weight on her bum leg.

I started to walk away with Sidney and Shadrach as Joanna started to take Romy back inside, but Sidney kept looking back, as if to say, "where's my walking buddy?" I looked over at Romy, who was planting her tripod into the ground as Joanna tried to go inside, Romy's eyes crying out, "Daddy, why can't I go with you?"

"Romy, *this* way," Joanna said, lightly tugging on her leash.

Romy took one step towards Joanna's direction, then looked back at me again to say, "please take me with you, I don't care how much I hurt." It wasn't just disappointment in her eyes; she was panicked.

She took one step towards Joanna again, then turned around and pulled Joanna my direction. Joanna gently called to her, and Romy turned around again. Suddenly, as if it was a novel thought that had just occurred to her, Romy remembered *"I want to go for a walk!"* and turned around, pulling Joanna towards me a third time.

Romy and I linked sad, sad eyes. This image gets seared into my mind, becoming one of the most upsetting memories of my lifetime, one that I'd ruminate over the next several years and beyond, pierced to my core as her heavy eyes speak to me.

"Daddy. I want to be with you."

"You have to stay here," I called out to her. "At least for now. We'll roam again."

My words didn't seem to comfort her. I walked up to Romy, fell to my knees, held her close, and cooed in her ear, "We'll walk again."

"Death is not the way it ought to be.
It is abnormal,
it is not a friend,
it isn't right.
This isn't truly part of the circle of life.
Death is the end of it.
So grieve.
Cry.
We have a lot of crying to do."
- Timothy Keller

THE VALLEY ROSE.

God spoke, and it's how
The mountain calls for you now.
Not me –
The Valley Rose.
And it was my beloved who was always
Bound to suffer.
The Lord was the One who was
So focused on growing His garden,
That He left us to wither on this side.
That God is actually not good.
Never again will I think
Faith is the most important pillar of life.
Contrary to my prior beliefs,
Prayer has no place in the logical man's life.
Now I know that it's foolish to say
God is sovereign.
For all of eternity,
I will never see Romy again.
I erroneously believed
This pain will pass;
And also that
God sent Yeshua as Messiah.
I've instead learned to trust
My old pragmatic way of thinking.
I've been forced to surrender
My family, after all.
I never deserved
Anything less than this confidence:
Our suffering is meaningless, and
Now I know it's a lie to say
God sees our pain.
After a bitter season of contemplation
I have come to the sobering conclusion
God does not change.
Give me a break;
I prayed so hard for change;
We can't stay in that place.
Come into the valley with me.

Come into the valley with me.

לג
December 1, 2020

I read your bible chapter, and I think it's pretty obvious that it's about Yeshua. But I know there has to be a twist otherwise you wouldn't have asked me to play the game.

Yes, I believe it's about Yeshua. But you're also right, there is a twist.

Okay. Bated breath over here.

The twist is that it's from OUR Bible, not just mine. It's from Isaiah.

I'm not sure I believe that. Where in Isaiah?

Isaiah 53.

Okay, I see it now, but it's not really fair.

How come?

You said it was from YOUR bible. So I didn't even consider it might be from mine.

If I hadn't given it any introduction, wouldn't you still have assumed it was talking about Yeshua?

I don't know. We can't know, because that's not how you presented it. You kind of cheated here.

Okay, well I'm sorry.
Remember when I said this game will force me into asking forgiveness from you?
Here it is.

And the prophecy has been fulfilled. I forgive you.
But you owe me a Romy.

That's fair.

The siege at the Church of the Nativity ended after 40 days, when negotiations were made to exile the offenders to Europe rather than stand trial in Israel. Even still, the curfew never fully lifted and it became a tiresome fact-of-life for Palestinians in Bethlehem.

"We won't make it," Okhti said, glancing to the back of the car where Claire's and Okhti's children were all asleep, all four of them packed together in the back seats.

"Yes, we will," Claire responded, stepping on the gas and feeling the pressure of the imminent curfew. "Can you try calling one more time?"

Okhti grabbed Claire's brand-new Nokia – the first cell phone she'd ever had – and dialed in.

"Still, nothing," she said.

"Don't hang up. I will leave a message this time," Claire said, grabbing the phone from her sister's hand. "Hi Zuji, it's me. We're on our way home from the birthday party. It wrapped up late. I will be home soon, but can you call me? I'm nervous that you are not picking up the phone. I love you, bye."

Claire sighed, finished down Hebron Road, and turned onto Caritas Street, but was immediately halted by a Turai. Beyond the soldier were a group of Jewish teenagers, all wearing knee-long kittels and spinning in circles as they danced to boisterous music as the clock crept past midnight.

"Okhti, what is the date?" Claire asked while the Tzahal jogged towards her car.

"It's... now? It's October 17th. Why?"

"The 11th of Cheshvan. It is Mother's Day in Judaism."

"Oh."

"Rachel Imenu is venerated today," she said, rolling down the window for the soldier to speak.

"You cannot pass," he said. "You must turn around and go home."

"That *is* my home," Claire replied, pointing beyond the soldier.

"I'm sorry, we have many problems today. I cannot allow you to drive your car near Rachel's Tomb."

"So the six of us must sleep in our packed car tonight?"

Oh those precious eyes. What a beautiful baby.
Thanks for this. It makes it worth suffering through your bogus game.

It's a common evangelism tactic, when Christians talk to Jews. They present Isaiah 53 as I did, and it generally blows the Jew's mind to find that it's actually a part of their Scripture.

Well, again. You kind of manipulated the way I was going to think about it.

I already apologized! You can't hold it against me anymore!

Lol fine, fair.

I do think it's interesting, though. This feels like a supremely critical, supremely compelling Messianic verse for a Jew to somehow not be familiar with. I mean, it's not just some random passage in a minor prophet book. This is one of the most important prophetic books, not just a one-off verse in Leviticus.

Lol ummm I learnt Leviticus twice. You're talking to an ortho jew. I actually haven't cracked open the book of Isaiah since high school. But even then, I don't remember ever reading this chapter in my life.

That's so interesting. I mean, if this chapter isn't about Yeshua, then who do you think it's about? So many of the things described in this chapter happened literally as they happened to Yeshua. And that's not just based on the New Testament / my Bible, but history.

I don't know who this would be about. I'll have to think about it and read some commentary.

It just strikes me as strange that you wouldn't be familiar with this chapter. I mean, even if you were to reject it as being about Yeshua, it's just so poetic, I'd say maybe even the most poetic chapter in the entire Old Testament. It seems like there is literary value for anyone who reads it.

Well I can't attest to why it's not more familiar to jews, but I will say that prophecies should take a back seat in the bible. The bigger deal is how god called us to the land of Israel.
Us = the collective jews. Not god calling us individually for anything. The individual call is that we would cling to our ancestors and become the best versions of ourselves in the land we've been given. The bible is narrative, yes, but it's not just some linear story that all connects together, as I think you see it. It's a bunch of interesting anecdotes in a collection of essays, not a novel.
Where christians see the bible as a story promising a future, jews see it as a testament to the past. It's why when a loved one dies, we don't say "may they be in heaven" but "may their memory be a blessing."

So what's the cosmic purpose of a Jew (or any human) then? Even if you don't believe God calls us to a specific purpose, surely you believe there's purpose for everyone. Even on the individual level. Right?

The idea (from my perspective, I'm not speaking for all jews remember) is that you're born a diamond in the rough. And that when you die, you should theoretically be the best version of yourself.

"Please just turn around," the soldier said. Claire noticed bags under his eyes so heavy that they might leave a wrinkled mark the next day.

"As you wish," she said, then backed her car out and headed back towards Hebron.

"What will we do?" Okhti asked.

"I have a plan," Claire responded, intently looking ahead.

"Which is…?"

"I will park and we will walk to our house."

"No," Okhti fiercely protested. "We will die. We will immediately be shot. They are not messing around tonight."

"Trust the Lord. We will be fine," Claire said, finding an abandoned lot with some emaciated dogs scurrying past her headlight.

"The Lord does not promise us such protection!"

"Yes, He is, Okhti. We will be fine."

"How can you know that?"

"He is speaking to me. I feel the warmth of the Holy Spirit. If you cannot trust the Lord, at least trust me."

Okhti sighed, but then was the first to open the car door and called behind, "children, wake up. It is time to go."

The six of them made their way out and approached Caritas by its side street. As immediately as they stepped foot onto the street, they found dozens of soldiers patrolling the corridor to Rachel's Tomb. And as quickly as they made it to Caritas, one Tzahal pointed them out and several soldiers turned their way.

The music from the feast was deafening, and yet not loud enough to mask the sound of multiple guns discretely clicking.

Abni whimpered, and Claire turned around to find both Abni and Ebnahty a shade of squash.

"Are you scared?" Claire asked Abni.

"Yes, Mama," Abni admitted.

"Then you're not trusting the Lord enough. He will see us through. I promise."

When Claire turned back around, there were four Tzahal standing before her. She looked to the heavens, sighing.

It was almost a full moon, but the overcast clouds had shrouded any of the moon's illumination and Claire couldn't even see the faces of the soldiers in front of her. While the other dozen Tzahal looked on, three of the soldiers kept their hands on their triggers while one approached Claire close enough that she could see his face. He began to open his mouth, but Claire promptly interrupted him before he uttered a sound.

"I do not wish to catch your cold. Bring me your commander."

Ha! That's timely. This morning, I discovered my third Metroid principle, which is kind of in line with the idea that the final version will be the best one. The version God wants us to be. The "right" version. The second principle was to confess sin, but you know what's better than confessing sin?

Just not sinning at all?

Exactly.
3. Ask to be spared from temptation so that you can resist sin and be delivered from evil - both your own and others'.

Hmm. I actually wouldn't put this up there as important with the other two you've mentioned. I mean, it's not bad, just doesn't seem too important to pre-empt sin from happening.

Well it goes back to the last principle. Sin is serious, and I think that because we don't see the immediate consequences of it, we forget that truth.

I don't want to sit here and say "sin isn't bad" but honestly I think it seems to be a bigger deal in your head than it actually is. There's no way for us to keep all the laws.

Please don't take this the wrong way, but sometimes I feel like some Jews lose perspective of the cost of sin.

Yeah I'm not sure how I'm supposed to take that the right way.

Sorry, there was probably a better way to say that. I didn't mean it maliciously. We don't need to get into this.

Well, we're here now. Please keep going

I just mean to say, Yeshua said that if we are under the Law, it's better to cut our hands off or gouge our eyes out rather than using those appendages to sin. I feel like a lot of Jews I've encountered have this mindset of "we'll do our best and God can sort it out." I guess I don't understand how any of us could expect sin - any sin at all - to not lead to death? I feel like when we don't take sin seriously, we're undercutting the Law.

One big assumption you're making here, that god is not merciful. God IS merciful. On Yom Kippur, we're commanded to purify ourselves by forgiving others and repenting our sins. Love as an act of mercy, mercy as a gift from god. If after our sincere effort, we still have fallen short, then we're still forgiven. And why? Because god is merciful.
God is mercy.
And: I care about sin. I avoid it at all costs. I have kept the Law, for the most part.

Really? You believe that you as an individual, and Jews as a people, have been faithful to the Law?

Absolutely. More than any other people, especially christians.

Okay. Let's accept everything you just said as true, for argument's sake. You said you kept most of the Law. But what about the rest of the Law you haven't kept?

From the shadows, one of the soldiers stepped forward and announced himself.

"I am in charge. Why are you here?"

"Sir, I have been trying to get home since before curfew began. Nobody told us that we could not get to our house, which stands right behind you."

"How did you even get here? Everything is supposed to be blocked off."

"None of your checkpoints had any personnel," Claire said.

"That is impossible!" the Segen argued, though he knew full well that it was quite possible given all the extra security that had been assigned to Rachel's Tomb.

"Sir," Claire continued, "I know you can shoot us and nobody would ever question you for it. Or you can have mercy, and escort us home right now and you will not have blood on your hands."

The Segen laughed, though it felt almost like a vulnerable laugh.

"Follow me," he said.

Upon entering the house after waving the Segen off, Claire called out for her husband.

"Zuji?"

Silence.

"Children, I know it's loud, but please go to bed, even if you can't fall sleep."

"Yes, Mama," Ebnahty agreed, and the kids shuffled upstairs to their rooms.

"Claire?" Okhti called. "There's a couple voicemails here."

Claire pressed the answering machine.

Beep.

"Hi Zuji, it's me. We're on our way home from the birthday party. It wrapped up late. I will…"

"Okay, next one," Claire said.

Beep.

"Hi Claire, hoping you get this. I'm using Chauncey's phone, and couldn't remember our cell phone number. I'm behind schedule, and I don't think I will make it back by curfew. Can you please tell the Tzahal that I am being driven home in a red Nissan? I will be home in 45 minutes. Thank you, dear."

Beep.

"He called after you did," Okhti noted. "He must be on his way right now."

"Okhti, please tuck the kids into bed and watch over them. I need to tell the commander to not shoot my husband."

Nobody can keep all of the Law. It's impossible. Not even Moses or Abraham or David could.

That's my point. All of us - including our shared Jewish heroes - stand condemned. I believe that's not only a message in Christianity, but in Judaism.

Honestly, your super pessimistic position is definitely not the message of jewdism. Hello?

Sorry. Just... I'll be honest. Kinda at an impasse here. I can tell you're angry. I don't like it. I don't want to upset you.

Don't mistake my bluntness for anger.
The problem here is I don't think that having Yeshua makes you a better person. That's all.

If I have led you to believe that being a Christian makes someone a "good person," then I've failed. Abysmally. Because the premise of Christianity is that you're such a broken person, you're in need of a Savior. If you think you're already a good person, then you need not apply. Christianity is the Official Religion of Bad People™. This is not like Islam and Judaism which the aim is to make you a good person. The aim of Christianity is to acknowledge that you're a shitty, broken person. At least in theory.

So in your religion, what can the jew do? You're telling me that god won't save a jew (his chosen race) just because they don't accept they're bad people, as your negative outlook does?

I'm not asking you (or any other Jew) to call yourself a bad person. Esther, you, more than any other culture or people-group, know the Law. You have studied it more than literally any other ethnic group. Your Scriptures are constantly crying out for a Messiah, for salvation, for atonement and redemption.

And the meshiach will come to restore the kingdom, don't worry.

What I'm trying to point to is our inability to keep the Law. How often have you failed to avoid sin, and then just forgotten about it later? Those sins that we don't feel guilty about, they're still repulsive to a Holy God, no? They don't just go away. If Judaism is right, then that sin is going to follow you forever, until it's atoned.

God is so much more merciful than you or I can comprehend. Abraham, Moses, David - all of them sinned, but found favor yet.

That's a good point.
All of this was just to say: asking God to keep me from temptation? I think it's worthwhile. And I've found that the request actually works.
We can stop here.

What do you mean, "works?"

I mean, I think I've seen this prayer answered more than any other prayer in my life. I've had several times in my life where I've been at a crossroads and prayed for God to spare me from sin, and I've actually seen one path close, and it's almost always the path that would have been a bad choice.

"Is the Holy Ghost telling you to do this?"

"No," Claire shook her head. "But there is no other way."

Okhti marched Claire's children upstairs so they wouldn't be privy to whatever fate was about to befall their mother for leaving the house past curfew. Claire opened her front door and was surprised to find a soldier with his back to her doorstep, who immediately spun around and shouted at her.

"No! Go back inside!" he demanded. "You cannot leave your house again tonight!"

"Boy," Claire said, tenderly, "how old are you?"

The soldier began to tremble, his composure crumbling at the first sign of Claire not cooperating.

"I am almost 18."

"You are almost old enough to be a soldier. Almost. Please get your commander."

The soldier fetched his superior, and when the Segen returned, Claire expected him to be indignant. But surprisingly, he was calm with her.

"Why have you not gone to bed?" the Segen asked, though it was less of an accusation and more of a genuine concern.

"My husband just left a message," she responded. "He does not know it is the day of Rachel Imenu, and he will be driving home in the next few minutes. I am begging you to spare his life."

"Hmmm. And does he know to drive slow?"

"Yes, he always drives as if a grandmother," she insisted, which probably would've driven Zuji into a fierce argument had he heard it.

"I will allow it," the Segen responded. "But there better be no tricks, or we will shoot. All 32 of us will shoot."

"I understand," Claire promised.

The Segen excused himself and spoke with a Samal, who promptly had all of his soldiers part to either side of the street and drop into the prone positions, watching the road through their scopes.

Oh, Zuji, Claire thought. *Please don't do anything stupid.*

Within a minute, a loud screech was heard as a red car careened down Caritas.

A couple soldiers strafed onto the street and pointed their rifles at the car, yelling "stop!" as the car drew closer.

Claire rushed onto the road and waved her hands, screaming, "Don't shoot! He's my family!"

The car continued speeding towards them, then in an instant, it jerked backwards and halted to a complete stop. Claire looked inside and found it was not her husband: it was a middle-aged Arab man with a girl,

I can't say I've seen that happen. Maybe that's why it isn't that forefront for me. But I also think that pre-empting sin often means pre-empting your thoughts, and thoughts can't be policed. It's too stressful.

You're telling me! I have no control over my thoughts. But Christianity emphasizes the value in taming one's thoughts, so I stand by the idea that this is important enough to pray about.

Probably just a difference between us, honestly. We have the law to guide us, and the law doesn't say a thing about minding your thoughts.
It has to be said, too: I've kept the law and its tenets. Or at least, I've done my best. But for you, the law is just a storybook. Part of a bigger narrative. And therefore you haven't kept it.

Yes. You've certainly got me there. I have done an atrocious job keeping the Law. If I believed the Law could save me, then I probably would be crippled by that fact. We can just boil this thing down to being the biggest difference between Jews and Christians. Between you and me.

I believe the law exists and you've thrown it out?

Jews meet at Sinai, Christians meet at Golgotha.

not even old enough to wear a hijab. Both the man and the young lady looked terrified, as if their lives were passing before their eyes.

"You know them?" the Segen asked.

"Yes," Claire lied to save the girl's life. "They're… lost?"

The car began to screech again as its wheels turned, and just as several soldiers raised their rifles to shoot, the car sped away in reverse and fishtailed back around the corner from where it came, as if a movie in rewind.

"Why did your family do that?" the Segen asked.

"I… don't know," Claire admitted.

"That was not your husband?" the Segen asked.

"No – he is in a different red car, then."

"Then who was that?"

"I can't testify to his behavior," Claire said, dodging the question.

"If your husband were to try to pull the same thing, then next time…"

The sound of a vehicle cut off the Segen's voice, and around the corner pulled a red Nissan, inching on the road as a pair of empty hands were raised out the passenger window.

"That's him," Claire said, breathing relief that Zuji knew to be cautious as he approached his home. "That's my husband."

The Samal approached the car, ordered Zuji to get out, and Chauncey slowly turned around and left after his friend was intercepted by the Tzahal.

"Go into your home," the Segen ordered Claire and Zuji. "This cannot happen ever again. If you find yourself in this situation once more, you won't be coming home. Understand?"

"Yes, sir," Zuji agreed, taking Claire's hand and rubbing it.

The 17-year-old soldier escorted the two of them to their home, still shaking from the whole encounter.

"Turai," Claire addressed the boy. "Don't be afraid. You are safe here. This is Caritas."

"We are in Palestine," the young soldier spoke. "There is so much danger here."

"Turai, who carries the weapons here? You're the danger. You're the one who holds the gun."

The soldier nodded, and Claire imparted a final urging for the soldier.

"Trust in the Lord. Be strong, as Joshua was."

> "The darker the night,
> the brighter the stars.
> The deeper the grief,
> the closer is God."
> - Fyodor Dostoevsky

"At least we know she won't die from this," I declared to Joanna as I rubbed Romy's belly. "Even if the surgery is terribly botched and everything goes wrong, she won't die from it. Doing this surgery can't be a mistake."

Joanna let out a "hmm," knowing that what I said was at least logical.

"Hey, Jo," I said, trying to throw some positivity into the mix. "What a champ Romy's been, right? For as much of a big baby as she normally is, we didn't even realize something was wrong until after that walk. She was in pain and didn't even let on. That's not like her."

Romy groaned in discomfort, but Joanna didn't respond to me, her hair dangling over her eyes as she stared into Romy's.

Romy Tono had been a champ, sure, but that didn't make her injury any less severe. When we took Romy to the ER in Minneapolis, the doctor took one glance at her x-rays and diagnosed her with a tear in her cranial cruciate ligament – the CCL. It's the doggy equivalent of the ACL, and it requires the low-risk TPLO surgery to repair it. There was no way to get it done before our ill-fated trip to Minny would conclude, so the doctor just told us to keep shoving these painkillers – carprofen – down her hatch to help manage the pain while we lugged the family back to Tulsa.

It was the most stressful drive of my life, but as long as Romy didn't put weight on her back leg and I didn't hit errant bumps while driving the 12-hour trip, the pain seemed manageable. Our first stop when we got home was to visit the most renowned TPLO specialist in Tulsa. He explained that, theoretically, dogs don't *need* the surgery, but the consequence of not doing it is they'll often be resigned to a life of limited mobility and quiet pain. We didn't want Romy to have to live this way: we wanted to see her jet and jump and juke again, so we had Romy undergo the reconstruction surgery.

The surgery itself seemed to be a great success, according to the doctor. The procedure was quick and without complication. Romy was sent home with her medications and I administered them dutifully, exactly as prescribed. Romy displayed some troubling symptoms like lethargy and lack of appetite and stumbling, but all of these could be explained by the fact that she was recovering from surgery.

461

"I don't like this," Jo replied. "She's going to waste away to nothing if she doesn't start eating."

"She'll be okay," I told her. Silly Joanna. Dogs don't die from knee surgery. Romy's not even seven years old and is completely healthy. She can bounce back.

"Hey," I reminded Joanna, nudging her chin with my fist, "God's got this." Be faithful, Joanna. Why aren't you trusting God? Don't you know that God sees every last sparrow that falls to the ground?

The next day, Romy could barely move. I called the vet and they squeezed in an appointment block to see her, so I brought her in to quell Joanna's fears... as well as mine that were secretly starting to manifest.

"She hasn't eaten anything since the surgery?" the veterinarian asked when I explained the issue.

"No, she has. Technically. We've been grinding up food and using a syringe to get it down her throat. It's messy and she doesn't get all of it, but she gets some of it."

"Have you tried cooking for her?"

"Yeah. Hamburger meat, turkey, mashed potatoes, rice, we've tried it all."

"I'm taking her fentanyl patch off. It's supposed to be silencing her pain, but these things can mess with appetite, too, and I suspect that's what's going on here. You should see her back to normal by tonight or, at worst, by tomorrow night. Do you want me to do another blood panel to make sure everything's peachy?"

"Those are like $40 or something, right? Nah. Let's just see if taking the patch off makes any difference."

Forty fucking dollars. #tulsalazy

I took Romy home. That night, we force fed her again with the syringe, and it seemed like she got a good chunk of it into her system – at least until she puked it all up 30 minutes later.

But the doc said it could take until tomorrow, so I didn't panic.

We put her in her kennel. She whined.

"Romy, stop," I yelled out. "I know you've been confined all day and your knee hurts, but there's nothing more we can do."

She didn't respond, having never learned English. The rest of us fell asleep as she continued to whine, which intermittently woke me up.

"Romy!" I'd snap, "you're fine!"

So much for not being a big baby about it.

Shortly after 3am, my phone buzzed. I had gotten a text from my little brother, Ben.

"Dawn of the Final Day: 24 Hours Remain" the text read. I laughed out loud and responded in kind.

"The countdown is on."

He didn't respond to that, but I didn't need any more context. The phrase, "Dawn of the Final Day: 24 Hours Remain" was a reference to one of my favorite video games, *Majora's Mask*, in which on the "dawn of the final day," the *Legend of Zelda* protagonist, Link, has 24 hours in gametime to prevent the villain from orchestrating his obliterative plan of crashing the moon into the terminal earth. (High drama!) The phrase had become an inside joke amongst Nintendo fans, something that was uttered anytime a highly-anticipated video game was about to be released.

In this case, "Dawn of the Final Day" referred to the imminent and eminent release of *Super Smash Bros. Ultimate*, one of the most highly-anticipated video games in the history of nerds.

It was for this reason that I'd been looking forward to December 7, 2018 for months. In fact, I tried to ensure that I had no work, no appointments, and no responsibilities that day. The plan was to wait until the clock struck midnight (which is when the digital version of the game would be available to play) and I'd sit around my TV with controller-in-hand and the volume barely audible so that I could pull an all-nighter without waking anyone in the house.

THE VALLEY ROSE

One appointment had snuck its way in – I had to take Romy back to the vet to get her staples out – but other than that, I was going to be able to relive my pre-pubescent days of sitting in front of the TV and controlling Mario (or preferably Luigi) all night and all day.

It was fitting that I'd be acting like a juvenile because, on top of *Smash* being released at midnight, it was December 6th: St. Nick's Day. We used to celebrate the holiday as kids, and every year, Mom still mailed us stockings filled with Silly Putty, candy, and oranges – always oranges for some reason, like any kid (or adult) wants that. Per the usual, Mom had packed a stocking and mailed it to Tulsa, which had arrived earlier that day.

It was also Kilmer's birthday. Joyce Kilmer, that is, if that wasn't clear: the namesake of Joanna's and my elementary school – the same school that had the monkeybars we met under, got engaged next to, and visited on our wedding day. I think there should still be an evergreen growing that we'd planted near the front entrance a few years ago. Granted, Kilmer's birthday had fallen on December 6th every year that I'd checked, but this Kilmer birthday was a little more poignant: Joyce Kilmer, born 1886 and died 1918 – arriving on scene exactly 100 years before me and this particular birthday was the centennial of his death. (Outlived you, old sport.)

Though, he and I certainly aren't identical in every way: he had a prolific urethra, siring five children before death. Perhaps his most beloved was his daughter, Rose Kilmer, born 1912 – in another eerie coincidence, that's exactly one century before Romy, *my* doghter, was born. Rose wasn't long for this world, dying after Kilmer deployed to fight in The Great War five years later. Rose had suffered from paralyzing polio since birth, and it's her tragedy that Joyce Kilmer credited as being the impetus for his blossoming faith. He told his priest that, before Rose, he'd always understood Catholicism intellectually, but he lacked a certain emotional conviction until Rose's condition brought him to his knees. I never understood how his daughter's pain could *increase* his faith, but it was enough to make him a full-fledged Catholic. Being Irish himself, he specifically enlisted in the "Fighting Sixty-Ninth," an infantry regiment known for its swarming Irish-Catholic soldiers. So it was: he went to war, Rose went to heaven, and the Kilmer legacy was seemingly snuffed out when he volunteered for a dangerous scouting mission in 1918 France. He'd be turning 132 today if not for that blasted bullet.

Kilmer was always one of two antecedents who I've come to recognize as a kindred spirit from a separate generation. (The other is Patrick McGoohan, another Irish-Catholic who'd been known by many names, including "Danger" and "Prisoner," at least until he officially licensed the monikers to me on January 13, 2009, after my first combat mission.)

This St. Nick's Day and Kilmer Birthday Bash was also more unusual than normal on account that it was the tenth anniversary of when I stepped into a war zone for my lone deployment with the Army. My unit relieved *none other* than the Fighting 69th – Kilmer's old troupe.

I texted Ben again.

"This'll be one of the best nights of my life."

"The night is nearly over; the day is almost here."
– Romans 13:12, NIV

לל

December 7, 2020

Can we talk?

Uh oh. I'm a millennial. You want to talk, like on the phone?

Lol no way, why would you even ask that? I'm a millennial too.

Okay good. Wow you gave me crippling anxiety there for a second.
What's up?

When I first met you, I asked if I could have an hour of your time. That was almost
2 years ago. I hate to tell you this, but you might not just be a participant
anymore, you might be my friend.

Ugh, how much time commitment does that require?

More than I'd ever tell you upfront.

Well, the way I see it, you have so many relationships in this life, only one or two
will last. You need to hold onto the ones who really care because in the end they'll
be the only ones there. :-p

That's... almost poetic?
I just appreciate the way you challenge me. You've taught me a lot, actually.

I'm flattered.
(✿ ಠ__ಠ)

I actually got you something

Huh?
What do you mean?

A small token of my appreciation for you

So. It is a gift. ┌(ಠ_ಠ)┘

Yes. Ready?

Huh? Yes? You're texting it?

שׁוֹן   q@q
    miii

Whut

You're welcome

Whut

That's it.
It's the gift

What's happening right now

It's a pair of Metroids fighting each other

Are you sure that's not Space Jam Michael Jordan trying to dunk?

No those are definitely Metroids
I tried really hard

That's what meteorid looks like?

Yep.

465

٣٤

<u>January 6, 2003</u>

Claire opened the door to her roof to find it still soaked from the downpour from the previous night. Earlier that morning, the sun's rays had finally broken through and the day was expected to be an oasis of shinedown before the weather snapped back to the rainy season by nightfall.

"If you go on that roof," Zuji had told her last night, his words echoing in her mind after she had detailed her plan, "you will be shot."

These words, in hot competition with the ones that came from Claire's mouth a few weeks ago:

"We are already living as a dead family, stuck in this house and being slaves to the war around us."

Besides: faith over fear.

Besides: women aren't shot at nearly as often as men are.

Besides: the kids need clean clothes.

Claire grabbed her bag of wet clothes and waded through the humidity permeating the roof to begin pinning her washed laundry on the clothesline.

What a beautiful white blouse, Claire thought to herself. *What a shame if Zuji is right, and my blood stains this.*

Claire glanced over at the watchtower, which was the only threat to her livelihood. This, in contrast to her balcony, which was in view of the soldiers at Rachel's Tomb, the nearby military camp, *and* the nearby watchtower – triple threat. She noticed the watchtower had a dirty window, hampered by the soot that came with the rainfall last night. And by the time she hung up the fourth of her five loads of laundry, she was convinced that the window must have been too dirty for the soldiers to see her. After all, she couldn't see any of the soldiers in the watchtower.

At one point during her fourth load, she heard two soldiers yell from inside the watchtower. And what seemed to be a mild argument between the two escalated to a screaming match.

My, someone ought to send a mediator for those two bickering!

You're sure?

A little.
Well... Idk. Well, maybe not.
No. I'm sorry. Upon closer inspection, I actually did terrible.

Why do they each look different?

One's Hebrew and the other is Anglican.

(⊙ ˏ ⊙)

Are you proud of me for trying?

I don't want to lie to you

I see.
Ugh I spent so long on that. I'll stick with words going forward.

That's appreciated. I'm glad I've taught you something. But I'm not sure what it is, because clearly it wasn't emoticon design.
So what does a Metroid actually look like?

You gotta google it

Can't you just show me a picture?

Absolutely not.

Why not?

Nintendo would sue me

Why would Nintendo sue you?

STOP! Shhhh.. If you say their name three times in the same conversation, Shigeru Miyamoto personally appears as a Boo to serve us papers.

Okay! I don't understand! But fine!
You're weird sometimes.

Can I tell you something I've been thinking about a lot?

Of course, friend.

In the Gospel of Matthew, Yeshua says that even the worst fathers wouldn't give his child a stone if he were to ask for bread.
So: Why would God Almighty give us a stone when we ask for bread?

Solid point

This verse has led me to question whether or not God is all-powerful.

My first thought wouldn't be to question god, but to question the claim that your bible is making. Why have you questioned god?

Well because a lot of our Bible verses talk about how great God's power is, but none explicitly state that it's infinite. And, because if God wasn't omnipotent, the world would start to become comprehensible.

But it's a cheap answer. God has unlimited power.
Even if that doesn't make things any simpler for you.

Exactly. It's a really bad, lazy answer.
So then, this means that it was HIS will for Romy to die the way she did, otherwise He could've and would've stopped it.
Meaning, it was not meaningless.

Okay.
First of all, if we're going to get into this, I need a deposit upfront.

Then, the window of the watchtower slid open and she found the two soldiers screaming at her: they weren't bickering, they were trying to get her attention.

"Are you talking to me?" Claire shouted across the roof, already knowing full well the answer to her question, but biding her time so she could at least finish collecting her fourth load.

The two soldiers climbed out of the window, shimmied along a shallow ledge, and hopped onto a small enclave that had a perfect view of Claire's roof. Here, one of the soldiers picked up his rifle and pointed it at Claire, while the other shouted at her.

"Go. Inside! Or he kill you!" the soldier yelled repeatedly, punching each of his words in broken English – the common language between Israelis and Palestinians.

"What did you say?" Claire shouted one more time as she grabbed her final piece of the fourth load.

"You. Die!"

She heard a mechanical snap – in fact, it might *not* have been the gun cocking, but it wasn't worth the chance, so Claire rushed back inside with her penultimate load of laundry. She crossed inside to the window on the third floor to find the soldiers edging their way back into their watchtower. Once she saw they slid the window shut, she grabbed her fifth and final load and headed back to the roof, quickly tossing each garment on a clothespin to dry.

As she sprinkled her family's clothes throughout the roof, she heard the watchtower window slide open and chuckled to herself as one of the soldiers sidled across the edge of the building again. When he made it to the concrete patch, he raised his rifle and shouted.

"Inside! Now!" he yelled, his voice cracking as he desperately sought control of the situation.

Claire turned to him, cupped her hands over her ear, and yelled, "Did you say something? I'm sorry, I did not hear you! I am doing laundry!"

The soldier rasped, "I shoot you!", losing his voice in the process.

"*Ohh*, okay," Claire said as she hung up the last piece of clothing. "I'll go inside now."

What deposit?
Oh.
You're weird sometimes.

Thanks.
So, you were saying, Romy's death had meaning?

I think so. When Romy died, God was NOT giving me a stone.
It can't mean that! It's not in His nature to do that.

That's how you wrap your head around it even now?

I think. For so long, I felt like I had been given a stone, without even considering
the possibility that maybe I had been given bread.
When I asked God for health for my family, I thought I was asking for bread, but
maybe I was being given a stone?

Well that would turn things on its head.

There's a book in the bible written by Yeshua's younger brother, and he says that
the prayer of a righteous man is heard, but only if you ask with right intentions.
Asking God to give good health for my family, and making it a pre-condition to
reconcile what He's doing in my life, I was actually asking for a stone. And that's
the difference between a God-fearer and those who don't care for God: the God-
fearer trusts that he wasn't given a stone.
Health is a miracle. It isn't a given. It isn't bread. And we need to be seeking
bread from God. I asked for a stone, and was given bread.

There's a lot to untie there.

Then I'll keep it knotted.

I just mean, it's kinda optimistic. It's, I don't know how to say it. Dissonant,
maybe? Like you're looking at the situation with rose-colored lens.

It only seems like a rose lens because I got blood in my eye.
I take comfort in this angle. Utmost comfort! Romy's life and death had meaning
to God. There is no greater solace than this, and lends way (the only way) to godly
grief. It's incomprehensible for anyone to imagine - and a syntax nightmare for
English majors to translate - how God could raise a valley. Yet the valley rose
under His instruction, just like the star rose into light.

Claire returned inside and couldn't help but laugh as she watched the soldier have to shimmy back into his watchtower. A couple hours later, as dusk began to set, the final set of clothes had been dried and, doing her best Usain Bolt impression, Claire sprinted back across her roof, collected the clothes, and made it back inside just as the soldier had finished shimmying across the building with his rifle.

Claire watched from her window inside to see the soldier screaming inaudibly and throwing his hands in the air as he realized Claire had already escaped by the time he negotiated across the chasm. As he carefully treaded across the edge, Claire leaned against her bedroom wall and was transported into a laughing fit, winsome tears streaming down her face as she found herself crying from laughter for the first time since the day her dad had died.

"*Claiirre,*" she heard a moan from the adjacent room.

"Yes, Umi?" Claire asked as she crossed to the next room, her heart crashing back to reality now that her frivolous escapades were achieved.

"Dear, I need my medicine and I'm too weak to get it," Umi said, looking directly at Claire, though her eyes didn't even seem like they were open.

"Of course," Claire told Umi, who really did look so frail and tired. Umi's wrinkled cheeks were stretched so tightly, her skin looked like a thin coat of cracked paint under those frail eyes.

Claire grabbed the pillbox on the dresser and popped it open, then wistfully sighed.

"Oh, Umi: you're out."

"I'm out of pills?"

"Yes, dear," Claire responded. "Did you know you were out?"

"Oh, I don't remember. Perhaps…" she said, then deployed another moan that needled Claire's heart into a state of helpless compassion.

"Hold on, Umi," Claire hustled back to the kitchen to grab her Nokia.

"Okhti? Yes, it's me. Yes, everything's fine. Do you still have Umi's leftover prescription? Okay, I need you to open your front door.

So you believe that the way Romy died was... bread?

Well, it couldn't have been a stone, right?

I'm not sure. Could it have been something in-between?

God doesn't give us processed sugar.

Of course not, but I don't know that I follow.

Last Lenten season, I tried a diet that no doctor would recommend: I only ate bread that was made from my own hands. I could put anything I wanted to into the bread, but for the 40 days, that was it. And I actually feel like I learned a lot, not just about bread, but about life, but the big thing I learned was how quickly bread goes bad.

You ate moldy bread?

No, never. Moldy bread is easy to throw out. But bread tends to go stale before it goes moldy. It's imperceptibly bad. And you eat it, thinking it's just as good as when it came out of the oven, but you forget how gratifying it was at first bite. The best bread is the bread that was made that same morning.

I smell a Metroid principle coming.

4. Ask for your daily bread every morning: this means asking for what you need on that particular day and not the things you need tomorrow.

I nailed it

Yes you did. But it's an important one. I believe that we were meant to live day-by-day. Not that we shouldn't think about the future and plan for what's coming, but we're not meant to worry about it.

And this: "Man does not live on bread alone."

I told you, no doctor would recommend this diet. Doctor nor prophet.

I think this a good principle, though. In a big way, I think that this is what the story of Job is getting at.

How so?

well, Job was so focused on explaining away the calamities in his life, and ultimately god said to him, "stop stressing about the implications of all of this. just trust that i'm god, and go about your day."

Hmm. Interesting. I've thought a ton about Job over the past months and I never made this connection once to it being about daily bread.

I know we've gone over this a little bit some time ago, but what's your understanding of the story of Job? Why is it in both our bibles?

Well, it's basically the Bible's look at theodicy. Job and Proverbs are 2 of the 7 "wisdom books" in the Bible, and Job is placed so close to Proverbs (i think) because it's an antithetical look at Proverbs.

Well that's a thought. Job and Proverbs being interlinked like that.

They are! Because they're at odds with each other, but paradoxically not in contradiction. They both have their specific purposes: Proverbs tells us why the righteous prevail, and Job tells us why the righteous don't prevail. Where Proverbs sets up the value of proverbial wisdom, Job emphasizes its limits in light of an all-powerful God.

Leave it wide open… yes, please, just listen to me, it's important. Yes, everything's fine! I promise! Just open your front door. Hey, trust me, okay? I need you to chill out and work with me, okay? Yes… thank you, dear."

Claire cracked her front door open and leaned her head out to see how many of the snipers were in their regular positions. There was one across the way monitoring Aida. And then there were the two soldiers she just mocked in the watchtower, but their vantage wasn't great and she was fairly confident that they couldn't get a good shot off if they wanted to. And then there was the third, Behruz, but he's a good boy and he knows Claire and he probably wouldn't shoot her unless he was commanded to. Of course, she had to worry now that her antics on the roof had been called in, too, so perhaps it was better to not count on any goodwill she had previously built up.

She stepped a little further in the street and tried determining how quickly she could get to Okhti's house across the road. It takes the average sniper – what? – about seven seconds to get a shot off on a day with no wind? This day wasn't particularly windy, and Claire could pop over to Okhti's house in about 40 seconds. Should she zig zag? No, that would add precious seconds to her excursion.

And then all of these scheming thoughts came to a head when a red dot appeared on Claire's nose. The sniper from Aida – who truly wasn't even that far away and probably didn't need to be using his sniper rifle – had locked onto her.

Claire beamed a wide, nervous smile, held her hands in the air, and yelled "Excuse me, dear! I need to get something from my sister."

"Go back," the sniper yelled, assigning his words with authoritative clarity as he knew the wind might carry the echo of his voice away. "Go. back. inside. *right*. now!"

Claire remained frozen, the red dot cementing Claire's feet to the ground.

"I repeat! Go inside! Or I will kill you in one second!"

But Umi needs her medicine… badly.

Claire heard the sliding of a window and sensed that the soldier in the watchtower – whom she had humiliated on the roof – was poking his

Yeah. I mean Job is all about trusting god, with the big things and the little things both. We need to worry about what's ahead of us and what we can control today. Daily bread.

I think though that worrying about the death of your family warrants some level of worry.

Sure. But you're faced with the same decision every day: trust god, or don't. Curse god, or don't.

I'm not like Job the man, but lately I do feel like I'm in the middle of a similar narrative arc. But the thing I don't understand about Job is it says that everything he lost was restored to him, and I don't think that's truly possible. for him, or for me. It's impossible - even for God - to write another line that would magically fix everything.

What do you mean? Why wouldn't it be possible?

Job lost his entire family. Sons, daughters, and wife. Sure, he remarried, and ended up having just as many children to "replace" what he lost, but you can't "replace" lost family members. Ever.

I don't know what word your bible uses, but the word "replace" isn't actually used in Job. Job's family is RESTORED. Not replaced.

Is there really any difference in this situation? Restore, replace, the kids are dead.

Danger. Brother. Friend. Are you ready for me to blow your mind?

I think

I want you to open to Job 1, hold your finger there, and simultaneously open to the last chapter of Job, I think it's Chapter 42.

K got it

In the last chapter of Job, what does it say? That god "restored" Job's fortunes, and gave Job twice as much as he had before. Correct?

Kosher.

Now answer my questions. How many sheep did Job have in chapter 1?

7000 sheep.

Chapter 42?

14,000 sheep.

Twice as many. Exactly twice as many. How many camels?

3000 in the first chapter, 6000 in the last.

Twice as many. Oxen?

500 in 1, 1000 in 42.

So, again: doubled.
And donkeys?

again: 500, then 1000.

Now, tell me. How many sons and daughters did Job have in Chapter 1?

7 sons and 3 daughters in Chapter 1.
But then also just another set of 7 sons and 3 daughters in Chapter 42.

So why is that? The author said that Job had been given twice as much of what he had as before. But he has 10 children in the first chapter, and 10 in the final chapter. Shouldn't he have 20 children in the final chapter?

head out. When he spotted that it was Claire who the sniper was yelling at, he began yelling in Hebrew – or more accurately, a new derivative language known as Angry Hebrew. He tried to aim his rifle at Claire himself to shoot her, but his angle was so rotten that he knew he couldn't safely pull off a shot. Instead, he began yelling to the other sniper in English – presumably so Claire could understand what he was saying.

"Kill that bitch right now! She is making us into freiers!"

The sniper didn't shoot, instead first shouting to the soldier, "*you, shaket!*", and then yelled to Claire, "and *you*, go back inside!"

The watchtower soldier began spewing again in Angry Hebrew at the sniper, then yelled in English so Claire again could hear him, "Kill this heap of pig-shit right now or I will leave my post and do it myself!"

But when the soldier looked back towards Claire, she had already slunk back inside, so he turned to the sniper and began yelling in Angry Hebrew.

Claire, with her back pressed against the wall in her foyer, exhaled sharply and said aloud to remind herself, "If you're scared, then you're not trusting the Lord enough."

Claire slid her body down against the wall and cradled her head in her hands.

"Lord, what shall I do? I have no way to get the medication. I need wisdom, Lord. Will you please protect me and send me the discernment I need today?"

As she prayed, Claire felt ethereal flame and frost come over her body. Sitting with the sublime presence for just a moment, she snapped her head back after a plan was hatched and marched to speak with her children.

Moments later, Claire was at the house entrance again. But instead of poking her head out, she pressed the intercom next to the front door.

"I'm ready," she spoke into it.

Three floors above her, Abni turned his head towards the back window.

"She says she's ready!" he yelled.

"Okay," Ebnahty said, watching the window. "The watchtower window is closed."

Maybe Jews are bad at math too?

Lol or maybe Job never "lost" his children in the first place. Yes, they died. But they weren't truly "gone." How is that? Because god still saw them. Just because they're gone from our view, doesn't mean they're out of god's sight.

...
Whoa.
So Job's children were waiting for him in the afterlife? That's what it means?

You tell me.

By that reading, I think so.
Yeah, it has to mean that Job would get his children back. Otherwise it doesn't make out to having been "doubled."

We see this from the prophet Joel, too. He says "the Lord restores the years that the locusts have eaten." How does god restore food that was lost during a famine? They still needed that food then, not now. People still died because they didn't have that food. How can god restore the dead?

Well. I guess God works in mysterious ways?

Job is a sad, sad story by itself. But when you read it in the context of there being an eternity, an eternity where god is sovereign over everything, it becomes a beautiful story. Because Job's brief suffering reconstructs the rest of his eternity, our eternity, into something that's more wonderful than he could've imagined.

Okay. Maybe you did blow my mind a little.

When you read Job, don't forget the main purpose of the story: Job is given a high honor, and that is to faithfully endure suffering for the purpose of god.
We can't be Job, but we can share in that purpose if we let god. And here's the kicker: eternity is now. It doesn't happen after you die. It's already started. You're living in it.

Thanks, Esther. Change like this is just hard, especially in such a short period.
Change of just a year.

What if there aren't any more lines to be written? What if you have everything you need already? You're right: 1+1 *can* equal 3 if god = x factor. What if you've been so hyperfocused on the valley, you don't see that god has created a route back up the mountain?
Change of just a year. Fine. But what's down can be up if you see it the right way.
And Danger?

Yes?

May her memory be for blessing.
May you be comforted by the eternal.
May beloved Romy know true Berakhah.
May her neshama rest with the eternal.

Hey. You remembered.
It's been a tough day.
That whole 24-hour period before she died... just, horrific.
I didn't think you'd remember or care.
So, thank you.
So much, actually. It actually means more than you know.

People care. Because god wired us to be like him.
Go light a candle for her.

"The watchtower window is closed," Abni yelled into the intercom.

"Abni, dear, you don't need to yell into it," Claire's gentle voice broadcasted through the system. "And what about the sniper by Aida?"

"What about Aida?" Abni called to Ebnahty.

"He's moving towards us," she yelled over to Abni.

"Stay still, Mama," Abni said.

"He's about to turn around," Ebnahty shouted.

"Get ready, Mama!" Abni yelled.

"Abni, dear, remember you don't need to yell. The speaker is very loud."

"Go!" Ebnahty yelled.

"Go!" Abni yelled.

At the front door, Claire winced as the words blasted through against her ear drums, then she cantered a couple steps into the street and, confirming the sniper was still walking the opposite direction, she gazelled to Okhti's house and burst through her open door.

"Claire!" Okhti blurted. "I almost closed the door! I thought you weren't coming."

"Please, Umi needs the medication right away," Claire said.

"Here, here," Okhti responded, handing Claire the prescription.

Claire returned to the front door and squinted towards her house.

"Ebnahty is giving me the thumbs up," she said. "Thank you, sister."

Claire raced back towards her house, but as if he had known her plan, the soldier in the watchtower flung the sliding window open and howled, "She's back! She's back! Kill her!"

Claire turned around and saw the sniper hurry to the edge of the elevated walkway he was manning and point his rifle towards the street, inspiring her to pick up the tempo and hustle into her home.

Slamming the door behind her, Claire leaned against the wall again and cachinnated so wildly that tears began falling from her face.

That's twice I've laughed until I cried today!

"Umi!" Claire yelled, clearing her throat. "I've got something for you!"

THE CURSE OF GENESIS

> "Nothing in the universe can travel at the speed of light,
> they say, forgetful of the shadow's speed."
> - Howard Nemerov

Spoiler alert: December 6th wasn't one of the best nights of my life.

On St. Nick's afternoon, Romy continued to show discomfort at home. I sat beside her and prayed on her behalf, pleading with God that surely this pain for such an innocent animal couldn't be part of His plan. I charismatically prayed in tongues, demanding the sickness to flee from Romy in the name of Yeshua. This was my chance – this was my big opportunity to pray with the kind of fervent faith that Claire talked about, the kind that stirred up the Holy Spirit to work miracles.

To my credit, Romy's condition did, indeed, change when I prayed for her: she got worse with each word that came out of my mouth. She shifted from showing signs of discomfort to showing signs of serious pain and confusion. She tried walking and fell on her chin, her front paws buckling over as she tried to amble around.

Romy's eyes were always full of expression, and in this moment, I could see her terror when I looked on her face. Utter, fierce terror. She tried to stand up again, but she had no control over her paws. She lost her composure as her legs wouldn't do what she wanted them to, frantically trying to stand up and falling over each time. She began to wildly fling her front paws every which way as she confronted the realization that her legs were no longer working.

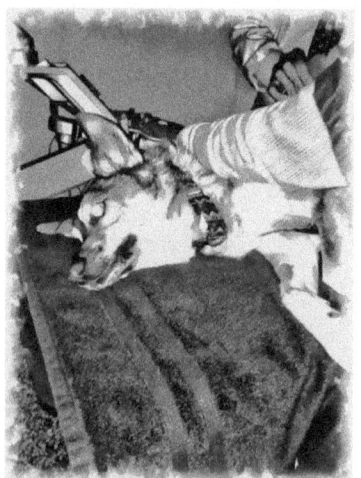

I clutched her front paws and calmly whispered "baby girl," masking my own terror. Her left and right paw were the difference between St. Petersburg, Florida and St. Petersburg, Russia: one was warm and lively, the other ice cold – and neither had been the leg that had been operated on.

I picked Romy up, tossed her into my Jeep, and sped off to the ER, where the doctors determined that the carprofen she had been prescribed had not only begun to tear her stomach (spawning an ulcer), but that she was suffering from a blood clot in her artery (which is why she had lost mobility of her leg).

"Joanna, you need to leave work.
The doctor says Romy is in critical condition."

Joanna rushed over to the ER where the doctor explained that Romy was basically dying a slow, painful, once-preventable death.

Ha, right. I didn't accept that. I already told you, that's not God's plan. Romy dying this way? Nope. That's the one thing we've regularly petitioned from God, multiple times a day. If He gave us this sharp desire in our heart, and He's a good God who "will give the desires of your heart" (Psalm 37:4), then surely this is the one thing He wouldn't overlook for us.

After we dropped Romy off at the ER and they told us they'd only call if she was worsening, Jo and I said our *temporary* goodbyes to her. I prayed once again for healing over her as she calmly rested in her kennel in the emergency room itself, then I put my face next to hers.

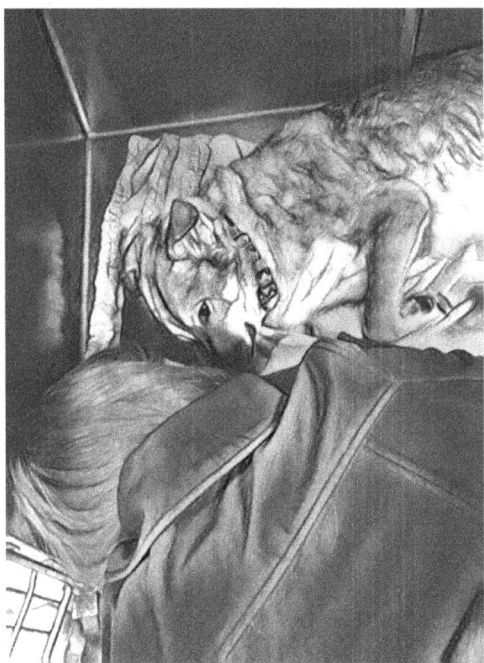

"Romy, give me kiss," I demanded.

She listlessly gazed out into space, almost as if my words had struck a stone and branched away from her.

"Okay," I conceded. "You're fine. We'll be back soon."

"We'll call if we need to," the vet told us as we left, "but no news is good news."

"Thanks," I said. "I hope to not hear from you."

Joanna and I drove home, then collapsed on the couch.

I pried my phone from the seat of my pants, then sent a text to one of my newest friends.

Do you pray for good health?

Me? Or Jews?

You. Personally.

No. Not really. I don't do initiated prayer like that usually. Usually I pray at temple, from a book.
Why? What's going on?

The doctor says Romy is going to die. I'm trying to have faith here, but I feel as desperate as David did when his son was stricken with sickness. Like, break out the sackcloth.

But what happened?!? Like how did this happen?

She tore her knee. She was put on an anti-inflammatory, Carprofen. The meds ripped a hole in her stomach, which created an ulcer. The ulcer is on the verge of rupturing. In fighting the ulcer, she's thrown a clot in her artery, which is preventing any blood from reaching her leg. She can't even stand up. Now, even if they can stop the ulcer from rupturing (a tall order), her blood clots might spark a stroke. Even if that doesn't happen and the blood clot dissolves, her leg could swell too quickly with blood (something called DIC), which is toxic and would put her into sepsis.

Oh. my. goodness. So she has to get past the ulcer, past the blood clots, and past DIC?

Yes

This just happened randomly? They couldn't see this was happening?

I could have gotten a blood panel when I suspected something was wrong. $40. Forty dollars. Four. Zero.

I'm sorry :(I hope that what is meant to be will happen.

"Do you want to open the St. Nick stocking?" Joanna interrupted my texting.

"No," I replied, setting the phone down. "Let's just go to bed."

"What about your *Smash* night?" she prodded me.

"Yeah, forget that. I won't spend a minute playing that until she's out of the ER."

"Okay. Let's just close our eyes for now."

"Before that, can we do one thing?"

"What's that?"

"I want to put up the 'our dogs love us' picture."

We were still moving out of our condo and into a new house at that point, and the only thing we hadn't set up in the home yet were the pictures on the walls.

A few years ago, we'd been gifted a wood-based canvas that said "We love our dogs and our dogs love us." This isn't the typical thing I like to hang in my house: it reeks of cheese, similar to any of those overly sentimental "Live Laugh Love" tchotchkes that had a popular surge during the 2010s.

Still, I've come to love not only this particular phrase, but also this wood canvas because it features two dogs who have striking similarities to Sidney and Romy. But in the weirdest of ways, the likenesses of the dogs are interchangeable. What I mean is that sometimes the left dog looks like Romy and the right dog looks like Sidney, but then other times I'll look at it and the left dog looks like Sidney and the right dog looks like Romy instead. It's like it's an optical illusion that was created specifically for our family.

I rummaged through all our framed art and canvasses, and I came across a Bible verse typed on a thick piece of paper.

"The prayer of a righteous man is powerful and effective."

It's from the Bible. James 5:16. Written by Christ's brother. And, sure, Yeshua had more "brothers" than Hulk Hogan on a caffeine high, but this epistle was written by Mr. Of-Nazareth's *literal* oldest little brother. And on a random Sunday about a year ago, it was the verse listed at the bottom of our church's bulletin. I silently deemed it "the verse of the year" for the Geist household, ripped it out of the bulletin, creased it so it had a fold to stand on, and prominently put it in our windowsill to reflect on it often. It was early December now, so still technically "the verse of the year." I walked to the kitchen and put it on our counter under the sole crucifix in the house.

The crucifix and a posted Bible passage: two of the more unusual sights in the Geist home. We always have several hanging crosses in the house, but not being Roman Catholic, they don't have the Messiah hanging on the cross. The crucifix is a keepsake from my childhood, the relic that used to hang above my twin-sized bed. I'd look at Christ's agonized face on the crucifix and reflect on the grief He must have felt during His abandonment, and it would center my teenage soul.

And tearing out a Bible verse and displaying it? Not my style. It wasn't anything I'd done before and isn't something I've done since. But tonight, as Romy set new heights of suffering, there were two things that I wanted her to take into passion: prayer and Christ.

I returned to the box of framed pictures, found the "our dogs love us" wood canvas, and hung it above the cage that Romy had been confined to after her surgery. But as I backed away to see if it was hanging level, I noticed an unfortunate mark: one of the dogs' faces had become scratched out, presumably during the actual move.

I let out a deep sigh and crawled into bed. Joanna and I forced ourselves to sleep, hoping that we wouldn't be woken up by a phone call.

"Did I purify my heart and
wash my hands in innocence for nothing?
For I am afflicted all day long
and punished every morning."
~ Psalm 73:13-14, CSB

לה
December 8, 2020

I've got a question for you. Maybe a sensitive one?

Well we've already talked about your urethra so it's only fair you get to ask a personal question

You usually don't capitalize the "G" in God. My teachers in Catholic school saw this as blasphemous. It's so ingrained in me that I even get anxiety if I don't refer to God as "He" without capitalizing His Pronouns. You're not like other Jews I've met. Some Jews are so worried about desecrating God's Name that they write it as "G-d." You don't seem to care at all. why?

It's english. English is not a holy language, and "God" is not his real name. The people who write god's name as "G-d" don't know Hebrew, I imagine.

Okay, fine, but you literally capitalize other names. Like Job. Even Ittai the Gittite!

"God" is a description. His title. That "name" doesn't count in my eyes. :) You would never catch me being laissez-faire with god's Hebrew name.

Okay. I think I got it, except that you literally just capitalized "Hebrew" and not God.

Autocorrect. :)

Gotcha. Well, it's a line between laissez-faire and anarchy.

Reminder that most Israelis are not religious, either. In fact I'd say most Jews aren't even religious. Most of them are Hiloni Jews, which is kind of basically 'secular Jew.'
It's like when you have your christians who say they're American, and Americans have historically been christian, so there's a bad assumption there that an american is christian until proven otherwise.

They still would refer to themselves as Jews though?

Yes. Many, many jews don't believe in the one true god, they only believe in the one true jewish ethnicity.

Got it.
I think.
While we're on this topic, why do you spell it "Jewdism." I assume that's just some transliteration thing?

How should it be spelled?

Judaism?

Lololol. On the record, let's just call it a transliteration thing. Off the record, I learned english when I was 14. And that word specifically, if I'm writing it, it's almost always in Hebrew. Apart from you, I can't recall a time I've ever written it in english

But you know so many other complicated English words!

Yeah, because that's what you're supposed to learn in school, not "jewdism."

Here I thought it was some ancient mystical beautiful thing you were doing

If you're relaying this in your book, please please fix my spelling

I don't know, I find it kind of endearing.

٣٥

Claire stood at the sink, drying the dishes she had just finished washing. She felt particularly exhausted this morning, so when she first heard the bullets whizzing by her window, she thought maybe she was imagining them, at least until Ebnahty confirmed they were, indeed, thwitting by.

"Mama, it's happening again," Ebnahty said.

"Okay, kids, time to go upstairs," Claire said, as if she was nonchalantly trying to herd her children to brush their teeth or comb their hair.

The obedient kids marched upstairs. Less than a beat later, Claire heard pounding on her door.

Claire checked the peephole to see a horde of soldiers in front of her house.

"Open the door!" screamed the soldier in front of the line, startling Claire as her face had been pressed against the wood, her cheek absorbing the reverberations from the bass in the man's voice.

Claire opened the door and found herself shocked to find that the group wasn't being led by a Samal or a Segen, but a *Seren*, the highest-ranking officer that operated in her corner of Bethlehem.

"What can I do?" Claire coyly asked.

"We need to get to your roof," the Seren dragooned.

This was a highly unusual request, at least given the time of day: in all the years of their occupation, the Tzahal never requested to use Claire's roof unless it was under the guise of night. This was the first time – and as she'd find, the only – that they wanted her roof during the day.

A female soldier emerged behind the Seren, nearly toppling him as she intruded into Claire's house, looked up the stairs, and announced, "We need to know where everyone in this house is, *right now*."

Claire looked at the woman's insignia and found, like the man, she had three bars on her collar.

Not just *a* Seren, but two! Two Serens!

"Oh, *my*, I didn't expect there to be two of you. I didn't even know there were two of you in Bethlehem! It is just me here, along with my children. My husband is at…"

"I did not stumble over my words," the female Seren monotonously replied, as if a robot devoid of human emotion. "I did not

Promise me you'll fix it.

I plomise I will fix it..

So it's my turn to ask something. What's your next Metroid principle?

I actually don't have a new one.

Aw but you were rolling. I was totally expecting you'd have a new one by now.

Sorry to disappoint! I'm still chewing on Job.

Does he taste like leather?

Well if it's the oldest book in the Bible, that's a fair description

What have you been thinking about?

Well, you're not going to like this because I'm kind of putting myself in Job's shoes again, but I'm wondering if the story of Job could happen in modern day. Like, why would I not think that God maybe had a discussion with "the adversary" about the events unfolding in my life? I feel like I'm just in the middle of my own version of God's story for my life, and I have to trust that I'll get to Chapter 42. BUT, in order to do that, I have to recognize that I didn't even get to see Chapter 1. I just popped into the middle chapters of my own life's story, where nothing makes sense. Had I been around for Chapter 1, I'd have an omniscience like God and Satan and even the reader had.

Right, you lack that insight. Job starts his story at chapter 2, and the rest of us get to see chapter 1. The characters of Job (besides god and the adversary) have no understanding of what's going on. As the reader, given the omniscience you've been afforded, you can't help but want to reach into the story and explain to Job why he's going through what he's going through.
Another big thing about Job that's easy to miss: you and I can sit down and read through Job in one sitting. We don't have to sit in it for very long. Job? Some people believe the trials he faced lasted over 40 years, if not twice that. Most people agree that it was at least 40 months.

That's a long time to live under that darkness.

It was silence, not darkness. Silence doesn't mean abandonment. That's important to differentiate.
Job cried out to god, and god still heard him, even if he chose not to intervene.
Malachi was our last prophet, and Josiah our last (good) king, then it's been silence while waiting for the meshiach.

Hmm. Interesting. For Christians, the period between the fall of Israel and Yeshua's arrival is known as the "400 Years of Silence." Even now, Christians are living in a period of...
Something. Idk. It's not silence, and it's not darkness, but it's not light. "2000 Years of Twilight?" I don't know.

Faithless is he that says farewell when the road darkens..

That's funny, given that I was at an all-time faith high when I left Israel, and immediately after, God highlighted my faithlessness. My "all-time faith high" was still a state of faithlessness.

Don't be too hard on yourself. God wouldn't have invented atonement if he didn't care about mercy.

True, but then you gotta wonder about those who didn't have a system of atonement before that.

ask you to account for your children. I am telling you to bring me to your fucking children."

Claire knew they were in for it now. In her experience, dealing with female soldiers was the worst. Claire felt that female soldiers had something to prove to the men, and overcompensated by being meaner, louder, scarier, and much quicker to rash decisions.

Claire marched the entourage upstairs: both Serens and a handful of junior enlisted, altogether eight of them.

As they reached the top floor, the female Seren asked, "Which room are the children in?"

Claire begun to walk towards one of the bedrooms, but was stunted when the Seren grabbed her shoulder and pushed her backwards.

"Did I ask you to fetch the children, or did I ask which room the children are in?"

"You know," Claire cheeked, "in ancient Rome, it was shameful for a woman to wear a toga."

"What does that mean?" the Seren asked.

Claire remained silent.

"What does *that* mean?" she repeated, her eyes shooting daggers into Claire's.

Claire remained silent still. The Seren pushed Claire into the stairwell.

"Get on your knees," the Seren said. "And tell me which room to find your children. Do not call for them, do not move. Tell me which room they are in."

Claire glanced at her nametape, hoping that addressing her personally may de-escalate her animosity and help remind her that she is a human.

"Seren Alon, dear. My children are just through that door, in the bedroom. But I beg you: please do not be rough with them."

Seren Alon walked into the bedroom and Claire immediately heard Ebnahty screaming. Claire began to lunge forward, but the male Seren put his hand out towards Claire, motioning her not to move.

Abni and Ebnahty marched out of the room and were ushered into the stairwell.

"Fall on your knees, all of you," Seren Alon told the Anastas family.

The children joined their mother with their knees on the hardwood. Three of the Tzahal raised their guns and pointed the ironsights toward Abni and Ebnahty.

What do you mean?

> The timespan from Adam to Aaron is maybe thousands (if not billions) of years. What about those who needed atonement in that time?

God doesn't need an excuse to have mercy.
Ok trivia question: who is the first priest mentioned in the bible?

> That's easy. I just said it: Aaron.
> 500 points to Danger.

Nope. Try again.

> Okay... if it's not Aaron, it has to be a trick question. Let me think on this for a second. I probably know the answer. It's sitting on the beach but right now it's high tide and the waves won't let me dig it from the sand.

Oh my goodness, Danger Poe. Are you even capable of using less than 3 words?

> No but thanks for asking.
> Was it technically Abraham or something?

Oooohhh getting closer! It's Melchizedek.
Mentioned only twice in scripture: Genesis and Psalms.
Gets a sentence of acknowledgement each time.

> Genesis is before the priesthood was ever established. Everything was anarchy back then.

There's a thin line between laissez-faire and anarchy. :-) Check it yourself though.
Melchizedek, a random guy that we don't get much detail on, gives Abraham a priestly blessing. Before there were priests.

> Looking it up.

It gets weirder. Melchizedek is said to be the "king of Salem." What's Salem?

> Jerusalem?

Correct. Salem was Jerusalem's first name.
Except, Jerusalem wasn't established yet! Not for another 1000 years or so.
Whatever "Salem" was, it wasn't Jewish.

> So Mel was a priest (before priests existed) who moonlighted as the king of Jerusalem (before Jerusalem existed)?

Yes.

> And we don't get any info beyond that?

Nope.

> It says that Melchizedek is mentioned three times, not just twice.

Where does it say that?

> Oh, nevermind. The third reference is in my Bible, in the book of Hebrews.
> The Googles says it.

You have a Hebrews book in your bible?

> Yes. And clearly I need to brush up on it because I don't remember the name Melchizedek at all, but Hebrews has an entire chapter dedicated to highlighting the mystery of this priest.

Typical. Christianity needing to close every loop that's ever existed in jewdism.
Judaism*

> Should there not be an attempt to answer these things?

"Is this an execution?" Claire asked.

Seren Alon scoffed, as if Claire's perception of the situation was somehow absurd.

"I need to get on your roof," Seren Alon responded.

Claire's heart sank. The roof was inaccessible. Ever since Marwan gained access to the Anastas roof years ago, they kept the key on Zuji's body at all times.

"Seren Alon, my husband is at work, and he has the key to the roof."

"That is fine," Seren Alon responded calmly, much to Claire's surprise.

"He will be home soon," Claire responded, though admittedly, "soon" was a relative term: he hadn't left for work but two hours ago.

"It is fine," Seren Alon repeated, then added, "we will just bomb it open."

Abni screamed.

"*Shaket!*" Seren Alon barked at Abni, then took her rifle and pressed it against Claire's head. "*Sha*-ket."

Abni stopped screaming and began to whimper.

"I need to grab the fuzes, but I will be back," Seren Alon informed everyone, pressing the muzzle of her rifle into Claire's temple. "None of you will move. If I come back and find you in a new position…"

She didn't finish her sentence, and stomped all the way downstairs with half the soldiers following her.

With Seren Alon gone, the room fell completely silent, save for the sniffles of the children. Claire closed her eyes and began to whisper inaudibly, the smacking of her lips shrouded by the sobs of Abni and Ebnahty.

"Yasue, Holy Spirit," Claire silently prayed, "I need You now. Come to my aid. Speak through me. Or if we are to die today, please have them take us all at once, so that these children will never know what it is to be orphaned. What do I say, Lord? Use my tongue for Your glory."

As expected, Claire felt heat at the top of her body, followed by the trademark chill as the polarized elements swirled around her body.

"*Ahim,*" Claire cleared her throat, then looked up at the male Seren and employed his name now. "Seren Vaknin, do you consider yourself a religious man? A real religious man, not in name only? Not just because you are Jewish. Are you a chosen man? A man of God?"

Can a mystery just be left a mystery?
Job, Ecclesiastes, Proverbs, Psalms all raise questions that aren't fully answered. That's part of their purpose, is to open a line of questions that we don't get to know the answer to. But each of them (Job, Solomon, David, etc) ultimately come to the same conclusion: God is sovereign. And worth trusting.

I do think one question deserves a solid answer, though: that of the Messiah.

Why would that need a definitive answer?

At the end of your canon, we're left with three big questions: (1) where is the relief from the evil of this world? (2) will this sacrificial system have to continue forever? (3) who is this suffering servant / conquering king that is the subject of so many prophecies?

And you absolutely need an answer for those? Right now? On your schedule?

Kind of, sure. It's like a TV plot arc that raises a bunch of questions it never intended to answer. It's how it gets viewership: ask bigger-than-life questions with no viable satisfying answers, leaving fans with disappointment and producers with wads of cash in their pockets. Judaism brings up these questions, and then completely falls away from even attempting to answer them. In mid-story, the story arc just stops. Judaism is a half-story.

Judaism is probably closer to a TV show that got abruptly cancelled, and only recently was renewed for a new season on a different network.

Can I share a Bible verse with you? From my Bible?

Okay

"Rejoice in hope, be patient in suffering, persevere in prayer." Romans 12:12 I recently noticed that this verse basically has three different storylines, across different spans of time, that are all trying to converge at the end.

What do you mean by that? It doesn't sound any edgier than your basic proverb.

We accidentally "rejoice in hope" all the time, it's natural. But we never sit in that state: Hope aggressively arrives and burns off even faster. It's not like suffering, which happens naturally too, but it takes much longer, and once it sets in, it stays. We allow suffering to slowly consume our being. If "rejoicing in hope" is a barrel explosion, then the second act is a longsuffering candle with thick wax and a stub of wick. We can end there, OR... work towards getting to the final and best "storyline." But we have to do something unnatural: pray. We need to intentionally work towards prayer. And it's a storyline that spans a lifetime, maybe more.

So. Okay. Help me here. Rejoicing in hope and being patient in suffering both have linear-esque end points, while persevering in prayer is more constant?

When you seek perseverance in prayer, you learn to settle into longsuffering, which amplifies hope. Suddenly, the act of rejoicing actually encroaches on your suffering, and we see things as God intended them to be.

I'm really, really trying to grasp your point but my brain is having a heart attack.

Here's the connection I'm trying to make: Why be patient in suffering? Because, maybe the hardest things, in the end, are the best things.

Got it.

There's something you said before that's really impacting me lately: Is there any way to really reconcile Romy's death outside of eternity? Because I don't think there is.

Seren Vaknin remained silent, opting not to respond to the onslaught of questions, nor would he even look at Claire as she asked them.

"Are you ashamed to answer me?" Claire continued her barrage of questions. "Are you not a religious man?"

This last pair of questions broke him.

"Yes!" Seren Vaknin shouted, almost with a twinge of pride in his response. "Yes, I am a religious man. I am a Jew! I love God."

"Do you have children?" Claire asked him.

"Yes," he replied, now with much more shame than pride as he understood where this conversation was going. "Three children."

"Imagine this," Claire pled, "that I would take your gun from you now and go to your home and point it at your children. What will you do with me?"

Seren Vaknin glanced down at Claire and found her wryly smiling.

"How dare you…" he began, only to find Claire's grin grow. "How dare you say that to me!"

"What would you do?" Claire repeated, demanding an actual response to her question.

"You'd never get anywhere near my house, because you would've been dead before you even got there, gutted twice before I let your corpse hit the floor."

"And yet you are inside mine, with three soldiers pointing their guns at my children," Claire continued, unvexed by the Seren's veiled threat. "I did not kill you, or try to kill you, before you came to my door. Perhaps I just didn't have the opportunity. But even if I had the chance to have killed you and your soldiers, I'd never have done it. Why, sir? Why would I not do that to you?"

Seren Vaknin inhaled deeply, then wheezed the air back out of his nose.

"I would not be able to kill you because, like you, I consider myself a religious person. Like you, my God is the God of Abraham, Isaac, and *Jacob*."

Claire let the words sink in.

"I belong to God," she continued her pitch. "And I do not understand, how do you expect me to allow you to blow up my house as you plan to?"

Claire continued to gaze at him, then saw his body loosen, Seren Vaknin easing into what almost appeared to be a hunched stance. Silence

What do you mean?

The sadness consuming me might last a lifetime. In fact, I think it will. The story doesn't improve, from that standpoint. UNLESS I consider that the story doesn't end after one lifetime. If it goes forever, then the years I WON'T have with Romy - or Sidney, or my parents or even Joanna - these are short, painful blips. For 'death is but a gardener,' no? Death is a quick little surgery, an excruciating rod down the urethra to stretch it out and make room for something more.

You have a certain grossness to you, sir.

Thanks

Again, not a compliment, sir

Thanks. Again.

(✿•ᴗ•)

Romy's death has me focusing on eternity, and how if we look at someone dying and beg God, "don't let it end like this," we're not realizing that it's not actually the end. Sure, the way it's presented bullies us into feeling like it's the end, at least at the time. And for some people, it's so convincing that we allow it to be the end. I think we often feel like God must be a sadist for what He puts us through. Like God revels in our suffering. But He's not looking at dying or suffering like it's a permanent thing. What if a baby losing their life is as significant to God as a baby losing their first tooth is to us? How unremarkable death must be in God's eyes. For us, it's the end of everything. For God, it's like watching us bear a child: significant, yes, but also on the other side of the spectrum from death.

I don't know that we know that much about what happens after our lives end, but I think I get what you're saying.

Relationships are the only thing you take into eternity. I mean, maybe only Christians will assume this to be true because Yeshua is the one who tells us that the only thing we're taking in is the righteousness poured upon us as a direct result of our relationship with Him.
Listen, Esther. you're born, you die.
How are you different between those 2 points? you have relationships. that's it.
relationships are the only thing on this earth that matter.

If I were a christian, I could buy into what you're saying. In the sense that I see where you're coming from.
If god has an ultimate purpose for mankind (I believe he does!), then we're certainly not there. Not yet. Which means pain, death, suffering still exists. BUT, god is also present in those moments with tears and sadness. And sometimes, those tears and sadness don't have to have a purpose beyond clinging to the hope of the resurrection.
And in the meantime, that just sucks.

Do you believe suffering is a part of God's plan?

I don't know. At least not for sure. But I lean towards suffering having a purpose for us as much as blessing does.

I'm resigned to believe that pain and suffering are *at least sometimes* a part of God's plan. Because what if those who sow in tears shall reap with shouts of joy? The idea that it's simply because we live in the "not yet" is predicated on the notion that God either can't make our suffering any less, or He won't... just because we're not in eternity yet. And as you told me once: eternity is now.

followed, at least until the front door on the ground floor opened and shut, and a stampede of steps thundered up the stairwell.

"I am asking you politely, now," Claire said, never loosing her eyes from Seren Vaknin's, "please leave. Go. I see your eyes. They are eyes that show me you are a man with a kind heart who seeks righteousness. But you need to prove that to yourself. But before you can prove it to yourself, you must prove it to God. And your moment is now at hand. You must prove it for Him, not for me."

"Everyone, vacate this building!" Seren Alon yelled as she ascended the final steps with a set of bombs in her grasp.

The Anastas children began to wail, prompting one of the soldiers to escort all the children down the stairs and outside their home.

"Are you not leaving too?" Seren Alon asked Claire. "Fine, stay kneeling there, if that's what you wish. But your blood will not be on my hands."

"So you will blow me and my house down? There may be no roof if you do this."

"Speak again, and I will tie you to this door first," Seren Alon riposted. "We have a right to defend Israel. And right now, this door is preventing us from being able to do just that."

Seren Alon slathered the paste on the four corners of the door, then slapped a C4 magnet to the top-left and bottom-left hinges. But as she worked on the next two corners, Seren Vaknin crept to the hinges and – without uttering a word – plucked the C4 off of the door.

"What in patriarchy's curse are you doing?" Seren Alon asked, snatching the magnets from Seren Vaknin's hands and re-positioning them on the door.

But without a word, Seren Vaknin pulled them off the door and tossed them to the ground.

Seren Alon grabbed him by the collar with one hand and threw her fist across his face with the other, a crack filling the air as his head snapped to the left. He calmly turned and looked directly at Seren Alon, but still did not say a word as a droplet of blood trickled down the corner of his lip.

"Don't touch these again," commanded Seren Alon. She picked up the two explosives off the ground and affixed them to the door, then grabbed two more magnets and appended them to the other corners.

But as Seren Alon plodded back to the other side of the room, Seren Vaknin picked off the four explosives again and dropped them at his feet.

I don't think it's vital to figure these types of things out right now. But if it's helping you cope, if that's what's helping you move forward, I'm here for it.

Hey! I didn't even have to ask for one! Thanks!

You've trained me to be Pavlov's dog I guess.

That's a fantastic picture, by the way. Your girls look like they're about to drop a debut album that's gonna be straight boss.

Red Hot Chili Puppers

Lol... Zoomie-DMC.

Two Human Night.

Canine Inch Nails.

Lick.

Lick?

Idk. Dogs like to lick.

And leave pawprints on our heart.

Hey: the Bible - mine - talks about this idea that Yeshua is written on our hearts. Doesn't the Old Testament talk about something like that?

Sure. Jeremiah says that god is going to write the law on the peoples' hearts. I believe in the context that we were about to go into exile, therefore we needed a way to remember the law.

If the Law is written on our hearts, and Yeshua is written on our hearts, then God's sovereignty must also be written on our hearts, right? As is God's persistence to peace, and His plan for redemption.
God's love for creation - dogs included - that is written on our hearts, too.

Most likely. Yeah, I can probably get behind that.

What if every dog goes to heaven? Then the overpopulation crisis is a GOOD thing. Every dog endures some pain, then spends eternity with Adonai.
That would be so beautiful, I could cry.

I'm glad I could help spur up some of this for you.

yeah. Thank you, Esther.

Anytime, gross little buddy.

At the sound of the magnets dropping, Seren Alon froze, tried to regain her composure, and then screamed and hurtled herself towards Seren Vaknin, clawing at him, only to be intercepted by the younger soldiers.

"Who changed your mind?" she shrieked. "I will kill them right now!"

Seren Vaknin held his hand out, "Tamar, quit."

Seren Alon stopped struggling as soldiers continued to hold her in place.

"You take your bombs," Seren Vaknin ordered, "and you get out of here."

Seren Alon, whose face could've been confused with an overgrown radish, huffed once more and then stomped her way down the stairwell, broadcasting her disgust.

"Everyone: leave," Seren Vaknin said, giving Claire a moment with him.

"Sir, thank you," she lauded the kind Seren. "Please, I have another favor to ask, and my hope is you're not void of goodwill yet."

Seren Vaknin looked at her, as silent as he had been with Seren Alon, and beckoned Claire to finish her request.

"I have been trying to gain an audience with the commander who oversees this area. These home invasions, they are simply torture for my family. It is a living nightmare, and you can't imagine what we have been put through. I wanted to speak with the head commander of Bethlehem to request that our house be spared from these home invasions, as we have never stirred up trouble for your soldiers, and…"

"I am the commander," Seren Vaknin interrupted her, and then as if reciting a decree from the Supreme Court of Israel, stated, "The commander you seek an audience with is me. Your request has been heard, and I am granting it to be so. This will stand as long as I am in authority over this jurisdiction: there will not be any more invasions in your house, nor will any of my soldiers bother you again."

And as he promised, there were no more and none did.

TRIGGER WARNING

> "In our times of suffering,
> God doesn't give answers
> as much as he gives himself."
> - Randy Alcorn

Shortly after 2am, I jolted awake to silence.

"Jo," I tapped on her shoulder. "Jo, I'm going to visit Romy. It's almost the Devil's Hour."

The Devil's Hour is the period between 3am and 4am local time. It is called this because, statistically, more people die during this one-hour period than any other time during the day (just ask a hospital nurse). Ancient legends say that evil and demons are most active during this time, and Christian mystics argue that it's because it's converse to 3pm, the "Holy Hour" in which Christ died on the cross. (I say that it's because the body usually goes into kind of a medical suspension during that time, and your organs are in a more vulnerable "maintenance" mode as you sleep.) Regardless of the reason, I wanted to be with Romy from before 3am to after 4am to see her through.

"I'll call you if anything happens," I told a groggy Joanna. "But try to get some sleep in the meantime."

I rushed out the door, not without grabbing some gum on the way out because my breath was atrocious, then tossed the gum aside when I remembered that one of Romy's favorite scents was bad morning breath. When I got to the ER, the staff set me in a room and told me it would be a couple minutes. The hospital rooms had a deep sadness about them – in the back room, I could hear one dog constantly yapping. You know, one of those annoying Yorkies or Poodles that constantly yips whether or not anything is wrong.

Drowning out the yaps, I waited patiently and looked around the room. I realized they had moved me into the "grieving room" – a room with tissues and pictures that volunteered pseudo-comforting phrases like "together forever, never apart" to eye-rolling clichés like "dogs leave pawprints on our heart" and a fold-down table that was presumably for putting dogs down. I was sitting in a room that probably thousands of dogs had been euthanized in. But that wasn't going to be the story today.

Not my girl.

Not my Romy.

Until they wheeled her in on a gurney. Romy glanced at me, and for the first time in her entire life, she wasn't excited to see me after an extended separation. And then I heard it. The yapping. The barking. That high-pitched "Yorkie" screeching? It was coming from Romy, who normally had one of the deeper barks I'd ever heard.

"How is she?" I solicited the doctor.

"Same status. Her vitals are slowly getting better, and her ulcer hasn't ruptured. We checked to see if she had any fluid buildup – the first sign of rupture – and there wasn't anything concerning. Before that, we checked her blood clot levels, and they looked fine too."

Exactly what I expected to hear. I thought we were out of the woods, the doctor's words having purled like a serene stream against a gentle eddy.

Yip. Yip. **YELP!**

Then we hit Romy's bay.

"However," the doctor paused just long enough to drop a log into the placid brook, "she *has* gotten quite vociferous in the last few minutes. I thought it might just be because she was excited to hear your voice at the front, but…"

She didn't finish her sentence. I nodded.

"I'll give you a few minutes," the doctor said.

I really only needed one minute. Romy kept squirming and shrieking in pain, nearly jumping off the gurney and onto the floor.

"Stop," I commanded my dog. And she stopped squirming for a few seconds, then would yelp and try again to get off the gurney.

"Stay," I commanded. "Good girl. Give me kiss."

She looked at me from the corner of her eye, unwilling to move an inch for her own sake, let alone give me a kiss for my sake.

I called home.

"Jo… you need to get here right away."

"No…" she said, as if words could cry.

"I'm sorry. Please get here."

After I got off the phone with Joanna, the doctors rushed back in to the room. I asked exactly how recently they last checked for a rupture; they said it was momentarily ago, and that they checked for blood clots immediately before that – all within the past 20 or 30 minutes.

"Can we do another blood clot test?" I appealed. I'm sure there was a medical term for it, but they knew what my layman term meant.

"Yes; we'll do it now and it'll take ten minutes to analyze. We can also give her some morphine if you want, but it's a little early to be doing so. Her last dose was six hours ago, and we were hoping to wait another six hours before her next dose. We can do it now, but there's risks involved."

Romy continued yelping, sounding like she had been shotgunned in the face by an errant hunter.

"Please. Give her more."

They lifted Romy from the gurney and onto a bed on the ground, then shot her up with the morphine and conducted the blood clot test. I was nuzzling Romy, praying that God spare her from this trial she was going through, when her tail wagged – just a single wag, but it was the first time I'd seen it move in days. Then I felt a delicate hand on my shoulder. I stood to greet Joanna.

"She's not dead," I said, mustering the best news I had to offer.

Not that it was much of a consolation. Joanna pinned herself against Romy, her tears soaking into Romy's thick Shiba Inu coat. Fortunately by this time, Romy had calmed down a bit. She still intermittently yelped, but she stopped twisting and was at least back in her own mind.

Joanna and I laid our hands on Romy. I cried out to Yeshua.

"Heal this girl, Jesus. Please don't let it end like this."

Romy whimpered.

"I know You hear our prayers, and that it would take less than a sliver of Your power to restore her."

Romy whimpered louder.

"I pray, in Your Holy Name, the precious Name of Jesus, the Name of Yeshua of Nazareth, that You bring Romy back to health."

Romy yelped.

"Christ, don't You hear us? Please hear our pleas! In the Name of Jesus, I command this sickness out of Romy's body!"

Romy yelped louder.

"Sickness, you have no place here. This is a family of God!"

Romy started twisting and yelping.

"Holy Spirit, come! Please come!"

I looked at Romy's face. She's in absolute, utter terror as she began to yip to high heaven.

"Come now Lord! Take this sickness away!"

Romy yapped as if she was being methodically stabbed by a serial killer.

"God, please take this soul from us!"

Yelp. Yap. Yap. Yelp.

"Don't burden us with this decision, Lord! Please! If you hear our prayers, please just let her soul pass on to you now, if that's what you want."

Yelp. Yap. YELP! YELP!

"Lord, I commend this spirit into your loving arms!"

YELP!

"Please welcome Romy into your Kingdom, Lord! Please don't make us do this. God, please."

The doctor walked back in.

"We got the results. Romy has thrown another blood clot. Her vitals indicate that she is about to, or has, slipped into DIC."

DIC, or disseminated intravascular coagulation, is exactly what the doctors had warned us could happen. It's where your body has spent so much of its clotting abilities in one bodily region that other areas are essentially becoming hemophilic. Not only do you have to worry about the coagulation where the blood clots have occurred, but now you're bleeding out in all the rest of the areas of your body. Most dogs who enter this stage don't recover.

"How long does she have if she's in DIC?"

"Hours. Maybe a day."

"But it would be pain like this for the remainder of that time?"

The doctor nodded, then added, "And she's already torn through that last dose of morphine in minutes."

I looked at Joanna.

"I can't do this," she gasped. "I can't handle this."

"It's your decision," the doctor said, "and it's a highly personal decision. But it isn't likely that Romy is going to come back from this."

More yelping, yipping, yapping, agony, torture, unbearable torture.

I looked at Joanna again. Our eyes caught each other's. I nodded at her. She buried her hands in her face and fell on Romy, weeping. I looked at the doctor; nodded.

"Okay," the doctor said.

And we began the process.

I ran my hands through Romy's fur, enough gentle force from my fingers for it to feel like a light massage between her shoulder blades.

"Romy, may I have one more kiss?" I cajoled her.

She didn't respond. It was as if the pain had cancelled out all other noise around her.

The doctor grabbed the foul needle and began prepping it.

"Romy, can you please give me a kiss?" I begged her.

Of course not. Why would she give me a kiss after what I've put her through?

"Romy," I instead said, "I have a question. Do you want... do you want to go..."

No tail wag this time.

"Romy, do you want to go to heaven?"

Romy raised her neck to see the doctor inserting the needle into her IV and flipped out, squirming to get away, like she knew exactly what we're doing to her.

"Romy, stay," I commanded.

She calmed down and whimpered.

"Why have you killed me?"

"Romy, do you want to go see Jesus? Yeah? See Jesus?"

Joanna wailed on Romy's side.

"Do you want... to go see Chiefy?"

Romy whimpered quietly, and her body relaxed a bit.

"Romy, can I have one more kiss?" I pleaded one more time.

She wasn't budging, just cringing from the pain.

"We'll see you again," I whispered to her. "You're being a good girl. Like you always are." Romy's breathing slowed. "Go scout out heaven for us. We'll catch up with you later. I love you, good girl. I love you forever."

I looked into Romy's eye and I saw it dilate for a brief moment, and then I watched as the life of my baby girl slipped out from time into eternity. The doctor pulled out her stethoscope and put it on Romy's chest.

"Her heart has stopped," the doctor announced.

Romy's dried tongue was hanging out, touching the hospital ground, so I stole a final kiss from her. It suddenly smelled like shit, and I looked over to see Romy's feces half-on-the-ground, half-still-in-her-body.

"I love you forever," I repeated in her ear again.

She can't hear me.

God's breath had departed.

I checked the time.

3:55am.

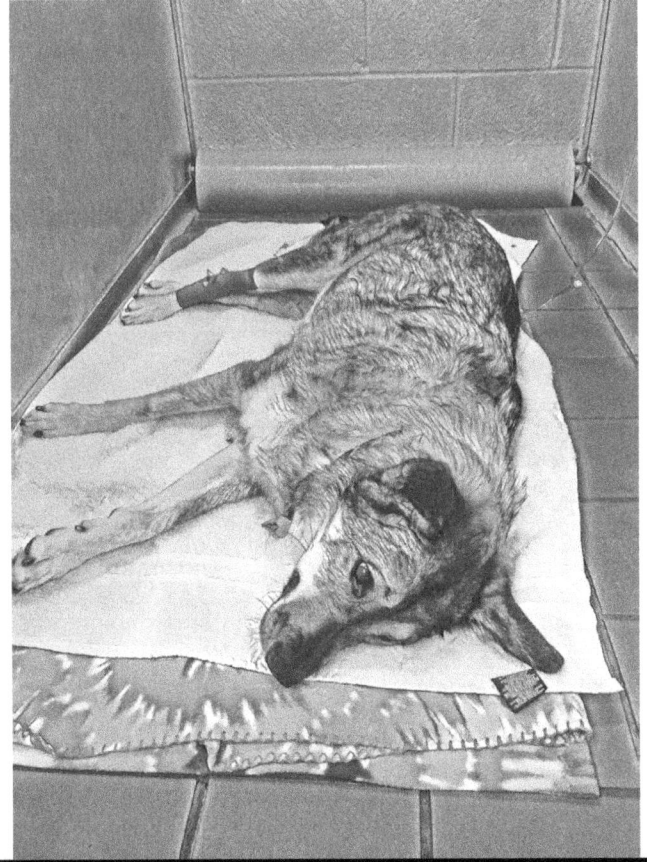

"The joy of our hearts has ceased; our dancing has turned to mourning."
~ Lamentations 5:15, ESV

You awake?

I'm awake. Listening.

Okay, I have a plothole to share.

Plothole in what? Lord of the Rings? because if so, you're wrong

No, in the Bible. my Bible.

oh okay, then yeah. what did you find

I'm thinking about eternity again. It helps me work through losing Romy. but it doesn't explain infertility. Not just "not explains" it, but it basically counteracts it.

How so?

Infertility is the first theodicy issue that I can't explain away. I mean, based on the logic we discussed before, wouldn't it be better to have kids and watch them die, rather than not have them at all? So why would God prevent faithful servants - people who will raise other faithful servants to live to honor Him - why prevent these people from having children?

Yeah, that's a tough one

The theodicy that I've landed on is centered around this idea that, even though suffering detracts from life on earth, it improves eternity.
Not the case when you shoot blanks! Why would He allow eternity to be less than it could be by disallowing the production of more faithful servants for His Kingdom?

Well, jews are uber fertile and americans are not, so maybe that goes to show whose theology is right?
I'm sorry, that was insensitive

No, I chuckled. I'm just thinking. Wasn't offended.
We don't get a ton of explanation - in either of our Bibles - about eternity's details.
So yeah, I think I'm going to be projecting a bit, but I can't fathom it any other way: if I don't get to share in God's Kingdom with my unborn children (or my dogs), then suffering follows me into eternity.

You're assuming eternity lives up to your standards, rather than god's.

Fair criticism. And let me pile on my self-critique: I'm coming at it from a purely individualistic angle.

Are you familiar with ל"ו (Lamed Vav Tzadikim)?

No. But maybe this'll help clear up any confusions going forward: whenever you start a question with "are you familiar with..." and that question ends with Hebrew, the answer will always be "no."

(⁻ ˏ˟) Oy vey iz mir.
There is this ancient Jewish myth that, in every generation, there are exactly 36 righteous people. They are the "Tzadikim Nistarim." And if you ever ask yourself, "might I be one of the 36 righteous?", then indeed you are not. The one who believes themself worthy of blessing deprives themself of blessing.

That's crazy. I've never heard of this.

‬ץ ד

"Mama, I don't want to go to school today," Abni told Claire, employing a trope galled by schoolchildren around the world since the advent of formal education.

"And why is that?" Claire asked as she buttoned his jacket.

"It's cold. It's rainy. There's soldiers. And I just want it to be Christmas."

Claire chuckled at her son's innocently honest statement.

"But what would Christmas be if we didn't wait for it? Imagine if it was Christmas every day. Sometimes, we need to wait in the in-between."

Abni sighed, knowing his mother was right.

"Besides, Christmas is a week away. You don't have to wait long. Just two more days of school, and you can play all day, every day."

Claire ushered the children out the front door. The rain was piercing cold, and Claire winced as the droplets iced over her skin.

Zuji, wearing a thick jacket, scarf, and gloves, approached his children.

"The car's all warmed up. Let's go," he said, rubbing his hands together. "Your cousin is already waiting."

The children hustled off and packed themselves into the idling Toyota.

Zuji gave his wife a quick embrace, and seeing Arab contractors continuing to dig trenches in front of their house, shook his head.

"Traitors," Zuji said. "The whole lot of them."

Job was believed to be the first Tzadik Nistar, and he's supposedly the one to pass out amulets that designate someone who is Tzaddik.

Wouldn't Abraham or someone in Genesis be the first?

Job is believed to be the oldest written book in the bible. Not sure why his book is placed where it is, but Job and Bereshit are believed by many to be written by Moses.

Is this Talmud?

Honestly it's more Kabbalah, which I don't ascribe to. Personally speaking here, but I don't believe 36 Lamed Vav actually exist.

Yeah. Me neither. 36 is a pretty rotten number.

Point is, there is a certain unrighteousness to individualism. This is just me speaking personally here again, but if they actually did exist, I can't imagine there ever being a Tzadik Nistar who wasn't more collectivistic rather than individualistic.

That's way interesting. I had been thinking about how, if I didn't know any better, I'd have guessed the Bible was a western invention because of how narrowly individualistic the concept of "hope" is. We're supposed to trust that the afterlife is good because it's good for ME, but not necessarily for loved ones who have rejected God. From a collectivistic angle, it seems like heaven could never be complete without our full earthly community restored with us.

But god can restore all things. Period. Whether we get it or not.
One seder tradition we do is the rabbi will say "if the Lord had brought us out of Egypt, but not split the Red Sea..." and then we as a congregation will respond "...it would have been enough for us."
Because it's not about ME. It's about US.

Wow.
One thing I've been realizing is that my Metroid principles are particularly "ME" focused. And the Bible is a collective story about a collective people brought together for a collective purpose. Not about "ME"

Yeah, the bible is collectivistic, and the US is the most individualistic country in the world. And Israel is a pretty individualistic-minded country, plopped right in the middle of a collectivistic-minded region.

Israel is the antithesis to the Middle East in a lot of ways.

True.

I think that I understand the Israeli-Palestinian Conflict less now than when I first studied it. The more I learn, the less I get it. But the more I learn, the one thing I understand better is that this world is so, so broken and in need of hope.

Also true.

Likewise, I'm feeling like I understand God less now than when I began my search. Just when I think I get it, I don't. But the more I pray and the more I navigate this muck, the one thing I understand better is that if the world is broken (it is), and God promised to send a messiah (He did), then He's good for the promise.

Still following

So my next Metroid principle, it's less about "me" and more about what's actually important for the world.

"Stop," Claire whispered. "They are human. We don't know what pressures they faced before agreeing to do this job."

"They've betrayed our people. I would have never agreed to this, no matter how much money they offered," Zuji said, Claire's tenderness not allaying his contempt. "Do you think they'll ever finish?"

She checked behind herself and joined in shaking her head.

"I don't know. After two months of digging, you would think they'd have something to show for it. I'd just as soon have them dig until the day we die."

"Why is it," Zuji mused, "that Jerusalem is considered the world's most sought-after city, when it is Bethlehem that has been the central point of all the death from this conflict?"

Claire hummed, pecked her husband on the cheek and the entourage left for school. Claire was there to receive the group when they returned nine hours later, but she was much less jovial. Zuji pulled up to the house and saw tears in Claire's eyes. He didn't have to guess why she was crying.

The kids hopped out of the car and converged to where their street used to be. But instead of it being a road where they could play with their cousins who lived across the way, it was a wall. A tall, crude concrete wall that blocked out the light from Israel.

Abni sieged the wall and vaulted into it, as if he could climb it.

"No!" he screeched.

"Mama," Ebnahty said, looking at Claire, "there are walls all around our house. When will they take this down?"

Oh goody! Another principle. Let's hear it.

5. Ask for God to be revealed to be holy, that all may see His holiness.

This one works for me. It's important, not just for outsiders to see that god is holy, but even for religious people to be reminded of it often.

One of our most famous prayers has the line, "hallowed be Your Name," but so often Christians treat Him like we've been pleading "hollowed be Your Name."

A less-holy god who doesn't demand piety would be a lot easier to work with, I guess.
Actually, that's what I've found Isaiah 53 to be about, I think that's where your interpretation goes off the rails

Oh, gloves off! You wanna tango with Isaiah 53 again?

(ﾉ ಠ_ಠ)ﾉ　　　　ᕦ(•_• ᕦ)
Now that you're not cornering me into a trap and I've had time to think it over. :-)
So, what I found is your interpretation is pretty off. Isaiah 53 is definitely just about Israel, as a collective nation.

I thought you'd say that. Mainly because it's the typical Jewish response.

Okay, first thing though. "Typical Jewish response." You dont seem to understand that jewishness is so vast and nuanced that you as a christian and an american don't even have a box to put it in. The gap between haredi to hiloni is wider than the gap from banana to olive. And clumping jews into one group is like putting a bunch of bananas and olives into a yogurt together because they both technically are fruit. We are a genetic race, an ethnicity, a culture, and a religion with different expressions and beliefs.

I'm so sorry. I don't even know what to say. I don't mean to make generalizations.

i'm not mad about it. :-) it's just important for you to know is all. I mean, youre talking about an identity that goes back, what, 4000 years? What other group of people have been more hated throughout history? When an Israeli is brusque to the point of being boorish, it's just because more than half our population was wiped out just 1 generation ago, and still we're dealing with being outnumbered and surrounded by enemies who relish the prospect of jewish annihilation.

Okay. Duly noted, I promise. And for the record, I'm not offended by your bluntness. I appreciate that I can talk to you and know that you're not going to beat around the burning bush. That's really why I lean on you for so much interpretation, I think.

Glad to be of service.

It's just, the thing I don't get about this interpretation - the bit about Isaiah 53 somehow being about Israel - is that the entire chapter speaks about this "mystery servant" in singular form. Meaning, it's not a body of people, it's clearly meant to be about an individual. I think the "mystery servant" is Yeshua, you think it's the people of Israel. But I don't get how it can be about all of Israel when the word is clearly singular. Is it different in Hebrew? Like, is it plural and we've mistranslated it?

No, it's singular in Hebrew too.
But I think the bigger point you're missing here is that it's about the people of Israel, being afflicted by Gentiles. Yes, it's about suffering, but the "suffering servant" is god's people.

"I don't know," Claire conceded, trying not to let her kids see how upset she was. "They claim the other side of the street – your home – it belongs to Israel."

Zuji stood near Claire, mouth gaped open and unable to comprehend what he was seeing. What had been a valley in the morning was a mountain in the evening.

"This…" he said, "this is… nine meters tall? Or ten? At least seven."

"It happened all today," Claire said. "Piece by piece, they brought concrete and snapped the pieces together, as if a Lego. The whole city is caged in."

"How will I get home?" asked Bent-Khalee, Claire and Zuji's niece.

Claire and Zuji exchanged glances. It was a great question: just this morning, the child could've skipped a few meters and been inside her home. But now she was cut off from her parents.

"I suppose…" Zuji said, then stalled as he devised a course of action. "I suppose we must go through the checkpoint? And I will have to drive along the wall and find a street that goes near your house."

"Zuji, that will take hours," Claire said. "And you will need to go get a permit first to enter Israel."

"Well, we can't very well lift her over the wall. And I don't think they're going to let us build a door."

Abni began pounding on the wall, getting drenched by the rainwater dripping off the top of the wall and off of the rogue cables jutting out from the wall.

See, this just doesn't work for me. It just doesn't pass the sniff test for me in context of the other chapters it's around.

Isaiah 49, Israel is always referred to in plural form, and it's about how shitty God's people have been to God.

Isaiah 50, plural form again, God's people (ie, Israel) are up to no good and push Him to tears.

Isaiah 51, plural, Israel is unfaithful.

Isaiah 52, plural, Israel is unfaithful.

Isaiah 54, plural, Israel is unfaithful.

Isaiah 55, plural, Israel is unfaithful.

Isaiah 56, plural, Israel is unfaithful.

And you're saying that Isaiah 53 randomly shifts into the singular form, and it's a celebration of how faithful Israel has been to God? It just doesn't hold water if that's the context.

Isaiah 49 through 56 is ALL about people being shitty. So yes, Isaiah 49 through 52 is about Israel's role as unfaithful servants, but the focus of Isaiah 53 isn't about Israel, but about how the Gentiles are even shitter than the Israelites. It's basically the prophet saying, "listen, I just hounded, expounded, and merry-go-rounded on and on and on about how unfaithful you are, but compared to those heathens, you guys are top notch."

This still doesn't work for me. Because when you read Isaiah 49, you see that the prophet is clearly identifying that there are two different servants who will be in play over the following chapters: the "shitty" servant and the "suffering" servant who is only suffering because of how shitty that first servant is.

And then you have that line in Isaiah 53: "He was wounded for our transgressions." That line is a nightmare to try to understand if this chapter is talking about Israel. Think about it, you'd be saying "Israel was wounded for Israel's transgressions." It's a super awkward syntax that you don't see anywhere else in the Bible. And then there's the question, why don't you read this in Temple at any point of the year?

Do you read every last sentence of the bible each year in church?

Of course not.

So this is the same thing: we just can't cover all of it. This is one that just gets cut out and we don't go over it.

I could buy what you're selling, except that you read Isaiah 49, 50, 51, 52, 54, 55, and 56 every year, don't you? So why pass up Isaiah 53? Why Esther? Why would you pass on this specific chapter every year, as if it's forbidden.

Oh, there you go. Calling it the "forbidden chapter," like christian evangelists do. Are you trying to proselytize now? Are you trying to prove that I need to think Isaiah 53 is about Yeshua? *We* are the chosen ones. We don't need anything else. God will send the meshiach when he wants to, and the world will clearly change when that happens. We don't need to consider other religions, which, remember, is kind of what you've been doing the past couple years.

But what if this isn't another religion? What if Christianity is just an offshoot of core Judaism, like Modern Ortho is an offshoot of Ultra Ortho?

Esther, our relationship was never built on me converting you. You know that. Do I think Isaiah 53 is about Yeshua? You bet I do, because you have to go around the barn to think of it as anything else.

"So this is the end?" Abni yelled, the combination of tears and rain nearly gagging him. "It's not enough that we live on curfew? We must now be buried alive in a big tomb for the rest of our days?"

"Mama," Ebnahty said, "he is right. They have traded the Tomb of Rachel for the Tomb of Anastas."

We have lived our whole lives next to the Tomb of Rachel. But now, this is the Tomb of Anastas."

Abni continued pounding the wall until his knuckles marooned, a massacre of the innocence for the well-mannered boy. Ebnahty wailed as she agonized with her brother's uncharacteristic rage.

"Children," Claire severed their fits, demanding their attention. "Look at me."

Abni dropped his fists and Ebnahty swallowed her grief.

Everyone, including Zuji, focused on Claire. Even though it wasn't yet sunset, it was darker than normal as the wall behind their house was blocking the low-hanging sun.

"Hey. What does the name 'Anastas' mean?"

"Resurrection," said Ebnahty.

"That's correct: resurrection. We are a family of resurrection," Claire said, then felt warmth on the tip of her head that slowly trickled to the rest of her body. "You are right: we are buried alive. Our home has become our tomb. This is to be expected: when God moves, Bethlehem suffers. You know who else had a disastrous first Christmas? Maryam, Youseph, and Yasue did, as did the families whose children are buried at the church. Bethlehem needs resurrection, yet there cannot be resurrection without burial. When Yasue returns, we will not be excluded just because

I guess I just don't get why you assume that. In the grand context of the bible being about jews' relationship to the land of Israel, it jives just fine for me.

I mean, you're telling me that Jews specifically go out of their way to read Isaiah 49, 50, 51, 52, 54, 55, and 56, which is focusing on the idea that Jews are a foolish people who can't stop committing idolatry, but then skip the one chapter in there that says "Jews are great people whose national longsuffering will redeem the rest of the world"? If your interpretation is the right one, that Isaiah 53 = Israel, then why not make it part of your yearly readings?? It's a super empowering chapter in that context, like a love letter! I'd want to read that every week, not just every year. But instead, you pass on that one chapter to instead read seven really deflating ones about Jewish unfaithfulness. I just don't get that part.

You don't have to get it, but you have to know that Isaiah 53 isn't a prediction of Yeshua. Yeshua is a postdiction of Isaiah 53.

Listen, I'm not asking you to accept that Isaiah 53 is about Yeshua. I'm just saying that it isn't logical to believe that it's about Israel. It's just too inconsistent. And I understand your skepticism towards Christians. Very few know Hebrew like you do. It's why I lean so much on your knowledge about Hebrew. I trust you. I believe you. But to just throw your hands up and say "Christians alter the meaning of Jewish Scripture" without thinking about where I'm coming from, it's like when Palestinians alter Jewish history to prove their own narrative. I think Jews are too quick to toss the Christian interpretation here. You know my frustrations with Christianity, but the Christian answer to Isaiah is too compelling to just throw out. You don't want to see Yeshua as the central figure here? Fine. But to me, it's clearly about the Messiah, whether or not you put that tag on Yeshua.

To believe that Isaiah 53 is about Yeshua, I'd have to believe that your bible isn't completely embellished and that Christians didn't deify him after-the-fact.

Of course that's a component. Definitely a pre-requisite to what I'm saying, sure. But is there any other major religious leader whose followers are accused of such a large-scale cover up? Is the story of Yeshua so groundbreaking that the only way to not accept it is to accuse of conspiracy? When Mohammad claimed to be divine, you can ignore it and Islam still could work. Buddha's followers (not even buddha himself) claimed he was divine, but you can just as easily ignore that if that helps you to become a buddhist. Yeshua claimed divinity, but neither followers nor detractors can ignore it - you have to either accept it or not, because it's too central to who He claims to be. You must say that either what the Bible says is true, or that the Bible was manipulated and given the world's greatest cover up. Either Yeshua is the world Messiah or the world con artist.

Or he was fictionalized by the same people who made up the two extra stories in your bible. I believe that there was a man named Yeshua who came from Nazareth and was crucified around 30 AD for claiming to be meshiach. But I think that's just about the only thing we know for sure about that guy.
You've also spent a lot of time thinking about this, and I haven't. It's like you set up this mind game, and I fell for it, and then you jumped out from behind the bush and yelled "gotchya!" when I tried to give you my opinion that you asked for.

I'm not trying to trick you. It's just, it doesn't work if it's not Him. How is it compatible to believe in the historical Yeshua of Nazareth, and then read Isaiah 53, and not draw the parallel? You're not going around the barn. You're burning it down, pissing on its ashes, and saying the barn never even stood there.
Hello?

there is a wall. Yasue conquered the grave in Jerusalem, and there *will be* resurrection in Bethlehem."

"When, Mama?" asked Abni.

"Soon," Zuji chimed in. "But, not today."

Ebnahty began to sob with Abni, and the two of them hugged as they wept. Claire allowed her tears to trickle, masked by the rain that was intensifying by the minute. Zuji rubbed Claire's back; he knew she was right.

"This is Truth," Zuji told his children. "Though we may no longer see the stars, we can still be the light."

The rain pattered the ground, turning the earth below their feet into a slopsink that could've easily been mistaken for quicksand.

"Holiness is pain," Claire reasoned. "It has been so, even since the birth of our faith here. Do we dare join Yasue in being light? Do we answer the call to be the light of Bethlehem?"

"Okay," Abni agreed, staunching the last of his resolve and tears. "I can do that."

"Me too," Ebnahty linked with her brother.

Claire nodded her head, then smiled through her weeping and answered the question she had posed to her children.

"We can be the light of this city, because He is the light of this world."

A HEALED KNEE

> "They poured out innocent blood,
> the blood of their sons and daughters."
> ~ Psalm 106:38, ESV

"This isn't real," Joanna muffled into the ground, lying prostrate on our carpet.

I had nothing to offer back. I was sitting on the floor, rubbing her back, staring straight ahead at the "Our Dogs Love Us" frame with the scratched-out dog silhouette.

When Romy yelped that fateful day, I'd thought it was just another Thursday. I didn't know it was the last time I'd see my sweetie-pie healthy and whole, and all the suffering that followed after we left my parents' garden in Zion escalated so abruptly and wounded so deeply that I was beginning to question everything I thought I knew.

"I yelled at her. I yelled at her for *whining*," Joanna moaned into the floor, soaking the carpet with saltwater. Joanna's body violently twitched, then when she settled, she turned her head to grab some air.

I know. We both did.

"I thought she was just being a big baby about her knee," Joanna lamented, then anthropomorphized, "She was just trying to tell us that we were killing her. That sound is going to scar me."

Her words cut to my core. She was right. We had to learn to reconcile ourselves to the fact that we yelled at Romy for dying. We ordered her to die silently, and disciplined her when she couldn't submit to our command.

God may be good, but He's not too good, at least not so much that He'd just let me have what suits me. I'd been *so* confident this wouldn't happen to me. I was assured that Romy wouldn't die like this. I thought that assurance came from God, but it didn't. My truth – or at least pieces of it – turned out to be a lie. So how much of my steadfast faith was actually rooted in denial?

At some point, every relationship fails, fizzles, or slits in half, and in particular, no dog's life ends in anything but tragedy. Either we go before them and they're alone, or the better option: they go first without the ability to let us know if they're ready or if they're not scared. So there's always pain from what we don't understand about the animal kingdom, and this mystery can intensify the agony of a beloved animal's death to becoming even more traumatic than a loved human's. Which scenario offers more closure: the child with cancer who proclaims "I'm ready to meet God" or the bleeding-out dog who cries out for death until you can't take it anymore and have to choose to kill her?

Romy's shrieks eclipsed all my other thoughts when Joanna abruptly grabbed a pillow, covered her face with it, and shrieked out her own bloodcurdle, prompting high-pitched tinnitus to pinball between my ears. Sidney scrammed into the closet. I followed and found her shaking. Sidney already knew something was afoot when, the day before, I'd tossed Romy in my Jeep and careened away. Sidney had been following us around every moment since we got home from the vet, panting and looking to us for assurance – something we couldn't offer. We'd just lost our own assurance. Trembling in the closet, I think it registered for Sidney that her world just changed.

I traipsed into the kitchen and found Shadrach cowering in the corner. She's an empath and easily adopted our grief. I knelt next to her and rubbed my thumb between her eyes, hoping to impute my tenderness instead of my anxiety. She licked her lips as a trial run, then snuck her tongue across my lips. I held her close and kissed her head.

I opened the pantry. There was little to eat; we were still in the process of moving, and we hadn't gone grocery shopping since coming back from holy Israel and cursed Minnesota. So I reached in and grabbed the St. Nick's stocking that Mom sent. I dumped the candy and Silly Putty on the table and gripped the two oranges weighing the bottom of the festive sock.

I'd started fasting when I realized how sick Romy was. What a short-lived fast that was: I barely missed one meal. David's words drowned out my tinnitus: "Why should I fast? Can I bring him back again? I shall go to him, but he will not return to me."

Why should I fast? Why should I pray?

"Will you eat this with me?" I insisted to Joanna, who was still on the floor, pale as a ghost. She nodded. She knew we needed it. We hadn't eaten anything since dropping Romy off at the ER.

We ate our oranges. They certainly weren't Jaffa oranges. Joanna told her boss she's not coming in. I had the whole day free, too. Well, except for my one appointment to bring Romy in to get her staples removed.

510

THE VALLEY ROSE

Oh, God, how I wish I could've kept that appointment.

Does anything better emphasize the brokenness of our world than when we take one of God's healthy creatures, give her the best medications our science has to offer, and it lands her in a freezer? Christians live in a false paradise when they believe that they can experience God's fullness on this earth.

"I'm sorry, Joanna," I said. "I should've listened to you."

"*Don't*. Don't do that. We both agreed for her to get the surgery."

"Yeah, but I was the one who insisted. You were the one who had a bad feeling, and I brushed it off. I just... I didn't want her to be in pain the rest of her life."

But fate had toyed with us for sport: by doing the surgery, we ended up spending thousands of dollars just to put Romy in horrific pain the rest of her life and cut it by half. Had we been bad parents and ignored Romy's knee pain, she'd still be alive. We rescued her from the animal shelter but couldn't save her from a little pill.

"You're not to blame," she said, putting her hand on my neck. Of course, she was wrong. Maybe I could accept that I wasn't *guilty* of Romy's death, but I certainly was at fault for it. Forty-dollars-worth, at least.

"Hey," Joanna said with her lip lifted ever-so-slightly, "remember when we'd let Romy out, how she liked to spin in circles and stop on a dime, grunt, then poop?"

I laughed. Indeed, Romy was a goofy pooper. The memory spurred a few other happy memories, and mere hours removed from Romy's death, I somehow found myself smiling. *Is that normal?* Then the other memories began to sneak in, the impish memories from when Romy would cower from me, her disaster of a dad. Romy had a deep, inherent fear of feet – we think she had been kicked a lot before she was rescued and ultimately adopted by our family. One of the most crushing memories in my thoughtbank is when I kicked Romy *because* I knew it was what she feared most. When I had become the personification of my own mental disorder, deadset on punishing my loved ones the way obsessive-compulsive disorder punished me.

Over the next few days, one of the most popular go-to consoling phrases from friends and family became "you gave Romy a good life." Sure, that was true for Joanna. Not for me. In the days following Romy's death, I don't know that I ever hated myself and my OCD more.

My brand of OCD is rooted in bad religion. It even has an ecclesiastical name: scrupulosity. One of the symptoms that had always been the hardest to deal with is the belief that if I pray for something, then the opposite may happen if I haven't prayed the prayer "right." It crippled my prayer life as a child and later again in adulthood. I spent years undergoing cognitive-behavioral therapy to convince myself that my prayer can't hurt my loved ones. Eventually, I had begun to believe that when I prayed for something, I may not get what I was asking for, but at least the opposite wasn't going to happen. I'd begun to believe that – for instance – if I prayed for my family's health, that my prayers weren't going to levy a fatal freak accident upon them. I prayed for my family's health every day, long before it was ever a medical emergency. Long before it was a prayer of desperation. The only other thing that Joanna and I collectively pled for with fervor across the years is for us to have children. Eight years into our marriage and six into trying to conceive, all that our prayers have produced is a dead dog. I had confided in God that I was afraid of feet, so He kicked me.

I received from Romy far more than I ever gave her. I don't want to treat Romy's staples as if they were nails, but why does it feel like she paid for my sins? Weren't the ancient Jews allowed to choose the animal who would die on their behalf?

Listen, I can accept that there was some cosmic reason that Romy had to die, and that I'll never get to know what that reason was. That's basic theodicy. But that first day our family spent without Romy – a date which will, indeed, live in infamy – was not only the day we lost our precious girl, but it's also the day my understanding of how the Lord operates was shot to shit. My assumptions about prayer – assumptions that, yes, had always been rooted in western Christian philosophy – were wrong. If you found out that which you thought was "grass" were actually "weeds," you would extirpate them from your lawn, no? So, if the one thing that I asked for on a multi-daily basis – perhaps the greatest innate desire of my heart if I'm praying about it that frequently – if that one thing doesn't happen, then what does that say about the power of my prayer?

I prayed for healing, for God to cast out Romy's sickness. Minutes after this, Romy began to die.

I prayed for healing at the ER, and she couldn't even stomach one night.

I prayed for Romy's soul to be taken, and we had to put her down.

The eyes are not here
There are no eyes here
In this valley of dying stars
In this hollow valley
This broken jaw of our lost kingdoms
In this last of meeting places
We grope together
And avoid speech
Gathered on this beach of this tumid river
Sightless, unless
The eyes reappear
As the perpetual star
Multifoliate rose
Of death's twilight kingdom
The hope only
Of empty men.

THE VALLEY ROSE

The ancient apostle Paul wrote to the early church in Corinth that, when the world is finally brought to completion, only three things would remain: faith, hope, and love. But Paul deliberately emphasized one caveat: of these three things, it was love that would endure the brightest. And for a long time, I couldn't really understand that. My faith and my hope had always outshone my love. I'm probably about to reveal too much of myself here, but on the day of Romy's cremation, it was my faith and hope that I carried into the funeral parlor. I asked the funeral director if I could see Romy one last time alone.

"Of course," she said, then wheeled Romy out on a gurney and left me with my girl.

Romy's eyes were closed, her tongue tucked back into her mouth.

"Hey, baby girl," I whispered. "It's Daddy."

I pulled out my tallit that I bought in Jerusalem's Old City and laid it over Romy's corpse. Then, I asked Romy's lungs to fill with God's breath again.

"*Talitha cumi*," I prayed in Aramaic. "Little girl, arise."

Still cold.

"*Talitha cumi*," I repeated over and over. "By Christ, rise!"

Lifeless.

"Talitha cumi, please!"

As I spoke my desperate words, I could see something was happening underneath the tallit! The tallit began cleaving to Romy's face, and it became damp as if dew was being breathed beneath the cloth – and then the innocuous moisture began to turn my tallit red, as if a rose melting and sullying the consecrated wool.

I lifted it to see what was happening; Romy's face was bleeding. A pool had collected on the gurney, and she was as cold as when we'd left her at the ER. There was no life in this corpse, though that reconstructed knee was looking tip-top at least.

"No. No, *nooooo*, Romy. Oh Romy," I wheezed. "I'm sorry."

I choked up.

"Romy," I mumbled. "I failed you. I'm so sorry."

Streams of living water came from my face as blood poured from hers.

"I've failed you in every way. I'm so sorry, baby girl."

I enveloped Romy in my arms, her nose and mouth continuing to drip as I cherished the last moment I'd see her worn body, and the embankment split from top to bottom: my old way of faith bled out until I was empty of all the things I once believed.

For Thine is
Life is
For Thine is the

This is the way the world ends
This is the way the world ends
This is the way the world ends
Not with a bang but with a whimper.

I noticed the funeral director had come back. I squeezed Romy's paw one more time – her nails still sporting pink nail polish from her doggy spa day with Grandma just two weeks ago. I nodded at the funeral director. She wheeled Romy's gurney towards the incinerator as I faltered out of the building, marooned-tallit in tow.

Love shone brightest. It was all that remained.

> "It's like in the great stories, Mr. Frodo.
> The ones that really mattered.
> Full of darkness, and danger, they were.
> And sometimes you didn't want to know the end,
> because how could the end be happy?
> How could the world go back to the way
> it was when so much bad had happened?
> But in the end, it's only a passing thing, this shadow.
> Even darkness must pass.
> A new day will come.
> And when the sun shines
> it will shine out the clearer."
> - Samwise Gamgee

לֹז

<u>December 11, 2020</u>

Esther, I miss talking to you. I'm sorry I upset you.

You're fine, I just don't like all this religion talk. There's no point in letting it put a wedge between us.

I understand. I just feel like it's important we share our differing views because, well, the Israeli-Palestinian Conflict shows what happens when people don't hash out the differences in their narratives, I guess.

And you want to get another jewel in your crown, too.

What? Who told you that was a thing?

My crystal ball named google.

So you think I'm trying to convert you?

I don't think you're not trying to convert me. You're "preaching the gospel," even if it isn't a direct attempt at conversion.

Okay. This is worth a discussion right now. What's hard for me is I feel like I understand your perspective really well at this point, but I don't know that you could say the same about mine.

I don't know, I think I have a pretty good grip on it.

That phrase that your crystal ball taught you, "earning a jewel in your crown?" Yes, some pastors use it when they bring someone to Christ. It's the motivation for some of them. But did you know it's nowhere found in the Bible? In fact that Bible says that we'll cast our crowns at Christ's feet, not keep ours.

That's so frustrating. Like, sure, we have our own superstitions that really aren't rooted in anything biblical, but if it's not from the bible, it's at least from the Talmud, or common sense. And it's definitely not coming from a place of manipulation.

I think it's almost an obsessive-compulsive thing, like pastors tell us to go through these motions so we have some kind of blessed insurance. Christians are easily wangled: they hear an axiom that has a twinge of divine dependence and then they'll assume it to be a biblical concept.

Jews, for their part, are pretty good at identifying when someone is impressing something that doesn't have rabbinic roots. But it's still hard sometimes to not confuse tradition with scripture.

I feel that. Christianity has that happening a lot in the western church. Like, there's a story in the Bible, in the Gospel of John. A woman is caught in adultery, which as you know, was punishable by death with stoning. Yeshua says "he who is without sin cast the first stone," and the accusers all scram. Nice story. Good moral lesson. May have even happened! But it wasn't in the original manuscripts. And still, most churches in the world will preach as if this is Gospel Truth, knowing that it wasn't in the original Scripture. The story persisted so long that we preach from it like it was in the earliest Bible manuscripts.

Christians seem to do that a ton.

Why do you say that?

٣٧

November 30, 2007

Claire found herself driving home after delivering the meager profits to one of her woodworkers along Manger Square, collecting a new set of freshly-carved nativity sets, which was her shop's bestseller.

As she drove down Hebron Road, she couldn't help but shake her head as she witnessed all the graffiti along the Separation Wall, which had become inundated with messages (mostly from tourists) over the past couple years. So many of the messages felt contrived and almost inappropriate, like the ones that read "women's rights are human rights" and "separation of church and state," as if either of those had anything to do with the occupation. Some of the simpler graffiti, though, was more heartfelt, like the plain, handwritten text that read "maybe leave the children out of this?" Though, this authentic message was perhaps overshadowed as it was adjacent to an oversized depiction of a pair of sandals with a painted-on museum placard that captioned, "Jesus wore these Air Bethlehems in game 6 against the Romans."

"Welcome to Disneyland," Claire muttered under her breath.

But as she continued along, she came upon a small commotion in front of the Palestinian Heritage Center. Slowing her car down so she could rubberneck, she noticed a group of about a dozen men huddling around a wall. In-between their bodies, she spotted glimpses of an art project they were completing against the wall. Claire gasped and screeched into park and jumped out of her car, rushing over to the crowd of people.

You already brought this up once before. You said that there's a line in your bible, one that says you can pick up snakes and not get bit, but that it wasn't in the earliest manuscripts, but still is accepted like it was. So it just seems like it happens a ton, given those two examples you've already shared.

In fairness, these are actually the only 2 places in the entire Bible that it happens. Here in John, and then again in Mark 16:9-20. Not in the earliest manuscripts, but still somehow canonized. So, probably not "a ton," but I do think it highlights the opinion that Christianity is being operated by people who purposely ignore facts to manipulate truth.
Which is incredibly ironic if you believe that Christianity is Truth, like I do.

Okay. But are you trying to convert me?

I have been given a commission by Yeshua: preach the Gospel. It is the highest calling of my life. And I will preach this Gospel unapologetically, and I will place that duty above every relationship, every identity-marker that I have.
Did I enter into relationship with you with the purpose to "win" you over to Christianity? No.
Did I enter into relationship with you with the hope that I could preach the Gospel to you? Yes, just as I do with every single one of my relationships with the aim of sharing the Gospel - whether they're Jewish, Muslim, Christian, Pastafarian, Jedi, Middle-earthers, flat-earthers, new age rebirthers, or Virgin Birthers. We all have things we stand for, and things we preach. You've preached to me about the Israeli perspective of the conflict, and about feminism, and about communism. You've influenced me to watch the Lord of the Rings trilogy. And you know what?
I even watched the entire Hobbit trilogy a couple months ago.

Oh, I'm so sorry. I didn't mean for that to happen.

Well it did. And it was the extended editions. I could've watched Wreck-It Ralph four times instead, but I didn't. Why? Because I care about you and I care about the things you care about.

I don't care at all about the Hobbit movies. They're not the prime trilogy.

So if I'm sharing the Gospel with you (and I hope I have), it's because I have a religious and/or spiritual duty to do it, but it's also because I care about you. I care about you enough to reveal that piece of me to you. And I hope I'm sharing it effectively. I hope it changes your life - now and eternally.

This makes me want to watch Wreck-It Ralph.

Lol. That's the takeaway you got from that?
My hope would be that I'm showing you that not all Christians try to heighten your emotional senses in order to drive home a point. But if you feel manipulated, I'm sorry. That's not my intention. And if I've manipulated you, I've failed you.

I don't feel manipulated. I don't think.

Let me be forthright. You want me to tell you what I'd like from you?

..what are you asking me to do?

There are 2 New Testament (i.e., Christian) books in the Bible. They were written specifically for Jews. I'd be so tickled if you read them.

And throw more on my plate? I can't promise that'll be happening.

Understandable. It's okay.
But this is what would be my "evangelism endgame" with any authentic Jew.

What do you mean, authentic?

517

"Excuse me?" Claire interrupted the crowd, of which she counted 13. "Who is doing this?"

Parting like the Red Sea, the crowd revealed a (partially-completed) gorgeous white dove carrying an olive branch in its mouth, protected by a bulletproof vest that had sniper crosshairs across its chest. A short man – the 14th of the group – was hunched over on his hammies, his hand holding up a stencil with one hand and a can of white spray paint in the other. Still squatting, the man turned his head to look at Claire, his nose rumpled in confusion. Revealing the incomplete dovetail, he dropped the stencil and paint, slapped his knees, and stood to greet Claire with a wide smile. He was wearing two layered black t-shirts, which seemed like a bad choice on this particularly warm autumn day. He had sweat streaming off his face and down the ends of his curly hair, which peeked out beneath a drenched ballcap.

"How are you going?" the man replied in a foggy British accent, taking off his thin-rimmed glasses as he rubbed his eyes and then extended his hand. "I am the artist."

"Mister, you must know, this is the most beautiful art I have ever seen in my life."

The man chuckled and took his hat off, revealing a thick head of black hair which culminated in a discernible widow's peak.

"Why, aren't you lambent! What is your name?"

"I am Claire Anastas. And you are a graffiti artist then?"

The man mumbled something inaudible to himself, then laughed, and said, "Quite right. I am. This is my team behind me. I do the main work, and they touch up the details so I can get out of the view of... the sun."

Someone who respects Mosaic Law and the TaNaKh, and appreciates the historical significance of the events recorded in Scripture. Someone whose sin is anything but acedia.

Acedia?

Sloth. But not just laziness, but an active indifference to religion. It was one of the original seven sins. Actually, they had 8 sins initially.

Who is "they"

John Cassian coined it originally. The "eight principal vices" I think he called them.
Gula (gluttony)
Luxuria/Fornicatio (lust, fornication)
Avaritia (avarice/greed)
Tristitia (sorrow/despair/despondency)
Ira (wrath)
Acedia (sloth)
Vanagloria (vanity)
Superbia (pride, hubris)

Sadness was a sin?

Yep. But then Pope Gregory combined that vice with acedia and called it sloth. He also combined vainglory with hubris, because he believed the root for both sins to be the belief "I deserve this."
So he took the 8, cut it to 6, then added envy.
Badabing-badaboom, you have your seven deadly sins.

And you think spiritual apathy is the worst sin?

No, but I think it's actually an offshoot of pride, which is the worst one. Laziness is giving yourself over to not thinking for yourself. It's worse than indifference: acedia is for the arrogant, those who think they know the answers.

Okay. So what are the bible books you think I should read?

I think the first must-read would be the Gospel of Matthew. There's a good chance you'll reject it. But you'll at least understand what I'm saying. It was written to non-believing Jews, to just kinda explain where Yeshua fit in with the Old Testament.
To help Jews understand the argument of why Christians put Yeshua as the suffering servant described in Isaiah 53.
Then there's the Book of Hebrews. It was written to Jews, but ones who believed that Yeshua was Christ. But they were so married to their Jewish customs that they were in danger of reverting back to believing the Law could save them, despite supposedly accepting Yeshua as Messiah.
And, if you read those two and don't outright reject those stories, I'd encourage you to go on and read the book of Romans.
Which was authored by the most zealous Pharisee in the Bible, written specifically to those in power who didn't believe they needed Yeshua in their lives.

Ok. Matthew, Hebrews, Roman.

And John.

John? Isn't that the book you said has fake scripture in it?

Fine. Skip John 7:53 through John 8:11 and read the rest. And only if you want.

"Where are you from?" Claire asked.

"Uhh…" he hesitated, then answered, "Bristol. England. Hence, the accent, that. And what is it that you do?"

"I own a guesthouse here, just down the way. The Anastas Walled-In."

"The Walled-In?" he exclaimed. "That's a brilliant name for an inn around here!"

"Yes, but we don't get visitors ever since this wall was put up. We are between three walls, and not even lost animals wander by our place anymore. We used to have the most beautiful view of Rachel's Tomb, and from the roof on our guesthouse, you could see for *miles*. Every dazzling sunset and sunrise would be ours to drink in! Now? It's the worst view in the world. My husband and I barely get by."

"Does your husband have work?"

"He helps with the guesthouse now. He lost his mechanic shop. The PLO and the Israelis both tax us, and it was also cut off by the wall, so we didn't get enough customers. So we just run the guesthouse. Oh, and we sell wood carvings like these," Claire said, reaching into a bag and pulling out a Nativity scene.

"*My*, what beautiful work. A manger tableau. You are an artist too!"

"I just sell these. Just to help the people that handcraft it. The design, though, is mine. You see Maryam and Youseph and the Christ?"

"Yeah."

"And you see the wise men?"

"Right."

"And here between them, it is the Separation Wall."

I'll see what I can do. But you should also understand this is borderline blasphemous for me to even explore this, as if I'm questioning my identity by doing this (when I'm clearly not).

I understand that. That anxiety isn't lost on me. With my brand of OCD, anytime I defy my gut, it feels like I'm instead defying God and rejecting my identity as a God-fearer. It feels like blasphemy. So any time I try to treat my OCD, there's an inherent requirement that I'm willing to put my firmest beliefs on ice and risk hell by giving into the treatment. And when I have doubts or anxiety about treatment, I have to remind myself that what I'm doing is informed by the newest research into my disorder and that I still exalt God. Many of the original Christians were also Jews, and they knew that they were suspending their firmest beliefs and risking hell by following Yeshua. But they did it because they felt like they could operate on the new information that was afforded them, and in the first year alone, thousands of them accepted that following Yeshua wasn't nullifying their Jewish identity, but actually advancing it. So, I don't mean to put you in a hard position, but I also think it's important to understand the staples of others' faiths, and for a Jew, you can't really understand Christianity without those 2 (or 3 (or 4)) books.

Ok. I hear you.

Can I share something else with you?

Do you really have to ask?

I have another collectivistic-minded Metroid principle. It's an important one, something I've prayed every day and just didn't even think about the fact that I was praying it.

So what is it

6. Pray that His will be done, not ours. Ask for any discrepancy between your own will and God's to be crushed. Ask Him to close that gap.

Tov. This is good too. I like this one.

I think it's important to let God know that we want to be a part of whatever it is He's doing. And we have to realize that if He lets us do that, our role is probably going to be a VERY, very small part in its bringing about.

Microcosmic. That's important. Really believing and accepting that you'd just be a blurry "extra" in god's story requires sincere humility. You have to not only be okay with that, but you have to want it that way.

Yeah. There are so many others that God can choose to work through besides you, and if you're not okay with that, then you actually don't want God's will. It's not Disney. You're not going to be "the one" who God chooses to do everything.

Even king david wanted to be used for more of god's plan and was deprived of it. He wanted to build the holy temple, and god said no.

Yeah. I think Christians forget this, and it's one reason they think of themselves as heroes in God's story. But even Yeshua wasn't used to His full potential. In fact, Yeshua beckoned the Holy Spirit to come and accomplish things that He could have achieved Himself, but wasn't meant to.
You know, I've been praying for years for God to "use me and my story, any way You see fit." He's doing that now and revealing to me that this wasn't my most sincere prayer, but it is my most important one.

We are to rest in god's sovereignty.

The Lord is sovereign.

"Oh, my, my, *my*! What subversive commentary!"

"Yes. Many people have since copied my design, but here is the thing about the ones that I have commissioned is you can do this," she said, plucking out the Separation Wall from the Nativity scene. "This is the true commentary: we have hope. Hope that one day, this wall and this division will not stand."

"Marvelous, I must tell you. I am so sorry for what your people have gone through. I can't even imagine the pain it has wrought."

"Yes," Claire scowled. "They put up the wall, and then my Umi had a stroke. It would have been okay, but it took the ambulance two hours to get through, because of the checkpoint. And... oh, we do miss our Umi."

"I'm very sorry."

"Well," Claire said, then cleared her throat. "I just wanted to stop by and tell you I loved your work. It is a strong symbol of peace, and a symbol of the Holy Spirit."

"Sure, I suppose," he pandered. "I don't suppose that was my intention necessarily, but, well. That's the delightful thing about art."

"May I take a picture of this dove? And perhaps sell pictures of it in my shop? For tourists?"

The man smiled again and nervously tittered.

"When it's done, of course," Claire added.

"I think that would be okay," he agreed. "I would like to support the Palestinian people. And art like this, it is for everyone, yeah? I don't suppose it would be fair for me to plaster this on a wall, force you to see it every day, and then tell you that you can't touch it. You shouldn't need to

Yes, that's what I just said.

I'm agreeing.

I've regrettably realized that I've allowed my Christian identity to be determined by whether or not I have kids. On one hand, I'm learning that faith cannot be tied to the expected outcome of prayer. On the other, what I'm asking for, it's not just a "I want this" type of thing. For God to give me this desire, even let me see my children in my mind's eye, and entrench it as my deepest and longest desire (aside from marrying Joanna), and for Him to tell us that it's HIS desire for us to have children? for it to not happen, that's an identity crisis.

So what do you do with that then? How do you NOT let your identity become fractured by this? How do you let "his will be done"?

That, I just don't know yet. That's basically asking for the answer to the problem of evil, the "why do we suffer?"

Yeah. I suppose so. And I don't have any simple answers for that.

What if pain, and suffering, and theodicy, and the entire problem of evil is actually an illustration of the coming judgment on sin and sinners?

I don't know. What if?

I've started to think that maybe Romy's death was a matter of God disciplining me for not seeking Him more earnestly in prayer. Several weeks ago, it seemed like He was telling me - the Shekhinah was telling me - that if I had been in prayer more often and seeking God's advice, that He could've told me exactly what was wrong with Romy and what steps to ensure her survival. But I didn't, and I therefore didn't have the wisdom I needed to figure out what was wrong with her.

No. You're going backwards here. You're sounding like Job's friends, blaming yourself for not being righteous enough.

It's not about "righteousness" per se. Maybe I'm not "guilty" of killing Romy as we think of the word "guilt," but I do bear a level of responsibility. And I can live with that, because at least God shows me that He sees the situation.

I don't know that you need to burden yourself with figuring out every aspect of the "why" here. Can't you live your life without reconciling this one event?

I wish I could. But I can't. Only the reconciled can bring reconciliation.

I need to get going, okay? Keep working on your Metroid principles. I like what you're finding there.

Noted. Have a good day. Or, good twilight.

Toda. Will do.

And Esther...
Have a wonderful chag!
Happy Chanukkah.

Toda.

523

ask for permission for something that's in your face. That's what I believe, at least."

Honk!

A man pulled up behind Claire's car and started yelling in Arabic.

"He is telling me I need to move my car," she replied. "I hope to see you again."

Honk! Honk!

"It's a pleasure, my Walled-In friend."

He took a step towards his dove, stopped for a moment, and turned around, shaking his head.

"Clever," he simpered. "Very clever."

> "Grieve, mourn, and wail.
> Change your laughter to mourning
> and your joy to gloom."
> ~ James 4:9, NIV

The Christmas tree sat in its box in the corner of the room. Neither of us cared to put it up. It'd taken every ounce of willpower to even drag it out of the closet the day before, and had been only one of two things we did all day – the other having been retrieving Romy from the crematorium. All 55 pounds of her – well, actually, she was only 45 pounds when she passed away – but our big, fluffy girl who loved to stretch out was now packed inside a ceramic room of 200 cubic inches.

Loss is hard any time of year. But during Christmastide, the grief weighs just a little more than it normally would. We'd already had gifts wrapped for Romy, and removing the label and replacing it with the name of a new designee – that is, someone living – felt like a cardinal betrayal. We needed the light from the Christmas star more than ever during this darkest time of the year, but setting up the tree that would host the star and the light felt insurmountable.

"Do you want to go for a walk?" I asked instead, the spark gone from my voice.

Sidney sensed it too. If it wasn't enough that her most beloved buddy was missing, someone who had been with her every single night for almost her entire life, Sidney could hear it in our voices. And she was depressed. Hopelessly, incurably depressed. Shadrach was excited about the walk and the sound of her tail slapping the leashes echoed down the hall. But for the first time in Sidney's life, our firstborn's answer was actually, "Not really, Daddy. No, I don't want to go for a walk."

"We'll bring Romy," I promised her.

"See?" Joanna offered a spark of enthusiasm as she held Romy's urn outstretched towards Sidney. The urn was a vibrant, iridescent mauve that seamlessly weaved purple with hints of pink, and it was so much heavier than it looked.

Sidney sniffed the urn, impressing her nose against the ombré alloy, then tracing each of the rosy contours with her snout. She audibly groaned, and then moved her head far enough away that the urn was out of her sight.

"She can't know that Romy's in there, can she?" I murmur. I glance at Jo, who doesn't respond except by biting her upper lip. It's the first time I've really looked at my wife today, and I notice she's wearing a familiar t-shirt.

I miss my dog.

Joanna handed Romy's urn to me and then knelt over Sidney, encompassing her with a tight hug. I put the top of Romy's urn against my lips and kissed it a few times as I watched Joanna mourn on Sidney.

"*Oh,* Sidney," Joanna pleaded, "You *know* we didn't just give Romy away, right? We would never do that. I know you're confused. You just want to know where your buddy is."

Joanna kissed Sidney's caramello-colored fur splotch on the top of her crown. We called it her "off button," though I think it was broken when she was a puppy.

"We want to know, too," Joanna whispered. "Come on, baby."

As if she could feel Mommy's desperation, Sidney begrudgingly moved off the floor and toddled towards her pink leash.

So we took Sidney, Shadrach, and Romy on their walk. It was frigid; the one-mile route was enough to lower the urn's temperature the same as Romy was when I saw her last. When we got home, I took the urn and cuddled up with it, trying to warm it up before setting it back on the shelf we installed in our living room for Romy to rest during the day. At night, we'd take her urn into the bedroom where we put it next to a picture of her, and that's where she'd rest while we slept – assuming I didn't spend the night snuggling her urn instead.

In the days leading up to Christmas week, I wanted to find out exactly how common it was for what happened to Romy to happen to others. The doctor had indicated that the phenomenon was quite extraordinary. "This is remarkably rare," he told us before we had to put Romy down. He'd been practicing medicine since before my oldest brother was even born, and yet "this would be only the second case in my 35 years of practicing medicine that I've seen a dog killed by carprofen." We're so lucky, we should buy a lottery ticket. It *was* on the 7th that Romy passed away, after all.

To the doctor's point, carprofen-instigated deaths were scarcely reported in official documents. But it didn't take too deep of a dive down the internet rabbit hole to find story after story of dogs dying in the way Romy had, only for Zoetis pharmaceuticals to attempt to pay off grieving pet parents from disclosing their story to anyone. So, sure, the type of death is so rarely reported that Zoetis isn't even required to list "death" as a potential side effect to their drug. But if a dog dies in a forest and nobody's there to report it, isn't that dog still dead?

I've often been thankful for medication. I take my own pills to wipe myself clean from the torment of obsessive-compulsive disorder, and it's ibuprofen that spares me from daily back pain and allows me to survive my suicide headaches. In less than a year, I'll be as old as Jesus and have yet to even worry about typhus, tuberculosis, or the plague. Civilization was once threatened because the drugs that were needed didn't exist, but thousands of years later and we're still finding new ways to kill ourselves, this time using the drugs that cure our ailments. From Eli Lilly to Zoetis, I may not need to worry about malaria or smallpox, but now there's carprofen and fentanyl.

Our hardest Christmas came and passed. Romy's presents were repurposed to her sisters and, yeah, it felt like Santa called in sick on Christmas Eve. I didn't want to face 2019 when it rolled in, and I found myself flooded with memories from New Year's Day 2018 when Joanna and I had taken Sidney and Romy to Turkey Mountain, a popular hilly hiking trail in Tulsa. Usually the craggy paths were teeming with journeyers, but on January 1, 2018, the hibernal weather kept most Tulsans indoors. For Chicagoland transplants, though, zero-degree weather was just another chilly spring morning, so we had the whole wilderness to ourselves. It was a rare opportunity to let Sidney and Romy off-leash without consequence, and I hid in the woods while my doghters would zoom around the forest looking for me as I whistled off clues to my location. We returned back to our warm condo that evening and all cuddled to thaw out each other's benumbed bones and the ice that had formed on the tips of my mustache. January 1, 2019 was only one year later, but so much – *so* much – had changed. It was now my spirit that had embrittled, and ice was forming on the tip of my faith.

Death is funny: a month into our grieving, it felt like we lost Romy yesterday and simultaneously like we hadn't seen her in years. At first, I didn't cry as much as you'd think I would have. Sure, I'd intermittently think of Romy and that memory would liquify, sneak out of my eye and roll down my cheek, but I'm not naturally lachrymose. Still, it was one Sunday morning when I opened the pantry door and saw Romy's favorite toy: a red rubber Kong that was usually filled with peanut butter. Visceral, physical pain ripped through my abdomen as the visual of Romy's black-and-blue Chow tongue getting out every ounce of peanut butter gushed through my memories, and then this wonderful image was replaced with one from the ER: Romy lying dead on the ground, her dry tongue resting on the hospital tile. And then it tore inside; I entered into whatever you would call the spiritual equivalent of Disseminated Intravascular Coagulation.

And I wailed.

Joanna came over and began to ask, "Is everything okay?" when she instead caught me falling to my knees and just held me. And I cried, I cried, I cried into Joanna's skinny arms and it took me until summer before I stopped crying again.

"I'll be fine," I responded to Joanna with more hope than truth.

"We're going to be late for church," she cooed in my ear as I wept onto the red rubber Kong.

"I don't care," I responded. "Let's skip it."

"Can we go to church please? If you don't do it for any other reason, will you do it for me?"

The value in going to church just wasn't there for me, just as there didn't seem to be any value in praying anymore. At least not in the way that the western church teaches us to pray. But all that aside, I really do love Joanna a lot.

"Can I bring Romy?" I asked.

"Please, no," she bucked. "Please. I'm not processing this the same way you are. I can't even look at her urn right now."

Plus, it was weird to be carrying around an urn. I recognize that. But I also don't care. I had always hated leaving our pups at home. There was a sense of guilt when Joanna and I were away from home too long, but the feeling that I was betraying Romy only intensified now whenever I'd leave home and her urn was all alone on her shelf. Especially now, in wintertide, when she'd just grow cold because of the imperceptible winter sun.

But this Sunday, at the appeal of Joanna, we left Romy behind and dragged ourselves to church. The congregation sang together:

> *"I raise a hallelujah, louder than the unbelief…*
> *I raise a hallelujah; Heaven comes to fight for me…*
> *I raise a hallelujah with everything inside of me;*
> *I raise a hallelujah, I will watch the darkness flee!"*

But not me. I couldn't sing those words.

> *"I raise a hallelujah in the middle of the mystery,*
> *I raise a hallelujah: fear, you lost your hold on me!"*

Praise God but perjure myself? A stench.

> *"I'm gonna sing in the middle of the storm,*
> *louder and louder, you're gonna hear my praises roar.*
> *Up from the ashes, hope will arise!*
> *Death is defeated…"*

My trust was conditional, less a worship song and more the title of an '80s era song title: "I Will Trust You (If I Can Make Sense Out of Whatever It Is You're Doing)." Or, a better, slightly more concise, more honest song title would be "I Plan to Trust You (But I Just Can't Know 'Til I Get There)." But that song will never have its time in the sun; churches don't sing country songs.

A few minutes later, my phone pinged during the sermon. Joanna looked over at me, probably to tell me that my vibration setting was too loud. I discretely checked my phone, then leaned over to Joanna.

"Claire landed in Dallas. She said I'm good to go on Wednesday."

Claire Anastas was visiting Texas to speak at a few churches. At least, that's what was put on paper so the Palestinian could get the clearance to leave through Israel. A big reason she was traveling to the United States was because she carved out some time for me to interview her in private. Later this week, I'd be driving south to meet her over the course of several days, at least until I got the bones of her story on paper. It wasn't a short drive, and it wasn't a short story, but I could stay as long as I needed because I certainly didn't have a job yet. Not even any prospects, for that matter. So what more financially responsible thing could I do other than travel to Dallas on a self-funded business trip for a book that's going to put us into debt to publish, and nobody's gonna read anyway?

"If you look for it, you can see God reveal Himself," the pastor preached as I slipped my phone back into my pocket. "How does God reveal Himself to you in your everyday life?"

How does God reveal Himself? It was an infuriating question for me because I always knew the answer: my family! My healthy, loving family. My family, whose health and happiness I prayed for multiple times a day for years. Before each and every meal – whether in public or at home – I would pray for blessings on my children. *My doghters.* I'd rub their backs, look heavenward, and thank God for them. I'd press my lips against Romy's corn-chip-scented ear and whisper, "you reveal God's goodness to me." *How does God reveal Himself?* This wasn't a sermon I needed. I *knew* my response to this specific question, and I reminded God of my answer often.

But without Romy? I didn't have that answer at my fingertips anymore. God took my answer anyway.

"Now you'll only understand this if you're a parent," the pastor continued, "but God reveals His majesty and glory and truth through our children."

Is God speaking to me or just rubbing it in?

In that pew, I stewed. I had no children; I couldn't even see my dogs to a full life. Why would God withhold this gift of children from me? And then why would He go as far as to take my consolation prize that served just as well as a reminder of His goodness?

"When you consider your child's smile," the pastor laid it on, "consider it one of God's greatest gifts to you."

Assuming nobody in the sanctuary was unable to have children.

Assuming nobody in the sanctuary had just laid their own to rest – furry or otherwise.

"I need to go," I whispered to Joanna, staring at our pastor with what almost felt like contempt.

She didn't respond.

"I need to leave now," I repeated, a little louder and on the verge of interrupting the pastor.

When she remained still this time, I looked over and saw she was trying to desperately hold back tears. She simply nodded and we got up and left – the first time I had ever left in the middle of church, let alone storm out of the sermon.

We got into the car. Joanna screamed. We got home. I hotfooted to the Bible verse.

"The prayer of a righteous man is powerful and effective."

I looked up at the Crucifix, zeroed in on Christ's anguished face, and grabbed the verse.

Look where Christ's prayers took Him.

I ripped-up the ripped-out verse.

Garden to the grave.

I found Joanna on the couch, holding Romy's urn.

"I don't want to write Claire's story."

"You *have* to, Nate," Joanna protested. "You promised her."

"I know I did. And I'm *gonna* do it. I'm just saying, I don't *want* to."

Joanna nodded once, then turned her attention back to the cremains in her mitts.

"Her birthday…" Joanna trailed off, then stroked the urn as if our beloved pet's fur would course through Joanna's fingers again by doing it. "It's going to be so hard this year."

I responded with a nod of my own. As if Christmas wasn't hard enough, Romy's birthday was only a few weeks away now: January 30th. She should be turning seven.

"Yeah," I started, then abruptly changed the subject. "We're not going to have children."

Jo looked at me with the bewilderment of a septuagenarian who just saw someone achieve a spare on a 7-10 split.

"That's not the tune you were singing about a month ago."

"You can learn a lot in 40 days."

She sighed. She didn't realize that I was coming at her with the boxing gloves.

"Nate…"

"I told you we shouldn't have gone to church."

"I don't regret going. I would've finished out the service if you hadn't wanted to leave."

"So it's my fault we didn't stay?"

"It's nobody's *fault*."

"Well, except God. God knew what the sermon was going to say. He knew how it would trigger us. So why did He send us?"

She didn't have an answer for that.

"In fact," I said, "why tell God 'I'll go where You go' or 'send me where You will' when He's going to send us to the slow burner? He has our future in His hands, and He sends us *here*?"

"I'm struggling, too. I feel just as unheard as you do right now."

"I knew it was a mistake to show up to church without giving ourselves time to grieve. You made us go, minutes after telling me how you're processing all of this differently. But did you stop to think that maybe I need to process this my way too? That it looks different than yours?"

"That's not fair."

"I know it's not. None of this is fair. I almost feel like that's the whole blessed point of this. Is it fair that I killed Romy?"

"Stop saying that."

"Saying what?"

"You 'killed her,' 'killed her.' I gasp for air when I hear that."

"I *did* kill her. I have to accept that. I know Romy would have forgiven me, because she's forgiven me for worse, and even if I'm not *guilty* for killing her, I'm surely *at fault* for her being dead, and I have to live with that much."

"If you killed Romy, then *I did*, too."

"Well, maybe we both did. But you weren't the one shoving poison down her throat. She knew I was killing her and she tried to tell me and I didn't listen to her. I thought she was being a crybaby about her leg. But no. She was saying, 'Daddy, that stuff is killing me.'"

"I can't take this right now," she replied, lip quivering.

"So we just stop talking about it? Because that's what *you* need? We keep her urn out of sight and pretend she's just sleeping under the bed, because that's what *you* need?"

"I want to *help* you, Nate," she said, her eyes swelling. "If you need to talk about it, then we'll talk about it. What is it that I can do? You can ask me for anything in the world, and I'll do it, if it helps you. What do *you* need from me? *Tell* me!"

"I *don't* have a fucking clue what you can do!" I snarled.

The words themselves didn't hurt, but the bite behind the bark clearly upset her.

"I can't do this right now," she said before getting up, putting Romy on her shelf, and then leaving the room, sobbing.

"I can't either," I yelled after her, following suit by cradling my head in my hands and letting the waterworks slip through my fingers.

"God," I redirected my enmity, "I can't do this."

Against every desire in my body, I stood up, grabbed Joanna's keys – the only keyring that still had the keys to our as-of-yet-unsold crammed condo – and got in her car and drove away across town, on my way chanting "God is sovereign, God is sovereign, God is sovereign," maybe as a prayer or a compulsion or a wish or all three.

January, with leaves yet falling. At 61ˢᵗ and Yorktown, I hopped out of the car, stamped the fronds with my grieved feet, and turned the handle to our old condo.

Death is an enemy, but not evil. Not any more evil than the whipping chill that rips the leaf from its source of life. The evil comes from me, when I don't stop to contemplate death, or don't consider who and where the enemy is, or don't care that the leaf has fallen. I am not evil because I've failed to keep the tree warm, I'm evil because I've never even cared enough to wonder if I ought to.

I stepped into the warmth and slammed the door shut, collapsing in the living room corner, sharing the space with a couple wolf spiders that had taken up residence since we left. I saw ghosts of Romy jouncing around the room, launching off the crowded furniture and spinning around whilst biting the air in excitement. I pressed one hand against my forehead and pounded my elbow into the wall, ignoring the deterioration it would do to the resale value.

> "I always stop for a minute,
> And look at the house,
> the tragic house,
> the house with nobody in it.
> I know this house isn't haunted,
> and I wish it were, I do;
> For it wouldn't be so lonely
> if it had a ghost or two."
> - Joyce Kilmer

In the month that had passed since Romy, I'd re-learned how to pray. I used to have a litany for Him, but now each night ended with me saying, "speak, Lord, for your servant is listening." And I'd listen until I fell asleep.

Only ever silence.

My hope was always in Christ. I'd always been able to deal with failure – governments flubbing, finances depleting, jobs terminating, pastors abusing. I could reel back when I'd misplaced hope. But this? Not this.

Christians leave Christianity because of Christians. If you apostatize because of something someone else did, then you weren't ever a part of a faith, you were a part of a club. Truly faithful people can't just turn their backs like that.

But my issue today wasn't with Christians.

"Lord," I cried out, my turn to speak. "You put me in the wrong existence. I'm like a flower adorned with every color of the rainbow on a planet that only values brown weeds.

"Yes, a seed must die if it will ever produce a flowerbed, but ought they not get a choice as to where they're tossed? Rose and wildflower die under the same shadow. Would you really sow me among rocky ground? Surely you know that only Christ was able to turn thorns into a throne! All seeds, Lord, all seeds pine for that good soil. Can the Creator of Earth run out of the Eden dirt He used to sculpt man?

"Are You short of breath, dear Lord? How can You accomplish the perfect through the incomplete? Who keeps Your Word accountable? If Job's job was not to question You, then how unworthy is Sakkanah's sukkah! I seek Your will by the wet fleece of the valley even as You sit atop the mountain in the burning bramble, for You are the High Priest from the order of Melchizedek and I am the impetuous stargazer from the order of Abimelech. What an affront my odor must be to You; so raze my rose – burn this stalk – skive these thorns – drown the plain.

THE VALLEY ROSE

"If you can't give me the desires of my heart, then the desire of my heart is that you take away the desires of my heart. Snuff my hopes and dreams so that I may live in peace.

"I ask for friends, and dogs surround me. They lick my hands and my feet; I am overfilled with joy. Yet the sun goes down, and they expire before the newborn rose. My sight cracks, darkness is my ally.

"But ask the dogs, and they will teach me; the pibbles of the shelter, and they will tell me; and the strays of the streets, they will declare to me. How can I ask any of these when you nip them from me? If this is how your glory gets revealed, why euthanize the healthy? They who would otherwise know the kindness of human hands, why set these under the rubber of the wheel?

"I would cleanse myself in the valley – swallow my catholicon of placebos and plunge myself in a pit of lye, but I'd be undefiled only until you shift the mud under my feet and dump me into a brook, forcing me to ditch my wears.

"And I'm naked. You burned the clothes right off my body. Stripped away of all the facades, I stand plainly before you. Do you like what you see? Shall I put a leaf over this corroding pile of bones?

"Do you bring me to the mountaintop only so it's a harder tumble into the valley?

"I thought I had a certified check, and it turned out to be a lottery ticket.
"I asked for encouragement, and you sent gloom.
"I asked for an answer, and you sent silence.
"I asked for life, and you sent death.
"I asked for fullness, and you sent barrenness.
"You have cursed my fig and shriveled my vine.
"You call me blessed and in the same breath declare, '*May no one ever eat fruit from you again.*'

"Blessed, blessed, blessed am I, with descendants as countless as the stars in the seashore,
                                                                      as the sand in the sky.
"You claim to rebuke the devourer, but are You not *He*?
"Is there a sacrifice that You would accept?
"What atonement could satiate Your hunger?
"Must you devour Your own creation until Your garden becomes a wasteland?

                              You...You shall consume.
                              Consume... consume everything.

"I'd ask you to kill me now, but I fear you'd curse me with more years. Now for wrath, now for ruin and the red dawn. The Scarlet Thread cried out to you, and you brought them into twilight. Now let him not vow to walk in the dark, who has not seen the nightfall. Will you bring me to completion, even now when the light has gone from my eyes?

Stone giver.   Cowshit planter.
       Frog greaser.   Beast anointer.
              Snail crusher.   Nurple twister.
Name changer.   Dog smasher.   Mud caver.
       Debt collector.   Olive slurper.   Mourning lover.
              Family slayer.   Jacob eater.   Night bringer.

WHO ARE YOU TO ME?
WHO AM I TO YOU?
THE VALLEY ROSE.
God spoke, and it's how
The mountain calls for you now.
Not me –
The Valley Rose.
And it was my beloved who was always
Bound to suffer.
The Lord was the One who was
So focused on growing His garden,
That He left us to wither on this side.
That God is actually not good.
Never again will I think
Faith is the most important pillar of life.
Contrary to my prior beliefs,
Prayer has no place in the logical man's life.
Now I know that it's foolish to say
God is sovereign.
For all of eternity,
I will never see Romy again.
I erroneously believed
This pain will pass;
And also that
God sent Yeshua as Messiah.
I've instead learned to trust
My old pragmatic way of thinking.
I've been forced to surrender
My family, after all.
I never deserved
Anything less than this confidence:
Our suffering is meaningless, and
Now I know it's a lie to say
God sees our pain.
After a bitter season of contemplation
I have come to the sobering conclusion
God does not change.
Give me a break:
I prayed so hard for change;
We can't stay in that place.
Come into the valley with me.
LORD, You alone can save the ending.
You alone level the crooked places.
Please move this mountain.
Don't let this poem end here.
Don't let the story end here.
Write me one more line."

לח

December 25, 2020

Guess what

What?

That's not a guess

You were at the store to find your favorite brand of juice, and you saw where it was supposed to be on the shelf, but they were out, and you really wanted it, so you jeeped to another store to find it, but along the way, you stopped to help a gypsy tie her shoes, so she granted you three wishes, and by the end of the three wishes, you had completely forgotten to grab juice.

Wow that's an amazing guess. That's the most amazing guess anyone's ever guessed in my lifetime. So, so wrong, but super impressive nonetheless.

Tell meeeeeee

We adopted Zero Suit Samus

(♩°♂°) ♩
Foster fail!! I knew you would adopt her!

What? how

I mean, you've only been fostering her for almost 2 years.

True. It's hard to find placement for a dog who screams like a pterodactyl and her butt smells like fish and metal and her neck always feels like sweaty garlic buns and she uses throw pillows as scoot paper.

She had a lot working against her.
U☉๏☉U
So: Sidney, Shadrach, and Samus.

Yep. I'm in bed and actually just peeled Zero Suit Samus off my chest. It's her favorite sleeping spot. I probably have about 10 minutes before it'll be the return of Samus and she'll sprawl across my face.

Lol and where's Sidney and Shadrach?

Sidney is spooning mommy, Shadrach is at my feet.

All in the same bed?

Yeah. Getting into bed is pretty dramatic, usually.

Hey, I have news too. Now you guess what

Your hostel is opening back up?

(☉!◎)
How did you know that?

I'm an excellent guesser.

Lies!

Okay, so I follow your hostel on Facebook. I saw the announcement about its re-opening and knew you'd tell me.

You're crafty

Just savvy enough to be a part of the social media cesspit. When does the hostel open again?

January 16, 2019

"He ducked?" I asked, my words landing somewhere between disbelief and unbelief. "Didn't know why? For no reason: just fell on his knees?"

"Yes," Claire unyielded. "If we had not called his name, his *first* name, he would have been hit. I know this to be true."

"Wow," I said, leaning back in my chair and slurping my coffee.

I looked past Claire's shoulder where there hung a shadow box, showcasing an American flag. Of course, that flag was folded, revealing neither the red nor the white stripes that are so associated with it. Instead, all that were visible were several stars. If I was Jewish, I'd be wanting a smoke right now. Appropriate, given that the American flag, when folded, is meant to symbolize the moment twilight sucks daylight through a straw until there's nothing left but bright stars amidst a sky of faint blue. Maybe it was because Claire's words had banded with the visual of the flag, but her story reminded me of a similar divine appointment that occurred when I was in Herat, Afghanistan a decade ago.

More immediately, though, the resting American flag was a poignant reminder that Claire, nor I, were anywhere near the danger of Bethlehem. We were guests in a house near Dallas, where she was the featured speaker at a Dallas church. Church happens on Sunday (at least in the United States of America), which meant that the rest of the week was ripe for a harvest of interviews.

"God spared your husband," I muffled, a statement more for myself than for Claire. I grabbed Romy's urn, which I'd set on a handkerchief on the kitchen table. A little weird to bring my dead dog to an interview? Maybe. But Claire was abreast of the trauma our family had just endured, and Romy always wanted to see Texas.

With my thumb and three inner fingers, I ever-so-slightly spun Romy's urn clockwise, then twisted back counter, my pinky extending laterally, perhaps for balance or perhaps for spright.

"Danger," Claire said, breaking up my thoughts, which I think she was probably mind-reading pretty easily, "why did God spare my husband, but take Mirna? I don't know. One is thrown into the most dangerous scenario possible, and lives; the other undergoes a most routine medical procedure, and dies. What do you do with that?"

"*Pangs of childbirth,*" I cited.

In 2 weeks. I go back to work in 1 though - the nick of time for me. The hostel's only open to local tourism to start, but I'm hoping international travelers will be allowed soon enough, after the vaccine is widely available next month.

That's wonderful news, Esther. For real.

Yeah. I was starting to get uncomfortable.

I know how that is.
I actually got my first interview since the pandemic.

Really?? Where?

Working in homeless advocacy. Outreach.
I'll go to homies' camps and try to help them navigate the ridiculously hard housing red tape.

Homies?

Homeless people. But apparently that's not politically correct anymore. You have to say "individuals experiencing homelessness."

Oh wow and they make you wear bifocals and a vest, too, then? You can smoke as long as it's from a pipe and you're wearing a top hat?

Or... you can call them "homies" and wear jeans.
But I still have to get the job. No guarantees there.

How's your writing going then?

It's getting there, I think. I hope? I've actually gotten to the point that I'm doing some editing, which is usually a good sign.

At least the hard part is over.

Writing? Actually that's the only part I enjoy. Editing is the least pleasant part of the process. If writing is giving birth, then editing is a bris. Or maybe even a castration. Either way, nobody likes performing it.
And this book is proving especially difficult.

Because of the subject matter?

I don't think so. I just feel my energy fizzling. Like, "what's the point."
It just requires so much discipline to write, edit, and publish a full-length book, especially when nobody knows about it and nobody's asking for it.

Well, I'll read it.

Super! You and my mom both!

Maybe you're the writing version of the Tzadikim Nistarim.

I'm certainly too much of an unrighteous clod for that.

I'm saying, what if the best writers are the ones who think their writing is bad?

Well if that's the case, it turns out Grandma's been right all along:
I really am a Dickens.

One point for Grandma Geist.

Maternal grandmother - so not a Geist. But that reminds me. There's something I wanted to tell you about, if you have time.

I've still got another week before work. I've got time.

You once told me about the Geists.

zeitgeist, weltgeist, volksgeist, yeah.
spirit of the age, spirit of the world, spirit of the nation.

"You can look at Mirna's death, and say, 'God did not provide.' Or you can look at this same narrative and say, 'science failed.'"

Well, I thought, *humans failed.* Neither science nor religion killed Mirna: that was human error, top to bottom. To be fair to her point, though, at the end of the day, science hadn't offered an ounce of salvation. And it certainly wasn't science that brought her out of her valley.

"Going back," I knuckled, remembering how much work was at hand, "back to your story about the nun. How much time was between when that happened, and when the wall was put up?"

"Oh, I think a year or two," she said. "I was 36 when the wall went up. My children were about... yes, I think I was 34 when talking to the nun. Why?"

Wild. I wasn't far off from being as old as Claire was when she watched the wall planted on her property.

"Just trying to get the chronology sorted," I said. "Americans struggle with books if they don't have a sense of time."

"I had not known this then," Claire expounded, "but there is a Bible story that is analogue to my night with the nun. When you have time, read the second chapter of James. It might amaze you."

I jotted her appeal sideways on my notepad, separate from the other notes I'd taken. I knew the book of James was famous for its exhortation that "faith without works is dead," but didn't recall anything about a family wearing camel-fur.

"It is a tragic story," she continued, "for a Christian to treat another Christian like that. We get taxed by Israel, yes, and this is crushing. But the PLO – our *own* people, our *own* government – taxed us. Between what we owed to Israel and to Palestine, we were paying more in taxes and 'fees' than what we made most months. And then the wall went up, and it was impossible to keep the business going. So we closed down the shop and opened the bed and breakfast."

"And, you still don't want to leave?"

"Want? It's hard to say what I *want.* Israel does not let us build on our guesthouse, and we are not allowed to sell it. We can leave it where it stands and become refugees in some Babylon, but our house will be taken over by Israel if we do. And that is bad for our people."

"That *is* tragedy."

"Palestinians are trying to escape Bethlehem, more and more every day. But it is so much more the case for Christian Palestinians. We are being pushed out. Pushed out of our home by Israelis, pushed out of our home by Muslims.

I think we forgot one. The most important one.
Heiliger Geist.
The Spirit of the Lord.
The Spirit that connects every other Geist.

Ah. Yes. Ruach HaKodesh again. Holy Geist in German. What brought this to your mind?

Just thinking about Bereshit and how I feel like we see the entire Trinity in the first three sentences of Genesis. First sentence, God. Second sentence, Holy Spirit. Third sentence, Yeshua.
But something kind of moving happened to me, which reminded me of the Geist of Geists, and His role in my life.

Let's hear it

Moving is an understatement. It was a big comfort, actually.
Romy died over two years ago now. But this week, I've just really been missing her more than normal. Not sure why.
Last night, I asked God to send me "supernatural comfort" that Romy is being taken care of. I told Him that I knew He didn't owe it to me, and that I know it isn't something He regularly does, that I would be so grateful for it.

Ok..

And then I remembered something this morning. I had written something down last April, the spring before Romy died. I had forgotten about it, but today it hit me like a freight train.

What did you write?

A scene; a dream; a vision; a prophecy. Whatever you want to call it. I wrote down all the details so I'd never forget it. And then it happened in real life.

You're going on again about these prophetic things, like you're touched by something special. I don't like it, it feels like nonsense to me. What's even the point of god telling you that something is going to happen? It's going to happen regardless.

I guess, seeing the events of my life play out as I had written it down, it just offered some comfort. Like. things happened the way they were supposed to.
Like God is in control.

Well he knows everything that would happen. Why would he need to reassure you of that? Things don't just happen, but we might never understand the meaning of what's happening. And even if we think we get it, it's just an interpretation of what it means because we can't get confirmation.

So you've never had a single dream that you felt like was on the edge of something divine? God trying to direct you or get your attention about something?

No! God doesn't need to "try" anything. He just does it, and does it well. Since when did you abandon reason for madness? I think more harm than good can come from giving dreams too much meaning and attention.
Ok, dreams can bring comfort, and sometimes it feels like they're telling you something, but eventually you need to wake up and let reality swallow it. It's just your subconscious doing subconscious things.

I'm sorry. I just have to disagree.
I can't look at Joseph and Elijah and Daniel and agree with you on this.

Bethlehem is thought of as a Christian city, but there are more Christian tourists in Bethlehem than there are Christian Palestinians. The last time there were fewer Christians in Bethlehem, Yasue was an infant."

I wonder what that looked like from a percentage standpoint. I had done research earlier this week and couldn't find any recent data, and even most of the older figures that were available were from unverified sources.

"Danger," she said, her voice somehow even more solemn than it was when she described the plight. "There is something I want to talk to you about."

Okay. Here we go. She must've googled my name.

"Do you know Bob Simon?"

"No," I said defensively, wondering what trash this Bob guy had to say about me. "Never met him."

"Bob Simon used to work for *60 Minutes* at CBS. He had interviewed us for his show. The whole family: we shared story after story. I shared the stories to him that I'm sharing with you now, and other family members shared their own."

"There are more stories than these?"

"Every Anastas has a story. Every Palestinian has one."

"When was this interview?"

"I can't remember," she said, shaking her head as if I was missing the point. "It was a few years ago, maybe five or ten. But after we filmed the segment, and it was to be featured, Israel called CBS and demanded they do not tell our stories."

"Who from 'Israel,' specifically?"

"I don't know. But Bob fought for us. He fought for our stories. And in the end, they cut our segment."

"It never aired?"

"It did, but they didn't share the most important stories. They talked about the conflict between Bob and the Israel ambassador almost as much as the conflict our family faced. Israel didn't even know what was going to be in the segment, and they still demanded this be not shown. It was like they knew that whatever was going to be shared was going to be very, very bad for Israel. That their oppression would become known. Bob – who's Jewish, by the way – Bob told the ambassador, the one who represented Israel, that this was the only time a country's leadership had ever intercepted one of his stories, demanding producers pull their segment without even knowing what had been said. And the ambassador, on national television, stared at Bob with so much contempt, it felt like a threat, and said 'There's a first time for everything, Bob.'"

AGAIN. With the p.r.o.p.h.e.t.s. No offense (but actually a little offense and I shouldn't tiptoe around it) but nobody is as close to god as they were in those days. If god wants something, He'll tell you straight up, not peep in and out and drive you nuts with hints. He's not a cryptic communicator. All visions and dreams had clear request and instruction, had a clear purpose, and were quick and concise. You have to have the ego of a narcissist to consider god is trying to communicate with you.

Christians believe that when Yeshua died, the veil in the second temple was ripped from top to bottom and God's presence poured out on the earth, and he made prophets and apostles out of the weakest.

It boggles my mind that people think this could be happening to them. It's some kind of mental disorder. The idea that the weakest become the strongest is just a mechanism to encourage the simplest, stupidest people who are low in social status to believe they could become great if they just become devout and don't question their leaders. It's a tool to keep everyone in line. It's why Yeshua used it. Christianity is nothing if not for this tool, because it's how you get a lot of gullible people who feel empty to suddenly feel important.
I know this is harsh but there's no value in sugarcoating it.

I believe Christianity is grounded in a lot more than that. My faith is weak, but the faith that is still there is based not only on belief, but historical veracity of this man, Yeshua, that lived in your city.
But, okay. I concede. To your point, I can't continue to gad about and speak prophecy. Because the reality is I've been wrong about this stuff in the past, and there's a deep level of sin in that. If I ever had that gift - and I know you think this is sacrilegious but I believe I once had this ability - but I don't have that gift anymore, I think. I don't know.

You don't have that gift. Because nobody does. And if you've spoken prophecy before, and it's been wrong, it proves that.

I hear what you're saying. I just can't get past the fact that this thing that I wrote down, it happened exactly as I saw it.

And so what? What now that it happened? It doesn't matter that it happened as you thought it might. It's not like you placed a large bet on it.

There is only one Lord, only one who can bend us to His will. And He shares His power with the Holy Spirit, who shares it with us.

That was the dream you had? The "prophecy dream?"

No. It didn't seem like you wanted to hear more about that, but my point is that I can have these dreams, and these special moments, because I believe the Shekhinah to be real. That's the difference between us. The same Spirit that David prayed upon while eluding King Saul, the same Spirit that convicted the Israelites of their sin in the face of exile, the same Spirit that led these same Israelites to repentance. This same Spirit is available to us today.
That's what I do believe.

Your imagination is so big. Stick to your Metroid principles.

No more Metroid principles.

No more? Why not?

I think I've covered the bases, the bare bones of what's critical for a comprehensive prayer. Anything more, and it's babble. At least in my opinion.

"So you're afraid that someone is going to come to me and want to censor your story?"

"During that same filming trip, Bob did another segment in Tel Aviv. He asked the mayor, 'how do you deal with knowing that terrorists can come at any time?' The mayor told to Bob, 'we all live with risks, even you. You can leave your home in New York and you might die in a car accident.'"

"Okay…"

"A few years after all this, Bob Simon was in a limo in New York City, where he lived. His limo driver was an Afghan immigrant named Abdul: a homeless man with a suspended license, one that had been suspended almost a dozen times. Abdul had just started with the company, but he was assigned as Bob's courier, even though he was new. With Bob as his passenger, Abdul began speeding, 15 miles over the limit, on a Manhattan highway."

In New York City traffic, that's like going the speed of light. My heart sank. I could tell where this was going.

"The limo struck another car, then accelerated more and crashed into metal barricades. Abdul survived. He claimed he had a heart attack. Doctors found no evidence of a heart attack. And the seat that Bob had been sitting on? It went missing by the time they investigated the crash."

"So," I spewed, at a loss for words, "how… how is Bob?"

The way Claire looked at me was the same way I'd imagined the Israeli ambassador looked at Bob.

"I will not say that there was corruption that caused this. It is probably all an accident. I hope it is! But I am obligated to tell you these facts. I am telling you that there are two wars going on," Claire said, convincing me that whatever story she was about to share would end with the punchline, *the one you feed.* "There is a war between Israelis and Palestinians. You see this war. The world sees this war. But I'm not a part of that war. I just want peace between men, and peace we will have. But there's another war. Do you know what this war is?"

"Is it, *the one you feed*?"

"What? No. The other war is a spiritual war. In the other war, if it bleeds, they're not the enemy. This war is between the powers of good and evil, and in that war, Israelis and Palestinians are the weapons. Not the enemies."

"Though," I reasoned, "how can you know if they bleed unless you cut them first?"

Claire shot me a blank. I forgot: humor doesn't translate. Perhaps especially when you're insinuating violence.

I'm actually disappointed to hear it. But you know better than me if this is where the story ends.

I wrote a prayer out. I try to pray it once every morning, just after waking, even if it's in the middle of the night. And what's funny about it is I have to admit that it's eerily similar to how Yeshua instructed us to pray.

Yeshua demands you pray a certain way?

Kind of. He had a lot of disciples asking him how we should pray, and He said, "okay, you idiots, this is what prayer looks like."

Nooooooo way! He really said that!?

No, that's just from the DSV.

dsv?

Danger Summarized Version. My commentary. I feel like maybe He was thinking it though when He told them how to pray? But to this day, most Christian churches pray that same prayer, almost verbatim, every time they get together. It's called the Lord's prayer. Or the Our Father. Yeshua instructed His disciples to pray like this, but now it's my own prayer, and that's critical.

Speaking of fathers. I've been meaning to ask. How's your dad?

He's well! Largely recovered from his stroke and is active again. Still slurs his speech, has some cognitive difficulties, but he's as healthy as you could ever expect from someone who suffered a stroke.

I'm so happy to hear that
~♡~ ٩(^ᵕ^)۶ ~♡~

They actually think he may have been one of the first Americans infected by COVID. Apparently, some people suffer strokes as a side effect. And he had his stroke in February 2020, after traveling internationally in January. So I personally think it's likely.

Is he still at risk you think?

I mean, we're always at risk. That's life. But he already got his vaccine, was one of the early eligibles. God spared him, and I love him a lot.

Love who?

Well, I was talking about my dad. But I guess both.

Has the pandemic slowed down by you?

Not a wink. Joanna's boss died last week. My uncle is on a ventilator in ICU. This month has had the highest fatality rate since the start. Death abounds. I think that's how it is everywhere at this point, including by you.

Yep. It's really, really bad. You wanna hear something crazy about December statistics though? Israel had its lowest terrorism rate.

Really? Lowest of the year?

No, friend. Lowest ever in the history of Israel. 3 Israelis murdered, 0 reported injuries. Still 3 more murders than there should be, but those stats are the lowest they've been since, like, the '60s I think.

Wow! Well, I guess the pandemic is doing enough killing on its own.

It's actually not because of that. Well, sure, a lockdown makes it harder to kill one another, sure, but there's been less animosity between Israelis and Palestinians.

Because you haven't had contact

"The point, Danger, is you need to know what you're in for. You believe in my story. But enough to ruin your name? Your entire publishing company?"

Ha! My publishing "company."

"Claire," I said, my turn to confess, "this is the first time I'll be publishing a story other than my own. I'm an indie publisher with a staff of dogs. I'm not Bob Simon. I'm nobody."

"Maybe nobody knows your company now. But I have good news. I had a prophecy. After you left Palestine, maybe a month ago, two tourists accidentally visited my guesthouse, much like how you found me. And they prophesied to me."

My body tensed up.

"They said that my book – our book, my story – it is going to fail."

"Oh," I said, my shoulders dropping.

"But after its first publication fails, it will be published again, and the second publication will be successful."

Great! At least for Claire. I wasn't sure how this was 'good news' for me. I'm that first publisher, destined to fail. So I'm going to put in the work, not get paid anything, and some better writer is going to swoop in and already have the bones of Claire's story, and they'll get the harvest I planted. *Ah, the indie publisher's dream!*

"Well," I rationalized, "a seed must die if a rose is to see the light of day."

"This will be the sign that the Holy Spirit will give. It will be like Gideon's fleece. You know this story of Gideon?"

Gideon's fleece.

A long time ago – a long, long time ago – in a galaxy flooded with campus geese, I had talked to my spiritual mentor about Gideon's fleece. The fact that most of those waterfowls had probably passed on actually had me feeling slightly sad, so I wrote a little rhyme down to honor their lives in my yellow writing pad.

"Do you know the story of Gideon's fleece?" Claire asked again, breaking up a ditty that was rattling about in my brain.

"Yes," I said. "God miraculously soaks Gideon's fleece one arid morning, then on the soggy morning that follows, the wool is lying there like a dry towel."

"My story will be like Gideon's fleece. First it will be overcome by saturation, too sopping wet for anyone to pick up. Then the next morning, the story will miraculously stand out from the dew, and many will wrap themselves in its warmth and will know the Spirit is surely with alive today."

No! That's what I'm trying to tell you. We had a common enemy and worked together to fight the virus. President Rivlin has been collaborating with President Abbas. They opened a joint operations center to help Palestinians. It's actually been really hard on them and sad to see their suffering.

I feel like I just walked into the Twilight Zone.

Better than being in the Danger Zone! This is all true. Israel has allowed for overnight permits for Palestinians who aren't normally eligible, just to help mitigate the amount of transportation going on. Some Palestinians who would never otherwise be allowed an Israeli sleep-over were given two months of such liberties.
And Israel delivered COVID test strips to Gaza and the West Bank so they could fight the spread, and Israelis were holding training for Palestinian medical workers. President Abbas - who hates Israelis and believes the Shoah never happened - has publicly praised Israel for helping out. I hate that cliche "unprecedented times," but the collaboration between enemies has been really, truly that definition.

That's incredible! Do you think it'll hold for long?

HA! No way. Wait until this plague passes, and it'll be business as usual. They'll attack us, we'll respond in kind, and then well-meaning but grievously misinformed idiots will call for a "ceasefire," not realizing that Israel's natural state is a ceasefire. We're not trying to conquer anyone.

But you do have those settlements...

We wouldn't have a single settlement if we felt safe. We know we're hated. We're not trying to provoke anyone. I don't want anyone to call on Israel for a ceasefire if they've never been the subject of a terrorist attack. Telling us to "ceasefire" is telling us to "stop exercising your right to defend yourself," as if the USA didn't chase down Bin Laden & the Squad of Terror after 9/11.

You tend to accidentally spew interesting band names when you talk.

Palestinians chant "from the river to the sea, Palestine will be free," referring to the lot between the Mediterranean and the Jordan. They think they came up with the witty phrase, but Israelis have a similar phrase that predates the Palestinians by thousands of years: "His rule shall be from sea to sea, and from the River to the ends of the earth."

But it doesn't rhyme.

True. Maybe that negates the whole thing.

Who is the "He" in that phrase

Meshiach. It's from Zechariah 9. Messianic verse. Just after the bit about the meshiach riding into Jerusalem on a donkey.

Just flipped the chapter open. Things seem to get pretty bloody there. And don't seem to end well for Damascus. Is this related to the Oracle of Damascus in Isaiah?

I don't think so. I'd have to look it up later. I'm not overly familiar with the Oracle of Damascus as it is.

It's considered by several scholars that it's the first and most obvious sign that the end times are on their way.

Well I'm sure that's what they've said anytime Damascus has been ransacked.

This assertion created a tension within me. Not because I was disheartened to be the writer of her failed first publication – writing a book that never gets read is a regular Tuesday for me (if Tuesday comes once every four years). But the idea that *I* had been commissioned to write a book that seeks to prove the Holy Spirit's presence? It was just over a month ago that I proved the inefficacy of my prayers, and I wasn't even sure that I believed the Holy Spirit actually worked in the way she was describing. When I had agreed to take on this project for Claire, I didn't know that God would be putting me through the most horrific experience of my life in less than a month's time. I don't think I would've accepted this consignment had I known what was about to do with Romy.

"I brought you a gift," Claire said, breaking through the acrimony inside my head by rummaging through the bag next to her feet. "It is from Bethlehem."

She handed me a small vial of oil.

"Thank you," I said, not sure why I was receiving this. "It's from the Church of the Nativity?"

"No," she said. "It is from St. George Monastery. George is important in Palestine, even to Muslims. They call him al-Khadr. He was martyred in Bethlehem because he refused to make a sacrifice to the Roman gods. He would not deny that there is only one God. In the church that was built on the spot where he was decapitated, there are shackles. And it is said that these chains can bring healing, even today. As so, I bring you healing oil from St. George, the patron saint of Palestinian Christians."

"This is kind, Claire. I appreciate it."

"Whenever and wherever you find yourself in need of healing, this oil can help."

How might I dip my faith in this oil?

"Thank you," I said, slipping the holy tube into my own bag. "Very much."

Claire bounced her head just once, her cool nod having the same impact as if it were a grizzled Robert Redford offering his approval.

Trying to exhale, I accidentally snorted.

"Might you make me a promise?"

"Sure," I said, "anything."

"When you have a child, if Joanna is able to have a child…," she hesitated as if she knew this was a sour topic, "…I need you to come back to Bethlehem for their Baptism."

"Baptism? Like, at your church?"

It's never happened there. Damascus is the longest-inhabited city in history. It's never been destroyed, not once. So when it goes down, it's going to be a big deal.

Where does the bible talk about any of this?

The oracle is in Isaiah 17. Jeremiah 49:27 also seems to have reference to it. It's a real thing. As real as any other prophecy in the Bible.

Is this related to your belief about Gog and Magog happening?

It's not "my belief." Both my Bible and yours go into great detail about Armageddon. And whether it's a place or a concept, doesn't matter.

I hate hate hate that I'm asking this. But who would Gog be and who would Magog be, according to your prophecy belief?

Gog is a person, who leads Magog. Magog is a bunch of countries, most often believed to be Russia, China, Iran, Turkey, and other Arab countries.

And where's the US on this?

Nowhere to be found. If anything, opponents to Israel. But they (we) don't help you guys.

You know, Russia used to be our closest ally.

I do know that. In your War of Independence, Russia was your sidekick. Within 20 years, during the Six-Day War, they sided with Palestine and the Arabs. So, a lot can change in a short period of time.

Where does Yeshua come in?

It's hard to tell what to take literally and what not with these prophecies. But Yeshua is likened to being like the flood in Noah's time: He's completely unexpected, but it's very, very clear that He's returned.
The story of Noah is sorta a pictorial prophecy for the Second Coming, according to the Gospel of Matthew. Not only will Yeshua be like the flood, but the people will act like the people acted in Noah's time.

Idolators?

No. For once in the Bible, that wasn't the big issue for God. Go ahead and read the text: Genesis 6.

Okay, so violence. It was a very, very violent time.
Actually, this is interesting. If you read it in Hebrew, there's an interesting word choice.

Where?

Genesis 6:11. The last word in the sentence.

"Violence?"

Yes. But the Hebrew word used there is "Hamas."

Okay so Hamas named themselves "violence."

Except they didn't. Hamas is an Arabic acronym. It means something like "The Islam Resistance Movement." It just so happens to also be the Hebrew word for "violence."

What. Looking this up now.
So you're saying "Islamic Resistance Movement" in Arabic means "violence" in Hebrew?

"Yes."

"*Infant* Baptism?"

"Yes."

"Okay," I said. "I promise. Claire, if that's what it takes – promising you and God that I'll bring my baby back to where the Messiah was born – that is a small thing."

But, if I was being honest, I didn't believe it would happen. What she was offering was a pie-in-the-sky dream. Covered in calorie-free whip with an everlasting gobstopper on top.

"I wish…" I said, then realized how fussy I sounded. "I… crave a story likes yours."

"In what way?" Claire asked.

"I want to be haunted."

"Haunted?" she said, almost as if the word had a language barrier. "By what? A ghost?"

"Not *what*, who. Not *a ghost*, but The Ghost."

"Mmm," Claire hummed, before repeating, "mmm."

"In all of this, this work we're doing and what we're putting onto pages, what do you want from any of this?" I asked Claire. "When your story is written and available to the masses, what do you want those with eyes to see? What do you want those with ears to hear?"

"It is the Holy Spirit who keeps you wrestling," she answered without missing a beat. "He's been poured out on us. Have you felt Him, head-to-toe like me? Maybe not. But keep in mind that I only felt Him – *physically* felt His presence – when I was living out my witness, and I was walking in step with Him, and I was in immediate need of Him."

Hmm. A three-switched circuit breaker to turn on the power of the Holy Spirit. Of course, He's not quite that formulaic, but Claire's experience resonated with me: the two times I could palpably feel the Holy Spirit – maybe not in Claire's unusual tingly sense, but times when I knew without doubt that He was with me – were in Afghanistan and in the Holy Land. The two places in my life where I was most seeking God on a daily basis, and the two times in my life where I needed His direct intervention.

Both times, I went home, let my faith get complacent, and my prayer's power went stale.

"I want another thing," Claire said. "I want people to know that we will have peace. Peace in Palestine. Peace in Israel."

Yes. They chose an innocuous name, because at first, they were considered a peacekeeping effort during the first intifada. Social justice organization. But it only took a couple years before they became full-on terrorists with the intent to wipe jews off the earth. "From the river to the sea."

I'm somewhat familiar with Hamas. Their whole intent is to bring the end times to fruition. That's in their constitution or whatever you want to call it, that they have a holy duty to jihad against Jews until the day of Magog.

Cool cool. So Hamas is doing their part to bring armageddon, Christians say that the end times will be like it was in Noah's days, and Genesis says that in Noah's days, "the earth was filled with hamas."

Lol. No concerns there.

And do you know where Hamas is headquartered?

Yes. Gaza.

No, that's where they operate. They have a literal HQ outside of Israel.

Where?

Syria.

Oh.

Damascus, Syria.

OH!

So in the oracle of Damascus, who actually destroys the city? Is it Israel or someone else?

It doesn't say. All it says is that Jews will be blamed for it.

Classic.

When I was interviewing for my dissertation, one of the questions I asked each person was what the outcome of this conflict would be.

Hello. Danger. I know this. Hi, I'm Israel Participant #1. Nice to meet you!

I bring it up because every single one of my participants said that this thing - the conflict - ends in full-scale war. Israelis and Palestinians alike. Nobody disagreed.

Well, yeah. How else can it end?

Joanna has always had the understanding that when Damascus is destroyed, I'm gonna drop everything and answer the call, no matter what's going on in life.

She agreed to that?

No. Not really. But she certainly understood it as a precondition to our relationship, I guess. She didn't agree to it any more than she agreed to let me go to Afghanistan. But until Damascus is destroyed, no focusing on Armageddon. No obsessing. We live our life and we don't make decisions around the far-fetched possibility of it happening in our lifetime.

So what if the end times do come, but Dasmascus is still standing? What if you got the precursor wrong?

Then I don't go. That simple. Because in that scenario, I don't even understand the little bits about the end times that I thought I understood. I'm of no value.

So do you still really believe you were called for this?

Well, I know what you think about it.

Nobody's asking what I think. What do YOU think?

549

"Hmm," I said, not quite sure how to tell her that *that's* just not gonna happen.

"There is hope. Yes, war will come. It always does here. I promise you that. But there will *also* be resurrection."

"*How* can you say that though?" I proffered my true feelings. "Claire, there is *no* solution to this thing. We've tried every angle of diplomacy. Don't get me wrong, I believe it *can* happen. My entire dissertation carries that hope! But if I were a betting man, that's one wager I'm not going up against the house on."

"Have faith," Claire said, using one of my least-favorite Christian tropes. "There was no solution to the brokenness in God's garden, either. He found a way and redeemed us through Yasue. Humans may *have* wisdom, but God *is* wisdom. Just because we don't see how it ends, doesn't mean God doesn't either."

That much was true. And hearing it? A small seed of hope sprouted.

"You can talk about the Holy Spirit," Claire continued, "and it's good to. But sometimes you just need to get up and see what He does. The flame of the early Church, spreading it to the rest of the world? It was the Holy Spirit carrying the flame. He *is* that flame. So we might not understand certain things about how He works or why He does things, but every person – Gentile or Jew – every person can understand the historical event of the Church bursting onto the scene against all odds."

"But *how*, Claire?" I asked, my skepticism starting to crack through what she was saying. "If I'm asking to see Him move, and He doesn't, then what?"

"You have to trust the Holy Spirit without doubt, but without begging. Don't be negative! Focus on the light, even if it's just one spot of light."

"Claire," I said, starting to get frustrated, "that sounds *new-agey*. Like, 'just be positive and good things will manifest.'"

"No," she closed her eyes and subtly – so, so gently – shook her head. "What I mean is you can talk about the negative things in life, but be thankful at the same time. Thank God that it isn't worse. It could be worse. It could *always* be worse. I knew women in Bethlehem who say they're cursed, and as a result, they're always sick. They lived as cursed women."

I felt cursed. I even vocalized to Joanna that I thought we must be cursed. Could I really be bringing the curse on myself by thinking that? That seems silly.

"Yasue said 'if you believe in Me, you shouldn't have fear.' After Mirna died, I felt that she in heaven and happier than she could've been with me in a war zone, and I hung onto that. I still grieved. Oh, I've grieved. I still missed her. Still

The Lord is sovereign. I rest in that.
I think the end is coming. Maybe sooner than we think. But I'm not going to obsess over it. Yeshua called these types of things "birth pangs." I'm supposed to be focusing on the creation that comes from the birth, not the pain from the contractions.

You're supposed to be. But I'm not sure that you're actually focusing on it.

I'm not focusing on it. Yes, it matters to me. But even if Russia and Iran joined forces, or Israel got in a land war with Hamas, or the United States completely abandoned Israel in her greatest time of need, none of those are enough to change my mind. I'm standing by this: my cue is the destruction of Damascus. And believe me when I say I'm not looking forward to that.

Alright. Well, you said it succinctly: God is sovereign.

Yep. I'll keep following that star to see where it leads.

Do Christians refer to god as their star?

No. That's just DSV commentary again. The concept of the North Star and the Bethlehem Star is important to me. I know it's sin to actually trust in the stars positioning and all that.

Right. Astrology is not kosher. No stargazing. At least not in the sense that you look at the stars for predictions of the future, especially trying to divinate from the position of the stars.
Avodat Kochavim U'Mazalot!

But you know how wild that is? Stargazing was illegal in ancient Hebrew law, especially around the time of Yeshua's birth, when Jews were getting back to their roots of following the law. When He arrived on scene, it was potentially the first time in history that Jews had been collectively agreeing and abiding by the Law long-term, which really emphasizes to me that the Law itself cannot save. Because it was the breaking of the Law that got the first pagans to find Him. God led astrologists to the Christ using a method that no good Jew would ever dream of dabbling in. The wise men followed a star, not certain what that journey looked like, but too compelled to ignore it.

Well, stars are pretty compelling. You and I can look in the sky and see the same star as one another. When it's twilight for you, you can see the same North Star that I'm seeing at dawn. Stars transcend time. Those stars we see may have died thousands of years ago!

Transcend time, and understanding. Two people can look at the same star and see something completely different. I was reading a book a bit ago, and the author, Eric Bargerhuff, talked about this. I wrote it down, hold on, let me find what he said.
"The word for 'star' by Matthew could mean any bright radiance or celestial light in the sky, and some have suggested this was either a comet, a supernova of some type, an alignment of planets, or better yet a supernatural manifestation of the Shekhinah, the glory of God (which led the Israelites through the desert under Moses in the Old Testament)."

That's cool. Mazel Tov just means "good constellation" in Hebrew.

I've heard that before, actually.

Yeah. It's basically "good luck." Like "have a good destiny," I guess.

do! But I had a peace. So: go ahead and cry. Cry, but don't curse. Grieve, but don't gripe. Negativity curses a house."

I felt something rising in my throat. Anger, sure, but I think something even more than that. A certain platitude of brine, maybe even venom.

"You lost Romy, and it's fine to cry," Claire said, cutting to the core of whatever had been stirring in my throat, her words as if a rebuke that sent a devil back to hell for a temporary imprisonment. "You have lost your daughter. *So have I*, and my dad. It hurts. But curse is the natural state of the world; anything good that comes from a cursed plane must be from God, no? So if your wife is crying and her tears and bringing you down, talk her through that. Bring her back to joy. Find joy."

I instinctively put my hand around the neck of Romy's urn again, unconsciously petting it like a genie might appear if I thumbed it lovingly enough.

"I'm angry with God," I admitted without looking at Claire. "And it makes me negative. How can I be happy when I feel like God's responsible for the bad in my life, as much as He is for the good?"

"When you're angry, speak in logic," she said, having her answer locked and loaded before I'd finished my question. "And, be careful about emotion. Emotion is fine, just like anger isn't a sin in itself, but it's often the vessel for sin. When you're angry at God, say, 'I love you, and I don't understand why You would do this or allow this.' Get out of the bitterness when you do it, though."

She paused, perhaps knowing she wasn't getting through to me in any meaningful way. After regrouping, she got awfully specific.

"To lose a child is to lose your heart. Lose your soul. I blamed God. First, when I lost my dad, I was angry even then. But then I prayed, 'God, take care of him,' and I trusted that He did. I was able to let it go. But I didn't go to the hospital when I lost my dad, and as a result of my decision, I lost my child. I blamed God, at least until I accepted that this wasn't His fault, and then I blamed myself. I failed Mirna; I'm sorry I failed Mirna. So I asked for forgiveness from God. Now, years removed from it, I believe Mirna would have died even if it hadn't been me that failed her."

I don't know whether I believed that. Frankly, I was exhausted, and I think my brain was fried from trying to mirror Claire's experience to my own, which is a lot like – well – it's a lot like taking an odd Bible passage and applying it to your life thousands of years after it was written in its original context.

"The Apostle Paul said that if you believe in God, God will take everything – *even* the bad stuff – and make it work for His good. It will be

One person looks, and they might see God's mighty hand. King Herod looks at a star and sees a threat. Another person sees a star from a scientific vantage. Ancient Egyptians lived their lives according to the stars and were reminded of Osiris. An ancient Greek may think of Zeus. The Aztecs and some Chinese astrologers believed some stars to even be deities. Others - like me and the wise men - see God guiding them to the Christ from the star's light.

You're sounding quite kabbalah. Can all religions be equally legitimate?

No. I don't think so. Maybe some of our beliefs overlap, but logically we can't all be right.

So what's the next step then? Especially in your case, where your religion... I mean, no nice way to put it, but it's been molested so much.

What if none of us are right?
What if your religion is made-up?
What if the wise men sought the Bethlehem Star, followed their mazel tov, and it was just a will-of-the-wisp? An ignis fatuus of biblical proportions?

Is that where you're at with this? Just throw your hands up and say "none of it is actually real"?

If no religion is right, that's awfully convenient. It's like a bad plothole. It just doesn't add up.

So Danger. You're frustrating me. Is religion real to you? If so, how do you figure out if anybody is right?

I think, to start, we need to research history well. If I could convince anyone to do anything in this life, it would be to look up the historical veracity of Christ's resurrection. Few of us do it, even Christians. We watch a 10-minute video on its history, maybe read a TIME article, and suddenly we become convinced of our stance. We're experts in our mind. It's agonizing to me when people dismiss Christianity because of its resemblance to Wikipedia's summary of the ancient Egyptian religion, but they never take the time to research the historical Yeshua - specifically His life, death, and life. The whole world was turned upside-down when Christ was born: the ones in power and with authority were the ones who were afraid, those who studied religious law and prophecy didn't care, and it was the pagans who were coming to worship in a way that ultimately pleased God. And if the Messiah really existed, then it's the only thing that actually matters in the world. We can't get enough of Lord of the Rings lore or who slept with who on the latest Netflix binge-worthy release. But when it comes to something that actually matters - like eternity - we become so lazy, so arrogant, that we'll spend 2 minutes looking at a meme and then become self-professed experts on religion.

How can anyone get there though? To actually becoming an expert?

I think we need to ask for that. Consistently. Pervasively. Wrestle with God like Jacob did. I think God can take a star - even one that, like the wise men, we're sinfully chasing - and God can take that star and re-contextualize it so that it's understood in a language we can understand.
Today, the "universe" is often credited with miracles. Even people who claim to have no spiritual bone or even an anti-religious bend, they'll say "the universe did this." It's like the worldwide new pagan religion.

Yeah. Whatever works, I guess. But it's silly to me. So many religions say that god has a personality, and so your response is to reject this notion and give the black expanse a personality instead?

meaningful. And Paul had been stoned, imprisoned, ridiculed, and cut off from his family and his tribe. He knew suffering. Everybody has Yasue written on their heart and the Lord decides which steps will be taken to come to Him."

Still not helpful. Or relevant.

"Here," she said. "If you throw a child into the wilderness, God will give that child wisdom about what's right and what's wrong. If they see a rabbit and decide to eat it, the child will know in his heart that he should kill the rabbit mercifully. But killing the rabbit needlessly would be sin."

I... think the Twelve Disciples probably would've been confounded by that parable. Maybe it was because I didn't have any bandwidth left to receive any more funky layered fables, or maybe Claire's mystifying allegory had me feeling like she was an ancient prophet, but I turned the chair I was sitting on into a confessional.

"Can I tell you my sin?" I asked.

"Yes," she said, her shortest sentence since I'd sat down to talk to her.

"I don't believe in the power of prayer."

"What is prayer?" she asked. "That's like saying you don't believe in the power of conversations with your wife. You can't just *talk* to your wife: you have to tune yourself to her frequency as you converse."

Hmm.

"Ask God for wisdom as to what's right or wrong, and what He is trying to tell you. Ask the Holy Spirit to let you understand God! Can I tell you a true story?"

"Of course," I said. "I'm here to hear the truth."

"There was a boy. At ten years old, he got cancer. At twelve, he went into hospice and fell into a coma. Of course, everyone assumed he would not wake up, but then he did. And when he did, they scanned and found his cancer was gone. They asked, 'how can this be?,' and the boy said, 'I know what happened.' He explained, during his coma, the boy saw an imam. He asked God, 'is that your religious leader?' God said, 'no, that is the devil.' The young boy then saw a nun and asked, 'is she from you?', and God said, 'no, that is also a devil.' The young boy saw a bishop adorned with grand vestments, and he said to God, 'this one must be from you.' God said, 'you see those seven diadems on his head? Those represent the seven devils that are inside of him.'"

I had to assume the bishop was Greek.

"Well, the young boy, still in his coma, sees a poor man who is growing a garden, and the man gives what's in his garden to those who are even poorer than

They're miscontextualizing God's blessing for them. But the blessing is still real even if God doesn't get the credit. and God can use that understanding to get them to where they need to be.

So do you feel you're where you "need to be"

Am I where I need to be? I'm trying. I don't know if I'm doing it right. I don't think I'll be where I need to be until the Kingdom is fully restored. Faith is like the Israeli-Palestinian Conflict: the more I study it, the less I understand.

Well, consider the wisdom we see in book of Job: what if god doesn't want you to understand certain things about him? What if he just wants you to be in awe of him?

What if God is all-powerful, chose not to save Romy, and He has His reasons that I'm not entitled to know?

Hey, now that's a thought experiment right there :-)

I have 2 choices: I can either rest in God's sovereignty, or not rest in God's sovereignty. The latter is a life of turmoil. I have to recognize that prior to Romy's death, my getting called to a PhD program, and our not being able to have kids, He had a pretty good track record. So there's optimism there, even though my faith and my praying has inflicted so much pain, anxiety, frustration, suffering.

What is it for you then? Why cling to something that causes so many negative reactions?

There's a thing that Yeshua says in the Gospel of John (which is the book I recommended checking out if you get through Matthew, Hebrews, and Romans). Yeshua says of his disciples, "I give them eternal life, and they shall never perish; no one can snatch them out of my hand." And I really believe that any God-fearing person - you, me, anyone that takes this stuff seriously - can't just step away and not be drawn back to it. Anybody who once had a seed of faith and truly felt it grow, you can't just rip out your entire belief system and turn away like you don't have gaping holes in your heart. It's the same reason that you stuck to your religion, even when so many other teenagers around you abandoned it. People like you and me, we're addicts for Truth. It's not a choice we're making. It's our lifeblood, and when we're done hemorrhaging for a time, we recycle what we lost.

Yeah, that's been true for me too. I agree with that part.

In the darkest times of my life, it's been impossible to just turn my back on what I know to be true about God. I can't just give up on faith. I mean, people who never actually had faith, then sure, I can see how they quit on it. But you can't rip out my faith without my roots unearthing the rest of the dirt under it. I'm not a baby plant. The mark of someone who truly has faith is that they don't abandon it in the face of contradictory evidence. They wrestle, not abandon.

So just believe it because it's what you've spent the most time with? Even as an ethnic jew, I don't like that philosophy.

No, it's not that. I mean, there have been so many times I've been angry at God, fed up with faith, and supposedly made the choice to kiss it goodbye like Judas did. But each time, I can't help but get drawn back to the altar.

Why though? That's what I'm trying to wrap my head around. I think it's easier for me to stay rooted because there's that ethnic component for me. It's an act of war for a jew to apostatize. Not for you. Why cling?

he is, and the gardener prays and weeps because he knows he is a sinner, and he confesses his sins, then praises and thanks God. God tells the boy, *'this one is mine.'* And that is when the boy woke up. Who hears God best? Will our wardrobe give us some kind of special power to hear God? Try as we may, none of us are ancient Levites. God dwelled with them in a holy tent. But that tent is gone, and is now given freely by the Holy Spirit."

"Okay, Claire," I said, trying to refocus her point. "After hearing your story, how can your reader feel the Holy Spirit? How can *I* feel the Holy Spirit?"

"You have never felt the Holy Spirit?" she gasped.

"Definitely not like you. I've had prophecy, some wild prophecies have come true, but I've been wrong on damaging levels, too. And healing? I don't think I've ever had anything that was divine healing, not like you've had."

"Do not fear," she said. "You, too, can have charisma from the Holy Spirit. The Holy Spirit belongs to Him who freely gives. He'll give power to who He wants to. All you can do is ask. You know, when I pray, I'm not asking for specific outcomes, as many do. I let God decide. The power of the Holy Spirit isn't the power for us to decide. If you try to invoke the Holy Spirit and try to determine the most favorable outcome, you will have neither. We just do our role. Can I tell you a true story?"

"Claire, I…"

"My cousin was sick," she battered on. "I prayed for him, and I felt the Holy Spirit empower me: head-to-toe, warm-to-cool, the same Holy Spirit who spared me so many times before. And I prayed over my cousin, in full strength of the Holy Spirit. God told me, 'I want him to be healed,' and my cousin breathed his last."

Wow. Not where I saw that story going.

"I wondered, what's the purpose of the Holy Spirit if He didn't revive my cousin? What's the difference between what I did and what anybody else might be able to do for my cousin? *This* is the difference: I have a relationship with God. The Holy Spirit empowers us to hear from God about our life situations: which decisions to make. And it might be the same decision and the same outcome as an atheist would have, except for the difference: we walk away from the situation, still knowing we are in continuing relationship with Him. And dying? That can be the healing."

"That's… it seems a bit cruel," I cross-examined.

"You have anger at the Church? That's fine, Danger. But you can't abandon her any more than you would abandon your wife if she did something

It's the evidence, Esther. When my faith fails, it's the facts that move me forward. I believe your Bible. Too much of it is rooted in history, and the stuff that seems too fabricated to be real - Jonah, the flood, Goliath, Shadrach Meshach Abednego, Methuselah, Enoch - nobody has any evidence to the contrary, either. And even if those stories are purely fables, their lessons aren't lost on me amidst the backdrop of a real, historical Jewish people.

So, we're aligned right there. So you're jewish-minded then?

I accept Judaism. It's real. Which means God is real. The prophets are real. And the Messianic prophecies are real. But does that mean Yeshua is the Christ?

No.

That's the easy answer, right? But there's a few questions about core Judaism that I can't get past.

Like what exactly?

The pictorial prophecies, those prophecies that mirrored Christ's life so clearly. You say the events of Yeshua's life didn't happen as they're recorded? Fine. But then you have to admit that the Gospel is the most finely-crafted piece of fan-fiction that's ever been penned, a story that is far more cohesive, a narrative far more interwoven, with an ending far more epic than anything Tolkien could've introduced into his Middle Earth mythology.

Well the Gospels took several decades to publish, so it's not out of the realm that they could've been carefully pieced together over that time.
And I haven't read your bible, but I can't imagine it actually being as legendary as Tolkien.

Five-hundred years from now, the Rings will be on the periphery consciousness at best. But even that aside, there's one thing that really, really has gotten under my skin. I don't have an answer for it. I don't think you have an answer for it.

You're talking Isaiah 53.

The obfuscation of that chapter is a big deal to me, yes. But it's not that. If you and I both believe in the history of Israel (we do), and we both believe that God's plan includes the sending of a Messiah (we do), then it has to mean that God's plan for the Messiah won't be thwarted.

Sure? Yes.

The prophecies say that the Messiah will come from the tribe of Judah, and the seed of David. That's not even tracked anymore. Even ancestry.com wouldn't be able to validate or invalidate if a self-proclaimed messiah alleged some genealogical connection to your Bible.

We did kind of talk about this already: you can't prove that Yeshua came from the tribe of Judah and/or the seed of David.

You're right: I can't. But I'm not trying to prove that to you. What I'm trying to say is that we agree on one thing here: that the seed can't be tracked.

Okay. So?

So maybe it's binary thinking on my part, but with this reality, I'm faced with only two possibilities to reconcile this:
either the Messiah has already come,
or the Bible isn't true and its prophecies will never be fulfilled.

Or maybe god will fulfill that prophecy in a way you don't expect?

repulsive. It would hurt you, but you can't ignore the love you have for her. The Church has not been faithful to Yasue. But like Hosea, Yasue comes right back to the unfaithful wife and seeks restoration. You must do the same. Be honest with God. It's a sin to hide your honest self and honest feelings. Have spiritual honesty. Deal directly with what you're feeling, like the psalmists do. And let me give you a tip: don't just pray in your head. You must pray out loud. And if possible, look at the sky as you pray. Find the sky."

"I'm just afraid," I confided, trying my hand at honesty.

"Of what?"

"I'm afraid of heaven," I said. "I don't want to commit to any kingdom without knowing if Romy's there. Heaven without Romy isn't heaven."

Claire reflected on what I'd said. I doubt she'd thought about the eternal state of pets as much as I did, if at all.

"I don't know if Romy is in heaven. But I'll ask a question I have thought about many times: how do I know that Mirna wasn't the one who whispered to me to ask for the Holy Spirit? I assume that voice I heard was from Yasue, but what if it wasn't? My life today would never have looked like it does now if I didn't have a posture of receiving the Holy Spirit. How can you know that Romy is not advocating for you in front of the Lord?"

"Well, she's a dog. She can't talk."

"Did the snake not talk to Eve in the perfect garden? Can dogs not talk in perfect heaven? Who says that?"

Fair.

"The point, Danger, is that we don't know what eternity is. We've only heard rumors about it. But that's the thing about rumors: a lot of them have Truth."

I sat in my thoughts for a moment, maybe even two moments. My chin dropped, setting my eyes on my notepad. I looked over my mad scribbles and my indistinct lines – blear glyphs that amounted to a secret code, intelligible to anyone but the scribe. Just a couple months ago, I was furiously penning participants' answers to my interviews.

Oh! But I didn't ask my favorite question.

"Claire," I said, "for fun, now. I won't put this in your book. What does your name mean?"

"Claire?" she asked. "Or Anastas?"

"Well, both!" I said, gleefully unmasking my affinity for the etymology of names.

I can't do it. Maybe I'm too much of a city boy, but that's a barn too wide for me. I know I don't pray well, I know I don't understand much about God, but I have to be intellectually honest. There are too many things about Yeshua that I can't get around. Yes, I'm biased. Yes, I'm rooting for Christianity to be true. But as unsatisfying as some of Christianity's answers are, its claims about the fulfillment of the Jewish Messiah are too compelling.

That's fine. We don't have to agree.

You and I both know: we're going to court someday, standing before The Judge. And I know you may not feel like the Law condemns you, but I certainly feel convicted. I'm guilty. I'm so guilty. I feel it in my soul.

I wouldn't put it that way but okay. Yes, there is judgment for all.

I need an expert penisologist just to urinate like a normal man. I can't even think clearly without a doctor handing me a tiny pill that resets my neurotransmitters. How incapable I am of doing anything! And if I can't even think or pee straight, then how much more I need an advocate in my religious walk.
Yeshua is my lawyer. Only fools go Pro Se. I need someone to appeal on my behalf. The Judge may love me, but He has His duties, too. And I know I broke the law. I've overslept when I needed to be alert. I've never kept a Mitzvah, not one. I have no reasonable defense for missing the targets. I wanted to get a perfect score, but I didn't even qualify.

So Yeshua is your lawyer who knows how to navigate the legal system?

I wouldn't put it that way either. Yeshua is the lawyer and the plea deal, wrapped in skin.

If you say so. He's also purportedly the son of god, who god killed, despite child sacrifice being strictly forbidden.

It's also forbidden for waters to part in two, for people to turn into salt, for fleeces to remain dry on a wet morning.

God transcends those laws, he doesn't break them.

Imagine a sci-fi movie, k? A man impregnates a woman, and instead of a new individual popping out, it was a baby version of himself, the father. Even though it's the same person, that father is still gonna call that second iteration his "son."

That's not sci fi, that's horror.

Well the Bible is full of horror.
I understand Yeshua to be the Son of God. For a long time, I struggled with this, especially when I noticed there aren't ancient Hebrew prophecies about the Messiah being the Son of God. But in the sci-fi/horror movie, how else would you relate to that child? He's the "son of the father" there. But what if "Son of God" is just terminology to give us cues as to how we should relate to Him?

So is he or is he not the "son of god?"

If Melchizedek was a priest before the priesthood, who came from nothing and was called "priest of the God Most High" before the Levites were even established, maybe Yeshua is "Son of God" in the same way. Melchizedek, a priest, but not in the way we assume it means. Yeshua, yes, Son of God, with no origin outside of the fact that He just is what it says He is: divine and of His own lineage to the Father, in the order of Melchizedek. What if the Messiah is divine, even if the prophecies didn't explicitly state so?

"Bright."

"What's bright?"

"My name."

"That's what it means? Or are you describing your name?"

"I am describing what it means."

"Are we... is this like a 'who's on first' routine?"

"What's 'first?'" she asked, then clarified, "My name, Claire, means 'bright.'"

"Ahh," I said. "Okay. Claire is bright."

"It may be a little different," she said, backpedaling like a politician caught in a lie. "I think it has a flair to it that is lost in English? A dash of soupçon, I think you say?"

Nobody says that.

"It is bright, as in clear," Claire clarified. "Except in one situation: if you say *'clair de lune,'* it literally means 'brightness of the moon,' yes?"

I have no idea.

"Now, I don't speak French," claimed the woman who just casually dropped *soupçon.* "But it is not actually 'brightness of the moon,' it is meaning 'light of the moon.' So Claire is 'bright,' but bright like starlight."

"Starlight?"

"Basically," she said. "Claire marks the light from the star. It's a light that makes everything clear."

"That is very, very cool," I said. "Thank you for sharing that."

"Danger, do you remember when I told you my story is a story of Resurrection?"

"Yes," I said, only vaguely recalling this.

"Well, I meant that. Anastas *means* Resurrection."

"Wow! That is just as cool!"

"The Anastas do not fear burial."

"How poetic. I'm *totally* putting that in your book. Did you have any second thoughts? About changing your name to Anastas, I mean, when you got married – given how close you were to your dad?"

"It's still there. Yes, I am Claire Anastas, but I am also Claire Bandak still."

"Does *Bandak* have significance?" I asked, geeking out at the potential onomastic weight that could possibly follow "bright light" and "resurrection."

"No, not really. I think its root comes from Arabic 'bunduq,' which is how you say *hazelnut.*"

Maybe. It's not convincing to me, but I'd rather you ascribe to it rather than enter into some state of nihilism. It would be a little more persuasive to me if god had ever communicated any of the things you just stated to jews. Even just once.

If the Law and/or Yeshua is written on our hearts, then doesn't that mean God has communicated it to us? There has to be some element of truth to "feeling" something spiritual inside, too.

What do you mean? I feel like you're doing a complete 180 here. You've spent all year railing against the american church for wending peoples' emotional responses for their own gain.

I hammer the church for artificially creating that "spiritual feeling" when it's only God who can create it.
Like, is there any place you've felt a spiritual transcendence? Some kind of link to the holy or the spiritual or the universe? If you ever do, ask that thing, "are you Yeshua?" And listen. I believe that if it's Yeshua, the voice will respond.

Uggghhhhhhhhhhhhh.
We've talked about this so many times before, I take up issue with the idea that god speaks directly to people. In any capacity.
Especially people who don't even attempt to adhere to the Law. If the Law was written on your heart, then you'd be obeying it.

All I'm getting at is that I have to recognize I won't ever have all the answers, but the task of the honest man is to continue wrestling like he might get the blessing anyway.
I believe that God promised a Messiah, that I can't save myself. So then I have to look at history and ask myself, has anyone even come close to being the Messiah?

And you see Yeshua as having been that historical person?

I do.
Cornelius Tacitus, Roman historian. Suetonius, Pliny the Younger, both Roman writers. Flavius Josephus, Jewish historian from the 1st century who had nothing to gain by writing about Yeshua, but he recorded the crucifixion and that hundreds of people were claiming they saw Yeshua long after His recorded death.
Hold on, let me find a quote I saw recently.

Just so you know, Flavius Josephus is considered a traitor to jews. He sowed dissension and division as the romans tore apart the Holy Temple. Jews break glass at weddings to symbolize that marriage holds both joys and sorrows, and that a lack of unity can destroy the marriage like the lack of unity destroyed the Temple.

Wow, I didn't know that.

You mentioned that when Yeshua died, the veil tore from top to bottom or whatever. And you know what? I haven't looked into that, but I think I can believe that to be true.

Wait. Really?

Weird things happened after Yeshua died. Weird things at first, then terrible things. Murder. Destruction of the temple. Diaspora.

We talked about the Scarlet Thread before, that after Yeshua died, it never turned white again (ie, Jewish sacrifices were rejected). Is that what you mean by "weird things?"

Well, that's a lot less sexy.

"Oh. So Claire Bandak is really Claire Hazelnut."

"I suppose so?" she affirmed. "I've been told our name is more related to Al-Bunduqíyya, though."

"Which is?"

"Al-Bunduqíyya is how you say 'Venice' in our language."

Claire Venice. Claire Canal-City-in-the-Shape-of-an-Italian-S.

"But," she perked up, "in Latin, it means 'blessed!'"

"Ohhh, that's… *cool*," I feigned enthusiasm over the generic significance her name had in a dead language.

"Hazelnut, Venice, and blessed: these are better meanings than what it means in Old Persian."

Cool. An embarrassing meaning from another dead language.

"What's that?"

"It is 'servant' in Persian, like a slave."

"Okay, that's something!"

"I have heard – I know not if this is true – but I have heard that King Darius…"

"Darius of the Bible?"

"…yes, Darius of the Bible. He had many generals as he conquered. They wore a kind of girdle, it was called a *bandaka*. And then after, bandaka became to mean someone who has a duty to serve. And today, even in modern Persian and Urdu, it means someone with a duty: a servant. Or slave. Someone who is bound. I do not like this meaning. It means Venice."

"I actually think I like 'slave' better."

"It is not just slave. It means slave, yes, but in Iran, you use this word in self-deprecation. When you want to emphasize the difference between you and a king. 'The king is king, but I am just his Bandak.' You use this word to mean how much you are not of importance."

"It sounds like it's almost an honorific name, then. A name of humility, one that helps you to remember your place."

"Yes, but maybe I don't explain it well. It's a very famous word in Arab cultures. It is like a man who has been put in jail or is bound to his lowly role. But, again, that is Persian. In Arabic, Bandak means Venice. And that is what it means. Not slave."

"So how do you say that same word – the slave of the king, or the man in jail – in Arabic?"

That's one of the things, yes. But there were other signs that the kingdom was falling apart because Yeshua turned jews on one another. For Yom Kippur, two goats had always been chosen, and the high priest would draw two stones: a black stone and a white stone. If the priest opened his left hand and it was a black stone, then the goat on the left would be the scapegoat; if black was on the right, then the right goat was the scapegoat.

What happened to the scapegoat?

He's the one who would get the scarlet thread tied to his horn. That thread symbolized the sins of the collective jews, so the scapegoat was led astray into the wilderness to starve to death or get mauled or whatever other malicious fate would befall him.
Tradition says that usually the scapegoat was pushed off a cliff to ensure he wouldn't accidentally wander back and carry the jewish sins back to camp.

That's barbaric.

Yep. Anyway, after the crucifixion, the system broke: whenever lots were cast for the goats, it was the goat on the left who'd get the black stone and become the scapegoat. 100% of the time. This happened for 40 straight years, which is a statistical impossibility. As if god was saying, "I'm not even entertaining your sacrifices anymore." And the scapegoat's scarlet thread would never turn white anymore. And after they'd tie the scarlet thread onto the doorknob of the Hekel (Temple), the temple doors would fly open at night, as if in protest.

Nuh uh..

So they say.

You wanna talk real horror...

And this was a really big deal, mind you. Those doors were to never ever be breached by anyone other than the priests. It was impossible to keep the Hekel from being defiled. Anyone, even gentiles and romans and the worst enemies of the jews were able to poke their head inside the holiest place on earth. It was devastating.

Is this oral tradition? Or is there any proof of this?

Talmudic. Here, gimme a sec.
"During the last forty years before the destruction of the Hekel, the Lot For The Lord did not come up in the right hand, nor did the crimson-colored strap become white, nor did the western most lights shine, and the doors of the Hekel would open by themselves."
That's from Soncino.

And is Sonic canon?

Canon is a tricky subject. Talmud is certainly authoritative, though.
Basically canon. Jews generally believe this happened.

Do you?

Idk. I doubt it matters.
What's the quote you wanted to show me?

"Independent accounts prove that in ancient times, even the opponents of Christianity never doubted the historicity of Jesus, which was disputed for the first time and on inadequate grounds at the end of the 18th, during the 19th, and at the beginning of the 20th centuries."
That comes from the New Encyclopedia Brittanica

"Abed, *Obb-ed*. It is where we get Abdul."

"Can you write it for me?"

"Of course," she said, sliding my notepad over with two fingers and then squiggling the pen with the same two.

"Do you know how it looks in Persian, too?"

The pen flicked in her hand once again, then she glid the notepad over the laminate wood table back to me with a little push.

In Arabic, عبد. In Persian, بنده.

"They don't look that different," I said, my eyes skating back and forth so rapidly that my body probably thought I'd entered REM. "They seem very similar."

"They are not," she expressed. "In Arabic, it is pronounced *'obb-ed.'* In Persian Farsi, and also Urdu or Dari or Pashto, it is *'ban-day.'*"

"Ban...," I stuttered, "*Bandee*?"

"Yes, *ban-day*. Bandee. I don't know how you say."

"Prisoner?"

"Yes, servant, slave, prisoner: Bandee."

"Your name... Bandak... would be *Bandee* in Dari?"

"But I am not Dari. I am Claire; I am Bandak."

I was frozen, floored, flustered, or flabbergust, not sure which, and leaving the possibility open for all four to be true at once.

"You are very surprised," she said.

"That name, *Bandee*," I said while focusing on holding back my tears, "Bandee is very important to me."

"Names mean a lot to you, I think. Or at least the meaning of names."

"Yeah," I said, "I think that's true of me."

"Is Danger your first name?"

"No, it's my third middle name."

"That is enough names that you can be an honorary Arab."

Ha!

"Thanks!" I smiled. "I'll take that. But most people do just call me Danger. *Danger Rose.*"

Nobody actually calls me Danger Rose.

"I thought your last name was Ghost," she said, genuinely confused.

"Okay, yes. I was kidding about the 'Rose' part. That's just a fun little name I made up for myself when I was in Israel."

"Because of Romy?"

"What? No. No connection there."

I'm not arguing you on that point. I just don't believe Yeshua fulfilled the prophecies, and I think the fact that christians have changed the translation to fit their narrative proves that.

Like Mary being called a virgin? And you believe it means "young woman?"

I don't *believe* it means that. It *is* that.

Again: there's no way I can argue with you about ancient Hebrew. Obviously. Goes without saying. I'm just an ignorant American who spent my entire life in one language. But, are we sure that my entire faith blows over in the wind if this one word, or a couple like it, are mistranslated?

It's a big deal to me, I'd say

Mary's virginity is not a prerequisite for Christ's divinity. Maybe Christians misconstrued the meaning of a certain word - "young" vs "virgin." Oh well. That doesn't change the rest of the narrative.
Getting caught up in this stuff is like when Israelis and Palestinians fight over what ancient texts say about land. Like, it's okay to go there, of course - sometimes we need to - but we miss the point when we dwell in that place. Those spaces are too low to the ground. My faith doesn't hinge on whether Mary was a virgin, or if God literally inseminated her, or if the Earth big banged, or if Job literally existed, or if Lot had angels come to his door. These questions were never meant to matter. The question is this and this alone: did Yeshua rise from the dead? And I've seen too much scholarly work that points to this actually happening. And that's not even including the instances of faith at work that I've experienced. Personal stuff that I can't argue against any more than I can argue ancient Hebrew. Purely from a research perspective, too many studies have pointed to this historical event where a man who was crucified was later seen alive. Which is unsettling until we learn to accept that the illogical happened. Saying that the historical Yeshua wasn't sighted after his documented crucifixion is like saying Abraham didn't appoint Isaac as his heir.

You would have to really go around the barn to believe that, huh?

Exactly.

Tell all your Palestinian friends!
ᕦ(ﾟ ｡•̀ ᴗ •́｡)⊃ ≡☆ ☆ °ﾟ

I think that's not a bad parallel: throwing out the historical facts of Yeshua is as offensive as when the Palestinian Authority throws out the historical facts of the Holocaust. And I think people hate the truth when they don't know how to resolve it with their hard-nosed beliefs. In that vein, I can see why so much of the world hates Yeshua. But for me, if the historical narratives about Yeshua are true (as I believe they are), it's near-impossible for me to look at the Old Testament and not see that it points to this man in history as the endgame. I can't ignore what historians have recorded about Yeshua. I can't ignore the historical records that a man named Yeshua of Nazareth was crucified, and then witnessed by hundreds of people in the months following. I can't ignore that dozens of those people refused to recant what they had seen, even in the face of death, when there was no benefit to them to push a lie.
That man was the Messiah. He is the Messiah.

That's okay.
We don't have to agree.

"But you *have* seen the rosemary in Bethlehem?"

"No? What do you mean, 'the rosemary?'"

"Oh, it is just a popular plant in Israel and in Palestine. You probably saw it all over during your trip, from Tel Aviv to Jerusalem to Bethlehem and beyond. That is, if you were looking for it. It is a small plant that grows purple and blue and pink flowers. You certainly smelled it, even if you did not know: it is different than the scent of a flower. It's still fragrant, but... it is like the smell of earth. It's like the aroma you might get from an evergreen pine that had a sweet perfume on it. But, as I was saying, rosemary comes first from Bethlehem."

"Really? The spice, rosemary? It's from Bethlehem? Is that... truth? Or is that legend?"

"Oh, it is truth, for sure," she patted. "Shortly after Maryam gave birth to Yasue, she hung her laundry to dry on a shrub. Her blue cloak miraculously stained the plant, and baby Yasue's swaddling linens gave the plant a heavenly smell. The plant became known as 'Mary's Rose,' or Rosemary. Rosemary does not live past 33 years or grow taller than six feet high because it does not want to outgrow or outlive Yasue."

Yes. Surely not a myth!

"This name, 'Rose Mary,' is famous in Palestine, but also Israel. You will see many shops and restaurants with some variant of this name."

"That seems odd," I said. "That story is a very... well, pro-Palestinian, pro-Christian view. Not tenets that I'd imagine Israelis would want to promote."

"Oh, but it has another meaning for them," she said. "It is another language – Latin, I believe – and to them, it means 'dew of the sea.' And which sea? It is the Mediterranean, next to Israel. You may have seen it."

I wasn't sure if the last piece there was supposed to be a joke, but I was too enthralled to laugh right now.

"Rosemary is not like other flora," Claire, formerly a French linguist and now a sudden botanist, explained to me. "When it is a drought, when the soil is crumbling and other plants are dying, rosemary can survive on the dew of the Mediterranean. But it is strange, for sometimes, when the soil is wet and the other plants are damp, rosemary will be brittle and wilting."

"What? That doesn't make sense. How is that even possible? It sounds like... it's... that's not natural."

"When you overwater, other plants might be happy, but it drowns the rosemary, and the roots shrivel, making it dry up."

"So," I wanted to point out the irony, "it dries up when there's flooding?"

You and I have bantered about theodicy. "Why do bad things happen to good people." But Luke 15:7 (Christian Bible, obvi) indicates that there is more beauty and rejoicing in restoration than there is in sustained wholeness. We are (or at least God is) always moving towards improvement and something better. So "Why do bad things happen to good people" is a much less important question than "why do bad things happen to a good God?"

That's a potent question.

My faith hurts me so much, and I may not have all the answers, but I do have a couple of them, and those are what get me through the toughest moments.
Faith is pleasure, faith is pain.

A rose.

A rose?

Rose: thorn and beauty. pleasure and pain.

Funny you say that. The state flower here is the Oklahoma Rose.

You're not any ol' ok rose. You're more like a dog rose.

A dog rose?

Dog rose: rosa canina. My aunt used to grow them in Europe. Literally symbolizes pleasure and pain.

Dog rose. Hm. Incredible. I didn't know this was a thing.

Dog roses are usually pink. Like, almost a purply pink. And colors mean something, too, in the flower world. You said Romy's "color" was purple. Well, the color purple is sometimes used to signify permanence during transition. I know for sure that's the case with tulips, I'm not sure about roses. But some purple flowers mean "eternal love." As in, no matter how long we must stay apart or how much things might change, this thing stays the same: I love you forever.

That's... really touching. Thank you.
I think I'll get to see Romy again. And I'll get to tell her how sorry I am for failing her so repeatedly. And I'll finally get the kiss I wanted as she was leaving this world, the one she wouldn't give because she was in so much pain and fear.

Do you really believe that?

That's my dogma. Relationships are the only thing we carry into eternity. Can our relationships and memories of a pet be ripped from heaven? If not, then there my Romy will be waiting for me.

I've been wanting to share something with you. Can I tell you a story?

of course

Two jews in ancient Egypt are given the same instructions: put a lamb's blood over your doorpost tonight. One jew gets it; he recognizes its significance, that the blood is a substitute atonement, so he spreads the blood and the Black Death passes over his house. The second jew doesn't get it; it sounds like the stupidest thing he's ever been instructed to do, but he spreads the blood anyway because he's learned that god is worth trusting. Black Death passes over his house too.

What's this mean?

Have faith. Don't stop praying, Danger, just because you don't get it. You've seen god act. So promise me: next time you see the valley, try going up it instead of down. Pray and watch him turn the path on its head. Even if you don't believe he will. Be that second jew who maintained a sliver of trust, which saved his family.

"Yes, it floods and dies like the people of Noah's time," she said, drawing up a strikingly dark Biblical allusion. "But it takes a *lot* of water to dry it up. It can survive anywhere, from the depths of the valley to the scorching mountaintop."

"Spunky!"

"Near the Jezreel Valley, especially, there are clusters of rosemary bushes. There is a city, Beisan, that is famous for rosemary. You may find walls of them there."

"Where is Beisan?" I wondered aloud.

"You have been to Caesarea? Or Haifa, maybe?"

"Yes. Both."

"East of Caesarea is Megiddo. Just east of Megiddo is Harod, where you may find Gideon's Spring. Just east of Gideon's spring is Beisan."

"Megid… what is Gideon's Spring?"

"It is where Gideon and his army refreshed before fighting the Midianites. There is a cave there, Gideon's cave. Gideon put the fleece outside of the cave where his army slept."

"Wait. That's where the rosemary bushes flourish?"

"Close to there, yes. Rosemary and Gideon's fleece have this in common: the ground is dry, but the herb and the wool remain wet. Other times, they are dry when everything around them are drenched. Maryam should have named it *Rose-Gideon*, instead?"

Again, I wasn't sure if she was attempting humor, but this time, it tickled me enough that I laughed.

"Well," I deliberated, "I think I prefer the Mary story. The bloodshed from Gideon's battle might put a damper on an otherwise bright history."

"Oh, but it is also a sad herb," Claire refuted. "Yes, the rosemary is used in weddings, because it is a symbol of fidelity. But it is a fidelity that goes beyond death: a faithfulness to what was lost; an eternal remembrance of those who have met the grave. For as often as it is used in weddings, rosemary is used in funerals."

"That's kind of poetic, I think."

"There is a city, north of Megiddo: Sheikh Abreik. I don't know how you say it in English. A city of graves?"

"Not sure."

"Like, a city that's for burial? A cemetery so large it has a postal code?"

"Hmm," I said, wanting to help her out, but not really sure how many dead people regularly need postal service. "I really don't know. The only thing I can think of is a necropolis, maybe?"

I just don't want to be stuck in-between forever.

Maybe that's where you're meant to be though? It's the Spirit of Danger. Ruach Sakana. Achtung Geist. There's beauty in the in-between. The day doesn't just go from bright to night, there's gloaming for a reason. In jewdism, we celebrate god as the bringer of dusk. It's a title we adorn him: He who mixes the twilight. Adonai, Ha'ma'ariv Aravim.

How do you say it?

Just like that.

I mean in Hebrew, what is it

I can't write it out in vain. It's too holy.

Wow.

Hey, I need to go. Shabbat is on its way.

But it's, like, only 4pm by you??

Yeah, that's kinda how the lunar cycle goes, ya know? The winter sun can't hold its liquor this time of year.
But my point earlier was that you're right: you're not entitled to know everything about god or the universe. And it's okay if you're operating off of a tiny strand of faith. It's okay to struggle. It's okay to wrestle. It's okay to be Jacob in the twilight.

In twilight, at least I can start to see the stars, even if they're not bright. Do you know how much I love stars, Esther? There's nothing better than looking up in the winter sky and clearly seeing a bright, beautiful star.
I don't know if you saw. I have one tattooed on my arm.

You're talking to one, you know.

Talking to what?

An esther. A star.

I'm not following.

You once asked what the meaning is behind my name.

Right. You didn't answer.

I'm answering it now.

Esther means Star??

Yes.

I'm at a loss for words. That's so meaningful to know that.

The fact that my name means star? That matters that much to you?

Absolutely. Yes, it does. Probably more than you realize.

Well, cool. Then may it be a light to you in dark places, when all other lights go out.

Esther, thank you for being a part of my bildungsromy.

Can you see clearly yet? God does love Romy. And your dad. And you. God is good.

Yeah. I think so.
Shabbat Shalom, Esther.

Merry Christmas.

Woe is the man who stands before God and thinks it best to speak.

"*Yes!*" she cheered. "Necropolis. And where else will you find rosemary? In Gethsemane, where Yasue prayed for deliverance. Rosemary is meant to bless the memory of a loved one."

"Wow," I said. "Is it too late to call myself Danger Rosemary?"

A rare laugh from Claire.

"That is why I thought this," she said, her radiantly beaming. "I thought it was for this maybe you named her Romy."

"Hmph," I chuckled. "No. Romy Tono was named after Tony Romo. Tony Romo was a man who played quarterback for the NFL, in this very city, in fact."

"So Tony Romo has gone on to rest?"

"In a way. But Romy was named after him. It worked out because Romy is a real name, short for Roman."

"No, but it is not."

"Not what?"

"Romy is *not* short for Roman. At least, it is not when it is a girl. This is what I have been saying: a boy named Romy might be Roman, but a girl named Romy is usually Rose Mary."

My heart palpitated, but for once, that broken-clock-of-a-ticker had nothing to do with my chronic arrhythmia.

"Rose… Rose Mary? Are you sure?"

"Of course I am sure. There are restaurants, they name their restaurants Rosemary, or sometimes, just Romy."

The palpitations soothed and my heart melted away, yet still somehow was heavier than ever before.

"I am sorry, maybe I shouldn't bring this up," she said. "It's fresh for you."

Yes, it was fresh, and, yes, it was painful, but that's not why I hadn't any words.

"It can be holy to grieve through the lens of someone else's tragedy," she said, "especially if their heartbreak concludes with the miracle of peace."

I still hadn't any words for Claire. Fighting skepticism while fleeing emotionalism had me frozen.

"I wish you could recognize what God is doing in your life," Claire persisted. "But someday, you will see it. Someday, you will see her. And peace you will have."

THE VALLEY ROSE.

God spoke, and it's how
The mountain calls for you now.
Not *me* –
The Valley Rose.
And it was *my beloved* who was always
Bound to suffer.
The Lord was the One who was
So focused on growing His garden,
That He left us to wither on this side.
That God is actually not good.
Never again will I think
Faith is the most important pillar of life.
Contrary to my prior beliefs,
Prayer has no place in the logical man's life.
Now I know that it's foolish to say
God is sovereign.
For all of eternity,
I will never see Romy again.
I erroneously believed
This pain will pass;
And also that
God sent Yeshua as Messiah.
I've instead learned to trust
My old pragmatic way of thinking.
I've been forced to surrender
My family, after all.
I never deserved
Anything less than this confidence:
Our suffering is meaningless, and
Now I know it's a lie to say
God sees our pain.
After a bitter season of contemplation
I have come to the sobering conclusion
God does not change.
Give me a break:
I prayed so hard for change;
We can't stay in that place.
Come into the valley with me.
Here's the thing: God intended you would
Crawl back to the mountaintop, because

VARIA

My eyes open. It's 3am and I'm back to reality in an instant. I don't have trouble falling asleep at night, but I never seem to stay down for more than a few hours.

I have dry tears crusted onto my eyelids. I don't remember crying, but it's hard to argue with the cloudy pressure on my eyes.

I'm still clutching Romy. Well, her urn anyway. I notice its color isn't as lively as it looked a couple years ago, but that's brass for you, I guess. Though, the only light in the room is the faint glow from the clock, so the darkness probably has something to do with that.

Still, I do wonder how long before the urn turns sea-green. The Statue of Liberty only took, *what*, 20 years or something? Though, Lady Liberty is actually true copper. That probably has something to do with that.

Sidney is stretched against my spine as if we're old war buddies leaning against each other for lumbar support. She tautens her body and all four of her paws reach for the ceiling; I probably woke her up by waking up. Her precious little head twists towards mine, and our eyes connect. Hers are particularly milky, Sidney's own brand of patina that's corporealized since we both lost Romy. She starts to sniff Romy's urn before giving her late sister a sweet, quick kiss. I'd flecked the anointing oil on the urn's brass a few hours ago. *That's* why Sidney licked it. She can't comprehend that Romy's former body is inside the urn. Right?

Sidney stands up, stretches once more for good measure, then jumps down to the floor to go rest in her pipsqueak-sized bed instead.

I set Romy back onto the makeshift pedestal I made for her, which is really just a glass-encased three-dimensional model of the map from one of the *Legend of Zelda* installments: a gift from Ben that Christmas after we lost Romy. That feels so long ago now. And, wow: Romy turns *nine* next week. Or, she would have.

I don't know why I'm awake now. From the night that Romy died, it's silence — not noise — that wakes me. Another good reason to want children, I suppose. As if I needed another reason. It frosts me that we're still childless in this *four*-bedroom house. I don't know why God doesn't allow it. We "prepared for the rain," and the rain never came.

To be fair, God may very well grant us children someday. Twins, even: one Baby Danger and one Baby Joanna. But I can't assume He will, and I have to hang onto the fact that God is good, even though I don't always feel it to be true. I'm a man of sorrow, sure, but I'm certainly *not* the only man who's been well-acquainted with grief.

I realize I never prayed before I dozed off. I still try to talk to God every night, even though I doubt my prayer's efficacy. I didn't skip praying on purpose last night. Like I said, I have no trouble falling asleep. I had actually started to pray, and like a baby easing into his father's safe chest, I slipped asleep.

I adjust my body onto its side, and then onto the other side, and then flip back facing the wall.

She's asleep but senses my struggle and strains her hands to rub my back with the tips of her fingers.

I can almost feel the exhaustion in her caress.

"I love you."

The lighthouse to my storm.

I find her hand, squeeze it, and she falls back asleep.

Lucky.

I really need the sleep. I'm in my first week of a new job, and I've been exhausted every day, even with a full night's rest. And it's a good job, too: I get to provide outreach services to those living on the streets. I don't earn much more money than I would if I were flipping burgers, but at least the work is meaningful.

But it's a moot point if I can't keep my eyes open on the job. I guess I'll just drink four coffees again.

Or maybe if I try praying again, I'll fall asleep.

I start praying in my head, but then remember one thing Claire – that woman I met in Bethlehem, if you remember her at all – told me: it's necessary to pray out loud. She didn't have any biblical support for this idea, except that Yeshua told His disciples to close their door when they pray (presumably so they can speak freely and in secret) , but He never outright commanded it. And, Claire says, there are extenuating circumstances when you can pray silently – like when an Israeli soldier is pressing a gun to your head – but she asserts that it's important to pray aloud.

Esther agrees with this idea, too. She said it doesn't count if you're not saying it out loud. Again, no real biblical support beyond an (albeit poignant) assertion that "God didn't *think* creation into existence." But when an Orthodox Jew and a Charismatic Christian agree on something, I think it's worth listening to.

I pull the sheets over my head, burrowing under the comforter to use it as a substitutionary tallit. I *could* just use my actual tallit, but I'd have to get out of bed to reach it, which would trigger Zero Suit Samus's wiggle butt, which would have her rat-tail slapping against the wall and wake up

Shadrach, who would become convinced that it's time for second breakfast, which means she'd get up and the two of them would start boisterously playing with each other, and if that sounds like an irrational slippery slope, then you need to start fostering more dogs.

More importantly, I'd taken my tallit out of its cloth case only once since that day I spread it over Romy's corpse and her blood transposed onto the fabric. When I had gotten home from the crematorium, I folded the shawl and put it into its sheath, and it stayed on a shelf for about a year. When I finally pulled it out again, I took a deep breath to prepare myself for what I was about to subject myself to. But when I unfurled it, the tallit was milkwhite – uncorrupted, chaste, worthy white.

"That's weird," one side of my brain muttered. "This had gotten stained."

"Probably not," the other half retorted. "You may have just imagined that blood had gotten on it."

"No, I know what I saw," righty responded. "It was crimson."

"Don't forget: you have a big imagination," lefty gaslighted. "Or it wasn't actually blood that had dripped out, but *plasma*. It's basically water: no red cells."

"Maybe," I said. "I don't practice medicine, so I can't tell the difference. But don't tell me this wasn't red before, because I *know* it was. And now I can't even tell where the stain used to be."

I slipped the tallit back in its pouch that day and haven't taken it out since. So, yes: I could use an actual prayer shawl instead of the bed covers, but I don't want to get out of bed, and the tallit feels a bit too holy for a wretch like me to even touch anymore. Like an orthodox gopher, I stay under the bed covers, and I'm content with that. I start my prayer over, now whispering to the Comforter.

"Lord, show me what I need so I can pray for those things instead of what I want. I pray for affliction upon my life that will strengthen my relationship with You. I pray that I get passed over for every incredible job opportunity that I'm not intended to get. Take my skull and crush it if that's what it takes to bring me to You. Take me through the horrific loss of my beloved Romy if that's what it takes to draw near to You, and each night as I cry out in anguish over this pain, may I remember that You are sovereign and You see my pain, You know my needs, and You love Romy more than even I do."

I grab Romy's urn again with both hands, then squeeze, as if she can feel my love for her. I stabilize the urn against my body more firmly than I'd ever clutched anything before. I feel my eyes grow wet, if only ever-so-slightly, so I shut my eyelids just as hard as I was squeezing the urn, forcing out a partially-formed tear before it could be consummated into completion. I bring Romy to my lips, give her a gentle peck, and then bow my head against the urn's bezel.

Oh, baby girl, my second baby! Did you even know how beloved you were? If each day had been a year, I still would have needed more time with you. Is it that I didn't love enough? How can it be that your blood would be on my own hands? How can the Lord ever restore me now?

Another tear snuck its way into existence and down my cheek, so I wipe it away and knuckle my eye before another could form, then sulk at the realization that I might be in for a night of restlessness.

Oh, God, please put me to sleep before 3:55.

I've tried to rationalize all the different reasons we lost Romy. It was God's plan. Or, it was God's judgment. Or, God had an agreement with Satan to let it happen. But right now, the theology doesn't even matter anymore, so long as she's safe and with God.

Seeing Romy carted towards the furnace pyre is one I won't soon forget. It's an obsessive thought that no compulsion has been able to swallow: believe me, I've tried. Romy was so beautiful, with the most gorgeous brown eyes I'd ever seen and an august coat that would almost trick you into thinking she was a maned mini-lion. It hurts my heart to think of her fur going up in flames, her body burnt whole, like an animal on the altar.

Esther told me about two ancient Jews on the night of the Passover, one who understood the relevance of God's instruction and one who didn't, both being spared by the Black Death because of their willingness to slaughter a lamb. Sacrifice is sacrifice because *it hurts*. Even if you've dodged the punishment, *someone* is still absorbing a cost. But slaughter – *zevakh* – is only one of the types of sacrifice. In fact, a slaughter offering is the weaker of the sacrifices: it had a silver lining (at least for us, as humans), that people were allowed to eat what remained of the animal after offering the fat and entrails to God. But the *Korban Olah* was the greatest form of sacrifice. The entire animal was immolated on an altar, creating a blaze so hot, so holy, so pure, that not even the devil dared dance on its flames. No meat was spared for consumption, only the smoke rising to the nostrils of the Lord. God got it *all*. Hebrews called it the burnt offering (*kaustos*); Greeks referred to it as the whole offering (*olos*). Nobody could agree on which term was better, so they just juxtaposed them together: a *holos kaustos*. Or, transliterated for dummies like me: a holocaust.

I have reason to believe that animals ritually sacrificed – holocaust or otherwise – are blessed with eternity in God's presence. (I'll have to save sharing my rationale for another day, *Enshallah*.) I don't know that I'd call Romy's tragedy a holocaust, but I can say with confidence that she was without blemish as she was wheeled to a stone slab to be burnt whole because of my failings. I can't imagine that I'll ever be able to think of Romy's death and not obsess over how she died and hate my role in it. And I don't like it when people spew the adage, "time heals all wounds." It's not helpful, and it almost implies that the only reason we're healing is because there's now a spatial distance from the event, as if you're only healing because there's a literal gap between you and your loved one.

The reason we heal over time is because our mind naturally figures out how to compartmentalize the event. When Romy died, I wanted to, too, because I couldn't imagine a life that wasn't marked by permanent sadness in every moment and every circumstance for the rest of my days. But my mind re-learned to separate the good and the bad into different boxes.

Romy's life: good.

Romy's death: bad.

Medications when they go right and help: good.

Medications when they go wrong and kill: bad.

God: good.

Me: not.

Then, focus on the good. Find joy.

"Please… Lord, please take care of her," I continue aloud. "Please take care of her for all eternity now. Thank You for letting us borrow her. Please let Romy know that we love her and that we miss her and that was think about her and that we're coming, too. I ask this in Yeshua's Name and through the Holy Spirit."

And then I transition into my scripted prayer. The prayer based on the Metroid principles, and the only thing I say when I just don't feel like praying but I know I ought to.

"Lord, thank You. Thank You for my family, for my health, for letting me survive the night. Today is a gift and I want to use it well. I ask that You give me my daily bread today; that is, please give me just what I need today and nothing more. Today, may You be revealed to be holy; may the world see and understand Your Glory better. Please spare me from temptation today; may I be able to resist sin and be delivered from evil – both my own and others'. Search my heart; reveal in me my sin so that I may confess to You how I've failed You and the purpose You've set out for me, and teach me how to forgive others as You do. Make me the person You've called me to be. Above all else, please see to it that Your will is achieved, not my will, and may I have even just a small part in the accomplishment of Your Will. I love You. And I trust You; teach me to trust You more. Thank You."

I set Romy back on my nightstand.

I miss my dog.

"Amen."

Well, I'm still not asleep. I'm still stuck between the night and the day. Between Genesis and Revelation. Between the end of the beginning and the beginning of the end. Between the star and its light.

Which is real? There's the star, which doesn't even exist anymore. We only see the light from it, and we clumsily name *that* "the star." The star is, in fact, a thing of the past. So are we just seeing a banana and calling it an olive? What's even real: the star that's a thing of the past, or the light that sprung from the star?

Plopped directly between the star and the light, like how I was plopped into the Valley of Jezreel by a 4x4 from Megiddo hill. But once you see the star and its light on the hill, it's impossible to unsee it. Even when you're in the valley, your neck twists and strains to get a glimpse of it again from below. Because it's that important to get a peek of, at least every once in awhile. We get two opportunities to experience twilight every day: the *crepuscular* twilight that beckons the night, and then the *diluculum* twilight is the herald of morning. Either twilight, whether daylight is getting sucked up through a straw or bubbled back out, you know you've got change a-coming. And Nicolas had been right: it grew cold after that day. Winter rolled in, and the sun became faint. I chided the sun for being so overbearing that day, but had I stayed in the valley a week longer, I would have cursed the sun for not being stronger. I may have even been convinced that the sun wasn't there. But the reality is that the winter sun is the only reason you or I have any light and any warmth at all. It's said that star differs from star in glory, but might a star differ from itself in glory depending on how hazy it looks during the dog days of winter? The sun is unchanging; it's *we* who shift. Beyond the earth's quietus remains the winter sun, our own personal star. The longer I stay in the valley, the more I've forgotten the glory of the winter sun.

Jews understand something that most others don't: your religion does *not* earn you a shortcut through the valley. It's the hope – *not* the fulfillment – of God's promise that gives you the stamina to scale the valley. Maybe I was meant to be there for a time, but I wasn't meant to stay in the vale. I need to get back to the top of the hill. I need to get back to my wife, to find rest. And rest only comes with trusting God's sovereignty. So I shoulder the hard decision to leave the valley, even though that's where I've found my comfort.

Life is seeking. Life is seeing. You will seek all your life and never get answers if those answers have never been revealed. And, man, I haven't talked to Esther in awhile. I used to talk to her several times a week, and now it's been a month without so much as a thought about her. It's funny how people move in and out of your life like that, how someone can be a daily part of your life for so long and then that just stops for no other reason than it just happened like that.

Esther doesn't believe in visions and prophecies, at least not in the sense that they can happen to people today like they did in the Bible. And she has good reason not to believe. Most "prophets" don't have a great track record, present company included. She rejected my "prophetic" dream before I even told her about it, and I'm not sure she was wrong to do it. It probably would've been a waste on my part to try to even explain it, because you can't describe the feelings of an experience to someone who has never encountered the same thing you did. For Esther, it's doubly true because she's already been exposed to people who tried to explain it and she decided then that it wasn't real.

But I still can't shake that dream I tried to tell her about, the one I wrote down many months before Romy's passing. I re-read the dream so many times, and it was as if the words had been written by a stranger, but I knew I was looking at my own handwriting.

In my dream, I was in a house. It was my house – the one I live in now – but I'd never seen it before. I had still been living in the stived condo when I wrote this down. But in this new house in my dream, I'm with my wife and our three dogs.

Except in reality at that time, we didn't have three dogs. We had two. But the third dog in the vision is a stray dog that we took in, and I'm looking at a brown dog dallying through the kitchen, and just as we're finishing unpacking things into our new house, this brown dog dies, and we're back to two dogs.

That's it. That's the whole vision, nothing out of the ordinary, really. A little morbid, maybe, but not wacky, as dreams can be.

Two weeks after this vision, though, Joanna and I took in a stray dog for the first time in our lives. An older, large, brown labrador with no collar, no tags, no chip. We named him Buddy. It's probably why I didn't remember this vision, because after we found Buddy, I'd mentally resolved my vision as being about him. I remember thinking that God sent me this vision to prepare me for the loss of Buddy.

Buddy didn't die, though. We took care of him for five days and then his owner came forward. Turns out, his name was really Jackson. So we returned Buddy Jack to his guardian, and we were back to two. A prophecy deferred. I took Sidney and Romy out to a coffee shop one early morning in May 2018, just to reward them for being such good girls around Buddy Jack. But apparently Buddy Jack had told the other dogs that the Geist family was offering free room and board, because when we pulled back up into our condo parking lot, there were three more stray dogs in front of our complex. Anemic, dehydrated, deathly hungry, scabby, scaly, ears full of mites, intestines full of worms, and one of them – the youngest one, a puppy – was showing signs of parvovirus. Of course, being Tulsa, there was nothing unusual about this sight. But, it was just too hard to look away this time, so we took them in: Shadrach, Meshach, and Abednego. Just like that, we upgraded from two dogs to five, at least until a Denver-based rescue took in Meshach and Abednego a month later.

Then we built a house, and a few months later, we shepherded our three dogs through that front door. A white one, a brown one, and a black-and-white one.

And the brown one died immediately after.

I reach out my hands to Romy's urn and start caressing it, as softly as Joanna's fingertips had done to my spine a few moments ago and as if Romy could physically feel it the same.

578

God created man – the pinnacle of creation – from dirt.
  Beauty out of ashes.

God transformed slaves – the "least of these" – into the chosen people.
        Acceptance out of rejection.

God selected fishermen and tax collectors – the scorned nobodies – to become the architects of the Christian Church.
                Wisdom out of regret.

God chose a violent zealot – the murderer of the earliest apostles – as the most influential courier to the message of Christ's peace.
                Lightness out of darkness.

Those are just the things that I inherently understand. Truth is, there's more that I don't know than I do. It's like I told Esther: each time God gives me an answer, it comes with two more questions. "Where's Romy? Where's Chiefy?" These are questions that, this side of eternity, I'm not ever guaranteed any answers to. God knows that there's no other question that keeps me more on edge than that one. And I don't know why He didn't afford us answers to some of the most distressing questions we could ask. And I don't know why God took Romy. I really don't. But I believe it to be an intentional act – Romy didn't die because God failed to act; Romy died *because* God acted. It was His choice and doing. There is purpose in Romy's death, and it happened at the will of God. And I'm so angry and hurt by that.

But He is still good.

Joy out of agony.

I check the clock. It's almost 4am now. I seal my eyes and see if I can start counting shooting stars.

I watch the galaxy on my eyelids – it starts as a lone globule, then two more join. The three double before tripling: a good constellation. The gloried expanse is anointed with luminous stones. The heavens animate. Stars rip from their assignments as if tears of the Kingdom, springing forth until dimensions crack open from the rims of the vault. One nova shoots west, another north, another southeast, if cardinal directions exist. Stars drip off the scaffold, seeking some kind of terrain to crash into, but no surface exists and they're caught in endless freefall. I follow their light until they dissolve and leave celestial streaks in their wake.

Then something rises. A new thing is happening. A figure approaches me. She has four legs and thick, sesamed fur.

It's a dream. I know it's a dream. But I don't mind because it's the first time I've seen Romy in two years. She's panting right before me, but she doesn't see me yet.

And then she does. Not head-on – she sees me out of her peripherals, pauses for a moment as she recognizes just the sliver of me that she can see, and then she sallies up to me and gives me the kiss I never got the morning she died.

And not just one kiss, but multiple. So many kisses. She's so excited to see me, wagging her butt and mewling a soft cry, all because I'm with her.

Then she spots something behind her, as if someone is calling for her, and Romy realizes she's spent too much time in my world already. She loves me, and she loves to spend time with me again, but there are more important things for her to do that I can never understand in my earthly plane.

I nod, and she produces a wide grin and exhales a lone pant before scooting away, juking into the distance.

Joy. She's so full of joy.

I want to wake Joanna up and tell her. But should I? It was just a dream. It didn't actually happen. Only people with their heads in the clouds and bad writers ever tell anyone about their dreams. So I don't. I turn over, and get back to sleep.

But it only lasts a few moments because just as I reach that in-betweenness when you've not fallen asleep but you're no longer awake, Joanna wraps her arms around me, startling me.

Now ought I tell her about my dream? Still, it was only a dream. But it felt so real and meant so much. I want to tell her, I dreamt of Romy and Romy's okay and Romy kissed me and Romy looked so happy. As if God gave us a glimpse to say, "don't worry. She's with Me."

But I don't want to upset her. It's been two years: two years since Israel, two years since Romy. And we still can't talk about it. Talking about Romy often leads Joanna to crying. But but but I want *so much* to tell her of my dream.

And then I hear her sniffle and realize she's already crying.

"In my dream," she chokes through her tears, "Romy came to me and gave me kisses."

Baruch ata Adonai, Ha'ma'ariv Aravim

ACKNOWLEDGMENT

Neil Armstrong famously declared on the moon, "That's one small step for a man; one giant leap for mankind." Except, no he didn't. What he really said was, "That's one small step for man; one giant leap for mankind," which is problematic because there's not a significant difference between the words "man" and "mankind." Ergo, history chose to rewrite the quote – adding an "A" before "man" – so that it would make sense.

Are you okay with this? Adding that one single letter captures the intention behind his verbatim quote, but it twists truth to get there. If it doesn't hurt anything, and it's a more fitting way to capture the essence of an event, are you comfortable with a little revisionist history being employed?

If so, if you're good with that, you can stop reading here. If not, then I'd like to take a few more pages to come clean with you. More, I'd like to defend the revisionist choices in this work, with the hope that you'll appreciate my position.

The valleys and the crests are easy to write about, but the largest chunk of any book are the mundane plains. Meaning, writers are tasked with filling in a lot of details to get readers to the next peak or dale. Unfortunately, I'm much less observant than the average word-keeper. So when I tell you that two men browbeat me onto their ATV so it wouldn't be on their conscience when they later found pieces of me in a caracal's litter box, that really happened, but Saleem wasn't actually quite that fat and he wasn't even wearing purple. When I say that Claire's brother had been arrested and tortured, that really happened, but his fingernails had actually filled back in by the time he returned to the Bandak home. When I describe the conversations I had with Esther after we lost Romy, those really happened, even if they were far less confrontational at times (though, not always).

My memory is on the back-knife. The conversations in this book are not verbatim (with some exceptions given that my dialogue with Esther is preserved in text messages). It seems to be the case that Albert Einstein, Mother Theresa, and Abraham Lincoln each had their own scribes assigned to follow them around and jot down their wittiest sayings into a notepad so that their best quotes could be uploaded to the Internet in due time. For the rest of us, however, when we recall things that have been said in conversation, we're not only remembering the conversation incorrectly, but we're only remembering the memory of the last time we thought about the conversation. More often than not, we only remember the zeitgeist of what was being discussed, not the literal words used. In the (actual, I think) words of essayist David Sedaris, "Memoir is the last place you'd expect to find the truth."

In this book, I've attempted to preserve the spirit of each conversation conveyed, or at the very least, the meaning I took from it. As such, aside from the Esther dialogues and the phrase, "Woe is the man who comes before Me, and thinks it best to speak," it's possible that there isn't a single sentence in this book that was delivered the way I said it was. If you found a striking quote within this book – a phrase that really stuck with you – there's a good chance that the person cited in the book as having spoken it was not the person who literally said it.

Therefore, I'd like to acknowledge the zhuzh within this work, with the hope that you'll appreciate that what might be one small sidestep for writer can be leaps-and-bounds better for readerkind.

FUSION SUITED

Several characters were composite (ie, several actual people fused into one), including Esther, Nicolas, Izzy, and Trae. They all existed, to be sure, but the conversations with them and the lessons I took from them sometimes happened through other people. For instance, I didn't learn about the Tulsa Race Massacre from Esther (though I did only learn about it in mid-2018). "If reading is ice-skating," then detailing that text exchange with a college friend about the history of Tulsa would've been akin to getting steamrolled by the zamboni.

Esther didn't work at a hostel – another Israeli participant did, and it was that participant who introduced me to Esther (and all of my other Israeli participants, for that matter). About half of Esther's thoughts and opinions came from other people: most of Esther's "Jewish rebuttals" came from rabbis, domestic and abroad. My relationship with Esther wasn't suspended between Romy's death and the 2020 pandemic. From the time I got home from Israel to the time of publication, I've kept in contact with Esther, almost weekly.

Esther's reaction to Isaiah 53 was far less visceral than depicted, but I was trying to fairly capture the arguments against the Christian perspective, which can become a very contested, heated discourse. That's not to say that Esther and I didn't share some confrontational rhetoric, but any animosity she had towards me was often in regards to my inceptive belief that my prayers *should* have rescued Romy. There never existed this seditious suspicion that I was trying to convert her to Christianity. I included that angle simply because it's often the natural trajectory when Christians discuss these things with Jews.

My conversations with Esther probably seem very egocentric. In reality, much of the dialogue with her centered around her life (her actual job, her family, etc.). But she adamantly desired to remain anonymous, so those details were purposely omitted so that she could not be identified.

Likewise, Izzy was real, and we did have a PlayStation night in Bethlehem (or was it Xbox?), but we played *Fifa*, not *The Show*. Including this would have meant I'd have to confess how badly he destroyed me, and I'd have to talk about soccer – two strikes! And if I went with soccer instead of baseball, then how might I include reference to one of the most iconic fights in baseball history?

I tried to convey the culmination of the Palestinian responses to my interviews through Izzy, though it felt less important to do that than conveying the Israeli responses, given that there were nearly 40 chapters' worth of the "Palestinian perspective" via Claire's narratives.

Trae-Beard, in fact, *was* one of my Israeli participants whom I met in Bethlehem. He was an amalgamation of a New Zealander woman I met in that hostel in Ramallah, as well as all the atheist Israelis I interviewed – which was most of them. By no means was Trae a connoisseur of American video games, a distinction that squarely falls to a few of my Palestinian participants (including Izzy).

Of all the characters, Nicolas was the most fabricated. This kind man, indeed, took me under his wing when I stumbled upon a life-saving fire in The Valley, but he was not very religious. He was far more spiritual, if you can appreciate the irony of me pointing that out. Many of the lessons and exhortations from Nicolas came from others who helped me through the odyssey of losing Romy, and, frankly, most of these lessons came from God Himself as revealed through Lectio Divina and my time reading Jewish commentary throughout 2019. As Scripture implores, "work out your own salvation with fear and trembling, for it is God who works in you" (Philippians 2:12-13). I would not be the man I am today without the Holy Spirit's revelations during Lectio Divina.

LIGHT ADJUSTMENTS

I'm a storyteller, not an investigative journalist. I didn't verify the facts of Claire's story, except that which was readily available with the click of a mouse. (But even if I tracked down the factkeepers to Claire's stories, would it make a difference to her objectors anyway?)

Several details (but never large ones) in her story were changed to protect the identities of specific people in Palestine, and I regret that I cannot go into further detail than that out of respect for the safety of those people. For whatever it's worth to you, Claire and I did work quite hard to keep her story as genuinely close to what literally happened.

One small-but-important detail is that Israelis weren't charging 5x for materials until *after* the First Intifada began. It was an act of suppression, not preemption. However, placing this later in the story slowed down the tempo of the higher-octane stories, and so it was inserted earlier instead.

The most processed element from Claire's narratives is that of her seemingly explaining the meaning of particular names to me. With the exception of Esther's (which she described after it had been hidden from me awhile), I usually discover the meaning behind peoples' names on my own. If the thought of me lying on my fur-covered couch, thumbing through my phone while slurping on my third coffee of the day sounds enticing to you, then I owe you an apology. Otherwise, you'll likely appreciate the fact that Claire was not the one who told me *Bandak* meant prisoner. Unearthing that factoid was an act of research that was spurred purely out of copious amounts of coffee and curiosity. Claire and I did discuss such name meanings, but it was over text exchanges and wasn't nearly as natural of a conversation as it appears in the book. But it was the meaning of the name Bandak — *not* the way I found out — that gave it its weight in the first place, and anyone who has read my first book understands the outright necessity of including it.

Likewise, Claire wasn't the one who told me about Rosemary, and in fact, that discovery happened at the tail-end of this five-year project. Claire's final narrative in this book was a chapter that I had long struggled to write. In the rough drafts I'd presented to beta readers, that chapter simply appeared with a placeholder note that I would get to it, someday, hopefully. On August 11, 2023, I was sitting in one of my favorite coffeeshops in one of my least-favorite cities in the world (ie, the one God called me to languish in). That day, less than four months away from final publication, I finally started working on Claire's final chapter — after the rest of the book had been written and endured rigorous edits, and after I had even started on the marketing already. I've since come to believe that this was a curious thought implanted by the Holy Spirit, but as I was working on that chapter, I wondered to myself if there was meaning behind the name of Rose Mary, the late school secretary at Joyce Kilmer Elementary. This is how I actually stumbled upon its meaning, a meaning for a name in which there existed no reason I shouldn't have previously known. It was as though a pall had previously covered my eyes, and in a holy moment I will never forget, I looked around at all the strangers in the coffeeshop, wishing to share with somebody that one of the most significant epiphanies of my entire lifetime had just happened in their midst, that a veil — like another, once upon a time — had just been torn top-to-bottom. For as a scarlet thread is woven throughout Scripture, so had a rose been planted time and again throughout my life. Oh, how many petals that have clung to my feet without the slightest appreciation for that which was gripping my sole.

I left the coffeeshop, cried for a quick moment in my car, stopped at a garden center on the way home, and began researching how to craft a rosemary bed in the front of my house.

Almost four months later, I've yet to experience clinical depression since that morning brew.

QUICK ACKNOWLEDGMENTS

Here are several other rapid-fire examples of facts that were altered, which, if you please, you may read like it's a legal disclaimer being rattled off by an auctioneer on a pharmaceutic commercial that you should talk to your doctor about:

- It was April 16, 2018 that I had dreamt (and wrote down) the dream that I shared in the final chapter (Varia), and it was April 2019 that I had stumbled upon it again.
- "Danger Rose" was a (semi-ironic) name I started calling myself in early October 2018 when describing my Holy Land exploits to friends. What was meant to be a humorous moniker ended up becoming an integral part of my life – not unlike how I came to be "Danger."
- I learned the meaning of Esther's name (via text, as depicted) in late October 2018, after my interview with her but before I left Israel.
- I learned the meaning of Claire's name (via text, not as depicted) in July 2020 – including Claire, Bandak, and Anastas.
- And, as pointed out, I only learned about the etymologies of Rosemary in August 2023.
- I didn't drive to Joanna's house to pick her up for Kilmer Prom. We both got ready at my house, and it was Mom who did her motherly duties in snapping our photos that day.
- I had an OCONUS deployment to Vicenza, Italy in June 2006, and it was on the 18th of that month – exactly four months after the first prophecy about marrying Joanna someday – that I heard the prophecy about Gog and Magog. The bit about the Hawkeye came shortly after that, and the process of listening to these separate prophecies and making sense of them happened across several months, not several minutes in a Burger King.
- My dissertation chair, Dr. Giddie, didn't threaten to destroy me, though his first name really was Lord.
- I knew about Megiddo (and its supposed significance to the end times) before I left for Israel: it wasn't some random "add on" to the itinerary. However, I would've had to establish Megiddo's importance early on, only to have to re-establish its relevance again later. That was a flow choice.
- None of the pictures I shared of Romy were from after she passed away. The picture of Joanna hovering over a frightened Romy on the night of St. Nick's is actually the last picture we have of Romy being alive. The picture shown in the fatal chapter that followed was taken hours before she died. When reflecting on that picture, it feels somewhat obvious in hindsight that Romy may have been aware (even more than we were) that her leash was loosening.
- For T.S. Eliot aficionados, it may seem like my book was intended to be some real-life adaptation of his unparalleled poem, *The Hollow Men*. In fact, I only learned about the poem on November 29, 2023 (and immediately lamented that I hadn't discovered it soon enough to put it into the book). On December 1st, six days before publication, I had a last-minute formatting crisis that required the chapter "A Healed Knee" to be a page longer. Eliot delivered.
- In my discussions with Esther, I made it seem like I had discovered the simple joys of supper popcorn during the pandemic. My friends, I have been eating popcorn for dinner long before the virus was a twinkle in the adversary's eye, and you can bet your pleated bippie that it's still the best meal that I make for my wife – now, with a dash of rosemary.

But the most brazen lie in this book comes on the front cover. In the space under Chris Beatrice's illustration, there's some text that says "by Danger Geist." Of all the claims made in this book, this is the most fabricated one as I've never written anything that's had more collaboration than this. In the preceding paragraphs, I've worked to acknowledge my untruths. Now it's time to acknowledge those who made this book truly possible, with the caveat that several of those who I would have liked to have named requested to not be identified.

I want to recognize the obvious ones first: Esther, Claire, James, Nicolas, Izzy, and Trae-Beard. Of these, Claire and James are the only ones who were not amalgamations, though the core of Esther, Nicolas, Izzy, and Trae were yet based on real, living people who agreed to let me talk about them in the book. I'm grateful for that, and for their input long after we first met in 2018.

There were several people who received the roughest (i.e., worst) edition of this book. They had the task of wading through the hot sludge to help me discern which material belonged inside the book and that which belonged outside the Dung Gate. This was no easy feat and they did it without compensation, and had I not had their conscientious feedback, this book wouldn't be as coherent as it is today. So if you hated this book, then please direct your fireballs to Dany Fitzgerald, Matt Ward, the S.S. Loucks, Luke Copeland, Dr. Michael Stevens, Kristin McAlister, Chris Tsotsoros (a Greek), Matt and Lara Archibald, Christy Anastas, David Aye, Mike Rancharan, and, of course, Bernie, Leanne, and Joanna Geist. If you liked this book, then thank them instead.

I also want to take a brief block to thank a few people who hadn't set eyes on this book prior to its publication, but offered some kind of practical help in its execution, or offered encouragement with it when I needed it most. In alphabetical order, that short list includes Chris Beatrice, Mac Eldridge, Hannah Goering, Jan Love, Yoav Newman, Trevor Niemann, Chuck and Janet Pearson, Dr. Yael Ron, Ido Viron, and Dr. Ada Zohar.

I hope I've established that the substance in this book remains. Melt the details, and you can still identify the story by its teeth: I did present Joanna with a doctored fortune cookie that led to us dancing on a beach. I did undergo a third-degree interrogation in Milan. (Pro tip: travel with your wife.) I did befriend many Israelis and many Palestinians and zero Greeks. I did meet Joe Manganiello (in his final Arab form). I did snap at custodians of the Manger of Christ, the Mount of Temptation, and the Temple Mount. I did fail to break down the walls of Jericho but my urologist sure didn't. I did receive a soul-crushing cluster headache that sidelined me for over 24 hours. Dr. Shalev did abandon me in my time of need. I did sneak into a kibbutz and then was nearly pounced by caracals. I did hitchhike (which is not an uncommon practice outside of the western world) and get picked up by Ido (who indeed is a very nice man). Joanna really did have a significant pregnancy "scare" when arriving to Israel. I did frequently deal with hucksters like the shopkeeper and Berakhah in Jerusalem. I did really shut off my phone service for a few months, which helped me to move toward healing. I did storm out of my church during a sermon. Tulsa really is as awful as I describe it. My stained tallit did turn white. God did follow me into Babylon.

Writing is like wine. Only the best ages well. Writers need help stamping out the grapes: it's cumbersome to take on by yourself, and if you try, you'll end up with gross chunks. But beware the inverse: get too many soles helping with the winepress, it starts to smell like feet.

In this particular piece, I had so many varying opinions on what I'd put together that it sometimes felt like a microcosm of the Israeli-Palestinian Conflict: there was no way to reconcile two opposing peoples' views on a certain matter. I was faced with having to make a hard choice that would leave one of my contributors feeling ignored, unappreciated, or invalidated, which stings a little more given that their claims almost always had some cogency. In times like these, I had a go-to approach: I went with whatever would make my dad proudest. In the end, this book is how Dad wanted it.

Hey, reader: hug your family. Time is not on your side.

It's not the mark of the beast.

I promise.

Milton Keynes UK
Ingram Content Group UK Ltd.
UKHW040636111223
434160UK00001B/215